"Composed in the style of the great medieval *catenae*, this new anthology of patristic commentary on Holy Scripture, conveniently arranged by chapter and verse, will be a valuable resource for prayer, study and proclamation. By calling attention to the rich Christian heritage preceding the separations between East and West and between Protestant and Catholic, this series will perform a major service to the cause of ecumenism."

Avery Cardinal Dulles, S.J.
Laurence J. McGinley Professor of Religion and Society
Fordham University

"The initial cry of the Reformation was *ad fontes*—back to the sources! The Ancient Christian Commentary on Scripture is a marvelous tool for the recovery of biblical wisdom in today's church. Not just another scholarly project, the ACCS is a major resource for the renewal of preaching, theology and Christian devotion."

Timothy George
Dean, Beeson Divinity School, Samford University

"Modern church members often do not realize that they are participants in the vast company of the communion of saints that reaches far back into the past and that will continue into the future, until the kingdom comes. This Commentary should help them begin to see themselves as participants in that redeemed community."

Elizabeth Achtemeier
Union Professor Emerita of Bible and Homiletics
Union Theological Seminary in Virginia

"Contemporary pastors do not stand alone. We are not the first generation of preachers to wrestle with the challenges of communicating the gospel. The Ancient Christian Commentary on Scripture puts us in conversation with our colleagues from the past, that great cloud of witnesses who preceded us in this vocation. This Commentary enables us to receive their deep spiritual insights, their encouragement and guidance for present-day interpretation and preaching of the Word. What a wonderful addition to any pastor's library!"

William H. Willimon
Dean of the Chapel and Professor of Christian Ministry
Duke University

"Here is a nonpareil series which reclaims the Bible as the book of the church by making accessible to earnest readers of the twenty-first century the classrooms of Clement of Alexandria and Didymus the Blind, the study and lecture hall of Origen, the cathedrae of Chrysostom and Augustine, the scriptorium of Jerome in his Bethlehem monastery."

George Lawless
Augustinian Patristic Institute and Gregorian University, Rome

"We are pleased to witness publication of the
Ancient Christian Commentary on Scripture. It is most beneficial for us to learn
how the ancient Christians, especially the saints of the church
who proved through their lives their devotion to God and his Word, interpreted
Scripture. Let us heed the witness of those who have gone before us in the faith."

METROPOLITAN THEODOSIUS
Primate, Orthodox Church in America

"Across Christendom there has emerged a widespread interest
in early Christianity, both at the popular and scholarly level. . . .
Christians of all traditions stand to benefit from this project, especially clergy
and those who study the Bible. Moreover, it will allow us to see how our traditions are
both rooted in the scriptural interpretations of the church fathers while at
the same time seeing how we have developed new perspectives."

ALBERTO FERREIRO
Professor of History, Seattle Pacific University

"The Ancient Christian Commentary on Scripture fills a long overdue need for scholars and
students of the church fathers. . . . Such information will be of immeasurable
worth to those of us who have felt inundated by contemporary interpreters and novel theories
of the biblical text. We welcome some 'new' insight from the
ancient authors in the early centuries of the church."

H. WAYNE HOUSE
Professor of Theology and Law
Trinity University School of Law

"Chronological snobbery—the assumption that our ancestors working without benefit of
computers have nothing to teach us—is exposed as nonsense by this magnificent
new series. Surfeited with knowledge but starved of wisdom, many of us are
more than ready to sit at table with our ancestors and listen to their holy
conversations on Scripture. I know I am."

EUGENE H. PETERSON
Professor Emeritus of Spiritual Theology
Regent College

"Few publishing projects have encouraged me as much as the recently announced Ancient Christian Commentary on Scripture with Dr. Thomas Oden serving as general editor.... How is it that so many of us who are dedicated to serve the Lord received seminary educations which omitted familiarity with such incredible students of the Scriptures as St. John Chrysostom, St. Athanasius the Great and St. John of Damascus? I am greatly anticipating the publication of this Commentary."

FR. PETER E. GILLQUIST
Director, Department of Missions and Evangelism
Antiochian Orthodox Christian Archdiocese of North America

"The Scriptures have been read with love and attention for nearly two thousand years, and listening to the voice of believers from previous centuries opens us to unexpected insight and deepened faith. Those who studied Scripture in the centuries closest to its writing, the centuries during and following persecution and martyrdom, speak with particular authority. The Ancient Christian Commentary on Scripture will bring to life the truth that we are invisibly surrounded by a 'great cloud of witnesses.'"

FREDERICA MATHEWES-GREEN
Commentator, National Public Radio

"For those who think that church history began around 1941 when their pastor was born, this Commentary will be a great surprise. Christians throughout the centuries have read the biblical text, nursed their spirits with it and then applied it to their lives. These commentaries reflect that the witness of the Holy Spirit was present in his church throughout the centuries. As a result, we can profit by allowing the ancient Christians to speak to us today."

HADDON ROBINSON
Harold John Ockenga Distinguished Professor of Preaching
Gordon-Conwell Theological Seminary

"All who are interested in the interpretation of the Bible will welcome the forthcoming multivolume series Ancient Christian Commentary on Scripture. Here the insights of scores of early church fathers will be assembled and made readily available for significant passages throughout the Bible and the Apocrypha. It is hard to think of a more worthy ecumenical project to be undertaken by the publisher."

BRUCE M. METZGER
Professor of New Testament, Emeritus
Princeton Theological Seminary

ANCIENT CHRISTIAN COMMENTARY ON SCRIPTURE

OLD TESTAMENT
IX

PROVERBS, ECCLESIASTES, SONG OF SOLOMON

EDITED BY

J. ROBERT WRIGHT

GENERAL EDITOR
THOMAS C. ODEN

InterVarsity Press
Downers Grove, Illinois

InterVarsity Press
P.O. Box 1400, Downers Grove, IL 60515-1426
Internet: www.ivpress.com
E-mail: mail@ivpress.com

InterVarsity Press* is the book-publishing division of InterVarsity Christian Fellowship/USA*, a student movement active on campus at hundreds of universities, colleges and schools of nursing in the United States of America, and a member movement of the International Fellowship of Evangelical Students. For information about local and regional activities, write Public Relations Dept., InterVarsity Christian Fellowship/USA, 6400 Schroeder Rd., P.O. Box 7895, Madison, WI 53707-7895, or visit the IVCF website at <www.intervarsity.org>.

Scripture quotations, unless otherwise noted, are from the Revised Standard Version of the Bible, copyright 1946, 1952, 1971 by the Division of Christian Education of the National Council of the Churches of Christ in the U.S.A., and are used by permission.

Selected excerpts from Fathers of the Church: A New Translation, copyright 1947-. Used by permission of The Catholic University of America Press. Full bibliographic information on individual volumes may be found in the Bibliography of Works in English Translation.

Selected excerpts from The Syriac Fathers on Prayer and the Spiritual Life, translated by Sebastian Brock, Cistercian Studies 101, ©1987; Bede the Venerable, Commentary on the Acts of the Apostles, translated by Lawrence T. Martin, Cistercian Studies 117, ©1989; Bede the Venerable, Commentary on the Seven Catholic Epistles, translated by David Hurst, Cistercian Studies 82, ©1985; Bede the Venerable, Homilies on the Gospels, translated by Lawrence T. Martin and David Hurst, Cistercian Studies 110 and 111, ©1991; Gregory the Great, Forty Gospel Homilies, translated by David Hurst, Cistercian Studies 123, ©1990; Pachomian Koinonia: The Lives, Rules, and Other Writings of Saint Pachomius, translated by Armand Veilleux, Cistercian Studies 45, 46 and 47, ©1980-1982. Used by permission of Cistercian Publications, Kalamazoo, Michigan.

Selected excerpts from John Cassian, Conferences, translated by Colm Luibheid, The Classics of Western Spirituality, ©1985; John Cassian, The Conferences, translated and annotated by Boniface Ramsey, Ancient Christian Writers 57, ©1997; Cassiodorus, Explanation of the Psalms, translated by P. G. Walsh, Ancient Christian Writers 51, 52 and 53, ©1990, 1991; Gregory the Great, Pastoral Care, translated by Henry Davis, Ancient Christian Writers 11, ©1950; John Chrysostom, Baptismal Instructions, translated by Paul W. Harkins, Ancient Christian Writers 31, ©1963; Origen, An Exhortation to Martyrdom, Prayer and Selected Works, translated by Rowan A. Greer, The Classics of Western Spirituality, ©1979; Origen, Prayer; Exhoration to Martyrdom, translated by John J. O'Meara, Ancient Christian Writers 19, ©1954; Origen, The Song of Songs Commentary and Homilies, translated by R. P. Lawson, Ancient Christian Writers 26, ©1957; Pseudo-Dionysius: The Complete Works, translated by Colm Luibheid, The Classics of Western Spirituality, ©1980; The Sermons of St. Maximus of Turin, translated and annotated by Boniface Ramsey, Ancient Christian Writers 50, ©1989; St. Gregory of Nyssa, The Lord's Prayer and The Beatitudes, translated and annotated by Hilda C. Graef, Ancient Christian Writers 18, ©1954; Symeon the New Theologian, The Discourses, The Classics of Western Spirituality, ©1980; by Paulist Press, Inc., New York/Mahwah, N.J. Used with the permission of Paulist Press, www.paulistpress.com.

Selected excerpts from Early Christian Fathers, translated and edited by Cyril C. Richardson, The Library of Christian Classics 1, ©1953; Christology of the Later Fathers, edited by Edward Rochie Hardy, The Library of Christian Classics 3, ©1954; Cyril of Jerusalem and Nemesius of Emesa, edited by William Telfer, The Library of Christian Classics 4, ©1955; Early Latin Theology, translated and edited by S. L. Greenslade, The Library of Christian Classics 5, ©1956; Augustine, Earlier Writings, translated by John H. S. Burleigh, The Library of Christian Classics 6, ©1953; Augustine, Confessions and Enchiridion, translated and edited by Albert C. Outler, The Library of Christian Classics 7, ©1955; Augustine, Later Works, translated by John Burnaby, The Library of Christian Classics 8, ©1955; Western Asceticism, translated by Owen Chadwick, The Library of Christian Classics 12, ©1958. Used by permission of Westminster John Knox Press.

Selected excerpts from St. Gregory of Nyssa, Commentary on the Song of Songs, translated by Casimir McCambley, ©1987. Used by permission of Helenic College Press.

Selected excerpts from Gregory of Nyssa, Homilies on Ecclesiastes: An English Version with Supporting Studies, translated by Stuart George Hall and Rachel Moriarty, ©1993. Used by permission of Verlag Walter de Gruyter.

Selected excerpts from The Works of Saint Augustine: A Translation for the 21st Century. Copyright 1990-. Used by permission of the Augustinian Heritage Institute.

Cover photograph: Scala/Art Resource, New York. View of the apse. S. Vitale, Ravenna, Italy.

Spine photograph: Byzantine Collection, Dumbarton Oaks, Washington D.C. Pendant cross (gold and enamel). Constantinople, late sixth century.

ISBN 0-8308-1479-5

Printed in the United States of America ∞

Library of Congress Cataloging-in-Publication Data has been requested.

P	25	24	23	22	21	20	19	18	17	16	15	14	13	12	11	10	9	8	7	6	5	4	3	2	1
Y	26	25	24	23	22	21	20	19	18	17	16	15	14	13	12	11	10	09	08	07	06	05			

ANCIENT CHRISTIAN COMMENTARY PROJECT RESEARCH TEAM

GENERAL EDITOR
Thomas C. Oden

ASSOCIATE EDITOR
Christopher A. Hall

OPERATIONS MANAGER AND TRANSLATIONS PROJECT COORDINATOR
Joel Elowsky

RESEARCH AND ACQUISITIONS DIRECTOR
Michael Glerup

EDITORIAL SERVICES DIRECTOR
Warren Calhoun Robertson

ORIGINAL LANGUAGE VERSION DIRECTOR
Konstantin Gavrilkin

GRADUATE RESEARCH ASSISTANTS

Jeffrey Finch	*Hsueh-Ming Liao*
Steve Finlan	*Michael Nausner*
Alexei Khamine	*Joel Scandrett*
Vladimir Kharlamov	*Baek-Yong Sung*
Susan Kipper	*Elena Vishnevskaya*
	Jeffery Wittung

ADMINISTRATIVE ASSISTANT
Judy Cox
Tod Bryant

Contents

General Introduction

The Ancient Christian Commentary on Scripture has as its goal the revitalization of Christian teaching based on classical Christian exegesis, the intensified study of Scripture by lay persons who wish to think with the early church about the canonical text, and the stimulation of Christian historical, biblical, theological and pastoral scholars toward further inquiry into scriptural interpretation by ancient Christian writers.

The time frame of these documents spans seven centuries of exegesis, from Clement of Rome to John of Damascus, from the end of the New Testament era to A.D. 750, including the Venerable Bede.

Lay readers are asking how they might study sacred texts under the instruction of the great minds of the ancient church. This commentary has been intentionally prepared for a general lay audience of nonprofessionals who study the Bible regularly and who earnestly wish to have classic Christian observation on the text readily available to them. The series is targeted to anyone who wants to reflect and meditate with the early church about the plain sense, theological wisdom and moral meaning of particular Scripture texts.

A commentary dedicated to allowing ancient Christian exegetes to speak for themselves will refrain from the temptation to fixate endlessly upon contemporary criticism. Rather, it will stand ready to provide textual resources from a distinguished history of exegesis that has remained massively inaccessible and shockingly disregarded during the last century. We seek to make available to our present-day audiences the multicultural, multilingual, transgenerational resources of the early ecumenical Christian tradition.

Preaching at the end of the first millennium focused primarily on the text of Scripture as understood by the earlier esteemed tradition of comment, largely converging on those writers that best reflected classic Christian consensual thinking. Preaching at the end of the second millennium has reversed that pattern. It has so forgotten most of these classic comments that they are vexing to find anywhere, and even when located they are often available only in archaic editions and inadequate translations. The preached word in our time has remained largely bereft of previously influential patristic inspiration. Recent scholarship has so focused attention upon post-Enlightenment historical and literary methods that it has left this longing largely unattended and unserviced.

This series provides the pastor, exegete, student and lay reader with convenient means to see what Athanasius or John Chrysostom or the desert fathers and mothers had to say about a particular text for preaching, for study and for meditation. There is an emerging awareness among Catholic, Protestant and Orthodox laity that vital biblical preaching and spiritual formation need deeper grounding beyond the scope of the historical-critical orientations that have governed biblical studies in our day.

Hence this work is directed toward a much broader audience than the highly technical and specialized scholarly field of patristic studies. The audience is not limited to the university scholar concentrating on the study of the history of the transmission of the text or to those with highly focused philological interests in textual morphology or historical-critical issues. Though these are crucial concerns for specialists, they are not the paramount interests of this series.

This work is a Christian Talmud. The Talmud is a Jewish collection of rabbinic arguments and comments on the Mishnah, which epitomized the laws of the Torah. The Talmud originated in approximately the same period that the patristic writers were commenting on texts of the Christian tradition. Christians from the late patristic age through the medieval period had documents analogous to the Jewish Talmud and Midrash (Jewish commentaries) available to them in the *glossa ordinaria* and catena traditions, two forms of compiling extracts of patristic exegesis. In Talmudic fashion the sacred text of Christian Scripture was thus clarified and interpreted by the classic commentators.

The Ancient Christian Commentary on Scripture has venerable antecedents in medieval exegesis of both eastern and western traditions, as well as in the Reformation tradition. It offers for the first time in this century the earliest Christian comments and reflections on the Old and New Testaments to a modern audience. Intrinsically an ecumenical project, this series is designed to serve Protestant, Catholic and Orthodox lay, pastoral and scholarly audiences.

In cases where Greek, Latin, Syriac and Coptic texts have remained untranslated into English, we provide new translations. Wherever current English translations are already well rendered, they will be utilized, but if necessary their language will be brought up to date. We seek to present fresh dynamic equivalency translations of long-neglected texts which historically have been regarded as authoritative models of biblical interpretation.

These foundational sources are finding their way into many public libraries and into the core book collections of many pastors and lay persons. It is our intent and the publisher's commitment to keep the whole series in print for many years to come.

Thomas C. Oden
General Editor

A Guide to Using This Commentary

Several features have been incorporated into the design of this commentary. The following comments are intended to assist readers in making full use of this volume.

Pericopes of Scripture

The scriptural text has been divided into pericopes, or passages, usually several verses in length. Each of these pericopes is given a heading, which appears at the beginning of the pericope. For example, the first pericope in the commentary on Proverbs is "1:1-7 Definitions, Purpose, Meaning." This heading is followed by the Scripture passage quoted in the Revised Standard Version (RSV) across the full width of the page. The Scripture passage is provided for the convenience of readers, but it is also in keeping with medieval patristic commentaries, in which the citations of the Fathers were arranged around the text of Scripture.

Overviews

Following each pericope of text is an overview of the patristic comments on that pericope. The format of this overview varies within the volumes of this series, depending on the requirements of the specific book of Scripture. The function of the overview is to provide a brief summary of all the comments to follow. It tracks a reasonably cohesive thread of argument among patristic comments, even though they are derived from diverse sources and generations. Thus the summaries do not proceed chronologically or by verse sequence. Rather they seek to rehearse the overall course of the patristic comment on that pericope.

We do not assume that the commentators themselves anticipated or expressed a formally received cohesive argument but rather that the various arguments tend to flow in a plausible, recognizable pattern. Modern readers can thus glimpse aspects of continuity in the flow of diverse exegetical traditions representing various generations and geographical locations.

Topical Headings

An abundance of varied patristic comment is available for each pericope of these letters. For this reason we have broken the pericopes into two levels. First is the verse with its topical heading. The patristic comments are then focused on aspects of each verse, with topical headings summarizing the essence of the patristic comment by evoking a key phrase, metaphor or idea. This feature provides a bridge by which modern readers can enter into the heart of the patristic comment.

Identifying the Patristic Texts

Following the topical heading of each section of comment, the name of the patristic commentator is given. An English translation of the patristic comment is then provided. This is immediately followed by the title of the patristic work and the textual reference—either by book, section and subsection or by book-and-verse references. If the notation differs significantly between the English-language source footnoted and other sources, alternate references appear in parentheses. Some differences may also be due to variant biblical versification or chapter and verse numbering. Where there is a scriptural quotation directly from the pericope under consideration, it is not footnoted.

The Footnotes

Readers who wish to pursue a deeper investigation of the patristic works cited in this commentary will find the footnotes especially valuable. A footnote number directs the reader to the notes at the bottom of the right-hand column, where in addition to other notations (clarifications or biblical cross references) one will find information on English translations (where available) and standard original-language editions of the work cited. An abbreviated citation (normally citing the book, volume and page number) of the work is provided. A key to the abbreviations is provided on page xv. Where there is any serious ambiguity or textual problem in the selection, we have tried to reflect the best available textual tradition.

Where original language texts have remained untranslated into English, we provide new translations. Wherever current English translations are already well rendered, they are utilized, but where necessary they are stylistically updated. A single asterisk (*) indicates that a previous English translation has been updated to modern English or amended for easier reading. The double asterisk (**) indicates either that a new translation has been provided or that some extant translation has been significantly amended. We have standardized spellings and made grammatical variables uniform so that our English references will not reflect the odd spelling variables of the older English translations. For ease of reading we have in some cases edited out superfluous conjunctions.

For the convenience of computer database users the digital database references are provided to either the Thesaurus Linguae Graecae (Greek texts) or to the Cetedoc (Latin texts) in the appendix found on pages 369-79.

ABBREVIATIONS

ACD	St. Augustine. *On Christian Doctrine.* Translated by D. W. Robertson Jr. Library of Liberal Arts. Indianapolis: Bobbs-Merrill, 1958.
ACW	Ancient Christian Writers: The Works of the Fathers in Translation. Mahwah, N.J.: Paulist Press, 1946-.
AHSIS	Dana Miller, ed. *The Ascetical Homilies of Saint Isaac the Syrian.* Boston: Holy Transfiguration Monastery, 1984.
ANF	A. Roberts and J. Donaldson, eds. Ante-Nicene Fathers. 10 vols. Buffalo, N.Y.: Christian Literature, 1885-1896. Reprint, Grand Rapids, Mich.: Eerdmans, 1951-1956. Reprint, Peabody, Mass.: Hendrickson, 1994.
AOV	Ambrose. *On Virginity.* Translated by Daniel Callam, CSB. Toronto: Peregrina Publishing Co., 1996.
CCL	Corpus Christianorum. Series Latina. Turnhout, Belgium: Brepols, 1953-.
CGSL	Cyril of Alexandria. *Commentary on the Gospel of St. Luke.* Translated by R. Payne Smith. Long Island, N.Y.: Studion Publishers, Inc., 1983.
CMWM	Dwight W. Young. *Coptic Manuscripts from the White Monastery: Works of Shenoute.* 2 vols. Vienna, Austria: In Kommission bei Verlag Brüder Hollinek, 1993.
CS	Cistercian Studies. Kalamazoo, Mich.: Cistercian Publications, 1973-.
CSCO	Corpus Scriptorum Christianorum Orientalium. Louvain, 1903-.
CSEL	Corpus Scriptorum Ecclesiasticorum Latinorum. Vienna, 1866-.
ECS	Pauline Allen, et al., eds. Early Christian Studies. Strathfield, Australia: St. Paul's Publications, 2001-.
ECTD	C. McCarthy, trans. and ed. *Saint Ephrem's Commentary on Tatian's Diatessaron: An English Translation of Chester Beatty Syriac MS 709. Journal of Semitic Studies* Supplement 2. Oxford: Oxford University Press for the University of Manchester, 1993.
EKOG	Eznik of Kolb. *On God.* Translated by Monica J. Blanchard and Robin Darling Young. Louvain: Peeters, 1998.
FC	Fathers of the Church: A New Translation. Washington, D.C.: Catholic University of America Press, 1947-.
FEF	W. A. Jurgens, ed. *The Faith of the Early Fathers.* Collegeville, Minn.: Liturgical Press, 1970.
FGFR	F. W. Norris. *Faith Gives Fullness to Reasoning: The Five Theological Orations of Gregory Nazianzen.* Leiden and New York: E. J. Brill, 1991.
GCS	Die griechischen christlichen Schriftsteller der ersten Jahrhunderte. Berlin: Akademie-Verlag, 1897-.
GNHE	Stuart George Hall, ed. *Gregory of Nyssa Homilies on Ecclesiastes: An English Version with Supporting Studies.* Proceedings of the Seventh International Colloquium on Gregory of Nyssa (St. Andrews, September 5-10, 1990). Berlin: Walter de Gruyter, 1993.
GNSS	*Saint Gregory of Nyssa. Commentary on the Song of Songs.* Translated by Casimir McCambley. Brookline, Mass.: Hellenic College Press, 1987.
GTPE	John Jarick. *Gregory Thaumaturgos: Paraphrase of Ecclesiastes.* Society of Biblical Literature, Septuagint and Cognate Studies Series 29. Atlanta: Scholars Press, 1990.
HOP	Ephrem the Syrian. *Hymns on Paradise.* Translated by S. Brock. Crestwood, N.Y.: St. Vladimir's Seminary Press, 1990.
ITA	*Isaiah Through the Ages.* Compiled and edited by Johanna Manly. Menlo Park, Calif.: Monastery Books, 1995.

IWG   Macarius. *Intoxicated with God: The Fifty Spiritual Homilies of Macarius.* Translated by George A. Maloney. Denville, N.J.: Dimension Books, 1978.

JCC   John Cassian. *Conferences.* Translated by Colm Luibheid. Classics of Western Spirituality. New York: Paulist, 1985.

LCC   J. Baillie et al., eds. The Library of Christian Classics. 26 vols. Philadelphia: Westminster, 1953-1966.

LCL   Loeb Classical Library. Cambridge, Mass.: Harvard University Press; London: Heinemann, 1912-.

LF   A Library of Fathers of the Holy Catholic Church Anterior to the Division of the East and West. Translated by members of the English Church. 44 vols. Oxford: John Henry Parker, 1800-1881.

MFC   Message of the Fathers of the Church. Edited by Thomas Halton. Collegeville, Minn.: Liturgical Press, 1983-.

NPNF   P. Schaff et al., eds. A Select Library of the Nicene and Post-Nicene Fathers of the Christian Church. 2 series (14 vols. each). Buffalo, N.Y.: Christian Literature, 1887-1894; Reprint, Grand Rapids, Mich.: Eerdmans, 1952-1956; Reprint, Peabody, Mass.: Hendrickson, 1994.

OFP   Origen. *On First Principles.* Translated by G. W. Butterworth. London: SPCK, 1936. Reprint, Gloucester, Mass.: Peter Smith, 1973.

OSW   *Origen: An Exhortation to Martyrdom, Prayer and Selected Writings.* Translated by Rowan A. Greer with preface by Hans Urs von Balthasar. Classics of Western Spirituality. New York: Paulist, 1979.

PDCW   *Pseudo-Dionysius: The Complete Works.* Translated by Colm Luibheid. Classics of Western Spirituality. New York: Paulist, 1987.

PG   J.-P. Migne, ed. Patrologiae cursus completus. Series Graeca. 166 vols. Paris: Migne, 1857-1886.

PL   J.-P. Migne, ed. Patrologia cursus completus. Series Latina. 221 vols. Paris: Migne, 1844-1864.

PO   Patrologia Orientalis. Paris, 1903-.

POG   Eusebius. *The Proof of the Gospel.* 2 vols. Translated by W. J. Ferrar. London: SPCK, 1920. Reprint, Grand Rapids, Mich.: Baker, 1981.

PS   R. Graffin, ed. Patrologia Syriaca. 3 vols. Paris: Firmin-Didot et socii, 1894-1926.

PSt   Patristic Studies. Washington, D.C.: Catholic University of America Press, 1922-.

PTA   Dieter Hagedorn, Rudolf Kassel, Ludwig Koenen and Reinhold Merkelbach, eds. Papyrologische Texte und Abhandlungen. Bonn: Habelt, 1968–.

SC   H. de Lubac, J. Daniélou et al., eds. Sources Chrétiennes. Paris: Editions du Cerf, 1941-.

SNTD   *Symeon the New Theologian: The Discourses.* Translated by C. J. de Catanzaro. Classics of Western Spirituality. New York: Paulist, 1980.

TCC   Richard A. Norris Jr., ed. *The Christological Controversy.* Philadelphia: Fortress, 1980.

TCH   *Two Coptic Homilies Attributed to Saint Peter of Alexandria: On Riches, On the Epiphany.* Translation and commentary by Birger Pearson and Tim Vivian with the assistance of Donald B. Spanel. Rome: C.I.M., 1993.

TLG   L. Berkowitz and K. Squiter, eds. *Thesaurus Linguae Graecae: Canon of Greek Authors and Works.* 2nd ed. Oxford: Oxford University Press, 1986.

TMB   Dimitri Z. Zaharopoulos. *Theodore of Mopsuestia on the Bible: A Study of His Old Testament Exegesis.* New York: Paulist, 1989.

TTC   William G. Rusch, ed. *The Trinitarian Controversy.* Philadelphia: Fortress, 1980.

TTH   Clark, G., M. Gibson, and M. Whitby, eds. Translated Texts for Historians. Liverpool: Liverpool University Press, 1985–.

WSA   J. E. Rotelle, ed. *Works of St. Augustine: A Translation for the Twenty-First Century.* Hyde Park, N.Y.: New City Press, 1995.

Introduction to Proverbs, Ecclesiastes and Song of Solomon

In the early church the critical study of the books of the Bible was not so far advanced that the ancient commentators were preoccupied with the questions of date, authorship, setting, context, source, genre and structure that energize so many scholars today. There was a developing sense already then, however, that the books of Proverbs and Ecclesiastes, together with the book of Job and certain of the Psalms, did have some of the common features that over time would lead them to become known collectively as the Wisdom literature of the canonical Old Testament. The Song of Solomon (Heb *Song of Songs*) was also seen as closely related because of a reputed Solomonic authorship, whereas the apocryphal books of Wisdom and of Ecclesiasticus or Sirach were affiliated on the basis of a similar content. Early groupings of the three canonical books treated in the present volume were made by Origen in the east (in the prologue to his *Commentary on the Song of Songs*) and in the west by Augustine of Hippo (in *City of God* 17.20). They, like most other ancient commentators, were unified in their conviction that Solomon was the author of all three books,[1] an opinion that is held by very few scholars today.

There was also a consensus that the contents of these books represented some of the finest wisdom about the deeper meaning of life that was available prior to the time that God became incarnate in the Lord Jesus Christ. Wisdom at times was even conceived as a personification or personified agent of God (see Prov 8—9), and thus the Wisdom literature collectively, then as now, was seen as an acknowledgment of the limits of human understanding and of the difficulty for human beings to grasp the ultimate meaning of life, short of an intervention from God that Christians came to call the incarnation. Such ambiguities, even the futility, frustration and mere vanity of life, could be stated but not finally solved short of an understanding of Christian revelation, in the view of the ancient Christian commentators.

The early Christian writers are often known as the early church fathers, a description that is not here intended to exclude women but only to acknowledge as a fact that the vast preponderance of surviving literature is written by men. Their writings are of various sorts, and not all of the ancient Christian commentators covered here wrote running commentary on the Bible that proceeds line by line and verse by verse. For the purpose of this series they are all called commentators, although it must be stressed that much of the contents of this volume are taken from a myriad of occasional writings and not exclusively from serial commentaries. These writers and their comments have been identified as a result of extensive searches performed within patristic source collections of all sorts, in English and in the original languages, conducted initially by the editorial staff of the ACCS project at Drew University and subsequently by authors of each

---

[1]A legend from the Talmud asserted that Solomon had written the Song of Songs in his lusty youth, Proverbs during the maturity of his middle age and Ecclesiastes in the skepticism of his advancing years. Origen and Theodoret of Cyr linked Proverbs, Ecclesiastes and the Song as constituting a three-step ladder that Solomon had provided for ascent in the stages of the spiritual life, from moral to natural to mystical or contemplative.

volume in this series. No retrieval system is perfect, though, and it must be acknowledged that final choices from them have had to be made on the basis of my subjective judgment.

The principles of selection and arrangement that I have followed are the same general principles outlined in the preceding general introduction to the series, and they include enduring relevance of the passages chosen, their penetrating significance, their practical applicability and their consensual agreement with one another but balanced at times by noteworthy individuality.[2] In principle, all substantive comments found for every verse of these three biblical books are included within this volume, which means that for the relatively few verses where no comments are recorded here no comments could be found or only passing references of little significance. No such criteria can be absolutely objective, and it is also obvious that one volume of selected excerpts from several writers, such as the present, may tell less than several volumes devoted separately to each of them, but the latter would have necessitated a much more extensive process. Existing translations of the ancient writers have been utilized when appropriate, and in other cases fresh translations have been made from the original languages, usually Greek or Latin, especially when none existed. A single asterisk (*) indicates that a previous English translation has been modernized, whereas a double asterisk (**) indicates that a new translation has been made, such as for the sake of better syntax. Spelling, punctuation and capitalization have been standardized, archaisms generally eliminated and grammatical variables made uniform. Biblical quotations in each excerpted selection that are not footnoted as to source come directly or nearly from the particular verse of Scripture (usually the RSV, or the LXX or Vulgate in translation) under which they are gathered, thus indicating their direct relationship to it. Every section begins with an overview of single sentences that summarize the excerpts selected for inclusion. Each collective overview thus in effect affords a retrospective conversation between the various commentators and their different points of view. Readers who wish to dig deeper are urged to consult the hundreds of original sources that are referenced. Biographical sketches and dates for all of the writers are given in an appendix at the end of this volume.

It should be noted that the Scriptural texts that these early writers were commenting upon were frequently not the same as the precise English text of the Revised Standard Version that is often used today and that is given and printed as the basis for the present and all other volumes in this series. The Greek, or Septuagint, versions of these biblical books are especially different in many ways from the Hebrew text upon which the RSV translation was made, and the implications of this point need to be drawn finely. Usually, when the ancient Christian commentators wrote in Greek they were commenting upon the books of the Bible as they were known in the Septuagint version of the Hebrew Scripture, and when they wrote in Latin they were commenting upon the Vulgate or Old Latin of the same body of material. The Vulgate, or Latin translation of the Hebrew that is associated with Jerome in the fifth century, was therefore not the same as the Septuagint, nor is the RSV based upon either. Less attention, for these reasons, will be paid in this volume to commentaries upon texts or portions of either Septuagint or Vulgate that do not survive in the RSV, although some attention will be given to them in the footnotes. When a scriptural passage that varies from the RSV is cited within a patristic quotation, it is indicated in the footnote by "cf."; and when a

---

[2]See Christopher A. Hall, *Reading Scripture with the Church Fathers* (Downers Grove, Ill.: InterVarsity Press, 1998); and Carl E. Braaten and Robert W. Jenson, eds., *Reclaiming the Bible for the Church* (Grand Rapids, Mich.: Eerdmans, 1995).

scriptural passage is merely evoked or indirectly invoked by allusion and without quotation marks, it is indicated in the footnote by "see."

At the outset it should also be remarked that the very earliest Christian commentators on many books of the Old Testament were to be found among the writers of the New Testament. They are excluded from the excerpts in the pages that follow by the fixed boundaries of the series in which this volume must play its part. Nonetheless, it seems at least appropriate to take some notice of these instances by way of background in order to illustrate the biblical precedent they offer and the continuity they establish. Like the early Christian commentators, such New Testament passages relate to the books of the Old Testament largely by way of allusion or paraphrase rather than by direct quotation, but the parallels are striking and do seem to be intended.[3] By far the largest number of instances for the present volume are found in the New Testament's references to Proverbs, too many in fact to enumerate them all.

For each of the biblical books covered by this volume there are some verse-by-verse, or running, commentaries that survive but do not exhaust the evidence. For the book of Proverbs, there is the extensive sequential commentary written by the Venerable Bede (672-735), as well as portions of verse-by-verse or running commentaries written by Basil the Great, John Chrysostom and Didymus the Blind, as well as the *scholia* of Evagrius of Pontus[4] and surviving fragments of commentaries by Hippolytus and Origen. On Ecclesiastes, the most useful verse-by-verse commentaries have been those of Gregory of Nyssa, Didymus the Blind and Jerome, together with the paraphrase (or metaphrase) of Gregory Thaumaturgus and the *scholia* of Evagrius of Pontus. For the Song of Solomon, by comparison, the most useful running commentaries have been those of Origen, Gregory of Elvira (spanning only the first three chapters), Apponius (whose work is little known), Gregory of Nyssa (in fifteen homilies), Theodoret of Cyr, Nilus of Ancyra, Gregory the Great (treating only part of the first chapter) and the Venerable Bede (a work both extensive and profound). Notwithstanding, it will be obvious that the vast majority of the selections have been taken from early writings of other sorts that contain quotations or allusions, albeit somewhat uneven in contents. It should be underlined that the works of early Christian authors who wrote sequential commentaries on the biblical books, therefore, do not begin to exhaust the surviving corpus of early Christian commentary, even by the same writers, that has survived in various occasional writings and is included here.

From the book of Proverbs, the aggregate of New Testament passages containing direct quotations or allusions is fifty-eight, the total comprised of five by direct quotation and fifty-three by indirect allusion. Although a complete run of such instances will be given below for the book of Ecclesiastes, where the total is much less, it will suffice at this point merely to note the one instance in Proverbs that is arguably the most important. Proverbs 8:22, "The Lord created me at the beginning of his work,[5] the first of his acts of old,"[6] finds its resonance and completion within the latter half of Revelation 3:14: "The words of the Amen, the faithful and true witness, the beginning of God's creation." It is not without reason, therefore, that this typological correspon-

---

[3]The parallels are laid out in the index of such quotations that is printed at the back of many standard editions of the Greek New Testament. I thank my colleague Professor Robert J. Owens for drawing my attention to this index and for other assistance.

[4]Not to be confused with Evagrius of Antioch or Evagrius Scholasticus. May also be referred to as Evagrius Ponticus or simply Evagrius.

[5]Heb *way*.

[6]LXX adds "He established me before time was."

dence came to be given high christological meaning, Jesus Christ being seen as the beginning of God's creation in the biblical commentaries of the early church. The earliest Christian commentators on Scripture were thus following the precedent of the New Testament writers who were commenting upon the Scriptures of the Old Testament. Jesus in the Gospel of John (Jn 16:25) had said: "These things I have spoken to you in proverbs,[7] but the time is coming when I shall no longer speak unto you in proverbs but plainly."

For the book of Proverbs, as indeed for all three books under consideration in the present volume, there is no consensus among modern scholars as to dating, structure, authorship or historical setting, but these matters need not detain us overmuch because they were of no great concern to the ancient Christian commentators. Indeed, as we have already remarked, the one point upon which the ancients were agreed, Solomonic authorship, is the one assertion that the modern scholars are largely agreed in rejecting. Neither the references to Solomon's composition of "three thousand proverbs" in 1 Kings 4:32 nor the attributions of Solomon's authorship in Proverbs 1:1, Proverbs 10:1 and Proverbs 25:1 seem as convincing to authorities now as they did to the early Christian writers,[8] and estimates today for dating the composition of Proverbs range all the way from the late eighth century B.C. down to the fourth century B.C.

Although the book of Proverbs was early recognized to consist of different sorts of materials, today there seems to be at least some agreement that the largest block of this material (Prov 10—29), which is quite possibly the oldest section, consists of proverbs properly so called. These were short, pithy sayings, often in the form of poetic couplets that presented some memorable truth in a striking way, either by antithesis or by comparison. These sayings convey pragmatic advice for the conduct of daily life, possibly to give practical advice for the young, especially young courtiers, about how to live in a way that would please God. As the contents of this volume will indicate, in the early Christian commentaries such proverbs could be further understood as riddles or enigmas that pointed to some deeper meaning for the living of life, often by way of moral instruction or exhortation or wisdom (Origen, Clement of Alexandria, Hippolytus, Didymus). These proverbs could also be considered sayings that, under the guise of the physical, signified the intelligible (Evagrius) or as "dark sayings" that related to the hidden and mysterious nature of God's glory (Cassiodorus, Origen, Gregory of Nyssa). Many of these writers, especially Origen, Gregory of Nyssa, Evagrius and Jerome, go out of their way to emphasize that the true meaning of Scripture is deeper than the literal or historical. Still another sort of material in the book is the longer instructional discourses, such as Proverbs 1—9 and Proverbs 22:17—24:22, and there is a brief and miscellaneous appendix consisting of the last two chapters (Prov 30—31). Solomon was generally regarded as the author of most of this material by the ancient Christian commentators, in spite of the varied contents contained within the book.

"The fear of the Lord is the beginning of wisdom" is the recurrent theme of Proverbs: a basic wisdom that is presented as necessary not only for pragmatic success but also for life to be lived wisely, even wisdom that comes from God and that conveys God to us. It is in the third grouping of material within Proverbs (Prov 1:20-33 and Prov 8:1—9:6) that this theme gets its fullest development. And it is within this group-

---

[7]Gk *paroimiais*; RSV *figures*.
[8]Among the ancient writers, I was able to find these transitions noticed only in the commentary of the Venerable Bede at Prov 10:1 and only in the comment of Hippolytus at Prov 25:1.

ing, in Proverbs 8:22-31, that one finds the female figure of personified Wisdom[9] that became identified with Christ as God's Word incarnate in patristic Christology and over which there are many theories as to its origin and meaning. Although Wisdom rejoices to be present in the inhabited world and delights to be with human beings (Prov 8:31), she was also present with God when the world was made (cf. Jn 1:1), and her existence before creation is affirmed no fewer than six times in Proverbs 8:22-26. For Proverbs 8:22 alone, twenty-eight passages of commentary from sixteen ancient authors are presented in this volume, mostly in approximate chronological order from Justin Martyr to Bede, so that the historical development of this verse's exegesis can be more clearly pondered.[10] Wisdom in Proverbs 8 is not only personified but also virtually hypostatized and developed into an almost metaphysical idea as a constituent part of the universe and, indeed, of the very being of God. Not only has this development been called the "Hebrew thinkers' closest approach to Greek philosophy,"[11] but it also leads directly into the descriptions of Christ as the Wisdom of God in 1 Corinthians 1:24 and in Hebrews 1:3, which, as already suggested, provided a rich foundation for christological thought on the part of early Christian commentators upon Scripture.[12] Most of those writers, however, as the catena at Proverbs 8:22 in this volume often bears witness, tended to apply the statement in that verse merely to the created humanity of the incarnate Christ and did not regard the verse as literally meaning "created" in the normal sense.[13]

Perhaps inevitable in a biblical book that consists of great numbers of profound sayings not connected by any overall narrative plan, much of the comment that these verses begat in the ancient Christian writers was also of a similar nature, "proverbs begetting fresh proverbs" as it were. Such comments, disparate though they may be, have their own interest and profundity, as is apparent from even an abbreviated and selective enumeration of their varied themes: the emperor's command to turn an ape into a lion (Prov 1:5); the concept of spiritual marriage in love of wisdom (Prov 4:6-8); assertion that there is more than one path of salvation (Prov 4:10-11); the case of an expert theologian who is also a shameless fornicator (Prov 5:3-4); the similarities of bees and ants and a description of "the ant of God" (Prov 6:6-8; 30:24-28); comment on "the hangover of God after his inebriation" (Prov 9:1); Christ as the true host and the food at every Eucharist (Prov 9:1; 23:1); early comment on "the Triad" or Trinity and interesting references to Plato, "who provided not the drink of faith but of unbelief" (Prov 9:2-5, 23:13-14); significance of a "golden ring in the snout of a pig" (Prov 11:22); a good husband as "the crown of the wife" rather than the other way around (Prov 12:1); advocacy of corporal punishment and even the discipline of the rod for the young (Prov 13:24; 23:13-14; 29:19); the bees that produced honey in the mouth of Ambrose (Prov 16:24); the theme that "money given to the poor is money lent to God" (Prov 19:17; 28:27); scorn at the emperor Julian the Apos-

---

[9]Such a positive personification in feminine terms, and the prominence of women in Prov 1—9 and Prov 30—31, has not gone without notice.

[10]For one interpretation of this development at the height of the Arian controversy, but only one, see Charles Kannengiesser, "The Bible in the Arian Crisis," pp. 217-28 of *The Bible in Greek Christian Antiquity*, ed. Paul M. Blowers (Notre Dame, Ind.: University of Notre Dame Press, 1997), esp. pp. 221, 224. For a perceptive analysis, see Manlio Simonetti, *Biblical Interpretation in the Early Church* (Edinburgh: T & T Clark, 1994), pp. 123, 127-28, 133-35.

[11]Robert C. Dentan in *The Interpreter's Dictionary of the Bible*, 4:305. For this and some other observations here I am indebted to the late Professor Dentan, my former mentor, and to Roland E. Murphy, O.Carm., in *The New Jerome Bible Commentary*, p. 450.

[12]See, for example, the identification of God's Son as Christ, the Wisdom of God, in Augustine's comment on Prov 30:3-4.

[13]Further see Robert J. Owens, "The Early Syriac Text of Ben Sira in the Demonstrations of Aphrahat," *Journal of Semitic Studies* 34:1 (1989), esp. p. 47.

tate, whose heart was not in the hand of God (Prov 21:1); development of early Christian theology of wealth and almsgiving (Prov 21:13; 22:1-2; 28:27; 30:8-9; 31:20); the canonicity and text of the Scriptures and their relationship to the Apocrypha as well as discussion of the Nicene Creed, divinity of the Holy Spirit and doctrine of the Trinity as ancient boundaries that must not be altered (Prov 22:28); historical examples of persons humiliated by their own pride (Prov 29:23); and the church, as the bride of Christ, standing at the gate of heaven (Prov 31:10-12, 31). The foregoing are but samples of the rich fare that the early Christian commentators provide to accompany and explain this book.

Overall, some 671 selections from some 64 ancient authors who wrote on the book of Proverbs have been chosen for inclusion here, this being by far the longest of the three books covered by this volume. Nine writers are represented by 30 or more selections each, the greatest numbers being from Augustine, who is the author of 74 of them; John Chrysostom, who authored 66; Origen with 55; and Ambrose with 45; followed by the Venerable Bede, Clement of Alexandria, Gregory the Great and Caesarius of Arles, each with 33. A second and smaller group represented by fewer than 30 down to 20 selections each is comprised of Jerome with 29, Basil the Great with 28 and John Cassian with 23. Behind them and showing fewer than 20 selections each down to 10 are Hippolytus and Cyril of Alexandria each with 18, Athanasius with 16, Evagrius Ponticus and the Apostolic Constitutions with 13 each and Gregory of Nyssa with 11. And after them comes a variegated group of 47 additional writers represented by fewer than 10 selections each, for a total of 131 selections.

The book of Ecclesiastes, and indeed the name, for those ancient writers then as for us today, posits the existence of an office or officer whose function is to assemble and to teach an assembly. The name *Ecclesiastes*, coming from the Greek Septuagint and Latin Vulgate translations of the Hebrew *Koheleth* or *Qoheleth*, a name not found in biblical literature outside the book itself, has come to identify such a person who has been known and rendered in English variously as "the Preacher," "the Teacher," "the Speaker," "the Convenor" or "the Ecclesiast." This person is no longer seen today as being Solomon, except in the sense of a personification or literary device, an acknowledgment that Solomon was renowned in the ancient world for his wisdom. The name *Solomon* does not appear anywhere in that book. Nonetheless, the relationship of Ecclesiastes to a collective gathering or congregation or even church by means of the similar words *qāhāl* in Hebrew, *ekklēsia* in Greek, and *ecclesia* in Latin, all meaning "assembly," was not lost on the ancient Christian writers, and the ascription to Solomon may have helped to facilitate the acceptance of these books within the Christian canon of Scripture. The translation as "Preacher" seems to go back ultimately to the Latin commentary on this book in the late fourth century by Jerome, who rendered the same word as *concionator* and led the sixteenth-century Reformers along his line of reasoning, although it is hardly the case that this person in the biblical book of Ecclesiastes can be said to be preaching in any sense generally accepted either then or now.

The structure and message of Ecclesiastes are not clear, and various modern commentators generally fail to agree about them with each other. Its structure, its historical setting and even its probable modern dating to the third century B.C. (around 350-250 B.C.) were not of much interest or concern to the ancient Christian commentators, and their views as to its message will gradually unfold in this volume as readers survey and reflect upon the excerpts from the early Christian writings that are presented. The apparent contradictions in its message were as apparent to those patristic exegetes then as they still are to scholars today. One consistent message within Ecclesiastes does seem to be an implication that traditional wisdom is inadequate, that the conventional values of secularized religion are generally not worth the effort, that illusions are easily shattered and that simplistic pronouncements inherited from the past must always be questioned. The fact that, in spite of such challenging assertions, this book did find a place in the Christian canon of Scripture as early as the list compiled by Melito of Sardis in the late second century A.D. and retained that place in spite of doubts raised by Theodore of Mopsuestia as late as the fifth century, may well indicate that already in Christian history such skeptical thought was nevertheless seen to merit a place within, rather than outside, the Christian community in the same way as the book came to be included within the canon. It presents a "wisdom of the heart" that needs to be pondered. It reminds us that life is empty without a firm faith in God, and it signals for us that, for the early Christian commentators, the ultimate answer to such assertions of meaninglessness was none other than Jesus Christ.

Who then were the early Christian commentators on the book of Ecclesiastes and what were some of their perspectives? It has already been noted that the earliest Christian commentators on many books of the Old Testament were the writers of the New Testament, and in the case of Ecclesiastes there are six comments on it located in the New Testament that constitute the earliest stratum of evidence. We now survey this evidence, each passage from Ecclesiastes being followed by the words of the New Testament in which it finds its echo and comment.

Ecclesiastes 1:2, "Vanity of vanity, all is vanity," is to be compared with Romans 8:20, "The creation was subjected to futility, not of its own will but by the will of him who subjected it in hope."

Ecclesiastes 5:15, "As he came from his mother's womb he shall go again, naked as he came, and shall take nothing for his toil, which he may carry away in his hand," finds resonance in 1 Timothy 6:7: "We brought nothing into the world, and we cannot take anything out of the world."

Ecclesiastes 7:9, "Be not quick to anger," is paralleled in James 1:19: "Let every man be quick to hear, slow to speak, slow to anger."

Ecclesiastes 7:20, "Surely there is not a righteous man on earth who does good and never sins," is echoed in Romans 3:10-12: "None is righteous, no, not one; no one understands, no one seeks for God. All have turned aside, together they have gone wrong; no one does good, not even one."

Ecclesiastes 11:5, "As you do not know how the spirit comes to the bones in the womb of a woman with child, so you do not know the work of God who makes everything," finds its match in John 3:8: "The wind blows where it wills, and you hear the sound of it, but you do not know whence it comes or whither it goes; so it is with every one who is born of the Spirit."

Ecclesiastes 12:14, "God will bring every deed into judgment, with every secret thing, whether good or evil," needs to be read alongside 2 Corinthians 5:10: "We must all appear before the judgment seat of Christ, so that each one may receive good or evil, according to what he has done in the body."

Moving on after the time of the Bible, we encounter the ancient Christian commentators, the principal subject of this volume. Broadly speaking, for the book of Ecclesiastes a total of some fifty commentaries of a more intentional sort (including catenas but not including other occasional comments in scattered writings) have been identified from the patristic period. This total includes those that still survive and those that do not, those only known in fragments or by reference, and some that have and others that have not been edited, translated or published.[14] The earliest is that of Melito of Sardis from the late second century, of which little is known. The writing of Origen on Ecclesiastes had a particular influence in the ancient Christian Greek world, especially from the way that he classified the books attributed to Solomon, and it was Origen who set the highest standards for deeply perceptive exegesis and verse-by-verse running commentary in the early church. His disciple Gregory Thaumaturgus paraphrased the book to give it a more directly Christian meaning, especially so as not to make God seem responsible for the human predicament.[15] Ecclesiastes was of less interest to Latin writers in the early Christian West, although the commentary of Jerome was not without significance. Following the example of Thaumaturgus, Jerome also proceeded to correct some of the pre-Christian wisdom that was thought to come from Solomon and to give it Christian meaning. The most profound of the ancient commentaries, at least of those that survive in print, seems to have been the eight homilies of Gregory of Nyssa, even though they cover somewhat less than the first three chapters of the book. For Nyssa, as for Jerome, there was an attempt to portray Solomon as more reserved and less affirmative regarding the carefree enjoyment of temporal goods. Still more sophisticated, however, was the Greek commentary of Gregory of Agrigentum, of which a critical edition is in preparation at this time of writing.[16]

Overall, some 346 selections from some 46 ancient authors who wrote on Ecclesiastes have been chosen for inclusion in the present volume, the most frequent in choice being Didymus the Blind (69 selections), Gregory of Nyssa (35), Ambrose (27), Augustine (26), Gregory the Great (20), Origen (18), Evagrius of Pontus (15), John Cassian (13), Chrysostom (12), Athanasius (11), Bede (11) and Jerome (11). Beyond these 12 authors, each of whom represents 10 or more selections, there are only 6 more writers from whom the numbers of selections range from 9 down to 5: Gregory Nazianzus (7), Basil the Great (7), Gregory Thaumaturgus (8), Olympiodorus (6), Cyril of Jerusalem (5) and Apostolic Constitutions (5). Beyond them, there are still many more.

The Song of Solomon, our third biblical book for consideration in this volume, came to be called by this title in English versions from the time of the King James Version down through the RSV and NRSV under the influence of a previously supposed Solomonic authorship, now generally discounted, that also gave it a certain tangential affiliation with the literature of wisdom. The book is also known as Song of Songs (from the first two words of the first verse of the Hebrew text) and, in Roman Catholic tradition, usually as Canticle of Canticles, the last two titles being translations of the Hebrew superlative and thus indicating that it was regarded as "the greatest song" or "the song sublime." All three titles, as well as the more literal Songs of Songs that is used to translate Bede's Latin plural Cantica Canticorum, refer to the same scriptural reality in the excerpts chosen here. All such titles impute to the book a certain unity of theme and content, even an affiliation with the literature of wisdom, in spite of a lack of clear structure and the probability of plural authorship, and many of the ancient authors comment upon the book's title. Unity is also suggested by the

---

[14]An extensive list is given by the Polish scholar Marek Starowieski in his superb essay "Le Livre de l'Ecclésiaste dans l'antiquité chrétienne," *Gregory of Nyssa: Homilies on Ecclesiastes: An English Version with Supporting Studies*, Proceedings of the Seventh International Colloquium on Gregory of Nyssa (St. Andrews, September 5-10, 1990), ed. Stuart George Hall (Berlin and New York: Walter de Gruyter, 1993), pp. 405-40. See also Marc Hirshman, "The Greek Fathers and the Aggada on Ecclesiastes: Formats of Exegesis in Late Antiquity," *Hebrew Union College Annual* 59:1 (1988): 137-65.

[15]There is merit in the translation of this paraphrase by Michael Slusser published in 1998 (FC 98), but on the whole I have preferred that of John Jarick (1990). Their subdivisions are numbered differently.

[16]PG 98:741-1181, forthcoming in *Corpus Christianorum, series Graeca*, edited by Gerard H. Ettlinger, S.J.

dialogical interplay of the voices of two lovers, one male and one female, and their professions of erotic love for each other. The book seems to be a loose collection or anthology of songs, poems or lyrics, counted as anywhere from six to as many as forty in number by individual scholars who think they know, and modern authorities tend to believe that this material was composed, or at least revised, at various times perhaps over the fifth and fourth centuries B.C.

Such agonizing questions of modern scholarship were not paramount in the minds of most early Christian commentators, any more than the obvious and literal meaning of the contents as all having to do with sensual, sexual love between a man and a woman. Even in Judaic tradition as well as generally in the early Christian world, the book's contents were treated allegorically or figuratively, although the book does not mention God or purport to be telling its readers a sacred history. Rabbi Akiba at the rabbinical council of Jamnia in the late first century of the common era is famous for his remark that "the Song of Songs is the Holy of Holies." When the book is treated allegorically or spiritually, as most patristic commentators did, its mosaic of love stories is seen as suggestive of the relationship between a bride and a bridegroom, between God and Israel as God's chosen people, between God and the individual soul, between Christ and the individual soul, or between Christ and the church.

Unlike in Ecclesiastes, the name of Solomon does appear in the Song, some six times, but not as the speaker. An early endorsement of Solomonic authorship, which is not demanded by the book's references to him, was given by Origen in the third century, as is attested in some of the excerpts that are included here. This endorsement, together with the early Christian tradition of allegorical interpretation, has worked to ensure the book's place within the Wisdom literature and its location within the Christian canon. It was, however, one of the last books to be so included. Gregory of Nyssa and Augustine remarked, each in their own ways, that if a literal reading of Scripture is without spiritual profit, then a more allegorical or figurative interpretation must be pursued.

The earliest surviving Christian commentary on the Song was by Hippolytus of Rome, surviving in fragments that span only the first three chapters, but it was Origen who wrote the commentary whose influence was all-pervasive.[17] Origen's spiritual interpretation of the Song as an allegory of Christ and the church seems in its own way to draw upon the one reference to the Song in the New Testament, where Paul says of marriage in Ephesians 5:32: "This mystery is a profound one, and I am saying that it refers to Christ and the church." Only three books of Origen's complete commentary, as well as two additional homilies, are extant, each fragment covering just slightly more than the same first two chapters of the Song, and all of these survive not in their Greek originals but only in the Latin translations of Jerome or Rufinus. More so than those of Hippolytus, the writings of Origen display the fertile imagination of allegory in interpreting the Song's contents, and his principles of exegesis are set forth with special clarity in his remarks on the Song's first two verses from the prologue of his commentary in the excerpts that follow. Origen's methodology is generally to expound first the literal or "superficial" meaning and then to proceed

---

[17]For his approach, interpretation and influence, see E. Ann Matter, *The Voice of My Beloved: The Song of Songs in Western Medieval Christianity* (Philadelphia: University of Pennsylvania Press, 1990), esp. chap. 2. See also Joseph W. Trigg, "Commentary on the Song of Songs," in *Origen*, The Early Church Fathers (London and New York: Routledge, 1998), pp. 45-49; and Mark W. Elliott, *The Song of Songs and Christology in the Early Church 381-451* (Tübingen: Mohr Siebeck, 2000).

to the "inner meaning" or "mystical explanation," as he calls it.[18] In the profundity of Origen's thought, the church already existed from the creation of the world, and Christ's mystical union with it at the incarnation marked the transition in time from law to grace. In many ways, Origen's use of allegory is at its most profound in his exposition of the Song's famous "black and beautiful" passages at Song 1:5 and Song 1:6, excerpted below, in lines of interpretation that were evidently developed and augmented by his followers and that constitute the most sophisticated Christian commentary on race and skin color in the legacy of the ancient church. It is a pity that they are not better known and used in today's well-intentioned but theologically somewhat impoverished discussions of the same subject.

Nearly a century and a half after Origen, a similar profundity and methodology but with some difference of terminology and approach and with a greater emphasis upon mysticism and spiritual progress, is found in the fifteen surviving homilies of Gregory of Nyssa on the Song, whose commentary extends into the middle of the sixth of the book's eight chapters.[19] With Gregory as earlier with Origen, his commentary even in its side comments is capable of surprising depth, as in his observations about the inadequacy of religious language, the interchangeability of divine genders and the absence of sexuality in God, made almost at random in his passing remarks upon Song 3:11 that are excerpted below. Ranking close behind Origen and Gregory in originality, and close to them even in profundity, is the commentary of Nilus of Ancyra, represented here by only a few selections and still in the process of being edited as this essay is written.[20] Traces of Origen are also clearly evident in the virtually complete, sequential commentary of Theodoret of Cyr from the mid-fifth century, spiritual and allegorical in approach (even christological and ecclesiological), in spite of his Antiochene background.[21] In the patristic west of the later fourth century, traces of Origen's approach are evident in various scattered writings of Ambrose, and similarities to Origen can also be found in the verse-by-verse commentary of Aponius, possibly an early Italian abbot, who wrote twelve books on all of the Song's eight chapters. The allegorical approach of Origen was also spread and popularized by Jerome (c. 347-420), Augustine of Hippo (354-430) and others.

The single writer in the early church favoring a literal and rationalizing exegesis of the Song was Theodore of Mopsuestia (360-429) of the school of Antioch, a sample of whose comment is presented below, who clearly implied that the literal is all there is, and whose views were condemned by the Fifth Ecumenical Council (Constantinople II, 553). Theodore's literal interpretation of the Song as an account of the marriage of Solomon to Pharaoh's daughter also finds echoes in his contemporary Julian of Eclanum, a Pelagian theologian and bishop, fragments of whose commentary are also presented here, although Theodore's literal interpretation is not followed in Theodoret of Cyr, who nearly matched Theodore in time and place. Located in the West and less easy to categorize are Gregory the Great (590-604), who wrote two homilies containing important and at times

---

[18]Further see Ronald Heine, "Reading the Bible with Origen," in *The Bible in Greek Christian Antiquity*, ed. Paul M. Blowers (Notre Dame, Ind.: University of Notre Dame Press, 1997), pp. 131-48.

[19]On this work see Ronald E. Heine, "Gregory of Nyssa's Apology for Allegory," *Vigiliae Christianae* 38 (1984):360-70.

[20]Of special interest may be his comments on the "bow and arrow" method of scriptural interpretation, at Song 2:7 *ad loc.*

[21]Theodoret also tells us (at Song 1:1, excerpted below) why he can borrow from his predecessors and not consider it to be plagiarism. Further see Jean-Noel Guinot, "Theodoret of Cyrus: Bishop and Exegete," in *The Bible in Greek Christian Antiquity*, ed. Paul M. Blowers (Notre Dame, Ind.: University of Notre Dame Press, 1997), pp. 163-93.

even mystical commentary that survive covering the first eight verses,[22] and the Venerable Bede (672-735), who composed a verse-by-verse explication that covers most of the Song's text in five books.[23]

Today, with the decline of allegory in scriptural exegesis, there seems a widespread consensus that the Song's contents, for a start, should be read as a literal appreciation of human love and the joys of mutuality in sex, but, paradoxically, there is also a lingering conviction among scholars that no mere literal reading can exhaust their meaning.[24] As they review the biblical and patristic evidence there is more here, they say, than a collection of simple human love songs. Certainly the book's final remarks, such as the declaration in Song 8:6-7 that love is stronger than death, natural catastrophe or wealth, and the admonition in Song 8:14 to ascend rapidly upon the scented mountains, give a positive and even transcendent note to the book's message about fidelity and mutual enjoyment in sex and marriage, whether the biblical text and the patristic commentators are read literally or figuratively and whether that message is seen as being more about desire than about satisfaction.

Overall, some 368 selections from some 34 ancient authors who wrote on the Song of Solomon have been chosen for inclusion here. Eleven writers are represented by 10 or more selections each, by far the greatest numbers being from Ambrose, who is the author of 81 of them, and Theodoret of Cyr, who is the author of 45. Ambrose was obviously quite familiar with the book's contents, although there is no evidence that he ever wrote a running commentary upon it, whereas Theodoret did. Others represented by the greatest numbers include Augustine with 33, Origen and Jerome with 25, Gregory of Nyssa with 23, Gregory the Great and Bede each with 19, Cyril of Alexandria with 18 and Gregory of Elvira and Aponius with 12 each. Behind them are Cyril of Jerusalem with 8, Nilus of Ancyra with 7 and Hippolytus and Cassiodorus with 5 each. All the rest have fewer than five.

In retrospect, since the purpose of this series is not to provide a commentary upon the commentators, much less to become immersed in the thicket of modern critical studies about the biblical text, it seems best to refrain from any more seemingly erudite observations upon the various methods of exegesis that these various writers employed. It is often remarked, although the distinction may be overdrawn, that commentators from the school of Alexandria, such as Origen, were generally more interested in the deeper and spiritual, or allegorical, meaning of the sacred page and were more ready to interpret one passage of Scripture by a direct application of some other passage to it. Writers of the school of Antioch, such as Chrysostom or Theodore of Mopsuestia, tended to eschew allegorizing in favor of seeking moral

---

[22]Cf. Joan M. Petersen, "The Influence of Origen upon Gregory the Great's Exegesis of the Song of Songs," *Studia Patristica* 18:1 (1985):343-47.

[23]A fresh translation of blocks of excerpts from many of the patristic and medieval writers who wrote running commentaries on the Song will be found in the helpful book edited by Richard A. Norris Jr., *The Song of Songs: Interpreted by Early Christian and Medieval Commentators* (Grand Rapids, Mich.: Eerdmans, 2003) which appeared just as the present volume was nearing completion. An earlier work from the last century, of similar scope, was Richard F. Littledale, *A Commentary on the Song of Songs from Ancient and Medieval Sources* (London: Joseph Masters and Son, 1869). A modern survey and critique of such early writers is provided by Marvin H. Pope, *Song of Songs: A New Translation with Introduction and Commentary* (Anchor Bible; Garden City, N.Y.: Doubleday. 1977). pp. 112-25. Making its appearance too late for consideration in the present volume was Russell J. DeSimone, *The Bride and the Bridegroom of the Fathers: An Anthology of Patristic Interpretations of the Song of Songs* (Sussidi Patristici 10; Rome: Istituto Patristico Augustinianum, 2000).

[24]For a collection of recent scholarly essays that affirm the literal meaning of the Song but do not regard the literal as the only or primary meaning, see Richard W. Corney, "What Does 'Literal Meaning' Mean? Some Commentaries on the Song of Songs"; R. A. Norris, "The Soul Takes Flight: Gregory of Nyssa and the Song of Songs"; and Ellen F. Davis, "Romance of the Land in the Song of Songs," all in *The Anglican* 25:2 (October 1996), all republished in the *Anglican Theological Review* 80:4 (fall 1998). For a recent disagreement with them, see Tremper Longman III, *Song of Songs*, New International Commentary on the Old Testament (Grand Rapids, Mich.: Eerdmans, 2001), esp. p. 35.

lessons that could be drawn from the text.[25]

All told, considering the three biblical books under review, there are some 1,385 passages of patristic commentary selected and excerpted from some 84 different patristic authors for inclusion within the present volume. Very few of these ancient commentators, however, offered comments upon the works of their predecessors by name, in spite of an amazing degree of consensus that is often evident in the particular interpretations that they offered. For the most part, these writers seem little concerned to place their own works in the context of their predecessors, rarely naming them by name or discerning a consensus among them or even showing awareness that there was a historical continuum of interpretation, even though occasional instances can be detected such as the influence of Origen. It should be emphasized, above all, that most of the patristic writers, of whatever school of exegesis, were so thoroughly imbued with Scripture that much of their commentary thereupon must be extracted from works whose primary intention was to discuss other subjects of Christian faith and teaching rather than to be independent running commentaries written upon particular biblical books.

Another way to state the above is to observe that Christian theology in the early history of the church was written with extensive and constant reference to what the Bible had said, and biblical commentators then, in some contrast to the present, were not seeking to establish their academic reputations by becoming the leading published authorities solely upon one or two biblical books by writing technical commentaries upon them. Modern theologians and biblical scholars may well claim, as many do, that the necessities of the world and worldview and context of scholarship in which we now live demand that they write their futuristic theologies and their critical commentaries in the ways that they often do. It is not the purpose of this series to take issue with what they do but only to indicate that there was also an earlier way, closer to the time of the Bible and lasting for several hundreds of years, that still has much to say to us and need not be rejected in order to be truly modern. Whereas today the Old Testament is often presented as the Hebrew Scriptures and taught historically only within an ancient Near Eastern context, the material from these earlier commentaries dates from a period when the entire Bible was thought to be a book about Christ and for the church—past, present and to come. It is this older wisdom that this series seeks to recover from the earliest Christian times down to the mid-eighth century, drawing from the doctrinal treatises, paraphrases, catechetical instructions, pastoral writings, letters, homilies, and other works of all those writers, as well as from their running commentaries whenever they happen to survive.

Therefore, the excerpts here presented constitute the best catena, or chain, of interpretation that could be identified, extracted and assembled from these classical writers who have clarified and interpreted the sacred text for the church over the centuries, especially insofar as this rich Christian heritage can be useful today for purposes of preaching, teaching, prayer, reflection and meditation. The overviews that precede each group of passages attempt to establish links within each chain. The material is not presented primarily for a technical academic readership, although one may hope that it will also be of use to the increasing num-

---

[25]Today the two schools tend to be regarded more as complementary than as opposed to each other, and their dichotomy has been challenged. Cf. Joseph W. Trigg, *Biblical Interpretation* (Message of the Fathers of the Church 9; Wilmington, Del.: Michael Glazier, 1988), esp. pp. 31, 34; and Robert Wilken, *Remembering the Christian Past* (Grand Rapids, Mich.: Eerdmans, 1995), esp. p. 107. For a description of the two schools more in terms of reaction and polemic, see Karlfried Froehlich, *Biblical Interpretation in the Early Church* (Philadelphia: Fortress, 1984), esp. pp. 19-22, and for the same in terms of rivalry and opposition, see Rowan A. Greer, pp. 176-99 of "The Christian Bible and Its Interpretation," in *Early Biblical Interpretation*, ed. James L. Kugel and Rowan A. Greer (Philadelphia: Westminster Press, 1986).

ber of scholars today who believe that modern exegesis must give some consideration to the meanings that Scripture has received from successive ages of committed Christians throughout the history of the church. This material is not presented as an alternative to modern or so-called postmodern critical scholarship but as a much-needed and long-neglected adjunct or supplement to it, offering earlier Christian perspectives that have sometimes been forgotten, sometimes ignored and perhaps sometimes even suppressed.

In the preparation of this volume, I have been greatly assisted by two teams of invaluable assistants: my own research team, as well as the editorial team from the offices of the Ancient Christian Commentary on Scripture at Drew University. Among the former I want to give thanks for the research of Victor Gorodenchuk, Richard Mammana and the Reverend Barrington Bates, all of whom did so much of the initial investigation into the sources under my direction. Likewise my gratitude is due also to the editorial supervision of the Reverend Joel Elowsky, who headed the ACCS team from the offices at Drew, as well as to Calhoun Robertson for his extensive editorial work and to Jeffrey Finch, Alexei Khamine, Michael Nausner, Dr. Mark Sheridan and Dr. Marco Conti for their valued assistance in the professional translation of various texts from other languages. Above all, however, my appreciation goes to Dr. Thomas Oden for his conceptualization of this project and for inviting me to be a part of it.

The fact remains, let it be underlined in conclusion, that the writers from this early period in Christian history believed that God was still speaking to them in Scripture as they prayerfully studied it and wrote about it. The modern historical-critical method of biblical scholarship, insofar as it tends to locate the "real" meaning of Scripture only in an academic past and not within the church's broader tradition of interpretation, was not an approach that they would have particularly recognized or comprehended. All too often, modern biblical commentaries seem to posit a necessary gap between the then and the now, focusing overmuch on the distant textual origins or upon the immediate present and choosing to ignore the intervening centuries of foundation and development. It is possible for a first-rate commentary to be written that speaks to us today and avoids an endless fixation upon modern textual and critical analysis, although even here the gap can remain because the long and distinguished tradition of exegesis from the early Christian centuries has not been readily available.[26]

The present volume, as indeed this entire series, seeks to give easy access to this older material, as it seeks to span the gap of hundreds of years of interpretation that have elapsed between manuscript and modern application. As we now invite these ancient commentators to speak to us today, I pause to dedicate this volume to one who has most inspired me in the scholarly study of the early church and its history and who needs no other introduction: Professor Henry Chadwick.

J. Robert Wright
St. Mark's Professor of Ecclesiastical History
General Theological Seminary
New York City
Easter 2004

---

[26]A fine modern commentary upon the three books under discussion that speaks well to modern readers and neither ignores modern critical exegesis nor is overcome by it, but whose scope and intention does not include extensive consideration of the early Christian commentaries, is Ellen F. Davis, *Proverbs, Ecclesiastes and the Song of Songs* (Louisville, Ky.: Westminster John Knox Press, 2000).

PROVERBS

1:1-7 DEFINITIONS, PURPOSE, MEANING

¹*The proverbs of Solomon, son of David, king of Israel:*

²*That men may know wisdom and instruction,*
  understand words of insight,
³*receive instruction in wise dealing,*
  righteousness, justice, and equity;
⁴*that prudence may be given to the simple,*
  knowledge and discretion to the youth—
⁵*the wise man also may hear and increase in learning,*
  and the man of understanding acquire skill,*
⁶*to understand a proverb and a figure,*
  the words of the wise and their riddles.

⁷*The fear of the LORD is the beginning of knowledge;*
  fools despise wisdom and instruction.

*Vg *A man of understanding shall possess governments.*

OVERVIEW: A proverb is a riddle or enigma that points to a deeper meaning, often by way of moral instruction or exhortation or wisdom for the living of life (ORIGEN, CLEMENT OF ALEXANDRIA, HIPPOLYTUS). It is even a sign or roadmap (DIDYMUS). It is also a saying that, under the guise of the physical, signifies the intelligible (EVAGRIUS). A proverb is called a parable in Greek and a simile in Latin (BEDE).

The authorship of this book has long been ascribed to Solomon (ORIGEN), who is also understood as a type of Christ the Lord (HIPPOLYTUS). The wisdom in Solomon's proverbs comes from secular as well as religious sources (AUGUSTINE), and it is closely related to the true justice and wisdom by which a just ruler is meant to govern (JEROME). Such wisdom can be subtle in its meaning, as "the wisdom of a serpent" (JEROME, AUGUSTINE), but to the faithful heart it can become clear (CHRYSOSTOM). Even the wise can increase in wisdom (ORIGEN), but they must take care not to fall in the process of doing so (GREGORY THE GREAT).

Proverbs can also be called "dark sayings," because they relate to the hidden and mysterious nature of God's glory (CASSIODORUS, ORIGEN). They contain hidden meanings that carry indirect signification (GREGORY OF NYSSA). Even the fear of

---

God, which is the beginning of wisdom, is God's free gift to us, for which no prior wisdom is necessary (Prosper of Aquitaine). The fear of God can dissolve our human pride (Augustine), as we practice self-restraint in an effort for something better in life (Clement of Alexandria). Wherever God exists, there also God is feared (Tertullian). The fool lacks fear and denies God (Theodoret of Cyr). To fear the Lord is to renounce sin (Ambrose), but the true source of wisdom is virtuous living (Chrysostom). Knowledge without practice is insufficient (Didymus). The beginning of discernment is piety (Chrysostom). Servile fear, however, differs from friendly fear (Bede).

1:1-2 Solomon and His Proverbial Wisdom

A Proverb Has a Deeper Meaning. Origen: [Solomon] entitles this very book "Proverbs." That word means something that is said openly but points to something deep within. Even the ordinary use of proverbs teaches this, and John in his Gospel writes that the Savior said this, "I have spoken to you in proverbs; the hour will come when I shall no longer speak to you in proverbs but tell you plainly of the Father."[1] So much for the title of the book itself. Commentary on the Song of Songs, Prologue.[2]

A Cryptic Saying with an Indirect Meaning. Origen: A proverb is a cryptic saying that has an indirect meaning. [Solomon] ruled in Israel, in order to understand wisdom and instruction. Wisdom is the spiritual knowledge pertaining to God, bodiless hosts and judgment; it also includes teaching about providence and unveils contemplation on the subjects of ethics, natural sciences and theology. Or rather, wisdom is the knowledge of both physical and spiritual worlds and of the judgment and providence pertaining to them. On the other hand, instruction is the disciplining of the passions of that passionate or unreasonable part of the soul. One who has advanced to the level of theology has learned wisdom. Exposition on Proverbs, Fragment 1.1.[3]

Like a Sign or Map. Didymus the Blind: A proverb is a saying such as, "War is pleasant to the inexperienced," or "A drop constantly falling hollows a stone." The name *proverb* derived from the fact that once roads were marked off with no signs. Now there are signs, which are called *miliaria* (milestones) by the Romans, while they were just called signs before. Ancient people set them in certain places and then inscribed them with certain information and questions. So they fulfilled two purposes. On the one hand, they indicated to the traveler the length of the journey. On the other, when one read the inscription and kept busy comprehending it, one was relieved of weariness. Therefore a road is called in Greek *oimos*, from which is derived the word *paroimia*, which means "proverb." Commentary on the Proverbs of Solomon, Fragment 1.1[4]

Moral Instructions from the King in Israel. Origen: Solomon, who apparently served the will of the Holy Spirit in these three books, is called in Proverbs "Solomon, son of David, who ruled in Israel.". . .

Therefore, in the first book, Proverbs, when he establishes us by moral instructions, he is said to be "king in Israel" but not yet in Jerusalem, because although we are called Israel because of faith, that does not yet mark an attainment by which we should appear to have arrived at the heavenly Jerusalem. Commentary on the Song of Songs, Prologue.[5]

Proverb a Mode of Prophecy. Clement of Alexandria: The proverb, according to barbarian philosophy, is called a mode of prophecy, and the parable is so called, and the enigma in addition. Further also, they are called wisdom; and again, as something different from it, "instruction and words of prudence," and "turnings of words" and "true righteousness"; and again, "teaching to direct judgment" and "subtlety to the simple," which is the result of training, and

---

[1]Jn 16:25. [2]*OSW* 232. [3]*PG* 17:161. [4]*PG* 39:1621. [5]*OSW* 240.

"perception and thought," with which the young catechumen is imbued. STROMATEIS 6.15.[6]

WHAT PROVERBS ARE AND HOW TO UNDERSTAND THEM. HIPPOLYTUS: Proverbs, therefore, are words of exhortation serviceable for the whole path of life; for to those who seek their way to God, these serve as guides and signs to revive them when wearied with the length of the road. These, moreover, are the proverbs of "Solomon," that is to say, the "peacemaker," who, in truth, is Christ the Savior. And since we understand the words of the Lord without offense, as being the words of the Lord, that no one may mislead us by likeness of name, he tells us who wrote these things and of what people he was king. [He does this] in order that the credit of the speaker may make the discourse acceptable and the hearers attentive, for they are the words of that Solomon to whom the Lord said, "I will give you a wise and an understanding heart, so that there has been none like you upon the earth, and after you there shall not arise any like unto you,"[7] and as follows in what is written of him. Now he was the wise son of a wise father; wherefore there is added the name of David, by whom Solomon was begotten. From a child he was instructed in the sacred Scriptures and obtained his dominion not by lot, nor by force, but by the judgment of the Spirit and the decree of God.

"To know wisdom and instruction." One who knows the wisdom of God receives from him also instruction and learns by it the mysteries of the Word; and they who know the true heavenly wisdom will easily understand the words of these mysteries. Wherefore he says, "To understand the difficulties of words,"[8] for things spoken in strange language by the Holy Spirit become intelligible to those who have their hearts right with God. FRAGMENTS ON PROVERBS.[9]

MEANING OF "PROVERB." EVAGRIUS OF PONTUS: A proverb is a saying that, under the guise of physical things, signifies intelligible things. SCHOLIA ON PROVERBS 1.1.1.[10]

PROVERB IS CALLED PARABLE IN GREEK AND SIMILE IN LATIN. BEDE: "The parables of Solomon, son of David, the king of Israel." What are called "parables" in Greek are called "similes" in Latin. Solomon gave this title to the book to encourage us to understand more deeply, not only according to the literal sense, because the Lord would speak to the crowds in parables,[11] just as he also announces the everlasting kingdom of Christ and the church both in his own name and through the peaceful state of his kingdom, about which it is written: "His rule will be multiplied and there will be no end to peace upon his throne and upon his kingdom."[12] Likewise, by the construction and dedication of the temple, he insinuates the building up of holy church, which will be dedicated for eternity at the time of the resurrection. He was also declared to be the son of David himself and the spiritual king of Israel by the testimony of the crowds of people who greeted him with praises and palm branches upon his entry to Jerusalem.[13] It must be noted, however, that the common translation of "parables," which in Hebrew is *māšlôt*,[14] is called *parhoemias*[15] [in Greek], that is, "parables." But this term is not inconsistent with the truth. For what are rightly called parables because they are mysterious can also not incongruously be called proverbs because such matters, often found in the course of conversation, ought to be contemplated and retained in memory. Proverbs are frequently so full of mystery that they can also be known as parables, as the Lord attests when he says, "I have said these things to you in proverbs; the hour is coming when I will no longer speak to you in proverbs, but I will announce the Father to you plainly."[16] COMMENTARY ON PROVERBS 1.1.1.[17]

SECULAR WISDOM IS NOT REJECTED IN PROVERBS. JEROME: You ask me . . . why it is that sometimes in my writings I quote examples from

---

[6]ANF 2:510. [7]1 Kings 3:12. [8]Prov 1:6. [9]ANF 5:172*; TLG 2115.015.33.2. [10]SC 340:90. [11]See Mt 13:34. [12]Is 9:7. [13]See Mt 21:8-9; Jn 12:13. [14]Femine plural; it should be *mĕšālîm*, masculine plural. [15]Or *paroimiai*. [16]Jn 16:25. [17]CCL 119B:23.

secular literature and thus defile the whiteness of the church with the foulness of heathenism. I will now briefly answer your question. . . . Both in Moses and in the prophets there are passages cited from Gentile books, and . . . Solomon proposed questions to the philosophers of Tyre and answered others put by them. In the commencement of the book of Proverbs he charges us to understand prudent maxims and shrewd adages, parables and obscure discourse, the words of the wise and their dark sayings; all of which belong by right to the sphere of the dialectician and the philosopher. LETTER 70.2.[18]

KNOWING WISDOM AND DISCIPLINE FOR THE SAKE OF JUSTICE. AUGUSTINE: The purpose for which the royal Father gave to the royal Son his judgment and his justice is sufficiently shown when he says, "To judge your people in justice,"[19] that is, for the purpose of judging your people. Such an idiom is found in . . . the Proverbs of Solomon, for the purpose of knowing wisdom and discipline. EXPLANATIONS OF THE PSALMS 72.3.[20]

1:3-4 Foundations for Instruction in Wisdom

THE WISDOM OF TRUE JUSTICE. JEROME: Even as there is one true God, and as there are many who are called gods by participation in him, and as there is one begotten Son of God, but others are called sons by adoption; so also there is one true justice—as it is written in the introduction of the Book of Proverbs—but the Lord loves the many acts of righteousness that are pronounced just because of their participation in true justice. HOMILIES ON THE PSALMS, ALTERNATE SERIES 60 (PSALM 10).[21]

TRUE JUSTICE ALSO IMPLIES THE OPPOSITE. JEROME: To confess that we are imperfect; that we have not yet laid hold of it; and that we have not yet obtained it. This is true wisdom in man: to know that he is imperfect; and, if I may so say, the perfection of all the just, living in the flesh, is imperfect. Whence, also, we read in Proverbs:

"To understand true justice." For unless there were also false justice, the justice of God would never be referred to as true justice. AGAINST THE PELAGIANS 1.14A.[22]

CONTRARY MEANINGS NECESSITATE SOPHISTICATION OF UNDERSTANDING. JEROME: According to Proverbs, "That resourcefulness may be imparted to the simple, to the young man knowledge and discretion" [is a statement that may be taken in a good sense but also] in a bad sense, as in the letter of the apostle: "But I fear lest, as the serpent seduced Eve by his guile, so your minds may be corrupted and fall from a single devotion to Christ."[23]

What the Lord is saying, therefore, is this: My knowledge, deepest thought and the inmost desire of my heart was with me, not only in my heavenly mansions but also when I dwelt in the night of this world and in darkness. It remained in me as man, and it instructed me and never left me, so that whatever the weakness of the flesh was unable to achieve, divine thought and power accomplished. HOMILIES ON THE PSALMS, ALTERNATE SERIES 61 (PSALM 15).[24]

EXAMPLE IS THE WISDOM AND SUBTLETY OF THE SERPENT. AUGUSTINE: There are, as you know, certain vices forming contraries to the virtues by a clear distinction, as imprudence to prudence. There are also some which are only contrary because they are vices but which have a sort of deceptive resemblance to virtues, as when we set against prudence, not imprudence, but craftiness. I am now speaking of that craftiness which is more commonly understood and expressed in an evil sense, not as our Scripture ordinarily uses it, which often gives it a good meaning; hence we have "wise as serpents"[25] and "to give subtlety to little ones." . . .

In the same way, injustice is contrary to justice by an evident antithesis, whereas the craving for

---

[18]NPNF 2 6:149. [19]Ps 72:2 (71:2 LXX, Vg). [20]NPNF 1 8:327**. [21]FC 57:13. [22]FC 53:252. [23]2 Cor 11:3. [24]FC 57:27-28. [25]Mt 10:16.

vengeance puts on a show of justice but is a vice. LETTER 167.6.[26]

HOW PARABLES BECOME CLEAR TO US. CHRYSOSTOM: Those concepts which are expressed by the Holy Spirit in parables through their counterpart of speech become quite clear when one brings them before God with a faithful heart. For they understand the true righteousness which was announced by Christ. COMMENTARY ON THE PROVERBS OF SOLOMON, FRAGMENT 1.3.[27]

1:5 Self-Advancement in Wisdom

MINISTRY OF HIGHER POWER COMMITTED TO A WEAK AGENT. GREGORY THE GREAT: There are indeed many who know how so to control their outward advancement as by no means to fall inwardly thereby. Whence it is written, "God casts not away the mighty, seeing that he also himself is mighty."[28] And it is said through Solomon, "A man of understanding shall possess governments." But to me these things are difficult, since they are also exceedingly burdensome, and what the mind has not received willingly it does not control fitly. Lo, our most serene lord the emperor had ordered an ape to be made a lion. And, indeed, in virtue of this order it can be called a lion, but a lion it cannot be made. Wherefore his piety must . . . himself take the blame of all my faults and shortcomings, having committed a ministry of power to a weak agent. LETTER 5.[29]

EVEN THE WISE MAY INCREASE IN WISDOM. ORIGEN: He who accepts the doctrines of wisdom, sometimes, in addition to the first doctrines because of which he is already wise, takes up second doctrines in reference to which he was not formerly wise, and [then] he will be wiser, just as also it is said, "For when a wise man has heard these things, he will be wiser." COMMENTARY ON THE GOSPEL OF JOHN 32.172.[30]

1:6 Riddles, Enigmas or Dark Sayings

DARKNESS IN THE GOOD SENSE. CASSIODORUS: "And he made darkness his covert, his pavilion round about him: dark waters in the clouds of the air."[31] . . . Take "darkness" in the good sense, as in the following passage from Solomon's Proverbs: "He understands also a parable and dark sayings." All the divine things of which we are unaware are dark to us, in other words, deep and obscure, even though they enjoy undying light. His covert is the hidden seat of his majesty, which he reveals to the just when they are allowed to gaze face to face on the glory of his divinity. [By] "his pavilion round about him" here is expounded the splendid dignity of the blessed, whereby those who faithfully continue in his church dwell close to him. "Round about him" signifies proximity, for he goes round and enters all things and is not encompassed by anything, for he cannot be confined in any place. EXPOSITION OF THE PSALMS 17.12.[32]

DARK, HIDDEN, INVISIBLE TREASURES. ORIGEN: We must observe that not every time something is named "darkness" is it taken in a bad sense; there are times when it has also been used in a good sense. It is because the heterodox did not make this distinction that they accepted the most irreverent doctrines concerning the Creator and withdrew from him and abandoned themselves to the fictions of myths. We must now point out, therefore, how and when the term *darkness* is understood in a good sense.

Darkness, storm clouds and thunderstorms are said to surround God in Exodus,[33] and in Psalm 17 it says, God "made darkness his hiding place, his tent around him, dark water in the clouds of the air."[34] . . .

But if someone takes offense at such interpretations, let him be persuaded both from the dark sayings and the dark, hidden, invisible treasures

---

[26]FC 30:37. [27]PG 64:660. [28]Job 36:5. [29]NPNF 2 12:75-76. [30]FC 89:375*. [31]Ps 18:11 (17:12 LXX, Vg). [32]ACW 51:181*. [33]See Ex 9:23, 16:10, 24:15-18. [34]Ps 18:11 (17:12 LXX, Vg).

given to Christ by God.[35] COMMENTARY ON THE GOSPEL OF JOHN 2.171-73.[36]

HIDDEN MEANING THAT CARRIES AN INDIRECT SIGNIFICATION. GREGORY OF NYSSA: It is universally admitted that the name of "proverb," in its scriptural use, is not applied with regard to the evident sense but is used with a view to some hidden meaning, as the Gospel thus gives the name of "proverbs" to dark and obscure sayings. So the "proverb," if one were to set forth the interpretation of the name by a definition, is a form of speech which, by means of one set of ideas immediately presented, points to something else which is hidden. Or [it is] a form of speech which does not point out the aim of the thought directly but gives its instruction by an indirect signification. AGAINST EUNOMIUS 3.2.[37]

1:7 Fear of the Lord and What It Means

EVEN THE FEAR OF GOD IS GOD'S GIFT TO US. PROSPER OF AQUITAINE: Since, therefore, the fear of God is the beginning of wisdom, and this virtue can be had without wisdom, to whom belongs the beginning of fear? The blessed apostle Peter says, "Grace to you and peace be accomplished in the knowledge of God, and of Christ Jesus our Lord," who has now given "us all things of his divine power, which appertain to life and godliness."[38] Does he say, "Who has excited in us by his help the seeds of virtues which we had naturally implanted"? Rather, he says, "Who has now given us all things which pertain to life and godliness." And in saying this, of what virtue has he placed the beginning in nature, which was not conferred by him who gave all things?[39] Wherefore, St. Paul also says, "For what have you that you have not received? And if you have received, why do you glory as if you had not received?"[40] GRACE AND FREE WILL 13.4.[41]

HUMAN PRIDE IS BROKEN DOWN BY RELIGIOUS FEAR. AUGUSTINE: You should regulate your life and conduct by the commandments of God, which we have received to enable us to lead a good life, beginning with a religious fear, for "the fear of the Lord is the beginning of wisdom," whereby human pride is broken down and weakened. Second, with a mild and gentle piety you should refrain from objecting to passages of the holy Scriptures which you do not yet understand and which seem to the uninstructed devoid of sense and self-contradictory. And you should not try to impose your ideas on the meaning of the holy books but submit and hold your mind in check rather than savagely attack its hidden meaning. LETTER 171A.[42]

SELF-RESTRAINT IS AN EFFORT FOR SOMETHING BETTER. CLEMENT OF ALEXANDRIA: There are things practiced in a vulgar style by some people, such as control over pleasures. For as among the heathen there are those who, from the impossibility of obtaining what one sees and from fear of men, and also for the sake of greater pleasures, abstain from the delights before them, so also, in the case of faith, some practice self-restraint, either out of regard to the promise or from fear of God. [Indeed] such self-restraint is the basis of knowledge, and an approach to something better, and an effort after perfection. For "the fear of the Lord," it is said, "is the beginning of wisdom." STROMATEIS 7.12.[43]

VIRTUOUS LIVING IS THE TRUE SOURCE OF WISDOM. CHRYSOSTOM: Virtuous living is really the source and root of wisdom, just as all wickedness has its source in folly. I say this because the braggart and the slave of passion are taken captive by these vices as a result of a lack of wisdom. For this reason the prophet has said, "There is no health in my flesh. My sores are foul and festering because of my folly,"[44] to indicate that all sin takes its beginning from a lack of wisdom; just as the virtuous person who fears God is wisest of all.

---

[35]See Col 2:3. [36]FC 80:140-41. [37]NPNF 2 5:137-38*. [38]2 Pet 1:2. [39]See 1 Cor 12:6. [40]1 Cor 4:7. [41]FC 7:384-85. [42]FC 30:69. [43]ANF 2:543*. [44]Ps 38:3, 5 (37:4, 6 LXX).

That is why a certain wise man also says, "The fear of the Lord is the beginning of wisdom." If, then, to fear God is to have wisdom, and the evildoer does not possess this fear, he is really bereft of wisdom; and he who is bereft of wisdom is truly the most foolish of all. HOMILIES ON THE GOSPEL OF JOHN 41.[45]

KNOWLEDGE WITHOUT PRACTICE IS INSUFFICIENT. DIDYMUS THE BLIND: To know goodness is not sufficient to reach blessedness, if one does not put goodness into practice with works. Piety toward God is actually the beginning of knowledge. COMMENTARY ON THE PROVERBS OF SOLOMON, FRAGMENT 1.7.[46]

BEGINNING OF DISCERNMENT. CHRYSOSTOM: Piety toward God is a beginning [of discernment]. It acts as a fountain and source for discerning the divine, according to our inner being, so that we may see the true light, hear the secret oracles, be nourished with the bread of life, obtain the fragrance of Christ and learn the doctrine of this life. When we have piety, our senses too are allied with us, when neither our eyes see nor our mouth speaks evil. COMMENTARY ON THE PROVERBS OF SOLOMON, FRAGMENT 1.7.[47]

TO FEAR THE LORD IS TO RENOUNCE SIN. AMBROSE: He who fears the Lord departs from error and directs his ways to the path of virtue. Except a man fear the Lord, he is unable to renounce sin. SIX DAYS OF CREATION 1.4.12.[48]

THE FOOL LACKS FEAR AND DENIES GOD. THEODORET OF CYR: To the atheist is the name *fool* most accurately applied in truth and nature: if the fear of God is the beginning of wisdom,[49] lack of fear and denial of him would be the opposite of wisdom. COMMENTARY ON PSALM 14.3.[50]

WHEREVER GOD EXISTS, THERE ALSO GOD IS FEARED. TERTULLIAN: How extremely frequent is the intercourse which heretics hold with magicians, with mountebanks, with astrologers, with philosophers. The reason is that they are people who devote themselves to curious questions. "Seek and you shall find," is everywhere in their minds. Thus, from the very nature of their conduct may be estimated the quality of their doctrine. They say that God is not to be feared; therefore all things are in their view free and unchecked. Where, however, is God not feared, except where he is not present? Where God is not, there truth also is not. Where there is no truth, then, naturally enough, there is also such a discipline as theirs. But where God is, there exists "the fear of God, which is the beginning of wisdom." PRESCRIPTIONS AGAINST HERETICS 43.[51]

SERVILE FEAR DIFFERS FROM FRIENDLY FEAR. BEDE: "The fear of the Lord is the beginning of knowledge." Two things constitute the fear of the Lord: first, the servanthood which is called the beginning of knowledge or wisdom and, second, the friendship which accompanies the perfection of wisdom. Servile fear is the beginning of wisdom because whoever begins to taste it after the error of sins is corrected by this first divine fear, lest he be led into torments. But perfect love casts this fear out.[52] Holy fear of the Lord then follows, remaining forever,[53] and is augmented by charity, not removed by it. This is the fear with which the good son is afraid, lest he offend the eyes of his most loving father in the least degree. For the soul is still afraid with elementary servile fear, lest it suffer punishment from an angry Lord. But each fear will come to an end in the future life. Charity, however, never passes away,[54] but will remain perpetually in the fulness of wisdom, which is to know the one, true God and Jesus Christ whom he has sent.[55] COMMENTARY ON PROVERBS 1.1.7.[56]

---

[45]FC 33:422. [46]PG 39:1624. [47]PG 64:661-64. [48]FC 42:12. [49]Ps 111:10 (110:10 LXX). [50]FC 101:108. [51]ANF 3:264. [52]See 1 Jn 4:18. [53]See Ps 19:9 (18:10 LXX, Vg). [54]See 1 Cor 13:8. [55]See Jn 17:3. [56]CCL 119B:25.

1:8-19 WARNINGS AGAINST
EVIL AND VIOLENCE

⁸*Hear, my son, your father's instruction,*
  and reject not your mother's teaching;
⁹*for they are a fair garland for your head,*
  *and pendants for your neck.**
¹⁰*My son, if sinners entice you,*
  do not consent.
¹¹*If they say, "Come with us, let us lie in*
    wait for blood,
  let us wantonly ambush the innocent;
¹²*like Sheol let us swallow them alive*
    and whole, like those who go down to
    the Pit:
¹³*we shall find all precious goods,*
  we shall fill our houses with spoil;[†]
¹⁴*throw in your lot among us,*

  we will all have one purse"—
¹⁵*my son, do not walk in the way*
    with them,
  hold back your foot from their paths;
¹⁶*for their feet run to evil,*
  and they make haste to shed blood.
¹⁷*For in vain is a net spread*
  in the sight of any bird;
¹⁸*but these men lie in wait for their own*
    blood,
  they set an ambush for their own
    lives.
¹⁹*Such are the ways of all who get gain*
    by violence;
  it takes away the life of its possessors.

*LXX You will receive a crown of graces upon your head.   †Vg Come with us, let us share innocent blood: let us unjustly hide away in the earth the just man, let us swallow him up alive like hell. Let us abolish his memory from the earth, let us lay hands upon his precious possession.

OVERVIEW: God is our Father and the church our Mother (DIDYMUS). Our parents' teachings, coming from God the Father but in the name of mother church, should direct us away from evil and violence (BEDE), for we shall not go wrong if we follow the general teachings of the church (FULGENTIUS). The transient laurel wreath of the Olympic games is nothing compared with the eternal crown offered us by the Lord (CHRYSOSTOM). By contrast, the desire of the wicked to ambush and bury the innocent is a reference to Christ and the church (AUGUSTINE) as well as a prediction of the Lord's passion (CLEMENT OF ALEXANDRIA). Jesus the Savior is the way of forgiveness, and our feet should run to the gospel rather than to mischief and evil (APOSTOLIC CONSTITUTIONS, GREGORY OF NAZIANZUS). Nets even for birds are spread for a purpose, and therefore

temptation is to be avoided (BARNABAS, ORIGEN).

1:8-9 The Teaching of Our Parents

GOD IS OUR FATHER AND THE CHURCH OUR MOTHER. DIDYMUS THE BLIND: God is Father of the righteous. Whoever practices justice was born from God. Our mother is the church, whose bridegroom is our Lord Jesus Christ. Our laws are the apostolic constitutions. Even though the concepts expressed above have a sublime meaning, they also apply to earthly parents when they educate their children in how to live piously before God. Since that teacher, who generates his children through the gospel, is a man, his wife and mother of his children is the church, or rather the ecclesiastical doctrine and way of life. If you, he says, listen to me as the author of the

Proverbs—first in my role as the narrator of the father, and then as the narrator of wisdom and virtue (that is, of the mother)—you will be encircled with a crown of grace and your neck will be adorned with a necklace fashioned of intellectual gold and jewels. The material of the crown, with which the head of the interior man is encircled, is the circle of virtues, which are called graces. Accordingly, the golden necklace put around the neck of the soul (that is, around one's obedience) must be understood as a part of the intellectual crown. COMMENTARY ON THE PROVERBS OF SOLOMON, FRAGMENT 1.8.[1]

COMING FROM GOD THE FATHER IN THE NAME OF MOTHER CHURCH. BEDE: "Listen, my son, to the discipline of your father, and do not reject your mother's law." Thus far, it argues proverbially from each side. From here on, it begins assiduously to admonish whoever is faithful that he prefer the discipline of the divine law to the flatteries of the reprobate, for eternal death surely follows their crimes, while a crown is given to those who keep the law. Hence, it rightly calls him son whom the father was careful to instruct with solicitude. This statement can be accepted as coming from the person of God the Father but in the name of mother church, who was then called the synagogue, I understand. Observe also that it commands us to listen to the father's instruction that we not reject the mother's law for any reason. For it is not adequate that anyone claims to love God and to comply with his precepts if he does not also pursue the unity of the church with fraternal charity, or if he denies that the mother herself receives any of the grace of God whereby we are saved. Even among the Hebrews the spirit that grants grace is known by the feminine gender. COMMENTARY ON PROVERBS 1.1.8.[2]

PATERNAL INSTRUCTION AND MATERNAL LAW. BEDE: Through listening to paternal instruction and through observance of maternal law, grace is put on our head and a neck ring on our neck. For the more one gives heed to divine

commands [and] strives to observe with greater diligence what one has learned in the unity of mother church, the more one may now ascend with greater worthiness to the honor of preaching and may in the future ascend with greater exaltation to the blessedness of reigning with Christ for ever. HOMILIES ON THE GOSPELS 1.19.[3]

THIS INSTRUCTION IS THE TEACHING OF THE CHURCH. FULGENTIUS OF RUSPE: The church is not truly called the "pillar and foundation of truth"[4] if it is found unsound in the most basic mystery of human salvation. But because it is truly called the "pillar and foundation of truth" by the apostle, whatever according to the canons of the church itself is given and received within it, among the holy mysteries of human redemption and reconciliation, is given with firm truth and received with firm truth.

It is so commanded in Proverbs: "Hear, my child, your father's instruction and do not reject your mother's teaching," so that we may never reject the general canons of holy mother the church, that is, those which the most harmonious assent of all the bishops confirms. LETTER TO FERRANDUS 12.21-22.[5]

UNFADING CROWN OF GLORY. CHRYSOSTOM: Our Lord . . . offers us his hand, takes part in the struggle, and seemingly in every way hands over our adversary to us in defeat, striving might and main that we may prevail and wrest the victory, so that he may place on our head the unfading crown. Scripture says, remember, "You will receive a crown of graces upon your head." Whereas in the Olympic games the crown after victory is nothing more than a laurel wreath, or applause, or acclamation of the crowd, all of which disappears and is lost with the coming of evening, the crown for virtue and its struggles has nothing material about it. It is not subject to decay in this world but is everlasting, immortal,

---

[1]PG 39:1624. [2]CCL 119B:26. [3]CS 110:189-90. [4]1 Tim 3:15. [5]FC 95:490-91.

enduring for all ages. HOMILIES ON GENESIS 42.4.[6]

REWARD FOR FAITHFULNESS. CHRYSOSTOM: If you preserve in your faithful heart the law of your Father and observe the commands of your mother, you will receive the crown of graces on your head and the golden necklace in the resurrection of the righteous ones. You will be glorified in the heavenly and imperishable kingdom and crowned by Christ if you fight in a manner worthy of such a crown. No athlete is crowned unless such a person has contended strongly and legitimately.[7] COMMENTARY ON THE PROVERBS OF SOLOMON, FRAGMENT 1.9.[8]

1:11-13 To Ambush and Bury the Innocent

REFERENCE TO CHRIST AND THE CHURCH. AUGUSTINE: There is one text in Proverbs so far from being obscure that its relationship to Christ and his possession, the church, can be grasped without any such trouble. Wicked men are speaking: "Let us unjustly hide away in the earth the just man, let us swallow him up alive like hell. Let us abolish his memory from the earth, let us lay hands upon his precious possession." This is very like what the Lord Jesus himself, in one of the Gospel parables, puts into the mouths of the wicked vinedressers: "This is the heir; come let us kill him, and we shall have his inheritance."[9] CITY OF GOD 17.20.[10]

PREDICTION OF THE LORD'S PASSION. CLEMENT OF ALEXANDRIA: In the words of Solomon, "My son, let not sinners lead you astray, do not walk in their ways. Do not walk if they entice you saying: Come with us, let us share innocent blood: let us hide the just man in the earth unjustly, let us swallow him up alive as in hell." This last passage is also a prophecy of the passion of the Lord. CHRIST THE EDUCATOR 1.10.94-95.[11]

1:16 Sinners Whose Feet Run to Evil

THE WAY OF JESUS IS FORGIVENESS. APOSTOLIC CONSTITUTIONS: It is not fair to be too hasty in casting out an offender but slow in receiving him when he returns; to be forward in cutting off but unmerciful when he is sorrowful and ought to be healed. For of such as these speaks the divine Scripture: "Their feet run to mischief; they are hasty to shed blood.". . . Now the way of peace is our Savior Jesus Christ, who has taught us, saying, "Forgive, and you shall be forgiven. Give, and it shall be given to you,"[12] that is, give remission of sins, and your offenses shall be forgiven you. CONSTITUTIONS OF THE HOLY APOSTLES 2.3.21.[13]

FEET SHOULD RUN TO THE GOSPEL. GREGORY OF NAZIANZUS: It is good for the . . . feet . . . that they be not swift to shed blood or to run to evil, but that they be prompted to run to the gospel and the prize[14] of the high calling, and to receive Christ who washes and cleanses them. ON HOLY BAPTISM, ORATION 40.39.[15]

1:17 Nets Are Spread for a Purpose

THE WAY OF DARKNESS IS TO BE AVOIDED. EPISTLE OF BARNABAS: The Scripture says, "Not unjustly are the nets spread out for the birds." This means that a man shall perish justly, who, having knowledge of the way of righteousness, thrusts himself into the way of darkness. EPISTLE OF BARNABAS 5.4.[16]

TEMPTATION IS LIKEWISE TO BE AVOIDED. ORIGEN: If, then, "not unjustly are nets spread for birds," as is said in Proverbs, and it is just that God should lead men into the net, as it is said, "You have brought us into the net,"[17] and if not even the sparrow, the most insignificant of birds, falls into the net without the will of the Father[18] (for what falls into the net falls into it for the sim-

---

[6]FC 82:419-20*. [7]See 2 Tim 2:5. [8]PG 64:664. [9]Mt 21:38. [10]FC 24:75. [11]FC 23:84. [12]Lk 6:37-38. [13]ANF 7:405-6. [14]See Phil 3:14. [15]NPNF 2 7:374. [16]FC 1:197**. [17]Ps 66:11 (65:11 LXX). [18]Mt 10:29.

ple reason that it fails to use properly the power of its wings given it to bear it aloft): then let us pray not to do anything which would demand that in God's just judgment we be led into temptation. Such is the fate of the one who is given up by God to the desires of his heart unto uncleanness; and of him who is delivered up to shameful affections; and of him who, as he liked not to have God in his knowledge, is delivered up to a reprobate sense, to do those things which are disgraceful.[19] ON PRAYER 2.29.16.[20]

---

[19]Rom 1:24, 26, 28. [20]ACW 19:124-25.

1:20-33 WARNINGS THAT WISDOM BE NOT NEGLECTED

[20]*Wisdom cries aloud in the street;*
*in the markets she raises her voice;**
[21]*on the top of the walls[a] she cries out;*
at the entrance of the city gates she
speaks:
[22]*"How long, O simple ones, will you love*
being simple?
How long will scoffers delight in their
scoffing
and fools hate knowledge?
[23]*Give heed[b] to my reproof;*
behold, I will pour out my thoughts[c]
to you;
I will make my words known to you.
[24]*Because I have called and you refused to*
listen,
have stretched out my hand and no one
has heeded,
[25]*and you have ignored all my counsel*
and would have none of my reproof,
[26]*I also will laugh at your calamity;*
I will mock when panic strikes you,

[27]*when panic strikes you like a storm,*
and your calamity comes like a
whirlwind,
when distress and anguish come upon you.
[28]*Then they will call upon me, but I will*
not answer;
they will seek me diligently but will not
find me.
[29]*Because they hated knowledge*
and did not choose the fear of the LORD,
[30]*would have none of my counsel,*
and despised all my reproof,
[31]*therefore they shall eat the fruit of their*
way
and be sated with their own devices.
[32]*For the simple are killed by their turning*
away,
and the complacence of fools destroys
them;
[33]*but he who listens to me will dwell*
secure
and will be at ease, without dread of evil."

---

a Heb uncertain **b** Heb *Turn* **c** Heb *spirit* *LXX *Wisdom is made known in death*

OVERVIEW: The praise of the dead is preferable to the praise of the living (HILARY), for wisdom is appropriately proclaimed at the moment or point of departure (HILARY, SALVIAN THE PRESBYTER). The one Word of God is distinct from the words of God's commands (ATHANASIUS), but we must always obey what God has decreed (CLEMENT OF ROME). We must also take heed when God reaches out to us (ORIGEN), for the correction of God is beneficial (CLEMENT OF ALEXANDRIA). But God will not hear those who refuse his call (GREGORY THE GREAT), and there is no room for complaint if we do not hear or look (SALVIAN THE PRESBYTER). After all, not every prayer is really a call to God, seeing that our minds fluctuate between the extremes of hope and despair (AUGUSTINE). The rejection of wisdom, therefore, can be the ruin of small minds or of fools (GREGORY THE GREAT).

1:20 *Wisdom Proclaimed at a Place or Point of Departure*

PRAISE OF THE DEAD PREFERABLE TO PRAISE OF THE LIVING. HILARY OF ARLES: It is written: "Wisdom is made known in death," that is to say, the life of the wise man is praised at the end of his life. Wherefore we read also in another place: "Do not praise a man during his lifetime "and again, "Praise not any man before death."[1] Now suppose someone says: praise a man after death, for in the praise of the living there is a possible occasion of vain exultation for the object of the laudation and a note of flattery is attached to the one bestowing it. In many ways, however, it is useful to praise the dead: in the first place, because, while the one is absent who might be gratified by our praise, it is necessary that the whole glory be referred to the bestower of grace; second, because only admiration for his virtue remains when the suspicion of flattery is removed. Therefore, praise of the dead which is proclaimed in the holy congregation of the faithful is full of edification and utterly free from ostentation. LIFE OF ST. HONORATUS, PREFACE 3.[2]

WISDOM PROCLAIMED AT DEATH. SALVIAN THE PRESBYTER: What about this saying: "He who shall have persevered to the end, shall be saved,"[3] or that oracle of the divine word in the sacred proverbs: "Wisdom is proclaimed at the moment of departure"? These sayings show that, though wisdom is helpful in every age, all people should be particularly wise when they are leaving this world, because the wisdom of past years will not fully deserve praise if it does not terminate in a good end. Wisdom is proclaimed at the moment of departure. FOUR BOOKS OF TIMOTHY TO THE CHURCH 4.1.[4]

1:23 *My Words Known*

THE ONE WORD OF GOD IS DISTINCT FROM THE WORDS OF GOD'S COMMANDS. ATHANASIUS: For where at all have they found in divine Scripture, or from whom have they heard, that there is another Word and another wisdom besides this Son, that they should frame to themselves such a doctrine? True, indeed, it is written, "Are not my words like fire, and like a hammer that breaks the rock in pieces?"[5] and in the Proverbs, "I will make known my words unto you." But these are precepts and commands, which God has spoken to the saints through his proper and only true Word, concerning which the psalmist said, "I have refrained my feet from every evil way, that I may keep your words."[6] Such words accordingly the Savior signifies to be distinct from himself, when he says in his own person, "The words which I have spoken unto you."[7] For certainly such words are not offsprings or sons, nor are there so many words that frame the world, nor so many images of the one God, nor so many who have become men for us, nor as if from many such there were one who has become flesh, as John says. He was preached by John as being the only Word of God: "the Word was made flesh," and "all things were made by him."[8]

---

[1]Cf. Sir 11:26-28. [2]FC 15:362-63*. [3]Mt 10:22. [4]FC 3:355. [5]Jer 23:29. [6]Ps 119:101 (118:101 LXX). [7]Jn 6:63. [8]Jn 1:14; 1:3.

Wherefore of him alone, our Lord Jesus Christ, and of his oneness with the Father, are written and set forth the testimonies, both of the Father signifying that the Son is one, and of the saints, aware of this and saying that the Word is one, and that he is Only-begotten. Four Discourses Against the Arians 2.39.[9]

Let Us Obey What God Has Decreed. Clement of Rome: So, then, let us obey his most holy and glorious name and escape the threats which wisdom has predicted against the disobedient. In that way we shall live in peace, having our confidence in his most holy and majestic name. Accept our advice, and you will never regret it. For as God lives, as the Lord Jesus Christ lives and the Holy Spirit (on whom the elect believe and hope), the man who with humility and eager considerateness and with no regrets does what God has decreed and ordered will be enlisted and enrolled in the ranks of those who are saved through Jesus Christ. Through him be the glory to God for ever and ever. Amen. 1 Clement 58.[10]

1:24-28 Refusal to Heed God's Call

Beneficial Correction. Clement of Alexandria: The correction of the Lord is very beneficial. He calls the same people, through David, also, "a perverse and exasperating generation, a generation that set not their heart aright: and whose spirit was not faithful to God. They kept not the covenant of God: and in his law they would not walk."[11] These are the reasons for his exasperation, and for these reasons he will come as judge to pass sentence on those who are unwilling to preserve goodness in their lives. Therefore, he treats them severely in the hope that perhaps he might curb their impulse toward death.... He knew that they repented out of fear, after neglecting his love; as a general rule, men always neglect the good that is kind, but serve it with loving fear if it keeps recalling justice. Christ the Educator 85-86.[12]

We Must Take Heed When God Stretches Out to Us. Origen: If there is someone who meditates on the law of the Lord day and night[13] and someone who is like the mouth of the righteous that meditates on wisdom,[14] he will be able to inquire more carefully and to find. This is so, provided he seeks rightly and in seeking knocks on the door of wisdom to ask God that it may be opened to him and that he be worthy to receive through the Holy Spirit the word of wisdom and the word of knowledge and to become a fellow of Solomon's wisdom. For it was the latter that said, "I stretched out my words and you did not hear."[15] And he rightly says that he stretched out words in his heart, because, as we said a moment ago, God gave him largeness of heart.[16] For that person's heart is enlarged who can explain what is briefly said in mysteries by a broader teaching with assertions taken from the divine books. Commentary on the Song of Songs, Prologue.[17]

Stretching Forth. Origen: How then is the heaven stretched forth? Wisdom stretches it forth. For it is clear that wisdom stretches it forth in the text: "Since I stretched forth words and you did not pay attention." He speaks of words being stretched forth; in this way the heaven is stretched forth. Homilies on Jeremiah 8.2.3.[18]

Sinners Unknown to God. Gregory the Great: "Then they will call upon me, and I will not listen; they will arise early in the morning and will not find me." You see how they cry out that it be opened for them; driven by sorrow at their rejection, they call twice upon him who has dominion over them, saying, "Lord, Lord, open to us."[19] They offer entreaties, but they are unknown to him. God abandons them as unknown persons. He does not recognize them now because of their sins. Forty Gospel Homilies 10 (12).[20]

---

[9]NPNF 2 4:369*. [10]LCC 1:70. [11]Ps 78:8,10 (77:8,10 LXX). [12]FC 23:76-77. [13]Ps 1:2. [14]Ps 37:30 (36:30 LXX). [15]Cf. Col 4:3. [16]1 Kings 4:29. [17]OSW 233-34**. [18]FC 97:77. [19]Mt 25:11. [20]CS 123:73.

Not Every Prayer Is Really a Call to God. Augustine: What is it then which Scripture says in many places: "They shall call, and I will not hear them"? Yet surely you are merciful to all who call upon you. . . . Some call, yet call not upon him of whom it is said, "They have not called upon God."[21] They call, but not on God. You call upon whatever you love: you call upon whatever you draw to yourself, whatever you wish to come to you. Therefore if you call upon God for this reason, in order that money may come to you, that an inheritance may come to you, that worldly rank may come to you, then you are calling upon those things that you desire may come to you; but you are making God the helper of your desires, not the listener to your needs. God is good, if he gives what you wish. What if you wish ill, will he not then be more merciful by not giving? Then if he gives not, then is God nothing to you; and you say, How much I have prayed, how often I have prayed, and have not been heard! Why, what did you ask? Perhaps that your enemy might die. What if he at the same time was praying for your death? God who created you, created him also. You are a human, your enemy also is human. But God is the judge: he hears both, and he grants the prayer to neither. You are sad, because you were not heard when praying against your enemy. But be glad, because his prayer was not heard against you. Explanations of the Psalms 86.7.[22]

No Room for Complaint If We Do Not Hear or Look. Salvian the Presbyter: What room is there for just complaint when each suffers according to his deeds? There is this exception which I can easily prove, namely, we never suffer in proportion to our deeds, and God deals with us much more leniently than we deal with him. But, in the meantime, let me [continue]. . . . Thus spoke the Lord himself: "I have cried unto you, and you have not heard me; and you shall cry unto me, and I shall not hear you."[23] What is more suitable and just than this? We have not heard; therefore, we are not heeded. We have not looked; therefore, we are not noticed.

The Governance of God 3.9.[24]

Extremes of Hope and Despair. Augustine: The mind fluctuates between hope and despair. It must be feared lest hope slays you; and when you hope for too much from mercy, you fall into judgment. Again, it must be feared lest despair slays you; and when you think that you cannot now be forgiven for grave sins you have committed, you do no penance and you encounter the judge, wisdom, which says, "And I will laugh at your doom."

What, then, has the Lord to do with those endangered by these diseases? To those who are endangered by hope, he says this: "Delay not to be converted to the Lord; and put it not off from day to day; for suddenly his wrath will come, and in the time of vengeance he will destroy you."[25] To those who are endangered by despair, what does he say? "On whatever day the wicked man is converted, I shall forget all his iniquities."[26] Therefore, because of those who are endangered by despair, he has proposed the harbor of forgiveness; because of those who are endangered by hope and deluded by delays, he has made the day of death uncertain. You do not know when the last day may come. Are you ungrateful because you have today, in which you may be corrected? Tractates on the Gospel of John 33.3-4.[27]

1:32 The Foolishness of Those Who Neglect Wisdom

The Ruin of Small Minds and of Fools Who Reject Wisdom. Gregory the Great: Solomon says, "The turning away of little ones shall kill them, and the prosperity of fools shall destroy them." Hence Paul admonishes, saying, "They that buy shall be as though they possessed not, and they that use this world, as if they used it not."[28] That is, the things which suffice us

---

[21]Ps 53:4 (52:5 LXX, Vg). [22]NPNF 1 8:412**. [23]See Jer 11:11. [24]FC 3:83**. [25]Cf. Sir 5:8-9. [26]See Ezek 18:21-22; 33:14-15. [27]FC 88:58-59. [28]See 1 Cor 7:29.

should so serve us outwardly as not to take away our minds from the pursuit of supernal delight, and the things that merely support us in our [earthly] exile, must not abate the mourning of our soul's pilgrimage. We who see ourselves miserable in our present state of separation from the eternal must not rejoice as though we were happy in the possession of what is transitory. PASTORAL CARE 3.26.27.[29]

---

[29]ACW 11:183*.

2:1-22 UNDERSTANDING THE FEAR OF THE LORD

[1]My son, if you receive my words
  and treasure up my commandments
  with you,
[2]making your ear attentive to wisdom
  and inclining your heart to understanding;
[3]yes, if you cry out for insight
  and raise your voice for understanding,
[4]if you seek it like silver
  and search for it as for hidden treasures;
[5]then you will understand the fear of the
  LORD
  and find the knowledge of God.
[6]For the LORD gives wisdom;
  from his mouth come knowledge and
  understanding;
[7]he stores up sound wisdom for the
  upright;
  he is a shield to those who walk in
  integrity,
[8]guarding the paths of justice
  and preserving the way of his saints.
[9]Then you will understand righteousness
  and justice
  and equity, every good path;
[10]for wisdom will come into your heart,
  and knowledge will be pleasant to your

soul;
[11]discretion will watch over you;
  understanding will guard you;
[12]delivering you from the way of evil,
  from men of perverted speech,
[13]who forsake the paths of uprightness
  to walk in the ways of darkness,
[14]who rejoice in doing evil
  and delight in the perverseness of evil;
[15]men whose paths are crooked,
  and who are devious in their ways.

[16]You will be saved from the loose[d]
  woman,
from the adventuress[e] with her smooth
  words,
[17]who forsakes the companion of her youth
  and forgets the covenant of her God;
[18]for her house sinks down to death,
  and her paths to the shades;
[19]none who go to her come back
  nor do they regain the paths of life.

[20]So you will walk in the way of good
  men
  and keep to the paths of the righteous.

^{21}*For the upright will inhabit the land,*
  and men of integrity will remain in it;
^{22}*but the wicked will be cut off from the*

land,
  and the treacherous will be rooted out
  of it.

d Heb *strange*　　e Heb *foreign woman*

OVERVIEW: The union of soul and spirit produces life, and inward perception leads to reverence (CLEMENT OF ALEXANDRIA). Although Scripture encourages us to seek wisdom like we seek money, this is not to say that Scripture is praising avarice, but rather it is to say that money and God are competing for our love (AUGUSTINE). Wisdom and understanding must precede the fear of God (EVAGRIUS). There is a divine sense, higher than human sense, that enables those of a pure heart to see God (ORIGEN). It is necessary not only to study the Scriptures but also to pray to understand them, that we may obtain not only learning but also the wisdom that comes from the Lord (AUGUSTINE). Those who do seek salvation will be guided by holy counsel (CAESARIUS). Jesus mourns for evildoers, although they should mourn for themselves (GREGORY THE GREAT). Straightforwardness of the mind makes for a straight path (CYRIL OF ALEXANDRIA). In the end, though, it is we ourselves who cause the smooth paths to become rough (JOHN CASSIAN).

2:1 *Spiritual Growth*

UNION OF SOUL AND SPIRIT PRODUCES LIFE. CLEMENT OF ALEXANDRIA: Wisdom is open to all and loves humankind.[1] Anyway, Solomon says, "My son, if you accept my words of instruction and keep them deep within you, your ear will listen to wisdom." This means that the word is sown and kept deep in the soul of the learner as if in the ground. This is spiritual growth.

So he adds, "You shall direct your heart to understanding and direct it towards instruction for your son." For in my view, the union of soul with soul and spirit with spirit in accordance with the sowing of the word brings growth to the seed sown and produces life. Everyone who is educated in obedience to his educator becomes a son. STROMATEIS 1.1.3-2.1.[2]

2:3 *Cry Out for Insight*

INWARD PERCEPTION LEADS TO REVERENCE. CLEMENT OF ALEXANDRIA: God's wisdom ... [works] "in many forms and many ways"[3] through technical skill, scientific knowledge, faith, prophecy; it shows us its power to our benefit, because "all wisdom comes from the Lord and is with him to all eternity," as the wisdom of Jesus puts it.[4] "For if you call for practical wisdom and perception at the top of your voice, if you seek it as you would a treasure of silver, and if you track it down ardently, then you will realize the meaning of reverence for God and you will grasp the perception of God." The prophet spoke to distinguish this from the philosophic approach to perception. He is teaching us with great dignity and solemnity to search it out in order to progress toward reverence for God. So he opposed to it perception made in reverence for God, alluding to revealed knowledge in these words: "For God grants wisdom from his mouth together with perception and practical wisdom, and stores up help for the righteous."[5] When people are made righteous by philosophy, they have stored help for themselves and inward perception which leads to reverence for God. STROMATEIS 1.27.1-3.[6]

2:4 *Seek Wisdom Like Silver*

DOES HOLY SCRIPTURE PRAISE AVARICE? AUGUSTINE: Another passage of Scripture exhorting us to love of wisdom says it should be

---

[1]See Tit 3:4.　[2]FC 85:23-24.　[3]Heb 1:1.　[4]Jesus the son of Sirach; Sir 1:1.　[5]Prov 2:6-7.　[6]FC 85:41.

sought after like money. Must we therefore think holy Scripture praises avarice? It is well known to what great efforts and pains lovers of money will patiently subject themselves, from what great pleasures they abstain, in their desire to increase their wealth or in their fear of diminishing it. With what great shrewdness they pursue gain, and how prudently they avoid losses; how they are usually afraid to take the property of others, and sometimes despise loss to themselves lest they lose more in its quest and litigation. Because these traits are well known, it is right for us to be exhorted so to love wisdom that we most eagerly seek it as our treasure, acquire more and more of it, suffer many trials, restrain desires, ponder the future, so that we may preserve innocence and beneficence. Whenever we act in this way we are in possession of true virtues, because our objective is true, that is, is in harmony with our nature in reference to salvation and true happiness. AGAINST JULIAN 4.3.18.[7]

LOVE GOD AS MUCH AS MONEY. AUGUSTINE: It's unfitting, it's insulting, that wisdom should be compared with money, but love is being compared to love. What I see here, after all, is that you all love money in such a way that when love of money gives the order, you undertake hard labor, you put up with starving, you cross the sea, you commit yourselves to wind and wave. I have something to pick on in the matter of what you love, but I have nothing to add to the love with which you love. "Love like that, and I don't want to be loved any more than that," says God. "I'm talking to the riffraff, I'm speaking to the greedy: You love money; love me just as much. Of course, I'm comparably better; but I don't want more ample love from you; love me just as much as you love money." SERMON 399.11.[8]

2:5 Divine Perception

WISDOM AND UNDERSTANDING MUST PRE-CEDE THE FEAR OF GOD. EVAGRIUS OF PONTUS: Wisdom and understanding must precede, in

order for the fear of God to coexist along with them. SCHOLIA ON PROVERBS 20.2.5.[9]

DIVINE SENSE HIGHER THAN HUMAN SENSE. ORIGEN: Solomon says, "You will find a divine sense." For he knew that there were in us two kinds of senses, the one being mortal, corruptible and human, and the other immortal and intellectual, which here he calls "divine." By this divine sense, therefore, not of the eyes but of a pure heart, that is, the mind, God can be seen by those who are worthy. ON FIRST PRINCIPLES 1.1.9.[10]

2:6 Knowledge and Understanding Come from the Lord

ZEAL FOR STUDY, ENDOWED WITH PIETY. AUGUSTINE: Students of these revered writings should be advised not only to learn the kinds of expressions in the holy Scriptures, to notice carefully how they are customarily expressed there, and to remember them but also to pray that they may understand them, and this is chiefly and especially necessary. Indeed, in these books which they are studying earnestly, they read that "the Lord gives wisdom; and out of his mouth comes prudence and knowledge." It is from him that they have received that zeal for study, if it is endowed with piety. CHRISTIAN INSTRUCTION 3.37.59.[11]

2:11 Discretion and Understanding

THE GUIDANCE OF HOLY COUNSEL. CAE-SARIUS OF ARLES: We read in sacred Scripture, dearly beloved, that holy counsel should keep those who are solicitous for their soul's salvation, as the divine Word puts it: "Holy counsel shall keep you." If holy counsel keeps a soul, that which is unholy not only fails to keep it but even kills it. Perhaps someone says, Who can always be thinking of God and eternal bliss, since all people

---

[7]FC 35:183. [8]WSA 3 10:465. [9]SC 340:112. [10]OFP 14. [11]FC 2:166-67.

must be solicitous for food, clothing and the management of their household? God does not bid us be free from all anxiety over the present life, for he instructs us through his apostle: "If anyone will not work, neither let him eat."[12] The same apostle repeats the idea with reference to himself when he says, "We worked night and day so that we might not burden any of you."[13] Since God especially advises reasonable thought of food and clothing, so long as avarice and ambition which usually serve dissipation are not linked with it, any action or thought is most rightly considered holy. The only provision is that those preoccupations should not be so excessive that they do not allow us to have time for God, according to the words: "The burdens of the world have made them miserable."[14] Since bodily necessities are satisfied with little, while ambition is never appeased even if it obtains the whole world, let us reject wicked thoughts which spring from the poisonous root of passion. Let us, on the other hand, love only those which will help us obtain an eternal reward, so that what was said before may be fulfilled in us: "Holy counsel shall keep you." Sermon 45.1.[15]

2:14 Evildoers

Should Mourn for Themselves. Gregory the Great: "Seeing the city, [Jesus] wept over it, saying, 'If only at least you had known.'"[16] He did this once when he proclaimed that [Jerusalem] would perish. Our Redeemer has not stopped doing this daily through his elect when he observes that certain persons have adopted corrupt habits after having lived good lives. He mourns for those who do not know why they are mourned for, who, in Solomon's words, "rejoice in doing evil, and delight in what is worse." If they recognized their impending condemnation, they would mourn for themselves! Forty Gospel Homilies 39.[17]

2:15 Those Whose Paths Are Crooked

The Mind Like the Path Must Be Made Straight. Cyril of Alexandria: What is the meaning of "Prepare the way of the Lord"?[18] Make ready for the reception of whatever Christ may wish to enact; withdraw your hearts from the shadow of the law; cease from the types; think no more perversely. . . . "Make the paths of our God straight." For every path that leads unto good is straight and smooth and easy; but the other is crooked that leads down to wickedness those who walk therein. For of such it is written, "Whose paths are crooked, and the tracks of their wheels awry." Straightforwardness, therefore, of the mind is as it were a straight path, having no crookedness. Commentary on Luke, Homily 6.[19]

2:20 Keep to the Paths of the Righteous

It Is We Who Have Made the Smooth Paths Rough. John Cassian: It is clearly we, I say, who make rough the straight and smooth paths of the Lord with the wicked and hard rocks of our desires, who very foolishly abandon the royal road paved with apostolic and prophetic stones and made level by the footsteps of all the holy ones and of the Lord himself, and who pursue byways and brambly roads. Blinded by the seductions of present pleasures, we crawl along the dark and obstructed trails, our feet lacerated by the thorns of vice and our wedding garment in tatters, and we are not only pierced by the sharp needles of thorny bushes but also brought low by the stings of the poisonous serpents and the scorpions that lie in wait there. Conference 24.24.5.[20]

---

[12]2 Thess 3:10. [13]1 Thess 2:9. [14]The source is unknown. [15]FC 31:226-27*. [16]Lk 19:41-42. [17]CS 123:359*. [18]See Mt 3:3. [19]CGSL 69. [20]ACW 57:845.

3:1-10 TEACHING THAT
MUST NOT BE FORGOTTEN

[1]*My son, do not forget my teaching,*
but let your heart keep my command-
ments;
[2]*for length of days and years of life*
and abundant welfare will they give you.

[3]*Let not loyalty and faithfulness forsake you;*
bind them about your neck,*
write them on the tablet of your heart.
[4]*So you will find favor and good repute[f]*
in the sight of God and man.

[5]*Trust in the LORD with all your heart,*

and do not rely on your own insight.
[6]*In all your ways acknowledge him,*
and he will make straight your paths.
[7]*Be not wise in your own eyes;*
fear the LORD, and turn away from evil.
[8]*It will be healing to your flesh[g]*
and refreshment[h] to your bones.

[9]*Honor the LORD with your substance*
and with the first fruits of all your
produce;
[10]*then your barns will be filled with plenty,*
and your vats will be bursting with wine.[†]

f Cn: Heb *understanding*   g Heb *navel*   h Or *medicine*   *LXX *mercy and faith may not forsake you*   †LXX *Honor the Lord from your righteous labors, and give to him from the fruits of your righteousness, so that your barns may be full of an abundance of wheat and your winepresses may be overflowing with wine.*

OVERVIEW: Even those who forget God's law are violating it (EVAGRIUS). God has given us free will, but we must exercise it by choosing to keep God's commandments (AUGUSTINE). Loyalty and faithfulness will not forsake you if your fasting for the sake of the gospel precept is accompanied by the act of anointing your head with the oil of mercy (ORIGEN). Ignorance accompanied by rashness, however, breeds false self-importance (CYRIL OF ALEXANDRIA), when in fact you should fear the Lord and depart from evil because the name of "catholic" on its own is not enough to guarantee salvation (FULGENTIUS). We do not honor the Lord with our substance if we provide alms that have been procured at the cost of another (AUGUSTINE). Nor do we honor the Lord by our good works if we attribute them to our merits rather than to God's grace (BEDE). It is not enough to fulfill the righteousness of the old law without the moderating force of judgment (JOHN CASSIAN), and it is no honor to God to take evilly in order to give well

(GREGORY THE GREAT). After all, we hold our possessions by the revocable will of God, who gave them to us. God is willing to call them our own, so that we may be the ones who give them to others (SALVIAN THE PRESBYTER).

3:1 *Keeping God's Commandments*

HEARERS AND FOLLOWERS OF THE LAW. EVAGRIUS OF PONTUS: Those who forget the law are the ones who violate it; yet those who remember the law are the ones who live in accordance with the law. Likewise, those who observe the sayings of God are those who keep them, and those who destroy them are those who do not want to follow them. "For it is not the hearers of the law who are righteous before God, but it is the doers of the law who will be justified."[1] SCHOLIA ON PROVERBS 27.3.1.[2]

---

[1]Rom 2:13.   [2]SC 340:120; cf. Scholia on Prov 343.28.4, SC 340:434.

HUMANS DO HAVE FREE WILL. AUGUSTINE: What of this fact, that God in so many passages commands that all his precepts be kept and carried out? How can he command if there is no free choice? And what of that "blessed man" about whom the psalmist says that "his will has been according to the law of the Lord"?[3] Does he not make it perfectly clear that it is by the will that a man takes his stand on the side of God's law? Finally, there are many commandments that in one way or another refer by name to the will. For example, "Be not overcome by evil, but overcome evil with good."[4] And there are similar passages, such as, "Do not become like the horse and the mule, who have no understanding";[5] and, "Do not cast off the counsels of your mother";[6] and, "Be not wise in your own conceit";[7] and, "Do not fall away from the correction of the Lord";[8] and, "Neglect not the law"; and, "Do not refrain from helping the needy";[9] and, "Plan no evil against your friends";[10] and, "Mind not the deceit of a woman";[11] and, "He would not understand that he might do well";[12] and, "They were unwilling to take correction."[13] What do such numerous passages from the books of the Old Testament show, except that a person's will is possessed of free choice? ON GRACE AND FREE WILL 2.4.[14]

3:3 Loyalty and Faithfulness

OIL OF MERCY. ORIGEN: If you wish to fast according to the precept of the gospel, observe the evangelical laws on fasting in which the Savior commands this about fasting: "But if you fast, anoint your head and wash your face."[15] But if you ask how "to wash your face," the apostle Paul teaches how "with uncovered face, you will contemplate the glory of the Lord and be transformed to this same image from glory to glory as by the Spirit of the Lord."[16] "Anoint even your head," but take care that it not be with the oil of sin. For "the oil of the sinner will not anoint your head."[17] But "anoint your head" with the oil of exultation, "the oil of joy,"[18] the oil of mercy, so

that, according to the command of wisdom, "mercy and faith may not forsake you." HOMILIES ON LEVITICUS 10.2.4.[19]

3:7 Be Not Wise in Your Own Eyes

IGNORANCE ACCOMPANIED BY RASHNESS BREEDS FALSE SELF-IMPORTANCE. CYRIL OF ALEXANDRIA: Ignorance is constantly, so to speak, accompanied by rashness and leads people on to attach great importance to their wretched fancies. Thus those who are the victims of this malady entertain a great idea of themselves and imagine themselves possessed of such knowledge as no one can gainsay. For they forget, it seems, Solomon, who says, "Be not wise in your own eyes," that is, according to your own single judgment; and again, that "wisdom not put to the proof goes astray." For we do not necessarily possess true opinions upon every individual doctrine that we hold, but often perhaps abandoning the right path, we err and fall into that which is not fitting. But I think it right that exercising an impartial and unprejudiced judgment, and not rendered rash by passion, we should love the truth, and eagerly pursue it. COMMENTARY ON LUKE, HOMILY 136.[20]

FEAR THE LORD AND DEPART FROM EVIL. FULGENTIUS OF RUSPE: If there are any who are even in the catholic church and live evil lives, before they finish this life, let them hasten to give up the evil life, and let them not think that the catholic name is enough for salvation, if they do not do the will of God. . . . In Proverbs each one of us is commanded both to fear the Lord and to depart from evil. There it is said, "Fear the Lord and turn away from evil. It will be a healing for your flesh and a refreshment for your body." ON THE FORGIVENESS OF SINS 1.26.2.[21]

---

[3]Ps 1:2. [4]Rom 12:1. [5]Ps 32:9 (31:9 LXX, Vg). [6]Prov 1:8. [7]Prov 3:7. [8]Prov 3:11. [9]Prov 3:27. [10]Prov 3:29. [11]Prov 5:2. [12]Ps 36:3 (35:4 LXX). [13]Prov 1:30. [14]FC 59:253. [15]Mt 6:17. [16]2 Cor 3:18. [17]Ps 141:5 (140:5 LXX). [18]See Ps 45:7 (44:8 LXX). [19]FC 83:206. [20]CGSL 540. [21]FC 95:143.

3:9 Honor the Lord with Your Substance

GOD DOES NOT APPROVE ALMS FURNISHED AT ANOTHER'S COST. AUGUSTINE: God approves of that alms which is furnished by just labors, as is written: "Honor the Lord with your labors and sacrifice to him with the fruits of your justice." For God abominates and refuses that alms which is furnished to him at the cost of another's tears. What profit accrues to you if one person blesses you while many curse you; what good does an alms bring to you when it is furnished from the possessions of another? In truth, need we fear that God does not have the goods with which you may feed his poor without plundering your neighbor? ON THE CHRISTIAN LIFE 12.[22]

NOT BY MERIT BUT BY GRACE. BEDE: We are commanded to honor the Lord not only with the substance of money that we extend to the poor and with all the good works we do, with the substance or fruits of the universal heavenly grace we receive, which is to seek his praise in all things rather than our own. [Not only the aforesaid,] but one honors the Lord with his substance and first fruits who attributes every good work not to his own powers and merits, but to supernatural grace, mindful of the word: "For without me, you can do nothing."[23] COMMENTARY ON PROVERBS 1.3.9.[24]

FULFILLING ALL RIGHTEOUSNESS. JOHN CASSIAN: "Honor the Lord from your righteous labors, and give to him from the fruits of your righteousness, so that your barns may be full of an abundance of wheat and your winepresses may be overflowing with wine." Know that when you exercise this devout practice in faith you have fulfilled the righteousness of the old law, which those who were under it then transgressed, unavoidably incurring guilt, while even when they did fulfill it they were unable to attain to the summit of perfection. CONFERENCE 21.2.1.[25]

MODERATING FORCE OF JUDGMENT. JOHN CAS-SIAN: Our Lord wants nothing to be done for his worship and honor without the moderating force of judgment, because "the king's honor loves judgment."[26] Therefore, so that we might tip to neither side by an erring judgment, the most wise Solomon says by way of admonition: "Honor God from your righteous labors, and give to him from the fruits of your righteousness." For there is in our conscience an incorrupt and true judge, who alone is never mistaken about the state of our impurity, even though all others may be misled. CONFERENCE 21.22.2.[27]

TAKING EVILLY DOES NOT HONOR GOD. GREGORY THE GREAT: It is written, "Honor the Lord from your just labors." It is no honor to the Lord to take evilly in order to give well. Hence also it is said through Solomon, "Whoever offers a sacrifice of the substance of the poor is as though he slew a son in his father's sight."[28] LETTER 106.[29]

STEWARDSHIP. SALVIAN THE PRESBYTER: We receive only the use of those possessions which we hold. We make use of the wealth loaned to us by God. We are, as it were, tenants by the revocable will of the grantor. When departing from this world, whether we like it or not, we leave everything behind on earth. Since we are tenants only of this sort, why do we attempt to take away and alienate from God's ownership what we cannot take with us? Why do we not use in good faith the little things given us by God? We hold property so long as he has allowed, we hold so long as he has permitted, he who has given us all.

What is more right, what is more proper, than when a thing is separated from him who had its use, that its possession revert to him who granted it for usage? Even the very words of God through the tongue of sacred Scripture order this, saying to one and all of us, "Honor the Lord from out of

---

[22]FC 16:33-34. [23]Jn 15:5. [24]CCL 119B:40. [25]ACW 57:720. [26]Ps 99:4 (98:4 LXX). [27]ACW 57:735. [28]Sir 34:24. [29]NPNF 2 13:25**.

your substance." And elsewhere he says, "Repay your debt."[30] How tender and condescending is our Lord God, who invites us to expend the wealth of our earthly substance! He says, "Honor the Lord from out of your substance." Though all we have received from God is his own property, he calls it ours so that we may be the ones who give it to others. Thus, he calls the proprietorship of possession ours so that there may be a greater reward for work, because, wherever effort spent seems to be on what is one's own, the worker necessarily has a greater return. FOUR BOOKS OF TIMOTHY TO THE CHURCH 1.5.[31]

---

[30]See Sir 4:8. [31]FC 3:278-79**.

3:11-12 GOD'S DISCIPLINE

[11]My son, do not despise the LORD's
discipline
or be weary of his reproof,

[12]for the LORD reproves him whom he
loves,
as a father the son in whom he delights.

OVERVIEW: Because God's grace complements our free will, punishment often comes to us for a good purpose and suffering often comes for the sake of justice (AUGUSTINE). We must be patient at God's chastisement (TERTULLIAN), for the Lord disciplines whom he loves and then makes all well (CLEMENT OF ROME). God did not spare from discipline even his only Son (AUGUSTINE). Illness, too, can be a punishment for sin (BASIL), and discipline from the Lord enables our progress toward salvation (CASSIODORUS) just as chastisement from priests can also enable our correction (CYPRIAN). Even the continuation of discipline, moreover, can mean that hope is not terminated or lost (JEROME). Opposition to sound doctrine, however, breeds opposition to discipline (VALERIAN).

3:12 The Lord Reproves Those Whom He Loves

GOD'S GRACE COMPLEMENTS OUR FREE WILL. AUGUSTINE: What clearer evidence is there for pointing to God's grace than in the case where we receive what we ask for in prayer? For if our Lord had said, "Watch that you enter not into temptation,"[1] he would appear to have merely given an admonition to man's will, whereas when he added the words "and pray," he made it clear that it is God who helps us so that we do not fall into temptation. It is to human free will that these words have been directed: "Son, do not fall away from the correction of the Lord."[2] ON GRACE AND FREE WILL 4.9.[3]

PUNISHMENT FOR A GOOD PURPOSE. AUGUSTINE: What here and now is the punishment of those who go astray? Some affliction perhaps, and some scourging that is for the purpose of either correcting or testing. Either, you see, people are corrected for their sins to avoid their incurring, uncorrected, severer punishments, or else their faith is being tested, to see with what endurance or what patience it remains intact under the Father's chastisement. [In either case,]

---

[1]See Mt 26:41; Mk 14:38; Lk 22:40. [2]Prov 3:11 Vg. [3]FC 59:261.

not grumbling angrily at the Father when he chastises and rejoicing at his caresses; but so rejoicing at his caresses that one also thanks him for chastising; because "he chastises every son whom he receives."[4] SERMON 113A.4.[5]

SUFFERING FOR THE SAKE OF JUSTICE.

AUGUSTINE: "Whom the Lord loves, he chastises; and he scourges every son whom he accepts."[6] . . . For, it is just that we who were dismissed from the pristine happiness of paradise because of our bold appetite for pleasures should be taken back through the humble endurance of difficulties, fugitives through our own evildoing, returning through suffering evils, there acting contrary to justice, here suffering for justice sake. ON PATIENCE 14.11.[7]

BE PATIENT AT GOD'S CHASTISEMENT. TER-

TULLIAN: If we believe some blow of misfortune is struck by God, to whom would it be better that we manifest patience than to our Lord? In fact, more than this, it befits us to rejoice at being deemed worthy of divine chastisement: "As for me," he says, "those whom I love I chastise."[8] Blessed is that servant upon whose amendment the Lord insists, at whom he deigns to be angry, whom he does not deceive by omitting his admonition! ON PATIENCE 11.4.[9]

THE LORD DISCIPLINES WHOM HE LOVES.

CLEMENT OF ROME: We must accept correction, dear friends. No one should resent it. Warnings we give each other are good and thoroughly beneficial. For they bind us to God's will. This is what the holy Word says about it: "The Lord has disciplined me severely and has not given me up to death. For the Lord disciplines the one he loves, and punishes every son he accepts."[10] . . . Do not refuse the Almighty's warning. For he inflicts pain and then makes us all well again. He smites, but his hands heal. 1 CLEMENT 56.[11]

GOD DID NOT SPARE HIS ONLY SON. AUGUS-

TINE: It is written, after all, "The Lord disciplines the one he loves, and scourges every son whom he receives."[12] Let us not fall away, then, under the lash, so that we may rejoice in the resurrection. So true is it, after all, that he scourges every son whom he receives, that he did not spare his only Son but handed him over for us all. So fixing our gaze on him, who was scourged without any sin to deserve it, and who died for our offenses and "rose again for our justification,"[13] let us not be afraid of being cast aside when we are scourged, but rather [let us] be confident that we will be received when we are justified. SERMON 157.3.[14]

ILLNESS AS PUNISHMENT FOR SIN. BASIL THE

GREAT: Not all sicknesses for whose treatment we observe medicine to be occasionally beneficial arise from natural causes, whether from faulty diet or from any other physical origin. Illness is often a punishment for sin imposed for our conversion. . . . Consequently, when we who belong to this class [of sinners] have recognized our transgressions, we should bear in silence and without recourse to medicine all the afflictions which come to us, in accordance with the words, "I will bear the wrath of the Lord because I have sinned against him."[15] THE LONG RULES 55.[16]

ENABLING PROGRESS TOWARD SALVATION.

CASSIODORUS: [The Lord] visits with a rod when he imposes stern punishment. In the same spirit Paul when writing to the Corinthians said, "What will you? Shall I come to you with a rod? Or in charity and in the spirit of meekness?"[17] He also visits us with stripes when he takes lighter vengeance on us; for a rod strikes us in one way, but whips flick us in another. Clearly each of these befalls Christian people according to the nature of their sin, enabling them to make progress toward salvation. As Solomon puts it: "For whom the Lord loves, he chastises; he whips every son whom he

---

[4]See Heb 12:6. [5]*WSA* 3 4:173*. [6]See Heb 12:6. [7]FC 16:248. [8]See Rev 3:19; Heb 12:6. [9]FC 40:212. [10]See Ps 118:18 (117:18 LXX); Heb 12:6. [11]LCC 1:69. [12]See Heb 12:6. [13]Rom 4:25. [14]*WSA* 3 5:111. [15]Mic 7:9. [16]FC 9:334-35. [17]1 Cor 4:21.

accepts."[18] EXPOSITION OF THE PSALMS 88.33.[19]

PRIESTS ALSO CHASTISE FOR THE SAKE OF CORRECTION. CYPRIAN: If God chastises whom he loves, and chastises that he may correct, brethren also, and priests particularly, do not hate but love those whom they chastise that they may correct, since God also prophesied before through Jeremiah and pointed to our own time saying, "I will give you pastors according to my own heart, and they shall nourish you, feeding you with discipline."[20] THE DRESS OF VIRGINS I.[21]

HOPE IS NOT TERMINATED. JEROME: The father schools only him whom he loves. The master rebukes only the pupil who he sees has a more zealous talent. Once the doctor stops trying to cure, he gives up hope. Your response may well be, "As Lazarus endured evils in his life, so I shall gladly endure torments now, so that glory may be stored up for me in the future; for the Lord will not punish the same sin twice."[22] The reason why Job, a holy and spotless man, a man just in his own day, suffered so grievously, is described in his book. LETTER 68.[23]

OPPOSITION TO SOUND DOCTRINE BREEDS OPPOSITION TO DISCIPLINE. VALERIAN: Many persons opposed to sound doctrine find fault with justice. They regard disciplinary control as haughtiness and attribute a just punishment to an overbearing nature. However, there is no haughtiness unless something unjust is ordered; and there is no overbearance except in the one who spurns discipline. Discipline, therefore, is a teacher of religion and of true piety; she does not threaten in order to inflict pain or chastise in order to work injury.

In fact, when discipline is angered she corrects the habits of people, and when she is aroused she keeps them under control, as Solomon tells us. . . . Indeed, there is nothing which correction fails to remedy or save. If anyone is wise enough to accept correction, he neither loses the pleasantness of friendship [with his corrector] nor runs the risk of condemnation. HOMILY 1.1.[24]

---

[18]See Heb 12:6. [19]ACW 52:362-63. [20]Jer 3:15. [21]FC 36:31-32. [22]Nah 1:9 LXX. [23]MFC 17:97. [24]FC 17:299.

3:13-20 WISDOM IS MORE PRECIOUS THAN JEWELS

[13]Happy is the man who finds wisdom,
　and the man who gets understanding,
[14]for the gain from it is better than gain
　　from silver
　and its profit better than gold.
[15]She is more precious than jewels,
　and nothing you desire can compare
　　with her.

[16]Long life is in her right hand;
　in her left hand are riches and
　　honor.
[17]Her ways are ways of pleasantness,
　and all her paths are peace.
[18]She is a tree of life to those who lay hold
　　of her;
　those who hold her fast are called happy.*

*[19]The LORD by wisdom founded the earth;
by understanding he established the
heavens;*

*[20]by his knowledge the deeps broke
forth,
and the clouds drop down the dew.*

*LXX and she is a safe [help] to them that lean on her, as on the LORD.

OVERVIEW: Eternal rewards, such as length of life, are in wisdom's right hand, whereas the things that perish, such as riches and glory, are in the left (CASSIODORUS, JEROME). Likewise the left hand of God symbolizes earthly prosperity, whereas the right hand of God stands for eternal happiness (GREGORY THE GREAT). The left hand of Christ, however, can refer to the church in its present life here and now (BEDE). The tree of life, by contrast, can indicate wisdom, or Christ (ORIGEN, JEROME), or Jesus (EPHREM), or the Bread by which humankind lives forever (ORIGEN). It also indicates the knowledge of good and evil (HILARY) as well as the cross and baptism (CAESARIUS). Likewise Christ, as God's wisdom, is known by many different names (ORIGEN). The Father did not make the heavens without the Son (AMBROSE), a process that also involved the Word or Christ, as proper Son of God (ATHANASIUS). Even the establishing of the church is related to God's creative activity (BEDE).

3:13-15 Those Who Find Wisdom and Understanding

THE NECESSARY PREREQUISITE TO FINDING WISDOM. BASIL THE GREAT: The souls of those who are about to speak with wisdom should first be cleansed through divine fear. For to distribute the mysteries of salvation to the general public and to receive all persons equally, including those whose life is not adorned with purity and those who have not been examined and prepared to make reasonable use of the mysteries, is like pouring one's most precious ointment into a filthy vessel. HOMILY ON THE BEGINNING OF PROVERBS 4.[1]

3:16 Riches of Virtue and Glories of Faith

LEFT AND RIGHT. CASSIODORUS: As Proverbs has it, "Length of days and years of life are in his[2] right hand," and this means eternal blessedness, whereas "In his[3] left hand are riches and glory," denoting the good things of this world, though there is no doubt that these can be bestowed by him. Moreover, it is his right side to which the saints are allotted when separated from the rest to obtain their rewards, whereas the left side is that mentioned when sinners are to be condemned to eternal punishment; for the saints have longed for things heavenly, whereas sinners have sought worldly goods. We also read that sinners have given the left hand's role to their right hand; our prophet is to say of them in Psalm 143: "Their mouth has spoken vanity, and their right hand is the right hand of iniquity."[4] But the true use of the right hand is where the bestowal of the Lord's grace is demonstrated. EXPOSITION OF THE PSALMS 120.5.[5]

A GREAT DIFFERENCE BETWEEN LEFT AND RIGHT. JEROME: The careful reader will easily perceive how great a difference there is between the right and the left side of wisdom when he has taken note of what she is reported to hold in her right hand and in her left, for Scripture says, "Long life is in her right hand, in her left are riches and honor." You see eternity and everlasting life in wisdom's right hand. But the perishable and fleeting things of time, creatures that are gone the very instant we think we have them in our grasp— riches and honor—are in her left. This is consistent with the fact that on the day of judgment, some will stand on the right and others on the left: sheep, naturally, and saints on his right, but goats

---

[1]PG 31:393. [2]KJV, RSV "her," i.e., wisdom. [3]KJV, RSV "her," i.e., wisdom. [4]Ps 144:8 (143:8 LXX). [5]ACW 53:268-69.

and sinners on his left.[6] HOMILIES ON THE PSALMS, ALTERNATE SERIES 61 (PSALM 15).[7]

GOD'S RIGHT HAND EMBRACES THE CHURCH. GREGORY THE GREAT: The church says by the voice of the elect, "His left hand is under my head, and his right hand shall embrace me."[8] She has put under her head, as it were, the left hand of God, that is, the prosperity of the present life, and presses it down in the rapture of supreme love; but the right hand of God embraces her, because in her complete devotion, she is enfolded with his eternal happiness. Wherefore, it is said again by Solomon, "Length of days is in her right hand, and in her left hand, riches and glory." He showed, then, how riches and glory are to be regarded, inasmuch as he recorded them as placed in the left hand. Wherefore, the psalmist says, "Save me with your right hand."[9] He does not say, "with the hand" but "with the right hand," to indicate by using the words "right hand," he is seeking eternal salvation. For this reason it is written again, "Your right hand, O Lord, has destroyed the enemy."[10] For the enemies of God, though prosperous in his left hand, are destroyed by his right hand, because very often the present life raises up the wicked, but the coming of eternal bliss condemns them. PASTORAL CARE 3.26.27.[11]

CHRIST'S LEFT HAND INDICATES THE CHURCH. BEDE: When the left hand of Christ is interpreted as referring to something good, the present life of holy church is understood. Hence it is written, "Length of days is in her right hand, in her left riches and glory." Length of days in her right hand [refers to] our Redeemer's wisdom because in the fatherland of the dwelling on high unfailing light is granted to the elect of both angels and human beings. Riches and glory are in her left hand, because we are restored during [our time of] exile in our journey [on this earth] by both the riches of the virtues and the glory of our faith, until we come to our eternal [resting place]. Of his glory the apostle says, "And we glory in our hope of

the glory of the children of God, and not only this, but we also glory in our tribulations";[12] and of these riches he says, "Because in everything you have become rich in him, with all speech and knowledge."[13] HOMILIES ON THE GOSPELS 2.21.[14]

3:18 The Tree of Life

THE TREE OF LIFE IS WISDOM. ORIGEN: I turn to the most wise Solomon as a witness when he said about wisdom, "The tree of life is for all who embrace it." Therefore, if "wisdom is the tree of life," without a doubt, there is another tree of prudence, another of knowledge and another of justice. For logically it is not said that only wisdom, of all the virtues, was worthy to be called "the tree of life" but that the other virtues by no means received names of a similar sort. Therefore, "the trees of the field will give their fruit."[15] HOMILIES ON LEVITICUS 16.4.3.[16]

THE TREE OF LIFE IS CHRIST. ORIGEN: These things must be understood to be said figuratively; for Christ himself is called "the tree of life." Just as by other things Christ is disclosed to be priest and victim and altar, and one understanding is not prevented by the other, and in their own passages each thing is perceived figuratively concerning him, so also now in the figures of mysteries a diversity of roles taken from one and the same thing will not get in our way.[17] HOMILIES ON JOSHUA 8.6.[18]

WATER'S BITTERNESS IS REMOVED BY BAPTISM. CAESARIUS OF ARLES: What is that tree which the Lord pointed out? Solomon shows us when he says of wisdom, "She is a tree of life to all who embrace her." If the tree of Christ's wisdom is put into the law, showing us how circumcision should be spiritually understood and how the sabbath and the law are to be observed, then

---

[6]See Mt 25:33. [7]FC 57:30. [8]Song 2:6. [9]Ps 108:6 (107:7 LXX). [10]Ex 15:6. [11]ACW 11:183-84. [12]Rom 5:2-3. [13]1 Cor 1:5. [14]CS 111:213-14. [15]Lev 26:4. [16]FC 83:268. [17]Heb 5:6; 1 Cor 5:7. [18]FC 105:92*.

the bitter water becomes sweet. When the bitterness of the law is changed into the sweetness of spiritual understanding, then the people of God can drink. . . . For this reason it is certain that if one wants to drink of the letter of the law without the tree of life, that is, without the mystery of the cross, the faith of Christ or spiritual understanding, he will die because of the excessive bitterness. Paul the apostle knew this when he said, "The letter kills."[19] In other words, the bitter water plainly kills if it is not changed into sweetness by the Spirit. For this reason the tree is cast into the water, so that it may be turned into sweetness. It is true, brethren, the bitterness is removed from the water when the tree of the cross is joined to the sacrament of baptism. SERMON 102.2.[20]

JESUS IS THE TREE OF LIFE. EPHREM THE SYRIAN: Risen is the light of the kingdom, in Ephrata the city of the king. The blessing wherewith Jacob blessed, to its fulfillment came today! That tree likewise, [the tree] of life, brings hope to mortal men! Solomon's hidden proverb had today its explanation! Today was born the child, and his name was called Wonder![21] For a wonder it is that God as a babe should show himself. HYMNS ON THE NATIVITY 1.[22]

THE TREE OF LIFE IS ALSO THE SUPERSUBSTANTIAL BREAD. ORIGEN: This supersubstantial bread, so it seems to me, has another name in Scripture, namely, "tree of life." If a person stretches out his hand and takes of it, he lives forever.[23] This tree is also given a third name, "wisdom of God," by Solomon when he says, "She is a tree of life to them that lay hold on her, and safe to them that lean on her as on the Lord." ON PRAYER 2.27.10.[24]

TREE OF THE KNOWLEDGE OF GOOD AND EVIL. HILARY OF POITIERS: In the book of Genesis,[25] where the lawgiver depicts the paradise planted by God, we are shown that every tree is fair to look upon and good for food. It is also

stated that there stands in the midst of the garden a tree of life and a tree of the knowledge of good and evil. Next, [we are told] that the garden is watered by a stream that divides into four heads. The prophet Solomon teaches us what this tree of life is in his exhortation concerning wisdom: "She is a tree of life to all them that lay hold upon her and lean upon her." This tree then is living; and not only living, but, furthermore, guided by reason. Guided by reason, that is, in so far as to yield fruit, and not casually nor unseasonably, but in its own season. And this tree is planted beside the rills of water in the domain of the kingdom of God, that is, of course, in paradise and in the place where the stream as it issues forth is divided into four heads. HOMILIES ON THE PSALMS 1.14.[26]

THE TREE OF LIFE IS NOT ONLY WISDOM BUT ALSO CHRIST. JEROME: This tree of life was planted in the Garden of Eden, and in Eden there rose a river that separated into four branches.[27] . . . Likewise, we read in Solomon, . . . "She is a tree of life to those who grasp her," [and here] he is speaking of wisdom. Now, if wisdom is the tree of life, wisdom itself, indeed, is Christ. You understand now that the man who is blessed and holy is compared to this tree, that is, he is compared to wisdom. Consequently, you see, too, that the just man, that blessed man who has not followed in the counsel of the wicked—who has not done that but has done this—is like the tree that is planted near running water.[28] He is, in other words, like Christ, inasmuch as he "raised us up together, and seated us together in heaven."[29] You see, then, that we shall reign together with Christ in heaven; you see, too, that because this tree has been planted in the Garden of Eden, we have all been planted there together with him. HOMILIES ON THE PSALMS 1 (PSALM 1).[30]

3:19 By Wisdom the Lord Founded the Earth

---

[19]2 Cor 3:6. [20]FC 47:104-5. [21]Is 9:6. [22]NPNF 2 13:223. [23]See Gen 2:9; 3:22. [24]ACW 19:99. [25]Gen 2:9. [26]NPNF 2 9:239*. [27]Gen 2:9-10. [28]See Ps 1:1-3. [29]Eph 2:6. [30]FC 48:7.

CHRIST, AS GOD'S WISDOM, IS UNDERSTOOD BY MANY DIFFERENT NAMES. ORIGEN: You will find it said in Proverbs, "God by wisdom founded the earth, and by prudence he prepared the heaven." Thus there is a certain prudence of God which one does not seek [except] in Christ Jesus. For all such [virtues], insofar as they are of God, are Christ: he is the wisdom of God, he is the power of God, he is the righteousness of God, he is sanctification, he is redemption.[32] In this way he is the prudence of God. But though there is one substance, for differences in the aspects the names are many. You do not understand the same thing about Christ when you understand him as wisdom and when you understand him as righteousness. For when he is wisdom, you mean the knowledge of things divine and human, but when he is righteousness, he is that power which allots to every person according to worth. And when he is sanctification, he is what enables those faithful and dedicated to God to become holy. In this way also then you will understand him as prudence, when he is the knowledge of what is good and evil, and what is neither. HOMILIES ON JEREMIAH 8.2.1.[33]

THE FATHER AND THE SON MADE THE HEAVENS. AMBROSE: Paul declares that it was said of the Son: "You, Lord, in the beginning laid the foundation of the earth, and the heavens are the work of your hands."[34] Whether therefore the Son made the heavens, as also the apostle would have it understood, while he himself certainly did not alone spread out the heavens without the Father; or as it stands in the book of Proverbs, "the Lord in wisdom has founded the earth, in understanding he has prepared the heavens," it is proved that neither the Father made the heavens alone without the Son, nor yet the Son without the Father. ON THE CHRISTIAN FAITH 5.2.29.[35]

WISDOM IS THE WORD OR CHRIST, THE PROPER SON OF GOD. ATHANASIUS: Solomon says, "The Lord by wisdom founded the earth; by understanding he established the heavens." And this wisdom is the Word, and by him, as John says, "all things were made"[36] [and without him not one thing was made]. This Word is Christ, "for there is one God the Father, from whom are all things. We are for him, and one Lord Jesus Christ, through whom are all things, and we are through him."[37] If all things are through him, he himself should not be reckoned with the "all things." Whoever dares to say that he, through whom are all things, is one of all the things surely will have the same speculation about God, from whom are all things. If anyone flees from this as absurd and excludes God from the "all things," it would follow that even the only-begotten Son, since he is proper to the Father's substance, must be excluded from the "all things." And if he is not one of the "all things," then it is not right to say about him "There was once when he was not" and "He was not before he was begotten." Such terms are fittingly used of creatures, but the Son himself is such a one as is the Father, of whose substance the Son is a proper offspring, Word and wisdom. This is peculiar to the Son in relation to the Father, and this shows that the Father is peculiar to the Son; so that we may neither say that God was ever wordless or that the Son was ever nonexistent. For how else could he be a Son, unless from God? Or how could he be Word and wisdom unless he is always peculiar to [God]? FOUR DISCOURSES AGAINST THE ARIANS 1.6.19.[38]

ESTABLISHING HIS CHURCH. BEDE: God the Father created all things through the Son. But he founded the earth by wisdom figuratively[39] when he established his holy church in firmness of faith through the Son. COMMENTARY ON PROVERBS 1.3.19.[40]

---

[32]See 1 Cor 1:24, 30. [33]FC 97:76-77. [34]Heb 1:10; cf. Ps 102:25 (101:26 LXX). [35]NPNF 2 10:288*. [36]Jn 1:3. [37]1 Cor 8:6. [38]TTC 82-83**. [39]Latin *typice*. [40]CCL 119B:42.

3:21-35 THE WISE INHERIT HONOR, BUT FOOLS DISGRACE

²¹My son, keep sound wisdom and
    discretion;
    let them not escape from your sight,ⁱ
²²and they will be life for your soul
    and adornment for your neck.
²³Then you will walk on your way securely
    and your foot will not stumble.
²⁴If you sit down,^j you will not be afraid;
    when you lie down, your sleep will be
    sweet.
²⁵Do not be afraid of sudden panic,
    or of the ruin^k of the wicked, when it
    comes;
²⁶for the LORD will be your confidence
    and will keep your foot from being caught.
²⁷Do not withhold good from those to
    whom it^l is due,
    when it is in your power to do it.

²⁸Do not say to your neighbor, "Go, and

come again,
    tomorrow I will give it"—when you
    have it with you.
²⁹Do not plan evil against your neighbor
    who dwells trustingly beside you.
³⁰Do not contend with a man for no
    reason,
    when he has done you no harm.
³¹Do not envy a man of violence
    and do not choose any of his ways;
³²for the perverse man is an abomination
    to the LORD,
    but the upright are in his confidence.
³³The LORD's curse is on the house of the
    wicked,
    but he blesses the abode of the righteous.
³⁴Toward the scorners he is scornful,*
    but to the humble he shows favor.
³⁵The wise will inherit honor,
    but fools get^m disgrace.

i Reversing the order of the clauses   j Gk: Heb *lie down*   k Heb *storm*   l Heb *Do not withhold good from its owners*   m Cn: Heb *exalt*   *LXX *God resists the proud*

OVERVIEW: Just as philosophy was to the Greeks what the law was to the Hebrews, a guide to righteousness, so now it serves as a tutor escorting persons to Christ (CLEMENT OF ALEXANDRIA). If one believes in God's providence, there is no reason to be anxious (ISAAC OF NINEVEH). Virtually every page of Scripture attests that God offers grace to the humble (AUGUSTINE). To be obedient to God, for example, one should be careful not to oppose the bishop (IGNATIUS). Arrogance must be countered by humility (CLEMENT OF ROME). God's grace is greater than worldly friendship (BEDE), and God is stern to the arrogant but kind to the humble

(JEROME). The wise inherit, but the wicked are disgraced like fools (HIPPOLYTUS).

3:23 Your Foot Will Not Stumble

GREEK PHILOSOPHY IS STILL A USEFUL GUIDE. CLEMENT OF ALEXANDRIA: Before the Lord's coming, philosophy was an essential guide to righteousness for the Greeks. At the present time, it is a useful guide toward reverence for God. It is a kind of preliminary education for those who are trying to gather faith through demonstration. "Your foot will not stumble," says Scripture, if you attribute good things, whether

Greek or Christian, to Providence. God is responsible for all good things: of some directly, like the blessings of the Old and New Covenants, of others indirectly, like the riches of philosophy. Perhaps philosophy too was a direct gift of God to the Greeks before the Lord extended his appeal to the Greeks. For philosophy was to the Greek world what the Law was to the Hebrews, a tutor escorting them to Christ. So philosophy is a preparatory process; it opens the road for the person whom Christ brings to his final goal. STROMATEIS 1.5.28.1-3.[1]

3:25 Be Not Afraid of Panic or Ruin

GOD MAKES PROVISIONS FOR US. ISAAC OF NINEVEH: If you believe that God makes provision for you, why be anxious and concerned about temporal affairs and the needs of your flesh? But if you do not believe that God makes provision for you, and for this reason you take pains to provide for your need separately from him, then you are the most wretched of all. Why even be alive or go on living in such a case? "Cast your care upon the Lord, and he will nourish you,"[2] and you shall never be dismayed at any terror that overtakes you.

One who has dedicated himself once and for all to God goes through life with a restful mind. Without nonpossessiveness the soul cannot be freed from the turmoil of thoughts; and without stillness of the senses it will not perceive peace of mind. Without entering into temptations, no one will ever gain the wisdom of the Spirit; and without assiduous reading, no one will know refinement of thought. Without tranquility of thoughts the intellect will not be moved in hidden mysteries; and without the confidence that comes through faith, the soul cannot dare to withstand temptations with boldness. Moreover, without actual experience of God's protection, the heart cannot hope in God; and if the soul does not taste Christ's sufferings consciously, it will never have communion with him. ASCETICAL HOMILIES 5.[3]

3:34 God Shows Favor to the Humble

SCRIPTURE TESTIFIES. AUGUSTINE: There is hardly a page in the holy books in which it is not shown that God resists the proud but to the humble offers grace.[4] CHRISTIAN INSTRUCTION 3.23.33.[5]

SUBMISSION TO GOD AND THE CHURCH. IGNATIUS OF ANTIOCH: Make no mistake about it. If a person is not inside the sanctuary, he is deprived of the Bread [of God]. For if the prayer of one or two has great avail, how much more is that of the bishop and of the whole church. Anyone, therefore, who fails to assemble with the others has already shown his pride and set himself apart. For it is written, "God resists the proud."[6] Let us be careful, therefore, not to oppose the bishop, so that we may be obedient to God. EPISTLE TO THE EPHESIANS 5.[7]

ARROGANCE MUST BE RESISTED BY HUMILITY. CLEMENT OF ROME: Since, then, we are a holy portion, we should do everything that makes for holiness. We should flee from slandering, vile and impure embraces, drunkenness, rioting, filthy lusts, detestable adultery and disgusting arrogance. "For God," says Scripture, "resists the arrogant but gives grace to the humble." We should attach ourselves to those to whom God's grace has been given. We should clothe ourselves with concord, being humble, self-controlled, far removed from all gossiping and slandering, and justified by our deeds, not by words. 1 CLEMENT 30.[8]

GOD GIVES GRACE GREATER THAN WORLDLY FRIENDSHIP. BEDE: The Lord gives greater grace than does the friendship of the world, because this grants earthly goods for a time and things that are to be lost with sorrow; he bestows the

---

[1]FC 85:41-42*. [2]Ps 55:22 (54:23 LXX). [3]AHSIS 45*. [4]See Jas 4:6; Mt 23:12; 1 Pet 5:5. [5]ACD 99. [6]Cf. Jas 4:6; 1 Pet 5:5. [7]FC 1:89**. [8]LCC 1:57.

eternal joy of life. On what sort he bestows this grace, however, he explains in succession. Wherefore he says, "God resists the proud but gives grace to the humble." God indeed punishes thieves, perjurers, dissolute persons, and other sinners, as despisers of his commandments. But he is said particularly to resist the proud, because they certainly are punished with a greater penalty who trust in their own strength, who neglect to be made subject to divine power by repenting, who refuse to seek the help of grace from above, as if they are sufficient by themselves to achieve salvation. But, on the other hand, he gives grace to the humble, because they who in the midst of the wounds of their vices humbly put themselves in the hands of the true physician rightly receive the gift of the hoped-for cure. . . . He will give grace, however, to the meek, because he bestows both the perfection of their good work and the gifts of a blessed everlasting life on those who humbly follow him. COMMENTARY ON JAMES 4.6.[9]

GOD IS STERN TO THE ARROGANT BUT KIND TO THE HUMBLE. JEROME: Candidly, I say to you, God hates all sin without exception: lying, perjury, theft, robbery, adultery, fornication; and if anyone should be caught in any of these acts, he would not be able to raise his eyes, and we would look upon him as one accursed. Yet, the proud man commits a far worse sin than adultery, and still we continue to converse with him. The fornicator may say, My flesh overcame me; youth was too much for me. I am not advocating that you yield to such a sin, for God hates that as well as any other; but, in comparing evils, I maintain that whatever other wrong

a man may commit, theft, for example, he can always find an excuse for it. What excuse does he give? I committed the theft because I was in need, I was dying from hunger, I was sick. What can the proud man say? Realize how evil pride is from the very fact that there is no excuse for it. Other vices harm only those who commit them; pride inflicts far more injury upon everyone. I am saying all this lest you consider pride a trifling sin. What, in fact, does the apostle say? "Lest he incur the condemnation passed on the devil."[10] The one who is puffed up with his own importance falls into the judgment of the devil. On the strength of Holy Writ, therefore, I declare, "When God is dealing with the arrogant he is stern, but to the humble, he shows kindness," so that we may shun all sin, most of all pride. HOMILY ON OBEDIENCE.[11]

3:35 Honor and Disgrace

THE WISE INHERIT, BUT THE WICKED ARE DISGRACED LIKE FOOLS. HIPPOLYTUS: They will not simply obtain glory but inherit wisdom. The wicked, again, even though they are exalted, are exalted only so as to have greater dishonor. For as one does not honor someone who is ugly and misshapen, if he exalts him, but only dishonors him the more by making his shame manifest to a larger number; so also God exalts the wicked, in order that he may make their disgrace obvious. For pharaoh was exalted, but only to have the world as his accuser. FRAGMENTS ON PROVERBS.[12]

---

[9]CS 82:50-51. [10]See 1 Tim 3:6. [11]FC 57:256. [12]ANF 5:172**; TLG 2115.053.

4:1-9 THE COMMAND TO OBTAIN WISDOM

[1]*Hear, O sons, a father's instruction,*
  and be attentive, that you may gain

insight;
[2]*for I give you good precepts:*

> do not forsake my teaching.
> [3]When I was a son with my father,
> tender, the only one in the sight of my
> mother,
> [4]he taught me, and said to me,
> "Let your heart hold fast my words;
> keep my commandments, and live;
> [5]do not forget, and do not turn away from
> the words of my mouth.
> Get wisdom; get insight.[o]
> [6]Do not forsake her, and she will keep

> you;
> love her, and she will guard you.
> [7]The beginning of wisdom is this: Get
> wisdom,
> and whatever you get, get insight.
> [8]Prize her highly,[p] and she will exalt
> you;
> she will honor you if you embrace her.
> [9]She will place on your head a fair
> garland;
> she will bestow on you a beautiful crown."

n Heb *know*   o Reversing the order of the lines   p The meaning of the Hebrew is uncertain

OVERVIEW: The command to follow wisdom comes from Paul as well as from Solomon (ATHANASIUS). Both the stag and the serpent, in their own ways, serve as models in the search for wisdom. We must therefore pray the Lord to open this treasury to us (EPHREM THE SYRIAN). Wisdom increases with age, whereas all other bodily excellences decay with longevity (JEROME). To observe the virtues is to honor wisdom (HIPPOLYTUS). To yearn for wisdom is to love it (PSEUDO-DIONYSIUS). Wisdom is capable of tasting and apprehending the quality of spiritual foods (ORIGEN). "Spiritual marriage" in love of wisdom, therefore, is a commendable alternative (GREGORY OF NYSSA).

4:1-2 Listen and Follow

SAME SORT OF TEACHING AS FROM PAUL.
ATHANASIUS: Paul wrote to the Corinthians, "You, therefore, follow me."[1] Let us follow him then, because that commandment has been passed down to us. The admonition originally given to the church at Corinth reaches to all Christians of all time in every place. For the apostle Paul was "a teacher of all nations in faith and truth."[2]

As a matter of fact, we get the same sort of teaching from all the saints of old. Solomon, for example, used proverbs, saying, "Hear, my children, the instruction of a father and pay attention to get understanding, for I give you a good gift. Do not forsake my word, for I was an obedient son to my father, and beloved in the sight of my mother." LETTER 2.1.[3]

THE GENTLE DISPOSITION OF THE STAG.
AMBROSE: Many indeed have complained over human weakness and frailty, but the holy Job and holy David have done so in a fashion superior to the rest. The former is straightforward, forceful, sharp, and displays a loftier style, as one who has been provoked by severe afflictions. The other is ingratiating and calm and mild, of a gentler disposition, so that he truly reflects the disposition of the stag which he set out as a model for his imitation.[4] And do not be disturbed if I should appear to praise such a mighty prophet under the likeness of a wild animal, when there is read to you the maxim given to the apostles, "Be wise as serpents, guileless as doves."[5]

But granted that likenesses of that sort find support from holy models, and that the stag is by nature harmless and gentle, still, I think that the stag which the prophet is setting out for imita-

---

[1]1 Cor 4:16.   [2]1 Tim 2:7.   [3]NPNF 2 4:510**.   [4]See Ps 42:1 (41:1 LXX).
[5]Mt 10:16.

tion in this passage is that stag of which Solomon, that apologist for paternal thought, said in Proverbs: "Let the loving stag and the graceful fawn confer with you."[6] THE PRAYER OF JOB AND DAVID 4.1.1-2.[7]

4:5 Get Wisdom and Insight

OPEN UP AND PAY ATTENTION. EPHREM THE SYRIAN: Open up the treasury door for us, Lord, at the prayers of our supplications; let our prayers serve as our ambassador, reconciling us with your Divinity. Listen, all who are wise, pay attention, all who are learned, acquire understanding and knowledge, seeing that you are instructed and wise. HYMNS PRESERVED IN ARMENIAN 1.1.[8]

WISDOM ALONE INCREASES WITH AGE. JEROME: Almost all bodily excellences alter with age, and while wisdom alone increases all other functions decay. Fasting, sleeping on the ground, moving from place to place, hospitality to travelers, pleading for the poor, perseverance in standing at prayer, the visitation of the sick, manual labor to supply money for almsgiving—all acts, in short, of which the body is the medium decrease with its decay.

Now there are young men and men of riper age who, by toil and ardent study, as well as by holiness of life and constant prayer to God, have obtained knowledge. I do not speak of these, or say that in them the love of wisdom is cold, for this withers in many of the old by reason of age. What I mean is that youth, as such, has to cope with the assaults of passion, and amid the allurements of vice and the tinglings of the flesh is stifled like a fire fed with wood too green and cannot develop its proper brightness. But when men have employed their youth in commendable pursuits and have meditated on the law of the Lord day and night, they learn with the lapse of time, fresh experience and wisdom come as the years go by, and so from the pursuits of the past their old age—their old age, I repeat—reaps a harvest of delight. Hence that wise man of

Greece,[9] perceiving, after the expiration of one hundred and seven years, that he was on the verge of the grave, is reported to have said that he regretted extremely having to leave life just when he was beginning to grow wise. LETTER 52.3.[10]

4:6-8 To Love and Embrace

TO OBSERVE THE VIRTUES IS TO HONOR WISDOM. HIPPOLYTUS: What is meant by "exalt her"? Surround her with holy thoughts, for you have need of larger defense, since there are many things to imperil such a possession. But if it is in our power to fortify her, and if there are virtues in our power which exalt the knowledge of God, these will be her bulwarks, as, for example: practice, study, and the whole chain of other virtues. The one who observes these honors wisdom, and the reward is to be exalted with her and to be embraced by her in the chamber of heaven. FRAGMENTS ON PROVERBS.[11]

YEARNING FOR WISDOM. PSEUDO-DIONYSIUS: Some of our writers on sacred matters have thought the term *yearning* to be more divine than "love." The divine Ignatius writes, "He for whom I yearn has been crucified." In the introductory Scriptures you will note the following said about the divine wisdom: "I yearned for her beauty."[12] So let us not fear this title of "yearning" or be upset by what anyone has to say about these two names, for, in my opinion, the sacred writers regard "yearning" and "love" as having one and the same meaning. DIVINE NAMES 4.12.[13]

DEEPER MEANING OF LOVE. ORIGEN: In these and a great many other places you will find that divine Scripture has avoided the term *love* and has put down "affectionate love" and "loving affection." Nevertheless, sometimes, granted it is rare, Scripture calls love by its own term and

---

[6]See Prov 5:19 LXX. [7]FC 65:389. [8]CS 101:36. [9]Theophrastus. [10]LCC 5:316-17*. [11]ANF 5:172**; TLG 2115.053.4.1. [12]Wis 8:2. [13]PDCW 81*.

summons and impels souls to it. For example, in Proverbs it says of wisdom, "Fall in love with her, and she will keep you . . . put her around you, and she will exalt you; honor her that she may embrace you." Moreover, in the book called the Wisdom of Solomon this is what is written about the same wisdom: "I became a lover of her beauty."[14] Now I think that where there is no apparent opportunity for error, Scripture in these cases introduces the word *love*. For what can any one find changeable or shameful in the love of wisdom or in the person who professes himself a "lover" of wisdom? But if it had said that Isaac fell in love with Rebekah or Jacob with Rachel, passion as something certainly shameful could have been understood through these words by the holy people of God, especially among those who do not know how to ascend from the letter to the Spirit. Commentary on the Song of Songs, Prologue.[15]

The Role of Taste and Sight in Spiritual Love. Origen: Just as taste and sight are different perceptions so far as the body is concerned, so, in accordance with the divine perceptions mentioned by Solomon, the visual and contemplative power of the soul is one thing, but that which is capable of tasting and apprehending the quality of spiritual foods is another.[16]

And . . . the Lord is capable of being tasted, being food for the soul, insofar as he is the bread of life which came down from heaven,[17] and is capable of being seen, insofar as he is wisdom, of

whose beauty he confesses to be a lover who says, "I became a lover of her beauty,"[18] and he commands us, "Love her, and she will preserve you.," For this reason it is said in the Psalms, "Taste and see that the Lord is good."[19] Commentary on the Gospel of John 20.405-6.[20]

Wisdom Will Honor You If You Embrace Her. Gregory of Nyssa: If anyone is going to obey Solomon and take true wisdom as the companion and sharer of his life, concerning which he says, "Love her, and she will safeguard you," and "Honor her, in order that she may embrace you," he will worthily prepare himself for this longing, keeping festival in a pure garment, rejoicing with those in this marriage, in order not to be rejected because of being clothed as a married person.

It is clear that the eagerness for this kind of marriage is common to men and women alike, for since, as the apostle says, "There is neither male nor female,"[21] and Christ is all things for all human beings, the true lover of wisdom has as his goal the divine One who is true wisdom, and the soul, clinging to its incorruptible bridegroom, has a love of true wisdom which is God. Now, what spiritual marriage is and toward what goal the pure and divine love looks has been sufficiently revealed in what we have said before. On Virginity 20.[22]

---

[14]Wis 8:2. [15]OSW 224-25. [16]See Wis 7:22-23. [17]See Jn 6:51. [18]Wis 8:2. [19]Ps 34:8 (33:9 LXX). [20]FC 89:288**. [21]Gal 3:28. [22]FC 58:64.

4:10-27 THE STRAIGHT PATH OF THE RIGHTEOUS

[10]*Hear, my son, and accept my words,*
  that the years of your life may be many.
[11]*I have taught you the way of wisdom;*

I have led you in the paths of uprightness.
[12]*When you walk, your step will not be*
  hampered;

and if you run, you will not stumble.
¹³*Keep hold of instruction, do not let go;*
guard her, for she is your life.
¹⁴*Do not enter the path of the wicked,*
and do not walk in the way of evil men.
¹⁵*Avoid it; do not go on it;*
turn away from it and pass on.
¹⁶*For they cannot sleep unless they have*
done wrong;
they are robbed of sleep unless they have
made some one stumble.
¹⁷*For they eat the bread of wickedness*
and drink the wine of violence.
¹⁸*But the path of the righteous is like the*
light of dawn,
which shines brighter and brighter
until full day.
¹⁹*The way of the wicked is like deep*

darkness;
they do not know over what they stumble.
²⁰*My son, be attentive to my words;*
incline your ear to my sayings.
²¹*Let them not escape from your sight;*
keep them within your heart.
²²*For they are life to him who finds them,*
and healing to all his flesh.
²³*Keep your heart with all vigilance;*
for from it flow the springs of life.
²⁴*Put away from you crooked speech,*
and put devious talk far from you.
²⁵*Let your eyes look directly forward,*
and your gaze be straight before you.
²⁶*Take heed to*[q] *the path of your feet,*
then all your ways will be sure.
²⁷*Do not swerve to the right or to the left;*
turn your foot away from evil.

q The meaning of the Hebrew word is uncertain

OVERVIEW: There is only one way of truth, but different paths come from different places (CLEMENT OF ALEXANDRIA). To follow this path, one should gird oneself with purity (PETER CHRYSOLOGUS) and follow the way of light (GREGORY OF NYSSA), keeping out the demons (ORIGEN). The real enemies are not flesh and blood (ATHANASIUS) but sins of the mind (GERONTIUS OF PETRA). We must not listen to the serpent within (MACARIUS), for evil thoughts are the source of all sin (ORIGEN). Therefore we must guard our heart and our mouth (AMBROSE) and sever the old bonds of attachment. We must guard our heart with constant vigilance (BASIL), neither lusting nor lingering (CAESARIUS), and seeking others' help if needed (BEDE). We should follow the divinely inspired Scriptures and fix our gaze straight ahead (CYRIL OF ALEXANDRIA), forseeing what outcome awaits (BEDE) but remembering always that sin lies within us (CYRIL OF JERUSALEM). The straight paths run toward our goal, the prize of our heavenly calling in Christ

(CYRIL OF ALEXANDRIA), and they are available even to those who limp (ORIGEN). God gives us grace and free will to make our paths straight (AUGUSTINE), so we must neither swerve nor deviate in either direction (AUGUSTINE, JOHN CASSIAN). Indeed, the good Shepherd will guide us (GREGORY OF NAZIANZUS).

4:10-11 One Way, Many Paths

MORE THAN ONE PATH OF SALVATION? CLEMENT OF ALEXANDRIA: There is only one way of truth, but different paths from different places join it, just like tributaries flowing into a perennial river. So these are really inspired words: "Hear, my son, and accept my words, to have many paths of life. I am teaching you the ways of wisdom, so that its springs may never fail you"—that is, those which spurt from the same soil. He is not merely affirming that there is more than one path of salvation for a single righteous person. He adds that there are plenty of righteous people and plenty of routes for them. He explains this as follows: "The paths of the righteous shine like light."[1] Stromateis 1.5.29.1-3.[2]

4:16 *Sleeplessness of the Wicked*

Cincture of Purity. Peter Chrysologus: Let your loins be girded about. Virtue should serve as a girdle in the place where passion should be checked. One who drops off the girdle of virtue cannot overcome the vices of the body. So girded with the cincture of purity—it is the badge of membership in the Christian army—let us cut away the dissolute cowardice of the flesh. Alert while watching our king, let us have no part in the restless sleep of worldly-minded people. For the wicked, Scripture says, "cannot sleep unless they have done wrong." Sermon 22.[3]

4:18 *The Path of the Righteous Is the Way of Light*

Participation in the True Light. Gregory of Nyssa: The person who removes himself from all hatred and fleshly odor and rises above all low and earthbound things, having ascended higher than the whole earth in his aforementioned flight, will find the only thing that is worth longing for. Having come close to beauty, he will become beautiful himself. Through his participation in the true light, he will himself be in a state of brightness and illumination. For just as at night the multitudinous glowing objects of the air which certain people call "shooting stars"... just as this earthly air, when it is forced upwards by the wind, becomes light-like, being changed in the clarity of the ether, so it is with the mind of man. After leaving this muddy and dusty life, it is purified through the power of the Spirit, becomes light-like, and is mixed with the true and lofty purity, and glows and is filled with rays and becomes light in accordance with the promise of the Lord who declared that the just will shine like the sun. On Virginity 11.[4]

4:23 *Keeping the Heart with Vigilance*

Necessary to Exclude the Demons. Origen: We who knew these and similar sayings wish to observe this precept with the mystical meaning, namely, "Keep your heart with all diligence," that nothing of a demoniacal nature may enter into our minds or any spirit of our adversaries turn our imagination whither it chooses. But we pray that the light of the knowledge of the glory of God may shine in our hearts, and that the Spirit of God may dwell in our imaginations, and lead them to contemplate the things of God; for "as many as are led by the Spirit of God, they are the sons of God."[5] Against Celsus 4.95.[6]

Our Enemies Are Not Flesh and Blood. Athanasius: Living thus, let us watch constantly and, as it is written, keep our heart with all watchfulness, for we have terrible and crafty enemies, the wicked demons, and we wrestle against them, as the apostle said: "For our wrestling is not against flesh and blood, but against the principalities and the powers, against the world rulers of this darkness, against spiritual forces of wickedness on high."[7] Life of St. Anthony 21.[8]

Guard Your Heart. Gerontius of Petra: Many people who are tempted by bodily delights do not sin with the body but lust with the mind: they keep their bodily virginity but lust in the soul. It is good then, my beloved, to do what is written: "Let everyone keep a close guard upon his heart." Sayings of the Fathers 5.2.[9]

Do Not Listen to the Serpent Within. Macarius: Scripture enjoins everyone to "guard his own heart with all diligence," so that anyone, guarding the word within him like a paradise, may enjoy the grace not to listen to the serpent

---

[1]Prov 4:18; RSV "path," LXX "paths" (*hodoi*). [2]FC 85:42*. [3]FC 17:68*. [4]FC 58:40-41*. [5]See Rom 8:14. [6]ANF 4:539. [7]Eph 6:12. [8]FC 15:155. [9]LCC 12:60.

that creeps around inside, enticing him with things that lead to pleasure whereby anger that slays a brother is engendered and the soul, that gives birth to it, itself dies. But may he have the grace rather to listen to the Lord saying, "Be concerned with faith and hope through which love of God and of man is engendered which bestows eternal life." . . .

For in a proportionate measure the word of God comes to each person. As long as a person possesses the word, he is held by the word and as long as he keeps it, so long he is guarded. FIFTY SPIRITUAL HOMILIES 37.1.[10]

EVIL THOUGHTS ARE THE SOURCE OF ALL SIN.

ORIGEN: The spring and source, then, of every sin are evil thoughts; for, unless these gained mastery, neither murders nor adulteries nor any other such thing would exist. Therefore, each person must keep his own heart with all watchfulness; for when the Lord comes in the day of judgment, "He will bring to light the hidden things of darkness and will make manifest the counsels of the hearts."[11] COMMENTARY ON MATTHEW 11.15.[12]

GUARDING OUR HEART AND OUR MOUTH.

AMBROSE: Let us then guard our hearts, let us guard our mouths. Both have been written about. In this place we are bidden to take heed to our mouth; in another place you are told, "Keep your heart with all diligence." If David took heed, will you not take heed? If Isaiah had unclean lips—who said, "Woe is me, for I am undone, for I am a man, and have unclean lips"[13]—if a prophet of the Lord had unclean lips, how shall we have them clean? . . .

Your possession is your mind, your gold your heart, your silver your speech: "The words of the Lord are pure words, as silver tried in the fire."[14] A good mind is also a good possession. And, further, a pure inner life is a valuable possession. Hedge in, then, this possession of yours, enclose it with thought, guard it with thorns, that is, with pious care, lest the fierce passions of the flesh should rush upon it and lead it captive, lest strong emotions should assault it, and, overstepping their bounds, carry off its vintage. Guard your inner self. DUTIES OF THE CLERGY 1.3.10-11.[15]

THE NEED TO SEVER THE OLD BONDS.

BASIL THE GREAT: Whoever, therefore, would be truly a follower of God must sever the bonds of attachment to this life, and this is done through complete separation from and forgetfulness of old habits. We must wrest ourselves from both fleshly ties and worldly society, being transported, as it were, to another world in our manner of living, as the apostle said: "But our commonwealth is in heaven."[16] Without this it is impossible for us to achieve our goal of pleasing God, inasmuch as the Lord said specifically, "So likewise every one of you that does not renounce all that he possesses cannot be my disciple."[17] And having done this, we should watch over our heart with all vigilance. THE LONG RULES 5.[18]

CONSTANT VIGILANCE IS NEEDED.

BASIL THE GREAT: Believe these words of mine that proceed from the fraternal charity of my heart. Have recourse to older men who make themselves difficult of access and in no way harm the young by their charm of countenance but animate them to virtuous deeds by sayings from Proverbs. "With all watchfulness, keep your heart"; for, like golden treasure, it is the object of the constant vigilance of thieves, night and day, and in an unguarded moment it is stolen without your being aware of it. See that the adversary does not seduce you into the sin of our first parent and cast you with all speed out of the paradise of delight. ON RENUNCIATION OF THE WORLD.[19]

NEITHER LUST NOR LINGER.

CAESARIUS OF ARLES: Let us listen to the prophet when he says, "With all watchfulness keep your heart," and

---

[10]IWG 188. [11]1 Cor 4:5. [12]ANF 9:444*. [13]Is 6:5. [14]Ps 12:6 (11:7 LXX, Vg). [15]NPNF 2 10:2-3. [16]Phil 3:20. [17]Lk 14:33. [18]FC 9:242-43**. [19]FC 9:24.

"Turn away my eyes that they may not behold vanity."[20] When someone lays hold of coals of fire but immediately throws them away they do not hurt him. But if he wants to hold on to them longer, he cannot get rid of them without injury. Similarly, if a man gazes lustfully and by lingering over it allows the evil of lust in his heart to get a hold on his thoughts, he cannot shake them off without injury to his soul. SERMON 41.5.[21]

BE VIGILANT AND SEEK OTHERS' HELP IF NEEDED. BEDE: Solomon convinces us to chastise all these kinds of evil thoughts when he says, "Guard your heart with all vigilance, for life comes forth from it." Following his suggestion, let us act quickly, that if we transgress in any way in our thoughts by consenting to carry out something wicked, we may swiftly wipe away this [transgression] by confession and fruits worthy of repentance.[22] If we perceive that we are being tempted by delight in committing sin, let us drive away this noxious delight by our frequent prayers and tears and by our frequent recollection of everlasting bitterness. If we see that we are not capable of ridding ourselves of it on our own, let us seek the help of our brothers, that we may accomplish by their advice and intercession what we are unable to do by our own strength. HOMILIES ON THE GOSPELS 2.12.[23]

4:25 Looking Directly Forward

FOLLOW THE SCRIPTURES. CYRIL OF ALEXANDRIA: It is necessary that, before other things, you have a sound mind within yourselves and that you are mindful of holy Scripture addressing you and saying, "Let your eyes look straight ahead." . . . To slip away from the rightness of holy doctrines would be nothing else except to sleep in death. We depart from this rightness when we do not follow the divinely inspired Scriptures. LETTER 55.3.[24]

FORESEE WHAT OUTCOME AWAITS. BEDE: Solomon, advising the wise hearer, says, "And let

your eyes anticipate your footsteps," which is to declare clearly that in all our actions we should take care to foresee with earnest intent what outcome awaits us, we should examine skillfully what is done according to the will of God and what opposes it. COMMENTARY ON 2 PETER 1:9.[25]

BUT SIN IS WITHIN US. CYRIL OF JERUSALEM: Someone will say, "What, then, is sin? Is it an animal? An angel? A demon? What is this which infects us?" Rest assured it is not an enemy attacking from without but an evil springing up within you. "Let your eyes look straight ahead," and there exists no evil desire. If you do not steal the property of others, robbery is at an end. Be mindful of the judgment and neither fornication nor adultery nor murder nor any wickedness will prevail over you. It is when you forget God that you begin to entertain evil thoughts and commit wicked deeds. CATECHETICAL LECTURES 2.2.[26]

4:26 Watch Where You Step

STRAIGHT PATHS FOR THOSE WHO LIMP. ORIGEN: "Invite the poor,"[27] he says, those who are poor in words, so that you can make them rich. Invite "the crippled," those whose minds are injured, so that you can heal them. Invite "the lame," those who limp in their reason, so that they can make "straight paths."[28] Invite the blind, who do not have the faculty of contemplation, so that they can see the true light.[29] FRAGMENTS ON LUKE 209 (LK 14:12-14).[30]

THE STRAIGHT PATHS RUN TOWARD THE GOAL. CYRIL OF ALEXANDRIA: We remember holy Scripture crying out, "Make straight the path for your feet, and direct your ways." They who honor the straight paths "run toward the goal to the prize of the heavenly calling in Christ."[31] But those who pay no heed to the apos-

---

[20]Ps 119:37 (118:37 LXX). [21]FC 31:207-8*. [22]Mt 3:8; Lk 3:8. [23]CS 111:116*. [24]FC 77:16. [25]CS 82:128**. [26]FC 61:97*. [27]Lk 14:13. [28]Cf. Heb 12:13. [29]Jn 1:9. [30]FC 94:211. [31]Phil 3:14.

tolic and evangelical tradition and honor the newer, useless and truly ridiculous invention of their own mind, let them hear from all, "Pass not beyond the ancient bounds which your fathers have set."[32] LETTER 31.3.[33]

4:27 Do Not Swerve

GOD GIVES US GRACE AND FREE WILL. AUGUSTINE: Mark well the counsel which the Holy Spirit gives us by Solomon: "Make straight paths for your feet, and order your ways aright. Turn not aside to the right hand nor to the left, but turn away your foot from the evil way; for the Lord knows the ways on the right hand, but those on the left are perverse. He will make your ways straight, and will direct your steps in peace." Now consider, my brothers, that in these words of holy Scripture, if there were no free will, it would not be said, "Make straight paths for your feet, and order your ways; turn not aside to the right hand, nor to the left." Nor yet, were this possible for us to achieve without the grace of God, would it be afterwards added, "He will make your ways straight and will direct your steps in peace." LETTER 215.5.[34]

TURN TO NEITHER HAND. AUGUSTINE: Let us hold fast, then, the confession of this faith, without faltering or failure. One alone is there who was born without sin, in the likeness of sinful flesh, who lived without sin amid the sins of others, and who died without sin on account of our sins. "Let us turn neither to the right hand nor to the left." For to turn to the right hand is to deceive oneself, by saying that we are without sin; and to turn to the left is to surrender oneself to one's sins with a sort of impunity, in I know not how perverse and depraved a recklessness. ON

THE MERITS AND FORGIVENESS OF SIN AND ON INFANT BAPTISM 2.57.[35]

THE GOOD SHEPHERD WILL GUIDE US. GREGORY OF NAZIANZUS: We must really walk on the King's highway[36] and take care not to turn aside from it either to the right hand or to the left, as the Proverbs say. For such is the case with our passions, and such in this matter is the task of the good shepherd, if he is to know properly the souls of his flock, and to guide them according to the methods of a pastoral care which is right and just, and worthy of our true Shepherd. IN DEFENSE OF HIS FLIGHT, ORATION 2.34.[37]

DO NOT DEVIATE IN EITHER DIRECTION. JOHN CASSIAN: And so one who wishes to go along the King's highway by means of the "arms of righteousness which are on the right hand and on the left" ought by the teaching of the apostle to pass through "honor and dishonor, evil report and good report."[38] And with such care [such a person ought] to direct his virtuous course amid the swelling waves of temptation, with discretion at the helm and the Spirit of the Lord breathing on us, since we know that if we deviate ever so little to the right hand or to the left, we shall presently be dashed against most dangerous crags. And so we are warned by Solomon, the wisest of men: "Turn not aside to the right hand or to the left." That is, do not flatter yourself on your virtues and be puffed up by your spiritual achievements on the right hand; nor, swerving to the path of vices on the left hand, seek from them for yourself (to use the words of the apostle) so as to "glory in your shame."[39] INSTITUTES 11.4.[40]

---

[32]Prov 22:28. [33]FC 76:123. [34]NPNF 1 5:440*. [35]NPNF 1 5:67. [36]Num 20:17. [37]NPNF 2 7:212*. [38]2 Cor 6:7-8. [39]Phil 3:19. [40]NPNF 2 11:276*.

5:1-14 WARNINGS TO EXERCISE DISCRETION

¹My son, be attentive to my wisdom,
    incline your ear to my understanding;
²that you may keep discretion,
    and your lips may guard knowledge.
³For the lips of a loose woman drip honey,
    and her speechʳ is smoother than oil;
⁴but in the end she is bitter as wormwood,
    sharp as a two-edged sword.
⁵Her feet go down to death;
    her steps follow the path toˢ Sheol;
⁶she does not take heed toᵗ the path of life;
    her ways wander, and she does not know it.

⁷And now, O sons, listen to me,
    and do not depart from the words of
    my mouth.

⁸Keep your way far from her,
    and do not go near the door of her house;
⁹lest you give your honor to others
    and your years to the merciless;
¹⁰lest strangers take their fill of your
    strength,ᵘ
    and your labors go to the house of an
    alien;
¹¹and at the end of your life you groan,
    when your flesh and body are consumed,
¹²and you say, "How I hated discipline,
    and my heart despised reproof!
¹³I did not listen to the voice of my teachers
    or incline my ear to my instructors.
¹⁴I was at the point of utter ruin
    in the assembled congregation."

r Heb *palate*   s Heb *lay hold of*   t The meaning of the Hebrew word is uncertain   u Or *wealth*

OVERVIEW: Your heart will not slip away if you guard your thoughts (GREGORY THE GREAT). At the beginning righteousness can seem bitter, but it will be sweet at the end (ORIGEN). Even the knowledge of doctrines can seem like honey dripping from a smooth tongue, when in reality it may be only the vanity of an expert theologian who is also a shameless fornicator (CYRIL OF JERUSALEM). It is possible to commit adultery with one's eyes (CLEMENT OF ALEXANDRIA). There are only two roads, one leading to death and one to life (CAESARIUS). What promises to be love may result only in slavery (CHRYSOSTOM). It is better to seek rest as the result of labor rather than to settle for labor as the result of rest (CAESARIUS). Practical advice assists us on the flight away from evil (AMBROSE). Immediate gratification lasts only an instant (ATHANASIUS). We are created in the image and likeness of our Creator, so we must not waste our honor or our years (GREGORY THE GREAT).

5:1 Be Attentive to Wisdom

GUARD YOUR THOUGHTS. GREGORY THE GREAT: "Attend to my wisdom, and incline your ear to my prudence, that you may guard your thoughts." Truly, there is nothing in us more fugitive than the heart that deserts us as often as it slips away in evil thoughts. Therefore, the psalmist says, "My heart has forsaken me."[1] So, too, returning to himself, he says [that he has found his heart to pray to you]. When thought is guarded, the heart so accustomed to flee away, is found. PASTORAL CARE 3.14.15.[2]

5:3-4 Dripping with Honey but Bitter as Wormwood

[1]Ps 40:12 (39:13 Vg). [2]ACW 11:130.*

Righteousness Is Bitter at the Beginning, Sweet at the End. Origen: "In the end," [Solomon] says, "you will find what seemed sweet in the beginning to be more bitter than gall and sharper than the edge of a sword." But the nature of righteousness is the opposite: In the beginning, it seems more bitter, but in the end, when it produces fruits of virtue, it is found to be sweeter than honey. Homilies on Joshua 14.2.[3]

The Expert Theologian Who Is Also a Shameless Fornicator. Cyril of Jerusalem: What does it profit a man to be an expert theologian if he is a shameless fornicator; or to be nobly temperate but an impious blasphemer? The knowledge of doctrines is a precious possession. There is need of a vigilant soul, since many there are who would deceive you by philosophy and vain deceit.[4] The Greeks, indeed, by their smooth tongue lead men astray, for honey drops from the lips of a harlot. Catechetical Lectures 4.2.[5]

Sinners Are Pleased for a While. Athanasius: Even when the sinner looks for gratification, he doesn't find the fruit of his sin pleasant. As the wisdom of God says in another place, "Bread of deceit is pleasant to a man, but after he eats it, his mouth will be filled with gravel."[6] And, "Honey drips from the lips of an adulteress, and for a time it tastes sweet, but in the end you will find it more bitter than gall and sharper than a two-edged sword." So he eats and is quite pleased for a little while. Then, when it is too late, when he has cut off his soul from God, he rejects it. But the fool does not know that those who are cut off from God shall perish. Letter 7.5.[7]

Two Roads Leading to Death or Life. Caesarius of Arles: In a very short time [the devil] leads the proud and wicked to death on a broad and spacious path. Christ our Lord, on the contrary, leads the humble and obedient to life on the straight and narrow path. Both of these roads, the wide one and the narrow one, have an end and are very short. Labor is not long on the narrow road, nor is joy lengthy on the broad one. Those whom the broad way of wickedness delights, after brief joy will have endless punishment. Those who follow Christ on the narrow way, after brief tribulations will merit to reach eternal rewards. If a layman who is in the world possesses pride, it is a sin for him. If a monk is proud, it is a sacrilege. You ought to show yourselves living so holy a life, so justly and piously in such a way that your merits may not only suffice for you but also find pardon in this world for other sinners. If we do not bridle our tongue, our religion is not true but false;[8] and it would have been better not to have made a vow than after the vow not to do what was promised. Sermon 233.7.[9]

Not Love, but Slavery. Chrysostom: The harlot knows not how to love, but only to ensnare. Her kiss has poison, and her mouth a pernicious drug. And if this does not immediately appear, it is the more necessary to avoid her on that account, because she veils that destruction, and keeps that death concealed, and does not permit it to become manifest from the outset. So if any one pursues pleasure and a life full of gladness, let him avoid the society of fornicating women, for they fill the minds of their lovers with a thousand conflicts and tumults, setting in motion against them continual strifes and contentions, by means of their words and all their actions. And just as it is with those who are the most virulent enemies, so the object of their actions and schemes is to plunge their lovers into shame and poverty and the worst extremities. And in the same manner as hunters when they have spread out their nets, they try to drive the wild animals into them, in order that they may put them to death. So also it is with these women. Homilies Concerning the Statues 14.10.[10]

---

[3]FC 105:133. [4]See Col 2:8. [5]FC 61:120*. [6]Prov 20:17. [7]NPNF 2 4:525**. [8]See Jas 1:26. [9]FC 66:198*. [10]NPNF 1 9:435*.

REST AS A RESULT OF LABOR RATHER THAN LABOR AS A RESULT OF REST. CAESARIUS OF ARLES: Let us reflect on what is written concerning dissipation and evil desires: "The lips of an adulteress are sweet for a time," it says, "but in the end she is more bitter than gall." Now since our life in this world is known to be, as it were, a road, it is necessary for us to reach rest as the result of our labor rather than labor as the result of rest. It is better for us to work for a short time on the way, in order that afterwards we may be able happily to reach eternal joy in our [home country], with the help of our Lord Jesus Christ, who lives and reigns with the Father and the Holy Spirit for ever and ever. SERMON 231.6.[11]

5:8 Do Not Even Go Near

ADULTERY WITH THE EYES. CLEMENT OF ALEXANDRIA: We should also be particularly careful of our eyes, for it is better to slip with the feet than with the eyes. The Lord offers a remedy for this weakness, indeed, with curt words: "If your eye scandalizes you, cut it out,"[12] thereby tearing lust up by the roots. Melting glances, and sly looks out of the corner of the eye, which is what is also called winking, are nothing more than adultery with the eyes, since lust operates at a distance through them. The sight sins before the rest of the body does. "The eye, seeing beautiful things, gladdens the heart," that is, when it knows how to see what is right it gives joy, "but he that winks with the eye deceitfully shall cause men sorrow."[13] CHRIST THE EDUCATOR 3.11.69-70.[14]

A GOOD FLIGHT FROM EVIL. AMBROSE: Your flight is a good one if your heart does not act out the counsels of sinners and their designs. Your flight is a good one if your eye flees the sight of cups and drinking vessels, so that it may not become envious as it lingers over the wine. Your flight is good if your eye turns away from the woman stranger, so that your tongue may keep the truth. Your flight is a good one if you do not answer the fool according to his folly.[15] Your flight is good if you direct your footsteps away from the countenance of fools. Indeed, one swiftly goes astray with bad guides; but if you wish your flight to be a good one, remove your ways far from their words. FLIGHT FROM THE WORLD 9.56.[16]

5:9 Honor and Years Wasted

IMAGES OF THE CREATOR, OR BODIES OF SLIME? GREGORY THE GREAT: Who are more strange to us than the evil spirits, separated from the lot of the heavenly fatherland? What else is our honor but to have been created in the image and likeness of our Creator, though we are made in bodies of slime? And who else is more cruel but that rebel angel who through pride smote himself with the punishment of death and who, though himself lost, has deliberately brought death on the race of humankind? He, therefore, gives his honor away to strangers, who, being created in the image and likeness of God, devotes the span of his life to the commands of the malignant spirits. He, too, gives his years to the cruel, who expends the span of the life which he has received obeying the will of an adversary who dominates him for evil. PASTORAL CARE 3.12.13.[17]

---

[11]FC 66:188-89. [12]Mt 5:29. [13]Prov 15:30. [14]FC 23:252-53. [15]Cf. Prov 26:4. [16]FC 65:322. [17]ACW 11:121*.

5:15-23 INTIMATE AFFECTION
SHOULD NOT BE DISPERSED

¹⁵*Drink water from your own cistern,*
flowing water from your own well.
¹⁶*Should your springs be scattered abroad,*
streams of water in the streets?
¹⁷*Let them be for yourself alone,*
and not for strangers with you.
¹⁸*Let your fountain be blessed,*
and rejoice in the wife of your youth,
¹⁹ *a lovely hind, a graceful doe.*
Let her affection fill you at all times
with delight,
be infatuated always with her love.

²⁰*Why should you be infatuated, my son,*
with a loose woman
and embrace the bosom of an adventuress?
²¹*For a man's ways are before the eyes of*
the LORD,
and he watches^v all his paths.
²²*The iniquities of the wicked ensnare*
him,
and he is caught in the toils of his sin.
²³*He dies for lack of discipline,*
and because of his great folly he is lost.

v The meaning of the Hebrew word is uncertain

OVERVIEW: Drink from your own cistern, and make use of your own resources (AMBROSE, ORIGEN, BASIL, JOHN CASSIAN). You are not merely watering the earth but enlightening human souls (CYRIL OF JERUSALEM). Since love is a gift of the Spirit, even if you appear pious yet follow evil ways, you cannot love (AUGUSTINE). The hind and the doe indicate a bond of affection that should be imitated by humans (HIPPOLYTUS). To run with a foreign woman is like being content with secular education rather than the Word of the Lord (CLEMENT OF ALEXANDRIA). We can easily be caught in our own sin (AUGUSTINE), in which case we are punished by ourselves (SALVIAN THE PRESBYTER). Therefore we ourselves must wash ourselves clean, and then we shall be happy (CYRIL OF JERUSALEM). But those who sin and have no discipline will perish (CHRYSOSTOM).

5:15-17 *Your Cistern for Yourself Alone*

SEARCH YOURSELF AND BEAR YOUR OWN

FRUIT. AMBROSE: Bear fruit for your own joy and delight. In yourself lies the sweetness of your charm, from you does it blossom, in you it sojourns, within you it rests, in your own self you must search for the jubilant quality of your conscience. For that reason he [Solomon] says, "Drink water out of your own cistern and the streams of your own well." SIX DAYS OF CREATION 3.12.49.[1]

YOUR OWN WELL. ORIGEN: Attempt, O hearer, to have your own well and your own spring, so that you too, when you take up a book of the Scriptures, may begin even from your own understanding to bring forth some meaning, and in accordance with those things which you have learned in the church, you too attempt to drink from the fountain of your own abilities. You have the nature of "living water" within you.[2] There are within you perennial veins and streams flowing with rational understanding, if only they have

---

[1]FC 42:103-4. [2]See Gen 26:19.

not been filled with earth and rubbish. But get busy to dig out your earth and to clean out the filth, that is, to remove the idleness of your natural bent and to cast out the inactivity of your heart. HOMILIES ON GENESIS 12.5.[3]

USE YOUR OWN RESOURCES. BASIL THE GREAT: "Drink water out of your own cistern," that is, examine your own resources, do not go to the springs belonging to others, but from your own streams gather for yourself the consolations of life. Do you have metal plates, clothing, beasts of burden, utensils of every kind? Sell them; permit all things to go except your [soul's] liberty. HOMILIES ON THE PSALMS 12 (PSALM 14).[4]

YOU WILL BE LIKE A FLOWING SPRING. JOHN CASSIAN: "Drink the waters from your own wells, fresh water from your own source." . . . As the prophet Isaiah declares, "You will be like a well-watered garden, like a flowing spring whose waters will never fail. And places emptied for ages will be built up in you. You will lift up the foundations laid by generation after generation. You will be called the builder of fences, the one who turns the pathways toward peace."[5] . . . And so it will happen that not only the whole thrust and thought of your heart but even all the wanderings and the straying of your thoughts will turn into a holy and unending meditation on the law of God. CONFERENCE 14.13.[6]

NOT MERELY WATERING THE EARTH. CYRIL OF JERUSALEM: Let us return to the sacred Scriptures and "drink water from our own cisterns and running water from our own wells." Let us drink of the living water, "springing up unto life everlasting."[7] . . . Not visible rivers merely watering the earth with its thorns and trees, but enlightening souls. CATECHETICAL LECTURES 16.11.[8]

THOSE WHO DO NOT LOVE REMAIN STRANGERS TO GOD. AUGUSTINE: "Let the fountain of

your water be your own and let no stranger share with you." For all who do not love God are strangers, are antichrists. And although they enter the basilicas, they cannot be numbered among the sons of God. That fountain of life does not belong to them. Even an evil person can have baptism; even an evil person can have prophecy. We find that king Saul had prophecy; he was persecuting the holy David and was filled with the Spirit of prophecy and began to prophesy.[9] Even an evil person can receive the sacrament of the body and blood of the Lord, for about such it has been said, "He who eats and drinks unworthily eats and drinks judgment to himself."[10] Even an evil person can have the name of Christ, that is, even an evil person can be called Christian; and about these it has been said, "They profaned the name of their God."[11] Therefore, even an evil man can have all these mysteries. But he cannot have love and be evil. This, then, is the peculiar gift; it is the unique fountain. For drinking of this the Spirit of God encourages you; for drinking of himself the Spirit of God encourages you. TRACTATES ON THE GOSPEL OF JOHN 7.6.[12]

5:19 The Hind and the Doe

BOND OF AFFECTION AND CONSTANCY. HIPPOLYTUS: He shows also, by the mention of the creature [the hind], the purity of that pleasure; and by the doe he intimates the quick responsive affection of the wife. And whereas he knows many things to excite, he secures them against these, and puts upon them the indissoluble bond of affection, setting constancy before them. And as for the rest, wisdom, figuratively speaking, like a stag, can repel and crush the serpentine doctrines of the heterodox. FRAGMENTS ON PROVERBS.[13]

5:20 Be Not Infatuated with a Loose Woman

---

[3]FC 71:183*. [4]FC 46:184. [5]Is 58:11-12. [6]JCC 168. [7]Jn 4:14. [8]FC 64:81. [9]See 1 Kings 19:20-24. [10]1 Cor 11:29. [11]See Ezek 36:20. [12]FC 92:221. [13]ANF 5:173*; TLG 2115.013.10.2.

DO NOT SETTLE FOR SECULAR EDUCATION.
CLEMENT OF ALEXANDRIA: When Scripture says, "Do not keep going steady with a foreign woman," it is advising us to make use of secular education but not to settle there permanently. Each generation received beneficial gifts at the appropriate points, but they were in preparation for the Word of the Lord. STROMATEIS 1.5.29.9.[14]

5:22 Snared by Our Iniquity

THE INDIVIDUAL CAUGHT IN HIS OWN SIN.
AUGUSTINE: Let those who are bound fear, those who are loosed fear. Let those who are loosed be afraid of being bound; those who are bound pray to be loosed. "Each one is tied up in the threads of his own sins." And apart from the church, nothing is loosed. SERMON 295.2.[15]

PUNISHED BY OURSELVES. SALVIAN THE PRESBYTER. I have previously said that we are punished by God because of our sins, and now I say that we are punished by ourselves. Both are true. We are, indeed, punished by God, but we act so that he has to punish us. Since we ourselves cause our own punishment, who doubts that we punish ourselves for our own crimes? For, whoever gives cause for his punishment punishes himself, according to the saying, "Each one is bound by the rope of his own sins." Therefore, if evil people are bound by the ropes of their own sins, each and every sinner, doubtless, binds himself when he sins. THE GOVERNANCE OF GOD 8.1.[16]

WASH YOURSELVES CLEAN! CYRIL OF JERUSALEM: Clothed as you are in the rotten garments of your offenses and "held fast in the meshes of your own sins," listen to the prophet's voice saying, "Wash yourselves clean! Put away the misdeeds of your souls from before my eyes,"[17] that the angelic choir may chant over you: "Happy [are] they whose faults are taken away, whose sins are covered."[18] CATECHETICAL LECTURES 1.1.[19]

5:23 Death for Lack of Discipline

FATE OF THOSE WHO SIN AND HAVE NO DISCIPLINE. CHRYSOSTOM: "He will perish here with those who have no discipline; and he will be driven out of the abundance of his fatness."[20] One who becomes the prey of sin and lacks discipline will experience the same things. Indeed the one who consorts with murderers becomes a murderer. See what bitter kind of death he [Solomon] designates when he says that he [the wicked person] will die with such companions. It is indeed horrible to depart from life with a bad reputation. Depravity—what he [Solomon] calls "fatness"—multiplies so that the flesh is destroyed completely by the works of flesh, keeping one away from the very kind of life that could save him. He [the wicked person] perishes because of imprudence, not because of lustful desires: he had a legitimate means to satisfy his desire, that is, his wife. Therefore nobody is allowed to accuse nature, but only human intemperance which is not proper to nature. COMMENTARY ON THE PROVERBS OF SOLOMON, FRAGMENT 5.23.[21]

---

[14]FC 85:43. [15]*WSA* 3 8:198. [16]FC 3:226. [17]See Is 1:16. [18]Ps 32:1 (31:1 LXX). [19]FC 61:91*. [20]Chrysostom diverges from LXX. [21]PG 64:669-72.

6:1-15 A FATHER TO HIS SON

¹My son, if you have become surety for
    your neighbor,
  have given your pledge for a stranger;
²if you are snared in the utterance of your
    lips,^w
  caught in the words of your mouth;
³then do this, my son, and save yourself,
  for you have come into your neighbor's
    power:
  go, hasten,^x and importune your neighbor.
⁴Give your eyes no sleep
  and your eyelids no slumber;
⁵save yourself like a gazelle from the hunter,^y
  like a bird from the hand of the fowler.

⁶Go to the ant, O sluggard;
  consider her ways, and be wise.
⁷Without having any chief,
  officer or ruler,
⁸she prepares her food in summer,

and gathers her sustenance in harvest.*
⁹How long will you lie there, O sluggard?
  When will you arise from your sleep?
¹⁰A little sleep, a little slumber,
  a little folding of the hands to rest,
¹¹and poverty will come upon you like a
    vagabond,
  and want like an armed man.

¹²A worthless person, a wicked man,
  goes about with crooked speech,
¹³winks with his eyes, scrapes^z with his
    feet,
  points with his finger,
¹⁴with perverted heart devises evil,
  continually sowing discord;
¹⁵therefore calamity will come upon him
    suddenly;
  in a moment he will be broken beyond
    healing.

w Cn Compare Gk Syr: Heb *the words of your mouth* x Or *humble yourself* y Cn: Heb *hand* z Or *taps* *LXX adds *Or go to the bee, and learn how diligent she is, and how earnestly she is engaged in her work; whose labors kings and private men use for health, and she is desired and respected by all; though weak in body she is advanced by honoring wisdom.*

OVERVIEW: There is a responsibility involved in watching over the soul of one's neighbor. Indeed, to be watchful means going without sleep or slumber, being vigilant with eyes both within and round about (GREGORY THE GREAT). Imitate the industry of the ant (AMBROSE). Labor in proportion to your strength (BASIL). Store up for the winter (AUGUSTINE). A monastery is in many ways like a colony of "the ants of God" (AUGUSTINE, JEROME). Moreover, the ant and the bee are similar (CLEMENT OF ALEXANDRIA). Both are worth imitating (CYRIL OF JERUSALEM), both are models of selflessness, and the bee also is serious about the future (CHRYSOSTOM). The bee repre-sents a unique situation (SHENOUTE), whereby one can even speak of "spiritual honey" (CYRIL OF ALEXANDRIA). The wax symbolizes creation, the honey contemplation (EVAGRIUS). The consequences of idleness are poverty and trouble (CHRYSOSTOM).

6:1-2 To Become Surety for Your Neighbor

RESPONSIBILITY INVOLVED IN GIVING SURETY. GREGORY THE GREAT: To be surety for a friend is to take charge of the soul of another on the guarantee of your own conduct. You are in charge of a responsibility which did not exist before. Your hand is bound fast to another's. One is ensnared with the words of his own mouth and caught with his own words. While he is obliged to speak what is good to those under his charge, he must first himself observe the matters of which he speaks. He is, therefore, ensnared with the words of his mouth, in that he is constrained by the exigency of right reason not to allow his way of life to be relaxed in a way that does not accord with his teaching. In other words, in the presence of the strict Judge he is constrained to accomplish in his own conduct what he clearly prescribes in words to others. PASTORAL CARE 3.4.5.[1]

6:3-4 To Be Watchful Means No Sleep and No Slumber

VIGILANT EYES WITHIN AND ROUND ABOUT.
GREGORY THE GREAT: Whoever is responsible for others for an example of living is admonished to be watchful not only over himself but also to arouse his friend. Indeed, it is not sufficient for him to keep watch by a good life, if he does not remove from the torpor of sin the person over whom he is set, for it is well said: "Give not sleep to your eyes, neither let your eyelids slumber." To give sleep to the eyes is to cease from care and thus to neglect altogether the charge of subjects. The eyelids slumber when our thoughts, weighed down by sloth, connive at what we know should be reproved. To be in deep sleep is neither to know, nor to correct, the actions of those committed to us. To slumber but not to sleep is to be well aware of what should be reprehended but not to amend it with proper reproof, owing to mental sloth. Yet by slumbering, the eye is induced to sleep profoundly, because commonly the superior who does not eradicate the evil which he observes, comes to that state which his negligence deserves, namely, not even to recognize the sins of his subjects. Therefore, those who [care for others' souls] must be warned to be earnestly on the watch, to have vigilant eyes within and round about, and to strive to become living

creatures of heaven. PASTORAL CARE 3.4.5.[2]

6:6 The Tiny Ant

IMITATE THE INDUSTRY OF THE ANT.
AMBROSE: The ant is a tiny creature, yet it ventures to achieve things beyond its strength. It is not driven to labor as a slave is. Rather, without compulsion and with freedom of foresight, it lays up provision for a future day. Scripture admonishes us to imitate the industry of the ant: "Go to the ant, you sluggard, and consider her ways and be wiser than she." [The ant] has no land under cultivation. Yet, without a taskmaster to urge it on as it looks after its stock of food, what a harvest has it in store for itself—a harvest gathered from the results of your labors! While you may frequently be in need, it wants for nothing. There are no granaries closed to the ant, no guards impassable, no stores of grain untouchable! The guard sees and dares not prohibit the theft. The owner gazes on his loss and exacts no punishment! Over the plain moves the dark column. The paths are aglow with the concourse of voyagers and particles of grain which cannot be seized by their narrow jaws are being heaved along by their shoulders! The owner of the crop beholds all this and blushes to refuse such trifles to cooperative industry such as this! SIX DAYS OF CREATION 6.4.16.[3]

LABOR IN PROPORTION TO YOUR STRENGTH.
BASIL THE GREAT: Why should we dwell upon the amount of evil there is in idleness, when the apostle clearly prescribes that he who does not work should not eat.[4] As daily sustenance is necessary for everyone, so labor in proportion to one's strength is also essential. . . . The Lord couples sloth with wickedness, saying, "Wicked and slothful servant."[5] Wise Solomon, also, praises the laborer not only in the words already quoted, but also, in rebuking the sluggard, associating

---

[1]ACW 11:97-98**. [2]ACW 11:98-99*. [3]FC 42:236*. [4]2 Thess 3:10. [5]Mt 25:26.

him by contrast with the tiniest of insects: "Go to the ant, O sluggard." We have reason to fear, therefore, lest, perchance, on the day of judgment this fault may also be alleged against us, since he who has endowed us with the ability to work demands that our labor be proportioned to our capacity. THE LONG RULES 37.[6]

THE PARABLE OF THE ANT OF GOD. AUGUSTINE: [The sluggard] has not imitated the ant. He has not gathered to himself grains while it was summer. What do I mean by "while it was summer"? While he had quietude of life, while he had this world's prosperity, when he had leisure; when he was being called happy by all, while it was summer. He should have imitated the ant, he should have heard the Word of God, he should have gathered together grains, and he should have stored them within. But there came the trial of tribulation, there came upon him a winter of numbness, a tempest of fear, the cold of sorrow, whether it were loss, or any danger to his safety, or any bereavement of his family; or any dishonor and humiliation. In winter; the ant falls back upon that which in summer it has gathered together; and within its secret store, where no one can see, it is replenished by its summer toils. When for itself it was gathering together these stores in summer, every one saw it: when on these it feeds in winter, no one sees. What does this mean?

See the ant of God. He rises day by day, he hastens to the church of God, he prays, he hears a reading, he chants a hymn, he digests that which he has heard, he thinks to himself about all this, and inside he is storing up grains gathered from the threshing floor. You who hear those very things which even now are being spoken, do just this. Go forth to the church, go back from church, hear a sermon, hear a reading, choose a book, open and read it. All these things are seen when they are done. That ant is treading his path, carrying and storing up in the sight of those who see him. But in due time there comes the winter. For whom does it not come? There happens to be

loss, or bereavement. Others perchance, who know not what the ant has stored up inside to eat, pity the ant as being miserable. EXPLANATIONS OF THE PSALMS 67.3.[7]

A COLONY OF ANTS IS LIKE A MONASTERY. JEROME: [Let us ponder] Solomon's sending us to learn wisdom from the ants, urging the sluggard to profit by their example. I began to weary of my capacity and to yearn for the cells of the monastery and to desire the comfort of the solicitude of those ants in whose community all worked together and where, since nothing belonged to anyone, all possessed all things in common. LIFE OF MALCHUS 7.[8]

6:8 The Ant and the Bee

HOW TO ORDER A MONASTERY AND DISCIPLINE A KINGDOM. JEROME: Construct also hives for bees, for to these the proverbs of Solomon send you, and you may learn from the tiny creatures how to order a monastery and to discipline a kingdom. LETTER 125.11.[9]

THE ANT AND THE BEE COMPARED. CLEMENT OF ALEXANDRIA: Scripture says, "Go to the ant, you sluggard, and become wiser than he." The ant at the time of harvest lays up an ample and varied store of food against the threat of winter. "Or go to the bee and learn her diligence." For she feeds over the whole meadow to produce a single honeycomb. STROMATEIS 1.6.33.5-6.[10]

THE ANT AND THE BEE ARE WORTH IMITATING. CYRIL OF JERUSALEM: There is the busy ant to rouse the indolent and sluggish; for when a man spends an idle youth, then he is instructed by the irrational creatures, being chided by the sacred Scripture, which says, "Go to the ant, O sluggard, and considering her ways, emulate her and become wiser than she." For when you

---

[6]FC 9:307. [7]NPNF 1 8:282*. [8]FC 15:294. [9]NPNF 2 6:248. [10]FC 85:46.

observe [the ant] treasuring up food for itself in good season, imitate it, and treasure up for yourself the fruits of good works for the world to come. And again, "Go to the bee and learn how industrious she is"; how, hovering above flowers of all kinds, it gathers the honey for your use, that you also, by ranging over the sacred Scriptures, may lay hold of salvation for yourself. Catechetical Lectures 9.13.[11]

Both Are Models of Selflessness. Chrysostom: Are you unwilling to learn from the Scriptures which teach that it is good to labor, and that he who will not work ought neither to eat?[12] Learn this lesson from the irrational creatures! . . . You should receive from this creature [the ant] the best exhortation to industrious living. Marvel at your Lord, not only because he has made heaven and the sun, but also because he has made the ant. For although this creature is small, it affords much proof of the greatness of God's wisdom. Consider then how prudent the ant is, and consider how God has implanted in so small a body such an unceasing desire for work!

But while you learn industry from this creature, you should take from the bee at the same time a lesson of neatness, industry and social concord! For it is not more for itself, than for us, that the bee labors and toils every day, which is indeed a thing especially proper for a Christian: not to seek his own things but the things of others. As then the bee traverses all the meadows that it may prepare a banquet for others, so also, O man, you should do likewise. Homilies Concerning the Statues 12.5.[13]

The Bee Is Serious about the Future. Chrysostom: "Go to the bee." Run to the church and learn the works of light which are done in it, and how the church in holiness accomplishes what it does. See how sensible and chaste it represents itself before kings and private citizens alike. Both the rich and the poor respect its prescription for their own salvation—although it is certainly weak and despised in this world. But when the church puts its faith in Christ it is exalted. In Christ, in fact, there is a rich and luxurious banquet for the time which he has appointed. The church does not look so much at what is present but rather envisions plans for the future. It prepares supplies in the summer and stores a great crop at harvest. Notice, I say, how the bee is solicitous about the future. You also should enjoy security in this life, but be careful lest, with the coming of winter, your house may be found empty and deprived of food. Notice how the bee treats everyone equally: not only is it useful to kings but to private citizens as well. Its medicine cures both alike; it serves nature but does not look for reward. You also should imitate it by valuing not so much the person but the nature of the works done. And does the bee have any beauty in its body? Not at all! For this reason, in order that lazy people might not find excuses in their weakness, Solomon chose the weakest among animals so that he might take away from them any excuses. The bee is pleasing to everybody, even to those who have no means or properties. Every day in the fields and in the cities we hear everyone speak countless praise of this insect. Commentary on the Proverbs of Solomon, Fragment 6.8.[14]

Unique Situation of the Bee. Shenoute: The bee alone, however, is collected and honored, as divine wisdom says: "It is in honor and in love among all." . . . Furthermore, the bee is loved by merit, for his labors are given for the delight of kings and [all] humans. To the Gentile Philosopher.[15]

Spiritual Honey. Cyril of Alexandria: Come, therefore, and let us also, wandering, as it were, around some intellectual meadow, gather the dew let fall by the Holy Spirit upon the divine message of the gospel, that so being enriched in mind we may bring forth the spiritual honey, even

---

[11]FC 61:192. [12]2 Thess 3:10. [13]NPNF 1 9:420*. [14]PG 64:672-73. [15]CSCO 96:23.

the word profitable and useful to all who thirst after the communication of the divine doctrines, whether they be noble and illustrious, or obscure and private persons in a humble rank of life. For it is written, "Good words are as honeycomb; and their sweetness is healing to the soul."[16] Commentary on Luke, Homily 62.[17]

The Practical and the Contemplative. Evagrius of Pontus: By "ant" Solomon seems to indicate the practical way, while the "bee" designates contemplation of creation and of the Creator. Both the pure and the impure, the wise and the foolish apply [this saying] for the benefit of their souls. It seems to me that the wax corresponds to the realities of creation, while the honey symbolizes the contemplation thereof. And while wax perishes, as it is written, "Heaven and earth will pass away,"[18] the honey does not perish. By the same token, the words of Christ our Savior do not pass away, about which Solomon says, "Pleasant words are like a honeycomb, their sweetness is health to the soul."[19] Also, David says, "How sweet are your words to my taste, sweeter than honey to my mouth!"[20] Scholia on Proverbs 72.6.8.[21]

6:11-14 Consequences of Idleness

Poverty Comes from Idleness. Chrysostom: "And poverty will come upon you like an evil traveler, and want like a good runner." Nothing is worse than poverty. It comes immediately to the idle and even overtakes strong runners in its speed. Poverty is just like need: poverty is lack of knowledge; need is lack of virtue. Can you see the absolute excellence of work? Will you not be taught by instinct? Learn then from an attempt at doing something. Or, do you want to appear even more irrational? Then run away from poverty. Is work at first difficult? Then look to its results. Is idleness sweet? Then consider what comes out of it in the end. So let us not look at the beginning of things, but let us also see where they end up. The one who goes out of his house does not want to stop along the way, but already at the beginning of his journey is thinking about the end. Because he starts out this way, his beginning will bring him to the end. But you do quite the opposite. Commentary on the Proverbs of Solomon, Fragment 6.11.[22]

Troubles Are Instigated. Chrysostom: "All the time this kind of man stirs up troubles in the city." Indeed! The words "all the time" are quite strong! In fact, even when such a person intends to command something good, his method of command is still full of suspicion. He leads people to fight and troubles secure cities with riots. This kind of a person has no peaceful spirit, nor has he listened to Jesus, who said, "How blessed are the peacemakers."[23] Commentary on the Proverbs of Solomon, Fragment 6.14.[24]

---

[16]Prov 16:24. [17]CGSL 266. [18]Mt 24:35. [19]Prov 16:24. [20]Ps 119:103 (118:103 LXX). [21]SC 340:168-70. [22]PG 64:673. [23]Mt 5:9. [24]PG 64:673.

6:16 — 7:27 WARNINGS AGAINST SINS AND MISDEEDS

[16]*There are six things which the Lord hates,*

seven which are an abomination to him: [17]*haughty eyes, a lying tongue,*

and hands that shed innocent blood,
¹⁸a heart that devises wicked plans,
  feet that make haste to run to evil,
¹⁹a false witness who breathes out lies,
  and a man who sows discord among
    brothers.

²⁰My son, keep your father's commandment,
  and forsake not your mother's teaching.
²¹Bind them upon your heart always;
  tie them about your neck.
²²When you walk, they^a will lead you;
  when you lie down, they^a will watch
    over you;
  and when you awake, they^a will talk
    with you.
²³For the commandment is a lamp and the
    teaching a light,
  and the reproofs of discipline are the
    way of life,
²⁴to preserve you from the evil woman,
  from the smooth tongue of the adven-
    turess.
²⁵Do not desire her beauty in your heart,
  and do not let her capture you with her
    eyelashes;
²⁶for a harlot may be hired for a loaf of
    bread,^b
  but an adulteress^c stalks a man's very life.
²⁷Can a man carry fire in his bosom
  and his clothes not be burned?
²⁸Or can one walk upon hot coals
  and his feet not be scorched?
²⁹So is he who goes in to his neighbor's wife;
  none who touches her will go unpunished.
³⁰Do not men despise^d a thief if he steals
  to satisfy his appetite when he is hungry?
³¹And if he is caught, he will pay seven
    fold;

he will give all the goods of his house.
³²He who commits adultery has no sense;
  he who does it destroys himself.
³³Wounds and dishonor will he get,
  and his disgrace will not be wiped away.
³⁴For jealousy makes a man furious,
  and he will not spare when he takes
    revenge.
³⁵He will accept no compensation,
  nor be appeased though you multiply gifts.

7 My son, keep my words
  and treasure up my commandments
    with you;
²keep my commandments and live,
  keep my teachings as the apple of your
    eye;
³bind them on your fingers,
  write them on the tablet of your heart.
⁴Say to wisdom, "You are my sister,"
  and call insight your intimate friend;
⁵to preserve you from the loose woman,
  from the adventuress with her smooth words.

⁶For at the window of my house
  I have looked out through my lattice,
⁷and I have seen among the simple,
  I have perceived among the youths,
  a young man without sense,
⁸passing along the street near her corner,
  taking the road to her house
⁹in the twilight, in the evening,
  at the time of night and darkness.

¹⁰And lo, a woman meets him,
  dressed as a harlot, wily of heart.^e
¹¹She is loud and wayward,
  her feet do not stay at home;
¹²now in the street, now in the market,
  and at every corner she lies in wait.

¹³*She seizes him and kisses him,*
    and with impudent face she says to him:
¹⁴*"I had to offer sacrifices,*
    and today I have paid my vows;
¹⁵*so now I have come out to meet you,*
    to seek you eagerly, and I have found you.
¹⁶*I have decked my couch with coverings,*
    colored spreads of Egyptian linen;
¹⁷*I have perfumed my bed with myrrh,*
    aloes, and cinnamon.
¹⁸*Come, let us take our fill of love till*
        morning;
    let us delight ourselves with love.
¹⁹*For my husband is not at home;*
    has gone on a long journey;
²⁰*he took a bag of money with him;*
    at full moon he will come home."

²¹*With much seductive speech she*

    persuades him;
    with her smooth talk she compels him.
²²*All at once he follows her,*
    as an ox goes to the slaughter,
    *or as a stag is caught fast*ᶠ
²³   *till an arrow pierces its entrails;*
    as a bird rushes into a snare;
        he does not know that it will cost him
        his life.

²⁴*And now, O sons, listen to me,*
    and be attentive to the words of my
        mouth.
²⁵*Let not your heart turn aside to her ways,*
    do not stray into her paths;
²⁶*for many a victim has she laid low;*
    yea, all her slain are a mighty host.
²⁷*Her house is the way to Sheol,*
    going down to the chambers of death.

a Heb *it* b Cn Compare Gk Syr Vg Tg: Heb *for because of a harlot to a piece of bread* c Heb *a man's wife* d Or *Men do not despise* e The meaning of the Hebrew is uncertain f Cn Compare Gk: Heb uncertain

---

Overview: Sin can come from evil actions or an impure heart (Chrysostom). Discord is the worst of the seven sins (Bede). God's law will be our lamp and our light (Cyril of Alexandria). Concerning adultery, there are as many snares as there are sins, and as many hunters as there are snares (Jerome). There is a natural attraction of opposite sexes (Leander of Seville), but danger can come even from mere touch (Jerome). Fire and hot coals can bring trouble, but a cheap harlot even more (Caesarius). Temptations first enter one's mind, then into one's prayer life, and then into reality (Isaac of Nineveh). Brief pleasure is not worth eternal punishment (Caesarius), and God is never pleased with an outward display of goodness and daring (Babai). Some misdeeds are worse than others, as stealing for avarice is worse than stealing for hunger (Salvian the Presbyter). Also, destruction of the soul by adultery must be distinguished from satisfaction of hunger by theft. (Chrysostom). Yet the creed remains on the table of our hearts, collected out of Scripture (Cyril of Jerusalem), and wisdom, our sister, is widely available to us (Origen). The seduction of the innocent but foolish young man, however, continues to remind us that worldly pleasure is contrary to nature (Ambrose, Bede).

6:16-19 *Warnings Against Seven Sins*

Evil Actions Through Members of the Body. Chrysostom: "A proud eye, an unjust tongue, hands that shed just blood." He [Solomon] emphasizes evil actions through members of the body used wickedly. As the eye, the tongue and the hands act in the body, in the same manner reflection, impulse and decision act in the soul. And, he [Solomon] did not enumerate these things to us without reason, but in order that we might learn to be moderate through them. Those who, while drinking the blood of the Lord, yet remain polluted with iniquity are shedding the blood of the just. COMMENTARY ON THE PROVERBS OF SOLOMON, FRAGMENT 6.17.[1]

AN IMPURE HEART MAKES THE LIMBS IMPURE. CHRYSOSTOM: "A heart that forges evil thoughts." Indeed, since the heart was impure, it also made the limbs impure, so that it shed the poison to its extremities. . . . By "brothers" he [Solomon] means those who have obtained the grace of adoption and are subjected to Christ our father. When unjust or lustful thoughts come to them, these thoughts try to trouble them. In fact, they inflame them to anger which causes hatred, and to evil desires which bring about immoral actions. COMMENTARY ON THE PROVERBS OF SOLOMON, FRAGMENT 6.18.[2]

DISCORD IS THE WORST OF THE SEVEN. BEDE: The six capital crimes enumerated here are nevertheless like minor faults when compared with the sowing of discord, since the deed that fractures the unity and fraternity which were achieved by the grace of the Holy Spirit is surely a greater sin. For anyone can raise his eyes boastfully, lie with the tongue, pollute himself with murder, plot to harm his neighbor, subject his members to other offenses, and give false testimony against another. But it must not be thought that what he names with his lying tongue is all the same, for he is able to tell a lie without doing so against a neighbor. For, in his book about lying,[3] blessed Augustine teaches that there are eight kinds of lies. Each reprobate, I say, can bring evil upon himself or upon others yet without harming the peace of the church. But what Donatus and Arius and their followers do is more serious, who destroy the harmony of fraternal unity by sowing discord. COMMENTARY ON PROVERBS 1.6.17-19.[4]

6:23 A Lamp and a Light

THE LAW OF GOD ILLUMINATES US. CYRIL OF ALEXANDRIA: Solomon also writes that "the commandment of the law is a lamp and a light." This sensible light that is in the world, by falling on our bodily eyes, dispels the darkness. So also the law of God, when admitted into the mind and heart of people, illuminates it thoroughly and does not allow it to fall against the stumbling blocks of ignorance or be caught in the thickets of sin. COMMENTARY ON LUKE, HOMILY 55.[5]

6:26-28 Warnings Against Adultery

AS MANY SNARES AS SINS, AS MANY HUNTERS AS SNARES. JEROME: We read in Proverbs, "The eyes of the harlot, the snare of the sinner." "Anyone who even looks with lust at a woman has already committed adultery in his heart."[6] There are as many snares as there are sins; as many hunters as there are snares. HOMILIES ON THE PSALMS, ALTERNATE SERIES 68 (PSALM 90).[7]

ATTRACTION OF OPPOSITE SEXES. LEANDER OF SEVILLE: When different sexes are placed together, they derive pleasure from those instincts with which they were born, and the natural flame is lighted by unnatural contact if it touches something inflammable. Who can ever take fire to his bosom and not be burned? Fire and tow[8] are as objects naturally opposite, but when brought together, they nourish flames. The sex of a man and of a woman is different, but, if they are brought together, the result will be what is provoked by the law of nature. THE TRAINING OF NUNS 2.[9]

DANGER COMES FROM THE MERE TOUCH. JEROME: We must notice the apostle's prudence. He did not say, it is good not to have a wife, but it is good not to touch a woman: as though there were danger even in the touch, as though he who

---

[1]PG 64:673. [2]PG 64:673-76*. [3]*Ad Consentium Contra Mendacium* (CSEL 41:469-528). [4]CCL 119B:55. [5]*CGSL* 240**. [6]Mt 5:28. [7]FC 57:83. [8]See Is 1:31. [9]FC 62:198.

touched her would not escape from her who "hunts for the precious life" and causes the young man's understanding to fly away. Can a man take fire in his bosom, and his clothes not be burned? Or can one walk upon hot coals, and his feet not be scorched? As then he who touches fire is instantly burned, so by the mere touch the peculiar nature of man and woman is perceived, and the difference of sex is understood. AGAINST JOVINIANUS 1.7.[10]

FIRE AND HOT COALS BRING TROUBLE. CAESARIUS OF ARLES: Solomon warns us against familiarity with such people when he says, "Can a man hide fire in his bosom, and his garments not burn? Or can he walk upon hot coals, and his feet not be burned?" And again: "The price of a harlot is scarce the half of one loaf: but the woman catches the precious soul of a man." Oh, how great is the wickedness and how deplorable the perversity, when a dissolute man for the sake of momentary lustful pleasure sells to the devil the soul which Christ redeemed with his blood! Truly lamentable and miserable is the condition whereby what brings delight passes away at once, while what causes torture endures without end. The assault of passion disappears in a moment, but the shame of the unfortunate soul abides. SERMON 41.3.[11]

FIRST IN ONE'S MIND, THEN IN ONE'S PRAYER LIFE, THEN IN REALITY. ISAAC OF NINEVEH: Do not voluntarily make trial of your mind with lewd reflections which tempt you, because in this way wise men have been darkened and made fools. Do not store a flame in your bosom.

Without harsh tribulations of the flesh it is difficult for untrained youth to be held under the yoke of sanctification. The beginning of the intellect's darkening (once a sign of it is visible in the soul) is to be seen, first of all, in slothfulness with regard to the services[12] and prayer. For except the soul first fall away from these, it cannot be led in the way of error; but as soon as it is deprived of

God's help, it easily falls into the hands of its adversaries. And again, whenever the soul becomes heedless of virtue's labors, it is inevitably drawn to what is opposed to them. ASCETICAL HOMILIES 2.[13]

BRIEF PLEASURE IS NOT WORTH ETERNAL PUNISHMENT. CAESARIUS OF ARLES: "The price of a loose woman is scarcely a loaf of bread; but if she is married, she is a trap for your life." Notice how great sin is, that on account of the space of one hour, in which an unhappy soul is joined to a prostitute, he renders himself alien to eternal life and makes himself liable to punishment by eternal fire. Even if that unfortunate delight of pleasure should stretch out over the space of a hundred years, it would not be right, and the unhappy soul would suffer eternal punishments in return for the pleasure of a hundred years. SERMON 189.4.[14]

GOD IS NOT PLEASED BY THE OUTWARD DISPLAY OF GOODNESS AND DARING. BABAI: "Can someone put fire in his lap without his clothes getting burned? Or can he walk over coals of fire without his feet getting scorched?"

Do not do anything out of the ordinary or adopt a singular way of life as long as you are with many brothers in the monastery. Otherwise when you imagine you are making progress you are in fact retrogressing, and you will be like the man who harvests and then scatters the grain, or the man who plants and then pulls up.

Try to ensure as far as possible that it is not men but God who sees your labors and good works. If they are visible to your fellow men, then the moment they are seen, they are flawed. For there is a path which appears to men to be good, but its tracks are those of death. Your religious life will be unacceptable if you show someone your good deeds.

It is very easy for someone to hide bread in the grass and then eat it, but to hide grass in bread

---

[10]NPNF 2 6:350*. [11]FC 31:206. [12]Liturgical services in church. [13]AHSIS 12. [14]FC 66:19*.

and live off that is something only the discerning is able to do. It is good to hide one's good deeds: a man whose actions only God sees has reached a high [level]. LETTER TO CYRIACUS 27-30.[15]

6:30-32 Some Misdeeds Are Worse Than Others

STEALING FOR AVARICE IS WORSE THAN STEALING FOR HUNGER. SALVIAN THE PRESBYTER: If slaves are thieves, they are perhaps forced to steal through want. Even though the customary allowances are given, these allowances satisfy custom rather than sufficiency and thus fulfill the law without fulfilling the need. Their indulgence makes their fault less blameworthy, because the guilt of the thief who is unwillingly forced into theft is excusable. Holy Scripture seems to excuse in part the offense of the needy when it says, "The fault is not so great when a man has stolen, for he steals to feed his hungry soul." THE GOVERNANCE OF GOD 4.3.[16]

SATISFACTION OF HUNGER BY THEFT BUT DESTRUCTION OF SOUL BY ADULTERY. CHRYSOSTOM: Not every sin brings the same penalty, but those which are easiest to be amended bring upon us the greatest punishment. Solomon indeed intimated this when he said, "It is not wonderful if anyone be taken while stealing, for he steals that he may satisfy his soul that is hungry, but the adulterer by lack of understanding destroys his own soul." But what he means is to this effect. The thief is a grievous offender, but not so grievous a one as the adulterer. For the former, though he has a sorry reason for his conduct, yet at the same time has to plead the necessity arising from indigence. But the latter, when no necessity compels him, by his mere madness rushes into the abyss of iniquity. HOMILIES CONCERNING THE STATUES 10.11.[17]

7:3 The Tablet of Your Heart

THE CREED IS COLLECTED FROM SCRIPTURE. CYRIL OF JERUSALEM: These articles of our faith were not composed out of human opinion but are the principal points collected out of the whole of Scripture to complete a single doctrinal formulation of the faith. And in like manner as the mustard seed contains numbers of branches-to-be within its tiny grain, so also this creed embraces in a few phrases all the religious knowledge contained in the Old and New Testaments together. Look now, brethren, and "hold the traditions,"[18] which are now being imparted to you, and "write them on the table of your hearts." CATECHETICAL LECTURES 5.12.[19]

7:4 Wisdom Our Sister

WISDOM NO LONGER EXCLUSIVE. ORIGEN: It is proper that until we reach maturity, virtue of the soul be within us and personal, but when we reach full maturity so that we are capable also of teaching others, let us then no longer enclose virtue within our bosom as a wife but as a sister, let us unite her also with others who wish her. For to those who are perfect the divine Word says, "Say that wisdom is your sister." HOMILIES ON GENESIS 6.1.[20]

7:6-23 An Innocent but Foolish Young Man

THE SEDUCTION OF WORLDLY PLEASURE CONTRARY TO NATURE. AMBROSE: She endeavors to steal the hearts of young men—a woman restless at home, a wanderer in the public squares, prodigal of kisses, indifferent to shame, gaudy in her dress and countenance. Since she is unable, indeed, to assume a beauty that is true to nature, she affects what is the opposite to truth—an external show of meretricious arts. . . . She attacks the citadels of men's hearts while uttering such words as these as a war cry: "I have vowed victims for peace, this day I have paid my vows. Therefore I am come out to meet you, desirous to see you, and I have found you. I have

---

[15]CS 101:148.* [16]FC 3:95. [17]NPNF 1 9:411*. [18]2 Thess 2:15. [19]LCC 4:124. [20]FC 71:122-23.*

woven my bed with cords. I have covered it with tapestry from Egypt. I have perfumed my bed with saffron and my home with cinnamon. Come and let us wrestle with desire." Here in the words of Solomon we behold the very picture of a wanton [woman]. What other than worldly pleasure is more characteristic of a prostitute who makes her entrance stealthily into the house, first making tentative explorations with her eyes and then entering quickly, while you concentrate the gaze of your soul outward on the public square, that is, on the streets frequented by passersby and not inward on the mysteries of the law? She has contrived to trap us in a room devoted to the associations of common life by such solid chains that a person, although held in bondage, finds herself at ease there. As she reclines there she covers her body with coverlets of fraud and deceit so as to allure the souls of young men, alleging the absence of a husband, that is to say, her disregard for the law. The law does not exist for sinners, for, if it were present, it would not have been ignored. Hence we read: "For my husband is not at home, he is gone a very long journey. He took with him a bag of money." What is the meaning of this, if not that the rich believe that there is nothing that money cannot control and that the law is something that can be sold for profit? Pleasure dissipates its fragrance because it has not the fragrance of Christ.[21] Pleasure looks for treasures, it promises kingdoms, it assures lasting loves, it pledges undreamed of intimacies, instruction without a guardian and conversation without

hindrance. Pleasure promises a life bereft of anxiety, a sleep devoid of disturbance and wants that cannot be satiated. We read: Entangling him with many words and alluring him with the snares of her lips, she led him even to her home. He was beguiled and followed her. . . . Everything there was confused and contrary to the order of nature. CAIN AND ABEL 1.4.14.[22]

HE WILL COME HOME. ORIGEN: In these words, "after many days he will return home," Paul (who in the spirit perceived the plan of the divine economy) refers to the last enemy which is to be destroyed, that is, death.[23] That enemy is the man of wickedness that Solomon will describe as one who took in his hand "a bag of money," that is, humanity. When [humanity] sins again and again, it allows itself to disregard the fear of God. It [only] becomes distressed when the human race is brought to the point of trials. Otherwise, if it never envisioned any fear of God at all, it would have perished in an instant. EXPOSITION ON PROVERBS, FRAGMENT 7.20.[24]

A FINAL COMMENT. BEDE: Uncircumcised in smell and touch are those who are steeped in ointment and various odors, who pursue the embraces of a harlot, sprinkling their bed with myrrh, aloes and cinnamon. HOMILIES ON THE GOSPELS 1.11.[25]

---

[21]2 Cor 2:15. [22]FC 42:370-71*. [23]1 Cor 15:26. [24]PG 17:181. [25]CS 110:110.

8:1-21 THE CALL OF WISDOM

¹Does not wisdom call,
Does not understanding raise her voice?

²On the heights beside the way,
in the paths she takes her stand;

³*beside the gates in front of the town,*
   at the entrance of the portals she cries
      aloud:
⁴*"To you, O men, I call,*
   and my cry is to the sons of men.
⁵*O simple ones, learn prudence;*
   O foolish men, pay attention.
⁶*Hear, for I will speak noble things,*
   and from my lips will come what is right;
⁷*for my mouth will utter truth;*
   wickedness is an abomination to my lips.
⁸*All the words of my mouth are righteous;*
   there is nothing twisted or crooked in
      them.
⁹*They are all straight to him who*
      understands
   and right to those who find knowledge.
¹⁰*Take my instruction instead of silver,*
   and knowledge rather than choice gold;
¹¹*for wisdom is better than jewels,*
   and all that you may desire cannot
      compare with her.
¹²*I, wisdom, dwell in prudence,ᵍ*
   and I find knowledge and discretion.*

¹³*The fear of the LORD is hatred of*
      evil.
   Pride and arrogance and the way of
      evil
   and perverted speech I hate.
¹⁴*I have counsel and sound wisdom,*
   I have insight, I have strength.
¹⁵*By me kings reign,*
   and rulers decree what is just;
¹⁶*by me princes rule,†*
   and nobles governʰ the earth.
¹⁷*I love those who love me,*
   and those who seek me diligently find
      me.
¹⁸*Riches and honor are with me,*
   enduring wealth and prosperity.
¹⁹*My fruit is better than gold, even fine*
      gold,
   and my yield than choice silver.
²⁰*I walk in the way of righteousness,*
   in the paths of justice,
²¹*endowing with wealth those who*
      love me,
   and filling their treasuries.

g Heb *obscure* **h** Gk: Heb *all the governors of* *LXX *I, wisdom, have dwelt with counsel and knowledge, and I have called upon understanding* †LXX *became great*

OVERVIEW: Meanings of words are distinct and different (HILARY). Wisdom examines the levels of advice, aware of the usefulness of varied methods of persuasion (CLEMENT OF ALEXANDRIA). We are indebted to the Greeks and the barbarians, to the wise and the foolish (ORIGEN). There is a concord and harmony in the law and the prophets (CLEMENT OF ALEXANDRIA), and in the gospel, which presents words and symbols, having outward and inward significance (ORIGEN). Wisdom, which is better than precious jewels, is an incomparable blessing that comes to us from above by means of holy Scripture (CYRIL OF ALEXANDRIA). Even kings and rulers have nothing without wis-

dom (BEDE). Those who deny the truth of faith have not even received salvation in baptism (FULGENTIUS). Discipline, even instruction and knowledge, is always to be preferred to silver or gold (BASIL).

8:4 The Call Goes Out

MEANINGS OF WORDS ARE DISTINCT AND DIFFERENT. HILARY OF POITIERS: In the first place, while wisdom addresses everyone, it warns the simple to understand subtlety and the unlearned to apply their heart, in order that the zealous and attentive reader may evaluate the meanings of words that are distinct and different. It teaches, therefore, that all things are to be done, understood, praised and grasped according to its methods and plans. On the Trinity 12.44.[1]

Three Methods of Advice and Persuasion. Clement of Alexandria: When the educator says in one of the passages of Solomon's work, "O men, to you I call, and my voice is to the sons of men. Hear, for I will speak of great things," and the rest of the passage, he is making use of persuasion—persuasion to something that is useful. Since advice is called for when there is a question of free acceptance or rejection, he is here advising what will lead to salvation. . . . There are three possible methods of giving advice. The first is to take examples from times gone by, such as the punishments the Jews met with after they had worshiped the golden calf,[2] or when they had committed fornication,[3] or after similar misdeeds. The second method is to call attention to some conclusion drawn from present events, as a conclusion readily grasped by the mind, such was the answer given by the Lord to those who asked him, "Are you the Christ, or should we look for another?" "Go," he said, "report to John that the blind see, the lame walk, the lepers are cleansed, the dead rise, and blessed is he who is not scandalized in me."[4] . . . Finally, the third method of advice is drawn from future events, in which things that are to come put us on our guard; an example is that saying that those falling into sin "will be put forth into the darkness outside, there will be weeping and the gnashing of teeth,"[5] and sayings of the same import. Therefore, it can be clearly seen that the Lord calls humankind to salvation by using progressively every kind of treatment. Christ the Educator 1.10.90-91.[6]

8:5-7 Learn Prudence and Pay Attention

We Are Debtors. Origen: Those among us who are ambassadors of Christianity sufficiently declare that they are debtors to Greeks and barbarians, to wise men and fools (for they do not deny their obligation to cure the souls even of foolish persons), in order that as far as possible they may lay aside their ignorance and endeavor to obtain greater prudence, by listening also to the words of Solomon: "O fools, be of an understanding heart," and "Whoever is the most simple among you, let him turn unto me."[7] Wisdom exhorts those who are empty of understanding in the words, "Come, eat of my bread, and drink of the wine which I have mixed for you. Forsake folly that you may live, and correct understanding in knowledge."[8] Against Celsus 3.54.[9]

Denial of Salvation in Baptism. Fulgentius of Ruspe: "For my mouth will utter truth; wickedness is an abomination to my lips." Therefore, they who do not hold the truth of the faith in heart and mouth do not receive salvation in baptism. Because of this, although they have the appearance of piety which consists in the sacrament of baptism, by refusing the power of piety they receive neither life nor salvation. Letter 7.[10]

8:9-11 All Things Are Right in Scripture

Concord and Harmony of Law and Prophets. Clement of Alexandria: [Jesus] "spoke all things in parables, and without a parable he spoke nothing" [to the apostles];[11] and if "all things were made by him, and without him was not anything made that was made,"[12] consequently also prophecy and the law were by him and were spoken by him in parables. "But all things are right," says the Scripture, "before those who understand," that is, those who receive and observe, according to the church's rule of faith, the exposition of the Scriptures explained by him. And the church's rule is the concord and harmony of the law and the prophets in the cove-

---

[1]FC 25:532*. [2]See Ex 32:26-28. [3]See Num 25:4-9. [4]Mt 11:3-6. [5]Mt 8:12. [6]FC 23:79-80. [7]Prov 9:4. [8]Prov 9:5-6. [9]ANF 4:485-86*. [10]FC 95:480. [11]Mt 13:34. [12]Jn 1:3.

nant delivered at the coming of the Lord. Knowledge is then followed by practical wisdom and practical wisdom by self-control, for it may be said that practical wisdom is divine knowledge and exists in those who share in God's life, while the self-control that is mortal, which is present in those who philosophize, is not yet wise. STROMATEIS 6.15.[13]

CIRCUMCISION AND BAPTISM. ORIGEN: That which John calls an eternal gospel,[14] which would properly be called a spiritual gospel, clearly presents both the mysteries presented by Christ's words and the things of which his acts were symbols, to those who consider "all things face to face" concerning the Son of God himself. Consistent with these matters, we understand that just as one is a Jew outwardly and circumcised, there being both an outward and inward circumcision, so it is with a Christian and baptism. COMMENTARY ON THE GOSPEL OF JOHN 1.40.[15]

PREFER DISCIPLINE OVER SILVER. BASIL THE GREAT: "Accept discipline, not silver," so that at a time of calamity or physical illness or domestic trouble, you would think nothing at all perverse of God, but accept the blows meted out by him with great patience as though you were being castigated for your sins. Thus, conscious of being disciplined, say, "I will bear the wrath of the Lord because I have sinned against him."[16] HOMILY ON THE BEGINNING OF PROVERBS 5.[17]

INCOMPARABLE BLESSING. CYRIL OF ALEXANDRIA: It is written that "wisdom is better than stones of costly price; and all precious things are not comparable to her." For the wisdom that comes from above, from God, is an incomparable blessing. When we attain to it by means of the holy Scripture, which is inspired of God, and gain the divine light to dwell in our minds, we then advance without wandering, and we come toward whatever is useful for our spiritual profit. Come, therefore, and let us now also scrupulously examine the meaning of the Gospel lessons. COMMENTARY ON LUKE, HOMILY 133.[18]

8:15 By Me Kings Reign

EVEN KINGS AND RULERS HAVE NOTHING WITHOUT WISDOM. BEDE: Those whom it calls "kings" are the apostles and other saints, like the lawmakers and authors of both Testaments and the subsequent writers of the church. They have learned first how to rule themselves, and then the church that was put under their care. Those whom it calls "rulers" are governors and other powerful leaders of the faithful. But none of these would have anything were it not through wisdom, for he says, "Without me, you can do nothing."[19] COMMENTARY ON PROVERBS 1.8.15-16.[20]

---

[13]ANF 2:509*. [14]See Rev 14:6. [15]FC 80:42*. [16]Mic 7:9. [17]PG 31:397. [18]CGSL 525*. [19]Jn 15:5. [20]CCL 119B:60.

8:22 THE LORD CREATED WISDOM AT THE BEGINNING

[22]The LORD created me at the beginning of his work,[i]
    the first of his acts of old.[*]

i Heb way   *LXX The Lord made me as the beginning of his ways for his works, he established me before time was.

OVERVIEW: During the Arian controversy, this verse was among the most contested passages of Scripture.[1] The classic Christian consensus rejected the Arian view that the Son was a creature, and not of the same substance as God. The Son was begotten of the Father before all creatures (JUSTIN MARTYR). Just as the world was created by Christ, so wisdom was created by God (APOSTOLIC CONSTITUTIONS). The Son is the first offspring from the Father but was not created (ATHENAGORAS). God's Word or reason is a Second Person called wisdom, who is first-begotten and only-begotten and who created all things "in" or "of" the beginning but not "at" the beginning (TERTULLIAN).

There are two natures of Christ, human and divine, that correspond to Christ as wisdom and as firstborn, for in him we have an invisible image of the invisible God, whose likeness has always existed. His existence is incorporeal, yet living and animate, comprised of the principles of the universe, according to which creation has come into existence by participation in wisdom—which is Christ. But the spiritual beauty of this wisdom can be seen only by spiritual eyes (ORIGEN). It is a key question, however, whether this wisdom is made or begotten (MARIUS VICTORINUS). He was indeed begotten before all ages, but this is not the same as the unbegotten (EUSEBIUS OF CAESAREA). From the very beginning God the Word was self-sufficient. God the Word and the human who was raised from the dead are distinguishable but not separable (EUSTATHIUS OF ANTIOCH).

"Creation," however, is a term indicating relationship and need not imply material substance (DIDYMUS). By the prophecy of the incarnation, in fact, creation was for the sake of creation (AMBROSE). That which was assumed in the incarnation was our created nature (GREGORY OF NYSSA). The cause of the Lord's manhood was absolute and unoriginate (GREGORY OF NAZIANZUS), but this was not merely a higher class of creation (HILARY OF POITIERS). Creation, therefore, was a corporeal and visible thing, yet still

the wisdom of the Father. If he was the Son he could not have been a creature, whereas if he was a creature then he could not have been the Son. Another way of putting this is to say that he was the creator of things created, true God in the flesh and true flesh in the Word. There never was a "when" when he did not exist (ATHANASIUS). A distinction must be made between birth and creation, although they both pertain to wisdom (HILARY OF POITIERS). The Word by which all things were made was created man in the beginning of his ways (AUGUSTINE). Already at the beginning of creation, therefore, wisdom had a role in it (BEDE).

8:22 *The First of His Acts of Old*

THE SON WAS BEGOTTEN OF THE FATHER BEFORE ALL CREATURES. JUSTIN MARTYR: If you have followed me closely, you can see that Scripture declares that the Son was begotten of the Father before all creatures, and everybody will admit that the Son is numerically distinct from the Father. DIALOGUE WITH TRYPHO 129.[2]

THE WORLD CREATED BY CHRIST, AND WISDOM CREATED BY GOD. APOSTOLIC CONSTITUTIONS: O Lord Almighty, you have created the world by Christ, and . . . you have also appointed festivals for the rejoicing of our souls, that we might come into the remembrance of that wisdom which was created by you; how he submitted to be made of a woman on our account; he appeared in life, and demonstrated himself in his baptism; how he that appeared is both God and man; he suffered for us by your permission, and died, and rose again by your power: on which account we solemnly assemble to celebrate the feast of the resurrection on the Lord's day and rejoice on account of him

---

[1]In the book of Proverbs, this verse received the greatest volume of comments from the writers of the early church, especially because of its implications for Christian doctrine. A representative selection is presented here in approximate chronological order so that the historical development can also be traced, and further observations are offered in the introduction to this volume. [2]FC 6:348-49.

who has conquered death and has brought life and immortality to light. CONSTITUTIONS OF THE HOLY APOSTLES 7.2.36.[3]

THE SON, THE FIRST OFFSPRING FROM THE FATHER, WAS NOT CREATED. ATHENAGORAS: [The Son] is the first offspring of the Father. I do not mean that he was created, for, since God is eternal mind, he had his Word within himself from the beginning, being eternally wise.[4] Rather did the Son come forth from God to give form and actuality to all material things, which essentially have a sort of formless nature and inert quality, the heavier particles being mixed up with the lighter. The prophetic Spirit agrees with this opinion when he says, "The Lord created me as the first of his ways, for his works."

Indeed we say that the Holy Spirit himself, who inspires those who utter prophecies, is an effluence from God, flowing from him and returning like a ray of the sun. Who, then, would not be astonished to hear those called atheists who admit God the Father, God the Son and the Holy Spirit, and who teach their unity in power and their distinction in rank? ... We affirm, too, a crowd of angels and ministers, whom God, the maker and creator of the world, appointed to their several tasks through his Word. He gave them charge over the good order of the universe, over the elements, the heavens, the world, and all it contains. A PLEA REGARDING CHRISTIANS 10.[5]

GOD'S WORD OR REASON IS A SECOND PERSON CALLED WISDOM WHO IS FIRST-BEGOTTEN AND ONLY-BEGOTTEN. TERTULLIAN: This power and disposition of the divine intelligence is set forth also in the Scriptures under the name of *sophia*, "wisdom," for what can be better entitled to the name of wisdom than the reason or the Word of God? Listen therefore to wisdom herself, constituted in the character of a Second Person: "At the first the Lord created me as the beginning of his ways, with a view to his own works, before he made the earth, before the mountains were settled; moreover, before all the hills he

begat me"—that is to say, he created and generated me in his own intelligence.... By proceeding from himself he became his first-begotten Son, because begotten before all things;[6] and his only-begotten also, because alone begotten of God, in a way peculiar to himself, from the womb of his own heart. AGAINST PRAXEAS 6-7.[7]

CREATION "IN" OR "OF" THE BEGINNING. TERTULLIAN: Since all things were made by the wisdom of God, it follows that when God made both the heaven and the earth *in principio*, that is to say "in the beginning," he made them in his wisdom. If, indeed, beginning had a material signification, the Scripture would not have informed us that God made so and so *in principio*, at the beginning, but rather *ex principio*, of the beginning, for he would not have created "in," but "of," matter. When wisdom, however, was referred to, it was quite right to say, "in the beginning." AGAINST HERMOGENES 20.[8]

HUMAN AND DIVINE NATURES OF CHRIST, WHO IS ALSO CALLED "WISDOM." ORIGEN: First we must know this, that in Christ there is one nature, his deity, because he is the only-begotten Son of the Father, and another human nature, which in very recent times he took upon him to fulfill the divine purpose.... He is called "wisdom," as Solomon said.... He is also called "firstborn," as the apostle Paul says: "who is the firstborn of all creation."[9] The firstborn is not, however, by nature a different being from wisdom but is one and the same. Finally, the apostle Paul says, "Christ the power of God and the wisdom of God."[10] ON FIRST PRINCIPLES 1.2.1.[11]

AN INVISIBLE IMAGE OF THE INVISIBLE GOD. ORIGEN: If he is an "image of the invisible God,"[12] he is an invisible image, and I would dare to add that as he is a likeness of the Father there is no

---

[3]ANF 7:474. [4]Gk *logikos*, adjectival form of *logos*, "Word." [5]LCC 1:309. [6]Col 1:15. [7]ANF 3:601*. [8]ANF 3:488*. [9]Col 1:15. [10]1 Cor 1:24. [11]OFP 15. [12]Col 1:15.

time when he did not exist. . . .Let the man who dares to say "There was a time when the Son was not" understand that this is what he will be saying: "Once wisdom did not exist, and word did not exist, and life did not exist." ON FIRST PRINCIPLES 4.4.1.[13]

CREATION HAS COME INTO EXISTENCE BY PARTICIPATION IN THE WISDOM THAT IS CHRIST.

ORIGEN: But if someone is able to comprehend an incorporeal existence comprised of the various ideas which embrace the principles of the universe, an existence which is living and animate, as it were, he will understand the wisdom of God which precedes all creation, which appropriately says of herself, "God created me the beginning of his ways for his works." It is because of this creation that the whole creation has also been able to subsist, since it has a share in the divine wisdom according to which it has been created, for according to the prophet David, God made "all things in wisdom."[14]

Many creatures, on the one hand, have come into existence by participation in wisdom, while they do not apprehend her by whom they have been created. Very few, however, comprehend not only the wisdom concerning themselves, but also that concerning many beings, for Christ is all wisdom.

But each of the wise participates in Christ to the extent that he has the capacity for wisdom, insofar as Christ is wisdom, just as each one who possesses power has obtained greater power to the extent that he has shared in Christ, insofar as Christ is power. COMMENTARY ON THE GOSPEL OF JOHN 1.244-46.[15]

A SPIRITUAL BEAUTY SEEN ONLY BY SPIRITUAL EYES.

ORIGEN: What must we say of wisdom which "God created as the beginning of his ways for his works"? Her Father rejoiced at her, rejoicing in her manifold spiritual beauty which only spiritual eyes see. Wisdom's divine heavenly beauty invites the one who contemplates it to love. COMMENTARY ON THE GOSPEL OF JOHN 1.55.[16]

MADE OR BEGOTTEN?

MARIUS VICTORINUS: Solomon says, "You have made me above your ways." For, concerning spiritual generation, he immediately adds, "He has begotten me before all things."[17] LETTER TO CANDIDUS 4.29.[18]

BEGOTTEN BEFORE ALL AGES, BUT NOT THE SAME AS UNBEGOTTEN.

EUSEBIUS OF CAESAREA: The divine and perfect essence existing before things begotten, the rational and firstborn image of the unbegotten nature, the true and only-begotten Son of the God of the universe, being one with many names, and one called God by many titles, is honored in this passage under the style and name of wisdom, and we have learned to call him Word of God, light, life, truth, and, to crown all, "Christ the power of God and the wisdom of God."[19] Now, therefore, in the passage before us, he passes through the words of the wise Solomon, speaking of himself as the living wisdom of God and self-existent, saying, "I, wisdom, have dwelt with counsel and knowledge, and I have called upon understanding," and that which follows. He also adds, as one who has undertaken the government and providence of the universe: "By me kings reign, and princes decree justice. By me princes become great." Then saying that he will record the things of ages past, he goes on to say, "The Lord created me as the beginning of his ways for his works, he established me before time was." By which he teaches both that he himself is begotten, and not the same as the unbegotten, one called into being before all ages, set forth as a kind of foundation for all begotten things. And it is probable that the divine apostle started from this when he said of him: "Who is the image of the invisible God, the firstborn of every creature, for all things were created in him, of things in heaven and things in earth."[20] For he is called "firstborn of every creature," in accordance with the words "The Lord created

---

[13]OFP 314-15. [14]Ps 104:24 (103:24 LXX). [15]FC 80:83. [16]FC 80:45. [17]Prov 8:25; Jn 1:3-4. [18]FC 69:80. [19]1 Cor 1:24. [20]Col 1:15.

me as the beginning of his road to his works." And he would naturally be considered the image of God, as being that which was begotten of the nature of the unbegotten. And, therefore, the passage before us agrees when it says, "Before the mountains were established, and before all the hills, he begets me."[21]

Hence we call him only-begotten Son, and the firstborn Word of God, who is the same as this wisdom. Proof of the Gospel 5.1.[22]

God the Word Was Self-Sufficient from the Beginning. Eustathius of Antioch: If, therefore, the Word began to exist at the time he passed through the mother's womb and wore the bodily framework, it is clear that he was born of a woman. But if God the Word was from the very beginning with the Father, and we say that all things were made through him,[23] then the one who is and is the cause of all things that are made was not born of a woman but is, by nature, God, self-sufficient, unlimited and incomprehensible. But from a woman was born a human being, who was implanted in the virgin's womb by the Holy Spirit. Discourse on the Text "The Lord Created Me in the Beginning of His Ways."[24]

Distinction Between God the Word and the Human Who Was Raised. Eustathius of Antioch: For the human being who died rises up on the third day; but when Mary strives with longing to touch his holy limbs, he objected and says to her, "Do not touch me, for I have not yet ascended to my Father; go to my brothers and tell them, 'I am ascending to my Father and your Father, my God and your God.'"[25] God the Word, who comes from heaven and lives in the bosom of the Father, did not utter the phrase "I have not yet ascended to my Father." The Wisdom that embraces all things that exist did not say it either; this was spoken by the very human being who was formed out of all kinds of limbs, who had been raised from the dead, and who after death had not yet ascended to his Father but

reserved for himself the firstfruit of his passage. Discourse on the Text "The Lord Created Me in the Beginning of His Ways."[26]

"Creation" Indicates Relationship. Didymus the Blind: Since wisdom is already eternal, it is not subjected to time. The "beginning," then, is yoked together with created things. But having existed before creation as wisdom, the Son of God—even though, he says, "The Lord created me"—this assertion ["The Lord created me"] must be understood as referring not to substance but to his relationship toward creatures. For [wisdom] says that its works were at the beginning of the creative and providential ways of God, that is, a "cause," introducing still another way of speaking. The Son of God was made man when he assumed the form of a servant. He is eternal before the ages, as he is God the Word. It says he was "created" because he was born of Mary and was made flesh. For those desiring to walk like God and with God, consult this teacher, an example of perfect life, who gives his teaching to those who follow him. The fact that the word "to create" does not mean everywhere "to make substance" is confirmed by David, who says, "Create in me a pure heart, O God."[27] He asks for such a creation not as if he does not have a heart; but since he had polluted it, he desires to have it back pure. Also Paul, when he speaks about creating out of the two a single new man,[28] does not mean from [two] human substances but rather the unity that results from concord. And so the interpreters proclaimed, "He created me." Commentary on the Proverbs of Solomon, Fragment 8.22.[29]

Prophecy of Incarnation Meant That Creation Was for the Sake of Creation. Ambrose: Hereby we are brought to understand

---

[21]Cf. Prov 8:25. [22]POG 1:231-32. [23]See Jn 1:1-3. [24]Quoted in Theodoret of Cyr, *Eranistes*, Dialogue 1.32; FC 106:74. [25]Jn 20:17. [26]Quoted in Theodoret of Cyr, *Eranistes*, Dialogue 3.12; FC 106:225-26. [27]Ps 51:10 (50:12 LXX). [28]Eph 2:15. [29]PG 39:1632.

that the prophecy of the incarnation, "The Lord created me the beginning of his ways for his works," means that the Lord Jesus was created of the Virgin for the redeeming of the Father's works. Truly, we cannot doubt that this is spoken of the mystery of the incarnation, forasmuch as the Lord took upon him our flesh, in order to save the works of his hands from the slavery of corruption, so he might, by the sufferings of his own body, overthrow him who had the power of death. For Christ's flesh is for the sake of things created, but his Godhead existed before them, seeing that he is before all things, while all things exist together in him. His Godhead, then, is not by reason of creation, but creation exists because of the Godhead. ON THE CHRISTIAN FAITH 3.7.46-47.[30]

ASSUMED FROM OUR CREATED NATURE. GREGORY OF NYSSA: The phrase "created me" refers not to the divine and the uncompounded but, as has been said, to that which had been assumed, in accordance with the divine plan, from our created nature. AGAINST EUNOMIUS 3.1.50.[31]

CAUSE OF THE MANHOOD WAS ABSOLUTE AND UNORIGINATE. GREGORY OF NAZIANZUS: In their eyes [of the Arians] the following is only too ready to hand: "The Lord created me at the beginning of his ways with a view to his works." How shall we meet this? Shall we bring an accusation against Solomon or reject his former words because of his fall in afterlife? Shall we say that the words are those of wisdom herself, as it were of knowledge and the creator-word, in accordance with which all things were made? For Scripture often personifies many even lifeless objects; as, for instance, "the sea said" so and so;[32] and, "the heavens declare the glory of God"; and again a command is given to the sword; and the mountains and hills are asked the reason of their skipping.[33] We do not allege any of these, though some of our predecessors used them as powerful arguments. But let us grant that the expression is used of our Savior himself, the true wisdom. Let us consider one small point together. What among all things that exist is unoriginate? The Godhead. For no one can tell the origin of God, that otherwise would be older than God. But what is the cause of the manhood, which for our sake God assumed? It was surely our salvation. What else could it be? Since, then, we find here clearly both the "created" and the "begets me," the argument is simple. Whatever we find joined with a cause we are to refer to the manhood, but all that is absolute and unoriginate we are to reckon to the account of his Godhead. ON THE SON, THEOLOGICAL ORATION 4(30).2.[34]

NOT MERELY A HIGHER CLASS OF CREATION. HILARY OF POITIERS: They attempt by a distortion of the sense and meaning to maintain that God was created rather than born because it was said, "The Lord created me for the beginning of his ways, for his works," so that he belongs to the common order of created things, although in a higher class of creation, nor does he enjoy the glory of the divine birth, but the power of a mighty creature. ON THE TRINITY 1.35.[35]

A CORPOREAL, VISIBLE THING, YET THE WISDOM OF THE FATHER. ATHANASIUS:[36] Salvation proceeds from the Savior, just as illumination does from the light. The salvation, then, which was from the Savior, being created new, did, as Jeremiah says, "create for us a new salvation,"[37] and as Aquila renders: "The Lord created a new thing in woman," that is, in Mary. For nothing new was created in woman, save the Lord's body, born of the Virgin Mary without intercourse, as also it says in the Proverbs in the person of Jesus, "The Lord created me, a beginning of his ways for his works." Now he does not say "created me before his works," lest any should take the text of

---

[30]NPNF 2 10:249. [31]Quoted in Theodoret of Cyr, *Eranistes*, Dialogue 1.52; FC 106:82. [32]Job 28:14. [33]Ps 19:1 (18:1 LXX); Zech 13:7; Ps 114:6 (113:6 LXX). [34]LCC 3:177-78. [35]FC 25:32. [36]May be attributed to Marcellus of Ancyra; cf. TLG 2041.004, 3.7.2-4.5.5. [37]Jer 31:22.

the deity of the Word.

Each text then which refers to the creature is written with reference to Jesus in a bodily sense. For the Lord's humanity was created as "a beginning of ways," and he manifested it to us for our salvation. For by it we have our access to the Father. For he is the way[38] which leads us back to the Father. And a way is a corporeal visible thing, such as is the Lord's humanity. Well, then, the Word of God created all things, not being a creature but an offspring. For he created none of the created things equal or like unto himself. But it is the part of a Father to beget, while it is a workman's part to create. Accordingly, that body is a thing made and created which the Lord bore for us, which was begotten for us,[39] as Paul says, "wisdom from God, and sanctification and righteousness, and redemption," while yet the Word was before us and before all creation, and is, the wisdom of the Father. STATEMENT OF FAITH 3-4.[40]

IF SON THEREFORE NOT CREATURE, OR IF CREATURE THEN NOT SON. ATHANASIUS: Let them tell us, from what teacher or by what tradition they derived these notions concerning the Savior? We have read in the Proverbs, they will say, "The Lord created me a beginning of his ways unto his works." This Eusebius and his fellows used to insist on, and you write me word, that the present men also, though overthrown and confuted by an abundance of arguments, still were putting about in every quarter this passage, and saying that the Son was one of the creatures, and reckoning him with things originated. But they seem to me to have a wrong understanding of this passage. . . . If then Son, therefore not creature; if creature, not Son; for great is the difference between them, and Son and creature cannot be the same, unless his essence be considered to be at once from God and external to God. DEFENSE OF THE NICENE DEFINITION 3.13.[41]

THE HUMAN AND DIVINE ATTRIBUTIONS ARE REASONABLE. ATHANASIUS: "The Lord

created me in the beginning of his ways for his works.". . . He is called also in the Scriptures "servant," and "son of a handmaid," and "lamb" and "sheep," and it is said that he suffered toil and thirst and was beaten and has suffered pain. But there is plainly a reasonable ground and cause why such representations as these are given of him in the Scriptures. It is because he became man and the Son of man, and took upon him the form of a servant, which is the human flesh, for "the Word," says John, "was made flesh."[42] And since he became man, no one ought to be offended at such expressions, for it is proper to man to be created and born and formed, to suffer toil and pain, to die and to rise again from the dead. And as, being Word and wisdom of the Father, he has all the attributes of the Father, his eternity, and his unchangeableness, and the being like him in all respects and in all things. And [he] is neither before nor after, but coexistent with the Father. And [he] is the very form of the Godhead, and is the creator and is not created (for since he is in essence like the Father, he cannot be a creature but must be the creator, for he himself has said, "My Father works hitherto, and I work."[43]) So being made man, and bearing our flesh, he is necessarily said to be created and made, and that is proper to all flesh. LETTER TO THE BISHOPS OF EGYPT 17.[44]

THE CREATOR OF THINGS CREATED. ATHANASIUS: The fact is, then, that the Word is not from things created but is rather himself their creator. For this reason did he assume a body created and human: so that, having renewed it as its creator, he might deify it in himself and thus might introduce all of us in that likeness into the kingdom of heaven. A man would not have been deified if joined to a creature, nor if the Son were not true God; neither would a man have been brought into the Father's presence if he had not been the

---

[38]Jn 14:6. [39]See 1 Cor 1:30. [40]NPNF 2 4:85. [41]NPNF 2 4:158*. [42]Jn 1:14. [43]Jn 5:17. [44]NPNF 2 4:232*.

Father's natural and true Word who had put on the body. Since we could have had nothing in common with what is foreign, we would not have been delivered from sin and from the curse if that which the Word put on had not been natural human flesh. So also, the man would not have been deified if the Word which became flesh had not been by nature from the Father and true and proper to him.

The union, therefore, was of just such a kind, so that he might unite what is man by nature, to him who is in the nature of the Godhead, thereby assuring the accomplishment of salvation and his deification. Let those, therefore, who deny that the Son is by nature from the Father and proper to his essence, deny also that he took true human flesh from the ever-virgin Mary. In neither case would it have been profitable to us men: if the Word were not by nature true Son of God, or if the flesh which he assumed were not true flesh. Four Discourses Against the Arians 2.70.[45]

True God in the Flesh and True Flesh in the Word. Athanasius: Although the Word did indeed become flesh, it is to the flesh that affections are proper; and although the flesh bears divinity in the Word, it is to the Word that grace and power belong. He performed the Father's works, then, through the flesh; but nonetheless the affections of the flesh were exhibited in him. Thus, he inquired and then raised Lazarus; he chided his mother, saying, "My hour is not yet come";[46] and immediately he turned the water into wine. Indeed, he was true God in the flesh, and he was true flesh in the Word. Out of his works, therefore, he made known both his own Father, and himself, the Son of God. By the affections of the flesh he demonstrated that he bore a true body and that it was proper to him. Four Discourses Against the Arians 3.41.[47]

There Was Never a "When" When He Did Not Exist. Athanasius: The Lord is God's true and natural Son, and he is known to be not just eternal but one who exists concurrently with the eternity of the Father. There are things which

are called "eternal" of which he is the creator, for in Psalm 23 it is written, "Lift up your gates, O rulers, and be lifted up, O everlasting doors."[48] It is apparent, though, that these everlasting doors also came into being through his agency. But if he is himself the creator of the things which are "everlasting," which of us can any longer doubt that he is more noble than these everlasting things and that he is made known as Lord not so much from his being eternal as from his being the Son of God? Being Son, he is inseparable from the Father, and there was never a "when" when he did not exist. He always existed. Moreover, since he is the image and radiance of the Father, he also possesses the Father's eternity. . . .

What is the basic meaning and purport of holy Scripture? It contains, as we have often said, a double account of the Savior. It says that he has always been God and is the Son, because he is the Logos and radiance and wisdom of the Father. Furthermore, it says that afterwards for us he took flesh of the Virgin Mary, the bearer of God, and became man. Four Discourses Against the Arians 3.28-29.[49]

Both God and Servant. Augustine: According to the form of God it was said, "Before all the hills he has begotten me,"[50] that is, before all the most exalted creatures, and, "Before the morning star I have begotten you,"[51] that is, before all the ages and temporal things. But according to the form of a slave it was said, "The Lord created me in the beginning of his ways." Because according to the form of God he said, "I am the truth," and according to the form of a slave, "I am the way." For since he himself, "the firstborn of the dead,"[52] has laid out the road for his church to the kingdom of God, to eternal life, of which he is the head even to the extent of giving immortality to the body. He was, therefore, created in the beginning of the ways of God for his works. On the Trinity 1.12.24.[53]

---

[45]FEF 1:330. [46]Jn 2:4. [47]FEF 1:332*. [48]Ps 24:7 (23:7 LXX). [49]TCC 86-87*. [50]Prov 8:25. [51]Ps 110:3 (109:3 LXX). [52]Rev 1:5. [53]FC 45:36.

THE HEAD OF THE CHURCH, THE ROAD TO GOD'S KINGDOM. AUGUSTINE: The beginning of his ways is the head of the church, which is Christ incarnate, through whom there was to be given us an example of living, that is, a certain way by which we might reach God. . . . So the Word by which all things were made was created man in the beginning of his ways. ON FAITH AND THE CREED 4.6.[54]

THE ROLE OF WISDOM AT THE BEGINNING OF CREATION. BEDE: The Lord's "ways" are his works, through contemplation of which man has arrived at faith or knowledge of him. "For his invisible nature was seen by the rational creatures of the world through what he had made."[55] His ways are the illuminations through which he showed himself both to angelic spirits and to human minds. He possessed[56] wisdom at the beginning of his ways because he had the Son with whom he arranged all things at the beginning of the nascent created order. Yet, lest anyone think that the Son began to exist at the beginning of his ways or at any other time, it adds vigilantly, . . . "In the beginning was the Word and the Word was with God and the Word was God; all things were created through him."[57] Let them perish, therefore, who deny that "the power of God and the wisdom of God,"[58] clearly Christ, was begotten by the Father himself from the beginning and indeed before any beginning that could be thought or expressed. In another translation, this passage begins, "The Lord created me at the beginning of his ways in his works." The fathers understand this saying to be about the Lord's incarnation, maintaining that by the grace of a certain mystery it said "the Lord created me," and not "the Father created me." The flesh, they say, acknowledges the Lord, glory indicates the Father, creation confesses the Lord, and charity knows the Father who is the beginning.[59] It could also read "in the beginning of his ways"; for he himself said, "I am the way,"[60] because he began the journey of his church to the kingdom of God,

to eternal life, when he rose from the dead. It adds "in his works" because he was born from a virgin for the purpose of redeeming the works of the Father, receiving flesh to liberate the Father's works from slavery to corruption, for the flesh of Christ exists for the sake of his works, whereas his divinity precedes them. COMMENTARY ON PROVERBS 1.8.22-30.[61]

THE DISTINCTION BETWEEN BIRTH AND CREATION. HILARY OF POITIERS: Ignorance of prophetic diction and lack of skill in interpreting Scripture has led them into a perversion of the point and meaning of the passage, "The Lord created me for a beginning of his ways for his works." They labor to establish from it that Christ is created rather than born, as God, and hence partakes the nature of created beings, though he excel them in the manner of his creation and has no glory of divine birth but only the powers of a transcendent creature. We in reply, without importing any new considerations or preconceived opinions, will make this very passage of wisdom display its own true meaning and object. We will show that the fact that he was created for the beginning of the ways of God and for his works, cannot be twisted into evidence concerning the divine and eternal birth, because creation for these purposes and birth from everlasting are two entirely different things. Where birth is meant, there birth, and nothing but birth, is spoken of; where creation is mentioned, the cause of that creation is first named. There is a wisdom born before all things, and again there is a wisdom created for particular purposes. The wisdom which is from everlasting is one, the wisdom which has come into existence during the lapse of time is another. ON THE TRINITY 1.35.[62]

---

[54]LCC 6:357. [55]Rom 1:20. [56]Latin *possedit*. [57]Jn 1:1-3. [58]1 Cor 1:24. [59]Latin *caritas patrem novit principium*. Cf. Ambrose *De fide* 1.15. [60]Jn 14:6. [61]CCL 119B:61-62. [62]NPNF 2 9:50*.

8:23-36 THE ONE WHO FINDS WISDOM OBTAINS FAVOR FROM GOD

²³*Ages ago I was set up,*
at the first, before the beginning of the earth.
²⁴*When there were no depths I was brought forth,*
when there were no springs abounding with water.
²⁵*Before the mountains had been shaped,*
before the hills, I was brought forth;*
²⁶*before he had made the earth with its fields,^j*
or the first of the dust^j of the world.
²⁷*When he established the heavens, I was there,*
when he drew a circle on the face of the deep,
²⁸*when he made firm the skies above,*
when he established^j the fountains of the deep,
²⁹*when he assigned to the sea its limit,*
so that the waters might not transgress his command,
when he marked out the foundations of the earth,
³⁰*then I was beside him, like a master workman;^l*
and I was daily his^m delight,
rejoicing before him always,
³¹*rejoicing in his inhabited world*
and delighting in the sons of men.

³²*And now, my sons, listen to me:*
happy are those who keep my ways.
³³*Hear instruction and be wise,*
and do not neglect it.
³⁴*Happy is the man who listens to me,*
watching daily at my gates,
waiting beside my doors.
³⁵*For he who finds me finds life*
and obtains favor from the LORD;[†]
³⁶*but he who misses me injures himself;*
all who hate me love death."

j The meaning of the Hebrew is uncertain   l Another reading is *little child*   m Gk: Heb lacks *his*   *LXX *Before all the hills he begets me*   †LXX *The will itself is prepared by the Lord*

OVERVIEW: Heretics have misinterpreted these passages of Scripture to their own ends (ATHANASIUS). He who created all things in himself submitted to become human so that the church might be constituted in him (DIDYMUS). The facts are that wisdom was established before time was begotten (HILARY OF POITIERS), the nature of divine begetting is continuous (Origen), and there was a beginning but will never be an ending (GREGORY OF NAZIANZUS). Father, Son and Spirit are equal in creation and in worship (AMBROSE). The utterance of God's wisdom made the sky (PRUDENTIUS). In form and outline the creation was always present (ORIGEN) and constituted one harmonious whole (AMBROSE). God gave us free will to find life in finding wisdom (AUGUSTINE).

8:23 *Ages Ago*

MISINTERPRETATION BY HERETICS. ATHANASIUS: Since the heretics, reading the next verse, take a perverse view of that also, because it is written, "He founded me before the world," namely, that this is said of the Godhead of the

Word and not of his incarnate presence, it is necessary, explaining this verse also, to show their error.

It is written, "The Lord in Wisdom founded the earth;[1] if then by wisdom the earth is founded, how can he who founds be founded? Indeed, this too is after the manner of proverbs. . . .

He says not, "Before the world he founded me as Word or Son," but simply, "He founded me," to show again, as I have said, that not for his own sake but for those who are built upon him does he here also speak, after the way of proverbs. FOUR DISCOURSES AGAINST THE ARIANS 2.22.72-74.[2]

HE SUBMITTED TO BECOME HUMAN. DIDYMUS THE BLIND: [Solomon] says, "He laid down both the cause and foundation of creation." Also it is written, "He created all things in himself, and he is before all things."[3] And the Lord says as well, "I am the beginning of the creation of God."[4] Indeed, desiring to be the foundation of the church, he submitted to becoming human so that the church might be constituted firmly in him. Desiring to give existence to creation, he adjusted himself to its rule by introducing the relationship we mentioned above, when he was made the beginning and cause of future things. However, it says, even if he was created according to these things, still "God begat me before everything," the very one who is his Son. COMMENTARY ON THE PROVERBS OF SOLOMON, FRAGMENT 8.23.[5]

8:25 Brought Forth Before the Mountains Were Shaped

WISDOM WAS ESTABLISHED BEFORE TIME. HILARY OF POITIERS: He who was established before time was already begotten, not only before the earth but also before the mountains and the hills. And because wisdom is certainly referring to itself in this passage, it says more than is heard. ON THE TRINITY 12.37.[6]

ONE SO BEGOTTEN IS ALWAYS BEGOTTEN.

ORIGEN: Let us consider [that] our Savior is a "reflection of glory."[7] The reflection of glory has not been begotten just once and no longer begotten. But just as the light[8] is an agent of reflection, in such a way the reflection of the glory of God is begotten. Our Savior is the wisdom of God.[9] But the wisdom is the reflection of everlasting light.[10] If then the Savior is always begotten—because of this he also says, "Before all the hills he begets me" (and not "Before all the hills he has begotten me," but "Before all of the hills he begets me")—and the Savior is always begotten by the Father, and likewise also if you have the Spirit of adoption,[11] God always begets you in him according to each work, according to each thought. And may one so begotten always be a begotten son of God in Christ Jesus, "to whom is the glory and the power for the ages of ages. Amen."[12] HOMILIES ON JEREMIAH 9.5.[13]

THE SOUL HAD A BEGINNING BUT WILL NEVER HAVE AN END. GREGORY OF NAZIANZUS: Whether he is eternally begotten or not, I do not yet say, until I have looked into the statement, "Before all the hills he begets me" more accurately. But I cannot see the necessity of their conclusion. For if, as they say, everything that is to come to an end had also a beginning, then surely that which has no end had no beginning. What, then, will they decide concerning the soul or the angelic nature? If it had a beginning, it will also have an end; and if it has no end, it is evident that according to them it had no beginning. But the truth is that it had a beginning and will never have an end. Their assertion, then, that that which will have an end had also a beginning, is untrue. ON THE SON, THEOLOGICAL ORATION 3(29).13.[14]

8:27-28 Creator of the Skies and the Deep

---

[1]Prov 3:19. [2]NPNF 2 4:388*. [3]Col 1:16-17. [4]Jn 8:25. [5]PG 39:1632. [6]FC 25:526. [7]Heb 1:3. [8]Cf. Wis 7:26; 1 Jn 1:5. [9]See 1 Cor 1:24. [10]Wis 7:26. [11]See Rom 8:15 KJV. [12]1 Pet 4:11. [13]FC 97:93*. [14]LCC 3:169.

EQUAL IN CREATION AND IN WORSHIP.
AMBROSE: Learn also that the Father was with him, and he with the Father, when all things were being made. Wisdom says, "When he was preparing the heavens I was with him, when he was making the fountains of waters." And in the Old Testament the Father . . . showed that the Son was to be worshiped with himself as the maker of all things. As, then, those things are said to have been created in the Son, of which the Son is received as the Creator, so too when God is said to be worshiped in truth by the proper meaning of the word itself often expressed after the same manner it ought to be understood, that the Son too is worshiped. So in like manner is the Spirit also worshiped because God is worshiped in Spirit. Therefore the Father is worshiped both with the Son and with the Spirit, because the Trinity is worshiped. ON THE HOLY SPIRIT 3.11.85.[15]

THE UTTERANCE OF GOD'S WISDOM MADE THE SKY. PRUDENTIUS:

This Wisdom uttered made the sky,
The sky and light and all besides;
All by the Word's almighty power
Were fashioned, for the Word was God.

HYMNS FOR EVERY DAY 11.[16]

8:30-31 Beside Him and Rejoicing in His Inhabited World

IN FORM AND OUTLINE THE CREATION WAS ALWAYS PRESENT. ORIGEN: We can therefore imagine no moment whatever when that power was not engaged in acts of well-doing. Whence it follows that there always existed [in God's wisdom] objects for this well-doing, namely, God's works or creatures, and that God, in the power of his providence, was always dispensing his blessings among them by doing them good in accordance with their condition and deserts. It follows plainly from this, that at no time whatever was God not creator, nor benefactor, nor providence. . . .

God the Father always existed, and he always had an only-begotten Son, who at the same time, according to the explanation we have given above, is called wisdom. This is that wisdom in whom God delighted when the world was finished, in order that we might understand from this that God ever rejoices. In this wisdom, therefore, who ever existed with the Father, the creation was always present in form and outline, and there was never a time when the prefiguration of those things which hereafter were to be did not exist in wisdom. ON FIRST PRINCIPLES 1.4.3-4.[17]

ONE HARMONIOUS WHOLE. AMBROSE: We have that general seemliness; for God made the beauty of this world. We have it also in its parts; for when God made the light, and marked off the day from the night, when he made heaven, and separated land and seas, when he set the sun and moon and stars to shine upon the earth, he approved of them all one by one. Therefore this comeliness, which shone forth in each single part of the world, was resplendent in the whole, as the book of Wisdom shows, saying, "I existed, in whom he rejoiced when he was glad at the completion of the world." Likewise also in the building up of the human body each single member is pleasing, but the right adjustment of the members all together delights us far more. For thus they seem to be united and fitted into one harmonious whole. DUTIES OF THE CLERGY 1.46.233.[18]

8:35 Finding Life in Wisdom

FREE WILL. AUGUSTINE: Man in paradise was capable of self-destruction by abandoning justice by an act of will; yet if the life of justice was to be maintained, his will alone would not have sufficed, unless he who made him had given him aid. But, after the fall, God's mercy was even more abundant, for then the will itself had to be freed from the bondage in which sin and death are the mas-

---

[15]NPNF 2 10:147. [16]FC 43:79. [17]OFP 42. [18]NPNF 2 10:38.

ters. There is no way at all by which it can be freed by itself, but only though God's grace, which is made effectual in the faith of Christ. Thus, as it is written, even the will by which "the will itself is prepared by the Lord" so that we may receive the other gifts of God through which we come to the Gift eternal—this too comes from God. Enchiridion 28.106.[19]

---

[19]LCC 7:403-4*.

9:1-18 WISDOM CONTRASTED TO A FOOLISH WOMAN

[1]*Wisdom has built her house,*
she has set up[n] her seven pillars.
[2]*She has slaughtered her beasts, she has*
mixed her wine,
she has also set her table.
[3]*She has sent out her maids to call*
from the highest places in the town,
[4]*"Whoever is simple, let him turn in*
here!"
To him who is without sense she says,
[5]*"Come, eat of my bread*
and drink of the wine I have mixed.
[6]*Leave simpleness,[o] and live,*
and walk in the way of insight."

[7]*He who corrects a scoffer gets himself abuse,*
and he who reproves a wicked man
incurs injury.
[8]*Do not reprove a scoffer, or he will hate*
you;
reprove a wise man, and he will love you.
[9]*Give instruction[p] to a wise man, and he*
will be still wiser;
teach a righteous man and he will increase

in learning.
[10]*The fear of the Lord is the beginning of*
wisdom,
and the knowledge of the Holy One is
insight.
[11]*For by me your days will be multiplied,*
and years will be added to your life.
[12]*If you are wise, you are wise for yourself;*
if you scoff, you alone will bear it.

[13]*A foolish woman is noisy;*
she is wanton[q] and knows no shame.[r]
[14]*She sits at the door of her house,*
she takes a seat on the high places of
the town,
[15]*calling to those who pass by,*
who are going straight on their way,
[16]*"Whoever is simple, let him turn in here!"*
And to him who is without sense she says,
[17]*"Stolen water is sweet,*
and bread eaten in secret is pleasant."
[18]*But he does not know that the dead[s] are*
there,
that her guests are in the depths of Sheol.

---

n Gk Syr Tg: Heb *hewn*   o Gk Syr Vg Tg: Heb *simple ones*   p Heb lacks *instruction*   q Cn Compare Syr Vg: The meaning of the Hebrew is uncertain   r Gk Syr: The meaning of the Hebrew is uncertain   s Heb *shades*

OVERVIEW: The house of wisdom is the new Jerusalem, as well as the temple of Christ's body (HIPPOLYTUS). Wisdom's seven pillars indicate the seven spirits mentioned by the prophet Isaiah (CHRYSOSTOM). But eating the bread and drinking the wine have a deeper meaning that relates to the church (AUGUSTINE). The sacrifice of bread and wine is a type of the Lord's sacrifice (CYPRIAN). In a deeper sense, also, the house that wisdom built is the Lord's flesh (GREGORY OF NYSSA), for the body was flesh from a real body, the same flesh as our own (LEO THE GREAT). The seven pillars, seven sacraments, sevenfold grace and seven churches are all connected (GREGORY THE GREAT). Thus, the house that wisdom built is the church and the pillars are its doctors (BEDE). The beasts that are killed are the prophets and martyrs slain by unbelievers, and the bread and wine at the table indicate the spiritual divine supper of the Christian eucharist (HIPPOLYTUS). The table that wisdom has prepared, the wine that is mixed, have the capacity to restore the mind to its perfect state (ORIGEN). We can even speak of an "inebriation of grace," as contrasted to the drink of unbelief that was provided by Plato. At this banquet, however, Christ comes when you call upon him even if you are sleeping (AMBROSE). The heavenly food indicates not only the commandments and holy Scripture (DIDYMUS) but also Christ's body and blood (BEDE).

In the meantime, if a wise person is instructed or reproved, he will take the opportunity to learn from his correction and to profit from it (AUGUSTINE), and this is especially so if the admonition is done in charity (CAESARIUS). Although wisdom's beginning is the fear of the Lord, nonetheless the only place where God is not feared is where God is excluded (TERTULLIAN). The wise person must be useful to many; else he is not wise (HIPPOLYTUS). The heretics, sad to say, use merely bread and water in their eucharists (CLEMENT OF ALEXANDRIA). Another foolish example is that brazen woman who offers stolen waters and hidden bread, for in this case "bread" is being used in a bad sense

(AUGUSTINE). That woman's true desire, however, was for the bread that comes from heaven (JEROME), and thus a literal interpretation of Scripture does not suffice (GREGORY THE GREAT).

9:1 *Wisdom Has Built Her House*

HOUSE OF WISDOM IS THE NEW JERUSALEM.
HIPPOLYTUS: He intends the new Jerusalem, or the sanctified flesh. By the seven pillars he means the sevenfold unity of the Holy Spirit resting upon it. FRAGMENTS ON PROVERBS.[1]

HOUSE OF WISDOM IS THE TEMPLE OF CHRIST'S BODY. HIPPOLYTUS: Christ, [Solomon] means, the wisdom and power of God the Father, has built his house, that is, his nature in the flesh derived from the virgin, even as [John] said beforetime: "The Word became flesh and dwelt among us."[2] [As likewise the wise prophet Solomon] testifies: Wisdom that was before the world, and is the source of life, the infinite "wisdom of God, has built her house" by a mother who knew no man—to wit, as he assumed the temple of the body. "And has raised her seven pillars," that is, the fragrant grace of the all-holy Spirit, as Isaiah says: "And the seven spirits of God shall rest upon him."[3] [But others say that the seven pillars are the seven divine orders which sustain the creation by his holy and inspired teaching: namely, the prophets, the apostles, the martyrs, the hierarchs, the hermits, the saints and the righteous.][4] FRAGMENTS ON PROVERBS.[5]

SEVEN PILLARS INDICATE SEVEN SPIRITS.
CHRYSOSTOM: "Wisdom has built her house, and has set seven pillars." Since wisdom is the Son of God, once he became man he built his house, that is, the flesh from the Virgin. He [Solomon] calls the seven pillars "the spirit of God, the spirit of wisdom and understanding, the spirit of counsel

---

[1]ANF 5:173; TLG 2115.044.37-38. [2]Jn 1:14. [3]Is 11:2. [4]Portions in brackets are not extant in the critical Greek text. [5]ANF 5:175**; TLG 2115.045.37-38.

and strength, the spirit of knowledge and piety, the spirit of the fear of God,"[6] as Isaiah says. [Solomon] also calls the church "house" and the apostles "pillars." The wise individual is the one who is safe and self-sufficient, lacking nothing. As the house of wisdom is the church, the pillars are those who appear to be pillars in the church.[7] COMMENTARY ON THE PROVERBS OF SOLOMON, FRAGMENT 9.1.[8]

COME, EAT AND DRINK. AUGUSTINE: [Wisdom said] to the unwise, "Come, eat my bread, and drink the wine which I have mingled for you." In these words, surely, we recognize that the wisdom of God, the Father's coeternal Word, has built a house for himself, namely, a body in the virgin's womb. And to this body, as to the head, he has united the church as his members, has "slain" his martyrs as "victims," set his "table" with bread and wine in allusion to the priesthood according to Melchizedek, and called the weak and unwise. CITY OF GOD 17.20.[9]

A TYPE OF THE LORD'S SACRIFICE. CYPRIAN: The Holy Spirit through Solomon shows forth the type of sacrifice of the Lord, making mention of the immolated victim and of the bread and wine and also of the altar and of the apostles. "Wisdom," he says, "has built a house and she has set up seven columns. She has slain her victims, mixed her wine in a chalice, and has spread her table." . . . He declares the wine is mixed, that is, he announces in a prophetic voice that the chalice of the Lord is mixed with water and wine. LETTER 63.5.[10]

THE HOUSE IS THE LORD'S FLESH. GREGORY OF NYSSA: We say, therefore, that when he said in his previous discourse that wisdom built a house for itself, he is speaking enigmatically about the formation of the Lord's flesh. For true wisdom did not live in someone else's building but built a home for itself from the Virgin's body. AGAINST EUNOMIUS 3.1.44.[11]

THE BODY WAS FLESH FROM A REAL BODY.

LEO THE GREAT: It was the Holy Ghost that gave fecundity to the Virgin, but it was from a body that a real body was derived. And when "Wisdom was building herself a house," "the Word was made flesh and dwelt among us,"[12] that is, in that flesh which he assumed from a human being and which he animated with the spirit of rational life. TOME 2.[13]

FROM THE SAME FLESH AS OUR OWN. LEO THE GREAT: We are his flesh, the flesh that had been taken up from the Virgin's womb. If this flesh had not been from ours, that is, had it not been truly human, the Word made flesh would not have dwelt among us. "He did" in fact "dwell among us,"[14] however, for he made the nature of our body his own. "Wisdom built itself a house," not from just any material but from the substance that is properly ours. The fact that he had taken it on has been made clear from when it was said, "the Word became flesh and dwelt among us."[15] SERMON 30.3.1.[16]

SEVEN PILLARS, SEVEN SACRAMENTS, SEVEN-FOLD GRACE, SEVEN CHURCHES. GREGORY THE GREAT: We may also not inappropriately interpret the "pillars of heaven" as the churches themselves. Being many in number, they constitute one catholic church spread over the whole face of the earth. So, too, the apostle John writes to the seven churches, meaning to denote the one catholic church replenished with the Spirit of sevenfold grace, and we know that Solomon said of the Lord, "Wisdom has built her a house; she has hewn out her seven pillars." And to make known that it was of the seven churches he had spoken, which sedulously introduced the very sacraments themselves also, he says, "She

---

[6]Cf. Is 11:2. The "spirit of piety," included by Chrysostom here and in LXX and Vg, is omitted from KJV and RSV. Thus, in addition to the spirit of God, the LXX and Vg enumerate seven spirits, as does Chrysostom, whereas the KJV and RSV name only six. [7]Cf. Gal 2:9. [8]PG 64:680. [9]FC 24:75*. [10]FC 51:205. [11]Quoted in Theodoret of Cyr, *Eranistes*, Dialogue 1.50; FC 106:81. [12]Jn 1:14. [13]LCC 3:363. [14]Jn 1:14. [15]Jn 1:14. [16]FC 93:127.

has killed her sacrifices, she has mingled her wine, she has also set forth her table." MORALS ON THE BOOK OF JOB 4.17.43.[17]

HOUSE THAT WISDOM BUILT IS THE CHURCH. BEDE: Because it had spoken sufficiently of the divinity of Christ, it goes on to speak of the humanity he assumed. "Wisdom has built her house," therefore, because the Son of God created the man whom he received into the unity of his person.

"She has set up her seven pillars." She erected churches throughout the world by the sevenfold grace of the Spirit to be his home, that is, the mystery of his incarnation, lest the memory for believing, worshiping and preaching be destroyed by the wickedness of the faithless, as though they remained together by supporting each other.[18] Or at least the house of wisdom is the church of Christ, while the pillars are the doctors of the holy church filled by the sevenfold Spirit, such as James, Peter and John.[19] Wisdom undoubtedly "raised up these pillars because it elevated the minds of preachers who were detached from love of the present age for the purpose of bearing the work of his church."[20] COMMENTARY ON PROVERBS 1.9.1.[21]

9:2-5 Come and Eat

THE SPIRITUAL SUPPER OF THE CHRISTIAN EUCHARIST. HIPPOLYTUS: The phrase "she has killed her beasts" denotes the prophets and martyrs [who in every city and country] are slain like sheep every day by the unbelieving, in behalf of the truth, and cry aloud, "For your sake we are killed all the day long, we were counted as sheep for the slaughter."[22] And again, "she has mingled her wine in the bowl" [by which is meant that the Savior, uniting his Godhead like pure wine with the flesh in the Virgin, was born of her at once God and man without confusion of the one in the other].[23] And the phrase "She has furnished her table" [denotes the promised knowledge of the Triad[24]].[25] . . .

And again, "She has sent forth her servants." Wisdom, that is to say, has done so, [and it is Christ] who summons them with lofty announcement. "Whoever is simple, let him turn to me," she says, alluding manifestly to the holy apostles who journeyed the whole world and called the nations to the knowledge of him [in truth, with their lofty and divine preaching]. And again, "To those who lack understanding she said" [denotes] those who have not yet obtained the power of the Holy Spirit. "Come, eat of my bread, and drink of the wine I have mingled for you" [indicates that he gave his divine flesh and honored blood to us to eat and drink it for the remission of sins].[26] FRAGMENTS ON PROVERBS.[27]

RESTORATION TO A PERFECT STATE. ORIGEN: "Wisdom has prepared her table, she has slain her victims, she has mingled her wine in the bowl and cries with a loud voice, Turn in to me and eat the bread which I have prepared for you, and drink the wine which I have mingled for you." The mind, when nourished by this food of wisdom to a whole and perfect state, as man was made in the beginning, will be restored to the "image and likeness"[28] of God. [Thus], even though a man may have departed out of this life insufficiently instructed but with a record of acceptable works, he can be instructed in that Jerusalem, the city of the saints. That is, he can be taught and informed and fashioned into a "living stone," a "stone precious and elect,"[29] because he has borne with courage and endurance the trials of life and the struggles after piety. There, too, he will come to a truer and clearer knowledge of the saying already uttered here, that "man does not live by bread alone but

---

[17]LF 21:306*. [18]Latin *quasi sustendando continerent*. [19]Cf. Gal 2:9. [20]Gregory the Great *Morals on the Book of Job* 7.33.32; LF 31:587. [21]CCL 119B:62. [22]Ps 44:22; Rom 8:36. [23]Alternate reading: "[Wisdom] gave the Holy Spirit in the church as wine." [24]Gk *triados*. [25]Alternate reading: "He calls the table 'truth' because of the holy prophets." [26]Portions in brackets either exist in alternate readings or are not extant in the critical Greek text. [27]ANF 5:175-76**; TLG 2115.045.39-44. [28]Gen 1:26. [29]1 Pet 2:4-6.

by every word that proceeds out of the mouth of God."[30] On First Principles 2.11.3.[31]

Inebriation of Grace. Ambrose: "Come, eat my bread and drink my wine which I have mingled for you." Do you find delight in songs which charm the banqueter? Listen to the voice of the church, who exhorts us not only in canticles but in the Canticle of Canticles, "Eat, O friends, and drink and be inebriated, my brethren."[32] But this inebriation makes people sober. This inebriation is one of grace, not of intoxication. Cain and Abel 1.5.19.[33]

Plato Provided the Drink of Unbelief. Ambrose: "Come and eat of my bread and drink the wine which I have mixed for you." Plato judged that the discourse over this bowl should be copied into his books,[34] he summoned forth souls to drink of it, but did not know how to fill them, for he provided not the drink of faith but that of unbelief. Flight from the World 8.50.[35]

He Comes Even If You Are Sleeping. Ambrose: And so he comes; whether you eat or drink, if you call upon Christ he is present, saying, "Come, eat of my bread and drink of my wine." Even if you are asleep, he is knocking at the door. He comes, I say, frequently and reaches in through the window. Frequently (but not always and not to everyone) he comes to that soul which can say, "At night I had put off my garment."[36] For in this night of the world the garment of corporeal life is first to be taken off as the Lord divested himself in his flesh that for you he might triumph over the dominions and powers of this world. On Virginity 9.55.[37]

Indicating the Commandments and Scripture. Didymus the Blind: The same food is called "meat," "bread," "milk" and "wine." However, fools say that they take it as [simply] bread and mixed wine. But if it were really taken in that manner, how would we interpret the words:

"So men ate the bread of angels"?[38] Now "bread," it seems to me, should be understood as the firm commandments of God and "wine" as the knowledge of God through meditation on holy Scripture; similarly also [the knowledge of] his divine body and his precious blood. Commentary on the Proverbs of Solomon, Fragment 9.5.[39]

The Sacrament of Christ's Body and Blood. Bede: By divine eloquence, the nature of his divinity and humanity conjoined in Christ's one person is expressed through this bread and mixed wine, as was said above. Or at least the sacrament[40] through which we are satiated at the table of his altar is clearly shown in the bread of his body and in the mixed wine of his most holy blood. Commentary on Proverbs 1.9.5.[41]

9:8 Reprove the Wise, for They Then Become Wiser

Reflecting in Solitude. Augustine: It happens regularly and it happens often that a man is cast down for a short time while he is being reproved, that he resists and fights back. But afterwards he reflects in solitude where there is no one but God and himself, and where he does not fear the displeasure of others by being corrected, but does fear the displeasure of God by refusing correction. Thereafter, he does not repeat the act which was justly censured but now loves the brother, whom he sees as the enemy of his sin, as much as he hates the sin itself. Letter 210.[42]

Admonish in Charity. Caesarius of Arles: Let us always admonish each other in charity. As often as any one of us sins, let us willingly and patiently accept the reproof of a neighbor or a friend, because of what is said: "Reprove a wise

[30]Mt 4:4. [31]OFP 149. [32]Song 5:1. [33]FC 42:377. [34]Cf. Plato Symposium 213E. [35]FC 65:320. [36]Song 5:3. [37]AOV 27. [38]Ps 78:25 (77:25 LXX). [39]PG 39:1633. [40]Latin mysterium. [41]CCL 119B:63. [42]FC 32:37.

man, and he will love you; rebuke a foolish man, and he will hate you." Therefore I beseech you, brethren, to chide, rebuke and reprove those who you know are dancing, leading songs, uttering disgraceful words voluptuously or drunkenly on the holy feasts. SERMON 225.5.[43]

9:10 Wisdom's Beginning Is the Fear of the Lord

WHERE GOD IS EXCLUDED. TERTULLIAN: Discipline is an index to doctrine. [The heretics] say that God is not to be feared. So everything is free to them and unrestrained. But where is God not feared, except where he is not present? Where God is not present, there is no truth either; and where there is no truth, discipline like theirs is natural. But where God is present, there is the fear of God, there are decent seriousness, vigilant care and anxious solicitude, well-tested selection, well-weighed communion and deserved promotion, religious obedience, devoted service, modest appearance, a united church, and all things godly. PRESCRIPTIONS AGAINST HERETICS 43.[44]

9:12 Wise for Oneself

THE WISE PERSON MUST BE USEFUL TO MANY. HIPPOLYTUS: Observe that the wise man must be useful to many, so that he who is useful only to himself cannot be wise. For great is the condemnation of wisdom if she reserves her power simply for the one possessing her. FRAGMENTS ON PROVERBS.[45]

9:17 The Sweetness of Stolen Water

BREAD AND WATER ARE USED BY HERETICS. CLEMENT OF ALEXANDRIA: Scripture sets down bread and water in clear reference simply to the heresies that use bread and water in their offertory contrary to the rules of the church. There are some who actually celebrate the Eucharist with plain water. "Jump up; do not linger in her place." Scripture is using the ambiguous word

place to designate the synagogue rather than the church. Then it adds, "In this way you will be crossing a foreign water," regarding heretical baptism as foreign and improper, "and traversing a foreign river"—one which takes you astray and dumps you in the sea, where everyone who allows himself to be led away from the firm ground of the truth is deposited. STROMATEIS 1.19.96.1-4.[46]

THE SEDUCTION OF THE SENSES. AUGUSTINE: I came upon that brazen woman, empty of prudence, who, in Solomon's obscure parable, sits on a seat at the door outside her house and says, "Stolen waters are sweet, and bread eaten in secret is pleasant." This woman seduced me, because she found my soul outside its own door, dwelling externally in the eye of my flesh and ruminating within myself on such food as I had swallowed through my physical senses. CONFESSIONS 3.6.11.[47]

AN EXAMPLE OF "BREAD" USED IN A BAD SENSE. AUGUSTINE: Bread is used in a good sense in "I am the living bread which came down from heaven,"[48] but in a bad sense in "hidden bread is more pleasant." Many other things are used in the same way. Those examples that I have mentioned create little doubt as to their meaning, for things ought not to be used as examples unless they are clear. There are, however, instances in which it is uncertain whether the signification is to be taken in a good sense or in an evil sense. CHRISTIAN INSTRUCTION 25.36.[49]

TRUE DESIRE. JEROME: "The foolish and bold woman comes to want bread." What bread? Surely that bread which comes down from heaven. And he immediately adds, "The earth-born perish in her house, rush into the depths of hell." Who are the earth-born that perish

---

[43]FC 66:155. [44]LCC 5:63*. See also Ancient Christian Commentary on Eccles 12:13. [45]ANF 5:173; TLG 2115.053.16.1. [46]FC 85:96. [47]LCC 7:68**. [48]Jn 6:51. [49]ACD 100.

in her house? They of course who follow the first Adam, who is of the earth, and not the second, who is from heaven. AGAINST JOVINIANUS 1.28.[50]

LITERAL INTERPRETATION DOES NOT SUFFICE. GREGORY THE GREAT: What does water signify but human knowledge? This is in accord with Solomon's words implying the voice of heretics: "Stolen waters are sweeter." What does the Lamb's raw flesh indicate but his humanity that

has been thoughtlessly and irreverently disregarded? Everything which we think of profoundly we cook, as it were, in our minds. The flesh of the Lamb was not to be eaten raw or boiled in water, because our Redeemer is not to be judged merely a human being, nor are we to use human science to explain how God could have been made man. FORTY GOSPEL HOMILIES 22.[51]

---

[50]NPNF 2 6:367*. [51]CS 123:171.

10:1-32 PROVERBS ABOUT THE RIGHTEOUS AND THE WICKED

[1]The proverbs of Solomon.
  A wise son makes a glad father,
    but a foolish son is a sorrow to his mother.
  [2]Treasures gained by wickedness do not profit,
    but righteousness delivers from death.
  [3]The LORD does not let the righteous go hungry,
    but he thwarts the craving of the wicked.
  [4]A slack hand causes poverty,
    but the hand of the diligent makes rich.
  [5]A son who gathers in summer is prudent,
    but a son who sleeps in harvest brings shame.
  [6]Blessings are on the head of the righteous,
    but the mouth of the wicked conceals violence.
  [7]The memory of the righteous is a blessing,
    but the name of the wicked will rot.
  [8]The wise of heart will heed commandments,
    but a prating fool will come to ruin.
  [9]He who walks in integrity walks securely,
    but he who perverts his ways will be found out.
  [10]He who winks the eye causes trouble,
    but he who boldly reproves makes peace.[t]
  [11]The mouth of the righteous is a fountain of life,
    but the mouth of the wicked conceals violence.
  [12]Hatred stirs up strife,
    but love covers all offenses.
  [13]On the lips of him who has understanding wisdom is found,
    but a rod is for the back of him who lacks sense.
  [14]Wise men lay up knowledge,
    but the babbling of a fool brings ruin near.
  [15]A rich man's wealth is his strong city;

the poverty of the poor is their ruin.

[16] The wage of the righteous leads to life,
the gain of the wicked to sin.

[17] He who heeds instruction is on the path
to life,
but he who rejects reproof goes astray.

[18] He who conceals hatred has lying lips,
and he who utters slander is a fool.

[19] When words are many, transgression is
not lacking,*
but he who restrains his lips is prudent.

[20] The tongue of the righteous is choice
silver;
the mind of the wicked is of little worth.

[21] The lips of the righteous feed many,
but fools die for lack of sense.

[22] The blessing of the LORD makes rich,
and he adds no sorrow with it.[u]

[23] It is like sport to a fool to do wrong,
but wise conduct is pleasure to a man
of understanding.

[24] What the wicked dreads will come upon
him,
but the desire of the righteous will be
granted.

[25] When the tempest passes, the wicked is
no more,
but the righteous is established for ever.

[26] Like vinegar to the teeth, and smoke to
the eyes,
so is the sluggard to those who send
him.

[27] The fear of the LORD prolongs life,
but the years of the wicked will be short.

[28] The hope of the righteous ends in
gladness,
but the expectation of the wicked
comes to nought.

[29] The LORD is a stronghold to him whose
way is upright,
but destruction to evildoers.

[30] The righteous will never be removed,
but the wicked will not dwell in the land.

[31] The mouth of the righteous brings forth
wisdom,
but the perverse tongue will be cut off.

[32] The lips of the righteous know what is
acceptable,
but the mouth of the wicked, what is
perverse.

t Gk: Heb *but a prating fool will come to ruin*   u Or *and toil adds nothing to it*   *LXX *In a multitude of words you will not escape sin*

OVERVIEW: This chapter begins a new title and a new approach, no longer discussing individual components of good and bad but now describing each action in alternate verses (BEDE). For example, you should obey the bishop as a wise son to a glad father, and he should recognize that he has chosen such persons to be his priests (JEROME). Money payments, though, will not free anyone from sin (CHRYSOSTOM), and affluence does have its pitfalls (CYRIL OF ALEXANDRIA). The just, however, should be generous with their inheritance (CYPRIAN), and at some point the wickedness of the wicked will no longer remain because the Lord will overturn and reverse their life (EVAGRIUS). Prayer for the departed benefits the living (CHRYSOSTOM), and there is a reward for humility. The memory of John the Baptist will be blessed, as contrasted to the name of Herod (CAESARIUS). There is also a contrast between Absalom, who was treacherous, and David, who walked in integrity without guile (CHRYSOSTOM). To speak openly and boldly in refutation of error is to make peace (CLEMENT OF ALEXANDRIA). Without charity nothing pleases God (CLEMENT OF ROME), and education, like charity, is an antidote to hatred (CLEMENT of ALEXANDRIA). Alms given in love are a way to cancel guilt (LEO THE GREAT), for riches in themselves are not evil (AMBROSE). The complete Word of God is not a multitude of words but a single Word of truth (ORIGEN). Silence is a virtue, especially in church (AMBROSE), and a discipline to be cultivated (EPHREM THE SYRIAN), because prolixity of words is an invitation to sin (BENEDICT). To speak many words, however, if they are in praise of God, is not sinful. Nonetheless, the tongue of the wicked is highly polluted and not choice silver at all (SHENOUTE). The righteous are saved, however, because they know how to avoid the storm (CHRYSOSTOM).

10:1-3 Contrasts Between Good Actions and Bad Actions

NEW TITLE SIGNIFIES A CHANGE OF APPROACH. BEDE: "The parables of Solomon." He provides a new title because he begins a new type of argumentation, one that will no longer discuss individual components of the good and the bad, as he had done previously, but will now describe the act of each one in alternate verses. COMMENTARY ON PROVERBS 2.10.1.[1]

OBEY THE BISHOP AS A WISE SON TO A GLAD FATHER. JEROME: Be obedient to your bishop and welcome him as the parent of your soul. . . . In your case the bishop combines in himself many titles to your respect. He is at once a monk, a prelate and an uncle who has before now instructed you in all holy things. This also I say that the bishops should know themselves to be priests, not lords. Let them render to the clergy the honor which is their due that the clergy may offer to them the respect which belongs to bishops. . . . It is a bad custom which prevails in certain churches for presbyters to be silent when bishops are present on the ground that they would be jealous or impatient hearers. "If anything," writes the apostle Paul, "be revealed to another that sits by, let the first hold his peace. For you may all prophesy one by one that all may

learn and all may be comforted; and the spirits of the prophets are subject to the prophets. For God is not the author of confusion but of peace."[2] "A wise son makes a glad father," and a bishop should rejoice in the discrimination which has led him to choose such for the priests of Christ. LETTER 52.7.[3]

MONEY PAYMENT WILL NOT FREE ANYONE FROM SIN. CHRYSOSTOM: "Treasures bring no profit to the unrighteous." What then? Did not many avoid death by paying money? Certainly, but they did not get free from sin and in fact they prepared for themselves a life much worse than death. Therefore let us not put our confidence in wealth but in virtue. Indeed when justice comes to deadly sins, people are taken away by death. Would they not rather receive profit from being righteous than from treasures amassed on the earth, "where they grow rusty and moth-eaten, and thieves break in to steal them?"[4] Thus, justice not only saves those who possess it but also leads many others to desire it, and always transports them from death to eternal immortality. COMMENTARY ON THE PROVERBS OF SOLOMON, FRAGMENT 10.2.[5]

PITFALLS OF AFFLUENCE. CYRIL OF ALEXANDRIA: If a man cast his seed in ground that is fertile [only] in thorns, and fruitful in briars, and densely covered with useless stubble, he sustains a double loss; of his seed first, and also of his trouble. In order, therefore, that the divine seed may blossom well in us, let us first cast out of the mind worldly cares and the unprofitable anxiety which makes us seek to be rich. "For we brought nothing into the world, nor can we take anything out."[6] For what profit is there in possessing superfluities? "Treasures profit not the wicked," as Scripture says, "but righteousness delivers from death." For immediately upon the possession of affluence, there run up, and, so to speak, forth-

---

[1]CCL 119B:66. [2]1 Cor 14:30-33. [3]NPNF 2 6:93*. [4]Mt 6:19. [5]PG 64:681. [6]1 Tim 6:7.

with hem us in, the basest wickednesses; profligate banquets, the delights of gluttony and carefully prepared sauces; music and drunkenness, and the pitfalls of wantonness; pleasures and sensuality, and pride hateful to God. But as the disciple of the Savior has said, "Everything that is in the world is the lust of the flesh, and the lust of the eye, and the pride of the world; and the world passes away, and its lust; but he that does the will of God abides for ever."[7] Commentary on Luke, Homily 41.[8]

Let the Just Be Generous with Their Inheritance. Cyprian: Do you fear that your patrimony may fail if you begin to act generously from it? For when did it happen that resources could fail a just person, when it is written, "The Lord will not afflict the soul of the just with famine." Works and Almsgiving 11.[9]

The Great Reversal. Evagrius of Pontus: If the life of the wicked is malicious and the Lord will overturn it, then it is clear that at some point the wicked will no longer be wicked. For, after that "reversal," "the Lord will pass the kingdom over to God the Father,"[10] so that God may be "all in all."[11] Scholia on Proverbs 118.10.3.[12]

10:7 Memory of the Blessed

Remembering the Departed Benefits the Living. Chrysostom: "The memory of the just man will be praised." But he did not say this because he meant that the departed souls are helped by our praise. He said it because those who praise the departed derive the greatest benefits from remembering them. Since, therefore, we have so much to gain from keeping their memory sacred, let us not reject the wise man's words but rather let us heed them. Against the Anomoeans, Homily 6.3.[13]

The Reward for Humility. Caesarius of Arles: Those who are humble should thank God and remain in humility to the end of their lives.

Thus, the blessing of the angels and patriarchs and prophets and apostles and all the Scriptures will come upon them, as is given to all who persevere in humility. With those blessings they will reach eternal rewards, while there will be fulfilled in them the words "The blessing of the Lord is upon the head of the just." Sermon 48.6.[14]

The Memory of John the Baptist Will Be Blessed. Caesarius of Arles: What wonder is it, dearest brethren, that a dancing girl killed the prophet [John the Baptist]? For we know that dissipation is always the enemy of justice and that error ceaselessly persecutes the truth. Wantonness, moreover, associates with cruelty. The head of the prophet is brought to the table of Herod; this dish was due to his inhumanity. Blessed John had told him that it was not right for him to take the wife of a man who was still living, and for this one admonition Herod had him thrown into prison. O how bitter reproof is to sinners! In order that wickedness may not be rebuked, it is multiplied. . . . Truly "the memory of the just will always be blessed, but the desire of the wicked shall perish." Sermon 218.4.[15]

10:9-10 To Walk in Integrity and Speak Boldly

Contrast Between Absalom and David. Chrysostom: Absalom was a treacherous man and "stole all men's hearts."[16] Observe how great was his treachery. It is recorded, "He went about, and said 'Have you no judgment?'" wishing to conciliate everyone to himself. But David was guileless. What then? Look at the end of them both, look, how full of utter madness was the former! For inasmuch as he looked solely to the hurt of his father, in all other things he was

---

[7]Cf. 1 Jn 2:16-17. [8]CGSL 180*. It has been noticed that Cyril in this commentary, whenever quoting 1 Jn 2:16, always omits the second half of the verse: "is not of the Father but is of the world." [9] FC 36:237*. [10]See 1 Cor 15:24. [11]1 Cor 15:28. [12]SC 340:216. [13]FC 72:165. [14]FC 31:248-49. [15]FC 66:126. [16]2 Sam 15:6.

blinded. But not so David. For "he that walks uprightly, walks securely." HOMILIES ON EPHESIANS 15.[17]

TO REFUTE ERROR IS TO MAKE PEACE. CLEMENT OF ALEXANDRIA: It follows that we must move rapidly to matters concerning what they call the standard educational curriculum, showing the extent of its usefulness, and concerning astrology, mathematics, magic and wizardry. The whole of Greece prides itself on these as supreme sciences: "Anyone who speaks openly to refute error is a peacemaker." STROMATEIS 2.1.2.3-4.[18]

10:12 Love Covers All Wrongs

WITHOUT CHARITY NOTHING PLEASES GOD. CLEMENT OF ROME: Who can explain the bond of the charity of God?[19] Who can express the splendor of its beauty? The height to which charity lifts us is inexpressible. Charity unites us to God, "Charity covers a multitude of sins."[20] Charity bears all things, is long-suffering in all things. There is nothing mean in charity, nothing arrogant. Charity knows no schism, does not rebel, does all things in concord.[21] In charity all the elect of God have been made perfect. Without charity nothing is pleasing to God. 1 CLEMENT 49.[22]

EDUCATION, LIKE CHARITY, IS AN ANTIDOTE TO HATRED. CLEMENT OF ALEXANDRIA: Ignorance involves a lack of education and learning. It is teaching which implants in us the scientific knowledge of things divine and human. It is possible to live uprightly in poverty. It is also possible in wealth. We admit that it is easier and quicker to track down virtue if we have a preliminary education. It can be hunted down without these aids, although even then those with learning, "with their faculties trained by practice,"[23] have an advantage. "Hatred," says Solomon, "stirs up strife, but education guards the paths of life." STROMATEIS 1.6.35.3-5.[24]

ALMS GIVEN IN LOVE CANCEL GUILT. LEO THE GREAT: This remedy has been granted by God to human weakness: If someone contracts any guilt while living on this earth, almsgiving wipes it away. Almsgiving is a work of love, and we know that "love covers a multitude of sins." SERMON 7.1.[25]

10:15 A Strong City

RICHES THEMSELVES ARE NOT EVIL. AMBROSE: Riches themselves are not to be censured. "The ransom of a man's life are his riches,"[26] for one who gives to the poor ransoms his soul. Therefore, even in riches there is scope for virtue. You are like helmsmen on a great sea. If one steers his course well, he passes quickly over the sea to reach harbor. But one who does not know how to manage his property is drowned by his load. Thus it is written: "The wealth of the rich is a very strong city." LETTER 59.[27]

10:19 Sinfulness Usually Present When Words Are Many

THE COMPLETE WORD OF GOD IS A SINGLE WORD OF TRUTH. ORIGEN: How can teaching accomplish anything without a multitude of words,[28] understood in the simpler sense, since even wisdom herself declares to the perishing, "I stretched out words, and you did not heed."[29] Paul appears to have continued teaching from early morning till midnight, when indeed Eutychus, overcome with deep sleep, fell down and troubled the audience since they thought he was dead.[30]

If, then, the statement is true, "In a multitude of words you will not escape sin,"[31] and it is also true that Solomon did not sin when he recited the many words about the subjects mentioned earlier, nor did Paul when he extended his teaching until midnight, one must inquire what the

---

[17]NPNF 1 13:122-23**. [18]FC 85:158. [19]See Col 3:14. [20]Cf. 1 Pet 4:8; Jas 5:20. [21]See 1 Cor 13:4-7. [22]FC 1:47. [23]Heb 5:14. [24]FC 85:47. [25]FC 93:36. [26]Prov 13:8. [27]FC 26:355. [28]Cf. Eccles 12:12. [29]Cf. Prov 1:24 LXX. [30]See Acts 20:7-10. [31]Prov 10:19 LXX.

multitude of words is, and from there make a transition to see what the many books are.

The complete Word of God which was in the beginning with God is not a multitude of words, for it is not words. It is a single Word consisting of several ideas, each of which is a part of the whole Word. . . .

Consequently, according to this understanding, we would say that he who utters anything hostile to religion is loquacious, but he who speaks the things of truth, even if he says everything so as to leave out nothing, always speaks the one Word. The saints are not loquacious, since they cling to the goal which accords with the one Word. COMMENTARY ON THE GOSPEL OF JOHN 5.4-5.[32]

SIN ENTERS WHEN VERBAL OUTPUT IS NOT LIMITED. AMBROSE: How does sin find entrance? We read, "In the multitude of words you shall not escape sin." When a multiplicity of words has come forth, sin has found an entrance, for in this very multiplicity of words what we utter is not in the slightest degree subject to measure. Because of lack of prudence we fall into error. In fact, to give expression to our thoughts without duly weighing our words is in itself a grave sin. CAIN AND ABEL 1.9.36.[33]

SILENCE IS A VIRTUE, ESPECIALLY IN CHURCH. AMBROSE: The virtue of silence, especially in church, is very great. Let no sentence of the divine lessons escape you. If you give ear, restrain your voice, utter no word with your lips which you would wish to bring back, but let your boldness to speak be sparing. For in truth in much speaking there is abundance of sin. To the murderer it was said, "You have sinned, be silent,"[34] that he might not sin more; but to the virgin it must be said, "Be silent lest you sin." For Mary, as we read, kept in heart all things that were said concerning her Son.[35] So when any passage is read where Christ is announced as about to come or is shown to have come, do not make a noise by talking, but attend. Is anything more

unbecoming that the divine words should be so drowned by talking, as not to be heard, believed or made known, that the sacraments should be indistinctly heard through the sound of voices, that prayer should be hindered when offered for the salvation of all? CONCERNING VIRGINS 3.3.11.[36]

SILENCE IS A DISCIPLINE TO BE CULTIVATED. EPHREM THE SYRIAN: Stir up your soul, so that, by his wisdom, you may know what is fitting, and that, by his will, what is in the commandment may come to pass. One who is pleasing to the wicked is more evil than they. Impure words are only verbiage and empty noise. "Abundance of words will not go blameless." Abundance of words is the sign of no discipline. COMMENTARY ON TATIAN'S DIATESSARON 22.4.[37]

PROLIXITY OF WORDS IS AN INVITATION TO SIN. BENEDICT: If, for the sake of silence, we ought sometimes not to speak what is good, then even more are we obliged to avoid all evil talk, for fear of the punishment due to sin. Therefore, frequent leave to talk is not to be granted to those who are advanced in perfection, even if the subject is good and holy and edifying. Because it is written, "In much talk you shall not avoid sin," and elsewhere, "Life and death are in the power of the tongue."[38] It belongs to the master to speak and teach, and it is the duty of the disciple to hear and obey. RULE OF ST. BENEDICT 6.[39]

SPEAKING MANY WORDS IN PRAISE OF GOD IS NOT SINFUL. AUGUSTINE: I know that it is written, "In much speaking you shall not escape sin." Would that all my speaking were only the preaching of your word and the praise of you! Then I would not only escape sin, no matter how many words I spoke, but also obtain a good reward. For it could not have been sin that a man blessed of you commanded upon his own son in

[32]FC 80:162-63. [33]FC 42:392-93. [34]Gen 4:7. [35]Lk 2:19. [36]NPNF 2 10:382-84*. [37]ECTD 335. [38]Prov 18:21. [39]LCC 12:300**.

the faith, to whom he wrote, "Preach the word, be instant in season, out of season."[40] In him who neither in season nor out of season kept back your word, none can say that there was not much speaking. And yet it was not much, when so much was needed. [But] deliver me, O God, from the multitude of words within my own soul. ON THE TRINITY 15.51.[41]

10:20 The Tongue of the Righteous and the Mind of the Wicked

THE TONGUE OF THE WICKED IS HIGHLY POLLUTED. SHENOUTE: When I read the Proverbs today, I began with this sentence: "The tongue of the righteous is tried silver." I said, If the tongue of the righteous is choice silver, the tongue of the wicked is most polluted. What is more choice or what is holier than the tongue of a man who uses it to confess and preach God and his Christ and to give him praise, but then also to read his laws and to meditate on them day and night,[42] and also to speak every good word? ON LANGUAGE.[43]

10:25 The Wicked Cannot Withstand the Tempest

THE RIGHTEOUS ARE SAVED BY AVOIDING THE STORM. CHRYSOSTOM: "When the storm has passed by, the wicked are destroyed: the righteous, by avoiding it, are saved forever." When temptation attacks, the wicked easily sin. On the other hand, the righteous are saved for eternity when they conquer temptation through patience and a soul of gratitude toward God. Notice how safe righteousness is: the righteous are saved when they avoid evil, are on the defensive and stand firm constantly. The wicked, on the other hand, are thrown to the ground even when the disturbance or temptation has not attacked completely. Therefore those who ignore the just judgment of God easily sin. COMMENTARY ON THE PROVERBS OF SOLOMON, FRAGMENT 10.25.[44]

---

[40]2 Tim 4:2. [41]LCC 8:180**. [42]Cf. Ps 1:2; Josh 1:8. [43]CSCO 96:66. [44]PG 64:685.

11:1-31 PROVERBS ABOUT THE GODLESS AND THE UPRIGHT, THE TRUSTWORTHY AND THE TALEBEARERS

[1]A false balance is an abomination to the
LORD,
but a just weight is his delight.
[2]When pride comes, then comes disgrace;
but with the humble is wisdom.
[3]The integrity of the upright guides them,
but the crookedness of the treacherous
destroys them.
[4]Riches do not profit in the day of wrath,
but righteousness delivers from death.
[5]The righteousness of the blameless keeps
his way straight,
but the wicked falls by his own
wickedness.
[6]The righteousness of the upright delivers
them,
but the treacherous are taken captive
by their lust.

⁷When the wicked dies, his hope perishes,
  and the expectation of the godless comes
    to nought.
⁸The righteous is delivered from trouble,
  and the wicked gets into it instead.
⁹With his mouth the godless man would
    destroy his neighbor,
  but by knowledge the righteous are
    delivered.
¹⁰When it goes well with the righteous,
    the city rejoices;
  and when the wicked perish there are
    shouts of gladness.
¹¹By the blessing of the upright a city is
    exalted,
  but it is overthrown by the mouth of
    the wicked.
¹²He who belittles his neighbor lacks sense,
  but a man of understanding remains
    silent.
¹³He who goes about as a talebearer
    reveals secrets,
  but he who is trustworthy in spirit
    keeps a thing hidden.
¹⁴Where there is no guidance, a people falls;
  but in an abundance of counselors there
    is safety.
¹⁵He who gives surety for a stranger will
    smart for it,
  but he who hates suretyship is secure.
¹⁶A gracious woman gets honor,
  and violent men get riches.
¹⁷A man who is kind benefits himself,
  but a cruel man hurts himself.
¹⁸A wicked man earns deceptive wages,
  but one who sows righteousness gets a
    sure reward.
¹⁹He who is steadfast in righteousness will

live,
  but he who pursues evil will die.
²⁰Men of perverse mind are an
    abomination to the LORD,
  but those of blameless ways are his delight.
²¹Be assured, an evil man will not go
    unpunished,
  but those who are righteous will be
    delivered.
²²Like a gold ring in a swine's snout
  is a beautiful woman without discretion.
²³The desire of the righteous ends only in
    good;
  the expectation of the wicked in wrath.
²⁴One man gives freely, yet grows all the
    richer;
  another withholds what he should give,
    and only suffers want.
²⁵A liberal man will be enriched,
  and one who waters will himself be
    watered.
²⁶The people curse him who holds back
    grain,
  but a blessing is on the head of him
    who sells it.
²⁷He who diligently seeks good seeks favor,
  but evil comes to him who searches for it.
²⁸He who trusts in his riches will wither,ᵛ
  but the righteous will flourish like a green
    leaf.
²⁹He who troubles his household will
    inherit wind,
  and the fool will be servant to the wise.
³⁰The fruit of the righteous is a tree of life,
  but lawlessnessʷ takes away lives.
³¹If the righteous is requited on earth,
  how much more the wicked and the
    sinner!

v Cn: Heb *fall*   w Cn Compare Gk Syr: Heb *a wise man*

OVERVIEW: A false balance can defraud one's soul of eternal life (AMBROSE). Disgrace comes with pride, whereas the wise are known for humility (BEDE). Money will not avert eternal punishment (BASIL). Those who have wealth should use it for mercy (SHENOUTE). Repetition of repentance, however, is pointless and superficial (CLEMENT OF ALEXANDRIA). Although the hope of the wicked perishes when they die, the righteous can look forward to eternal glory (CHRYSOSTOM). For the correction of one's deeds many heads are better than one (BEDE). Money spent on others carries its own reward (LEO THE GREAT). Neither pierce your ears nor your nose, for such would be as inconsistent as a golden ring in a pig's snout (CLEMENT OF ALEXANDRIA). One's entire life can be stained by a single disorder of the soul (GREGORY OF NYSSA). The study of Scripture is pointless if one's works and thoughts are muddied (JOHN CASSIAN). The appellation of the name *Christian*, if used unworthily, is like a golden ring in the snout of a swine (SALVIAN THE PRESBYTER). To withhold from those in need is to decline to render mercy (SHENOUTE). To refrain from preaching is just like hiding corn, and it will be cursed by the people (GREGORY THE GREAT). Let your focus be upon the future rather than upon the present or the past (BEDE). Christ is the fruit of righteousness and the tree of life (HIPPOLYTUS). The righteous are those who organize their lives in terms of righteousness (CHRYSOSTOM). Total conversion, from impiety and iniquity, is expected of us all (FULGENTIUS). Retribution on earth may be difficult for the righteous, but for sinners the penalty is damnation (BEDE).

11:1 A False Balance or a Just Weight?

A DECEITFUL BALANCE CAN DEFRAUD ONE'S SOUL OF ETERNAL LIFE. AMBROSE: Let each one weigh his words without fraud and deceit: "A deceitful balance is an abomination before the Lord." I do not mean that balance which weighs out another's pay (in trivial matters the flesh is deceitful). Before God that balance of words is

detestable which simulates the weight of sober gravity while practicing at the same time cunning fraud. God condemns especially the man who deceives his neighbor with treacherous injustice. He will have no gain from his clever skill. For what does it profit a man if he gains the wealth of the whole world but defrauds his own soul of the payment of eternal life?[1] LETTER 15.[2]

11:2 Disgrace Comes with Pride, but Wisdom Comes with Humility

MANY REASONS WHY PRIDE BRINGS DISGRACE. BEDE: "Where there is pride, there will also be disgrace" because the proud conduct themselves disgracefully through contempt or ignorance of discipline, or because they bring disgrace upon their neighbors, or, in any event, "because all who exalt themselves will be humbled."[3] COMMENTARY ON PROVERBS 2.11.2.[4]

11:4 Riches Do Not Profit, but Righteousness Delivers from Death

MONEY WILL NOT AVERT ETERNAL PUNISHMENT. BASIL THE GREAT: [Solomon] leads toward understanding especially when he says, "Possessions are of no advantage in the day of wrath." For he infused your heart with the knowledge that an abundance of money will be of no help to you in that day, nor will it remove eternal punishment. And when he says, "The innocent will inherit the earth,"[5] he clearly means the earth of which the meek are also heirs, for first the psalmist said, "But the meek will inherit the earth,"[6] and then the Lord, when preaching about beatitude, said, "Blessed are the meek, for they will possess the earth."[7] HOMILY ON THE BEGINNING OF PROVERBS 14.[8]

WEALTH SHOULD BE USED FOR MERCY. SHENOUTE: I know why it is written: "Wealth will not

---

[1]See Mt 16:26. [2]FC 26:82. [3]Lk 14:11. [4]CCL 119B:70. [5]Cf. Prov 2:21. [6]Ps 37:11 (36:11 LXX). [7]Mt 5:4. [8]PG 31:416.

profit in the day of wrath." This was said about the one who does not employ his wealth for mercy. Is not the power of wealth to be brought forth and used at a time of need? At the hour in which you return your spirit to the hands of God, you will understand that the full utility of your riches is to use them for the sake of mercy. For they were given to you by Jesus Christ, God and the Son of God. ON LANGUAGE.[9]

11:5 Righteousness Keeps One in the Straight Way

REPEATEDLY REQUESTING FORGIVENESS. CLEMENT OF ALEXANDRIA: To be repeatedly requesting forgiveness for offenses repeatedly committed is not repentance, only its appearance. "The righteousness of the blameless keeps their way straight," proclaims Scripture, and again, "The righteousness of the innocent will set straight their way." STROMATEIS 2.13.59.1.[10]

11:7 Hope Perishes When the Wicked Dies

THE RIGHTEOUS CAN LOOK FOR GLORY AFTER DEATH. CHRYSOSTOM: "When a righteous man dies, hope does not perish." He hopes that his children will do well; he hopes to be provided with great things. This passage also transports us to thoughts of the resurrection or of our posterity. Or, since one who is righteous has delighted in all these things already, he will also enjoy their future consummation; or, finally, that he would have enjoyment of glory after death. COMMENTARY ON THE PROVERBS OF SOLOMON, FRAGMENT 9.7.[11]

11:14 Failure for Lack of Guidance

MANY HEADS ARE BETTER THAN ONE. BEDE: Lest you think that a friend's crime which you are unable to correct should be concealed, it rightly says that a people are corrupted without a governor but are saved where there is abundant counsel. [This is said] in order to show that the deed

you are unable to amend alone should be revealed to many, so that it may be corrected by the unanimous diligence of all. COMMENTARY ON PROVERBS 2.11.14.[12]

11:17 Kindness Benefits the Self, but Cruelty Hurts the Self

MONEY SPENT ON OTHERS CARRIES ITS OWN REWARD. LEO THE GREAT: Prayer rises up quickly to the ears of God when lifted up by the recommendation of [alms and fasting]. Since, as it has been written, "the merciful man benefits his own soul," nothing belongs to each individual more than what has been spent on one's neighbor. Part of those physical resources which are used to help the poor become transformed into eternal riches. Born from this generosity are funds which will not be able to be diminished through use nor damaged through decay. "Blessed are the merciful, for God will have mercy on them."[13] He who constitutes the very exemplar of this precept will also be the sum of their reward. SERMON 16.2.[14]

11:22 A Golden Ring in a Pig's Snout

PIERCE NOT YOUR EARS OR YOUR NOSE. CLEMENT OF ALEXANDRIA: Reason also forbids us to do violence to nature by piercing the lobes of the ear. Why not pierce the nostrils also? The Scriptures would then be accomplished indeed: "As a ring in the nose of the swine, so is beauty in a foolish woman." To conclude, if anyone thinks he is decorated when he wears gold, then he is less than his gold, and he who is less than gold is not its master. CHRIST THE EDUCATOR 3.11.56.[15]

DISORDER OF THE SOUL. GREGORY OF NYSSA: Let eagerness for virginity be put down as the foundation for the life of virtue, but let there be built upon this foundation all the products of virtue. If this is believed to be precious and befitting

---

[9]CSCO 96:67. [10]FC 85:198. [11]PG 64:685. [12]CCL 119B:71. [13]Mt 5:7. [14]FC 93:59-60. [15]FC 23:244*.

to God, as it is, but one's whole life does not conform to it and is stained by the rest of the soul's disorder, then this is "the golden ring in the swine's snout" or the pearl trampled under the feet of the swine.[16] ON VIRGINITY 18.[17]

IF ONE'S WORKS AND THOUGHTS ARE MUDDIED. JOHN CASSIAN: As for those who seem to have some semblance of knowledge and those who do not abandon the sins of the flesh even when they apply themselves diligently to the reading and memorizing of Scripture, Proverbs has the following well-put statement: "The beauty of a woman of evil ways is like a golden ring in the snout of a pig." What use is it for a man to possess the jewel of heaven's words and to give himself over to that most precious loveliness of Scripture if he himself is stuck fast in muddied works and thoughts? CONFERENCE 14.16.[18]

THE APPELLATION CHRISTIAN USED UNWORTHILY. SALVIAN THE PRESBYTER: What is a holy appellation without merit but an ornament set in the mud? The holy Scriptures have testified to this in writing: "A golden ring in a swine's snout, a woman fair and foolish." And in us the appellation *Christian* is like a golden ornament. If we use it unworthily, we seem to be swine with an ornament. THE GOVERNANCE OF GOD 4.1.[19]

11:26 Holding Back Grain

TO WITHHOLD IS TO DECLINE MERCY. SHENOUTE: It is written, "Men speak evil of him who withholds wheat." One who withholds is without mercy. He does not gather for the sake of mercy. For, unless he gathers, with what can he bestow mercy? Is it not also true that men bless the person who expends and gives, as it is written here and there in the pages of sacred Scripture?[20] ON LANGUAGE.[21]

REFRAINING FROM PREACHING IS LIKE HIDING CORN. GREGORY THE GREAT: It is well said by Solomon, "He that hides corn shall be cursed among the people." To hide corn is to retain with oneself the words of sacred preaching. Among the people any such one is cursed, since, for the fault of mere silence, he is condemned in the punishment of the many whom he could have corrected. PASTORAL CARE 3.25.26.[22]

11:28 Trust Not in Riches but in Righteousness

LET YOUR FOCUS BE ON THE FUTURE. BEDE: He who does not think of the future because he is longing for present goods will finally be lacking in both. But they who do good deeds in the present for the hope of future rewards will justly receive that for which they hope. The green leaf in the tree that does not yet have fruit to display surely signifies the future. And the righteous flourish like green leaves because, having been saved in hope through faith,[23] they do not cease to make progress in virtue by grace until they attain the fruit of their desired reward. COMMENTARY ON PROVERBS 2.11.28.[24]

11:30 Tree of Life Is the Fruit of the Righteous

CHRIST IS THE FRUIT AND THE TREE. HIPPOLYTUS: The fruit of righteousness and the tree of life is Christ. He alone, as man, fulfilled all righteousness. And with his own underived life[25] he has brought forth the fruits of knowledge and virtue like a tree, whereof they that eat shall receive eternal life and shall enjoy the tree of life in paradise, with Adam and all the righteous. But the souls of the unrighteous meet an untimely expulsion from the presence of God, by whom they shall be left to remain in the flame of torment. FRAGMENTS ON PROVERBS.[26]

11:31 Even the Righteous Receive Their Due

---

[16]Mt 7:6. [17]FC 58:56. [18]JCC 170-71. [19]FC 3:90. [20]Cf. Acts 20:35. [21]CSCO 96:67. [22]ACW 11:177*. [23]See Rom 8:24. [24]CCL 119B:73. [25]Gk *autozōē*. [26]ANF 5:173; TLG 2115.053.17.1.

THOSE WHO ORGANIZE THEIR LIVES IN RIGHTEOUSNESS. CHRYSOSTOM: "If the righteous are saved with difficulty, where will the impious and sinners appear?" Consider that life is long, a lasting residence with many dangers. And he [Solomon] does not say these words about those who lived righteously. But if by any chance he said something about them, he would speak in the best of terms. Indeed if God has bestowed something upon us, what we have done with it will be examined, and who will be justified except the one who is purer than the sun? By "righteous" he [Solomon] means the one who organizes his life in righteousness. The one who hates God is "impious." The "sinner" is the one who acts wickedly. COMMENTARY ON THE PROVERBS OF SOLOMON, FRAGMENT 11.31.[27]

TOTAL CONVERSION IS COMMANDED OF US. FULGENTIUS OF RUSPE: Conversion from both impiety and iniquity is commanded. For both provoke the wrath of God against one, because God detests and condemns both, as Paul says,

"The wrath of God is indeed being revealed from heaven against every impiety and human wickedness."[28] And Solomon says, as the blessed Peter had also inserted among his own words, "And if the righteous one is barely saved, when will the godless and the sinner appear?"[29] ON THE FORGIVENESS OF SINS 1.13.1.[30]

DIFFICULTY FOR THE RIGHTEOUS BUT DAMNATION FOR SINNERS. BEDE: "If the righteous receives [retribution] on earth, how much more the wicked and sinner?" This is to say clearly, "If the frailty of mortal life is so great that not even the righteous who are to be crowned in heaven pass through this life without tribulations on account of the countless slips of [our] flawed nature, how much more do those who are cut off from heavenly grace await the certain outcome of their everlasting damnation? COMMENTARY ON 1 PETER 4:18.[31]

---

[27]PG 64:689. [28]Rom 1:18. [29]Cf. 1 Pet 4:18. [30]FC 95:125-26. [31]CS 82:113-14.

12:1-28 THE DISCIPLINE
OF KNOWLEDGE AND WISDOM

[1]Whoever loves discipline loves
    knowledge,
  but he who hates reproof is stupid.
[2]A good man obtains favor from the
    LORD,
  but a man of evil devices he condemns.
[3]A man is not established by wickedness,
  but the root of the righteous will never
    be moved.
[4]A good wife is the crown of her husband,

but she who brings shame is like rot-
    tenness in his bones.
[5]The thoughts of the righteous are just;*
  the counsels of the wicked are treacherous.
[6]The words of the wicked lie in wait for
    blood,
  but the mouth of the upright delivers men.
[7]The wicked are overthrown and are no
    more,[†]
  but the house of the righteous will stand.

^{8}A man is commended according to his
　　good sense,
　　but one of perverse mind is despised.
^{9}Better is a man of humble standing who
　　works for himself
　　than one who plays the great man but
　　lacks bread.
^{10}A righteous man has regard for the life
　　of his beast,
　　but the mercy of the wicked is cruel.
^{11}He who tills his land will have plenty of
　　bread,
　　but he who follows worthless pursuits
　　has no sense.
^{12}The strong tower of the wicked comes to
　　ruin,
　　but the root of the righteous stands firm.^{x}
^{13}An evil man is ensnared by the
　　transgression of his lips,
　　but the righteous escapes from trouble.
^{14}From the fruit of his words a man is
　　satisfied with good,
　　and the work of a man's hand comes back
　　to him.
^{15}The way of a fool is right in his own
　　eyes,
　　but a wise man listens to advice.
^{16}The vexation of a fool is known at once,
　　but the prudent man ignores an insult.
^{17}He who speaks the truth gives honest
　　evidence,

　　but a false witness utters deceit.
^{18}There is one whose rash words are like
　　sword thrusts,
　　but the tongue of the wise brings healing.
^{19}Truthful lips endure for ever,
　　but a lying tongue is but for a moment.
^{20}Deceit is in the heart of those who devise
　　evil,
　　but those who plan good have joy.
^{21}No ill befalls the righteous,
　　but the wicked are filled with trouble.
^{22}Lying lips are an abomination to the
　　LORD,
　　but those who act faithfully are his
　　delight.
^{23}A prudent man conceals his knowledge,
　　but fools^y proclaim their folly.
^{24}The hand of the diligent will rule,
　　while the slothful will be put to forced
　　labor.
^{25}Anxiety in a man's heart weighs him
　　down,
　　but a good word makes him glad.
^{26}A righteous man turns away from evil,^{z}
　　but the way of the wicked leads them
　　astray.
^{27}A slothful man will not catch his prey,^{a}
　　but the diligent man will get precious
　　wealth.^{b}
^{28}In the path of righteousness is life,
　　but the way of error leads to death.^{c}

x Cn: The Hebrew of verse 12 is obscure　y Heb *the heart of fools*　z Cn: The meaning of the Hebrew is uncertain　a Cn Compare Gk Syr: The meaning of the Hebrew is uncertain　b Cn: The meaning of the Hebrew is uncertain　c Cn: The meaning of the Hebrew is uncertain　*LXX *The reflections of the righteous are judgments.*　†Vg *Change the wicked, and they will not exist.*

OVERVIEW: The crown of the husband is a good wife, but the husband is also the crown of the woman (CLEMENT OF ALEXANDRIA). The wife should be a companion in virtue as well as in life (CHRYSOSTOM). Continue to be the person you have become by grace (GREGORY THE GREAT). Our attitude of mercy toward fellow human beings is paralleled by our merciful attitude toward animals (Chrysostom). Jesus has given us the way of reconciliation (Apostolic Constitutions), and for this reason we are called to love our enemies as well as our friends (Caesarius).

12:4-5 A Good Wife Is the Crown of the Husband

The Crown of a Husband Is His Marriage. Clement of Alexandria: The crown of the woman must be considered the husband, and the crown of the husband is his marriage. For both, the flower of their union is the child who is indeed the flower that the divine cultivator culls from the meadow of the flesh. "The crown of old men is their children's children and the glory of children is their father,"[1] it is said. Our glory is the Father of all, and the crown of the whole church is Christ. Christ the Educator 2.8.71.[2]

A Wife Should Also Be a Companion in Virtue. Chrysostom: When you are going to take a wife, do not only look for a companion in life but also for a companion in virtue. It is inevitable that the husband of a depraved wife perishes in the same way. Therefore look for virtue and not for money. And a well-behaved wife will become a crown of glory because she is strong; [whereas] an evil wife, as if a worm dwells inside her heart, will cause destruction gradually and silently. And what is even more dreadful is that this does not appear externally, but this sort of wife injects the poison inside and consumes an unhappy soul. In the opposite way, virtue adorns the one who follows it, whereas iniquity makes the iniquitous even more detestable. "The reflections of the righteous are judgments." They are, in fact, discreet and simple: either because the righteous always reflect on the judgments and commands of God or because they always turn judgments over inside their mind. Our mind sits like a judge, judging the different virtues and arguing with the opposing vices, approving one, condemning the other. Commentary on the Proverbs of Solomon, Fragment 12.4.[3]

12:7 When the Wicked Are Overthrown, They Are No More

Continue to Be the Person You Have Become by Grace. Gregory the Great: Let us abandon the selves we have made by sinning. Let us continue to be the selves we have become by grace. You see a person who was proud: if he has turned to Christ he has become humble, he has abandoned himself. If a person of unrestrained desires has changed to a life of self-restraint, he has certainly denied what he was. If a miser, one who previously seized what belonged to others, has ceased to go around looking for gain and learned to be generous with what belongs to him, beyond any doubt he has abandoned himself. He is the generous person he was created to be, not the one he would become through his wickedness. This is why it is written, "Change the wicked, and they will be no more." The wicked who have been changed will be no more, not because they will altogether cease to exist in their essential being. [Rather,] they will cease to exist in their guilty state of ungodliness. Forty Gospel Homilies 32.[4]

12:10 A Righteous Person Has Regard for Animals' Lives

One's Attitude Toward Animals. Chrysostom: "The righteous has pity upon the soul of his animals." It is an exercise of human charity when someone, by means of his animals, becomes accustomed to show mercy upon his fellow human beings. Indeed he who has pity upon animals tends to have much more pity upon his brothers. . . . Do the righteous have pity upon the souls of their animals? Absolutely. Certainly it is necessary to convey benevolence toward them, so that there may be a greater exercise [of benevolence] toward fellow human beings. Indeed with good reason God ordered that we carry hurt animals and take back those that stray, and not to

---

[1]Prov 17:6. [2]FC 23:154*. [3]PG 64:689-92. [4]CS 123:258-59*.

bind the mouth of an ox.[5] He absolutely wants us to preserve the health of animals: in the first place for our sake, second, in order that they may provide us with their menial service. At the same time it is an exercise of benevolence and care. Indeed the one who has pity upon strangers has much more pity upon those who are familiar to him. And the one who has pity upon his servants has much more pity for his brothers. But you may say: an animal provides you with a profitable service, but with what does a brother provide you? He is helpful to you, I say, much more from the viewpoint of God. You can see that when we offer care such as we do for our animals we do not consider this demeaning. For, in doing so we are not only serving them but also ourselves. COMMENTARY ON THE PROVERBS OF SOLOMON, FRAGMENT 12.10.[6]

12:28 Righteousness Tends Toward Life, but Error Leads to Death

JESUS HAS GIVEN US THE WAY OF RECONCILIATION. APOSTOLIC CONSTITUTIONS: "The souls of those that bear a settled hatred are to death," says Solomon. But our Lord and Savior Jesus Christ says in the gospels: "If you bring your gift to the altar, and there remember that your brother has anything against you, leave there your gift before the altar, and go your way; first be reconciled to your brother, and then come and offer your gift to God."[7] CONSTITUTIONS OF THE HOLY APOSTLES 2.6.53.[8]

STRIVE TO LOVE YOUR ENEMIES. CAESARIUS OF ARLES: "The paths of those who harbor resentment for an injury lead to death." Are these my words, dearest brothers? They are taken from the canonical sacred Scriptures. Therefore in order that we may not be murderers or among the living dead, let us strive to love not only our friends but also our enemies. Then we will be able to meet a kind and merciful Lord with a conscience at ease, in accord with the bond of his pledge. SERMON 223.4.[9]

---

[5]See Deut 22:1-4. [6]PG 64:692. [7]Mt 5:23-24. [8]ANF 7:419*. [9]FC 66:146-47*.

13:1-25 A WISE SON LISTENS

[1]A wise son hears his father's instruction,
  but a scoffer does not listen to rebuke.
[2]From the fruit of his mouth a good man
    eats good,
  but the desire of the treacherous is for
    violence.
[3]He who guards his mouth preserves his
    life;
  he who opens wide his lips comes to ruin.
[4]The soul of the sluggard craves, and gets
    nothing,
  while the soul of the diligent is richly
    supplied.
[5]A righteous man hates falsehood,
  but a wicked man acts shamefully and
    disgracefully.
[6]Righteousness guards him whose way is
    upright,
  but sin overthrows the wicked.
[7]One man pretends to be rich, yet has

nothing;
    another pretends to be poor, yet has
       great wealth.
[8]The ransom of a man's life is his wealth,
    but a poor man has no means of
       redemption.[d]
[9]The light of the righteous rejoices,
    but the lamp of the wicked will be put out.
[10]By insolence the heedless make strife,
    but with those who take advice is wisdom.
[11]Wealth hastily gotten[e] will dwindle,
    but he who gathers little by little will
       increase it.
[12]Hope deferred makes the heart sick,
    but a desire fulfilled is a tree of life.
[13]He who despises the word brings
       destruction on himself,
    but he who respects the commandment
       will be rewarded.
[14]The teaching of the wise is a fountain of
       life,
    that one may avoid the snares of death.
[15]Good sense wins favor,
    but the way of the faithless is their ruin.[f]
[16]In everything a prudent man acts with
       knowledge,
    but a fool flaunts his folly.

[17]A bad messenger plunges men into
       trouble,
    but a faithful envoy brings healing.
[18]Poverty and disgrace come to him who
       ignores instruction,
    but he who heeds reproof is honored.
[19]A desire fulfilled is sweet to the soul;
    but to turn away from evil is an
       abomination to fools.
[20]He who walks with wise men becomes wise,
    but the companion of fools will suffer
       harm.
[21]Misfortune pursues sinners,
    but prosperity rewards the righteous.
[22]A good man leaves an inheritance to his
       children's children,*
    but the sinner's wealth is laid up for
       the righteous.
[23]The fallow ground of the poor yields
       much food,
    but it is swept away through injustice.
[24]He who spares the rod hates his son,
    but he who loves him is diligent to
       discipline him.
[25]The righteous has enough to satisfy his
       appetite,
    but the belly of the wicked suffers want.

d Cn: Heb *does not hear rebuke,* LXX *bears not reprehension*　　**e** Gk Vg: Heb *from vanity*　　**f** Cn Compare Gk Syr Vg Tg: Heb *is enduring*　　*LXX *A good man shall inherit children's children*

OVERVIEW: Pride is the disease of riches, and Christians should avoid both of them (AUGUSTINE). Do not, for lack of discipline, store your profits in a bag that has holes in it (JOHN CASSIAN). Moderation in either wealth or poverty does not necessarily prevent sin (ORIGEN). Because wealth is the ransom of a person's life, wealth must be shared for the sake of salvation (CLEMENT OF ALEXANDRIA), and it is even proper to despise money for the sake of one's soul (PETER OF ALEXANDRIA). Wealth is for the sake of redemption, not of destruction (AMBROSE). Poverty is not an evil thing, but neither is honest wealth (CHRYSOSTOM). If the poor feel dejected, they should look around and count their blessings (BASIL). Souls are more valuable to the Lord than riches (JEROME), and wealth that redeems the soul may be either temporal or spiritual (BEDE). The property of the ungodly, however, is not transmitted to their children (CHRYSOSTOM). Parents must give account if they fail to discipline their children (APOSTOLIC CONSTITUTIONS). There are, after all, good reasons not to spare the rod (THEODOTUS), and correction by the rod is especially useful for teaching obedience to the precepts of salvation (AMBROSE). Temporal scourging is sometimes necessary for eternal life (AUGUSTINE). Nonetheless, the greed of the wicked can never be quenched (CLEMENT OF ALEXANDRIA), although the hunger of the righteous is satisfied by the food of the soul (ORIGEN). Overall, the just are satisfied with the heavenly food of God's Word and Wisdom (ORIGEN, CAESARIUS).

13:7 The Pretenses of Wealth and of Poverty

THE DISEASE OF RICHES IS PRIDE. AUGUSTINE: It is simply not to be credited that holy Scripture is concerned to advise us on these riches which the proud get such swollen heads about. I mean these visible, earthly riches, of course, as though we should either think they are very important or fear not to have them. "After all," someone will say, "what good does a man get from pretending to be rich when in fact he has nothing?" Scripture has taken note of such a person and found fault with him. . . .

It is not improper, nor is it unseemly or useless that the holy Scriptures should wish to commend rich people to us for being humble. The thing really to be afraid of with riches, you see, is pride. In fact, the apostle Paul has advice on this point for Timothy: "Command the rich of this world," he says, "not to have proud thoughts."[1] It wasn't riches he went in dread of but the disease of riches. The disease of riches is great pride. A grand spirit it is indeed, that in the midst of riches is not prone to this disease, a spirit greater than its riches, surpassing them not by desiring but by despising them.

Great then indeed is the rich person who doesn't think he is great just because he is rich. But if that is why he does think he is great, then he is proud and destitute. He's a big noise in the flesh. In his heart of hearts he's a beggar. He has been inflated, not filled. If you see two wineskins, one filled, the other inflated, they each have the same bulk and extent, but they don't each have the same content. Just look at them, and you can't tell the difference; but weigh them, and you will find out. The one that has been filled is hard to move; the one that has been inflated is easily removed. . . .

I am not telling you to do away with your wealth but to transfer it, because there are many people who have refused to do this and have been very sorry indeed that they did not obey, when they not only lost their wealth but on account of it have lost themselves too. So, command the rich of this world not to have proud thoughts, and there will happen in them what we have heard in Solomon's proverb: "There are those who humble themselves though they are rich." It can happen even with these temporal riches. Let him be humble. Let him be more glad that he's a Christian than that he's rich. Don't let him be puffed up or become high and mighty. Let him take notice of the poor man his brother, and not refuse to be called the poor man's brother. After all, however rich he may be, Christ is richer, and he wanted all for whom he shed his blood to be his brethren. SERMON 36.1-2, 5.[2]

DO NOT PUT YOUR PROFITS IN A BAG WITH HOLES. JOHN CASSIAN: A person who, because of his undisciplined heart and daily distraction of mind, loses whatever he seemed to have acquired by the conversion of others truly puts his profits in a bag with holes. And so it is that, while believing themselves able to make greater profit by instructing others, they are deprived of their own betterment. For "there are those who make themselves out as rich, although they have nothing, and there are those who humble themselves in the midst of great wealth." CONFERENCE 24.13.6.[3]

13:8 Ransom of One's Life Is Wealth

[1]1 Tim 6:17. [2]WSA 3 2:174-75, 177*. [3]ACW 57:836-37.

MODERATION OF WEALTH OR OF POVERTY DOES NOT NECESSARILY PREVENT SIN.

ORIGEN: What is the use of counting the number of those who, because of their earthly riches which they did not use properly, have received the same punishment as the rich man in the gospel?[4] Or the number of the poor who have endured their poverty ignobly and conducted themselves in a lowly and servile manner—not as becomes saints—and who consequently have forfeited the hope laid up for them in heaven? Even those who occupy a middle station between riches and poverty are not because of their moderate estate entirely removed from sinning. ON PRAYER 2.29.6.[5]

WEALTH MUST BE SHARED FOR THE SAKE OF SALVATION.

CLEMENT OF ALEXANDRIA: Just as the foot is the measure of the sandal, so the physical needs of each person are the measure of what he should possess. Whatever is excessive—the things they call adornments, the trappings of the rich—are not adornments but a burden for the body. If one is to use violence to ascend to heaven,[6] it is necessary to carry the good staff of holy deeds and first to share our goods with the oppressed before laying hold of the true rest. Scripture declares that really "his own wealth is the redemption of the soul of man," that is, if a person is rich, he will obtain salvation by sharing his wealth. CHRIST THE EDUCATOR 3.7.39.[7]

DESPISE MONEY FOR THE SAKE OF ONE'S SOUL.

PETER OF ALEXANDRIA: Against those who have given money that they might be entirely undisturbed by evil, an accusation cannot be brought. For they have sustained the loss and sacrifice of their goods that they might not hurt or destroy their soul, which others for the sake of filthy lucre have not done. And yet the Lord says, "What is a man profited, if he shall gain the whole world, and lose his own soul?"[8] And again, "You cannot serve God and mammon."[9] In these things, then, they have shown themselves the servants of God, inasmuch as they have hated, trodden under foot and despised money, and have thus fulfilled what is written: "The ransom of a man's life are his riches." CANONICAL EPISTLES 12.[10]

WEALTH IS FOR THE SAKE OF REDEMPTION.

AMBROSE: The riches of a person ought to work to the redemption of his soul, not to its destruction. Wealth is redemption if one uses it well. It is a snare if one does not know how to use it. For what is a person's money if not provision for the journey? A great amount is a burden; a little is useful. We are wayfarers in this life; many are walking along, but a person needs to make a good passage. The Lord Jesus is with him who makes a good passage. LETTER 15.[11]

POVERTY IS NOT AN EVIL THING, BUT NEITHER IS HONEST WEALTH.

CHRYSOSTOM: "The redemption of the soul of a man is his own wealth." What are you saying? What do you mean by exalting so much wealth? First of all he [Solomon] did not speak about just any wealth but that which is produced through honest activities. Poverty is not, therefore, an evil thing. Rather, he says that no one who wants to may threaten someone who is poor; indeed how can some one terrify one who possesses nothing? For this reason this kind of life is devoid of afflictions. Or, maybe he [Solomon] calls "his own wealth" "righteousness" which snatches him away from death. So the one who is poor in virtue does not have a mind at peace when he suffers threats or the declaration of a punishment. COMMENTARY ON THE PROVERBS OF SOLOMON, FRAGMENT 13.8.[12]

THE POOR MUST COUNT THEIR BLESSINGS.

BASIL THE GREAT: Suppose you are an ignoble and undistinguished person, poor and of lowly origin, without home or city, sick, in need of daily

---

[4]See Lk 16:22-24. [5]ACW 19:116*. [6]See Mt 11:12. [7]FC 23:231-32.* [8]Mt 16:26. [9]Mt 6:24. [10]ANF 6:276-77*. [11]FC 26:80-81. [12]PG 64:696.

sustenance, in dread of the powerful, cowering before everyone because of your abject condition. "But he that is poor," says the Scripture, "bears not reprehension." Yet, do not despair or cast aside every good hope because your present state is quite unenviable. Rather, turn your thoughts to the blessings already granted you by God and to those reserved by promise for the future. HOMILY ON THE WORDS "GIVE HEED TO THYSELF."[13]

SOULS ARE MORE VALUABLE TO THE LORD THAN RICHES.

JEROME: The Lord yearns for believers' souls more than for their riches. We read in the Proverbs, "The ransom of a man's soul are his own riches." We may, indeed, take a person's own riches to be those which do not come from someone else or from plunder; according to the precept, "honor God with your just labors."[14] But the sense is better if we understand a person's "own riches" to be those hidden treasures which no thief can steal and no robber wrest from him.[15] LETTER 71.4.[16]

WEALTH THAT REDEEMS THE SOUL.

BEDE: As Solomon says, "A man's own wealth is the redemption of his soul." This might be temporal wealth which one distributes and gives to the poor so that one's righteousness may endure forever, or it might be spiritual wealth in the form of the righteousness that one has attained by taking pity on the poor or by doing other good things. ON THE TABERNACLE 3.13.[17]

13:22 A Good Person Leaves an Inheritance

THE PROPERTY OF THE UNGODLY NOT TRANSMITTED TO THEIR HEIRS.

CHRYSOSTOM: "A good man will inherit children's children." The verb "he will inherit" does not mean that he will take the inheritance from his sons; in fact, this would be the greatest curse. Rather, it means the opposite, that is, that he will transmit his riches to his posterity and will leave behind descendants. But the property of the ungodly is

not transmitted to their sons but to those who can use them properly. Another interpretation may be: the mind, almost like a parent, generates good thoughts; and these become parents of similar actions. COMMENTARY ON THE PROVERBS OF SOLOMON, FRAGMENT 13.22.[18]

13:24 Spare the Rod and Spoil the Child

PARENTS MUST GIVE ACCOUNT.

APOSTOLIC CONSTITUTIONS: You fathers, educate your children in the Lord, bringing them up in the nurture and admonition of the Lord, and teach them such trades as are agreeable and suitable to the Lord, lest they by such opportunity become extravagant and continue without punishment from their parents, and so become slack before their time and go astray from that which is good. Therefore do not be afraid to reprove them and to teach them wisdom with severity. For your corrections will not kill them but rather preserve them.... [Thus Solomon says,] "He that spares his rod hates his son," and afterwards, "Beat his sides while he is an infant, lest he be hardened and disobey you."[19] He, therefore, who neglects to admonish and instruct his own son, hates his own child. Teach, therefore, your children the word of the Lord. Bring them under with cutting stripes, and make them subject from infancy, teaching them the holy Scriptures, which are Christian and divine, and delivering to them every sacred writing, "not giving them such liberty that they get the mastery"[20] and act against your opinion. Do not permit them to club together with peer groups. For so they will be turned to disorderly ways and will fall into fornication. And if this happens by the carelessness of their parents, those who gave them birth will be guilty of their souls. For if the offending children get into the company of debauched persons by the negligence of those who gave them life, they will not be punished alone by themselves, but

---

[13]FC 9:441. [14]Prov 3:9. [15]See Mt 6:20. [16]NPNF 2 6:153. [17]TTH 18:157*. [18]PG 64:697. [19]Sir 30:12. [20]Sir 30:11.

their parents also will be condemned on their account. For this cause, endeavor at the time when they are of an age fit for marriage, to join them in wedlock and settle them together, lest in the heat and fervor of their age their course of life become dissolute and you be required to give an account by the Lord God in the day of judgment. CONSTITUTIONS OF THE HOLY APOSTLES 4.2.11.[21]

GOOD REASONS NOT TO SPARE THE ROD.
THEODOTUS THE VALENTINIAN: God, out of goodness, has mingled fear with goodness. For what is beneficial for each one, that he also supplies, as a physician to a sick man, as a father to his insubordinate child: "For he that spares his rod hates his son." And the Lord and his apostles walked in the midst of fear and labors. When, then, the affliction is sent in the person of a right-eous man, it is either from the Lord rebuking him for a sin committed before, or guarding him on account of the future, or not preventing by the exercise of his power an assault from without—for some good end to him and to those near, for the sake of example. EXCERPTS OF THEODOTUS 9.[22]

CORRECTION USEFUL FOR OBEDIENCE.
AMBROSE: The correction of the father who does not spare the rod is useful, that he may render his son's soul obedient to the precepts of salvation. He punishes with a rod, as we read, "I shall punish their offenses with a rod."[23] LETTER 45.[24]

TEMPORAL SCOURGING SOMETIMES NECESSARY. AUGUSTINE: "He that spares the rod hates his son." For, give us a person who with right faith and true understanding can say with all the energy of his heart, "My soul thirsts for God, for the living God: when shall I come and appear before God?"[25] For such a person there is no need of the terror of hell, to say nothing of temporal punishments or imperial laws, seeing that with him it is so indispensable a blessing to cleave to the Lord that he not only dreads being parted from that happiness as a heavy punishment but

can scarcely even bear delay in its attainment. But yet, before the good sons can say they have "a desire to depart, and to be with Christ,"[26] many must first be recalled to their Lord by the stripes of temporal scourging, like evil servants, and in some degree like good-for-nothing fugitives. THE CORRECTION OF THE DONATISTS 6.21.[27]

13:25 The Appetite of the Righteous Is Satisfied

THE GREED OF THE WICKED CAN NEVER BE QUENCHED. CLEMENT OF ALEXANDRIA: We have been created, not to eat and drink but to come to the knowledge of God. "The just man," Scripture says, "eats and fills his soul; but the belly of the wicked is ever in want," ever hungry with a greed that cannot be quenched. CHRIST THE EDUCATOR 2.1.14.[28]

FOOD OF THE SOUL SATISFIES THE HUNGER OF THE RIGHTEOUS. ORIGEN: We must consider the food promised in the law as the food of the soul, which is to satisfy not both parts of a person's nature but the soul only. And the words of the gospel, although probably containing a deeper meaning, may yet be taken in their more simple and obvious sense, as teaching us not to be disturbed with anxieties about our food and clothing, but, while living in plainness, and desiring only what is needful, to put our trust in the providence of God. AGAINST CELSUS 7.24.[29]

THE JUST ARE SATISFIED. ORIGEN: If you take [this verse] according to the literal sense that "when the just person eats he will fill his soul but the souls of the impious will be in poverty," it will appear false. For the souls of the impious take food with eagerness and strive after "satiety," but the just meanwhile are hungry. Finally, Paul was just, and he said, "Up to this hour we are hungry,

---

[21]ANF 7:435-36*. [22]ANF 8:44. [23]Ps 89:32 (88:33 LXX). [24]FC 26:234. [25]Ps 42:2. [26]Phil 1:23. [27]NPNF 1 4:641*. [28]FC 23:106. [29]ANF 4:620.

and thirsty, and naked, and we are beaten with fists."[30] And again he says, "In hunger and thirst, in many fastings."[31] And how does Solomon say, "when the just eats he will satisfy his soul"? But if you consider how "the just person" always and "without interruption" eats from "the living bread" and fills his soul and satisfies it with heavenly food which is the Word of God and his wisdom, you will find how the just person "eats his bread in abundance" from the blessing of God. HOMILIES ON LEVITICUS 16.5.4.[32]

---

[30]1 Cor 4:11. [31]2 Cor 11:27. [32]FC 83:270-71. Caesarius of Arles in a sermon offers the same comment; see FC 47:120-21.

14:1-35 WISDOM OPPOSED BY FOLLY

[1]Wisdom[g] builds her house,
  but folly with her own hands tears it
  down.
[2]He who walks in uprightness fears the
  LORD,
  but he who is devious in his ways
  despises him.
[3]The talk of a fool is a rod for his back,[h]
  but the lips of the wise will preserve them.
[4]Where there are no oxen, there is no[i]
  grain;
  but abundant crops come by the strength
  of the ox.
[5]A faithful witness does not lie,
  but a false witness breathes out lies.
[6]A scoffer seeks wisdom in vain,
  but knowledge is easy for a man of
  understanding.
[7]Leave the presence of a fool,
  for there you do not meet words of
  knowledge.
[8]The wisdom of a prudent man is to
  discern his way,
  but the folly of fools is deceiving.
[9]God scorns the wicked,[j]

  but the upright enjoy his favor.
[10]The heart knows its own bitterness,
  and no stranger shares its joy.
[11]The house of the wicked will be
  destroyed,
  but the tent of the upright will flourish.
[12]There is a way which seems right to a
  man,
  but its end is the way to death.[k]
[13]Even in laughter the heart is sad,
  and the end of joy is grief.
[14]A perverse man will be filled with the
  fruit of his ways,
  and a good man with the fruit of his
  deeds.[l]
[15]The simple believes everything,
  but the prudent looks where he is
  going.
[16]A wise man is cautious and turns away
  from evil,
  but a fool throws off restraint and is
  careless.
[17]A man of quick temper acts foolishly,
  but a man of discretion is patient.[m]
[18]The simple acquire folly,

but the prudent are crowned with
    knowledge.
¹⁹The evil bow down before the good,
    the wicked at the gates of the righteous.
²⁰The poor is disliked even by his
    neighbor,
    but the rich has many friends.
²¹He who despises his neighbor is a
    sinner,
    but happy is he who is kind to the poor.
²²Do they not err that devise evil?
    Those who devise good meet loyalty
    and faithfulness.
²³In all toil there is profit,
    but mere talk tends only to want.
²⁴The crown of the wise is their wisdom,ⁿ
    but folly is the garland^o of fools.
²⁵A truthful witness saves lives,
    but one who utters lies is a betrayer.
²⁶In the fear of the Lord one has strong
    confidence,
    and his children will have a refuge.
²⁷The fear of the Lord is a fountain of
    life,
    that one may avoid the snares of death.
²⁸In a multitude of people is the glory

of a king,
    but without people a prince is ruined.
²⁹He who is slow to anger has great
    understanding,
    but he who has a hasty temper exalts
    folly.
³⁰A tranquil mind gives life to the flesh,
    but passion makes the bones rot.
³¹He who oppresses a poor man insults his
    Maker,
    but he who is kind to the needy honors
    him.
³²The wicked is overthrown through his
    evil-doing,
    but the righteous finds refuge through
    his integrity.^p
³³Wisdom abides in the mind of a man of
    understanding,
    but it is not^q known in the heart of
    fools.
³⁴Righteousness exalts a nation,
    but sin is a reproach to any people.
³⁵A servant who deals wisely has the
    king's favor,
    but his wrath falls on one who acts
    shamefully.

---

g Heb *Wisdom of women*   h Cn: Heb *a rod of pride*   i Cn: Heb *a manger of*   j Cn: Heb obscure   k Heb *ways of death*   l Cn: Heb *from upon him*   m Gk: Heb *is hated*   n Cn Compare Gk: Heb *riches*   o Cn: Heb *folly*   p Gk Syr: Heb *in his death*   q Gk Syr: Heb lacks *not*

Overview: The house of wisdom built by the wise woman can easily be destroyed by words of the foolish (Besa the Copt). The house built upon doctrine and faith, likewise, can be destroyed by heresy (Chrysostom). The house built in heaven can be destroyed by the rebellion of the wicked (Bede). The phenomenon of fear can make people more religious (Chrysostom). Fools condemn themselves by their foolish talk (Ambrose), and a foolish preacher knows better how to reprove than how to sympathize (Gregory the Great). Martyrs are faithful witnesses worth believing (Apostolic Constitutions). Wisdom indicates three ways of friendship, of which the highest is virtue (Clement of Alexandria). In the end God's counsel does prevail, even though people may think otherwise (Jerome). Our true fear is not a fear of God but a fear of falling into evil (Clement of Alexandria). Life, however, is transformed by fear of punishment (Augustine), and strength is shown in adversity (Gregory the Great). Patience comes from resistance to anger

(JOHN CASSIAN), just as understanding, like strength, comes from patience and exercise (CHRYSOSTOM). The meek person can heal the heart, just as the tranquil give life to the flesh (AMBROSE). All notwithstanding, the commands of God must not be reduced to the triviality of jokes (CHRYSOSTOM).

14:1 Wisdom's House Destroyed by Folly

CONSTRUCTIVE WORK OF THE WISE WOMAN. BESA THE COPT: And it was also said, "A wise woman builds a house, but the foolish will destroy it with her hands." This means that the wise woman encourages her neighbor in the fear of God and the love which is in her heart toward her sister and her sisters. But, on the other hand, the foolish woman will destroy them by her words full of bitterness, hatred, wickedness and scorn, even as it is written, "A rod of scorn is in the mouth of the foolish,"[1] and that means you. FRAGMENT 29, LETTER TO ANTINOE 2.3-4.[2]

THE HOUSE BUILT ON DOCTRINE AND FAITH. CHRYSOSTOM: "The wise women built up their homes." The church built its house with its patience and hope in Christ, that is, it has roused and restored those entering it with its doctrine and faith. "The foolish destroyed it with her own hand." This is the heresy which becomes the cause for their eternal death. COMMENTARY ON THE PROVERBS OF SOLOMON, FRAGMENT 14.1.[3]

THE HOUSE BUILT IN HEAVEN. BEDE: Both each faithful soul and the catholic church throughout the world build a house for itself in the heavenly homeland through good works. The wicked, however, through their evil living and even, at times, through open rebellion, destroy what was well designed by the good. COMMENTARY ON PROVERBS 2.14.1.[4]

14:2 The Upright Fear the Lord

A FEAR FACTOR THAT FAVORS RELIGION. CHRYSOSTOM: "He who walks straight, fears the Lord." Not just any fear makes people walk straight, but the fear of God. . . . A life provided with virtue is quite illustrious, but the addition of fear makes persons more religious. COMMENTARY ON THE PROVERBS OF SOLOMON, FRAGMENT 14.2.[5]

14:3 The Talk of a Fool

FOOLS CONDEMN THEMSELVES BY THEIR FOOLISH TALK. AMBROSE: What judgment harder than that of our hearts, whereby each one stands convicted and accuses himself of the injury that he has wrongfully done against his brother? This the Scriptures speak of very plainly, saying, "Out of the mouth of fools there is a rod for wrongdoing." Folly, then, is condemned because it causes wrongdoing. Ought we not rather to avoid this, than death, or loss, or want, or exile or sickness? Who would not think some blemish of body or loss of inheritance far less than some blemish of soul or loss of reputation? DUTIES OF THE CLERGY 3.4.24.[6]

MOE READY TO REPROVE THAN TO ENCOURAGE. GREGORY THE GREAT: It is the way of haughty preachers that they are more desirous of strictly reproving their hearers even when distressed than they are to cherish them in a kindly manner. For they study more to chide and reprove faults than to encourage goodness with praise. They are anxious to appear superior to other people, and they are better pleased when anger raises their feelings than when love makes them equal. They always want to find something to smite sharply with reproof. As it is written, "In the mouth of the foolish is a rod of pride," because really he knows how to smite sharply but not to sympathize with humility. MORALS ON THE BOOK OF JOB 5.24.34.40.[7]

14:5 A Faithful Witness Does Not Lie

---

[1]Cf. Prov 14:3. [2]CSCO 157:96, 158:92-93. [3]PG 64:700. [4]CCL 119B:82. [5]PG 64:700. [6]NPNF 2 10:71. [7]LF 23:81*.

**Martyrs Are Faithful Witnesses Worth
Believing.** Apostolic Constitutions: These
things we have said concerning those that in
truth have been martyrs for Christ, but not concerning false martyrs, concerning whom the oracle speaks, "The name of the ungodly is
extinguished."[8] For "a faithful witness will not lie,
but an unjust witness inflames lies." For he that
departs this life in his testimony without lying,
for the sake of the truth, is a faithful martyr, worthy to be believed in such things wherein he
strove for the word of truth by his own blood.
Constitutions of the Holy Apostles 5.1.9.[9]

14:8 The Folly of Fools

**Virtue, Mutuality and Pleasure: Three
Ways of Friendship.** Clement of Alexandria: "The wisdom of able men will understand
the paths of wisdom, but the folly of fools goes in
the wrong direction." Prophecy says, "To whom
shall I look if not to the man who is gentle and
tranquil and who trembles at my words."[10] We
have been taught that there are three forms of
friendship. The first and best of these is based on
virtue, since the love which proceeds from reason
is firmly based. The second stands between the
others and is based on mutuality. It involves
mutual sharing and is beneficial to life. Friendship on the basis of free giving is mutual. The
third, and last, comes, as we put it, from habit.
Some say that it chops and changes, being based
on pleasure.[11] Stromateis 2.101.2-3.[12]

14:12 A Way That Leads to Death

In the End God's Counsel Prevails.
Jerome: We read in Proverbs, "There is a way
that seems just to men, yet the end of it leads to
the depths of hades." You see, ignorance is also
clearly condemned in this text, since man thinks
otherwise and he falls into hades, seemingly having the truth. "There are many thoughts," he
says, "in the heart of man."[13] But still, it is not his
will, which is uncertain and doubtful and change-

able, that prevails but the counsel of God.
Against the Pelagians 1.39.[14]

14:16 The Wise Are Cautious

**Not a Fear of God but a Fear of Falling
into Evil.** Clement of Alexandria: Awe is
fear of the divine. But if fear is a passion, as some
insist that fear is a passion, not every fear is a passion. Superstition is a passion, being the fear of
spiritual powers which are themselves agitated by
different passions. On the other side, the fear of
the God who is free from passions is itself free
from passions. It is really not a fear of God but a
fear of losing him. This fear is a fear of falling into
evil; it is a fear of evil. Fear of falling is a desire for
incorruptibility and for freedom from the passions. Stromateis 2.8.40.1-2.[15]

14:26 Strong Confidence Comes from Fear of
the Lord

Learn How to Fear. Augustine: "The fear
of the Lord is the hope of courage." When you
fear the punishment that is threatened, you learn
to love the reward that is promised; and thus
through fear of punishment you keep on leading a
good life, and by leading a good life you acquire a
good conscience, so that finally through a good
conscience you don't fear any punishment.
Therefore, learn how to fear, if you don't want to
be afraid. Sermon 348.1.[16]

Strength Is Shown in Adversity. Gregory the Great: Strength is never shown except
in adversity, and so patience is immediately made
to succeed to strength. For every person proves
himself in a much truer sense to have advanced in
strength in proportion as he bears with the
bolder heart the wrongs of other persons. Morals on the Book of Job 1.5.33.[17]

---

[8]Cf. Prov 10:7. [9]ANF 7:442*. [10]Is 66:2. [11]Cf. Aristotle *Nichomachaean
Ethics* 8.3.1156 A 6ff. [12]FC 85:224. [13]Prov 19:21. [14]FC 53:292*.
[15]FC 85:185-86. [16]*WSA* 3 10:91. [17]LF 18:266.

14:29 The Patience of Those Who Are Slow to Anger

PATIENCE COMES FROM RESISTANCE TO ANGER. JOHN CASSIAN: Everyone knows that patience is derived from passion and endurance and therefore that you cannot call anyone patient unless he endures indignities without annoyance. So Solomon rightly praised the patient person: "Better is the patient man than the strong, and he who restrains his anger more than he that takes a city,"[18] and "A long-suffering man is mighty in prudence, but a fainthearted man is very foolish." Therefore, if a wronged man flares up in anger, the wrongful abuse should not be thought of as the cause of his sin but the manifestation of a hidden weakness. CONFERENCE 18.13.[19]

UNDERSTANDING COMES FROM PATIENCE AND EXERCISE. CHRYSOSTOM: Do you not see the athletes, how they exercise when they have filled the bags with sand? But there is no need for you to practice this. Life is full of things that exercise you and make you strong. . . . For it is said, "One who is long-suffering abounds in wisdom, but he who is small of soul is strongly foolish." ON THE EPISTLE TO THE HEBREWS 19.5.[20]

14:30 A Tranquil Mind Gives Life

THE HEALER OF THE HEART. AMBROSE: While all our actions should be free from hidden malevolence, this is particularly the case in the selection of a bishop, whose life is the pattern for all his flock. Calm and pacific judgment is called for if you are to prefer to all his fellows a man who will be elected by all and who will heal all dissension. "The gentle man is the physician of the heart." In the gospel the Lord declared himself the physician of the heart when he said, "They that are whole have no need of a physician, but they that are sick."[21] LETTER 63.46.[22]

14:31 To Oppress the Poor Is to Insult God

THE COMMANDS OF GOD. CHRYSOSTOM: "He who slanders the poor irritates his own Maker." Here there are two sins: slander and opposition to the poor. Why does he irritate his Maker? His Maker certainly made him and made it easy for him to be subjected to a tongue of a slanderer. "He who really honors God has pity upon the needy." If God made the poor, why must the poor be pitied? Certainly I heard many saying: Is there any need to pity the poor man whom God would have not made poor if he loved him? How long will we play with our salvation? How long will we laugh at things in which the one who is wicked and loaded with countless sins should tremble and fear and be terrified? Tell me then whom God did favor: did he favor either Lazarus or the rich man? This is what ruins us, the fact that we easily slip into [bad] jokes. COMMENTARY ON THE PROVERBS OF SOLOMON, FRAGMENT 14.31.[23]

---

[18]Prov 16:32. [19]LCC 12:272*. [20]NPNF 1 14:456*. [21]See Mt 9:12; Mk 2:17; Lk 5:31. [22]LCC 5:269. [23]PG 64:701.

15:1-33 INSTRUCTIONS IN WISDOM

[1]A soft answer turns away wrath,
   but a harsh word stirs up anger.

[2]The tongue of the wise dispenses knowedge,[r]

but the mouths of fools pour out folly.
^{3}The eyes of the LORD are in every place,
    keeping watch on the evil and the good.
^{4}A gentle tongue is a tree of life,
    but perverseness in it breaks the spirit.
^{5}A fool despises his father's instruction,
    but he who heeds admonition is prudent.
^{6}In the house of the righteous there is
    much treasure,
    but trouble befalls the income of the
    wicked.
^{7}The lips of the wise spread knowledge;
    not so the minds of fools.
^{8}The sacrifice of the wicked is an
    abomination to the LORD,
    but the prayer of the upright is his delight.
^{9}The way of the wicked is an abomination
    to the LORD,
    but he loves him who pursues
    righteousness.
^{10}There is severe discipline for him who
    forsakes the way;
    he who hates reproof will die.
^{11}Sheol and Abaddon lie open before the
    LORD,
    how much more the hearts of men!
^{12}A scoffer does not like to be reproved;
    he will not go to the wise.
^{13}A glad heart makes a cheerful
    countenance,
    but by sorrow of heart the spirit is broken.
^{14}The mind of him who has understanding
    seeks knowledge,
    but the mouths of fools feed on folly.
^{15}All the days of the afflicted are evil,
    but a cheerful heart has a continual feast.
^{16}Better is a little with the fear of the
    LORD
    than great treasure and trouble with it.

^{17}Better is a dinner of herbs where love is
    than a fatted ox and hatred with it.
^{18}A hot-tempered man stirs up strife,
    but he who is slow to anger quiets
    contention.
^{19}The way of a sluggard is overgrown with
    thorns,
    but the path of the upright is a level
    highway.
^{20}A wise son makes a glad father,
    but a foolish man despises his mother.
^{21}Folly is a joy to him who has no sense,
    but a man of understanding walks aright.
^{22}Without counsel plans go wrong,
    but with many advisers they succeed.
^{23}To make an apt answer is a joy to a man,
    and a word in season, how good it is!
^{24}The wise man's path leads upward to life,
    that he may avoid Sheol beneath.
^{25}The LORD tears down the house of the
    proud,
    but maintains the widow's boundaries.
^{26}The thoughts of the wicked are an
    abomination to the LORD,
    the words of the pure are pleasing to him.^{s}
^{27}He who is greedy for unjust gain makes
    trouble for his household,
    but he who hates bribes will live.
^{28}The mind of the righteous ponders how
    to answer,
    but the mouth of the wicked pours out
    evil things.
^{29}The LORD is far from the wicked,
    but he hears the prayer of the
    righteous.
^{30}The light of the eyes rejoices the heart,
    and good news refreshes^t the bones.
^{31}He whose ear heeds wholesome admonition
    will abide among the wise.

³²*He who ignores instruction despises himself,*
but he who heeds admonition gains
understanding.

³³*The fear of the LORD is instruction in*
wisdom,
and humility goes before honor.

r Cn: Heb *makes knowledge good*   s Cn Compare Gk: Heb *pleasant words are pure*   t Heb *makes fat*

OVERVIEW: Jesus' way is persuasion, not admonition (EPHREM). Anger is one's own decision, not the Lord's (CHRYSOSTOM). God's eyes watch us and are present everywhere (BENEDICT). God listens to the heart, not to the voice (CYPRIAN). Often the tongue sins by speaking (CHRYSOSTOM), but the prudent person is always prepared and knows what to do. Indeed, prudence is useful for every beneficial activity (BASIL). The consistency of the wise stands in contrast to the inconsistency of fools (GREGORY THE GREAT). Good works, performed by the upright, constitute a prayer acceptable to God (CLEMENT OF ALEXANDRIA). Laughter, however, must be held in check (BASIL).

A cheerful countenance is reflected in the church's beauty (CASSIODORUS). Natural desires do have a limit set by self-sufficiency (CLEMENT OF ALEXANDRIA). On the whole it is better to prefer a simple and frugal meal offered in love and good conscience rather than a virtual feast that is characterized by hatred (ORIGEN). A livelihood of simplicity is sufficient (AMBROSE), and to the eyes of love even scraps from the table seem generous. Pleasure, however, is not found in abundance but abundance in pleasure (CHRYSOSTOM). The way of the slothful is strewn with thorns that are many and various (GREGORY OF NYSSA), but the royal highway of the upright points to the heavenly Jerusalem (JOHN CASSIAN). Denial of God is the greatest evil (ORIGEN). One who rejects instruction is the foe of his own soul (VALERIAN), for to reject instruction is to hate oneself (ORIGEN).

15:1 *Anger*

GENTLENESS PENETRATES DEEPER THAN HARSHNESS. EPHREM THE SYRIAN: Our Lord gave most of his assistance with persuasion rather than with admonition. Gentle showers soften the earth and thoroughly penetrate it, but a beating rain hardens and compresses the surface of the earth so that it will not be absorbed. "A harsh statement evokes anger," and with it comes injury. Whenever a harsh word opens a door, anger enters in, and on the heels of anger, injury. HOMILY ON OUR LORD 22.3.[1]

ANGER IS ONE'S OWN DECISION. CHRYSOSTOM: "Anger even ruins the prudent: a soft answer turns away anger, but a painful word arouses rage." All things depend on our decision, certainly also to raise anger or to soothe. It is not the Lord who gets angry, but it is in our power to cause his anger or the opposite. And if anger even ruins the prudent, how much more will it ruin those about whom it was said [that] anger destroys the imprudent? And this certainly happens also to the prudent because of some negligence. But "a soft answer turns away anger," that is, a way of answering in open humility and without any harshness. COMMENTARY ON THE PROVERBS OF SOLOMON, FRAGMENT 15.1.[2]

15:3 *Eyes in Every Place*

GOD IS WATCHING AND PRESENT. BENEDICT: We believe God is everywhere, and his eye beholds the good and wicked wherever they are: so we ought to be particularly assured of his special presence when we assist at the divine office. Therefore we must always remember the advice of the prophet, "To serve God in fear," "to sing wisely" and that "the angels are witnesses of what we sing."[3] Let us then reflect what behavior is

---

[1]FC 91:298-99. [2]PG 64:704. [3]Cf. Ps 2:11; 47:7 (46:8 LXX); 138:1 (137:1 LXX).

proper for appearing in the presence of God and the angels, and so sing our psalms that the mind may echo in harmony with the voice. RULE OF ST. BENEDICT 19.[4]

GOD LISTENS TO THE HEART. CYPRIAN: "In every place the eyes of the Lord behold the good and the evil." And when we are gathered together with the brethren in one place and celebrate divine sacrifices with a priest of God, we ought to be mindful of modesty and discipline and not toss our prayers about at random with uncouth voices and not cast forth with turbulent loquaciousness our petition. Rather, our petition should be commended to God in modesty, because it is our heart, not our voice, that will be heard. God, who sees our thoughts, is not to be admonished by shouts, as the Lord proves when he says, "Why do you think vainly in your hearts?"[5] And in another place, "And all the churches shall know that I am a searcher of the desires and the heart."[6] THE LORD'S PRAYER 4.[7]

15:4 A Gentle Tongue

THE ILLNESS OF THE TONGUE. CHRYSOSTOM: "Sanity of tongue is the tree of life." The tongue which does not sin by speaking makes use of sanity: indeed the illness of the tongue is its sin. The one who can check his tongue and does not sin with it is filled with the Holy Spirit. COMMENTARY ON THE PROVERBS OF SOLOMON, FRAGMENT 15.4.[8]

15:5 The Fool Lacks Prudence

THE PRUDENT ARE ALWAYS PREPARED. BASIL THE GREAT: True prudence is the knowledge of what to do and what not to do. One who possesses it never refrains from virtuous works and is never pierced by the deadly arrow of vice. Thus, he who understands words of prudence knows the difference between what is insidious, structured for deception, and what reminds us quietly about the best way to live life. Like the good prac-

tice of a banker, he will retain what is good and abstain from every form of evil.[9] Grant such prudence to the builder of his house, that he would lay its foundation upon rock, that is, support it on faith in Christ, so that it will remain unmoved when the winds and rains and thunderstorms attack.[10] For the Lord teaches us through this parable to remain immovable in the presence of temptations, both those of human and also of supernatural origin. Beyond this, he teaches us not to neglect the necessary things, but, having been equipped for the journey of life, to anticipate the coming of the bridegroom with eager hearts. HOMILY ON THE BEGINNING OF PROVERBS 6.[11]

PRUDENCE IS USEFUL FOR EVERY BENEFICIAL ACTIVITY. BASIL THE GREAT: Prudence is that quality by which all things are accomplished through skillful industry, in the same way that malice is that quality whereby only evil is perpetrated. Because, therefore, every activity admits prudence and because evils likewise occur in all things, the name of prudence signifies two realities. Whoever uses cleverness and skill for the destruction of others is evil, but one who acts cleverly and shrewdly to avoid the harm that others have in store for him, directly and wisely detecting his own good, possesses a prudence that is worthy of praise. Attend diligently, therefore, to the voice of the prudent soul, and you will know that it contains a center in which the prudence which uses healthy counsel for its own benefit and that of its neighbor is to be praised. But the prudence which applies itself to the neighbor's detriment, using its faculties for the purpose of destruction, becomes liable to condemnation. HOMILY ON THE BEGINNING OF PROVERBS 11.[12]

15:7 The Lips of the Wise and the Minds of Fools

---

[4]LCC 12:309. [5]See Mt 9:4. [6]See Rev 2:23. [7]FC 36:129-30**. [8]PG 64:704. [9]See 1 Thess 5:21. [10]See Mt 7:25. [11]PG 31:400. [12]PG 31:409.

CONSISTENCY AND INCONSISTENCY. GREGORY THE GREAT: The heart of the wise is always consistent, because, while it remains at peace in its upright convictions, it constantly urges itself to good deeds. But the heart of the fool is inconsistent, because, in exhibiting itself as variable and changeable, it never remains what it was. PASTORAL CARE 3.18.19.[13]

15:8 The Sacrifice of the Wicked and the Prayer of the Upright

AN ACCEPTABLE PRAYER TO GOD. CLEMENT OF ALEXANDRIA: We can discover many counsels about other things, also, as about prayer, for example: "Good works are a prayer acceptable to the Lord," Scripture says. The way to pray is prescribed: "If you see one naked, cover him, and do not look away from the members of your family. Then shall your light break forth as the morning, and your garments shall speedily rise, and your justice shall go before your face, and the glory of God shall encircle you."[14] CHRIST THE EDUCATOR 3.12.89.[15]

15:13 A Glad Heart Is Appropriate

REFLECTED IN THE BEAUTY OF THE CHURCH. CASSIODORUS: The church explains how it can please the Lord in the light of the living,[16] which means in the brightness of the saints, among whom [the church] is made beautiful, spotless and without wrinkle. Whatever befalls them shines from its face. Just as a man's healthy constitution makes his face more handsome, just as in Solomon's words, "When the heart rejoices the countenance flourishes," so the beauty of the features of holy church is diffused abroad when found in the merits of the blessed. EXPOSITION OF THE PSALMS 55.13.[17]

A CHEERFUL SMILE DISTINGUISHED FROM RAUCOUS LAUGHTER. BASIL THE GREAT: Those who live under discipline should avoid very carefully even such intemperate action as is com-

monly regarded lightly. Indulging in unrestrained and immoderate laughter is a sign of intemperance, of a want of control over one's emotions and of failure to repress the soul's frivolity by a stern use of reason. It is not unbecoming, however, to give evidence of merriment of soul by a cheerful smile, if only to illustrate that which is written, "A glad heart makes a cheerful countenance"; but raucous laughter and uncontrollable shaking of the body are not indicative of a well-regulated soul, or of personal dignity, or self-mastery. THE LONG RULES 17.[18]

15:17 A Meager Meal with Love Is Better Than a Feast with Hatred

THE MEAN BETWEEN EXTREMES. CLEMENT OF ALEXANDRIA: "Herbs with love are better than a fatted calf with deceit." This is reminiscent of what we said before, that herbs are not the Agape, but that meals should be taken with charity. A middle course is good in all things, and no less so in serving a banquet. Extremes, in fact, are dangerous, but the mean is good, and all that avoids dire need is a mean. Natural desires have a limit set to them by self-sufficiency. CHRIST THE EDUCATOR 2.1.16.[19]

PREFER SIMPLE AND FRUGAL HOSPITALITY. ORIGEN: "It is better to be invited to herbs with love and grace than to a fatted calf with hatred." Often, we prefer simple and frugal hospitality from hosts who receive us with good conscience—but who cannot offer us more—to lofty words, "exalted against the knowledge of God,"[20] which, with much persuasion, teach a doctrine foreign to the Father of our Lord Jesus, who gave us the law and the prophets.[21] ON PRAYER 2.27.6.[22]

A LIVELIHOOD OF SIMPLICITY IS SUFFICIENT.

---

[13]ACW 11:145.* [14]See Is 58:7-8. [15]FC 23:267*. [16]See Ps 56:13 (55:14 LXX). [17]ACW 52:37*. [18]FC 9:271*. [19]FC 23:108*. [20]2 Cor 10:5. [21]See Mt 5:17*. [22]ACW 19:96*.

AMBROSE: Be content with what is your own and do not let your well-being be based on doing harm to your neighbor. You may find your livelihood in the simplicity of innocence. The person in possession of his own good knows nothing of waylaying others. He is not inflamed by the desires of the avaricious person, whose every gain is at the expense of virtue and a further incentive to cupidity. Therefore, should he come to know his blessings, the poor person is truly happy who lives righteously in a manner which is to be preferred to all the treasures of the world, because "better a little with the fear of the Lord than great treasures without fear." How much under these circumstances does one need to support life? If you go beyond that little and seek that, also, which others find pleasure in possessing, that, too, has little to commend it: "It is better to be invited to herbs with love than to a fatted calf with hatred."

Let us use our talents, therefore, for the acquisition of grace and the attainment of salvation, not to circumvent others who do us no harm. SIX DAYS OF CREATION 5.8.23.[23]

TO THE EYES OF LOVE EVEN SCRAPS FROM THE TABLE SEEM GENEROUS. CHRYSOSTOM: When one invites to supper guests that are hungry and have an appetite, even if he lays a meager table it seems abundant owing to the anticipation of the guests who fall upon the dishes with great relish. In just the same way we too have confidence in your spiritual appetite and do not hang back, even if we have a poor and meager table, before laying it in customary manner before your good selves. This is what a certain sage also remarked: "Better a meal of vegetables with love than a beast from the manger with enmity," suggesting that love has a different view of what is set forth, and to its eyes ordinary things appear rich and scraps seem generous. HOMILIES ON GENESIS 45.1.[24]

PLEASURE IS NOT IN ABUNDANCE. CHRYSOSTOM: "It is better the hospitality with vegetables."

I will explain what [Solomon] says. If one fears God and also enjoys the benevolence of people, it is still better for him to have little property than an abundance. Indeed, pleasure is not in abundance, but abundance is in pleasure, as Hesiod says. One who neglects offenses settles the future judgments about them. A stupid person does nothing sensibly, whereas the judicious one directs, that is, displays actions of free opinion. Those who despise consulting other people about what must be done, despise advice. It then happens that those people, who think they are something when they are nothing, wander in error. COMMENTARY ON THE PROVERBS OF SOLOMON, FRAGMENT 15.17.[25]

15:19 Thorns Impede the Sluggard, but the Path of the Upright Is Level

THE WAY OF THE SLOTHFUL IS STREWN WITH MANY THORNS. GREGORY OF NYSSA: There are those who are called the slothful in the book of Wisdom, who strew their path with thorns, who consider harmful to the soul a zeal for deeds in keeping with the commandments of God, the demurrers against the apostolic injunctions, who do not eat their own bread with dignity, but, fawning on others, make idleness the art of life. Then, there are the dreamers who consider the deceits of dreams more trustworthy than the teachings of the Gospels, calling fantasies revelations. Apart from these, there are those who stay in their own houses, and still others who consider being unsociable and brutish a virtue without recognizing the command to love and without knowing the fruit of long-suffering and humility. ON VIRGINITY 23.[26]

THE ROYAL HIGHWAY TO THE HEAVENLY JERUSALEM. JOHN CASSIAN: In the words of Solomon, "The ways of those who do nothing are strewn with thorns, but the ways of the strong are well trodden." Thus, having turned aside from the royal path, they are unable to get

---

[23]FC 42:178.* [24]FC 82:469. [25]PG 64:705. [26]FC 58:71.

to that metropolis to which our journeying must ever and unswervingly be directed. Ecclesiastes also expressed this quite distinctly when he said, "The toil of fools afflicts those who do not know how to go to the city"[27]—namely, to "that heavenly Jerusalem, which is the mother of us all."[28] CONFERENCE 24.24.6.[29]

15:26 Wicked Thoughts Are an Abomination to the Lord

DENIAL OF GOD IS THE GREATEST EVIL. ORIGEN: If every evil word is an abomination to the Lord your God, how great an abomination must be supposed the evil word of denial and the evil word of publicly proclaiming another god and the evil oath by the fortune of people, something that has no existence.[30] EXHORTATION TO MARTYRDOM 7.[31]

15:32 To Ignore Instruction Is to Despise Oneself

ONE WHO REJECTS INSTRUCTION IS THE FOE OF HIS OWN SOUL. VALERIAN: If the prophet deems those guilty whom discipline has never reached, what should we think of those whom it has abandoned? Discerning between the acts of these two classes of people, the prophet authoritatively regards the fault of never having come to discipline as one less serious than that of having rejected her law. Notice his words: "He that rejects instruction despises his own soul." The case truly is just what he says. For the person who has spurned the warnings of discipline in order to occupy himself with the devil's business is indeed the foe of his own soul. HOMILY 1.4.[32]

TO REJECT INSTRUCTION IS TO HATE ONESELF. ORIGEN: We are not harsh to those who do not repent. Rather, such people are evil to themselves, for one who ignores instruction hates himself. Nevertheless, in the case of such people healing must be sought in every way possible, even for the person so completely perverted that he is not even conscious of his own evils and is drunk with a drunkenness more deadly than that caused by wine, the drunkenness that comes from the darkness of evil.[33] ON PRAYER 7.[34]

---

[27]Eccles 10:15 LXX. [28]Gal 4:26. [29]ACW 57:845. [30]Origen has been discussing idol worship. [31]OSW 45. [32]FC 17:304*. [33]Cf. Prov 20:1; Is 28:1, 7; Mt 24:49. [34]OSW 150.

16:1-33 THE LORD WEIGHS THE PLANS OF THE MIND

[1]The plans of the mind belong to man,
　　but the answer of the tongue is from the
　　LORD.
[2]All the ways of a man are pure in his
　　own eyes,
　　but the LORD weighs the spirit.
[3]Commit your work to the LORD,

　　and your plans will be established.
[4]The LORD has made everything for its
　　purpose,
　　even the wicked for the day of trouble.
[5]Every one who is arrogant is an abomination to the LORD;
　　be assured, he will not go unpunished.

⁶By loyalty and faithfulness iniquity is
atoned for,
and by the fear of the LORD a man
avoids evil.
⁷When a man's ways please the LORD,
he makes even his enemies to be at
peace with him.
⁸Better is a little with righteousness
than great revenues with injustice.
⁹A man's mind plans his way,
but the LORD directs his steps.
¹⁰Inspired decisions are on the lips of a king;
his mouth does not sin in judgment.
¹¹A just balance and scales are the
LORD's;
all the weights in the bag are his work.
¹²It is an abomination to kings to do evil,
for the throne is established by
righeousness.
¹³Righteous lips are the delight of a king,
and he loves him who speaks what is
right.
¹⁴A king's wrath is a messenger of death,
and a wise man will appease it.
¹⁵In the light of a king's face there is life,
and his favor is like the clouds that
bring the spring rain.
¹⁶To get wisdom is better^u than gold;
to get understanding is to be chosen
rather than silver.
¹⁷The highway of the upright turns aside
from evil;
he who guards his way preserves his life.
¹⁸Pride goes before destruction,
and a haughty spirit before a fall.
¹⁹It is better to be of a lowly spirit with
the poor

than to divide the spoil with the proud.
²⁰He who gives heed to the word will prosper,
and happy is he who trusts in the LORD.
²¹The wise of heart is called a man of
discernment,
and pleasant speech increases
persuasiveness.
²²Wisdom is a fountain of life to him who
has it,
but folly is the chastisement of fools.
²³The mind of the wise makes his speech
judicious,
and adds persuasiveness to his lips.
²⁴Pleasant words are like a honeycomb,
sweetness to the soul and health to the
body.
²⁵There is a way which seems right to a man,
but its end is the way to death.^v
²⁶A worker's appetite works for him;
his mouth urges him on.
²⁷A worthless man plots evil,
and his speech is like a scorching fire.
²⁸A perverse man spreads strife,
and a whisperer separates close friends.
²⁹A man of violence entices his neighbor
and leads him in a way that is not good.
³⁰He who winks his eyes plans^w perverse
things,
he who compresses his lips brings evil to pass.
³¹A hoary head is a crown of glory;
it is gained in a righteous life.
³²He who is slow to anger is better than
the mighty,
and he who rules his spirit than he who
takes a city.
³³The lot is cast into the lap,
but the decision is wholly from the LORD.

u Gk Syr Vg Tg: Heb *how much better*   v Heb *ways of death*   w Gk Syr Vg Tg: Heb *to plan*

OVERVIEW: We cannot take even the first step toward salvation without God's grace (AUGUSTINE). Everyone's light shines in its particular way, but God does not acknowledge the deeds of the proud (CHRYSOSTOM). Our ways are made straight by God's help and mercy (JEROME). God is not moved either by fear or hope of reward (JOHN CASSIAN). The tyranny of pride estranges us from God's mercy (CHRYSOSTOM). By faith with good works sins are cleansed (CYPRIAN). Wisdom, which is better than gold, is none other than Christ (DIDYMUS). Sloth leads to destruction (JOHN CASSIAN), and pride must be checked rather than given free license (GREGORY OF NAZIANZUS). Let us delight in the honey of wisdom (CYRIL OF ALEXANDRIA) and shun the hearing of worldly tales (BASIL). In fact, the words of Scripture are sweet like a honeycomb (AMBROSE), and bees in the mouth of Ambrose prefigured the sweetness of his message (PAULINUS). If you must be angry, let your anger be self-critical (AMBROSE). Anger can be contained by the discipline of reason (CASSIODORUS). There is an outstanding example of patience over anger in the story of the woman in 2 Maccabees who chose to give over to the executioner every one of her seven sons rather than to utter a single word of sacrilege (AUGUSTINE). If you seek a great victory, conquer yourself by patience rather than some city by force (GREGORY THE GREAT).

16:1 *The Answer of the Tongue*

HUMANITY'S PART CAN BE DONE ONLY WITH GOD'S GRACE. AUGUSTINE: Assuredly, as to what is written, "The preparation of the heart is man's part, and the answer of the tongue is from the Lord," they are misled by an imperfect understanding, so as to think that to prepare the heart—that is, to begin good—pertains to people without the aid of God's grace. Be it far from the children of promise thus to understand it! AGAINST TWO LETTERS OF THE PELAGIANS 2.19.[1]

16:2 *Pure Ways*

GOD DOES NOT ACKNOWLEDGE THE PROUD. CHRYSOSTOM: Besides being bright, certainly light (as it is) is conspicuous. As it does its work everyone observes it. In the same way, the humble person shows us in no small way what is right. For a contrite person will nevertheless excel in great things. But God does not desire to acknowledge the deeds of the proud. COMMENTARY ON THE PROVERBS OF SOLOMON, FRAGMENT 16.2.[2]

16:3 *Commit Your Work to the Lord*

OUR WAYS ARE MADE STRAIGHT BY GOD'S HELP AND MERCY. JEROME: We are commanded to show him our ways and make our ways to him, which are made straight, not by our own efforts but by his help and mercy. Whence it is written, "Make straight your way in my sight"[3] (or as other copies have it, "make straight my way in your sight"), so that what is straight to him may also appear straight to me. Solomon also says, "Lay open your works to the Lord, and your thoughts shall be directed." For our thoughts are directed then, and only then, when we lay open to the Lord, as to a firm and very stable rock, everything that we do and impute everything to him. AGAINST THE PELAGIANS 3.8.[4]

16:4 *Everything Has Its Purpose*

ONLY GOD IS MOVED BY NEITHER FEAR NOR HOPE OF REWARD. JOHN CASSIAN: Only God does what is good, acting from love of goodness for its own sake and not moved by fear or hope of reward. As Solomon says, "The Lord has done all things for his own sake." For the sake of his own goodness he bestows an abundance of goodness upon the worthy and the unworthy, because he can neither be wearied by wrongdoing nor provoked to painful emotion by human wickedness. He always remains what he is, perfect in goodness and unchanging in nature. CONFERENCE 11.6.[5]

---

[1]NPNF 1 5:400. [2]PG 64:708. [3]Ps 5:8 (5:9 LXX). [4]FC 53:360-61. [5]LCC 12:248-49**.

16:5 *Arrogance Is an Abomination*

THE TYRANNY OF PRIDE ESTRANGES US FROM GOD'S MERCY. CHRYSOSTOM: Nothing so estranges from the mercy of God and gives over to the fire of hell as the tyranny of pride. If we possess this within us, all our life becomes impure, even if we practice chastity, virginity, fasting, prayer, almsgiving, or any virtue whatsoever. "Every proud man," Scripture says, "is an abomination to the Lord." Therefore, let us check this puffing up of the soul, and let us cut out this tumor, if we wish to be pure and be rid of the punishment prepared for the devil. HOMILIES ON THE GOSPEL OF JOHN 9.[6]

16:6 *Atonement for Iniquity*

SINS ARE CLEANSED. CYPRIAN: The Holy Spirit speaks in the Scriptures, saying, "By alms and by faith sins are cleansed." Surely not those sins which had been contracted before, for they are purged by the blood and sanctification of Christ. Likewise again he says, "As water quenches fire, so do alms quench sin."[7] Here also it is shown and proved that just as with laver of the waters of salvation the fire of Gehenna[8] is extinguished, so by almsgiving and good works the flame of sin is quenched. And because the remission of sins is once granted in baptism, constant and continuous labor acting in the manner of baptism again bestows the mercies of God. This the Lord also teaches in the Gospel. For when it was noted that his disciples were eating without first having washed their hands, he replied and said, "He who made the inside made also the outside. Truly give alms, and behold all things are clean to you."[9] WORKS AND ALMSGIVING 2.[10]

16:16 *Wisdom Is Better Than Gold*

WISDOM IS CHRIST. DIDYMUS THE BLIND: As gold is better than silver, so wisdom is superior to prudence. The former pertains to knowledge, the latter to the interpretation of what is hidden.

Either you can interpret the nests of wisdom as the churches or as the dwelling places of the holy ones in heaven. But wisdom itself is Christ. COMMENTARY ON THE PROVERBS OF SOLOMON, FRAGMENT 16.16.[11]

16:18 *Destruction and Fall*

SLOTH LEADS TO DESTRUCTION. JOHN CASSIAN: "Injury precedes destruction, and an evil thought precedes ruin." In the same way a house never suddenly collapses except because of some old weakness in the foundation or because of extended disregard by its tenants. Thus the structure of the roof is eventually destroyed by what had begun as a tiny leak but into which, through long neglect, a stormy tempest of rain pours like a river, once a large breach has been made. For "by slothfulness a dwelling will be brought low, and through lazy hands a house will leak."[12] CONFERENCE 6.17.1.[13]

PRIDE MUST BE CHECKED. GREGORY OF NAZIANZUS: Do we commend hospitality? Do we admire brotherly love, wifely affection, virginity, feeding the poor, singing psalms, nightlong vigils, penitence? Do we mortify the body[14] with fasting? Do we through prayer take up our abode with God? Do we subordinate the inferior element in us to the better—I mean, the dust[15] to the spirit, as we should if we have returned the right verdict on the alloy of the two which is our nature? Do we make life a meditation of death? Do we establish our mastery over our passions, mindful of the nobility of our second birth? Do we tame our swollen and inflamed tempers? Or our pride, which "comes before a fall," or our unreasonable grief, our crude pleasures, our dirty laughter, our undisciplined eyes, our greedy ears, our immoderate talk, our wandering thoughts,

---

[6]FC 33:94. [7]See Sir 3:33. [8]Jeremiah warned that this place would be renamed the "Valley of Slaughter" (Jer 7:32, 19:6), because it was looked upon as a divinely appointed place of punishment for apostates and other great sinners. [9]See Lk 11:40-41 Vg. [10]FC 36:228*. [11]PG 39:1637*. [12]Eccles 10:18. [13]ACW 57:234. [14]1 Cor 9:27. [15]Gen 2:7.

our anything in ourselves which the evil one can take over from us and use against us, "bringing in death through the windows,"[16] as Scripture has it, meaning through the senses?

No. We do the very opposite: we offer freedom to the passions of others, like kings declaring an amnesty after a victory, on the sole condition that they give their assent to us—and thus rush against God more violently or more "piously" than before; for this discreditable purchase we pay them a dishonorable price, license in exchange for impiety. AGAINST THE EUNOMIANS, THEOLOGICAL ORATION 1(27).7.[17]

16:24 Good Words Are Like Honeycombs

DELIGHT IN THE HONEY OF WISDOM. CYRIL OF ALEXANDRIA: You who love instruction and are eager to listen, receive once again the sacred words: delight yourselves in the honey of wisdom; for so it is written, "Good words are honeycombs, and their sweetness is the healing of the soul." For the labor of the bees is very sweet and benefits in many ways the soul of man; but the divine and saving [honey] makes those in whom it dwells skillful in every good work and teaches them the ways of [spiritual] improvement. COMMENTARY ON LUKE, HOMILY 120.[18]

SHUN THE HEARING OF WORLDLY TALES. BASIL THE GREAT: This course . . . will bring you honor and true glory. With your ears opened to give heed and your hands ready to execute the command you have heard, let your tongue be silent and keep your heart under custody. Be slow and dull for idle talk but knowing and wise in hearkening to the saving words of the holy Scriptures. Let the hearing of worldly tales be to you as a bitter taste in your mouth but the discourse of holy men as a honeycomb. ON RENUNCIATION OF THE WORLD.[19]

THE WORDS OF SCRIPTURE ARE SWEET LIKE A HONEYCOMB. AMBROSE: The sea is holy Scripture which has within it profound meanings and the mysterious depths of the prophets. Into this sea many rivers have entered. Delightful and clear are these streams. These fountains are cool, springing up into life everlasting.[20] There, too, are "pleasant words, like honeycomb," and courteous conversations which water souls with the sweetness of moral commands. The streams of holy Scripture are diverse; you know that which you should drink from first, second, and last. LETTER 15.[21]

BEES IN THE MOUTH OF AMBROSE PREFIGURED THE SWEETNESS OF HIS MESSAGE. PAULINUS OF MILAN: It came to pass that our Ambrose was born while his father, Ambrose, was administering the prefectureship of the Gallic provinces. On one occasion, when the child had been placed in a cradle in his father's courtyard and was asleep with his mouth open, a swarm of bees suddenly approached and covered his face, so that they were continually flying in and out of his mouth. His father, who was strolling nearby with his wife and daughter, watched with fatherly affection to see in what way this miracle would terminate. Meanwhile, he restrained the maid from driving away the bees, for she had accepted the responsibility of feeding the child and was anxious lest they harm him. But, after a while, the bees flew away and rose so high in the air that they could in no way be seen by human eyes. The father, terrified by this event, said, "If this child lives, he will be something great." For, even then, the Lord was acting during the infancy of his servant in order that what was written might be fulfilled: "Well-ordered words are as a honeycomb." For that swarm of bees was implanting the honeycombs of his later works, which would proclaim the heavenly gifts and direct the minds of people from earthly to heavenly things. LIFE OF ST. AMBROSE 2.3.[22]

16:32 Be Slow to Anger

---

[16]Jer 9:21. [17]FGFR 221. [18]CGSL 480. [19]FC 9:21-22. [20]See Jn 4:14. [21]FC 26:77-78*. [22]FC 15:34-35.

RESTRAIN YOUR ANGER TOWARD OTHERS.
AMBROSE: If you are angry, be angry with yourselves, because you are roused, and you will not
sin. For he who is angry with himself, because he
has been so easily roused, ceases to be angry with
another. But he who wishes to prove his anger is
righteous only gets the more inflamed and
quickly falls into sin. "Better is he," as Solomon
says, "that restrains his anger than he that takes a
city," for anger leads astray even brave men.
DUTIES OF THE CLERGY 1.21.96.[23]

**ANGER CAN BE CONTAINED BY THE DISCI-
PLINE OF REASON.** CASSIODORUS: That anger is
less offensive which does not lead to indignant
actions. In the words of Scripture, "He that con-
quers his anger is better than he who takes a city."
So the injunction to control anger is extended, so
that if we are already angry we do not sin through
impulsive rashness. Because of human frailty we
cannot govern our hot emotions, but with the
help of God's grace we contain them with the discipline of reason. EXPOSITION OF THE PSALMS
4.5.[24]

**AN OUTSTANDING EXAMPLE OF PATIENCE
OVER ANGER.** AUGUSTINE: The Scriptures offer
the example[25] of a woman of astounding fortitude
and oblige me now to speak of her. This woman
chose to give over to the tyrant and executioner
every one of her seven sons rather than to utter a
single word of sacrilege. And after fortifying them
with her exhortations, at the same time suffering
cruelly in their tortures, she herself had to
undergo what she had called upon them to
endure. Could any patience be greater than this?

Yet what marvel is it that the love of God per-
vading her inmost soul should have withstood the
tyrant and the executioner, and bodily pain, and
the weakness of her sex, and her own human emotions? Had she not heard the words: "Precious in
the sight of the Lord is the death of his saints"?[26]
Had she not heard, "The one who is patient is better than the one who is the mightiest"? . . . She
most assuredly knew these and many other divine
precepts on fortitude written in the books of the
Old Testament (which were the only ones then in
existence) by the same Holy Spirit who wrote
those in the New Testament. THE CATHOLIC AND
MANICHAEAN WAYS OF LIFE 1.23.43.[27]

CONQUER YOURSELF BY PATIENCE. GREGORY
THE GREAT. Taking cities is a smaller victory
because the places we conquer are outside of ourselves. A greater [victory] is won by patience,
because a person overcomes himself and subjects
himself to himself, when patience brings him low
in bearing with others in humility. FORTY GOS-
PEL HOMILIES 35.[28]

---

[23]NPNF 2 10:17. [24]ACW 51:76**. [25]2 Macc 7:1-42. [26]Ps 116:15 (115:6 LXX). [27]FC 56:36**. [28]CS 123:306**.

17:1-28 THE ONE WHO RESTRAINS WORDS HAS KNOWLEDGE

[1]*Better is a dry morsel with quiet*
   than a house full of feasting with strife.
[2]*A slave who deals wisely will rule over a*
   son who acts shamefully,

and will share the inheritance as one of
   the brothers.
[3]*The crucible is for silver, and the furnace*
   is for gold,

and the LORD tries hearts.
⁴An evildoer listens to wicked lips;
and a liar gives heed to a mischievous
tongue.
⁵He who mocks the poor insults his
Maker;
he who is glad at calamity will not go
unpunished.
⁶Grandchildren are the crown of the aged,
and the glory of sons is their fathers.
⁷Fine speech is not becoming to a fool;
still less is false speech to a prince.
⁸A bribe is like a magic stone in the eyes
of him who gives it;
wherever he turns he prospers.
⁹He who forgives an offense seeks love,
but he who repeats a matter alienates a
friend.
¹⁰A rebuke goes deeper into a man of
understanding
than a hundred blows into a fool.
¹¹An evil man seeks only rebellion,
and a cruel messenger will be sent
against him.
¹²Let a man meet a she-bear robbed of her
cubs,
rather than a fool in his folly.
¹³If a man returns evil for good,
evil will not depart from his house.
¹⁴The beginning of strife is like letting out
water;
so quit before the quarrel breaks out.
¹⁵He who justifies the wicked and he who
condemns the righteous
are both alike an abomination to the
LORD.
¹⁶Why should a fool have a price in his

hand to buy wisdom,
when he has no mind?
¹⁷A friend loves at all times,
and a brother is born for adversity.
¹⁸A man without sense gives a pledge,
and becomes surety in the presence of
his neighbor.
¹⁹He who loves transgression loves strife;
he who makes his door high seeks
destruction.
²⁰A man of crooked mind does not
prosper,
and one with a perverse tongue falls
into calamity.
²¹A stupid son is a grief to a father;
and the father of a fool has no joy.
²²A cheerful heart is a good medicine,
but a downcast spirit dries up the bones.
²³A wicked man accepts a bribe from the
bosom
to pervert the ways of justice.
²⁴A man of understanding sets his face
toward wisdom,
but the eyes of a fool are on the ends of
the earth.
²⁵A foolish son is a grief to his father
and bitterness to her who bore him.
²⁶To impose a fine on a righteous man is
not good;
to flog noble men is wrong.
²⁷He who restrains his words has knowledge,
and he who has a cool spirit is a man
of understanding.
²⁸Even a fool who keeps silent is
considered wise;
when he closes his lips, he is deemed
intelligent.*

*LXX Wisdom will be credited to the fool who asks questions

113

OVERVIEW: Be liberal and benevolent but not wasteful or extravagant. The truly wealthy are those who are rich in faith (AMBROSE), but God also is the Creator of the poor (CHRYSOSTOM). Children bring a hundred times more riches than a field or a house (JOHN CASSIAN). Neither God nor the church rejoices in wicked children who reject divine wisdom (ORIGEN). God the Father is our glory, and Christ is the church's crown (CLEMENT OF ALEXANDRIA). Quarrels easily begin when the tongue is loosened (GREGORY THE GREAT). One who is prudent is sparing in words (HIPPOLYTUS). Account must be rendered for everything that comes from the mouth (PACHOMIUS). Opening the mouth may reveal an empty head (GREGORY THE GREAT). Even one who asks questions can also be credited with wisdom (JOHN CASSIAN).

17:1 Counsel of Moderation

BE LIBERAL AND BENEVOLENT. AMBROSE: The Scriptures teach us not to be wasteful but liberal. There are two kinds of free giving, one arising from liberality, the other from wasteful extravagance. It is a mark of liberality to receive the stranger, to clothe the naked, to redeem the captives, to help the needy. It is wasteful to spend money on expensive banquets and much wine. Therefore one reads, "Wine is wasteful, drunkenness is abusive."[1] It is wasteful to spend one's own wealth merely for the sake of gaining the favor of the people. This they do who spend their inheritance on the games of the circus, or on theatrical pieces and gladiatorial shows, or even a combat of wild beasts, just to surpass the fame of their forefathers for these things. All this that they do is only foolish, for it is not right to be extravagant in spending money even on good works. DUTIES OF THE CLERGY 2.21.108-9.[2]

17:5 To Mock the Poor Insults One's Maker

THE TRULY WEALTHY. AMBROSE: Let no one think that he is to be paid more deference because he is rich. In the church a person is rich if he is rich in faith, for the faithful person has a whole world of riches. Is it strange that the faithful person owns the world, since he owns Christ's inheritance, which is more priceless than the world? "You were redeemed with the precious blood,"[3] surely was said to all, not only to the rich. LETTER 59.[4]

GOD IS THE CREATOR OF THE POOR. CHRYSOSTOM: "He who laughs at the poor irritates his creator." Why? Because God is the creator of the poor. Who is so cruel, who is so inhuman, that when he should be moved to compassion he laughs instead? Certainly this too will have to be punished. That person will perish because he sins against the high and wise providence of God. COMMENTARY ON THE PROVERBS OF SOLOMON, FRAGMENT 17.5.[5]

17:6 Grandchildren Are the Crown of Their Grandparents

CHILDREN BRING RICHES. JOHN CASSIAN: Instead of the pleasure that a person has in possessing one field and house, he who has passed over into the adoption of the children of God[6] will enjoy a hundred times more all the riches that belong to the eternal Father and that he will possess as his own, and in imitation of the true Son he will proclaim by disposition and by virtue, "All that the Father has is mine."[7] No longer occupied with the criminal concern of distraction and worry, but secure and happy, he will enter everywhere as it were into his property, and every day he will hear it said to him by the apostle, "All things are yours, whether the world or things present or things to come."[8] And by Solomon, "The faithful man has a world of riches." CONFERENCE 24.4.4.[9]

GOD OUR GLORY AND CHRIST THE CHURCH'S

---

[1]Prov 20:1. [2]NPNF 2 10:60*. [3]1 Pet 1:18-19. [4]FC 26:353. [5]PG 64:713. [6]See Eph 1:5 KJV. [7]Jn 16:15. [8]See 1 Cor 3:22 KJV. [9]ACW 57:848.

CROWN. CLEMENT OF ALEXANDRIA: "The crown of old men is their children's children and the glory of children is their father," it is said. Our glory is the Father of all, and the crown of the whole church is Christ. CHRIST THE EDUCATOR 2.8.71.[10]

17:14 Beginning of Strife

QUARRELS EASILY BEGIN WHEN THE TONGUE IS LOOSENED. GREGORY THE GREAT: Commonly, since the slothful mind is brought gradually to a downfall by our neglect to guard against idle words, we come to utter harmful ones. At first we are satisfied to talk about the affairs of others, then the tongue gnaws with detraction the lives of those of whom we speak, and finally we break out into open slanders. Hence provocations are sown, quarrels arise, the torches of hatred are lit, peace of heart is extinguished. Therefore it is well said by Solomon: "The beginning of quarrels is as when one lets out water." For to let out water is to loose the tongue in a spate of words. PASTORAL CARE 3.14.15.[11]

17:21 A Stupid Son Is Grief to a Father

WICKED CHILDREN WHO REJECT DIVINE WISDOM. ORIGEN: God is called "father" and God's love to humankind "mother," which was the cause of the divine incarnation and his suffering for our sake. Although God is our Father, he does not rejoice in an adopted son who is uneducated in divine wisdom and knowledge and who is committed to wickedness and evil. But a reasonable son gladdens his mother, that is, God's love toward humankind. It is she who presents us to God the Father as undernourished children, longing for solid spiritual food. That is done in order that his son, Jesus Christ, who became like our brother,[12] could make us full citizens [of his kingdom] both in word and in deed. Also, our mother is the church who was betrothed to God the Father through the Holy Spirit. Eternally, she begets sons and daughters for him. And those who learned divine wisdom and knowledge gladden both God our Father and his church, our mother. But she grieves and laments over those uninstructed who do not want to repent and be saved but prefer to persevere in wickedness. EXPOSITION ON PROVERBS, FRAGMENT 17.21.[13]

17:27 One Who Restrains Words Has Knowledge

ONE WHO IS PRUDENT IS SPARING OF WORDS. HIPPOLYTUS: He asks of wisdom who seeks to know what is the will of God. And he will show himself prudent who is sparing of his words on that which he has come to learn. If one inquires about wisdom, desiring to learn something about wisdom, while another asks nothing of wisdom, as not only wishing to learn nothing about wisdom himself but even keeping back his neighbors from so doing, the former certainly is deemed to be more prudent than the latter. FRAGMENTS ON PROVERBS.[14]

ACCOUNT MUST BE RENDERED. PACHOMIUS: Let your words be measured and counted by yourself, knowing that you shall render an account to God of what comes out of your mouth, including a pleasantry or even a word that does not edify. . . . And do not become a stranger to such promises. Whatever you think and whatever you love, establish it firmly in the Lord. And keep in mind your departure from the body to go to God "who will reward each one according to his works."[15] FRAGMENT 2.3.[16]

17:28 Even a Fool Who Keeps Silent Is Considered Wise

OPENING THE MOUTH MAY REVEAL AN EMPTY HEAD. GREGORY THE GREAT: As in a

---

[10]FC 23:154. [11]ACW 11:132-33. [12]See Heb 2:17. [13]PG 17:201. [14]ANF 5:173; TLG 2115.053.19.1. [15]Cf. Mt 16:27; Prov 24:12; Rom 2:6. [16]CS 47:86.

house, when the door is shut, it is not known what members there are hidden within, so, generally speaking, if a fool holds his peace, it is hidden whether he is wise or foolish. This is only so, however, if no other works come to light that may speak the mind even of one who is silent. For this reason, the holy man, seeing that his friends were anxious to appear what they were not, charged them to hold their peace, so they might not appear what they were. And so it is said by Solomon, "Even a fool, when he holds his peace, is counted wise." MORALS ON THE BOOK OF JOB 3.11.35.[17]

EVEN ONE WHO ASKS QUESTIONS CAN ALSO BE CREDITED WITH WISDOM. JOHN CASSIAN: It falls to the intellect to discern the divisions and the outlines of questions, and understanding's highest function is to know that you do not know. Hence it is said, "Wisdom will be credited to the fool who asks questions,"[18] for although the questioner does not know the answer to his question, nonetheless, because he inquires prudently and comes to understand what he does not understand, this very thing— his having prudently acknowledged what he does not know—is credited to him as wisdom. CONFERENCE 4.9.1.[19]

---

[17]LF 21:24*. [18]Prov 17:28 LXX, apparently the opposite of RSV. [19]ACW 57:159.

18:1-16 FREQUENCY OF WICKEDNESS BRINGS CONTEMPT

[1]He who is estranged[x] seeks pretexts[y]
  to break out against all sound
    judgment.
[2]A fool takes no pleasure in
    understanding,
  but only in expressing his opinion.
[3]When wickedness comes, contempt comes
    also;*
  and with dishonor comes disgrace.
[4]The words of a man's mouth are deep
    waters;
  the fountain of wisdom is a gushing
    stream.
[5]It is not good to be partial to a wicked
    man,
  or to deprive a righteous man of justice.

[6]A fool's lips bring strife,
  and his mouth invites a flogging.
[7]A fool's mouth is his ruin,
  and his lips are a snare to himself.
[8]The words of a whisperer are like
    delicious morsels;
  they go down into the inner parts of
    the body.
[9]He who is slack in his work
  is a brother to him who destroys.
[10]The name of the LORD is a strong
    tower;
  the righteous man runs into it and is
    safe.
[11]A rich man's wealth is his strong city,
  and like a high wall protecting him.[z]

¹²*Before destruction a man's heart is
    haughty,
    but humility goes before honor.*
¹³*If one gives answer before he hears,
    it is his folly and shame.*
¹⁴*A man's spirit will endure sickness;*

but a broken spirit who can bear?
¹⁵*An intelligent mind acquires knowledge,
    and the ear of the wise seeks
        knowledge.*
¹⁶*A man's gift makes room for him
    and brings him before great men.*

x Heb *separated*   y Gk Vg: Heb *desire*   z Or *in his imagination*   *LXX *When a sinner shall have come into the depth of evil things he despises [them].*

OVERVIEW: The Arian heretics lend truth to the proverb that frequency of wickedness breeds contempt and a lack of ability to discriminate. The deeper people go into superstition, the more they advance in shamefulness (ATHANASIUS), and the deeper one becomes involved in sin, the harder it is to extricate oneself (AUGUSTINE). Those who sink to the depths of sin also infect others (FULGENTIUS). Daily penance is preferable to an accumulation of sins at the end of life. Despair and even crimes arise as sins build up (CAESARIUS), for, once our sins begin, they are difficult to stop (CHRYSOSTOM). An evil mind, once mired in sin, also begins to suspect others, and increasing frequency of sin easily leads to disregard for it (JOHN OF DAMASCUS). The waters of God's word are abundant and life-giving. Shun the wicked, even those in important positions (CHRYSOSTOM). Pride often precedes ruin (ORIGEN), but an upright life makes one worthy of the fullness of God (EVAGRIUS).

18:3 Frequency of Wickedness Breeds Lack of Ability to Discriminate

THE ARIAN HERETICS LEND TRUTH TO THIS PROVERB. ATHANASIUS: As to [the Arians'] blasphemous position that "the Son knows not the Father perfectly," we ought not to wonder at it; for having once set themselves to fight against Christ, they contradict even his express words, since he says, "As the Father knows me, even so I know the Father."[1] Now if the Father knows the Son but in part, then it is evident that the Son does not know the Father perfectly. It is not lawful to say this. The Father does know the Son

perfectly; then it is evident that as the Father knows his own Word, so also the Word knows his own Father whose Word he is.

By these arguments and references to the sacred Scriptures we frequently overthrew them; but they changed like chameleons and again shifted their ground, striving to bring upon themselves that sentence, "When an ungodly man comes into a depth of evils, he despises them." DEPOSITION OF ARIUS 4-5.[2]

THEY ADVANCE IN SHAMEFULNESS. ATHANASIUS: Just as men who plunge into the deep, the deeper they go down, they descend into darker and deeper places, so it is with humankind. For they did not keep to idolatry in a simple form, nor did they abide in that with which they began. But the longer they went on in their first condition, the more new superstitions they invented, and, not satiated with the first evils, they again filled themselves with others, advancing further in utter shamefulness and surpassing themselves in impiety. But to this divine Scripture testifies when it says, "When an ungodly man comes into a depth of evils, he despises them." AGAINST THE HEATHEN 8.4.[3]

HARD TO EXTRICATE ONESELF. AUGUSTINE: Confession dies with a dead man, but is always possible for one who is alive. There is this saying, "When a sinner shall have come into the depth of evil things, he despises [them]." For it is one thing to long for, another thing to fight against

[1]Jn 10:15.   [2]NPNF 2 4:71**.   [3]NPNF 2 4:8*.

righteousness. It is one thing to desire to be delivered from evil, another thing to defend one's evil doings rather than to confess. EXPLANATIONS OF THE PSALMS 68.7.[4]

THOSE WHO SINK TO THE DEPTH OF SIN.

FULGENTIUS OF RUSPE: The proud and recalcitrant who despair of the forgiveness of sins repudiate forgiveness. Not only do they with pitiable blindness reject the care for their own salvation, but they also do not rest from upsetting other faithful souls with deadly words, if they are unable to pervert them. Often, either the frightfulness of their sins or the length of a wicked life takes away from them the hope of salvation and drives them to perpetrate even worse things in such a way that in such people that statement of holy Scripture is fulfilled: "When wickedness comes, contempt comes also." LETTER TO VENANTIA 3.[5]

DAILY PENANCE PREFERABLE TO AN ACCUMULATION OF SINS.

CAESARIUS OF ARLES: Not only slight sins but even greater offenses try to overtake us day and night. So let us not hold back repentance until the end of life, but while we are living let us endeavor to do penance daily. This practice should be observed continuously, not only by the laity and clerics, but even by priests and monks. . . . Since we cannot spend a day without sin, what is the sense of gradually piling up slight offenses and thus making endless streams of tiny drops? Despair arises from a multitude of sins heaped up over time, according to the words: "The wicked man, when he has come into the depth of sins, despises [them]." Of course, you are all well aware that we can more easily uproot them when they are still young than cut them off when they are firm. SERMON 61.1.[6]

DESPAIR AND EVEN CRIMES ARISE AS SINS BUILD UP.

CAESARIUS OF ARLES: Believe this devoutly and firmly: God never abandons a person unless he himself has already deserted God.

Although a person may have committed serious sins once, twice and a third time, God still looks for him, as he says through the prophet, "that by his conversion he may live."[7] However, when he begins to continue in his sins, despair arises from the multitude of them, and hardening is caused by the despair. While careless people at first despise their own sins because they are small, if these slight offenses increase, crimes are even added; they heap up to finally overwhelm them, and when this happens there is fulfilled what is written: "With wickedness comes contempt." SERMON 101.2.[8]

SINS ARE DIFFICULT TO STOP.

CHRYSOSTOM: "When the godless fall to the depths of evil, they lose all sense of respect." It is a terrible thing, you see, dearly beloved, a terrible thing to fall into the clutches of the devil. I mean, the soul then, as though caught in a net, and like a boar trapped in the mire, is likewise caught up in pleasure and, swept along by its evil habits, it loses all sense of the foul odor of its sins. Consequently, we must be awake and on our guard so as never to allow the evil demon any entrance at the outset, lest he cloud our reasoning, blind the sharp vision of our mind, and thus as if robbing us of sunlight render us unable to see the rays of the sun of justice and cause us to fall into the abyss. HOMILIES ON GENESIS 22.12.[9]

AN EVIL MIND BEGINS TO SUSPECT OTHERS.

GREGORY THE GREAT: The evil mind is always set in pains and labors, since it is either contriving mischiefs that it may bring down or fearing lest these be brought down upon it by others. While hatching plots against neighbors, one becomes all the more afraid of plots being hatched by neighbors against oneself. . . . Even when there is peace, he suspects plots, in that he, who is always dealing craftily, calculates that there is no one who might deal honestly with himself. MORALS ON THE BOOK OF JOB 3.12.44.[10]

---

[4]NPNF 1 8:287*. [5]FC 95:355. [6]FC 31:300*. [7]Ezek 33:11. [8]FC 47:99*. [9]FC 82:78. [10]LF 21:72-73*.

Increasing Frequency of Sin. John of Damascus: The more those greater sins grow on them, the more does the soul become accustomed to them and think light of them. For it is said, "When the wicked comes to the depth of evil things, he thinks light of them." Barlaam and Joseph 19.172.[11]

18:4 The Words of the Mouth Are Deep Waters

The Waters of God's Word Are Abundant and Life-Giving. Chrysostom: "The word in the heart of man is a deep water, and a river and fountain of life spring forth." By "deep water" he [Solomon] means "abundant" water which can often produce many rivers instead of one. Or, he says: it contains it deeply hidden in itself. As water is immeasurable, so the word in the heart of the person who lives according to God is without limit. Therefore, he uses "word" for knowledge. This is the one in whose heart a fountain of water is made when he hears the words of Jesus. He [Solomon] then speaks of it "springing forth," raining upon or watering the fields which makes them fertile. Commentary on the Proverbs of Solomon, Fragment 18.4.[12]

18:5 Do Not Cater to the Wicked

Shun the Wicked. Chrysostom: "It is not good to admire those who are impious," even though one of them has an important position or covers up what is right with persuasive speech. To admire the behavior of the impious is to sanction iniquity inspired by the devil. Commentary on the Proverbs of Solomon, Fragment 18.5.[13]

18:12 A Haughty Heart Comes Before Destruction

Pride Often Precedes Ruin. Origen: There is nothing to be proud about. For to sink to the state of being proud has its consequences according to the text: "Before ruin the heart of man is exalted and before glory it is humble." These words [also] concern the text: "Hear and hearken, and do not be proud, because the Lord has spoken."[14] Homilies on Jeremiah 12.8.3.[15]

18:16 A Gift that Opens Possibilities

An Upright Life. Evagrius of Pontus: "A man's gift" is called an upright life. It is that gift that "makes room for him" and makes him worthy of the fullness of God.[16] It is that very thing which is called the "throne" of the holy powers. Indeed, the "throne" of the mind is that excellent state which they maintain who are seated in a position that is fixed or immovable. Scholia on Proverbs 184.18.16.[17]

---

[11]LCL 34:291*. [12]PG 64:717. [13]PG 64:717. [14]Jer 13:15. [15]FC 97:122. [16]See Eph 3:19. [17]SC 340:278.

18:17-24 THE ONE WHO STATES HIS CASE FIRST

[17]He who states his case first seems right,
　　until the other comes and examines him.
[18]The lot puts an end to disputes
　　and decides between powerful contenders.
[19]A brother helped is like a strong city,[a]
　　but quarreling is like the bars of a castle.

²⁰*From the fruit of his mouth a man is
       satisfied;*
   he is satisfied by the yield of his lips.
²¹*Death and life are in the power of the
       tongue,*
   and those who love it will eat its fruits.
²²*He who finds a wife finds a good thing,*

   and obtains favor from the LORD.
²³*The poor use entreaties,*
   but the rich answer roughly.
²⁴*There are*ᵇ *friends who pretend to be
       friends,*ᶜ
   *but there is a friend who sticks closer
       than a brother.*

a Gk Syr Vg Tg: The meaning of the Hebrew is uncertain   b Syr Tg: Heb *A man of*   c Cn Compare Syr Vg Tg: Heb *to be broken*

OVERVIEW: David is a model for confessing his sin (ORIGEN). Indeed, the just person anticipates his accuser in the admission of sin. It is an act of freedom to confess early. Pardon is sure to follow (AMBROSE). It is wise to anticipate the accusation of your adversary (PAULINUS OF MILAN). The true Christians are those who are willing to condemn their own sins (AMBROSE). Always be the first to accuse yourself (BASIL), because to do this allows you to correct any later accusation. Cain, however, delayed his confession until it was too late (CHRYSOSTOM). Paul promptly acknowledged his own sin, and so should we (JEROME). Neither despair of God's forgiveness nor defer your repentance to later (CAESARIUS OF ARLES). Some confess their sins in order to gain credit, however, and not for the sake of being honest (GREGORY THE GREAT). To settle a dispute by lot may reduce contentiousness (AUGUSTINE). The concord of two brothers bound together is unbreakable, for the disciples were united like brothers helping each other in a fortress (CHRYSOSTOM). But brotherhood is also a matter of spiritual affection (CYRIL OF ALEXANDRIA). The tongue, surrounded by teeth and lips, stands in the middle of the mouth like a sword (CHRYSOSTOM). But words can still cause deaths (VALERIAN).

18:17 He Who States the Case First

DAVID IS A MAJOR PRECEDENT IN CONFESSING HIS SIN. ORIGEN: David also speaks in the Psalms and says, "I made my iniquity known and did not cover my sin. I said, 'I will proclaim my

injustice against myself,' and you have forgiven the impiety of my heart."[1] You see, therefore, that "to proclaim the sin" is to deserve the forgiveness of sin. For the devil, having been anticipated in the accusation, will not be able to accuse us further. If we are our own accusers, this profits us to salvation. But if we delay so that we are accused by the devil, that accusation delivers us to punishment; for he will have as companions in hell those whom he will have convicted of complicity. HOMILIES ON LEVITICUS 3.4.5.[2]

THE JUST PERSON ANTICIPATES HIS ACCUSER. AMBROSE: The just person takes note of his own weakness . . . . The wise person recognizes it; the foolish one does not. Indeed, the wise person is moved to repentance by his own faults, while the foolish one takes pleasure in his. "The just man is the accuser of himself," while the unjust one is his own apologist. The just person wishes to anticipate his accuser in the admission of his sin, while the unjust one desires to conceal his. The one rushes on in the beginning of his speech to reveal his wrongdoing, the other attempts to lay the accusation to rest by the garrulousness of his speech, so as not to reveal his wrongdoing. THE PRAYER OF JOB AND DAVID 1.6.20.[3]

TO CONFESS FIRST TO THE LORD IS FREEDOM. AMBROSE: Let us who are free from sin, purchased, as it were, by the price of Christ's

---

[1]Ps 32:5 (31:5 LXX).   [2]FC 83:61.   [3]FC 65:342-43*.

blood, let us not be subject to the slavery of people or of passion. Let us not be ashamed to confess our sin. See how free is the one who could say, "I have not been afraid of a very great multitude, so that I would not confess my sin in the sight of all."[4] One who confesses to the Lord is freed from his slavery: "The just is the accuser of himself in the beginning of his speech." He is not only free but just, for justice is in liberty, and liberty in confession, and as soon as one has confessed he is pardoned. LETTER 54.[5]

THE TRUE CHRISTIANS. AMBROSE: Are not those who condemn their sin truer Christians than those who think to defend it? "The just accuses himself in the beginning of his words." He who accuses himself when he sins is just, not he who praises himself. LETTER 51.[6]

CONFESSION REQUIRES CORRECTION. PAULINUS OF MILAN: He is his own accuser who, instead of waiting, anticipates his accuser, so as to lighten his own sin by confession, lest he have something which his adversary may accuse. And for this reason, Scripture says, "The just is first accuser of himself." For he snatches away the voice of his adversary and by the confession of his own sins breaks to pieces the teeth prepared for the prey of hostile accusation. In so doing he gives honor to God, to whom all things are exposed, and who wishes the life rather than the death of the sinner.[7] Indeed, to the penitent himself confession alone does not suffice, unless correction of the deed follows, with the result that the penitent does not continue to do deeds which demand repentance. LIFE OF ST. AMBROSE 9.39.[8]

BE THE FIRST TO ACCUSE YOURSELF. BASIL THE GREAT: Speak not in your own praise, nor contrive that others do so. Do not listen to indecent talk. Conceal insofar as you can your own superior gifts. On the other hand, where sin is concerned, be your own accuser, and do not wait for others to make the accusation. Thus, you will be like a just man who accuses himself in the first speech made in court, or like Job who was not deterred by the crowd of people in the city from declaring his personal guilt before all.[9] ON HUMILITY.[10]

BE THE FIRST TO CONDEMN YOURSELF. CHRYSOSTOM: When you commit sin, do not wait for another man to accuse you but, before you are accused and indicted, you yourself had best condemn what you have done. Then, if someone accuses you later on, it is no longer a matter of your doing the right thing in confessing but of your correcting the accusation which he makes. And so it is that someone else has said, "The just man begins his speech by accusing himself." So it is not a question of accusing but of being the first to accuse yourself and not waiting for others to accuse you.

Peter certainly sinned gravely in denying Christ. But he was quick to remind himself of his sin and, before anyone accused him, he told of his error and wept bitterly.[11] He so effectively washed away his sin of denial that he became the chief of the apostles, and the whole world was entrusted to him. DISCOURSES AGAINST JUDAIZING CHRISTIANS 8.3.3-4.[12]

CAIN DELAYED HIS CONFESSION UNTIL IT WAS TOO LATE. CHRYSOSTOM: You see, when Cain was asked by the Lord, "Where is your brother Abel?" that was the time for him to confess his fault, fall on his knees, pray and ask pardon. At that point, however, he rejected the healing, whereas now, after the sentence, after all was over, after the accusation was leveled at him in a loud voice by the blood that had been shed, he made his confession only to gain nothing from it. That is why the inspired author also said, "He who accuses himself at the beginning of the speech is in the right." Accordingly, had Cain anticipated the Lord's accusation, perhaps he would have been

---

[4]Job 31:34. [5]FC 26:302-3*. [6]LCC 5:257. [7]Cf. Heb 4:13; Ezek 18:32. [8]FC 15:57*. [9]Job 31:34. [10]FC 9:485*. [11]Cf. Mt 26:69-75; Mk 14:66-72; Lk 22:54-62; Jn 18:16-18. [12]FC 68:213-14*.

granted some mercy on account of the Lord's unlimited goodness. I mean, there is no sin, no matter how grave, that can exceed his mercy provided we demonstrate our repentance at the proper time and beg pardon. "Cain said, 'My guilt is too great for me to be forgiven'"—an adequate confession, but too late. HOMILIES ON GENESIS 19.14.[13]

PAUL PROMPTLY ACKNOWLEDGED HIS SIN. JEROME: Blessed, therefore, is he who acknowledges that he is a sinner just as the apostle does: "I am not worthy to be called an apostle, because I persecuted the church of God."[14] If the apostle makes such a confession, how much more should the sinner? Scripture says, moreover, "If the just man is prompt to accuse himself, how much more should the sinner be?" HOMILIES ON THE PSALMS 47 (PSALM 135).[15]

NEITHER DESPAIR OF GOD'S FORGIVENESS NOR DEFER REPENTANCE. CAESARIUS OF ARLES: If you acknowledge your sins, God will forgive you. So, let no one despair, but, likewise, let no one entertain presumptuous hope. The one who believes that even if he does penance for his sins the divine mercy will not forgive him wrongly despairs, while one who defers the remedy of repentance to a much later day is presumptuous. SERMON 64.4.[16]

SOME CONFESS THEIR SINS TO GAIN CREDIT. GREGORY THE GREAT: Even those who do not believe that they have sinned, generally confess themselves sinners. For it is frequently the case that people openly confess themselves sinners, but on hearing a true account of their sins when other persons attack them, they boldly defend themselves and endeavor to appear innocent. Everyone of this character, then, if he says that he has sinned, speaks untruly, as he proclaims himself a sinner not from the inmost heart, but only in words. For since it is written, "The just man in the beginning accuses himself," he wished to gain credit, not to be humbled, by confessing his sin. He desired, by accusing himself, to appear humble

without being so. . . . The righteous, then, in passing sentence on his own conduct, knows from the bottom of his heart, by the examples of holier men, that he really is what he professes to be. MORALS ON THE BOOK OF JOB 5.24.22.[17]

18:18 Disputes Can Be Ended by Lot

TO SETTLE A DISPUTE BY LOT MAY REDUCE CONTENTIOUSNESS. AUGUSTINE: "The lot suppresses contentions and determines even between the mighty." For it is better for God to decide in uncertainties of this kind than for people, whether he deigns to call the better ones to a share in his passion and to spare the weak, or to strengthen the former to bear these evils and to withdraw from this life those whose survival cannot be as beneficial to the church as theirs would be. It will be an unusual thing to proceed in this matter by drawing lots, but, if it is done, who will dare to judge it adversely? Surely, everyone but the envious or those ignorant of this appropriate quotation will praise it. LETTER 228.[18]

18:19 Help for Brothers in a Strong City

THE CONCORD OF TWO BROTHERS. CHRYSOSTOM: Do you see the great strength which comes from concord? And do you see the great harm caused by contentiousness? A kingdom in revolt destroys itself. When two brothers are bound together and united into one, they are more unbreakable than any wall. DISCOURSES AGAINST JUDAIZING CHRISTIANS 3.1.3.[19]

THE DISCIPLES WERE UNITED LIKE BROTHERS. CHRYSOSTOM: "A brother helped by his brother is like a fortified and elevated city: and is as strong as a well fortified palace of kings." The disciples of Christ were of the same mind, like brothers, and were fortified like a royal palace

---

[13]FC 82:29-30. [14]1 Cor 15:9. [15]FC 48:353. [16]FC 31:310-11. [17]LF 23:65-66. [18]FC 32:150. [19]FC 68:48.

surrounded by many walls as they helped each other. They were firm in their unity, and their mutual aid made them stronger and stronger. COMMENTARY ON THE PROVERBS OF SOLOMON, FRAGMENT 18.19.[20]

THE BONDS OF SPIRITUAL AFFECTION WITHSTAND THE SIEGE. CYRIL OF ALEXANDRIA: Truly spiritual affection is a strong city not able to be overcome or besieged by the devil either by undermining or by scaling. For it does not give way to the siege machines of Satan because it is guarded by Christ, the Lord, by Christ who conquered the world and has prepared eternal blessings for you, by Christ, who said, "He who does not take up his cross and follow me is not worthy of me."[21] LETTER 30.2.[22]

18:21 Death and Life in the Power of the Tongue

THE TONGUE STANDS IN THE MIDDLE LIKE A SWORD. CHRYSOSTOM: Christ makes the same point when he says, "By your own words you will be condemned, and by your words you will be justified."[23]

The tongue stands in the middle ready for either use; you are its master. So also does a sword lie in the middle; if you use it against the enemy, it becomes an instrument for your safety; if you use it to wound yourself, it is not the steel but your own transgression of the law that causes your death. Let us think of the tongue in the same way, as a sword lying in the middle. Sharpen it to accuse yourself of your own sins, but do not use it to wound your brother.

Hence, God has surrounded the tongue with a double wall—with the barrier of the teeth and the fence of the lips—in order that it may not easily and heedlessly utter words it should not speak. BAPTISMAL INSTRUCTIONS 9.33-35.[24]

WORDS CAUSE DEATHS. VALERIAN: A wound arising from words is unbearable. . . . Truly, dearly beloved, if you look deeply, and diligently investigate the swelling tumor of an exasperated heart, you will discover that the wounds produced by words cause deaths. HOMILY 5.4.[25]

---

[20]PG 64:720. [21]See Mt 10:38. [22]FC 76:120 [23]Mk 12:27. [24]ACW 31:142*. [25]FC 17:332.

19:1-29 A POOR PERSON WALKS IN INTEGRITY

[1]Better is a poor man who walks in his
  integrity
    than a man who is perverse in speech,
    and is a fool.
[2]It is not good for a man to be without
    knowledge,
  and he who makes haste with his feet
    misses his way.
[3]When a man's folly brings his way to

  ruin,
    his heart rages against the LORD.
[4]Wealth brings many new friends,
  but a poor man is deserted by his friend.
[5]A false witness will not go unpunished,
  and he who utters lies will not escape.
[6]Many seek the favor of a generous man,
  and every one is a friend to a man who
    gives gifts.

[7] All a poor man's brothers hate him;
　　how much more do his friends go far
　　　from him!
He pursues them with words, but does not
　　have them.[d]
[8] He who gets wisdom loves himself;
　　he who keeps understanding will prosper.
[9] A false witness will not go unpunished,
　　and he who utters lies will perish.
[10] It is not fitting for a fool to live in
　　luxury,
　　much less for a slave to rule over princes.
[11] Good sense makes a man slow to
　　anger,
　　and it is his glory to overlook an offense.
[12] A king's wrath is like the growling of a
　　lion,
　　but his favor is like dew upon the grass.
[13] A foolish son is ruin to his father,
　　and a wife's quarreling is a continual
　　　dripping of rain.
[14] House and wealth are inherited from
　　fathers,
　　but a prudent wife is from the Lord.
[15] Slothfulness casts into a deep sleep,
　　and an idle person will suffer hunger.
[16] He who keeps the commandment keeps
　　his life;
　　he who despises the word[e] will die.
[17] He who is kind to the poor lends to the
　　Lord,
　　and he will repay him for his deed.
[18] Discipline your son while there is hope;
　　do not set your heart on his destruction.

[19] A man of great wrath will pay the
　　penalty;
　　for if you deliver him, you will only
　　　have to do it again.[f]
[20] Listen to advice and accept instruction,
　　that you may gain wisdom for the
　　　future.
[21] Many are the plans in the mind of a man,
　　but it is the purpose of the Lord that
　　　will be established.
[22] What is desired in a man is loyalty,
　　and a poor man is better than a liar.
[23] The fear of the Lord leads to life;
　　and he who has it rests satisfied;
　　he will not be visited by harm.
[24] The sluggard buries his hand in the dish,
　　and will not even bring it back to his
　　　mouth.
[25] Strike a scoffer, and the simple will
　　learn prudence;
　　reprove a man of understanding, and
　　　he will gain knowledge.
[26] He who does violence to his father and
　　chases away his mother
　　is a son who causes shame and brings
　　　reproach.
[27] Cease, my son, to hear instruction
　　only to stray from the words of
　　　knowledge.
[28] A worthless witness mocks at justice,
　　and the mouth of the wicked devours
　　　iniquity.
[29] Condemnation is ready for scoffers,
　　and flogging for the backs of fools.

d Heb uncertain　**e** Cn Compare 13.13: Heb *his ways*　**f** Heb obscure

OVERVIEW: Grace is not bestowed upon us according to our human merits (AUGUSTINE). The angels uphold spiritual friendship that comes from knowledge of God (EVAGRIUS). At the end there will be punishments for the false and crowns for the true (AUGUSTINE). A lack of patience indicates a lack of wisdom (GREGORY THE GREAT). God is with those who responsibly marry and with those who, living the single life, show self-control (CLEMENT OF ALEXANDRIA). God created marriage, indeed, but not every match of every man with a particular woman. At the end, it is better to have God as debtor, to whom alms have been lent, than as judge (CHRYSOSTOM), for money given to the poor is money lent to God (CYRIL OF ALEXANDRIA). So give to the poor now, and great will your reward be later in heaven (CAESARIUS). God's perfect purpose is greater than any human plan (AUGUSTINE). When a pestilent character is punished a simple one is made wiser, because sinners are punished for the education of others (ORIGEN).

19:3 Raging Against the Lord

GRACE IS NOT BESTOWED ACCORDING TO OUR DESERVING. AUGUSTINE: Grace is not bestowed according to human merits; otherwise grace would be no longer grace.[1] For grace is so designated because it is given gratuitously. ON GRACE AND FREE WILL 21.43.[2]

19:4 The Role of the Angels in Spiritual Friendship

RELATIONSHIP TO THE ANGELS COMES FROM KNOWLEDGE OF GOD. EVAGRIUS OF PONTUS: "Richness" of knowledge and wisdom "brings us many angels,"[3] but an impure person is even separated from the angel given to him at birth. Spiritual friendship is virtue and knowledge of God, through which we bind ourselves to friendship with the holy powers. Thus it is said that human beings who repent give cause for joy to the angels.[4] Thus also the Savior calls his servants "friends,"[5] since they are ready to receive greater wisdom. So also Abraham, rich in knowledge, offered that mystical table to the friends who appeared to him in the middle of the day.[6] SCHOLIA ON PROVERBS 189.19.4.[7]

19:5 True and False Witnesses

PUNISHMENTS FOR THE FALSE AND CROWNS FOR THE TRUE. AUGUSTINE: There are true martyrs and false ones, because there are true and false witnesses. But Scripture says, "The false witness shall not go unpunished." If the false witness will not escape punishment, neither will the true witness be denied a crown. And it was, indeed, easy to bear witness to the Lord Jesus Christ and the truth, because he is God; but to do so to the death, that was a great work. SERMON 286.1.[8]

19:11 Slow to Anger

LACK OF PATIENCE INDICATES LACK OF WISDOM. GREGORY THE GREAT: Each person shows himself to be less wise the more he proves to be less patient. He cannot truly impart good by his teaching if he does not know how to bear calmly the evils done him by another. FORTY GOSPEL HOMILIES 35.[9]

19:14 A Prudent Wife Is from the Lord

CHOICE BETWEEN SELF-CONTROL OR RESPONSIBLE MARRIAGE WITH CHILDREN. CLEMENT OF ALEXANDRIA: Who are the two or three who gather in the name of Christ with the Lord in their midst?[10] By three does he not mean husband, wife and child? "A wife is united with her husband by God." But if a man wishes to be unencumbered and prefers to avoid producing children because of the time it takes up, then, says the apostle, "he had better stay unmarried like me."[11] . . . God through his Son is with those who responsibly marry and produce children, and it is the same God who in the same way is with the man who shows self-control in the light of the Logos. STROMATEIS 3.10.68.1-4.[12]

---

[1]Rom 11:6. [2]NPNF 1 5:463*. [3]Evagrius reflects a different textual tradition. [4]See Lk 15:10. [5]See Jn 15:15. [6]See Gen 18:1-8. [7]SC 340:282. [8]WSA 3 8:101. [9]CS 123:305-6*. [10]Mt 18:20. [11]1 Cor 7:8. [12]FC 85:298.

GOD CREATED MARRIAGE. CHRYSOSTOM: When a certain wise man says, "It is by the Lord that a man is matched with a woman," he means this: God made marriage, and not that it is God that joins together every man that comes to be married with a woman. For we see many that come to be with one another for evil, even by the law of marriage, and this we should not ascribe to God. HOMILIES ON ROMANS 23.13.1.[13]

19:17 Be Kind to the Poor

IT IS BETTER TO HAVE GOD AS DEBTOR THAN AS JUDGE. CHRYSOSTOM: Let us lend to God almsgiving so we may receive from him clemency in exchange. Oh, how wise is this statement! "Whoever has mercy upon the poor lends to God." Why did he not say, "Whoever has mercy upon the poor gives to God" instead of "lends"? Scripture recognizes our greediness; it understood that our insatiate desire, which looks longingly toward greediness, asks for an excess. This is why it did not say simply, "Whoever has mercy upon the poor gives to God," so you may not think that the recompense will be customary; rather, it said, "Whoever has mercy upon the poor lends to God." Since God borrows from us, then, he is our debtor. How do we want to have him, as judge or debtor? The debtor is ashamed before his lender; the judge does not put to shame the one who borrows. HOMILIES ON REPENTANCE AND ALMSGIVING 7.6.23.[14]

MONEY GIVEN TO THE POOR IS MONEY LENT TO GOD. CYRIL OF ALEXANDRIA: The lesson, therefore, which he teaches us is love for the poor, which is precious in the sight of God. Do you feel pleasure in being praised when you have any friends or relatives feasting with you? I tell you of something far better: angels shall praise your bounty, and the rational powers above, and holy men as well; and he too shall accept it who transcends all, and who loves mercy and is kind. Lend to him fearing nothing, and you will receive with interest whatever you gave, for "he," it says, "who has pity on the poor lends unto God." COMMENTARY ON LUKE, HOMILY 103.[15]

GIVE TO THE POOR NOW. CAESARIUS OF ARLES: If a trustworthy man said to you, Give me one gold coin, and I will repay you one hundred solid gold coins, would you not gladly give him the one in order that you might receive the hundred? Now the God of heaven and earth says to you, "He who has compassion on the poor lends to God"; moreover, "As long as you did it for one of the least of these, you did it for me";[16] and in the Psalms, "Well for the man who is gracious and lends."[17] How much more, then, should you lend to God on earth, in order that you may receive a manifold return in eternal life? Then you will deserve to come before the tribunal of the eternal judge in the sight of the angels and can say with assurance and a clear conscience, Give, Lord, because I have given; have mercy because I have shown mercy. SERMON 158.6.[18]

19:21 The Purpose of God

GOD'S DESIGNS ARE GREATER THAN HUMAN JUDGMENTS. AUGUSTINE: What lies hidden in the designs of God I confess I do not know—I am only a man—but this I know with full certainty, that, whatever it is, it is more just, more wise, and more solidly based on incomparable perfection than all the judgments of people. LETTER 104.[19]

19:25 A Simple One Is Made Wiser

SINNERS ARE PUNISHED FOR THE EDUCATION OF OTHERS. ORIGEN: If you want to take Scripture as a witness that sinners are punished for the education of others, even if those unabashed may be beyond treatment, hear Solomon in the Proverbs who says, "When a pest is being whipped, the fool will be more astute." He did not say that he who is being whipped will be more astute and

---

[13]NPNF 1 11:511*. [14]FC 96:105. [15]CGSL 414*. [16]Mt 25:40. [17]Ps 112:5 (111:5 LXX). [18]FC 47:362-63. [19]FC 18:189.

more sensible through the whips, but he said that the fool will change from foolishness into common sense through whips employed on the pest. For this is signified here by the term *astute*, and the fool changes because he sees others who are whipped. Hence the punishment of others is use-

ful for us if we learn greater readiness for salvation through others who are punished. HOMILIES ON JEREMIAH 12.6.[17]

---

[20]FC 97:118-19

20:1-30 THE RIGHTEOUS AND THE SINNERS

[1]*Wine is a mocker, strong drink a brawler;*
and whoever is led astray by it is not wise.
[2]*The dread wrath of a king is like the*
growling of a lion;
he who provokes him to anger forfeits
his life.
[3]*It is an honor for a man to keep aloof*
from strife;
but every fool will be quarreling.
[4]*The sluggard does not plow in the autumn;*
he will seek at harvest and have nothing.
[5]*The purpose in a man's mind is like deep*
water,
but a man of understanding will draw
it out.
[6]*Many a man proclaims his own loyalty,*
but a faithful man who can find?
[7]*A righteous man who walks in his integrity—*
blessed are his sons after him!
[8]*A king who sits on the throne of judgment*
winnows all evil with his eyes.
[9]*Who can say, "I have made my heart clean;*
I am pure from my sin"?
[10]*Diverse weights and diverse measures*
are both alike an abomination to the
LORD.

[11]*Even a child makes himself known by*
his acts,
whether what he does is pure and right.
[12]*The hearing ear and the seeing eye,*
the LORD *has made them both.*
[13]*Love not sleep, lest you come to poverty;*
open your eyes, and you will have
plenty of bread.
[14]*"It is bad, it is bad," says the buyer;*
but when he goes away, then he boasts.
[15]*There is gold, and abundance of costly*
stones;
but the lips of knowledge are a precious
jewel.
[16]*Take a man's garment when he has*
given surety for a stranger,
and hold him in pledge when he gives
surety for foreigners.
[17]*Bread gained by deceit is sweet to a man,*
but afterward his mouth will be full of
gravel.
[18]*Plans are established by counsel;*
by wise guidance wage war.
[19]*He who goes about gossiping reveals secrets;*
therefore do not associate with one who
speaks foolishly.

²⁰*If one curses his father or his mother,*
his lamp will be put out in utter darkness.
²¹*An inheritance gotten hastily in the*
beginning
will in the end not be blessed.
²²*Do not say, "I will repay evil";*
wait for the LORD, *and he will help you.*
²³*Diverse weights are an abomination to*
the LORD,
and false scales are not good.
²⁴*A man's steps are ordered by the* LORD;
how then can man understand his way?
²⁵*It is a snare for a man to say rashly, "It*
is holy,"

and to reflect only after making his vows.
²⁶*A wise king winnows the wicked,*
and drives the wheel over them.
²⁷*The spirit of man is the lamp of the*
LORD,
searching all his innermost parts.
²⁸*Loyalty and faithfulness preserve the*
king,
and his throne is upheld by righteousness.^g
²⁹*The glory of young men is their strength,*
but the beauty of old men is their gray
hair.
³⁰*Blows that wound cleanse away evil;*
strokes make clean the innermostparts.

g *Gk: Heb* loyalty

OVERVIEW: Wine is a wasteful expenditure, and Scripture repudiates its intemperate use (CLEMENT OF ALEXANDRIA). Wine is a good thing only in moderation (PACHOMIUS). Wine teaches us, in that it makes him that is familiar with it like itself. Wine hates those who are most fond of it (EPHREM). One who offends God's holiness with sin, sins against his own soul (ORIGEN). There will be nothing in the summer for the sluggard who retreated from the cold in winter (GREGORY THE GREAT). The practice of mercy, so characteristic of our fathers in the faith (APHRAHAT), must characterize also the honorable person in our time (CHRYSOSTOM). No human is without sin (APOSTOLIC CONSTITUTIONS), no one's heart is perfectly clean (CHRYSOSTOM), there is no one without stain (GREGORY OF NYSSA), and hence no one can dispense with repentance (CYRIL OF ALEXANDRIA). After all, if even the stars are not pure, as Job says, then how can anyone's heart be entirely clean (JEROME)? Rectitude in judgment is evidence that one's soul is well disposed toward equity and law (BASIL). False weights and measures must be repudiated in every walk of life; indeed, equity must be observed, permitting neither excess nor defect (AMBROSE). And person-

ally, we must not tolerate lighter weights for ourselves than for others (JOHN CASSIAN). An immediate gain of wealth is not worth the loss of eternal blessedness (GREGORY THE GREAT). Ordered by God, our steps are guided toward the attainment of the kingdom of heaven and not merely for earthly gain (AUGUSTINE), for our steps as mortal sinners are nevertheless directed by the Lord (CHRYSOSTOM). Thus, we have free choice but we also have God's help (JEROME). There must be collaboration of the young and strong with the old and wise (BEDE). Through bodily affliction can come great gifts that lead to repentance and that avoid future sins (GREGORY THE GREAT).

20:1 Strong Drink Leads Astray

SCRIPTURE REPUDIATES INTEMPERATE USE.
CLEMENT OF ALEXANDRIA: Scripture always uses wine in a mystical sense, as a symbol of the holy blood, and always repudiates any intemperate use made of it. CHRIST THE EDUCATOR 2.2.29.[1]

---

[1]FC 23:119.

**WINE IS A GOOD THING ONLY IN MODERA-
TION.** PACHOMIUS: As it is said, "The priest and
the prophet were deranged by wine."[2] "Wine is
licentious, drunkenness is bold. The person who
indulges in them will not be exempt from sin."
Wine is a good thing if you drink it with moderation. "If you set your eyes on cups and goblets
you will walk naked as a pestle."[3] Therefore, all
who have prepared to become disciples of Jesus
should abstain from wine and drunkenness.
INSTRUCTIONS 1.45.[4]

WINE HATES THOSE WHO ARE FOND OF IT.
EPHREM THE SYRIAN: Those who eat the heavenly bread become heavenly without doubt!
Wine teaches us in that it makes those who are
familiar with it like itself: for it hates those who
are fond of it and is intoxicating and maddening
and a mocker of them. HYMNS ON THE NATIV-
ITY 3.[5]

20:2 An Angry King Is Like a Growling Lion

**CHRIST IS THE KING WHO SHOULD NOT BE
IRRITATED.** ORIGEN: In this place it openly
speaks of Christ as the king, for the one who irritates Christ with [his] sin, sins against his own
soul. EXPOSITION ON PROVERBS, FRAGMENT
20.2.[6]

20:4 The Sluggard Will Have Nothing at Harvest

**NOTHING IN THE SUMMER FOR THE SLUG-
GARD.** GREGORY THE GREAT: The slothful, in
neglecting to do what he ought, imagines to himself certain difficulties and harbors certain
unfounded fears; and when he discovers an
apparent reason for having fear apparently justified, he acts as if he were quite justified in being
inactive and indolent. . . . The sluggard does not
plough because of the cold, when he is held back
by the torpor of sloth and fails to do the good
that he ought to do. The sluggard does not

plough owing to the cold, when he fears trifling
evils that confront him and fails to do things of
the greatest moment. And it is well said, "He
shall beg in the summer, and it shall not be given
him." The person who does not toil in good
works now will receive nothing in the summer;
that is, when the scorching sun of judgment shall
appear, he will beg in vain to enter the kingdom.
PASTORAL CARE 3.15.16.[7]

20:6 Loyal for Oneself or Faithful for the Sake of Others?

**OUR FATHERS WERE FAITHFUL AS WELL AS
MERCIFUL.** APHRAHAT: All the righteous, our
fathers, in all that they did were victorious
through faith, as the blessed apostle also testifies
about them all, "They prevailed by faith."[8]
Solomon also said, "Many men are called merciful, but who can find a faithful man?" DEMON-
STRATIONS 1.16.[9]

**MERCY SHOULD CHARACTERIZE GOD'S
IMAGE.** CHRYSOSTOM: A human being is of great
value since he is made in the likeness of God. If
he adds to this the practice of mercy in practical
matters he then becomes an honorable man. He,
who does this wisely and faithfully, finds the
work [he was created to do]. COMMENTARY ON
THE PROVERBS OF SOLOMON, FRAGMENT 20.6.[10]

20:9 Pure from Sin

NO HUMAN IS WITHOUT SIN. APOSTOLIC
CONSTITUTIONS: No human, therefore, is
without sin. Labor therefore to the utmost of
your power to be unblamable; and be solicitous
of all the parts of your flock, lest any one be
scandalized on your account and thereby
perish. CONSTITUTIONS OF THE HOLY APOS-
TLES 2.3.18.[11]

---

[2]Is 28:7. [3]Prov 23:31 LXX. [4]CS 47:35*. [5]NPNF 2 13:232*. [6]PG
17:209. [7]ACW 11:135. [8]Heb 11:33, 39. [9]NPNF 2 13:351*. [10]PG
64:724. [11]ANF 7:403**.

TO FALL IS NOT AS BAD AS TO LIE WHERE FALLEN. CHRYSOSTOM: Let us not therefore give up in despair; for to fall is not so grievous as to lie where we have fallen. It is not so dreadful to be wounded as it is to refuse healing after being wounded. "For who shall boast that he has his heart chaste? or who shall say confidently that he is pure from sin?" These things I say not to make you more negligent but to prevent your despairing. HOMILIES ON 1 CORINTHIANS 8.8.[12]

IS THERE ANYONE WITHOUT STAIN? GREGORY OF NYSSA: Whose soul, then, is pure from stain? How has anyone not been struck by vanity or been trodden down by the foot of pride? Whose hand has never been touched by sin? Whose feet have never run toward evil? Who has not been polluted by a roving eye or been defiled by an undisciplined ear? Whose taste has never been preoccupied by its enjoyment, whose heart has remained unmoved by vain emotions? ON THE LORD'S PRAYER 5.[13]

NO ONE CAN DISPENSE WITH REPENTANCE. CYRIL OF ALEXANDRIA: The merciful God has provided for the inhabitants of earth repentance as the medicine of salvation. Some endeavor to dispense with repentance, saying of themselves that they are clean. In their great madness they do not understand that to entertain such an idea of themselves is full of all impurity. For "no man is free from defilement," as it is written. COMMENTARY ON LUKE, HOMILY 149.[14]

HOW CAN ANYONE'S HEART BE ENTIRELY CLEAN? JEROME: "Who can say," writes the wise man, "I have made my heart clean"? The stars are not pure in the Lord's sight; how much less people whose whole life is one long temptation.[15] LETTER 125.7.[16]

20:10 Inequalities in Weights and Measures

RECTITUDE IN JUDGMENT. BASIL THE GREAT: If there were two persons to be judged, one being

given more consideration and the other less consideration, with a judge standing between both and making them equal by depriving only the one who has more than enough, the judge can be said to have failed to the extent that the adjudged party is injured. He who does not first have true justice instilled in his soul, but is corrupted by money or favors his friends or seeks vengeance against his enemies or reveres power, is unable to effect justice. . . . For rectitude in judgment is evidence that someone's soul is well disposed toward equity and law. Hence, it prohibits this in what follows, saying, "Large weights and small weights are abominable before God," with inequality in judgment being indicated in Proverbs under the title of weights. HOMILY ON THE BEGINNING OF PROVERBS 9.[17]

FALSE WEIGHTS AND MEASURES MUST BE REPUDIATED. AMBROSE: Every kind of unfair action is shameful. Even in common things, false weights and unjust measures are accursed. And if fraud in the market or in business is punished, can it seem free from reproach if found in the midst of the performance of the duties of virtue? DUTIES OF THE CLERGY 3.9.65.[18]

EQUITY MUST ACCEPT NEITHER EXCESS NOR DEFECT. AMBROSE: He who commands must always keep to the exact scope of the commandments, and he who distributes tasks must observe equity in looking into them, for "a false balance is an abomination to the Lord."[19] There is, then, an excess and a defect in weight, but the church acccepts neither, for "excessive and defective weights and diverse measures, both of them are alike abominable in the sight of the Lord." CONCERNING WIDOWS 13.78.[20]

WE MUST NOT TOLERATE LIGHTER WEIGHTS FOR OURSELVES THAN FOR OTHERS. JOHN CASSIAN: We must be careful not to have either

---

[12]NPNF 1 12:47*. [13]ACW 18:79*. [14]CGSL 592*. [15]Job 25:5-6. [16]NPNF 2 6:246. [17]PG 31:405. [18]NPNF 2 10:78. [19]Prov 11:1. [20]NPNF 2 10:404-5.

unjust weights in our hearts or double measures in the storerooms of our conscience, not only in the way that we have spoken but also in the following way. That is, we must not burden those to whom we preach the word of the Lord with stricter and heavier precepts than we ourselves are able to bear, while taking it upon ourselves to lighten with a greater and more indulgent relaxation the things that pertain to our rule of strictness. If we do this, what are we doing but weighing and measuring the revenue and fruit of the Lord's precepts with a double weight and measure? For if we weigh them out in one way for ourselves and in another for our brothers, we are rightly rebuked by the Lord for having deceptive balances and double measures, according to the words of Solomon, where it is said, "A double weight is an abomination to the Lord, and a deceptive balance is not good in his sight." CONFERENCE 21.22.6.[21]

20:21 *An Inheritance Hastily Gained Will Not Be Blessed*

IMMEDIATE GAIN IS NOT WORTH THE LOSS OF ETERNAL BLESSEDNESS. GREGORY THE GREAT: When these people burn with the desire of being replete with all manner of wealth at once, let them hear what Scripture says: "He that makes haste to be rich, shall not be innocent."[22] Obviously, a person who strives to increase his resources is not interested in avoiding sin; and being caught after the way of birds, while looking greedily at the bait of earthly things, he does not perceive that he is being strangled in the noose of sin. When these long for the gains of this world and ignore the losses they will suffer in the future life, let them hear what Scripture says: "The inheritance gotten hastily in the beginning, in the end shall be without a blessing." Indeed, it is this our life from which we take our beginning, that we may come at the end to the lot of the blessed. They, therefore, who hasten to an inheritance in the beginning cut themselves off from the lot of the blessed in the end, because, while desiring increase here through evil cupidity, they become

hereafter disinherited of their everlasting patrimony. When they either aim at getting much, or are able to compass all they desired, let them hear what Scripture says: "What does it profit a man if he gain the whole world and suffer the loss of his own soul?"[23] PASTORAL CARE 3.20.21.[24]

20:24 *Steps Ordered by God*

GUIDED TOWARD THE ATTAINMENT OF THE KINGDOM OF HEAVEN. AUGUSTINE: Do they suppose, accordingly, that God moves the wills of those whom he has wished to the creation of earthly kingdoms but that he does not move them to the attainment of a heavenly kingdom? But I think that it was in reference to the kingdom of heaven, rather than to an earthly kingdom, that it was said . . . "The steps of a man are guided by the Lord, but how does a mortal understand his own ways?" Let them hear, "Every man seems just to himself, but the Lord directs the hearts."[25] Let them hear, "As many as were ordained to life everlasting believed."[26] Let them hear these words, and whatever others I have not quoted, by which it is shown that God prepares and converts people's wills also for the kingdom of heaven and for eternal life. And think how strange it would be for us to believe that God moves people's wills for the establishment of earthly kingdoms but that for the attainment of the kingdom of heaven people move their own wills. PREDESTINATION OF THE SAINTS 20.42.[27]

THE STEPS OF MORTALS ARE DIRECTED BY THE LORD. CHRYSOSTOM: "The steps of man are directed by God." A mortal, that is a sinner [as such], cannot [of himself] know the ways of the Lord; in fact, since he is mortal, he has [of yet] neither died nor lived with Christ. Therefore in the journey to the kingdom of heaven the steps of man are directed by the Lord. COMMENTARY ON THE PROVERBS OF SOLOMON, FRAGMENT 20.24.[28]

---

[21]ACW 57:736-37. [22]Prov 28:20. [23]Mt 16:26. [24]ACW 11:157*. [25]Prov 21:2. [26]Acts 13:48. [27]FC 86:268-69. [28]PG 64:724.

FREE CHOICE WITH GOD'S HELP. JEROME: You maintain that "all are governed by their own free choice." What Christian can bear to hear this? For if not one, or a few or many but all of us are governed by our own free choice, what becomes of the help of God? And how do you explain the text, "A man's goings are ordered by the Lord"? AGAINST THE PELAGIANS 1.27.[29]

20:29 The Contrast Between Young and Old

PLEA FOR COLLABORATION. BEDE: It calls gray hair wisdom. For only then will the city be well ordered, only then will the administration of the holy church be conducted properly, when all the strong men pursue the necessary works and when the elders, endowed with greater prudence, meditate advantageously on what must be done. COMMENTARY ON PROVERBS 2.20.29.[30]

20:30 Blows That Cleanse Evil

BODILY AFFLICTION CLEANSES SINS. GREGORY THE GREAT: The sick are to be admonished to consider that through bodily affliction can come great gifts. It may be the occasion for cleansing of sins committed or the restraint of those that could be committed and lead from a troubled mind toward penitence inflicted by outward stripes. Hence Scripture says, "The blueness of a wound cleanses evils, and stripes in the more inward parts of the belly." The blueness of a wound cleanses evil, that is, the pain of chastisement cleanses wickedness, whether meditated or perpetrated. . . .

That is, when we are outwardly smitten, we are recalled, silent and afflicted, to the memory of our sins, and we bring before our eyes all the evil we have done, and in proportion as we suffer outwardly, the more do we grieve inwardly for our deeds. PASTORAL CARE 3.12.13.[31]

---

[29]NPNF 2 6:462.   [30]CCL 119B:107.   [31]ACW 11:124-25**.

21:1-31 THE VICTORY BELONGS TO GOD

[1]The king's heart is a stream of water in
  the hand of the LORD;
he turns it wherever he will.
[2]Every way of a man is right in his own
  eyes,
  but the LORD weighs the heart.
[3]To do righteousness and justice
  is more acceptable to the LORD than
    sacrifice.
[4]Haughty eyes and a proud heart,
  the lamp of the wicked, are sin.
[5]The plans of the diligent lead surely to
  abundance,

but every one who is hasty comes only to
  want.
[6]The getting of treasures by a lying tongue
  is a fleeting vapor and a snare of death.
[7]The violence of the wicked will sweep
    them away,
  because they refuse to do what is just.
[8]The way of the guilty is crooked,
  but the conduct of the pure is right.
[9]It is better to live in a corner of the
  housetop
  than in a house shared with a contentious
    woman.

¹⁰The soul of the wicked desires evil;
   his neighbor finds no mercy in his eyes.
¹¹When a scoffer is punished, the simple
      becomes wise;
   when a wise man is instructed, he gains
      knowledge.
¹²The righteous observes the house of the
      wicked;
   the wicked are cast down to ruin.
¹³He who closes his ear to the cry of the
      poor
   will himself cry out and not be heard.
¹⁴A gift in secret averts anger;
   and a bribe in the bosom, strong wrath.
¹⁵When justice is done, it is a joy to the
      righteous,
   but dismay to evildoers.
¹⁶A man who wanders from the way of
      understanding
   will rest in the assembly of the dead.
¹⁷He who loves pleasure will be a poor
      man;
   he who loves wine and oil will not be rich.
¹⁸The wicked is a ransom for the
      righteous,
   and the faithless for the upright.
¹⁹It is better to live in a desert land
   than with a contentious and fretful woman.
²⁰Precious treasure remains[h] in a wise
      man's dwelling,
   but a foolish man devours it.

²¹He who pursues righteousness and
      kindness
   will find life[i] and honor.
²²A wise man scales the city of the mighty
   and brings down the stronghold in which
      they trust.
²³He who keeps his mouth and his tongue
   keeps himself out of trouble.
²⁴"Scoffer" is the name of the proud,
      haughty man
   who acts with arrogant pride.
²⁵The desire of the sluggard kills him
   for his hands refuse to labor.
²⁶All day long the wicked covets,[j]
   but the righteous gives and does not hold
      back.
²⁷The sacrifice of the wicked is an abomi-
      nation;
   how much more when he brings it with
      evil intent.
²⁸A false witness will perish,
   but the word of a man who hears will
      endure.
²⁹A wicked man puts on a bold face,
   but an upright man considers[k] his ways.
³⁰No wisdom, no understanding, no
      counsel,
   can avail against the LORD.
³¹The horse is made ready for the day of
      battle,
   but the victory belongs to the LORD.

h Gk: Heb *and oil*   i Gk: Heb *life and righteousness*   j Gk: Heb *all day long he covets covetously*   k Another reading is *establishes*

OVERVIEW: Good kings do reign over sin, but this is not true of despotic rulers and persecutors, whose hearts were not in God's hand. A literal interpretation of this verse is not sufficient. The hearts in the hand of God are those who govern their bodies and keep them in subjection (JEROME). The king yearns for godliness if his heart is in God's hand (ATHANASIUS). Our souls are in God's hands (AMBROSE). The king, however, will be saved by divine guidance, not by earthly power (BASIL). Even though the king's heart is in God's hand, Christians are bought by blood, not by money; otherwise their martyrdom would not bring glory to God if they had to pay

133

for their survival by taxes to the rulers of this world. After all, the kingdom for which we pray is God's reign (TERTULLIAN).

Only the merciful can merit God's mercy (CYPRIAN), and ill-gotten gains, even if offered to the poor, are unacceptable to God (BASIL). Those who give alms, however, will receive happiness that does not perish (CYRIL OF ALEXANDRIA). God repudiates offerings that have been stolen from the needy (GREGORY THE GREAT). Those who do evil without cause are perverse (CHRYSOSTOM). Wives should exhibit modesty and meekness to all outside the church (APOSTOLIC CONSTITUTIONS). It is better to ponder wisdom than to try to swallow it all at once (AUGUSTINE). Wisdom demolishes untruth (ORIGEN). Do not be double-minded or double-tongued (DIDACHE). All day long the wicked covet, which means their entire human life (EVAGRIUS), but the efforts of the righteous are directed to higher things (GREGORY THE GREAT).

21:1 The King's Heart and God's Hand

CHRISTIANS PAY BY MARTYRDOM RATHER THAN IN MONEY. TERTULLIAN: This is the will of God: Look at the situation of the kingdoms and empires as arranged by God, in whose hand the heart of the king lies. Every day they plan for future income, from the registration of property, taxes in kind, gifts and taxes payable in money. But never up to this time has there been procured any such income by bringing the Christians under some sales tax for the person and the sect, when that could be a tremendous source of income because of our vast numbers, known to all. We are bought with blood, we are paid for in blood, we owe no money for our head, because Christ is our head.[1] It is not fitting that Christ should cost us money. How could martyrdoms bring glory to God if by tribute we should pay for the liberty of our sect? And so, the one who bargains to have his freedom at a price goes counter to the divine dispensation. ON FLIGHT IN TIME OF PERSECUTION 12.8.[2]

THE KINGDOM WE PRAY FOR IS GOD'S REIGN. TERTULLIAN: The phrase "Thy kingdom come" also refers to the same end as "Thy will be done," namely, [that God's kingdom may come] in ourselves. For, when does God not reign, "in whose hand is the heart of every king"? But, whatever we wish for ourselves, we direct our hope toward him, and we attribute to him what we expect from him. . . . This is the prayer of Christians; this shall bring shame to the heathens; this shall bring joy to the angels. It is for the coming of this kingdom that we are harassed now, or rather, it is for this coming that we pray. ON PRAYER 5.1-4.[3]

THE KING YEARNS FOR HEAVENLY THINGS IF HIS HEART IS IN GOD'S HAND. ATHANASIUS: A desire to learn and a yearning for heavenly things is suitable to a religious emperor; for thus you will truly have "your heart" also "in the hand of God." Since then your piety desired to learn from us the faith of the catholic church, giving thanks for these things to the Lord, we counseled above all things to remind your piety of the faith confessed by the fathers at Nicea. LETTER TO JOVIAN 56.1.[4]

THE SOUL IS IN THE HANDS OF GOD. AMBROSE: Entrust your soul to the hands of the Lord. Not only when it departs from the body but also when it is in the body, it is in the hands of the Lord, because you do not see it, its source or its destination. It is both in you and also with God. Therefore "the heart of the king is in the hand of the Lord," who guides it and rules it. The heart is also filled with the spirit, because the spirit is the ruling part of the soul and the strength of the soul. I say that strength lies not in the arms but in counsel, temperance, piety and justice. If the heart of a man is in the hand of the Lord, much more is his soul. DEATH AS A GOOD 10.44.[5]

---

[1]See Eph 5:23. [2]FC 40:302. [3]FC 40:163*. [4]NPNF 2 4:567*. [5]FC 65:101*.

THE KING WILL BE SAVED BY DIVINE GUIDANCE. BASIL THE GREAT: If "the heart of the king is in the hand of God," he will not be saved through power of arms but through the divine guidance. Now, not any random person is in the hand of God but one who is worthy of the name of king. HOMILIES ON THE PSALMS 15.9 (PSALM 32).[6]

KINGS OF THE EARTH REIGN OVER SIN. JEROME: The kings of the earth are those who reign over sin; consequently, they who govern sin shall give thanks. The prophet is certainly not referring to the kings of this world, for it is written, "The king's heart is in the hand of the Lord." Do you for one moment suppose that the heart of Julian the Apostate was in the hand of God? God forbid! Or of Nero or of Maximianus and Decius, the persecutors? God forbid! No, he is speaking of those who have control over sin, who, because their heart is in the hand of God, have conquered the vices and passions of their soul and thereby prevail over sin. HOMILIES ON THE PSALMS 49 (PSALM 137).[7]

THE HEARTS IN THE HANDS OF GOD. JEROME: The heart of Julian, the persecutor, of Nero, of Decius, are their hearts in the hand of God? No, the hearts in the hand of God are those who govern their body, who bring it into subjection and compel it to servitude, lest preaching to others they themselves should be rejected.[8] These are the kings of whom Wisdom says in Proverbs, "He gives kingship to kings."[9] HOMILIES ON THE PSALMS 54 (PSALM 143).[10]

A LITERAL INTERPRETATION IS NOT POSSIBLE. JEROME: Was the heart of Julian, the persecutor, in the hand of God? The heart of Saul, was it in the hand of God? Was the heart of Manasseh in the hand of God? The heart of Ahab? Were the hearts of all the impious kings of Judah in the hand of God? Do you see that this verse does not admit of a literal interpretation? The kings, therefore, are the saints, and their hearts are in the hand of the Lord. . . . The following words of the apostle are appropriate here: "But I chastise my body and bring it into subjection, lest perhaps after preaching to others, I myself should be rejected."[11] May our soul be in command, our body in subjection. Then Christ will come at once to make his abode with us. HOMILIES ON THE PSALMS 9 (PSALM 75).[12]

21:6 A Lying Tongue

DO NOT BE DOUBLE-MINDED OR DOUBLE-TONGUED. DIDACHE: Do not be double-minded or double-tongued, for a double tongue is a "deadly snare." Your words shall not be dishonest or hollow but substantiated by action. Do not be greedy or threatening or hypocritical or malicious or arrogant. Do not plot against your neighbor. Do not hate anybody. Reprove some, pray for others, and still others love more than your own life. DIDACHE 2.4-7.[13]

21:8 The Way of the Guilty Is Crooked

HABITUAL EVILDOERS ARE PERVERSE. CHRYSOSTOM: "For God sends crooked ways to the perverse.". . . Indeed, nothing makes people so stupid as does habitual evildoing. When a person is deceitful, when he is unjust, when he is churlish (and these, to be sure, are different forms of evildoing), when, without having been wronged in any way himself, he inflicts pain, when he connives at trickery—how will he not be exhibiting signs of utter stupidity? HOMILIES ON THE GOSPEL OF JOHN 41.[14]

21:13 The Cry of the Poor

ONLY THE MERCIFUL CAN MERIT THE MERCY OF GOD. CYPRIAN: He will not be able to merit the mercy of God who himself has not been merciful, nor will [he] gain any request from the divine love by his prayers who has not been hu-

---

[6]FC 46:243.* [7]FC 48:362. [8]See 1 Cor 9:27. [9]Cf. Prov 8:15. [10]FC 48:385. [11]1 Cor 9:27. [12]FC 48:67*. [13]LCC 1:172. [14]FC 33:421.

mane toward the prayer of the poor. WORKS AND ALMSGIVING 5.[15]

ILL-GOTTEN GAINS ARE UNACCEPTABLE TO GOD. BASIL THE GREAT: Benefactions to the needy, financed by unjust gains, are not acceptable with God. Even one who refrains from committing injustices, and yet does not share the goods he possesses with anyone, is not deserving of praise.... If you will make an offering to God from the fruits of injustice and rapine, it would be better not to possess such wealth and not to make an offering. ON MERCY AND JUSTICE.[16]

THOSE WHO GIVE ALMS. CYRIL OF ALEXANDRIA: Do you not agree that poverty, as I said, is more cruel than any beast of prey? Therefore you must aid those who are fallen under it. Incline your ear to the poor and listen to them, as it is written: "For he who stops his ears that he may not hear the feeble shall also cry, and there shall be none to listen." Give so that you may receive; hear so that you may be heard; sow the little you have so that you may reap much. Besides, the pleasure of the body is short and temporary and ends in rottenness. But almsgiving and charity to the poor crown those who practice them with glory from God and lead to that incorruptible happiness which Christ bestows on those who love him. COMMENTARY ON LUKE, HOMILY 103.[17]

21:19 Better to Live in a Desert Land

WIVES SEEK MODESTY AND MEEKNESS. APOSTOLIC CONSTITUTIONS: "It is better to dwell in the wilderness than with a contentious and an angry woman." You wives, therefore, demonstrate your piety by your modesty and meekness to all outside the church, whether they are women or men, in order to their conversion and improvement in the faith. And since we have warned you and instructed you briefly, whom we do esteem our sisters, daughters and members, as being wise yourselves, persevere all your lives in a blameless course of life. Seek to know such kinds

of learning whereby you may arrive at the kingdom of our Lord, and please him, and so rest for ever and ever. CONSTITUTIONS OF THE HOLY APOSTLES 1.3.10.[18]

21:20 The Wise Are Frugal, but Fools Are Wasteful

BETTER TO PONDER WISDOM THAN TO SWALLOW IT ALL AT ONCE. AUGUSTINE: Another passage of Scripture speaks of the precious treasure of wisdom and describes ruminating on wisdom as clean and not ruminating as unclean: "A precious treasure rests in the mouth of a wise man; but a foolish man swallows it up." Symbols of this kind, either in words or in things, give useful and pleasant exercise to intelligent minds in the way of inquiry and comparison. But formerly people were required not only to hear [of food laws] but to practice many such things. For at that time it was necessary that, by deeds as well as by words, those things should be foreshadowed which were in after times to be revealed. After the revelation by Christ and in Christ, the community of believers is not burdened with the practice of the observances but is admonished to give heed to the prophecy. This is our reason for accounting no animals unclean, in accordance with the saying of the Lord and of the apostle, while we are not opposed to the Old Testament, where some animals are pronounced unclean. REPLY TO FAUSTUS THE MANICHAEAN 6.7.[19]

ENJOYING THE FLAVOR OF THE WORD. AUGUSTINE: So those who hear and out of carelessness forget, so to say swallow what they have heard, so that they no longer have a taste of it in their mouth but just bury what they hear under forgetfulness. But those who meditate on "the law of the Lord day and night"[20] are chewing the cud, as it were, and enjoying the flavor of the word with a kind of palate of the heart. SERMON 149.4.[21]

---

[15]FC 36:231. [16]FC 9:507-8. [17]CGSL 415**. [18]ANF 7:395*. [19]NPNF 1 4:171*. [20]Ps 1:2. [21]WSA 3 5:20.

21:22 Demolishing the Fortifications

Wisdom Demolishes Fortresses of Lies.
Origen: "The wise person assaults strong cities
and demolishes the fortifications in which the
ungodly trusted." Do you think when Solomon
said this he wanted to teach us that the wise person seized cities and demolished fortifications
built from stones? Or, rather, is he indicating that
the city and the walls are the doctrines of the
ungodly and the syllogisms of philosophers, with
which they augment every impiety that is contrary to the divine law and that is observed
among pagans or barbarians? And those things
that the heretics, with attestations from the
Scriptures, place as if in high mountains must
also be considered to be among these cities that
are both fortified and placed in the mountains.
Cities such as these, therefore, are demolished by
every wise person who proclaims the word of
truth. Homilies on Joshua 18.3.[22]

21:26 The Wicked Covet All Day

The Entire Human Life. Evagrius of Pontus: It belongs to angels never to have evil
desires; it is human sometimes to have evil
desires and other times not to have them; it
belongs to demons always to have evil desires.
The expression "all the day" signifies the entire

life. So also, "continue in the fear of the Lord all
the day"[23] applies to the whole life. Scholia on
Proverbs 231.21.26.[24]

The Soul's Effort. Gregory the Great:
When the soul does not direct its efforts to
higher things, neglecting itself, it stoops to concern itself with low desires, and when it does not
restrain itself by aiming vigorously at higher
things, it is wounded by the hunger of a base
cupidity. Consequently, as it neglects the con-
straints of discipline, it is the more distracted in
its craving for pleasure. Therefore, it is written by
the same Solomon, "The slothful man is given
utterly to desires." Pastoral Care 3.15.16.[25]

21:27 A Sacrifice Offered with Evil Intent

**God Repudiates Offerings Withdrawn
from the Needy.** Gregory the Great:" The
sacrifices of the wicked are abominable, because
they are offered of wickedness." These often go so
far as to offer to God what they withdraw from
the needy. But the Lord shows with what
reproach he disowns them. Pastoral Care
3.21.22.[26]

---

[22]FC 105:165*. [23]Prov 23:17. [24]SC 340:326. [25]ACW 11:134-35*. [26]ACW 11:161-62.

22:1-29 A GOOD NAME
IS BETTER THAN RICHES

[1]A good name is to be chosen rather than
    great riches,
  and favor is better than silver or gold.
[2]The rich and the poor meet together;

  the Lord is the maker of them all.
[3]A prudent man sees danger and hides
    himself;
  but the simple go on, and suffer for it.

⁴The reward for humility and fear of the
LORD
   is riches and honor and life.
⁵Thorns and snares are in the way of the
      perverse;
   he who guards himself will keep far from
      them.
⁶Train up a child in the way he should go,
   and when he is old he will not depart
      from it.
⁷The rich rules over the poor,
   and the borrower is the slave of the
      lender.
⁸He who sows injustice will reap calamity,
   and the rod of his fury will fail.
⁹He who has a bountiful eye will be blessed,
   for he shares his bread with the poor.
¹⁰Drive out a scoffer, and strife will go
      out,
   and quarreling and abuse will cease.
¹¹He who loves purity of heart,
   and whose speech is gracious, will have
      the king as his friend.
¹²The eyes of the LORD keep watch over
      knowledge,
   but he overthrows the words of the
      faithless.
¹³The sluggard says, "There is a lion
      outside!
   I shall be slain in the streets!"
¹⁴The mouth of a loose woman is a deep
      pit;
   he with whom the LORD is angry will fall
      into it.
¹⁵Folly is bound up in the heart of a child,
   but the rod of discipline drives it far from
      him.
¹⁶He who oppresses the poor to increase

his own wealth,
   or gives to the rich, will only come to
      want.
¹⁷Incline your ear, and hear the words of
      the wise,
   and apply your mind to my knowledge;
¹⁸for it will be pleasant if you keep them
      within you,
   if all of them are ready on your lips.
¹⁹That your trust may be in the LORD,
   I have made them known to you today,
      even to you.

²⁰Have I not written for you thirty sayings
   of admonition and knowledge,*
²¹to show you what is right and true,
   that you may give a true answer to those
      who sent you?

²²Do not rob the poor, because he is poor,
   or crush the afflicted at the gate;
²³for the LORD will plead their cause
   and despoil of life those who despoil them.
²⁴Make no friendship with a man given to
      anger,
   nor go with a wrathful man,
²⁵lest you learn his ways
   and entangle yourself in a snare.
²⁶Be not one of those who give pledges,
   who become surety for debts.
²⁷If you have nothing with which to pay,
   why should your bed be taken from under
      you?
²⁸Remove not the ancient landmark
   which your fathers have set.
²⁹Do you see a man skilful in his work?
   he will stand before kings;
   he will not stand before obscure men.

*LXX But you describe those things for yourself in threefold fashion according to the largeness of your heart.

OVERVIEW: The wise possess much more than riches, since a good name is better than wealth (AMBROSE). The wealthy are given wealth to help the poor, the poor are made to test the rich. The Lord helps the poor by the rich and tests the rich by the poor. Let the rich lighten their load by giving away some of their possessions to the needy (AUGUSTINE). A holy sharing of material substance and divine lessons between rich and poor can be of mutual benefit on the road of life (CAESARIUS).

The book of Proverbs offers training that children need and from which they are unlikely to waver in their adult years (BASIL); therefore, we should be zealous for virtuous habits in the young (BEDE). Those who persist in disobedience, however, should be dismissed from a monastic community (BASIL). A slanderer can easily fall into a deep pit and never escape (AMBROSE). Solomon advises that his wisdom be read in a threefold manner (ORIGEN), and indeed the wisdom literature has a threefold division of scriptural teaching, moving from Proverbs to Ecclesiastes to Songs, reflecting moral, physical and theological dimensions (EVAGRIUS). The meaning of Scripture also consists of body, soul, and spirit (CHRYSOSTOM), corresponding with three kinds of spiritual knowledge (JOHN CASSIAN).

When confronted by spiritual distraction, it is best to distance yourself from it (BASIL). The ancient landmarks should never be violated (ORIGEN). Indeed, we should beware of changing the apostolic testimony (EVAGRIUS). The Nicene Creed in particular is an everlasting boundary that must not be altered (CYRIL OF ALEXANDRIA). To demand constant change in religion is to transgress the ancient bounds (VINCENT OF LÉRINS), and recent teachings should be rejected (ACACIUS OF BEROEA AND JOHN OF ANTIOCH). Let us, therefore, be satisfied with the ancient boundaries that have been revealed (JOHN OF DAMASCUS).

22:1 A Good Name Is Better Than Silver or Gold

THE WISE POSSESS MUCH MORE THAN RICHES. AMBROSE: A good name is more excellent than money, and good favor is better than heaps of silver. Faith itself redounds to itself, sufficiently rich and more than rich in its possession. There is nothing which is not the possession of the wise person except what is contrary to virtue, and wherever he goes he finds all things to be his. The whole world is his possession, since he uses it all as his own. LETTER 15.[1]

22:2 Rich and Poor

THE LORD HELPS THE POOR BY THE RICH AND TESTS THE RICH BY THE POOR. AUGUSTINE: "The poor man and the rich have met each other." Where have they met each other? In this life. This one was born, that one was born, their lives were crossed, they have met each other. And who made them? The Lord. The rich man, to help the poor; the poor man, to test the rich. SERMON 39.6.[2]

AUGUSTINE: The rich and the poor meet together. In what way, except in this present life? The rich and the poor are born alike. You meet one another as you walk along the way together. The poor must not defraud the rich; the rich must not oppress the poor. The one has need, the other has plenty, but "the Lord is the maker of them both." The Lord helps the one in need by the one who has; by the one who has not the Lord tests the one who has. SERMON 35 (85).7.[3]

TO GIVE AWAY POSSESSIONS IS TO LIGHTEN THE LOAD OF THE RICH. AUGUSTINE: Both of you are traveling the same road; you are companions on the journey. Lightly laden are the poor man's shoulders, but yours are burdened with heavy luggage. Give away some of the load that is weighing you down; give away some of your luggage to the needy man—and you will thus afford

[1]FC 26:81.* [2]WSA 3 2:219. [3]NPNF 1 6:368**.

relief both to yourself and to your companion. The Scripture says, "The rich and the poor have met one another, but the Lord has made them both." Where have they met, except in this life? The one is now arrayed in costly garments, while the other is clad in rags. When did they meet? Both were born naked, and even the rich man was born poor. Let him disregard what he found when he had come; let him consider what he brought with him. SERMON 11.6.[4]

HOLY SHARING OF POOR AND RICH. CAESARIUS OF ARLES: I beseech you, beloved brethren, be eager to engage in divine reading whatever hours you can. Moreover, since what a person procures in this life by reading or good works will be the food of his soul forever, let no one try to excuse himself by saying he has not learned letters at all. If those who are illiterate love God in truth, they look for learned people who can read the sacred Scriptures to them. This even illiterate merchants have learned to do, for they hire literate mercenaries and through their reading or writing acquire great profits. Now, if people do this for earthly wealth, how much more should we do it for the sake of eternal life? It often happens that a learned person may be poor in food or clothing, while one who does not know letters has more abundant wealth. The illiterate person who abounds in earthly goods summons the poor learned one, and they mutually give each other what they need. The one by reading feeds the other with the sweet word of God, while the other by giving material substance does not allow his neighbor to suffer want. The learned man should satisfy the soul of the rich man, while the latter should warm the body of the poor man with clothing and refresh him with earthly food. If this is done with charity, there will be fulfilled what is written: "The rich and poor have met one another: the Lord is the maker of them both." Being pressed down with a heavy burden by possessing more than was necessary, the rich man was unable to walk, while

the poor man perhaps was learned but was failing because of not having the necessities of life. For this reason, there was holy sharing on the part of both men. While the rich man gave the poor material wealth from his possessions, the poor man imparted the sacred lessons to the rich, and they both happily reach the eternal country on the road of this life. SERMON 8.1.[5]

22:6 The Child Trained in Youth Will Not Waver as an Adult

PROVERBS OFFERS TRAINING THAT CHILDREN NEED. BASIL THE GREAT: Thus, here also it calls him a new child who was reborn through the washing of regeneration and educated and made childlike, who is made fit for the kingdom of heaven through this process in the same way. The book of Proverbs, therefore, provides training which imparts perception and understanding to the recently born child who is hungry for rational and genuine milk: a perception of present realities but an understanding of future realities. For the child is educated in human matters and given a perception of reality so that he would neither be enslaved to shameful desires nor long for the empty glory of this world. Beyond this, Proverbs confers an understanding of the coming age and encourages faith in the promises by its words. HOMILY ON THE BEGINNING OF PROVERBS 13.[6]

BE ZEALOUS FOR VIRTUOUS HABITS IN THE YOUNG. BEDE: It is well known that the Lord grants a great many in their old age to be changed and relieved of the vices that they had in their youth. It is also well known, on the other hand, that some abandon in their old age the virtues with which they were seen to be marked in their youth. But because people much more commonly follow the habits with which they were imbued as children for the rest of their lives, it became a proverbial saying that a man will not change in

---

[4]FC 11:364. [5]FC 31:49-50. [6]PG 31:413.

his old age whatever he began to do as a youth, even though it does not always happen that way. The proverb is formulated like this, therefore, to persuade its readers to be zealous for virtue in youth, lest they be unable as adults to learn the practices which they had despised to acquire at a tender age, for "the odor of that with which a new vessel is imbued will endure for a long time."[7] COMMENTARY ON PROVERBS 22.6.[8]

22:10 No Scoffer, No Strife

THOSE WHO PERSIST IN DISOBEDIENCE. BASIL THE GREAT: If some persist in their disobedience, finding fault in secret and not openly stating their grievance, thus becoming the cause of quarreling in the community and undermining the authority of the commands given, they should be dismissed from the community as teachers of disobedience and rebellion. For the Scripture says, "Cast out the scoffer from the council, and contention shall go out with him" and also, "Put away the evil one from yourselves, for a little leaven corrupts the whole lump."[9] THE LONG RULES 47.[10]

22:14 Take Care Not to Be Entrapped

A SLANDERER CAN FALL INTO HIS OWN PIT. AMBROSE: The mouth of one speaking ill is a great pit, a steep precipice for the innocent, but steeper for one of ill will. An innocent person, though easily credulous, falls quickly,[11] but when he has fallen rises again. The slanderer is thrown headlong by his own acts, from which he will never emerge or escape. LETTER 15.[12]

22:20 Numerical Divisions for Instructional Purposes

SOLOMON'S WISDOM IS READ IN A THREE-FOLD MANNER. ORIGEN: Solomon counsels that what we read "be transcribed in the heart in a threefold manner." I shall make known to your ears that which occurs to my mind, even beyond

the things that we have said, and you yourself [should] do what is written: "Let one speak and the rest judge."[13] Therefore, as I speak what I perceive, you consider and judge if it is correct or not correct. HOMILIES ON JOSHUA 21.[14]

THE THREEFOLD DIVISION OF WISDOM LITERATURE. EVAGRIUS OF PONTUS: He who has opened his heart through purity, contemplates the words of God in their practical, physical and theological sense. Accordingly, the whole corpus of Scripture may be divided into three parts: ethical, physical and theological. Consequently, Proverbs corresponds to the first part, Ecclesiastes to the second, and Song of Songs to the third.[15] SCHOLIA ON PROVERBS 247.22.20.[16]

THE MEANING OF SCRIPTURE ALSO CONSISTS OF BODY, SOUL AND SPIRIT. CHRYSOSTOM: As human beings consist of body, soul and spirit, so also Scripture consists of the body of letters, by which the ignorant man is benefited; and that is called "manual instruction." Second, it consists of soul, that is, a higher meaning,[17] which the one who is higher in learning understands. It also consists of spirit, that is, a more sublime and spiritual contemplation which those who are perfect understand and speak. COMMENTARY ON THE PROVERBS OF SOLOMON, FRAGMENT 22.20.[18]

THREE KINDS OF SPIRITUAL KNOWLEDGE. JOHN CASSIAN: Now, there are three kinds of spiritual knowledge—tropology, allegory and anagogy—about which it is said in Proverbs, "But you describe those things for yourself in threefold fashion according to the largeness of your heart." CONFERENCE 14.8.1.[19]

---

[7]Horace Epistle 1.2.69-70. [8]CCL 119B:112-13. [9]1 Cor 5:13, 6. [10]FC 9:325*. [11]Cf. Prov 14:15. [12]FC 26:82. [13]1 Cor 14:29. [14]FC 105:186-87*. [15]This threefold classification for the books of Scripture and its teaching in the wisdom literature, including the stages of spiritual progress, was early established by Origen in the prologue of his *Commentary on the Song of Songs* ("moral, natural and contemplative") and followed by other writers. See the present volume at Song 1:1. [16]SC 340:342. [17]Gk *anagōgē*. [18]PG 64:728. [19]ACW 57:509.

22:24 Do Not Befriend an Angry Person

Distance Yourself from Spiritual Distraction. Basil the Great: A secluded and remote habitation also contributes to the removal of distraction from the soul. Living among those who are unscrupulous and disdainful in their attitude toward an exact observance of the commandments is dangerous, as is shown by the following words of Solomon: "Do not be a friend to an angry man, and do not walk with a furious man, lest perhaps you learn his ways and take snares unto your soul." The Long Rules 5.[20]

22:28 Ancient Landmarks Should Not Be Disturbed

The Apocrypha Is Set Outside the Ancient Boundaries. Origen: It is, however, obvious that many examples exist of passages, taken by the apostles or by the Evangelists and put into the New Testament, which we never read among those Scriptures we hold to be canonical but which are found in the apocryphal writings and may be clearly demonstrated to have been taken from them. But not even this must be thought to argue for acceptance of the apocryphal writings, for "the ancient landmarks which our fathers have set must not be removed." It could have happened that the apostles or Evangelists, filled with the Holy Spirit, knew what ought to be taken from those writings and what ought to be refused. But for us, who do not have such a great fullness of the Spirit, it is not without danger to attempt such a discrimination. Commentary on the Song of Songs, Prologue.[21]

Ancient Landmarks Must Not Be Violated in Translating the Scriptures. Origen: Consider whether it would not be well to remember the words, "You shall not remove the ancient landmarks which your fathers have set." Nor do I say this because I hesitate to examine the Jewish Scriptures, comparing them with ours and noticing their differences. This, if it is not arrogant

to say it, I have already to a great extent done to the best of my ability, laboring hard to get at the meaning in all the editions and various readings. I paid particular attention to the Septuagint translation, lest I might be found to accredit any forgery to the churches which are under heaven and give an occasion to those who seek such a pretext for gratifying their desire to slander prominent persons and to bring forth some accusation against those who are outstanding in our fellowship. And I make it my endeavor not to be ignorant of their various readings, so that in my controversies with the Jews I may not quote to them what is not found in their copies and that I may make some use of what they accept, even if it is not found in our Scriptures. For if we are so prepared for them in our discussions, they will not, as is their manner, scornfully laugh at Gentile believers on the grounds that we do not know the true readings recorded in their texts. Letter to Julius Africanus 5.[22]

Beware of Changing the Ancient Boundaries. Evagrius of Pontus: The one who moves the boundaries of piety demonstrates either superstition or impiety. And the one who moves the boundaries of courage changes it into either audacity or cowardice. In the same manner, this applies to other virtues as well as to dogmas and other matters of faith. This especially pertains to the doctrine of the holy Trinity. Thus, whoever rejects the divinity of the Holy Spirit rejects baptism; and whoever names some others as gods introduces a whole pantheon of gods. Scholia on Proverbs 249.22.28.[23]

The Nicene Creed Is an Everlasting Boundary. Cyril of Alexandria: We do not permit the faith or the symbol of the faith defined by our holy fathers assembled in their day in Nicea to be shaken by anyone, and we do not trust ourselves or others to change a word of what was laid down there, or to depart from a

---

[20]FC 9:245-46*. [21]OSW 244. [22]ANF 4:387**. [23]SC 340:344.

single syllable of it. For we remember the one who said, "Do not alter the everlasting boundaries which your fathers set." LETTER TO JOHN OF ANTIOCH 39.7.[24]

VIOLATING THE ANCIENT BOUNDS. VINCENT OF LÉRINS: I cannot help wondering about such madness in certain people, the dreadful impiety of their blinded minds, their insatiable lust for error that they are not content with the traditional rule of faith as once and for all received from antiquity but are driven to seek another novelty daily. They are possessed by a permanent desire to change religion, to add something and to take something away—as though the dogma were not divine so that it has to be revealed only once. But they take it for a merely human institution, which cannot be perfected except by constant emendations, rather, by constant corrections. Yet, the divine prophecies say, "Pass not beyond the ancient bounds which your fathers have set," and "Judge not against a judge,"[25] and "he that breaks a hedge, a serpent shall bite him."[26] COMMONITORIES 21.[27]

RECENT TEACHINGS MUST GENERALLY BE REJECTED. ACACIUS OF BEROEA AND JOHN OF ANTIOCH: We reject all the doctrines introduced recently either through letters or through pamphlets as confusing the common people, since we are content with the ancient legislation of the fathers and obey the one who said, "Remove not the ancient landmarks which your fathers set up." LETTER TO CYRIL OF ALEXANDRIA 2.[28]

SATISFIED WITH THE ANCIENT BOUNDARIES. JOHN OF DAMASCUS: He has revealed to us what it was expedient for us to know, whereas that which we were unable to bear he has withheld. With these things let us be content, and in them let us abide, and let us not step over the ancient bounds or pass beyond the divine tradition. ORTHODOX FAITH 1.1.[29]

---

[24]TCC 144. [25]Sir 8:14. [26]Eccles 10:8. [27]FC 7:305-6*. [28]FC 77:183. [29]FC 37:166.

23:1-35 SURELY THERE IS A FUTURE FOR THOSE WHO ARE WISE

[1]*When you sit down to eat with a ruler,*
  observe carefully what[l] is before you;
[2]*and put a knife to your throat*
  if you are a man given to appetite.
[3]*Do not desire his delicacies,*
  for they are deceptive food.
[4]*Do not toil to acquire wealth;*
  be wise enough to desist.
[5]*When your eyes light upon it, it is gone;*
  for suddenly it takes to itself wings,
  flying like an eagle toward heaven.

[6]*Do not eat the bread of a man who is stingy;*
  do not desire his delicacies;
[7]*for he is like one who is inwardly reckoning.[m]*
  "Eat and drink!" he says to you;
  but his heart is not with you.
[8]*You will vomit up the morsels which you*
      have eaten,
  and waste your pleasant words.
[9]*Do not speak in the hearing of a fool,*
  for he will despise the wisdom of your
      words.

¹⁰Do not remove an ancient landmark
   or enter the fields of the fatherless;
¹¹for their Redeemer is strong;
   he will plead their cause against you.
¹²Apply your mind to instruction
   and your ear to words of knowledge.
¹³Do not withhold discipline from a
   child;
   if you beat him with a rod, he will not
   die.
¹⁴If you beat him with the rod
   you will save his life from Sheol.
¹⁵My son, if your heart is wise,
   my heart too will be glad.
¹⁶My soul will rejoice
   when your lips speak what is right.
¹⁷Let not your heart envy sinners,
   but continue in the fear of the Lord all
   the day.
¹⁸Surely there is a future,
   and your hope will not be cut off.

¹⁹Hear, my son, and be wise,
   and direct your mind in the way.
²⁰Be not among winebibbers,
   or among gluttonous eaters of
   meat;
²¹for the drunkard and the glutton will
   come to poverty,
   and drowsiness will clothe a man with
   rags.

²²Hearken to your father who begot you,
   and do not despise your mother when
   she is old.
²³Buy truth, and do not sell it;
   buy wisdom, instruction, and

understanding.
²⁴The father of the righteous will greatly
   rejoice;
   he who begets a wise son will be glad in
   him.
²⁵Let your father and mother be glad,
   let her who bore you rejoice.

²⁶My son, give me your heart,
   and let your eyes observeⁿ my ways.
²⁷For a harlot is a deep pit;
   an adventuress is a narrow well.
²⁸She lies in wait like a robber
   and increases the faithless among men.

²⁹Who has woe? Who has sorrow?
   Who has strife? Who has complaining?
Who has wounds without cause?
   Who has redness of eyes?
³⁰Those who tarry long over wine,
   those who go to try mixed wine.
³¹Do not look at wine when it is red,
   when it sparkles in the cup
   and goes down smoothly.*
³²At the last it bites like a serpent,
   and stings like an adder.
³³Your eyes will see strange things,
   and your mind utter perverse
   things.
³⁴You will be like one who lies down in the
   midst of the sea,
   like one who lies on the top of a mast.^o
³⁵"They struck me," you will say,^p "but I
   was not hurt;
   they beat me, but I did not feel it.
When shall I awake?
   I will seek another drink."

l Or *who* **m** Heb obscure **n** Another reading is *delight in* **o** Heb obscure **p** Gk Syr Vg Tg: Heb lacks *you will say* *LXX *If you set your eyes on cups and goblets, you will walk naked as a pestle.*

OVERVIEW: Scripture must be understood in a spiritual sense (EVAGRIUS). The passage on dining with a ruler, for example, pertains to Christ (CHRYSOSTOM), for it is from this regal table that we spiritually receive the body and blood of Christ. The table is Christ, and he is also the host, the food and drink, of the banquet (AUGUSTINE). Therefore, to understand this table both mental and spiritual perceptions are needed (ORIGEN). This table is also a table of Scripture from which we can pluck many flowers (JEROME). We should not be gluttonous for sweet foods (CLEMENT OF ALEXANDRIA).

We can become ensnared in envy if we establish contact with one who is envious (BASIL). Plato advised correction and chastisement for those who are undisciplined and degenerate (CLEMENT OF ALEXANDRIA). Indeed, the discipline of children is viewed under the analogy of God's discipline of humanity (BASIL). If evil will is given total freedom, there would be no point in rebuking careless shepherds (AUGUSTINE). After all, sins not corrected now will be punished in the future (CAESARIUS).

The soul is the mother of our mind, leading us to enlightenment by practical virtues (EVAGRIUS). Charity wants you to give her your heart, not just your money (AUGUSTINE). Beware, though, of an affair with a harlot, which can cause endless disaster (CHRYSOSTOM). Just as redness of the eyes can indicate death to God's Word (CLEMENT OF ALEXANDRIA), so also woe and sorrow can indicate transgression of one's baptismal covenant (BASIL).

The clergy, indeed, ought always to be sober (APOSTOLIC CONSTITUTIONS). The soul of a drunkard is like the flesh of a leper, and excuses for drunkenness are displeasing to God (CAESARIUS). Since the mind guides the soul in life as the pilot steers a ship at sea, it is a sad state to be asleep to pain but awake to wine (GREGORY THE GREAT).

23:1 When You Dine with a Ruler, Observe Carefully

SCRIPTURE MUST BE UNDERSTOOD IN A SPIRITUAL SENSE. EVAGRIUS OF PONTUS: The divine Scripture should be understood in an intellectual[1] and spiritual sense, because the knowledge of sense perception, literally understood,[2] is not the truth. SCHOLIA ON PROVERBS 251.23.1.[3]

DEEPER MEANING OF THIS VERSE PERTAINS TO CHRIST. CHRYSOSTOM: "If you sit at the dinner table of a prince, understand with prudence what is set before you." Christ is anticipated here as the prince. His table and food are the words of his doctrine and his eternal goods which he has prepared for those who love him. Each Christian sits at his dinner table. The one who understands with prudence what Jesus has taught with his works and words extends his hand, which means that with his works he begins to show that he is an imitator of Christ, made humble, a peaceful lover of all and patient in tribulations. The one who does not do this but instead gazes with eagerness at the pleasures of the world must give up any desire for eternal goods which at any rate he will never own. The pleasures of the world are characteristic of a false life, and those who love them will never enjoy eternal possessions. COMMENTARY ON THE PROVERBS OF SOLOMON, FRAGMENT 23.1.[4]

WE RECEIVE THE BODY AND BLOOD OF CHRIST. AUGUSTINE: What is "the table of a powerful man" except that one from which is taken the body and blood of him who has laid down his life for us? And what is to sit at it except to approach humbly? And what is to consider and understand the things that are set before you except to reflect worthily upon so great a grace? TRACTATES ON THE GOSPEL OF JOHN 84.2.[5]

THE TABLE IS CHRIST. AUGUSTINE: You are approaching the table of a potentate. You, the

---

[1]Gk *noētos.* [2]Gk *kata tēn historian.* [3]SC 340:346. [4]PG 64:729. [5]FC 90:133.

faithful, know what table you are approaching. . . . What regal table are you approaching? One who sets himself before you, not a table spread by the skill of cooks. Christ sets his table before you, namely, himself. Approach this table, and take your fill. Be poor, and you will have your fill. SERMON 332.2.[6]

CHRIST IS THE HOST, THE FOOD AND DRINK OF THE BANQUET. AUGUSTINE: It is certainly a great table where the lord of the table is himself the banquet. Nobody feeds his guests on himself, yet that is what the Lord Christ did, being himself the host, himself the food and drink. So the martyrs recognized what they ate and drank, so that they could give back the same kind of thing. SERMON 329.1.[7]

MENTAL AND SPIRITUAL PERCEPTION ARE NEEDED. ORIGEN: What therefore is "the table of the powerful one," except the mind of that one who says, "I can do all things in Christ who strengthens me";[8] and "when I am weak, then I am strong"?[9] On this "clean table of the powerful one," that is, in his heart, in his mind is offered "a loaf" to the Lord. At the table of this powerful apostle, if you sit to eat, "understand intelligently what is set before you," that is, perceive spiritually what is said by him. HOMILIES ON LEVITICUS 13.4.6.[10]

THE TABLE OF SCRIPTURE. JEROME: Holy writ warns us to partake of the feast prudently when we have been invited to dine at the table of a rich man. I might say that a rich man's table of Scripture has been laid before us. We enter a meadow filled with flowers; here the rose blushes; there the lilies glisten white; everywhere flowers abound in all varieties. HOMILIES ON THE PSALMS II (PSALM 77).[11]

23:3 Foods That Deceive

BUT DO NOT TURN INTO A GIANT MOUTH. CLEMENT OF ALEXANDRIA: There is no limit to

the gluttony that these people practice. Truly, in ever inventing a multitude of new sweets and ever seeking recipes of every description, they are shipwrecked on pastries and honey cakes and desserts.

To me, a man of this sort seems nothing more than one great mouth. . . . As for us, who seek a heavenly food, we must restrain the belly and keep it under the control of heaven. CHRIST THE EDUCATOR 2.1.4.[12]

23:6 Do Not Dine with One Who Is Stingy

WE CAN BECOME ENSNARED. BASIL THE GREAT: Wise, therefore, was he who forbids us even to dine in company with an envious man, and in mentioning this companionship at table, he implies a reference to all other social contacts as well. Just as we are careful to keep material which is easily inflammable as far away as possible from fire, so we must refrain insofar as we can from contracting friendships in circles of which envious persons are members. By so doing, we place ourselves beyond the range of their shafts. We can be caught in the toils of envy only by establishing intimacy with it. HOMILY CONCERNING ENVY.[13]

23:13-14 Punish Sinners and Even Children in Order to Save Them

PLATO ADVISED CORRECTION AND CHASTISEMENT. CLEMENT OF ALEXANDRIA: Correction and chastisement, as their very name implies, are blows inflicted upon the soul, restraining sin, warding off death, leading those enslaved by vice back to self-control. Thus, Plato, recognizing that correction has the greatest influence and is the most effective purification, echoes the Word when he claims that one who is notably lacking in purification becomes undisciplined and degenerate because he was left uncorrected, while one who is to be truly happy

---

[6]*WSA* 3 9:194-95*. [7]*WSA* 3 9:182*. [8]Phil 4:13. [9]2 Cor 12:10. [10]FC 83:241. [11]FC 48:79. [12]FC 23:95-96. [13]FC 9:468-69.

should be the most purified and virtuous.[14] CHRIST THE EDUCATOR 1.9.82.[15]

DISCIPLINE OF CHILDREN IS PARALLELED BY GOD'S DISCIPLINE OF US. BASIL THE GREAT: As small children who are negligent in learning become more attentive and obedient after being punished by their teacher or tutor, and as they do not listen before the lash, but, after feeling the pain of a beating, hear and respond as though their ears were just recently opened, improving also in memory, so likewise with those who neglect divine doctrine and spurn the commandments. For, after they experience God's correction and discipline, then the commandments of God which had always been known to them and always neglected are most readily received as though by ears freshly cleansed. HOMILY ON THE BEGINNING OF PROVERBS 5.[16]

IF EVIL WILL IS GIVEN TOTAL FREEDOM, THERE IS NO POINT IN REBUKING CARELESS SHEPHERDS. AUGUSTINE: If the evil will is always to be left to its own freedom, why are careless shepherds rebuked, and why is it said to them, "The wandering sheep you have not called back, that which was lost you have not sought"? LETTER 173.[17]

SINS NOT CORRECTED NOW WILL BE PUNISHED. CAESARIUS OF ARLES: When someone presumes to commit a sin against God, he ought to suffer a monastic penance. This should be done in a kind and devout spirit, so that through rebuke he may be corrected in this life in such a way that he may not perish in the future. For every sin which is not corrected in this world will be punished in the future life. Sacred Scripture speaks thus about the son and the servant: "Strike him with the rod," it says, "and you will save him from the nether world." SERMONS 235.3.[18]

23:22 Mother and Father Should Each Be Heeded

THE STRUCTURE OF THE HUMAN PSYCHE. EVAGRIUS OF PONTUS: As the ancient saying goes, soul[19] is the mother of the mind,[20] because it is the soul which leads the mind to enlightenment by means of practical virtues. SCHOLIA ON PROVERBS 258.23.22.[21]

23:26 Give Me Your Heart

CHARITY WANTS YOU TO GIVE YOUR HEART. AUGUSTINE: If you don't give yourself, you will lose yourself. Charity herself speaks through wisdom and tells you something to save you from panicking at being told, "Give yourself." If anyone wanted to sell you a farm he would say to you, "Give me your gold," and if it was something else, "Give me your coppers," "Give me your silver." Now listen to what charity says to you, speaking through the mouth of wisdom: "Give me your heart, son. Give me," she says. Give her what? "Your heart, son." It was ill when it was with you, when you kept it to yourself. You were being pulled this way and that by toys and trifles and wanton, destructive loves. Take your heart away from all that. Where are you to drag it to, where are you to put it? "Give me your heart," she says. "Let it be mine, and it won't be lost to you." SERMON 34.7.[22]

23:27 A Harlot Is a Deep Pit

AN AFFAIR CAN CAUSE ENDLESS DISASTER. CHRYSOSTOM: Solomon compared the love of [such a] woman with the deep pit. She calls a halt only when she sees that her lover has been stripped of all his possessions. Even more so, she does not stop then but decks herself out more elaborately and insults him in his humiliation, and draws ridicule upon him, and causes him so much misfortune that words are inadequate to describe it. HOMILIES ON THE GOSPEL OF JOHN 87.[23]

---

[14]Plato *Soph.* 230DE. [15]FC 23:73-74. [16]PG 31:396. [17]FC 30:75. [18]FC 66:206*. [19]Gk *psychē*. [20]Gk *nous*. [21]SC 340:352-54. [22]WSA 3 2:169*. [23]FC 41:469**.

23:29-31 Those Who Linger over Much Wine

DEATH TO GOD'S WORD. CLEMENT OF ALEXANDRIA: By the mention of redness of eyes—a sign of death—it is made clear that the wine-bibber is already dead to the Word and to reason. It declares his death to the Lord. If one forgets the motives that prompt him to seek the true life, he is dragged down to corruption. With good reason, then, the Educator, in his concern for our salvation, sternly forbids us, "Do not drink wine to drunkenness." CHRIST THE EDUCATOR 2.2.27-28.[24]

TRANSGRESSION OF THE BAPTISMAL COVENANT. BASIL THE GREAT: "Who has woe? Who has sorrow?" For whom is there distress and darkness? For whom eternal doom? Is it not for the transgressors? For those who deny the faith? And what is the proof of their denial? Is it not that they have denied their own confession? And when and what did they confess? Belief in the Father and in the Son and in the Holy Ghost, when they renounced the devil and his angels and uttered those saving words. What fit title, then, has been discovered for them, for [these former] children of light to use? Are they not addressed as transgressors, as having violated the covenant of their salvation? ON THE SPIRIT 11.27.[25]

CLERGY OUGHT ALWAYS TO BE SOBER. APOSTOLIC CONSTITUTIONS: Since you are the presbyters and deacons of Christ, you ought always to be sober, both among yourselves and among others, so that you may be able to warn the unruly. Now the Scripture says, "The men in power are passionate. But let them not drink wine, lest by drinking they forget wisdom and are not able to judge aright."[26] Wherefore, [the bishops][27] and the presbyters and the deacons are those of authority in the church next to God Almighty and his beloved Son, Jesus Christ, and the Holy Spirit. We say this, not that they are not to drink at all, otherwise it would be to the reproach of what God has made for cheerfulness, but that they not be disordered with wine. For the Scripture does not say, "Do not drink wine"; but what says it? "Drink not wine to drunkenness." CONSTITUTIONS OF THE HOLY APOSTLES 8.4.44.[28]

DRUNKENNESS LIKE LEPROSY. CAESARIUS OF ARLES: Understand this, brethren, that every drunkard who has made drinking a habit will have leprosy within, in his soul, because the soul of the drunkard is known to be such as the flesh of the leper is seen to be. Therefore one who wishes to free himself of the sin of drunkenness, where not only his soul is killed but even his body is weakened, should drink merely as much as suffices. If he is unwilling to observe this rule, he will be hateful to God and an object of reproach to people. SERMON 189.5.[29]

EXCUSES FOR DRUNKENNESS DISPLEASE GOD. CAESARIUS OF ARLES: People who want to be like this try miserably to excuse themselves. They say, My friend will be unpleasant if I do not give him as much as he wants to drink when I invite him to a banquet. [But I say to you,] Do not have a friend who is willing to make you displeasing to God, for he is both his own enemy and yours. If you make yourself and someone else intoxicated, you will have a man as your friend but God as an enemy. SERMON 46.4.[30]

23:34 The Pilot Asleep in the Midst of the Sea

THE MIND GUIDES THE SOUL IN LIFE. GREGORY THE GREAT: A person sleeps in the midst of the sea who in the temptations of this world neglects to provide against the attacks of vices that beset him, like waves threatening mountain-high. And the pilot loses the rudder, as it were,

---

[24]FC 23:117-18*. [25]NPNF 2 8:17**. [26]Prov 31:4-5 LXX. [27]According to some manuscripts. Cf. ANF 7:498, n. 12. [28]ANF 7:498*. [29]FC 66:20. [30]FC 31:233*.

when the mind loses all anxious solicitude for guiding the ship of the body. To lose the rudder at sea is to fail to keep attentive forethought amidst the storms of this world. But if a pilot carefully holds fast the rudder, he steers the ship, now against advancing billows, now by cleaving the impetuous winds aslant. So, when the mind vigilantly rules the soul, it now surmounts and treads down some things with forethought, turns aside from others. It thus overcomes the present dangers with great toil, and by looking forward, gathers strength to face future conflicts. PASTORAL CARE 3.32.33.[31]

23:35 Drunk and Beaten but Still Seeking More Wine

ASLEEP TO PAIN BUT AWAKE TO WINE. GREG-ORY THE GREAT: A mind sleeps with no care to worry it, and [it] is beaten and feels no pain when it does not foresee impending evils and so, too, is unaware of those it has committed. It is drawn . . . yet without feeling it. It is attracted by the allurements of vices, and yet [it] does not arouse itself to its self-defense. But at the same time it wishes to be awake in order to find wine, that is, though it is so weighed down in its languid sleep as not to keep watch over itself, nevertheless, it still tries to be awake to the cares of the world, so as ever to inebriate itself with pleasures. And when it is asleep to that whereto it should be vigilantly awake, it wishes to be awake to something else, in regard to which it might have been laudably asleep. PASTORAL CARE 3.32.33.[32]

---

[31]ACW 11:211-12. [32]ACW 11:211*.

24:1-34 LOOK AND RECEIVE INSTRUCTION

[1]Be not envious of evil men,
　　nor desire to be with them;
[2]for their minds devise violence,
　　and their lips talk of mischief.

[3]By wisdom a house is built,
　　and by understanding it is established;
[4]by knowledge the rooms are filled
　　with all precious and pleasant riches.
[5]A wise man is mightier than a strong man,[q]
　　and a man of knowledge than he who has strength;
[6]for by wise guidance you can wage your war,
　　and in abundance of counselors there is

　　victory.
[7]Wisdom is too high for a fool;
　　in the gate he does not open his mouth.

[8]He who plans to do evil
　　will be called a mischief-maker.
[9]The devising of folly is sin,
　　and the scoffer is an abomination to men.

[10]If you faint in the day of adversity,
　　your strength is small.
[11]Rescue those who are being taken away to death;
　　hold back those who are stumbling to the slaughter.

¹²If you say, "Behold, we did not know this,"
　does not he who weighs the heart perceive
　　it?
　Does not he who keeps watch over your
　　soul know it,
　and will he not requite man according to
　　his work?

¹³My son, eat honey, for it is good,
　and the drippings of the honeycomb are
　　sweet to your taste.
¹⁴Know that wisdom is such to your soul;
　if you find it, there will be a future,
　and your hope will not be cut off.

¹⁵Lie not in wait as a wicked man against
　　the dwelling of the righteous;
　do not violence to his home;
¹⁶for a righteous man falls seven times,
　　and rises again;
　but the wicked are overthrown by calamity.

¹⁷Do not rejoice when your enemy falls,
　and let not your heart be glad when
　　he stumbles;
¹⁸lest the LORD see it, and be displeased,
　and turn away his anger from him.

¹⁹Fret not yourself because of evildoers,
　and be not envious of the wicked;
²⁰for the evil man has no future;
　the lamp of the wicked will be put out.

²¹My son, fear the LORD and the king,
　and do not disobey either of them;ʳ
²²for disaster from them will rise suddenly,
　and who knows the ruin that will come
　　from them both?

²³These also are sayings of the wise.

Partiality in judging is not good.
²⁴He who says to the wicked, "You are
　　innocent,"
　will be cursed by peoples, abhorred by
　　nations;
²⁵but those who rebuke the wicked will
　　have delight,
　and a good blessing will be upon them.
²⁶He who gives a right answer
　kisses the lips.

²⁷Prepare your work outside,
　get everything ready for you in the field;
　and after that build your house.

²⁸Be not a witness against your neighbor
　　without cause,
　and do not deceive with your lips.
²⁹Do not say, "I will do to him as he has
　　done to me;
　I will pay the man back for what he has
　　done."

³⁰I passed by the field of a sluggard,
　by the vineyard of a man without
　　sense;
³¹and lo, it was all overgrown with thorns;
　the ground was covered with nettles,
　and its stone wall was broken down.
³²Then I saw and considered it;
　I looked and received instruction.
³³A little sleep, a little slumber,
　a little folding of the hands to rest,
³⁴and poverty will come upon you like a
　　robber,
　and want like an armed man.

q Gk Compare Syr Tg: Heb *is in strength*　　r Gk: Heb *do not associate with those who change*

OVERVIEW: Christ is Wisdom, and wisdom's house is Christ's church (CHRYSOSTOM). Not every strong person is also wise, but every wise person is strong if he possesses wisdom (BEDE). Caution is advised, however, and many counselors should be consulted to avoid conflicts. Captives should be redeemed, not merely enquired about (CHRYSOSTOM), and those who struggle should be encouraged with compassion (JOHN CASSIAN). The just person will not perish however often he falls, and whereas "falling" indicates tribulations, so "rising" signifies benefit or profit. When falls do occur, the wicked are weakened but the righteous are strengthened (AUGUSTINE). In fact, by little offenses most of us fall many times daily (JOHN CASSIAN). Nevertheless, multitudes of minor sins should be feared because they accumulate (CAESARIUS). "To rise again" has two senses, first by justification and second at the general resurrection (CASSIODORUS). The saints rise from sin with God's assistance, but the righteous do not cease to be righteous (BEDE). Count as your friends only those who fear Christ as true God and king (CHRYSOSTOM). In order first to prepare the work outside and ahead, it is well to remember that in the midst of life we must prepare for death (CYRIL OF ALEXANDRIA) and that in such preparation we should be sure to preserve the advantage of our good works (APOSTOLIC CONSTITUTIONS), for there is always a need to prepare for death (BESA THE COPT).

24:3 With Wisdom a House Is Built

CHRIST IS WISDOM, AND THE HOUSE IS THE CHURCH. CHRYSOSTOM: [Solomon] calls Christ wisdom, intelligence and reason. The house is [Christ's] church which he built and whose storerooms he filled with every kind of precious and splendid riches. The storerooms are the hearts of those who believe in Christ and live in imitation of him—those hearts, I mean, which abound in goodness in thoughts, words and deeds. For this reason, they are made worthy of eternal blessedness. COMMENTARY ON THE PROVERBS OF SOLOMON, FRAGMENT 24.3-4.[1]

24:5 Wisdom Is Mightier Than Strength

EVEN A WEAK WISE PERSON IS STRONG. BEDE: It must be said that not every strong person is also wise, but every wise person is strong, because although one may be physically weak, he will still be able to overcome every strength of the enemy, that is, the devil, if he has wisdom. COMMENTARY ON PROVERBS 24.5.[2]

24:6 War Should Be Waged Only with the Guidance of Many Counselors

CAUTION IS ADVISED BEFORE ENTERING WAR. CHRYSOSTOM: [Solomon] calls war a matter full of disorder, a matter in need of many hands. Or, he may be warning us not to rush to war inconsiderately. Behold, he says, When a decision must be taken, is it not always beneficial to have wisdom in the middle of things? COMMENTARY ON THE PROVERBS OF SOLOMON, FRAGMENT 24.6.[3]

24:11 Rescue Those Who Are Stumbling to Death

REDEEM THE CAPTIVES. CHRYSOSTOM: "Redeem those who are ready to be slain; spare no effort." [Solomon] did not say, "Enquire curiously, and learn who they are," and yet for the most part they who are led away to execution are wicked. This especially is charity. For he that does good to a friend does it not altogether for God's sake; but he that does good to one unknown acts purely for God's sake. Do not spare your money; even if it is necessary to spend all, yet give.

But we, when we see persons in extreme distress, bewailing themselves, suffering things more grievous than ten thousand deaths, and oftentimes unjustly, we [I say] are sparing of our money and unsparing of our brothers. We are careful of lifeless things but neglect the living soul! ON THE EPIS-

---

[1]PG 64:732**. [2]CCL 119B:121. [3]PG 64:732.

TLE TO THE HEBREWS 10.9.[4]

ENCOURAGE WITH COMPASSION THOSE WHO STRUGGLE.

JOHN CASSIAN: From your own example, therefore, learn to be compassionate toward those who struggle, and never frighten with bleak despair those who are in trouble or unsettle them with harsh words. Instead, encourage them mildly and gently and, according to the precept of that most wise Solomon: "Spare not to save those who are being led to death and to redeem those who are being slain." CONFERENCE 2.13.10.[5]

24:16 *The Righteous Fall and Rise Again*

THE JUST WILL NOT PERISH.

AUGUSTINE: The text, "For a just man shall fall seven times and shall rise again," means that he will not perish, however often he falls. There is here no question of falling into sins but of afflictions leading to a lower life. CITY OF GOD 11.31.[6]

TRIBULATIONS AND BENEFIT OR PROFIT.

AUGUSTINE: The words "falls seven times" are employed to express every kind of tribulation, whereby one is cast down in the sight of people; and the words "rises up again" signify that one profits from all these tribulations. EXPLANATIONS OF THE PSALMS 119.162.[7]

WHEN FALLS OCCUR.

AUGUSTINE: "The just falls seven times and rises again, but the wicked shall be weakened in evils." When evils befall the wicked, they are weakened by them. When evils befall the righteous, "the Lord strengthens all that are falling". . . "and lifts up all those that have been cast down"[8]: all, that is, who belong to him, for "God resists the proud."[9] EXPLANATIONS OF THE PSALMS 145.13.[10]

BY LITTLE OFFENSES WE FALL MANY TIMES DAILY.

JOHN CASSIAN: There will be no end of penance for those little offenses by which "the righteous person falls seven times," as it is written, "and gets up again." For we commit these frequently every day, unwillingly or willingly, whether through ignorance or forgetfulness or thought or word or surprise or necessity or weakness of the flesh or pollution during a dream. On account of these David asks the Lord in prayer for purification and forgiveness, saying, "Who understands his sins? From my hidden sins cleanse me, and from those of others spare your servant."[11] And the apostle says, "The good that I want, I do not do, but the evil that I do not want, this I do."[12] CONFERENCE 20.12.1-2.[13]

MULTITUDES OF MINOR SINS SHOULD BE FEARED.

CAESARIUS OF ARLES: With God's help we both can and should be without serious offenses, but no just person ever was or ever will be able to live without small sins. We are continuously troubled and tormented by these as by flies buzzing around. . . . Very often sins creep up on us through thoughts or desires or speech or action, as the result of necessity, through weakness or out of forgetfulness. If a person thinks only of serious sins and strives to resist only these but has little or no care about small sins, he incurs no less danger than if he committed more serious offenses. Therefore let us not think little of our sins because they are slight, but let us fear them because they are many. Drops of rain are small, but because they are very many, they fill rivers and submerge houses, and sometimes by their force they even carry off mountains. SERMON 234.4.[14]

"TO RISE AGAIN" HAS TWO SENSES.

CASSIODORUS: A Christian is said to rise again in two senses; first, when in this world he is freed by grace from the death of vices, and he continues being justified by God; in the words of the most wise Solomon, "A just man falls seven times and rises again." Second, there is the general resurrection, at which the just will attain their eternal

---

[4]NPNF 1 14:417**. [5]ACW 57:97. [6]FC 14:237*. [7]NPNF 1 8:587*. [8]Ps 145:14 (144:14 LXX). [9]Jas 4:6. [10]NPNF 1 8:660*. [11]Ps 19:12-13 (18:13-14 LXX). [12]Rom 7:19. [13]ACW 57:703*. [14]FC 66:203.

rewards. Expositions of the Psalms 19.9.[15]

The Saints Rise from Sin with God's Assistance.

Bede: Let no one, therefore, believe, as Pelagius teaches, that he can live without sins and debts, when he sees the apostles praying earnestly for their own transgressions, as the Lord teaches. And there is also written elsewhere, "The righteous falls seven times and rises again." For it is impossible even for the saints to live without occasionally incurring guilt in very small sins which are committed through talk, thought, ignorance, forgetfulness, necessity, will, surprise. But still they do not cease being righteous, because with the Lord's assistance they rise again more quickly from their guilty act. Commentary on 1 John 1.10.[16]

The Righteous Do Not Cease to Be Righteous.

Bede: Although the righteous may offend perhaps through the frailty of the flesh or through ignorance, nevertheless he does not cease to be righteous, because just as there is daily and unavoidable offense of this kind, so also there is the daily remedy of prayers and good works that quickly raises up the righteous offender, so that he may not tumble to the ground and befoul with the dust of vices the marriage dress of charity and faith. Commentary on James 3.2.[17]

24:21 Fear the Lord and the King

Count as Friends Only Those Who Fear Christ.

Chrysostom: "Fear God, my son, and the king," that is, fear Christ, the true God and king. Or by "king" [Solomon] means the one who, before ruling over others, rules himself. "Do not be disobedient to any of them." Indeed, the one who denies respect to the king elected by God dishonors God. The impious will be immediately punished: certainly nobody knows that hour or day. Often for those still living an unexpected punishment is taken. Therefore only the judge knows the opportunity and reason of the punishment to be inflicted, or somebody who is a very close friend. So never have a friend except for the Lord and the king: certainly if they are not friends of the Lord and the king, they are their enemies. In truth, do not consider as friends those who are not the friends of the king and the Lord. Commentary on the Proverbs of Solomon, Fragment 24.21.[18]

24:27 First Prepare the Work Outside and Ahead

In the Midst of Life We Must Prepare for Death.

Cyril of Alexandria: The sacred Scripture has somewhere said, "Prepare your works for your departure, and make yourself ready for the field." Now by our departure I imagine is meant our going from this world and removal from it. And this time must of course overtake every one; for, as the psalmist says, "What man is there that shall live and not see death, and that can save his soul from the hand of hell?"[19] For the nature of man was condemned in Adam and fell away unto corruption, because he foolishly transgressed the commandment given him. Commentary on Luke, Homily 118.[20]

Preserve the Advantage of Your Good Works.

Apostolic Constitutions: Therefore he who values the security of his soul will take care to be out of danger, by keeping free from sin, that so he may preserve the advantage of his former good works to himself. Constitutions of the Holy Apostles 2.3.13.[21]

The Need to Prepare for Death.

Besa the Copt: It is a day of shouting and the trumpet.[22] It is a day of grief and sighing for those who have not prepared their works well for the way, which means for their departure out of the body, so that they might meet God profitably. Sermon 3, On the Punishment of Sinners 10.2.[23]

---

[15]ACW 51:207. [16]CS 82:165-66*. [17]CS 82:36. [18]PG 64:733. [19]Ps 89:48 (88:49 LXX). [20]CGSL 470*. [21]ANF 7:400*. [22]Zeph 1:16. [23]CSCO 158:8-9.

25:1-28 THESE ALSO ARE PROVERBS OF SOLOMON

¹*These also are proverbs of Solomon which the men of Hezekiah king of Judah copied.*

²*It is the glory of God to conceal things,*
but the glory of kings is to search things out.
³*As the heavens for height, and the earth for depth,*
so the mind of kings is unsearchable.
⁴*Take away the dross from the silver,*
and the smith has material for a vessel;
⁵*take away the wicked from the presence of the king,*
and his throne will be established in righteousness.
⁶*Do not put yourself forward in the king's presence*
or stand in the place of the great;
⁷*for it is better to be told, "Come up here,"*
than to be put lower in the presence of the prince.

What your eyes have seen
⁸*do not hastily bring into court;*
for⁵ what will you do in the end,
when your neighbor puts you to shame?
⁹*Argue your case with your neighbor himself,*
and do not disclose another's secret;
¹⁰*lest he who hears you bring shame upon you,*
and your ill repute have no end.

¹¹*A word fitly spoken*
is like apples of gold in a setting of silver.

¹²*Like a gold ring or an ornament of gold*
is a wise reprover to a listening ear.
¹³*Like the cold of snow in the time of harvest*
is a faithful messenger to those who send him,
he refreshes the spirit of his masters.
¹⁴*Like clouds and wind without rain*
is a man who boasts of a gift he does not give.

¹⁵*With patience a ruler may be persuaded,*
and a soft tongue will break a bone.
¹⁶*If you have found honey, eat only enough for you,*
lest you be sated with it and vomit it.
¹⁷*Let your foot be seldom in your neighbor's house,*
lest he become weary of you and hate you.
¹⁸*A man who bears false witness against his neighbor*
is like a war club, or a sword, or a sharp arrow.
¹⁹*Trust in a faithless man in time of trouble*
is like a bad tooth or a foot that slips.
²⁰*He who sings songs to a heavy heart*
is like one who takes off a garment on a cold day,
and like vinegar on a wound.ᵗ
²¹*If your enemy is hungry, give him bread to eat;*
and if he is thirsty, give him water to drink;
²²*for you will heap coals of fire on his head,*
and the LORD will reward you.

²³*The north wind brings forth rain;*
    and a backbiting tongue, angry looks.
²⁴*It is better to live in a corner of the housetop*
    than in a house shared with a contentious
    woman.
²⁵*Like cold water to a thirsty soul,*
    so is good news from a far country.
²⁶*Like a muddied spring or a polluted*

fountain
    is a righteous man who gives way before
    the wicked.
²⁷*It is not good to eat much honey,*
    *so be sparing of complimentary words.*ᵘ
²⁸*A man without self-control*
    is like a city broken into and left without
    walls.

s Cn: Heb *lest*   t Gk: Heb *lye*   u Cn Compare Gk Syr Tg: Heb *searching out their glory is glory*

OVERVIEW: Many of the Proverbs of Solomon were selected and copied by friends of Hezekiah for the edification of the church (HIPPOLYTUS). Those whom Christ has set free are friends to one another (EVAGRIUS). A boastful exorcist should be evaluated by the love he manifests, not by the miracles he performs (JOHN CASSIAN). Bearing false witness, it must be remembered, is like a stroke of calumny (ATHANASIUS). Food and alms are to be given to everyone, even to enemies and sinners. To heap coals of fire upon your enemy, therefore, is a figurative expression that indicates burning lamentations of repentance by which one's pride is healed (AUGUSTINE). In other words, doing good to your enemy causes him or her to grieve and repent (CAESARIUS). The hunger and thirst involved, however, need not be limited to the physical (BEDE).

If a husband and wife quarrel, then it is better for the man to move to the housetop (JEROME). Knowledge of the Savior is like life-giving water (CYRIL OF ALEXANDRIA). It must not be forgotten that the good news is Christ's love and the church's increase in life, work and doctrine (FRUCTUOSUS). Walls are needed for self-control, however, in order to gather spiritual riches (JOHN CASSIAN).

25:1 The Men of Hezekiah Copied These

SOME BOOKS SELECTED FOR EDIFICATION OF THE CHURCH. HIPPOLYTUS: Moreover, in the days of Hezekiah, there were some of the books

selected for use, and others set aside. Whence the Scripture says, "These are the mixed proverbs of Solomon, which the friends of Hezekiah the king copied out." And from where did they take them but out of the books containing the three thousand parables and the five thousand songs? Out of these, then, the wise friends of Hezekiah took those portions which bore upon the edification of the church. FRAGMENTS ON SONG OF SONGS.[1]

25:8-10 The Friendship of a Neighbor

THOSE WHOM CHRIST HAS SET FREE ARE FRIENDS TO ONE ANOTHER. EVAGRIUS OF PONTUS: Solomon frequently mentions "friend" and "friendship." Therefore, it is fitting now to look into what he means by friendship. He says [in effect] that grace and friendship liberate. Also, the Savior in the gospels says to the Jews who had believed in him, "If you continue in my word, you are truly my disciples and you will know the truth, and the truth will make you free."[2] Again, Paul writes, "Christ freed us from the curse of the law."[3] Hence, if "friendship sets free" and "truth sets free" and the Savior sets free, then Christ is both truth and friendship. Therefore, all who possess the knowledge of Christ are friends to each other. Therefore, the Savior calls his disciples "friends,"[4] and John the Baptist is a friend of the bridegroom,[5] and so are Moses[6] and all the

---

[1]ANF 5:176*; TLG 2115.031.7. [2]Jn 8:31-32. [3]Gal 3:13. [4]Jn 15:15.
[5]Jn 3:29. [6]Ex 33:11.

saints. And it is in virtue of that friendship alone, that his friends are also friends to each other. SCHOLIA ON PROVERBS 304.25.10.[7]

25:14 One Who Boasts of a Gift He Does Not Give

BOASTFUL EXORCISTS SHOULD BE EVALUATED BY THEIR LOVE. JOHN CASSIAN: Humility, then, is the teacher of all the virtues; it is the most firm foundation of the heavenly edifice; it is the Savior's own magnificent gift. For a person may perform without danger of pride all the miracles that Christ worked if he strains after the meek Lord not because of his exalted signs but because of his patience and humility. But a person who itches to command unclean spirits, to bestow the gift of health on the sick, or to show some wondrous sign to the people is far from Christ even though he invokes the name of Christ in his displays, because by reason of his proud mind he does not follow the teacher of humility. . . . [Christ] did not say, "If you perform signs and mighty deeds," but, "If you have love for one another." Certainly no one can observe this but the gentle and the humble.

Therefore our forebears never considered those monks to be upright or free of the disease of vainglory who presented themselves as exorcists before men and who, in the midst of admiring crowds, proclaimed by a boastful display this grace that they had either deserved or arrogated to themselves. Hence, if someone does one of these things in our presence, we should think him praiseworthy not for his wonderful signs but for his splendid behavior, and we should not ask whether demons are subject to him but whether he possesses the parts of love that the apostle describes.[8] CONFERENCE 15.7.2-5.[9]

25:18 One Who Bears False Witness

LIKE A STROKE OF CALUMNY. ATHANASIUS: He that has been struck by a stone goes to a physician, but sharper than a stone are the strokes of calumny. For, as Solomon has said, "A false witness is a war club, and a sword, and a sharp arrow," and its wounds truth alone is able to cure. If truth is set at naught, the wounds grow worse and worse. DEFENSE BEFORE CONSTANTIUS 12.[10]

25:21-22 Feed Your Enemy and Heap Coals of Fire

FOOD AND ALMS ARE TO BE GIVEN TO EVERYONE. AUGUSTINE: The apostle Paul teaches us in the clearest possible way that alms are to be distributed to everybody, when he says, "Let us be tireless, while we have the time, in doing good to all, though supremely to those at home in the faith."[11] This indeed makes it plain enough that in works of this kind the just are to be given preference. Who else, after all, are we to understand by "those at home in the faith," since elsewhere it is stated plainly, "The just person lives by faith"?[12] That doesn't mean, though, that we must close our hearts to other people, even sinners, not even if they adopt a hostile attitude toward us. The Savior himself says, after all, "Love your enemies, do good to those who hate you."[13] Nor is the point passed over in silence in the books of the Old Testament; one reads there, you see, "If your enemy is hungry, feed him; if he is thirsty, give him a drink," a text the apostle also makes use of in the New.[14] SERMON 164A.2.[15]

COALS OF FIRE ARE BURNING LAMENTATIONS OF REPENTANCE. AUGUSTINE: This [scriptural passage] seems to prescribe a crime or a vice; therefore, it is a figure of speech directing that we are to participate in the Lord's passion and treasure up in grateful and salutary remembrance the fact that his flesh was crucified and wounded for us. Scripture says, "If your enemy is hungry, give him food; if he is thirsty, give him drink." This

---

[7]SC 340:396. [8]See 1 Cor 13:4-7. [9]ACW 57:542-43. [10]NPNF 2 4:242**. [11]Gal 6:10. [12]Cf. Hab 2:4; Rom 1:17; Gal 3:11; Heb 10:38. [13]Lk 6:27. [14]Rom 12:20. [15]WSA 3 5:198-99.

undoubtedly prescribes a kindness, but the part that follows—"For by so doing you will heap coals of fire upon his head"—you might suppose was commanding a crime of malevolence. So, do not doubt that it is a figurative expression. Although it can have a twofold interpretation, by one intending harm, by the other intending a good, charity should call you away from the former to kindness, so that you may understand that the coals of fire are the burning lamentations of repentance by which that person's pride is healed and he grieves that he has been an enemy of the one who relieves his misery. CHRISTIAN INSTRUCTION 3.16.24.[16]

DOING GOOD TO YOUR ENEMY. CAESARIUS OF ARLES: The Holy Spirit speaks in the same manner through Solomon: "If your enemy is hungry, give him to eat; if he is thirsty, give him to drink; in doing this you will heap coals of fire upon his head." At this point we must watch carefully, lest, perchance, we make wounds out of the remedies for us if we do not understand it well. Some people are even inclined to take this precept as if to satisfy their wrath. Indeed, they say within themselves, Behold, I will feed my enemy, so he may burn forever. May God keep an idea of this sort far from our minds! This point ought to be accepted as the saints and ancient fathers have explained it under the guidance of the Holy Spirit.... When you piously do good to your enemy, however wicked and cruel, savage and unfeeling he may be, he at length sometimes blushes and grieves, beginning to repent of what he has done. Then, when he has begun to do penance, his rational sense, that is, his head, begins to be kindled with the fire of charity. One who before was inclined to harbor wrath against you like a cold maniac now begins to love you with his whole heart through being kindled with spiritual warmth arising from your kindness. SERMON 36.5.[17]

THE HUNGER AND THIRST NEED NOT BE LIMITED TO THE PHYSICAL. BEDE: This can be understood both of corporeal food and of spiri-

tual nourishment. COMMENTARY ON PROVERBS 25.21.[18]

25:24 A Contentious Wife

IF HUSBAND AND WIFE QUARREL, THEN HE MUST MOVE TO THE HOUSETOP. JEROME: What necessity rests upon me to run the risk of the wife I marry proving good or bad? "It is better," [Solomon] says, "to dwell in a desert land than with a contentious and passionate woman."[19] He who is married knows how seldom we find a wife without these faults. Hence that sublime orator, Varius Geminus, says well, "The man who does not quarrel is a bachelor." [In fact], "it is better to dwell in the corner of the housetop than with a contentious woman in a house in common." If a house common to husband and wife makes a wife proud and breeds contempt for the husband, how much more if the wife is the richer of the two and the husband but a lodger in her house!

She begins to be not a wife but mistress of the house; and if she offends her husband, they must part. AGAINST JOVINIANUS 1.28.[20]

25:25 Good News

KNOWLEDGE OF THE SAVIOR IS LIKE LIFE-GIVING WATER. CYRIL OF ALEXANDRIA: Just as "waters are pleasant to the thirsty soul," as Scripture says, so to the mind that loves instruction is the life-giving knowledge of the mysteries of our Savior. Let us, therefore, draw from the sacred springs the living and life-giving waters, even those that are rational and spiritual. Let us take our fill, and weary not in the drinking; for in these things more than enough is still for edification, and greediness is great praise. COMMENTARY ON LUKE, HOMILY 65.[21]

GOOD NEWS IS CHRIST'S LOVE. FRUCTUOSUS

[16]FC 2:136*. [17]FC 31:179*. [18]CCL 119B:129. [19]Prov 21:19. [20]NPNF 2 6:367*. [21]CGSL 277*.

of BRAGA: We have learned from the story in sacred Scripture how pleasing to a man is "good news from a far country." And what other better news could we expect than the love of Christ, than the spotless profession and propagation of the catholic church, than the pure lives, successful work, and faithful doctrine of the friends of God and the bishops and priests of Christ? These, most blessed father, we confess that we vehemently yearn for and thirstily desire to learn. LETTER 43.[22]

25:28 A City Without Walls

WALLS ARE NEEDED FOR SELF-CONTROL.

JOHN CASSIAN: The example and image used in this text, which compares a person with a city that is broken down and without walls, demonstrates how dangerous it is for a monk to be deprived of [self-control]. Herein is wisdom; herein is knowledge and understanding. Without them can neither our interior dwelling be built nor spiritual riches be gathered, as it is written: "With wisdom a dwelling is built, and with knowledge it is set up again; with understanding its cellars are filled with all precious riches and good things."[23] CONFERENCE 2.4.2.[24]

---

[22]FC 63:96*. [23]Prov 24:3-4. [24]ACW 57:86-87.

26:1-28 HONOR IS NOT FITTING FOR A FOOL

[1]Like snow in summer or rain in harvest,
  so honor is not fitting for a fool.
[2]Like a sparrow in its flitting, like a
    swallow in its flying,
  a curse that is causeless does not
    alight.
[3]A whip for the horse, a bridle for the ass,
  and a rod for the back of fools.
[4]Answer not a fool according to his folly,
  lest you be like him yourself.*
[5]Answer a fool according to his folly,
  lest he be wise in his own eyes.
[6]He who sends a message by the hand of a
    fool
  cuts off his own feet and drinks violence.
[7]Like a lame man's legs, which hang
    useless,
  is a proverb in the mouth of fools.

[8]Like one who binds the stone in the sling
  is he who gives honor to a fool.
[9]Like a thorn that goes up into the hand
    of a drunkard
  is a proverb in the mouth of fools.
[10]Like an archer who wounds everybody
  is he who hires a passing fool or
    drunkard.[v]
[11]Like a dog that returns to his vomit
  is a fool that repeats his folly.
[12]Do you see a man who is wise in his own
    eyes?
  There is more hope for a fool than for
    him.
[13]The sluggard says, "There is a lion in
    the road!
  There is a lion in the streets!"
[14]As a door turns on its hinges,

so does a sluggard on his bed.

¹⁵The sluggard buries his hand in the dish;
    it wears him out to bring it back to his
      mouth.

¹⁶The sluggard is wiser in his own eyes
    than seven men who can answer
      discreetly.

¹⁷He who meddles in a quarrel not his own
    is like one who takes a passing dog by the
      ears.

¹⁸Like a madman who throws firebrands,
    arrows, and death,

¹⁹is the man who deceives his neighbor
    and says, "I am only joking!"

²⁰For lack of wood the fire goes out;
    and where there is no whisperer, quarrel-
      ing ceases.

²¹As charcoal to hot embers and wood to
    fire,
    so is a quarrelsome man for kindling
      strife.

²²The words of a whisperer are like
    delicious morsels;
    they go down into the inner parts of the
      body.

²³Like the glaze^w covering an earthen
    vessel
    are smooth^x lips with an evil heart.

²⁴He who hates, dissembles with his lips
    and harbors deceit in his heart;

²⁵when he speaks graciously, believe him
    not,
    for there are seven abominations in his
      heart;

²⁶though his hatred be covered with guile,
    his wickedness will be exposed in the
      assembly.

²⁷He who digs a pit will fall into it,
    and a stone will come back upon him
      who starts it rolling.

²⁸A lying tongue hates its victims,
    and a flattering mouth works ruin.

v The Hebrew text of this verse is uncertain   w Cn: Heb *silver of dross*   x Gk: Heb *burning*   *A variant reads, *Do not say anything in the ears of the foolish, lest when he hears he may mock your wise words*

OVERVIEW: The fool who does injustice to others for no reason or cause will bring it also upon himself (APOSTOLIC CONSTITUTIONS). God's Word turns us from idols to the cross, where physical beauty is disfigured but spiritual beauty is resplendent (EPHREM). There is a time for silence and a time to speak (AMBROSE), and fools, in particular, should be ignored in silence (CYPRIAN). Indeed, foolish and irreverent assumptions are unworthy of our response (MACRINA). There are thorns growing deep within all of us that must be burnt out by God's Word (ORIGEN). It was necessary to keep the tabernacle free of thorny barbs, just as thorns grow in the hands of a drunkard and sins in the works of a fool (BEDE). Vacillation will prompt the fool to return to the same sin like a dog to its own vomit (CHRYSOSTOM), and the same is true of those who vacillate on their vows (FRUCTUOSUS, CAESARIUS OF ARLES). Pagan philosophers are foolish when they consider themselves wise (CHRYSOSTOM), but a person unaware of his own ignorance is even worse (GREGORY OF NAZIANZUS). Silence after an altercation is dangerous without at least some attempt to make up (FRUCTUOSUS). In plotting against others, in fact we sharpen the sword against ourselves (CHRYSOSTOM).

26:2 The "Curse Causeless" Will Do No Harm

THE FOOL BRINGS REPROACH ON HIMSELF.
APOSTOLIC CONSTITUTIONS: "As birds and spar-

rows fly away, so the curse causeless shall not come upon any one."[1] And again [Solomon] says, "Those that bring reproaches are exceedingly foolish."[2] But as the bee, a creature as to its strength feeble, if it stings anyone, loses its sting and becomes a drone; in the same manner you also, whatsoever injustice you do to others, will bring it upon yourselves. CONSTITUTIONS OF THE HOLY APOSTLES 3.1.15.[3]

26:3 Whip, Bridle and Rod

GOD'S WORD TURNS US FROM IDOLS. EPHREM THE SYRIAN: The nations confess you because your word became a mirror before them in which they might see hidden death devouring their lives. Idols are ornamented by those who craft them, but they disfigure their crafters with their ornamentation. [The mirror] brought [the nations] directly to your cross, where physical beauty is disfigured but spiritual beauty is resplendent. The one who was God pursued the nations who were pursuing gods that were not gods at all. And [using] words like bridles, he turned them away from many gods [and brought them] to one.

This is the mighty one whose proclamation [of the gospel] became a bridle in the jaws of the nations,[4] turning them away from idols to the one who sent him. HOMILY ON OUR LORD 5.1-2.[5]

26:4 Do Not Imitate the Fool

A FOOL SHOULD BE IGNORED IN SILENCE. CYPRIAN: I had treated you with contempt, Demetrian, as you railed with sacrilegious mouth against God, who is one and true, and frequently cried out with impious words, thinking it more fitting and better to ignore with silence the ignorance of a man in error than to provoke with speech the fury of a man in madness. And I did not do this without the authority of the divine teaching, since it is written, "Do not say anything in the ears of the foolish, lest when he hears he may mock your wise words," and again, "Do not

answer the foolish according to his folly, lest you become like him." To DEMETRIAN 1.[6]

AVOID FOOLS IF YOU WISH A GOOD FLIGHT. AMBROSE: Your flight is a good one if you do not answer the fool according to his folly. Your flight is good if you direct your footsteps away from the countenance of fools. Indeed, one swiftly goes astray with bad guides; but if you wish your flight to be a good one, remove your ways far from their words. FLIGHT FROM THE WORLD 9.56.[7]

A TIME FOR SILENCE AND A TIME TO SPEAK. AMBROSE: [David] used not to answer the enemy that provoked him, the sinner that exasperated him. As he says elsewhere, "As though he were deaf he heard not them that speak vanity and imagine deceit, and as though he were dumb he opened not his mouth to them."[8] Again, in another place, it is said, "Answer not a fool according to his folly, lest thou also be like to him."

The first duty then is to have due measure in our speech. In this way a sacrifice of praise is offered up to God. Thus a godly fear is shown when sacred Scriptures are read. Thus parents are honored. I know well that many speak because they know not how to keep silence. But it is not often that any one is silent when speaking does not profit him. A wise person, intending to speak, first carefully considers what he is to say and to whom he is to say it; also where and what time. DUTIES OF THE CLERGY 1.10.34-35.[9]

FOOLISH AND IRREVERENT ASSUMPTIONS ARE UNWORTHY OF RESPONSE. MACRINA:[10] It is more agreeable to remain silent on such questions and to consider their foolish and irreverent assumptions unworthy of a response, since the divine words forbid it, saying, "Answer not a

---

[1]The power of a curse unmerited and pronounced for no good reason or cause is hereby denied. [2]Prov 10:18. [3]ANF 7:430-31*. [4]See Is 30:28. [5]FC 91:280-81. [6]FC 36:167. [7]FC 65:322; see also at Prov 5:8 above. [8]Ps 38:13 (37:14 LXX). [9]NPNF 2 10:6-7*. [10]As related by her younger brother Gregory of Nyssa.

fool according to his folly." But the fool, according to the prophet, is "the one who says there is no God."[11] ON THE SOUL AND THE RESURRECTION.[12]

26:9 A Thorn in the Hand of a Drunkard

THORNS MUST BE BURNED BY GOD'S WORD.
ORIGEN: The sin of all people is not taken away by the Lamb if they neither grieve nor are tormented till it be taken away. For since thorns have not only been sown but have also taken deep root in the hands of everyone who has become drunk because of evil, and has lost sobriety, according to what is said in Proverbs, "Thorns grow in the hand of the drunkard." So what must we say in addition regarding the extent of distress they produce in him who has received such plants into the body of his own soul? For he who has admitted evil into the depth of his own soul to such an extent that he has become thorn-producing earth has to be cut down by the living and effectual word of God which is more piercing than any two-edged sword and more capable of burning than any fire.[13]

That fire which discovers thorns, and which, because of its own divinity, will stop them and not in addition set the threshing floors or fields of grain on fire, will need to be sent to such a soul. COMMENTARY ON THE GOSPEL OF JOHN 6.297-98.[14]

THE TABERNACLE MUST BE KEPT FREE OF THORNY BARBS. BEDE: Now the boards [of the tabernacle] were made out of acacia wood, that is, a thorny sort [of wood], and according to the Savior's pronouncement thorns are the cares of this world, its pleasures, riches and false delights.[15] But the pricks of sins may also not incongruously be compared with thorns, for it is written here that thorns grow in the hands of a drunkard, that is, sins in the works of a fool. Because the holy preachers are eager both to expurgate themselves from the pricks of vices and to strip away all the cares and delights of the

world so that with a free mind they might be able to be expanded in the love of God and neighbor and to run far and wide to preach the word, it is therefore rightly said that the boards of the tabernacle were made out of acacia wood (that is, out of thorny [wood]), for they were indeed made of thorns, but thorns from which all the thorny barbs had been completely stripped away, so that they shone with a pure whiteness. ON THE TABERNACLE 2.5.[16]

26:11 A Fool Repeats Folly

THE FOOL RETURNS TO THE SAME SIN. CHRYSOSTOM: Don't you know that people so unconcerned about their own salvation and vacillating between attention to it and headlong course into the devil's net are compared in sacred Scripture with dogs? It says, remember, "The person who turns away from his sin and then goes back to it is like a dog returning to its vomit." HOMILIES ON GENESIS 6.2.[17]

TO WITHDRAW FROM MONASTIC RULE. FRUCTUOSUS OF BRAGA: We have learned that in some less observant monasteries, men have entered and brought their capital with them and later, losing their religious fervor, have made great trouble in demanding their property. Returning to the world which they had left, as dogs return to their vomit, with the aid of their relatives they have extorted what they had brought with them to the monastery and have sought the support of secular judges. With the help of magistrates they have [thus] destroyed the monasteries, so that we see many innocent men ruined by a single sinner. GENERAL RULE FOR MONASTERIES 18.[18]

THE RETURN TO SIN. CAESARIUS OF ARLES: These, no doubt, are the things suffered by clerics, monks or virgins who are proud, disobedient

---

[11]Ps 53:1 (52:1 LXX). [12]FC 58:203. [13]Cf. Heb 4:12; Sir 48:1. [14]FC 80:249. [15]Mt 13:22; Lk 8:14. [16]TTH 18:67. [17]FC 74:78*. [18]FC 63:202*.

and lukewarm. When at the beginning of their life they abandoned the ways of this world and with a fervent spirit fled to the service of holy religion, through the grace of God they were rid of all their sins. But afterwards, when they did not put forth zeal because of carelessness and sloth and were not filled with spiritual graces through the help of God, the vices which had departed found them empty and returned with many more[19] and compelled them to return to their vomit. Then was fulfilled in them what is written, "As the dog that returns to his vomit becomes hateful, so is the sinner that returns to his sin." SERMON 237.3.[20]

26:12 One Wise in His Own Eyes Is Dumber Than a Fool

PAGAN PHILOSOPHERS ARE FOOLISH WHEN THEY CONSIDER THEMSELVES WISE. CHRYSOSTOM: This is not a small fault either to consider oneself wise and to refer everything back to one's own judgment. . . . Paul addresses this same reproach to the pagan philosophers: "Professing to be wise, they become fools."[21] This is the reason for their folly. The author of the Proverbs said on his part, "Do you see a man wise in his own eyes? There is more hope for a fool than for him." Again, it is Paul who gives this advice: "Do not be wise in your own opinion."[22] COMMENTARY ON ISAIAH 5.21.[23]

EVEN WORSE IS ONE UNAWARE OF HIS OWN IGNORANCE. GREGORY OF NAZIANZUS: There is an evil which I have seen under the sun, a person wise in his own conceit; and a still greater evil is to charge with the instruction of others a person who is not even aware of his own ignorance. IN DEFENSE OF HIS FLIGHT, ORATION 2.50.[24]

26:24 Deceit Concealed in the Heart

SILENCE AFTER AN ALTERCATION IS DANGEROUS. FRUCTUOSUS OF BRAGA: If one of the brothers who agreed upon a common pact shall suddenly on one occasion only fall into altercation with another, he may, according to the gospel, ask and receive forgiveness.[25] But if he refuses to mend his ways, and if the one against whom a wrong has been done has not succeeded in changing the other's presumption after a first and second admonition, then he shall report it to the abbot, lest both he and his brother be endangered by this silence. As the prophet says, "He who hides his enmity maintains deceit." MONASTIC AGREEMENT 6.[26]

26:27 Digging a Pit for Oneself

IN PLOTTING AGAINST OTHERS WE SHARPEN THE SWORD AGAINST OURSELVES. CHRYSOSTOM: "He that digs a pit for his neighbor shall fall into it." And this happened even then. For they wished to destroy [Jesus] in order to suppress his preaching, but just the opposite took place.[27] His preaching flourished by the grace of Christ, whereas all their schemes have been snuffed out and have perished. Further, they have lost their homeland, and freedom, and security and worship, and have been deprived of all honor and glory, and become slaves and captives.

Accordingly, since we know these things, let us never plot against others, because we have learned that by so doing we are sharpening the sword against ourselves and wounding ourselves more deeply than others. HOMILIES ON THE GOSPEL OF JOHN 51.[28]

---

[19]Conjectural reconstruction of a small lacuna in the text. [20]FC 66:217. [21]Rom 1:22. [22]Rom 12:16. [23]ITA 78; SC 304:244-45. [24]NPNF 2 7:215. [25]See Mt 18:15-17. [26]FC 63:219*. [27]Chrysostom is commenting on Jn 7:37-44. [28]FC 41:40-41**.

27:1-27 DO NOT BOAST ABOUT TOMORROW

[1]Do not boast about tomorrow,
    for you do not know what a day may
        bring forth.
[2]Let another praise you, and not your own
        mouth;
    a stranger, and not your own lips.
[3]A stone is heavy, and sand is weighty,
    but a fool's provocation is heavier than
        both.
[4]Wrath is cruel, anger is overwhelming;
    but who can stand before jealousy?
[5]Better is open rebuke
    than hidden love.
[6]Faithful are the wounds of a friend;
    profuse are the kisses of an enemy.
[7]He who is sated loathes honey,
    but to one who is hungry everything
        bitter is sweet.
[8]Like a bird that strays from its nest,
    is a man who strays from his home.
[9]Oil and perfume make the heart glad,
    but the soul is torn by trouble.[y]
[10]Your friend, and your father's friend, do
        not forsake;
    and do not go to your brother's house in
        the day of your calamity.
    Better is a neighbor who is near
    than a brother who is far away.
[11]Be wise, my son, and make my heart glad,
    that I may answer him who reproaches
        me.
[12]A prudent man sees danger and hides
        himself;
    but the simple go on, and suffer for it.
[13]Take a man's garment when he has
        given surety for a stranger,
    and hold him in pledge when he gives
        surety for foreigners.[z]
[14]He who blesses his neighbor with a loud
        voice,
    rising early in the morning,
    will be counted as cursing.
[15]A continual dripping on a rainy day
    and a contentious woman are alike;
[16]to restrain her is to restrain the wind[a]
    or to grasp oil in one's right hand.
[17]Iron sharpens iron,
    and one man sharpens another.
[18]He who tends a fig tree will eat its fruit,
    and he who guards his master will be
        honored.
[19]As in water face answers to face,
    so the mind of man reflects the man.
[20]Sheol and Abaddon are never satisfied,
    and never satisfied are the eyes of man.
[21]The crucible is for silver, and the
        furnace is for gold,
    and a man is judged by his praise.
[22]Crush a fool in a mortar with a pestle
    along with crushed grain,
    yet his folly will not depart from him.

[23]Know well the condition of your flocks,
    and give attention to your herds;
[24]for riches do not last for ever;
    and does a crown endure to all generations?
[25]When the grass is gone, and the new
        growth appears,
    and the herbage of the mountains is
        gathered,

²⁶*the lambs will provide your clothing,*
   and the goats the price of a field;
²⁷*there will be enough goats' milk for your*
   food,
   for the food of your household
   and maintenance for your maidens.

y Gk: Heb *the sweetness of his friend from hearty counsel*   **z** Vg and 20.16: Heb *a foreign woman*   **a** Heb obscure

OVERVIEW: Baptism should not be delayed to the deathbed (APOSTOLIC CONSTITUTIONS). The time to act is now (BABAI). To procrastinate is to give advantage to the devil (CHRYSOSTOM). Turn to Christ, therefore, for this very day could be your last. Walk while it is light and do not delay your repentance, for death will come only once and we know not when. Moreover, we can never tell who may be joining us tomorrow in heaven, whether friend or enemy (CAESARIUS). Testimony to oneself is arrogant (AUGUSTINE). A book devoted to self-glorification is contrary to wisdom (GREGORY OF NYSSA), and God is aware of those who steal the honors that properly belong to others (CYRIL OF ALEXANDRIA). Open rebuke is better than hidden love (BASIL); therefore, we should prefer friendly rebukes over silent friendship (AMBROSE). Love mingled with severity is a mark of true friendship, and between friends it is possible to object without eliciting hatred (AUGUSTINE). The wounds of love are sweet (MAXIMUS OF TURIN). The wound of love is seen in Peter, not Judas . In matters of trust, it is better to prefer close friendship over kinship (AMBROSE). Spiritual carelessness can be compared with a neglected roof that leaks (JOHN CASSIAN). Various levels of spiritual maturity need different kinds of instruction (CYRIL OF ALEXANDRIA).

27:1 *You Know Not What Tomorrow May Bring*

DO NOT DELAY BAPTISM TO THE DEATHBED. APOSTOLIC CONSTITUTIONS: He that says, "When I am dying I will be baptized, lest I should sin and defile my baptism," is ignorant of God and forgetful of his own nature. For "do not delay to turn to the Lord, for you do not know what the next day will bring forth." Baptize also your infants, and bring them up in the nurture and admonition of God. For he says, "Suffer the little children to come to me, and forbid them not."[1] CONSTITUTIONS OF THE HOLY APOSTLES 6.3.15.[2]

THE TIME IS NOW. BABAI: Do not rely on tomorrow: your business belongs to today, for our time is not a time for just words or for acquiring property, or indeed to swagger about enjoying ourselves, or to relax in idleness. No, for the discerning it is time for action; it is the time to gather in fruits; it is the time for repentance, it is the time for everyone to supplicate Christ with all his heart. LETTER TO CYRIACUS 4.[3]

DO NOT PROCRASTINATE OR GIVE ADVANTAGE TO THE DEVIL. CHRYSOSTOM: Let us not then be procrastinating until tomorrow. For we "know not what the next day may bring forth," nor let us say "we shall conquer this habit "little by little," since this "little by little" will never come to an end. Therefore, dismissing that excuse, let us say, "If we do not reform the practice of swearing today, we will not delay until later, when ten thousand things press upon us. Though it were necessary to die, or to be punished, or to lose all that we have, we will not give the devil the advantage of slackness nor the pretext of delay." Thus if God should perceive your soul inflamed and your diligence quickened, then he also himself will lend his assistance to change you. HOMILIES CONCERNING THE STATUES 20.22.[4]

TURN TO CHRIST. CAESARIUS OF ARLES: Let us

---

[1]Mt 19:14. [2]ANF 7:457*. [3]CS 101:140. [4]NPNF 1 9:480**.

turn to him, dearly beloved, and not wish to defer our amendment until the end of our life. Let us listen to the prophet when he says, "Delay not your conversion to the Lord, put it not off from day to day,"[5] "for you know not what any day may bring forth." O man, why do you delay from day to day, when perhaps today you are going to have your last day? SERMON 109.2.[6]

DO NOT DELAY YOUR REPENTANCE. CAESARIUS OF ARLES: "You know not what any day may bring forth." "Between morning and evening the weather changes."[7] Elsewhere we are also advised with a salutary precept: "Let us walk while we still have the light, before darkness comes over us."[8] Now some careless person may say, When I reach old age, then I shall have recourse to the healing of repentance. The wretched person does not know that if one has been accustomed to commit sins with a promise of repentance, never or only with difficulty will he merit to obtain the fruit of repentance. SERMON 209.1.[9]

DEATH WILL COME, AND ONE KNOWS NOT WHEN. CAESARIUS OF ARLES: With what boldness does he put off his salvation to old age, when he cannot be certain of the space of one day? Therefore, if we do not want to fear death, we should always be ready. Then, when the Lord bids us come from this world, we may come before the sight of the eternal judge with a clear and free conscience; not with despair but with joy. SERMON 22.5.[10]

WE CAN NEVER TELL WHO MAY JOIN US TOMORROW IN HEAVEN. CAESARIUS OF ARLES: Therefore let us love our enemies. Perhaps the person who is your friend today will commit such sins that he cannot be with you in eternal life, "for you know not what tomorrow may bring." On the contrary, your enemy may be converted to repentance in such a way that he merits to be your fellow citizen in that heavenly Jerusalem; in fact, he might even become greater than you. SERMON 38.3.[11]

27:2 Let Your Praise Come from Another

PRAISEWORTHY TESTIMONY OF ONESELF IS ARROGANT. AUGUSTINE: If I seem arrogant to you, it is for this reason, that I bear testimony to myself. For every person, when he wishes to bear praiseworthy testimony to himself, seems arrogant and proud. So it has been written, "Let not your own mouth praise you, but let the mouth of your neighbor praise you." TRACTATES ON THE GOSPEL OF JOHN 36.3.2.[12]

SELF-GLORIFICATION IS CONTRARY TO WISDOM. GREGORY OF NYSSA: If we did anything in those struggles for our religion that redounds to our honor in the telling, wisdom commands us to leave it to others to tell. "Let another man praise you, and not your own mouth." And it is this very thing that our omniscient friend has not been conscious of in devoting the larger half of his book to self-glorification. AGAINST EUNOMIUS 1.12.[13]

GOD KNOWS THOSE WHO STEAL HONORS THAT BELONG TO OTHERS. CYRIL OF ALEXANDRIA: No one crowns himself, and that person is justly ridiculed who devises praises for himself, for it is written, "Let your neighbor praise you, and not your own mouth; a stranger, and not your own lips." Though hypocrites may be able possibly to remain undetected and thus to seize the honors that people bestow, yet God knows your hearts. The judge cannot be deceived. . . . He knows who steals by fraud the honor which another truly deserves. COMMENTARY ON LUKE, HOMILY 110.[14]

27:5 Open Rebuke Rather Than Hidden Love

DO NOT CONCEAL A SIN IN BEHALF OF ANOTHER. BASIL THE GREAT: It is surely clear

[5]Sir 5:7. [6]FC 47:141. [7]Sir 18:26. [8]See Jn 12:35. [9]FC 66:89-90. [10]FC 31:117-18*. [11]FC 31:191*. [12]FC 88:83*. [13]NPNF 2 5:48. [14]CGSL 448**.

that concealing sin contributes to the death of the sick person, "for the sting of death is sin," says the Scripture,[15] and also, "Open rebukes are better than hidden love." Let no one, therefore, conceal a sin in behalf of another, lest fratricide take the place of fraternal charity. The Long Rules 46.[16]

27:6 The Wounds of a Friend

A Friendly Rebuke Is Better Than Silent Friendship. Ambrose: Rebukes are good, and often better than a silent friendship. Even if a friend thinks himself hurt, still rebuke him; and if the bitterness of the correction wounds his mind, still rebuke him and fear not. "The wounds of a friend are better than the kisses of flatterers." Rebuke, then, your erring friend; forsake not an innocent one. For friendship ought to be steadfast and to rest firm in true affection. Duties of the Clergy 3.22.127.[17]

A Mark of True Friendship. Augustine: Not everyone who spares is a friend, nor is everyone who strikes an enemy. "Better are the wounds of a friend than the proffered kisses of an enemy." Love mingled with severity is better than deceit with indulgence. Letter 93.[18]

Between Friends It Is Possible to Object Without Begetting Hatred. Augustine: "More trustworthy are the wounds of a friend than the proffered kisses of an enemy." Let us, then, with all the insistence we can put into it, impress this upon our dearest friends, those who are most sincerely interested in our work, and let them know that it is possible between dear friends for something to be objected to in the speech of either, without charity being thereby diminished, without truth begetting hatred. This is something which is owed to friendship, even if what is objected to is true, or whatever it is, so long as it is uttered from a truthful heart, without keeping in the mind what is at variance with the words. Letter 82.[19]

Wounds of Love Are Sweet. Maximus of Turin: When one who is loved is chastised, a pious act is exercised in his regard, for love has its wounds as well, which are all the sweeter for the harshness of their infliction. For a religious chastisement is sweeter than easy forgiveness, which is why the prophet says, "Sweeter are the wounds of a friend than the freely offered kisses of an enemy." Sermon 80.1.[20]

The Wound of Love Came from Peter. Ambrose: The wounds of love are good too, better than kisses. For "useful are the wounds of a friend; profuse are the kisses of an enemy." Peter wounds, and Judas kisses. But the kiss condemned Judas because it carried a traitorous venom; the wound inflicted by Peter also cured him because he washed away his fault with tears. On Virginity 6.33.[21]

27:10 Prefer a Nearby Neighbor to a Distant Relative

Prefer Close Friendship over Kinship. Ambrose: Solomon says, "Better is a neighbor that is near than a brother far off." For this reason a person generally trusts himself to the good will of a friend rather than to the ties of relationship to his brother. So far does good will prevail that it often goes beyond the pledges given by nature. Duties of the Clergy 1.34.174.[22]

27:15 A Continual Dripping on a Rainy Day

Spiritual Carelessness. John Cassian: Solomon remarks that the same thing happens to the soul in a spiritual way when he says in other words, "Leaks drive a person out of his house on a stormy day." Neatly, then, does he compare spiritual carelessness with a neglected roof, through which as it were certain tiny leaks of passion penetrate to the soul. If these little and insignificant

---

[15]1 Cor 15:56. [16]FC 9:324. [17]NPNF 2 10:88. [18]FC 18:60. [19]FC 12:416*. [20]ACW 50:192*. [21]AOV 18. [22]NPNF 2 10:29-30.

leaks are let go unattended, they weaken the structure of the virtues, and afterward they pour in a heavy shower of sinfulness. As a consequence, on a stormy day—that is, in time of trial—the mind is expelled by the onrushing assault of the devil from the dwelling place of virtue, in which it had once reposed as if it were its own house when it maintained a careful watchfulness. CONFERENCE 6.17.2.[23]

27:23 Know Your Own Flock Well

VARIOUS LEVELS OF SPIRITUAL MATURITY.
CYRIL OF ALEXANDRIA: It is not fitting to address simply to all who have believed in Christ instruction upon all points, for it is written, "With knowledge learn the souls of your flock." For the way is very different by which we establish in the paths of truth one who has but just now become a disciple, from one more confirmed in mind and able to understand what is the height and depth, and what the length and breadth. In the former, use simple teaching, in which there is nothing profound or difficult to understand. Counsel him to escape from the error of polytheism and fittingly persuade him to discern by the beauty of things created, the universal creator and artificer, who is one by nature and truly God. COMMENTARY ON LUKE, HOMILY 93.[24]

---

[23]ACW 57:234. [24]CGSL 374*.

28:1-28 WHEN THE WICKED PERISH, THE RIGHTEOUS INCREASE

[1]*The wicked flee when no one pursues,*
but the righteous are bold as a lion.
[2]*When a land transgresses it has many*
rulers;
but with men of understanding and
knowledge
its stability will long continue.
[3]*A poor man who oppresses the poor*
is a beating rain that leaves no food.
[4]*Those who forsake the law praise the*
wicked,
but those who keep the law strive against
them. *
[5]*Evil men do not understand justice,*
but those who seek the LORD understand
it completely.

[6]*Better is a poor man who walks in his*
integrity
than a rich man who is perverse in his
ways.
[7]*He who keeps the law is a wise son,*
but a companion of gluttons shames his
father.
[8]*He who augments his wealth by interest*
and increase
gathers it for him who is kind to the
poor.
[9]*If one turns away his ear from hearing*
the law,
even his prayer is an abomination.
[10]*He who misleads the upright into an*
evil way

will fall into his own pit;
 but the blameless will have a goodly
  inheritance.
[11]A rich man is wise in his own eyes,
 but a poor man who has understanding
  will find him out.
[12]When the righteous triumph, there is
  great glory;
 but when the wicked rise, men hide
  themselves.
[13]He who conceals his transgressions will
  not prosper,
 but he who confesses and forsakes them
  will obtain mercy.
[14]Blessed is the man who fears the LORD
  always;
 but he who hardens his heart will fall
  into calamity.
[15]Like a roaring lion or a charging bear
 is a wicked ruler over a poor people.
[16]A ruler who lacks understanding is a
  cruel oppressor;
 but he who hates unjust gain will prolong
  his days.
[17]If a man is burdened with the blood of
  another,
 let him be a fugitive until death;
 let no one help him.
[18]He who walks in integrity will be
  delivered,
 but he who is perverse in his ways will
  fall into a pit.[b]
[19]He who tills his land will have plenty of

bread,
 but he who follows worthless pursuits
  will have plenty of poverty.
[20]A faithful man will abound with
  blessings,
 but he who hastens to be rich will not go
  unpunished.
[21]To show partiality is not good;
 but for a piece of bread a man will do
  wrong.
[22]A miserly man hastens after wealth,
 and does not know that want will come
  upon him.
[23]He who rebukes a man will afterward
  find more favor
 than he who flatters with his tongue.
[24]He who robs his father or his mother
 and says, "That is no transgression,"
 is the companion of a man who destroys.
[25]A greedy man stirs up strife,
 but he who trusts in the LORD will be
  enriched.
[26]He who trusts in his own mind is a fool;
 but he who walks in wisdom will be
  delivered.
[27]He who gives to the poor will not want,
 but he who hides his eyes will get many a
  curse.
[28]When the wicked rise, men hide
  themselves,
 but when they perish, the righteous
  increase.

b Syr: Heb *in one* *LXX *Scoundrels think nothing of the law, but those who love the law set it in front of them like a wall.*

OVERVIEW: If you ask why do the wicked flee when no one is pursuing them, the answer is that they flee from their own conscience (CHRYSOSTOM). The righteous, by contrast, do not fear but rather dare all things by faith (ISAAC OF NINEVEH). The Stoic doctrine of nature, however, was wrong, because it mistook "nature" for "God" (CLEMENT OF ALEXANDRIA). Read God's precepts in Scripture as if you expect God to hear your prayers (CAESARIUS). But do not be surprised that God is slow to hear if we have been slow to pay attention (GREGORY THE GREAT). Strive to be worthy, therefore, of being heard by the Lord (BEDE). God does have mercy on those who confess their sins (APHRAHAT); indeed, God cleanses those who acknowledge and confess their sins (JEROME). Fear God in all things; stand firm in the truth (BASIL). Let your worship be focused and attentive (CHRYSOSTOM). Trembling is a necessary prelude to eternal joy (GREGORY THE GREAT), for the wise and holy are always fearful about their salvation (SALVIAN). If we give to the poor, we may receive the kingdom (AUGUSTINE), and always we must heed the challenge that comes from a hungry throat (VALERIAN). Give of your excess, therefore, and your soul will rejoice (CAESARIUS).

28:1 The Wicked Flee, but the Righteous Are Bold

THE WICKED FLEE FROM THEIR OWN CONSCIENCE. CHRYSOSTOM: How do [the wicked] flee when no one pursues? He has that within which drives him on—an accuser in his conscience, and this he carries about everywhere. Just as it would be impossible to flee from himself, so neither can he escape the persecutor within; but wherever he goes, he is scourged and has an incurable wound! But not such is the righteous. HOMILIES CONCERNING THE STATUES 8.3.[1]

THE RIGHTEOUS DARE ALL THINGS BY FAITH. ISAAC OF NINEVEH: [The righteous] will fear none of the things here enumerated, as it is written, "The righteous man is bold as a lion," daring all things through faith, not as one who tempts the Lord but as one who has confidence in him and as one who is armed and arrayed in the power of the Holy Spirit. And because God is his constant concern, God will also say concerning him, I am with him in affliction, and I will rescue him and glorify him. ASCETICAL HOMILY 7.[2]

28:4 Those Who Keep the Law Strive Against Those Who Forsake It

STOIC DOCTRINE OF NATURE WAS WRONG. CLEMENT OF ALEXANDRIA: The Stoics laid down their doctrine on the basis that the goal is to live according to nature, using the word *nature* improperly rather than "God," since nature applies to plants, crops, trees and stones. At any rate, there is the clear statement, "Scoundrels think nothing of the law, but those who love the law set it in front of them like a wall." For "the wisdom of able men will understand the paths of wisdom, but the folly of fools goes in the wrong direction."[3] STROMATEIS 2.19.101.[4]

28:9 Those Who Turn from Hearing God's Law

LISTEN TO GOD IF YOU WANT GOD TO HEAR YOUR PRAYER. CAESARIUS OF ARLES: What is written in the book of Solomon we ought to read with great anxiety and fear, not with indifference: "He that hardens his ears from hearing the law, his prayer shall be an abomination." A person should first be willing to listen to God, if he wants to be heard by him. Indeed, with what boldness does he want God to hear him when he despises God so much that he refuses to read God's precepts?

How is it, my brothers, that some Christians and, what is worse, even clergy, at times, when they are about to make a journey, order bread, wine, oil, and different items to be provided for themselves, but, while such great preparations are being made for his earthly journey so that his body may live, a man does not bother to read a single book to refresh his soul both here and forever? SERMON 7.3-4.[5]

IF WE HAVE PAID NO ATTENTION. GREGORY THE GREAT: Just as Scripture says, "When one

---

[1]NPNF 1 9:396*. [2]*AHSIS* 65. [3]Prov 14:8. [4]FC 85:224**. [5]FC 31:48*.

turns away his ears from hearing the law, even his prayer is an abomination." Why should we be surprised, then, if God is slow to hear our petitions when we on our part are slow to hear God's command or pay no attention whatever to it? DIALOGUE 3.15.[6]

BE WORTHY OF BEING HEARD BY THE LORD. BEDE: Let [anyone] beg, however, in faith, in no way hesitating. Let him, by living well, show himself to be worthy of being heard when he begs. For anyone who remembers that he has not obeyed the Lord's commands rightly loses hope that the Lord pays attention to his prayers. For it has been written, "The prayer of one who closes his ear that he may not hear the law will be detestable." COMMENTARY ON JAMES 1.6[7]

28:13 Confess Your Transgressions Rather Than Conceal Them

GOD HAS MERCY ON THOSE WHO CONFESS THEIR SINS. APHRAHAT: I address you too, the penitents. You should not keep back from yourselves this means of healing [confession] that has been given you. For it says in the Scripture, "He who confesses his sins and abandons them, on him God has mercy." Look at the son who squandered his wealth. And when he returned to his father, he received him in joy and slew the fatted ox for him. And his father rejoiced at his repentance and even invited his friends to rejoice with him. And his father embraced him and kept on kissing him, saying, "This my son was dead and has come to life; he was lost and has been found."[8] And his father did not reprove him for the wealth he had squandered.[9] DEMONSTRATIONS 7.12.[10]

GOD CLEANSES THOSE WHO CONFESS THEIR SINS. JEROME: "As confession and beauty are in the sight of God,"[11] so a sinner who confesses his sins and says, "My wounds stink and are corrupt because of my foolishness"[12] loses his foul wounds and is made whole and clean. But "he that covers his sins shall not prosper." LETTER 122.3.[13]

28:14 Blessed Is the One Who Fears God

FEAR GOD IN ALL THINGS. BASIL THE GREAT: He who in all things stands in awe out of reverent timidity is called blessed, and he stands firm in the truth who is able to say, "I set the Lord always in my sight; for he is at my right hand that I shall not be moved."[14] THE LONG RULES, PREFACE.[15]

BE FOCUSED AND ATTENTIVE IN YOUR PIETY. CHRYSOSTOM: Let your requests be spiritual . . . let your mind be alert, let your attention be concentrated on the words. Ask for the kind of things it is usual to ask of God so that you may gain what you ask. To the same end maintain your constant vigil, alert, keeping your attention undimmed, no yawning or switching your mind in one direction and another, but working out your salvation in fear and trembling. "Blessed is the person," Scripture says, remember, "whose piety puts him in awe of everything." HOMILIES ON GENESIS 30.15.[16]

TREMBLING IS A NECESSARY PRELUDE TO ETERNAL JOY. GREGORY THE GREAT: You ought not, in this life, to have security, whereby you may be rendered careless. For it is written, "Happy is the one who always fears [the Lord]." And again, it is written, "Serve the Lord in fear, and rejoice in him with trembling."[17] In short, then, it must be that in the time of this life trembling will possess your soul, to the end that it may hereafter rejoice without end through the joy of security. LETTER 25.[18]

THE WISE AND HOLY ARE FEARFUL ABOUT THEIR SALVATION. SALVIAN THE PRESBYTER: Someone asks, "Is there, therefore, no difference between saints and sinners?" Certainly, there is a great and almost immeasurable difference. Scripture says, "Blessed is the man who is always fear-

---

[6]FC 39:140. [7]CS 82:10*. [8]Lk 15:32. [9]Lk 15:11-32. [10]SC 349:423. [11]Ps 96:6 (95:6 Vg). [12]Ps 38:5 (37:6 Vg). [13]NPNF 2 6:227*. [14]Ps 16:8 (15:8 LXX). [15]FC 9:227-28*. [16]FC 82:232*. [17]Ps 2:11. [18]NPNF 2 12:219**.

ful." The mind of a wise person is ever uneasy about his own salvation. Although there is a great difference between saints and sinners, still I ask all those who profess a religion, Who, according to his own conscience, is sufficiently holy; who does not tremble about the fearful severity of a future judgment; who is untroubled about his eternal salvation? If this is not the case, just as it should not be, I beg, let any one tell me why he does not strive with all the power of his goods to redeem, by a holy death, whatever sins he may have committed by transgression during his lifetime. FOUR BOOKS OF TIMOTHY TO THE CHURCH 2.3.[19]

28:27 *Those Who Give to the Poor Will Not Want*

GIVE TO THE POOR AND RECEIVE THE KINGDOM. AUGUSTINE: Don't forget that rule, where it says, "Whoever gives to the poor will never be in want." Have you already forgotten what the Lord is going to say to those who have given to the poor: "Come, blessed of my Father, receive the kingdom"? SERMON 198.3.[20]

WE MUST HEED THE CHALLENGE. VALERIAN: The cry of the hungry person is a challenge in your ears, and the sound of a failing voice from a hungry throat is striking at your door. Why do you not think of that phrase, "Blessed is he that

understands concerning the needy and the poor: the Lord will deliver him in the evil day."[21] The businessman who keeps stored away in a sack the money with which he could carry on gainful trading is recognized as being quite a fool. HOMILY 9.2.[22]

GIVE OF YOUR EXCESS, AND YOUR SOUL WILL REJOICE. CAESARIUS OF ARLES: Whenever you gather the harvest or vintage, calculate your expenses and those of all who pertain to you and include what you will put into your purse. Then, of what remains, because it was not really given to you, as was already said, but was transmitted to you for distribution among the poor, set it all aside or as much as God inspires your heart to give. The result thus will be as though you had put it in God's hand. If, as we believe, you are willing to do this devoutly, your soul will not only be exasperated and saddened by the captives and poor who come to you but will even rejoice and be glad. With the greatest willingness you will bestow what you set aside for the necessities of the poor out of love for God, and there will be fulfilled in you the words "God loves a cheerful giver"[23] and "He that gives to the poor shall never want." SERMON 30.6.[24]

---

[19]FC 3:296-97. [20]WSA 3 6:74-75. [21]Ps 41:1 (40:1 LXX). [22]FC 17:359*. [23]2 Cor 9:7. [24]FC 31:152.

29:1-27 RIGHTEOUSNESS GIVES STABILITY TO THE LAND

[1]*He who is often reproved, yet stiffens his neck,*
will suddenly be broken beyond healing.

[2]*When the righteous are in authority, the people rejoice;*
but when the wicked rule, the people

groan.

^{3}He who loves wisdom makes his father
glad,
but one who keeps company with harlots
squanders his substance.
^{4}By justice a king gives stability to the
land,
but one who exacts gifts ruins it.
^{5}A man who flatters his neighbor
spreads a net for his feet.
^{6}An evil man is ensnared in his
transgression,
but a righteous man sings and rejoices.
^{7}A righteous man knows the rights of the
poor;
a wicked man does not understand such
knowledge.
^{8}Scoffers set a city aflame,
but wise men turn away wrath.
^{9}If a wise man has an argument with a
fool,
the fool only rages and laughs, and there
is no quiet.
^{10}Bloodthirsty men hate one who is
blameless,
and the wicked^c seek his life.
^{11}A fool gives full vent to his anger,
but a wise man quietly holds it back.
^{12}If a ruler listens to falsehood,
all his officials will be wicked.
^{13}The poor man and the oppressor meet
together;
the LORD gives light to the eyes of both.
^{14}If a king judges the poor with equity
his throne will be established for ever.
^{15}The rod and reproof give wisdom,
but a child left to himself brings shame to
his mother.

^{16}When the wicked are in authority,
transgression increases;
but the righteous will look upon their
downfall.
^{17}Discipline your son, and he will give you
rest;
he will give delight to your heart.
^{18}Where there is no prophecy the people
cast off restraint,
but blessed is he who keeps the law.
^{19}By mere words a servant is not
disciplined,
for though he understands, he will not
give heed.
^{20}Do you see a man who is hasty in his
words?
There is more hope for a fool than for
him.
^{21}He who pampers his servant from
childhood,
will in the end find him his heir.^{d}
^{22}A man of wrath stirs up strife,
and a man given to anger causes much
transgression.
^{23}A man's pride will bring him low,
but he who is lowly in spirit will obtain
honor.
^{24}The partner of a thief hates his own
life;
he hears the curse, but discloses nothing.
^{25}The fear of man lays a snare,
but he who trusts in the LORD is safe.
^{26}Many seek the favor of a ruler,
but from the LORD a man gets justice.
^{27}An unjust man is an abomination to the
righteous,
but he whose way is straight is an
abomination to the wicked.

c Cn: Heb upright   d The meaning of the Hebrew word is uncertain

OVERVIEW: There are ways for one who loves wisdom to preserve it (CLEMENT OF ALEXANDRIA). The wise person tempers his anger with discretion (JOHN CASSIAN), but the fool has no interior discipline for restraining his anger (GREGORY THE GREAT). The undisciplined are corrected not by words but by stripes that bear fruit (AUGUSTINE). The wisdom you teach should be what you practice (JOHN CASSIAN). Israel, pampered from infancy, grew fat and went into captivity among the Gentiles (EPHREM). History provides many examples of persons who have been humiliated by their pride (APHRAHAT). Even perpetual continence, for example, can generate the pride of self-complacence (AUGUSTINE). Indeed, we should cultivate humility for our own good (BEDE).

29:3 He Who Loves Wisdom Makes His Father Glad

THERE ARE WAYS TO PRESERVE WISDOM.
CLEMENT OF ALEXANDRIA: In my view, the sketch of a soul which yearns to preserve the blessed tradition without losing a single drop runs something like this: "When a man loves wisdom, his father's heart will be warmed." Wells which are constantly baled out provide a clearer water; wells which no one draws from turn to rottenness. Use keeps iron brighter; disuse produces rust in it. In general, exercise produces fitness in souls and bodies. STROMATEIS 1.1.12.[1]

29:11 Give Not Full Vent to Anger

THE WISE PERSON TEMPERS ANGER WITH DISCRETION. JOHN CASSIAN: It behooves us, therefore, to contain every movement of wrath and to temper it with discretion as our guide lest, overcome with rage, we be swept up into what is condemned by Solomon: "The wicked person expends his anger all at once, but the wise person dispenses it gradually." That is to say, in the heat of his anger the fool is inflamed to revenge himself, but by mature deliberation and moderation the wise person slowly dimin-

ishes and releases his. CONFERENCE 16.27.1.[2]

THE FOOL HAS NO INTERIOR DISCIPLINE.
GREGORY THE GREAT: Let the impatient be told what is also said by Solomon: "A fool utters all his mind; a wise man defers and keeps it till afterwards." Under the impulse of impatience the whole spirit exposes itself, and its turbulence drives it out the more speedily, in that there is no interior discipline of wisdom to keep it in. The wise person, on the other hand, keeps back and lets the future take care of matters. When he is wronged, he does not wish to avenge himself at once, because in his forbearance he wishes others to be spared, though he is not ignorant of the fact that all things are punished justly at the last judgment. PASTORAL CARE 3.9.10.[3]

29:19 Verbal Discipline Does Not Suffice

THE UNDISCIPLINED ARE NOT CORRECTED BY WORDS. AUGUSTINE: In saying that "the servant will not be corrected by words," [Solomon] did not order him to be left to himself but implied an admonition as to the means whereby he ought to be corrected. Otherwise he would not have said, "He will not be corrected by words," but without any qualification, "He will not be corrected." For in another place he says that not only the servant but also the undisciplined son must be corrected with stripes, and that with great fruits as the result. For he says, "You shall beat him with the rod and shall deliver his soul from hell,"[4] and elsewhere he says, "He that spares the rod hates his own son."[5] THE CORRECTION OF THE DONATISTS 6.21.[6]

29:20 The Fool Is Hasty in Words

PRACTICE THE WISDOM YOU TEACH. JOHN CASSIAN: In all things be "quick to listen and slow to speak"[7] lest the remark of Solomon be

---

[1]FC 85:30. [2]ACW 57:573*. [3]ACW 11:109*. [4]Prov 23:14. [5]Prov 13:24. [6]NPNF 1 4:641**. [7]Jas 1:19.

fulfilled in you: "If you see a man too ready of speech, know that a fool has more hope than he." And never dare to teach someone what you have not practiced yourself. Conference 14.9.[8]

29:21 Pampered from Infancy

Israel Was Imprisoned among the Gentiles. Ephrem the Syrian: Formed, surrounded and coddled by delicacies and pleasures since its infancy, Israel, in spite of the [prefigured] images of the cross, "grew fat, became gross and recalcitrant,"[9] so that, finally, captivity imprisoned it among the Gentiles. "The one who is pampered in his infancy will be handed over to servitude." Commentary on Tatian's Diatessaron 38.[10]

29:23 The Humble Shall Increase in Honor

History Provides Examples of Persons Humiliated by their Pride. Aphrahat: Pride and arrogance have subverted many. Through pride Adam went forth from paradise, and dust became the serpent's meat. Through pride Cain killed his brother and became a trembler and a straggler on the earth. And Ham, because he was uplifted and mocked his father, became accursed and a servant of servants to his brothers. Because of his pride Esau lost the birthright of his primogeniture; and Pharaoh, because he was hardened and uplifted, was drowned in the Red Sea, he and his host. And the sons of Eli the priest, because they were lifted up against the people, were deposed from the priesthood of the Holy One. Goliath the Philistine, because of his arrogance against David, was humbled and put to shame, and fell by his pride. And upon Abimelech the son of Gideon, who was lifted up against his brothers and slew them, came the curse of Jotham his brother. Absalom, who was uplifted and seized the kingdom, fell and was humbled before the servants of David; and Adonijah the son of Haggith, who stole the kingdom, neither retained it nor prospered by his pride. As for Ahithophel

the counselor of iniquities, his pride was humbled by his own hands; and Jeroboam the son of Nebat, the servant of Solomon, who made division among the people, became an evil memory in Israel; and Ahab the son of Omri was overcome by covetousness in the inheritance of Jezreel and received retributions. To the king of Edom, who was lifted up against Ahab, there was not found anyone that should bind or that should loose. And Haman, who was lifted up against Mordecai, received retribution on the gallows, he and his sons. The men of Babylon who accused Daniel had their bones crushed by lions. And Judas, who betrayed our Savior, fell into the sea with a millstone about his neck. These all were humbled by their pride, as it was written, "The pride of a man shall humble him, and to him who is humble in spirit honor shall be increased." Demonstrations 14.10.[11]

Perpetual Continence Can Generate Self-Complacence. Augustine: Give me someone professing perpetual continence, and free from these and all similar vices and blemishes of conduct. For her I fear pride; for her I dread the swelling of self-conceit from so great a blessing. The more there is in her from which she finds self-complacence, the more I fear lest by pleasing herself she will displease him who "resists the proud but gives grace to the humble."[12] Holy Virginity 34.[13]

We Should Cultivate Humility for Our Own Good. Bede: That we ourselves may become worthy of following in his footsteps and ascending to heaven, let us in the meantime become humble on earth for our own good, always mindful that, as Solomon says, "Humiliation follows the proud, and honor follows the humble in spirit." Homilies on the Gospels 2.15.[14]

---

[8]JCC 163. [9]Deut 32:15. [10]ECTD 314. [11]SC 359:617-20. [12]Jas 4:6. [13]FC 27:184-85*. [14]CS 111:147.

30:1-9 PERSONAL OBSERVATIONS OF AGUR

¹*The words of Agur son of Jakeh of Massa.ᵉ*

The man says to Ithi-el,
to Ithi-el and Ucal:ᶠ
²*Surely I am too stupid to be a man.*
I have not the understanding of a man.
³*I have not learned wisdom,**
nor have I knowledge of the Holy One.†
⁴*Who has ascended to heaven and come*
down?
Who has gathered the wind in his fists?
Who has wrapped up the waters in a
garment?
Who has established all the ends of the
earth?
What is his name, and what is his son's
name?

Surely you know!
⁵*Every word of God proves true;*
he is a shield to those who take refuge in
him.
⁶*Do not add to his words,*
lest he rebuke you, and you be found a
liar.

⁷*Two things I ask of thee;*
deny them not to me before I die:
⁸*Remove far from me falsehood and lying;*
give me neither poverty nor riches;
feed me with the food that is needful for me,
⁹*lest I be full, and deny thee,*
and say, "Who is the LORD?"
or lest I be poor, and steal,
and profane the name of my God.

e Or the oracle f The Hebrew of this verse is obscure *LXX *God has taught me wisdom* †Vg *and I have not known the science of the saints*

OVERVIEW: Train your eyes on heaven, and the Spirit will lead you there (BASIL). The Wisdom spoken by Solomon is from God (GREGORY OF NYSSA). God's Son is Christ, the Wisdom of God (AUGUSTINE). Even the waters are guided by God's will (EPHREM), just as faith also has need of works (ISAAC OF NINEVEH). We must neither add to God's words nor subtract from them (APOSTOLIC CONSTITUTIONS). Pray for adequate resources, not excess either of poverty or riches (AMBROSE). Sufficiency does vary according to physical condition and present need (BASIL), but in essence it means the ability to live honorably and respectably (AUGUSTINE).

30:3-4 Wisdom Ascending and Descending

TRAIN YOUR EYES ON HEAVEN. BASIL THE

GREAT: Raise your eyes to heaven, therefore, like him who said, "To you who lives in heaven, I lift my eyes."[1] Look upon the sun of righteousness and, as you are directed by the commandments of the Lord, which resemble the most radiant of stars, have vigilant eyes. Do not allow the eyes [of the soul] to slumber or the eyelids to rest,[2] that the commandments might lead you perpetually. "For, your law is a lamp to my feet," he says, "and a light to my path."[3] Indeed, if you never fall asleep at the helm while steering through life, given the obviously unstable state of worldly affairs, you will obtain the cooperation of the Spirit, who will lead you beyond and transport you with gentle breezes and in peaceful security

[1]Ps 123:1 (122:1 LXX). [2]See Ps 132:4 (131:4 LXX). [3]Ps 119:105 (118:105 LXX).

until you arrive unharmed at that tranquil and serene gate by the will of God, to whom be glory and power forever and ever. Amen. HOMILY ON THE BEGINNING OF PROVERBS 17.[4]

THE WISDOM SPOKEN BY SOLOMON IS FROM GOD. GREGORY OF NYSSA: It is not mere human wisdom that is claimed for himself by Solomon, who says, "God has taught me wisdom," and who, where he says, "all my words are spoken from God,"[8] refers to God all that is spoken by himself. AGAINST EUNOMIUS 3.2.[9]

GOD'S SON IS CHRIST, THE WISDOM OF GOD. AUGUSTINE: "Surely," you say, "you will be kind enough to tell me whether Solomon truly said, 'God has no son.'" This is quickly answered: not only did he not say, "God has no son," but he did say that God has a Son. Wisdom speaking through him says, "Before all the hills, he begot me,"[5] and what is Christ but the wisdom of God?[6] Again, in a certain passage in Proverbs, he says, "God has taught me wisdom, and I have known the science of the saints. Who has ascended up into heaven and descends? Who has held the wind in his bosom? Who has changed the water as a garment? Who has held all the borders of the earth? What is his name? and what is the name of his son?" LETTER 102.5.[7]

EVEN THE WATERS ARE GUIDED BY GOD'S WILL. EPHREM THE SYRIAN:
Indeed, that Will
    for whom everything is easy
    constrains these abundant
    fountains of paradise,
    confining them with land,
    like water channels;
    he summoned them to issue forth
    in our direction,
    just as he bound up the waters
    in the bosom of his clouds,
    ready to be sent forth into the atmosphere
    at the bidding of his Will.

HYMNS ON PARADISE 9.[10]

FAITH ALSO HAS NEED OF WORKS. ISAAC OF NINEVEH: Do you believe that God provides for his creatures and is able to do all things? Let suitable labor, therefore, follow on your faith, and then he will hear you. Think not to grasp the winds in your fist, that is, faith without works. ASCETICAL HOMILIES 7.[11]

30:6 Do Not Add to God's Words

NEITHER ADD TO GOD'S WORDS NOR SUBTRACT FROM THEM. APOSTOLIC CONSTITUTIONS: You shall hate all hypocrisy; and whatever is pleasing to the Lord, that shall you do. By no means forsake the commands of the Lord. But you shall observe what things you have received from him, neither adding to them nor taking away from them. "For you shall not add unto his words, lest he convict you and you become a liar." You shall confess your sins unto the Lord your God; and you shall not add unto them, that it may be well with you from the Lord your God, who wills not the death of a sinner but his repentance. CONSTITUTIONS OF THE HOLY APOSTLES 7.1.14.[12]

30:8-9 Sufficiency Entails Neither Poverty Nor Riches

PRAY FOR ADEQUATE RESOURCES, NOT EXCESS. AMBROSE: The poor man and the rich man should therefore take heed, because there are temptations for the man of poverty as well as for the man of wealth. And so the wise man says, "Give me neither beggary nor riches." He tells you how this can be obtained. Man has enough when he has a sufficiency, because a wealthy man tends to distend his mind with cares and anxieties, just as he gorges his stomach with rich food. For that

---

[4]PG 31:421-24*. [5]Cf. Prov 8:25. [6]1 Cor 1:24. [7]FC 18:168-69*. [8]Cf. Prov 24; 31. [9]NPNF 2 5:140*. [10]HOP 88. [11]AHSIS 65. [12]ANF 7:468.

reason the wise man prays that he may have what is necessary and adequate. . . .

Shun and avoid, therefore, the temptations of the world, so that the poor may not despair and the rich may not grow proud. Six Days of Creation 6.53.[13]

Sufficiency Varies. Basil the Great: Solomon says, "Give me neither beggary nor riches; give me only what is necessary and sufficient," lest being filled I should deny and say, Who sees me? Or being poor, I should steal and forswear the name of my God; thus representing riches as satiety, poverty as a complete lack of the necessities of life, and sufficiency as a state both free from want and without superfluity. Suffi-

ciency varies, however, according to physical condition and present need. . . . In every case, care must be taken for a good table, yet without overstepping the limits of the actual need. The Long Rules 20.[14]

Sufficiency Means the Ability to Live Honorably and Respectably. Augustine: Surely you see that this sufficiency is not to be coveted for its own sake but to provide for health of body and for clothing which accords with one's personal dignity and which makes it possible for him to live with others honorably and respectably. Letter 130.[15]

---

[13]FC 42:267*. [14]FC 9:280. [15]FC 18:385-86.

30:10-33 PROVERBS OF NUMERICAL CONSTRUCTION

[10]Do not slander a servant to his master,
   lest he curse you, and you be held guilty.

[11]There are those who curse their fathers
   and do not bless their mothers.
[12]There are those who are pure in their
      own eyes
   but are not cleansed of their filth.
[13]There are those—how lofty are their eyes,
   how high their eyelids lift!
[14]There are those whose teeth are swords,
   whose teeth are knives,
   to devour the poor from off the earth,
   the needy from among men.

[15]The leech[g] has two daughters;*

   "Give, give," they cry.
   Three things are never satisfied;
   four never say, "Enough":
[16]Sheol, the barren womb,
   the earth ever thirsty for water,
   and the fire which never says, "Enough."[h]

[17]The eye that mocks a father
   and scorns to obey a mother
   will be picked out by the ravens of the valley
   and eaten by the vultures.

[18]Three things are too wonderful for me;
   four I do not understand:
[19]the way of an eagle in the sky,
   the way of a serpent on a rock,

the way of a ship on the high seas,
   and the way of a man with a maiden.
²⁰This is the way of an adulteress:
   she eats, and wipes her mouth,
   and says, "I have done no wrong."

²¹Under three things the earth trembles;
   under four it cannot bear up:
²²a slave when he becomes king,
   and a fool when he is filled with food;
²³an unloved woman when she gets a
       husband,
   and a maid when she succeeds her
       mistress.

²⁴Four things on earth are small,
   but they are exceedingly wise:
²⁵the ants are a people not strong,
   yet they provide their food in the summer;
²⁶the badgers are a people not mighty,

yet they make their homes in the rocks;
²⁷the locusts have no king,
   yet all of them march in rank;
²⁸the lizard you can take in your hands,
   yet it is in kings' palaces.

²⁹Three things are stately in their tread;
   four are stately in their stride:
³⁰the lion, which is mightiest among beasts
   and does not turn back before any;
³¹the strutting cock,ⁱ the he-goat,
   and a king striding before^j his people.

³²If you have been foolish, exalting yourself,
   or if you have been devising evil,
   put your hand on your mouth.
³³For pressing milk produces curds,
   pressing the nose produces blood,
   and pressing anger produces strife.

g The meaning of the Hebrew word is uncertain   h Heb obscure   i Gk Syr Tg Compare Vg: Heb obscure   j The meaning of the Hebrew is uncertain   *LXX *The horseleech had three dearly loved daughters.*

OVERVIEW: The proverbial expressions about the grave, woman's love, dry earth and eternal fire are enigmatic, but they have a deeper meaning: inordinate love is insatiable (JEROME). Sin grows continually and never gets enough of what it desires. The proverb about the eye mocking and scorning the parent can be understood in the deeper sense that blasphemy may be directed against God (HIPPOLYTUS).

Still another enigmatic proverb is about the way of an eagle, a serpent, a ship and a man; its meaning, also, must be discovered at a level deeper than the historical (BEDE). Just as a serpent leaves no mark of its track on a rock, so the church leaves no trace of sin in its course (HIPPOLYTUS), and the gates of hell will not prevail against the church just as the way of the serpent upon a rock cannot be found (ORIGEN). Doctri-

nally, as against the Arians, this means that there is but one Godhead and not two (AMBROSE).

In fact, the church was once an adulteress (HIPPOLYTUS), and thus the sinner who repents of fornication has more hope than one who does not (ORIGEN), just as the prostitute who renounces sin becomes a virgin by her faith in Christ (MAXIMUS OF TURIN). The three things by which the earth is moved are Father, Son and Holy Spirit (HIPPOLYTUS).

Regarding the four things on earth that are small but wise, the ants, badgers, lizards and locusts are all wiser than the wise especially because they store up for times of need (HIPPOLYTUS). Likewise humans, even those whose faith is as little as the weakness of such creatures, may nonetheless store up treasures for eternal life by their good works (DIDYMUS). To be prudent therefore we should copy the ants (AUGUSTINE), for their real meaning is hidden and not literal. As for the locusts, human beings are less orderly than they (ORIGEN) and know less about self-government than they (CAESARIUS). Four stately things that all go well are angels, saints, souls and God the Word incarnate (HIPPOLYTUS). Squeeze out the commandments of the two testaments, and they will become like butter for your bread (CHRYSOSTOM).

30:15-16 Four Things Never Satisfied

INORDINATE LOVE IS INSATIABLE. JEROME: Who can hide from himself what is thus enigmatically expressed? "The horseleech had three daughters, dearly loved, but they satisfied her not, and a fourth is not satisfied when you say Enough: the grave, and woman's love, and the earth that is not satisfied with water, and the fire that does not say Enough." The horseleech is the devil, the daughters of the devil are dearly loved, and they cannot be satisfied with the blood of the slain: "the grave, and woman's love, and the earth dry and scorched with heat." It is not the harlot or the adulteress who is spoken of, but woman's love in general is accused of ever being insatiable. Put it out, it bursts into flame; give it plenty, it is again in need. It enervates a man's mind and engrosses all thought except for the passion which it feeds. AGAINST JOVINIANUS 1.28.[1]

SIN NEVER ACQUIRES ENOUGH. HIPPOLYTUS: "The horseleech had three dearly loved daughters." Its daughters lead to sin: the daughters of fornication, murder and idolatry. These three did not satisfy her, for she is not to be satisfied. In destroying man by these actions, sin never varies but only grows continually. For the fourth, [Solomon] continues, is never content to say "enough," meaning that it is universal lust... . For as the body is one and yet has many members, so also sin, being one, contains within it many various lusts by which it lays its snares for men. FRAGMENTS ON PROVERBS.[2]

30:17 Mocking and Scorning

BLASPHEMY AGAINST GOD AND WISDOM. HIPPOLYTUS:"The eye that mocks at his father, and dishonors the old age of his mother." That is to say, one who blasphemes God . . . ravens from the caves may pluck from him the eye of gladness. FRAGMENTS ON PROVERBS.[3]

30:18-19 The Ways of an Eagle, Serpent, Ship and Man

THE CHURCH LEAVES NO TRACE OF SIN IN ITS COURSE. HIPPOLYTUS: As a serpent cannot mark its track upon a rock, so the devil could not find sin in the body of Christ. For the Lord says, "Behold, the prince of the world comes and will find nothing in me."[4] For as a ship, sailing in the sea, leaves no traces of its way behind it, so neither does the church, which is situated in the world as in a sea, leave her hope upon the earth, because she has her life reserved in heaven; and as it holds her way here only for a short time, it is not possible to trace out her course. . . . "There are three things which I cannot understand, and the fourth I know not: the tracks of an eagle flying," that is, Christ's ascension; "and the ways of a serpent upon a rock," that is, that the devil did not find a trace of sin in the body of Christ; "and the ways of a ship crossing the sea," that is, the ways of the church, which is in this life as in a sea and which is directed by its hope in Christ through the cross; "and the ways of a man in youth"—the ways of him, namely, who is born of the Holy Spirit and the Virgin. FRAGMENTS ON PROVERBS.[5]

THE GATES OF HELL WILL NOT PREVAIL. ORIGEN: Neither against the rock on which Christ builds the church nor against the church will the gates of hades prevail; just as the way of a serpent upon a rock, according to what is written

---

[1]NPNF 2 6:367*. [2]ANF 5:173-74*; TLG 2115.044.46. [3]ANF 5:174**; TLG 2115.045.49. [4]Jn 14:30. [5]ANF 5:174*; TLG 2115.013.22, 54.

in the Proverbs, cannot be found. Now, if the gates of hades prevail against any one, such cannot be a rock upon which Christ builds the church. COMMENTARY ON MATTHEW 12.11.[6]

NOT TWO GODS BUT ONE GOD. AMBROSE: An eagle and a ship and a serpent are not of one family and nature but of a distinguishable and different substance, and yet they are three. On the testimony of Scripture, therefore, [the Arians] learn that their arguments are against themselves.

Therefore, in saying that the substance of the Father and of the Son is diverse and their Godhead distinguishable, [the Arians] themselves assert there are two gods. But we, when we confess the Father and the Son, in declaring them still to be of one Godhead, say that there are not two gods but one God. And this we establish by the Word of the Lord. ON THE CHRISTIAN FAITH 5.3.40-41.[7]

EXPLANATION OF SUCH PARABLES IS DISCOVERED ONLY AT A DEEPER LEVEL. BEDE: With regard to history, it is as written thus. But because this speaks in parables, "the way of the eagle in the heavens" is discovered only with difficulty, referring as it does to the subtlety of the enemy whereby great effort is required to detect his flight around the hearts of heavenly people. The same is true for "the way of the serpent upon the earth," that is, the cunning of the venomous enemy with which he does not cease to plot against those whom he perceives to be founded upon the rock of faith. Likewise for "the way of the ship in the middle of the sea," that is, the way of iniquity whereby he moves with such subtlety through the bitter waves of this world, agitated by the winds of unclean spirits, that his journey can be hardly detected or not at all. For the prophet testifies that the eagle signifies this malignant adversary, saying, "Our persecutors were faster than the eagles of heaven,"[8] that is, the people who pursued us were so fierce that they appeared to be even more vicious than demons themselves. That a serpent often represents the devil was proven both in the sin of the first man

and when a wise man said, "Flee from sin as though from the face of a serpent."[9] And the prophet showed that a ship designates the inconstancy of those who are blown about by every wind of doctrine[10] when he referred to "the Chaldeans glorying in their ships,"[11] that is, the unclean of spirit exalting in the fragility and instability of the human mind and in their own destruction, as though they were rejoicing victors. Just as they are too clever to be found, therefore, so does the young person who has abandoned the way of truth have such difficulty in thinking that he continually every hour descends further into aimless, senseless considerations. COMMENTARY ON PROVERBS 30.18-19.[12]

30:20 The Way of an Adulteress

THE CHURCH WAS ONCE AN ADULTERESS. HIPPOLYTUS: "Such is the way of an adulterous woman, who, when she has done the deed of sin, wipes herself and will say that no wickedness has been done." Such is the conduct of the church that believes on Christ, when, after committing fornication with idols, she renounces these and the devil and is cleansed of her sins, and receives forgiveness, and then asserts that she has done no wickedness. FRAGMENTS ON PROVERBS.[13]

THE SINNER WHO REPENTS OF FORNICATION HAS MORE HOPE THAN ONE WHO DOES NOT. ORIGEN: I will describe two persons who have sinned the same abominable sin of fornication, yet between these two who have fornicated, the one is not aggrieved nor feels pain nor is vexed but experiences what was said in Proverbs concerning the adulterous woman "who having washed herself, if she does something, says she has done nothing wrong." See with me the other who after the mistake is unable to contain himself but punishes the conscience, tortures the heart, is

---

[6]ANF 9:456*. [7]NPNF 2 10:289-90. [8]Lam 4:19. [9]Sir 21:2. [10]See Eph 4:14. [11]Is 43:14. [12]CCL 119B:144-45. [13]ANF 5:174*; TLG 2115.044.56.1.

unable to eat and drink, who fasts not because of a judgment but because of grief of repentance. I will describe him as the kind of person who "appears sad all day long"[14] and who wears himself down with suffering and who goes "wailing from the groaning of his heart,"[15] who sees his sin reproved before himself on account of all which happened before. And see that this sort of person punishes himself not only for one day nor one night but for a long time. Who do you say has hope before God? Is it that first person who has fornicated and does not care but is callous and also has hardened himself just as one who has "given himself up to licentiousness"?[16] Or is it this latter person who after one sin goes into mourning, lamenting it?

This latter [has some grounds for hope]. The more such a one is burnt by the fire of grief, the more he is shown mercy, and there is for him such sufficient time for punishment, as there is a time of punishment given to that person who fornicated and was grieved.[17] HOMILIES ON JEREMIAH 20.9.1-2.[18]

THE PROSTITUTE WHO RENOUNCES SIN BECOMES A VIRGIN BY FAITH IN CHRIST. MAXIMUS OF TURIN: "Such is the way of a prostitute: when she has washed herself she says that she has done something wrong." Clearly this is said of her who, after having washed herself at the source, does not remember the vices of her sins, assumes the virtue of preaching, and, wiping away her stains with living water, has no more awareness of her sin but is urged on by the ardor of faith. For in a certain way she says that she has done nothing wicked now that she has become a messenger of the truth, and by forgetfulness she renounces her impurity now that she preaches chastity in her devotion. For this is the power of Christ the Lord, that even a sinner who washes himself in his water returns afresh to virginity and forgets what he had done before. And in his new birth he manifests the innocence of infancy, he does not know the sins of youth, and although he had been an adulterer because of the corrup-

tion of sin, he becomes a virgin because of faith in Christ. SERMON 22.3.[19]

30:21-23 The Earth Trembles and Moves

BY FATHER, SON AND HOLY SPIRIT THE WHOLE EARTH IS MOVED. HIPPOLYTUS: "By three things the earth is moved," namely, by the Father, the Son and the Holy Ghost. "And the fourth it cannot bear," namely, the last appearing of the Savior. . . .

The shaking [of the earth] signifies the change of things upon earth. Sin, then, which in its own nature is a slave, has reigned in the mortal body of people. Once, indeed, at the time of the flood; and again in the time of the Sodomites, who, not satisfied with what the land yielded, offered violence to strangers; and a third time in the case of hateful Egypt, which, though it obtained in Joseph a man who distributed food to all, that they might not perish of famine, yet did not take well with his prosperity but persecuted the children of Israel. "The handmaid casting out her mistress," that is, the church of the Gentiles, which, though itself a slave and a stranger to the promises, cast out the freeborn and lordly synagogue and became the wife and bride of Christ. By Father, Son and Holy Spirit, the whole earth is moved. The "fourth it cannot bear": for he came first by lawgivers, and second by prophets, and third by the gospel, manifesting himself openly; and in the fourth instance he shall come as the judge of the living and the dead, whose glory the whole creation will not be able to endure. FRAGMENTS ON PROVERBS.[20]

30:24-28 Four Things That Are Small but Wise

ANTS, BADGERS, LIZARDS AND LOCUSTS ARE ALL WISER THAN THE WISE. HIPPOLYTUS:

---

[14]Ps 38:6 (37:7 LXX). [15]Ps 38:8 (37:9 LXX). [16]See Eph 4:19. [17]See 2 Cor 2:5-11. [18]FC 97:240-41*. [19]ACW 50:55. [20]ANF 5:174-75*; TLG 2115.013.54.25, 26.1.

"There are four things which are least upon the earth, and these are wiser than the wise: The ants have no strength, yet they prepare their meat in the summer." And in like manner, the Gentiles by faith in Christ prepare for themselves eternal life through good works. "And the conies [badgers], a feeble folk, have made their houses in the rocks." The Gentiles, that is to say, are built upon Christ, the spiritual rock, who is become the head of the corner. "The spider [lizard], that supports itself upon its hands, and is easily caught, dwells in the strongholds of kings." That is, the thief with his hands extended [on the cross], rests on the cross of Christ and dwells in paradise, the stronghold of the three kings—Father, Son and Holy Ghost.

"The locust has no king and yet marches out in array as by one command." The Gentiles had no king, for they were ruled by sin; but now, believing God, they engage in the heavenly warfare. FRAGMENT ON PROVERBS.[21]

STORE UP TREASURES FOR ETERNAL LIFE. DIDYMUS THE BLIND: [Solomon] indicates here those people who have no strength but nonetheless store up treasures for eternal life on account of their good works. . . . The rock, in fact, is the refuge of badgers in which they live. You too, he says, even though you are weak, run to the rock of true faith, and with it restore life. The one who is supported by deeds enters the kingdom. Therefore, he says, do not despair of the kingdom of heaven because of the weakness of your faith; but believing in the promises, hasten to those works which are commanded. Christ is the lion: indeed all rational things are cattle in comparison with him. Moses, in fact, said, "I am a child." Because of its natural alacrity, the lion is said to walk unhindered. COMMENTARY ON THE PROVERBS OF SOLOMON, FRAGMENT 30.25.[22]

THE REAL MEANING OF THE ANTS. ORIGEN: I do not quote these words, however, as taking them in their literal signification, but, agreeably to the title of the book (for it is entitled "Proverbs"), I investigate them as containing a secret meaning. For it is the custom of these writers [of Scripture] to distribute into many classes those writings which express one sense when taken literally but which convey a different signification as their hidden meaning; and one of these kinds of writing is "Proverbs." . . . It is not, then, the visible ants which are "wiser even than the wise," but they who are indicated as such under the "proverbial" style of expression. And such must be our conclusion regarding the rest of the animal creation. AGAINST CELSUS 4.87.[23]

BE PRUDENT AND COPY THE ANT! AUGUSTINE: Be prudent, and provide for yourself against the future in heaven. Be therefore prudent, copy the ant, as Scripture says, "Store in summer, lest you be hungry in winter." The winter is the last day, the day of tribulation; the winter is the day of offenses and bitterness. Gather what may be there for you in the future. If you do not, you will perish, being both imprudent and unwise. EXPLANATIONS OF THE PSALMS 49.12.[24]

HUMAN BEINGS UNDER GOD ARE LESS ORDERLY THAN THE LOCUSTS. ORIGEN: Although the locusts do not have a king, as Scripture says, "He marches the well-ordered army in one line," but people, although they have been made rational by God, have been able neither to rule themselves orderly nor to endure patiently the control of God as king. HOMILIES ON EXODUS 4.7.[25]

HUMANS KNOW LESS ABOUT SELF-GOVERNMENT THAN DO THE LOCUSTS. CAESARIUS OF ARLES: "Although the locust has no king," as Scripture says, "he leads his army all in array"; but people who have been created rational neither know how to govern themselves nor how to endure with patience the guidance of their king and God. SERMON 99.2.[26]

---

[21]ANF 5:174-75*; TLG 2115.013.54.33. [22]PG 39:1641-44. [23]ANF 4:536*. [24]NPNF 1 8:173**. [25]FC 71:270. [26]FC 47:83.

30:29 *Four Stately Things*

ANGELS, SAINTS, SOULS AND GOD THE WORD INCARNATE: ALL GO WELL. HIPPOLYTUS: "There are three things that go well, and the fourth which is comely in going"; that is, the angels in heaven, the saints upon earth, and the souls of the righteous under the earth. And the fourth, that is, God, the Word incarnate, passed in honor through the Virgin's womb; and creating our Adam anew, he passed through the gates of heaven and became the firstfruits of the resurrection and of the ascension for all. FRAGMENTS ON PROVERBS.[27]

30:33 *Pressing Milk Produces Curds*

LIKE BUTTER PRESSED FROM THE MILK OF SCRIPTURE. CHRYSOSTOM: "Squeeze out the milk, and it will be butter." Squeeze out faithfully the two Testaments of Christ, and you will find the commandments to be as milk. Once you have been nourished with them, you may be transformed into perfect and faithful bread. COMMENTARY ON THE PROVERBS OF SOLOMON, FRAGMENT 30.33.[28]

---

[27]ANF 5:175*; TLG 2115.013.59.47. [28]PG 64:737.

31:1-31 THE WORDS OF LEMUEL

[1]The words of Lemuel, king of Massa,[k]
　　which his mother taught him:

[2]What, my son? What, son of my womb?
　　What, son of my vows?
[3]Give not your strength to women,
　　your ways to those who destroy kings.
[4]It is not for kings, O Lemuel,
　　it is not for kings to drink wine,
　　or for rulers to desire[l] strong drink;*
[5]lest they drink and forget what has been
　　　decreed,
　　and pervert the rights of all the afflicted.
[6]Give strong drink to him who is perishing,
　　and wine to those in bitter distress;
[7]let them drink and forget their poverty,
　　and remember their misery no more.
[8]Open your mouth for the dumb,
　　for the rights of all who are left desolate.[m]

[9]Open your mouth, judge righteously,
　　maintain the rights of the poor and needy.

[10]A good wife who can find?
　　She is far more precious than jewels.
[11]The heart of her husband trusts in her,
　　and he will have no lack of gain.
[12]She does him good, and not harm,
　　all the days of her life.
[13]She seeks wool and flax,
　　and works with willing hands.
[14]She is like the ships of the merchant,
　　she brings her food from afar.
[15]She rises while it is yet night
　　and provides food for her household
　　and tasks for her maidens.
[16]She considers a field and buys it;
　　with the fruit of her hands she plants a
　　　vineyard.

¹⁷*She girds her loins with strength*
    and makes her arms strong.
¹⁸*She perceives that her merchandise is*
        profitable.
    Her lamp does not go out at night.
¹⁹*She puts her hands to the distaff,*
    and her hands hold the spindle.
²⁰*She opens her hand to the poor,*
    and reaches out her hands to the needy.
²¹*She is not afraid of snow for her*
        household,
    for all her household are clothed in
        scarlet.
²²*She makes herself coverings;*
    her clothing is fine linen and purple.
²³*Her husband is known in the gates,*
    when he sits among the elders of the
        land.
²⁴*She makes linen garments and sells*
        them;

she delivers girdles to the merchant.
²⁵*Strength and dignity are her clothing,*
    and she laughs at the time to come.
²⁶*She opens her mouth with wisdom,*
    and the teaching of kindness is on her
        tongue.
²⁷*She looks well to the ways of her*
        household,
    and does not eat the bread of idleness.
²⁸*Her children rise up and call her*
        blessed;
    her husband also, and he praises her:
²⁹*"Many women have done excellently,*
    but you surpass them all."
³⁰*Charm is deceitful, and beauty is vain,*
    but a woman who fears the LORD is to be
        praised.
³¹*Give her of the fruit of her hands,*
    and let her works praise her in
        the gates.†

k *Or* King Lemuel, the oracle   l Cn: Heb *where*   m Heb *are sons of passing away*   *LXX *Princes are prone to anger; let them not drink wine.*   †LXX *And her husband will be praised in the gates.*

OVERVIEW: The wine of the flesh produces madness, whereas there is also a spiritual wine that gladdens the human heart (JEROME). Wine is a remedy for depression, unless intemperance results, but drunkenness comes from intemperance and not from wine itself (CHRYSOSTOM). Wine can turn grief or sorrow into joy (GREGORY OF NYSSA). To those who are regretful over their earlier lives, wine is the joy of spiritual knowledge that gladdens the heart (JOHN CASSIAN).

A prudent and loving wife is commendable in the sight of God (APOSTOLIC CONSTITUTIONS), and an ideal marriage is more a union of virtue than of bodies. Gregory eulogized his sister as just such a woman, whom to praise would be like praising a statue for its shadow (GREGORY OF NAZIANZUS). The church from the beginning is the bride of Christ, the good wife and valiant woman of whom

Solomon speaks in Proverbs (CAESARIUS). Jesus treats the church with confidence as his loving bride. A good housewife is concerned with planning for the future (AUGUSTINE). The church possesses the trees of knowledge and of life (ORIGEN).

This housewife is also a valiant woman, the good work she has done is already on the spindle (AUGUSTINE), and just as she puts her hands to the distaff and spindle so we too should not be ashamed to practice "holy works of wool" (CAESARIUS). As she makes herself clothing, there are two garments made of action and spirit, faith and works (AMBROSE). When wool and flax are compared, the wool implies fleshly and outward whereas the linen means spiritual and inward (AUGUSTINE). In fact, the priests of the Old Testament used linen to indicate chastity (CAESARIUS). Mercy, however, is always to be preferred over the law (AUGUSTINE).

This good woman praises God and all creation in their proper order (AUGUSTINE), and she does not eat the bread of idleness, which breeds evil (BASIL). This one woman who surpasses all others in excellence has many bad daughters, however, and these are heresies bearing a certain family likeness (AUGUSTINE). Thus, heresies are generated from Christian seed but nourished outside the church (LEANDER OF SEVILLE). At the end, all her works will praise her in the gates, and she as the church will dwell in God's house forever, praising her husband, seeing and praising God (AUGUSTINE).

31:4 Wine and Strong Drink

THERE ARE DIFFERENT KINDS OF WINE.
JEROME: The wine of the flesh does not cheer the heart of man but overpowers it and produces madness; it is written, in fact, that it is not for kings to drink wine. The apostle, too, writes that it is good not to eat meat and not to drink wine;[1] yet we are told that wine gladdens the heart of man.[2] This means, however, spiritual wine, by which, if one drinks, he immediately becomes inebriated. HOMILIES ON THE PSALMS 42 (PSALM 127).[3]

31:6 Only to Those Perishing or in Bitter Distress

WINE IS A REMEDY FOR DEPRESSION. CHRYSOSTOM: "Let people in distress have wine and those in pain strong drink," which shows that nothing can prove such a good remedy for depression as recourse to this, aside from the fact that in some cases intemperance undermines the benefit coming from it. HOMILIES ON GENESIS 29.6.[4]

DRUNKENNESS COMES FROM INTEMPERANCE. CHRYSOSTOM: "Give strong drink unto him who is ready to perish, and wine unto the bitter in soul." Justly so, because it can mitigate asperity and gloominess and drive away clouds from the brow. "Wine makes glad the heart of man,"[5] says

the psalmist. How then does wine produce drunkenness? For it cannot be that one and the same thing should work opposite effects. Drunkenness then surely does not arise from wine but from intemperance. Wine is bestowed upon us for no other purpose than for bodily health; but this purpose also is thwarted by immoderate use. HOMILIES ON EPHESIANS 19.5.17.[6]

A MEDICINE FOR SORROW. GREGORY OF NYSSA: Console each other with the following words. It is a good medicine that [Solomon] has for sorrow; for he bids wine be given to the sorrowful. He says this to us, the laborers in the vineyard, "Give," therefore, "your wine to those that are in sorrow," not that wine which produces drunkenness, plots against the senses and destroys the body, but such as gladdens the heart, the wine which the prophet recommends when he says, "Wine makes glad the heart of man."[7] Pledge each other in that liquor undiluted and with the unstinted goblets of the word, that thus our grief may be turned to joy and gladness, by the grace of the only-begotten Son of God, through whom be glory to God, even the Father, for ever and ever. Amen. FUNERAL ORATION ON MELETIUS.[8]

THE JOY OF SPIRITUAL KNOWLEDGE. JOHN CASSIAN: "Give strong drink to those who are in gloom and wine to those who are sad so that they may forget their poverty and be reminded no more of their grief." What [Solomon] means is this. To those filled with bitter regret and sadness over their earlier lives give abundantly the joy of spiritual knowledge like "a wine which gladdens the heart of a man."[9] Warm them with the headiness of saving words lest they sink into gloom and deadly despair. CONFERENCE 14.17.[10]

31:10 A Good Wife

---

[1]See Rom 14:21. [2]Ps 104:15 (103:15 LXX). [3]FC 48:322. [4]FC 82:203. [5]Ps 104:15 (103:15 LXX). [6]NPNF 1 13:138*. [7]Ps 104:15 (103:15 LXX). [8]NPNF 2 5:517*. [9]Ps 104:15 (103:15 LXX). [10]JCC 172.

GOD COMMENDS A PRUDENT AND LOVING WIFE. APOSTOLIC CONSTITUTIONS: A religious wife is blessed. Let her praise the fear of the Lord: give her of the fruits of her lips, and let her husband be praised in the gates. And again, "A virtuous wife is a crown to her husband."[11] And again, "Many wives have built a house."[12] You have learned what great commendations a prudent and loving wife receives from the Lord God. CONSTITUTIONS OF THE HOLY APOSTLES 1.3.8.[13]

A TRIBUTE TO A UNION OF VIRTUE. GREGORY OF NAZIANZUS: I have heard sacred Scripture saying, "Who shall find a valiant woman?" and also that she is a gift of God, and that a good marriage is arranged by the Lord. Those outside, too, have the same thought—if indeed the saying is theirs: "There is no greater boon for a man than a good wife, no worse, than the opposite."[14] It is impossible to mention anyone who was more fortunate than my father in this respect. For I believe that, if anyone, from the ends of the earth and from all human stocks, had endeavored to arrange the best possible marriage, a better or more harmonious union than this could not be found. For the best in men and women was so united that their marriage was more a union of virtue than of bodies. Although they surpassed all others, they themselves were so evenly matched in virtue that they could not surpass each other. ON THE DEATH OF HIS FATHER, ORATION 18.7.[15]

AN IDEAL SISTER. GREGORY OF NAZIANZUS: The divinely inspired Solomon in his instructive wisdom, I mean in his Proverbs, praises the woman who keeps her house and loves her husband. And in contrast to the woman who wanders abroad, who is uncontrolled and dishonorable, who hunts precious souls with wanton ways and words, he praises her who is engaged honorably at home, who performs her womanly duties with fearless courage, her hands constantly holding the spindle as she prepares double cloaks for her husband, who buys a field in season, and carefully provides food for her ser-

vants, and receives her friends at a bountiful table, and who exhibits all other qualities for which he extols in song the modest and industrious woman. If I were to praise my sister on such counts, it would be like praising a statue for its shadow. ON HIS SISTER ST. GORGONIA, ORATION 8.9.[16]

THE CHURCH IS THE BRIDE OF CHRIST, THE GOOD WIFE AND VALIANT WOMAN. CAESARIUS OF ARLES: The catholic church was not only preached after the coming of our Lord and Savior, beloved brethren, but from the beginning of the world, it was designated by many figures and rather hidden mysteries. Indeed, in holy Abel the catholic church existed, in Noah, in Abraham, in Isaac, in Jacob, and in the other saintly people before the advent of our Lord and Savior. Truly, Solomon says of her, "Who shall find a worthy wife?" What does he mean: "Who shall find"? Here, we should understand the difficulty, not impossibility, of finding her. That valiant woman is the church. SERMON 139.1.[17]

31:11-12 A Trusting Husband, for Whom She Does Good

CHRIST IS CONFIDENT IN HIS BRIDE, THE CHURCH. AUGUSTINE: "The heart of her husband is confident about her." He certainly is confident, and he has taught us to be confident too. He commissioned the church, you see, to the ends of the earth, among all nations, from sea to sea. If she was not going to persevere to the end, her husband's heart would not be confident about her. . . . So she despoils the world, spread throughout it everywhere; on all sides she plunders trophies from the devil. . . .

"For she works for her husband's good and not his harm, all the time." That is why this lady despoils the nations, working for her husband's good and not his harm. All the time she does

---

[11]Prov 12:4. [12]Prov 14:1. [13]ANF 7:394-95. [14]Cf. Hesiod *Works and Days* 1.700. [15]FC 22:124. [16]FC 22:106*. [17]FC 47:276.

good and not harm: not for herself either, but for her husband, "that whoever lives may live no longer for himself, but for the one who died and rose again for all."[18] SERMON 37.4-5.[19]

31:13 Wool and Flax

WOOL MEANS FLESH OR OUTWARD, LINEN MEANS SPIRIT OR INWARD. AUGUSTINE: The sacred text describes this housewife as a weaver of woolens and linen. But what we want to find out is what wool represents and what linen does. I think wool means something of the flesh, linen something of the spirit. I hazard this conjecture from the order we wear our clothes in; our underclothes or inner garments are linen, our outer garments woolen. Now everything we do in flesh is public, whatever we do in the spirit is private. Now to act in the flesh and not to act in spirit may seem good but is in fact worthless, whereas to act in spirit and not act in the flesh is downright laziness. SERMON 37.6.[20]

LINEN INDICATED CHASTITY. CAESARIUS OF ARLES: The sacred word describes that woman as working in wool and linen. Perhaps you will ask us what the wool and linen are. The wool signifies something carnal; the linen, what is spiritual. This interpretation is given because in the order of clothing inner garments are of linen, outer ones are of wool. Therefore, the wool signifies something carnal, because it is produced from a mingling or union, while the linen is brought forth from the earth without any carnal pleasure and for this reason seems to be an image of chastity. So true is this that by command of the law, priests of the Old Testament used linen bands as an indication of chastity. SERMON 139.2.[21]

31:16 To Buy a Field and Plant It

THE GOOD HOUSEWIFE PLANS FOR THE FUTURE. AUGUSTINE: After saying, "Being farsighted she has bought a field," as though you were to say, "What did she buy it with?" it adds,

"With the fruit of her hands she has planted a property." . . . The property it means, you see, lies in the future; that was suggested by the word *farsighted*. SERMON 37.9.[22]

THE WOMAN, AS THE CHURCH, POSSESSES THE TREES OF KNOWLEDGE AND LIFE. ORIGEN: [The text] speaks of the church as a virtuous soul possessing the tree of knowledge and the tree of life. [The church possesses] knowledge as the law, and life as the Word. For she herself [is the church] who came out of the rib of Christ and was found by her bridegroom to be a woman of sound mind and strength, guarding the faith of her bridegroom as she awaits his [return] again from heaven. EXPOSITION ON PROVERBS, FRAGMENT 31.16.[23]

31:17 Loins Girded with Strength

THE HOUSEWIFE IS A VALIANT WOMAN. AUGUSTINE: "Valiantly girding her loins, she has braced her arms." Valiant she is indeed. Now we see if she is not also a maidservant. With what devotion she serves, and how readily! To prevent the flapping folds of carnal desires from getting in the way of her work she girds her loins, and so avoids treading on overlong skirts as she hurries about her work. There lies the chastity of this lady, tightly bound by the girdle of the commandment and always ready for good work. SERMON 37.10.[24]

31:19 The Distaff and the Spindle

THE GOOD WORK SHE HAS DONE. AUGUSTINE: "She has also braced her arms on the spindle." About this spindle let me say what the Lord permits me to. After all, this business of spinning wool is not completely foreign to men. Listen to what it means to say, "She has braced her arms on the spindle." It could have said "on the distaff." It said spindle, not without reason, perhaps.

---

[18]2 Cor 5:15. [19]*WSA* 3 2:187*. [20]*WSA* 3 2:188. [21]FC 47:277. [22]*WSA* 3 2:190. [23]PG 17:252. [24]*WSA* 3 2:190.

Though you could, of course, take it, and it wouldn't be at all absurd, that the spindle seems to signify spinning, and spinning signifies the good works of a chaste woman and a busy and careful housewife. All the same I, dearly beloved, will not keep from you what I understand by this spindle. . . .

Look at these two instruments for spinning wool, the distaff and the spindle. The wool is wrapped round the distaff and has to be drawn and spun in a thread and so pass onto the spindle. What's wrapped on the distaff is the future; what's collected by the spindle is already past. So your good work is on the spindle, not on the distaff. On the distaff is what you are going to do; on the spindle is what you have done. So see if you have anything on the spindle, that's where your arms should be braced. SERMON 37.13.[25]

31:20 The Poor and Needy

BY CARING FOR THE POOR, YOU PRACTICE HOLY WORKS. CAESARIUS OF ARLES: Brethren, let us not be ashamed to practice holy works of wool. If anyone has a full storeroom or granary, all those things are on the distaff; let them pass over to the spindle. They are on the left side as long as you do not give to the poor, but as soon as you begin to practice almsgiving, they are transferred to the right side and become a work from which a garment may result. SERMON 139.4.[26]

31:22 Making Herself Clothing

TWO GARMENTS ARE MADE OF ACTION AND SPIRIT, FAITH AND WORKS. AMBROSE: The beauty of a good thing pleases the more, if it be shown under various aspects. For those are good things, whereof the texture of the priestly robe was the token, that is to say, either the Law or the church, which latter has made two garments for her spouse, as it is written[27]—the one of action, the other of spirit, weaving together the threads of faith and works. ON THE CHRISTIAN FAITH 2, INTRODUCTION 11.[28]

31:26 The Teaching of Kindness

MERCY IS ALWAYS TO BE PREFERRED OVER THE LAW. AUGUSTINE: There is mercy on [Jesus'] tongue, and so he teaches the Law mercifully, as was said about wisdom: "But she carries on her tongue the Law and mercy." Do not fear that you cannot fulfill the Law; flee to mercy. TRACTATES ON THE GOSPEL OF JOHN 7.10.2.[29]

THIS GOOD WOMAN PRAISES GOD AND ALL CREATION IN PROPER ORDER. AUGUSTINE: "She has opened her mouth with care, and imposed order on her tongue," praising creatures as creatures, the creator as creator, angels as angels, heavenly things as heavenly, earthly things as earthly, men as men, animals as animals. Nothing mixed up, nothing out of order. Not taking the name of the Lord her God in vain, not attributing the nature of a creature to the creator, speaking about everything so methodically that she doesn't put lesser things above the more important or subordinate the more important to the lesser. SERMON 37.23.[30]

31:27 She Does Not Eat the Bread of Idleness

IDLENESS BEGETS EVIL. BASIL THE GREAT: Why should we dwell upon the amount of evil there is in idleness, when the apostle clearly prescribes that he who does not work should not eat?[31] As daily sustenance is necessary for everyone, so labor in proportion to one's strength is also essential. Not vainly has Solomon written in praise: "and she has not eaten her bread idle." THE LONG RULES 37.[32]

31:29 One Woman Surpassing All Others in Excellence

HERESIES ARE BAD DAUGHTERS BEARING A

---

[25]WSA 3 2:191. Similar comments are found in Caesarius of Arles; see FC 47:278. [26]FC 47:279. [27]Cf. Prov 31:22 LXX. [28]NPNF 2 10:225. [29]FC 78:163. [30]WSA 3 2:197. [31]2 Thess 3:10. [32]FC 9:307.

CERTAIN FAMILY LIKENESS. AUGUSTINE:
"Many daughters have done mightily, but you
have surpassed and outdone them all." You, he
says, have surpassed them all, you have outdone
them all. So who are these other daughters who
have done mightily, whom this one has surpassed,
and whom this one has outdone? And again, how
have they done mightily, and in what way has this
one surpassed them? There are, you see, bad
daughters, namely, heresies. Why are they daughters? Because they too were born of this woman.
But bad daughters, daughters not in the family
likeness of their behavior but in the likeness of
their sacraments. They too have our sacraments,
they have our Scriptures, they have our Amen
and Alleluia, most of them have our creed, many
of them have our baptism. That's why they are
daughters.

But would you like to know what is said to
this lady somewhere else, in the Song of Songs?
"Like a lily in the midst of thorns, so is my darling in the midst of the daughters."[33] SERMON
37.27.[34]

**HERESIES ARE GENERATED FROM CHRISTIAN
SEED BUT NOURISHED OUTSIDE THE
CHURCH.** LEANDER OF SEVILLE: "Many women
have gathered together riches; you have excelled
them all." . . .

Heresies are generated from Christian seed;
they are thorns because they have been nourished
outside of God's paradise, that is, outside of the
catholic church. This is proved not by any conjecture of my own making but by the authority of
divine Scripture, when Solomon said, "As a lily
among thorns, so is my beloved among women."[35]
HOMILY ON THE TRIUMPH OF THE CHURCH.[36]

31:31 Let Her Works Give Praise in the Gates

**SHE WILL DWELL IN GOD'S HOUSE FOREVER,
SEEING AND PRAISING GOD.** AUGUSTINE: And
what occupation will she have from then on, her
labors being ended? "And her husband will be
praised in the gates." That will be the haven of
our labors, to see God and praise God. There
they will not say, "Get up, work, clothe the servants, clothe yourself too, put on your best purple, give food to the maids, see that the lamp does
not go out, be thorough, get up at night, open
your hand to the poor, draw the thread from the
distaff to the spindle." There will not be any
works of necessity, because there will not be any
necessity. There will not be any works of mercy,
because there will not be any misery. You will not
break your bread to the poor, because no one will
be begging. You will not take in the stranger,
because everyone will be living in their own home
country. You will not visit the sick, because everyone will be in good health for all eternity. You will
not clothe the naked, because everyone will be
clothed in eternal light. You will not bury the
dead, because everyone will be living life without
end.

You will not, however, be doing nothing, just
because you are not doing any of this. For you
will see the One you have desired, and you will
praise him without weariness or fatigue. That is
the fruit you will receive. Then will come to pass
that one thing you have asked for: "One thing I
have asked from the Lord, this will I seek: to
dwell in the house of the Lord all the days of my
life." And what will you do there? "To contemplate the delight of the Lord."[37] And her husband
will be praised in the gates. "Blessed are those
who dwell in your house, they will praise you forever and ever."[38] SERMON 37.30.[39]

---

[33]Song 2:2. [34]WSA 3 2:198-99. [35]Song 2:2. [36]FC 62:230**. [37]Cf. Ps
27:4 (26:4 LXX). [38]Ps 84:4 (83:5 LXX). [39]WSA 3 2:200-201*.

ECCLESIASTES

1:1-12 THE VANITY OF HUMAN LIFE

¹The words of the Preacher,ᵃ* the son of
David, king† in Jerusalem.
²Vanity of vanities, says the Preacher,
vanity of vanities! All is vanity.
³What does man gain by all the toil
at which he toils under the sun?
⁴A generation goes, and a generation comes,
but the earth remains for ever.
⁵The sun rises and the sun goes down,
and hastens to the place where it rises.
⁶The wind blows to the south,
and goes round to the north;
round and round goes the wind,
and on its circuits the wind returns.
⁷All streams run to the sea,
but the sea is not full;
to the place where the streams flow,
there they flow again.

⁸All things are full of weariness;
a man cannot utter it;
the eye is not satisfied with seeing,
nor the ear filled with hearing.
⁹What has been is what will be,
and what has been done is what will
be done;‡
and there is nothing new under the sun.
¹⁰Is there a thing of which it is said,
"See, this is new"?
It has been already,
in the ages before us.
¹¹There is no remembrance of former things,
nor will there be any remembrance
of later things yet to happen
among those who come after.
¹²I the Preacher have been king over
Israel in Jerusalem.

a Heb Qoheleth   *LXX Ecclesiastes   †LXX adds of Israel   ‡LXX what is it that has been made? The same that is to be. And what is it that has been created? The same that is destined to be created.

OVERVIEW: Ecclesiastes, "the Preacher," also understood as being Solomon, is also a type of Christ (DIDYMUS, ORIGEN, GREGORY OF NYSSA). In one sense, though, the Spirit is the real author of this book (DIDYMUS). In addition, the name Ecclesiastes indicates the church and the one who leads it (JEROME, GREGORY OF NYSSA). The church is true knowledge, and Christ is the author of that knowledge (EVAGRIUS). The book of Ecclesiastes must be understood spiritually and in light of other passages of sacred Scripture (GREGORY OF NYSSA), for this present world is not the ultimate end (EVAGRIUS). All things are vanity, and we must turn away from them toward God (AMBROSE, AUGUSTINE). All things are vanity even though God made them good (JEROME). But there are different kinds of vanities (DIDYMUS). Vanity is pointlessness or futility (GREGORY OF NYSSA), the possession of material bodies (ORIGEN), the pursuit of worldly pleasures (VALERIAN) and being busied with vain things (CHRYSOSTOM). Even the sun in the sky, compared with the true Sun, is vanity (OLYMPIODORUS). Prosperity does not profit our life, and we should not work for things that perish (AUGUSTINE), but those who toil for the eternal gain much. The earth remains, but generations go and come by death and birth (DIDYMUS). The stability of the earth depends on God (AMBROSE), and God's power is evident in the existence and movement of the sea (EPHREM, GREGORY OF NAZIANZUS), although a second enlightenment comes when sunrise follows sunset (DIDYMUS). That we are caught in an endless repetition of cycles, however, is an error of pagan belief (AUGUSTINE). The pattern of the sea indicates the pattern of our journey through life, and, just as it never exceeds its capacity, so never should we (GREGORY OF NYSSA).

1:1 The Name Ecclesiastes

ON THE SYMBOLISM OF THE NAME ECCLESI-ASTES (PREACHER). ORIGEN: We can also examine why Solomon, who apparently served the will of the Holy Spirit in these three books, is called in Proverbs "Solomon, son of David, who ruled in Israel,"[1] but in the second book "Solomon" is not written. Instead, it says, "The words of Ecclesiastes, the son of David, the king of Israel in Jerusalem." He writes that he is the son of David and the king of Israel, just as he did in the first book. But there he put down "Proverbs"; here, "words." And there he called himself Solomon; but here, Ecclesiastes. And whereas there he put down only the nation in which he ruled, here he both puts the nation and indicates the place of his rule as Jerusalem. . . .

I do not think it can be doubted that in a great many respects Solomon bears a type of Christ, either because he is called "peaceful" or because "the queen of the south came from the ends of the earth to hear the wisdom of Solomon."[2] Thus Christ also rules in Israel because he is called Son of David and because he rules over those kings in respect to whom he is called King of kings. Furthermore, the true Ecclesiastes is the one who, though he was in the form of God, emptied himself, taking the form of a servant[3] in order to assemble the church; for "Ecclesiastes" is derived from "to assemble the church.". . . Therefore, in the first book, Proverbs, when he establishes us by moral instructions, he is said to be "king in Israel" but not yet in Jerusalem, because although we are called Israel because of faith, that does not yet mark an attainment by which we should appear to have arrived at the heavenly Jerusalem. But when we have made enough progress for it to come to pass that we are brought into fellowship with the church of the firstborn, which is in heaven, and know by previous careful consideration and by natural reasons that the heavenly Jerusalem is our mother, then Christ is made for us, as well, our Ecclesiastes and is said to rule not only in Israel but also in Jerusalem. COMMENTARY ON THE SONG OF SONGS, PROLOGUE.[4]

ECCLESIASTES IS SOLOMON, SON OF DAVID. DIDYMUS THE BLIND: Solomon, who here appears as Ecclesiastes, that is, who preaches what is appropriate for the church,[5] is the son of David. He came after Saul, whose rule was destroyed and terminated. Solomon is son of this king David in two ways. . . . The first is according to nature and lineage; the second is according to his teaching. One has to understand Paul in this [second] way when he says, "For though you might have ten thousand guardians in Christ, you do not have many fathers. Indeed, in Christ Jesus I became your father through the gospel."[6] David thus was Solomon's father in both respects: according to nature—Solomon was his heir and "David begot Solomon"—but he was also his

---

[1]Prov 1:1. [2]Mt 12:42. [3]Phil 2:6-7. [4]OSW 240-41. [5]Gk ekklēsia. [6]1 Cor 4:15.

father in terms of instruction. David was wise as only few are—especially wise regarding God. . . .

But Solomon also became wise in a way that few achieve: he became wise through the wisdom [he received] and through his human lineage. According to both ways Solomon thus was the son of David.

But especially in terms of his words as Ecclesiastes is he the son of David, not so much according to nature as according to instruction. For the sons of the wise beget wise people, since they are wise themselves. But someone who is father of a son according to nature does not necessarily become a father again. Many were sons and did not become fathers. The sons according to the Spirit, however, become fathers themselves. COMMENTARY ON ECCLESIASTES 5.2.[7]

THE NAME ECCLESIASTES ALSO INDICATES THE CHURCH. JEROME: Solomon is here given the Greek name Ecclesiastes [Heb *Qōhelet*], for he gathers the assembly [*qāhāl*], that is, the church. But we can call him the Preacher because he speaks to the people and his word is directed not only to one person but to everyone. COMMENTARY ON ECCLESIASTES 1.1.[8]

VARIOUS POSSIBILITIES AS TO THE REAL AUTHOR. DIDYMUS THE BLIND: *Question:* [Are the] words of Ecclesiastes said by the author personally?

Answer: Actually the Spirit is the author of the divinely inspired Scriptures. The Spirit inspires so that words are expressed, but the wise man is also involved. For the Spirit has not himself invisibly written the letter and put down the text, but he breathes it into the soul. Either the real author is Solomon, or some [other] wise men have written it. Maybe we should opt for the latter so that nobody may say that the speaker talks about himself. COMMENTARY ON ECCLESIASTES 7.9.[9]

SPIRITUAL INTERPRETATION IS NECESSARY. GREGORY OF NYSSA: Before us for exposition lies

Ecclesiastes, which requires labor in spiritual interpretation quite as great as the benefit to be obtained. The thoughts of Proverbs [have] already prepared the mind by exercise. . . .

Then for those who have developed to the more advanced stages of learning there comes the ascent toward this truly sublime and God-inspired work of Scripture [i.e., the book of Ecclesiastes]. If then the exercise in expressions [from the book of Proverbs] which prepares us for these lessons is so painful and difficult to understand, how great an effort must be envisaged in these lofty thoughts which now lie before us for interpretation? . . .

Nevertheless, since it is also one of the Master's commands that we must search the Scriptures,[10] there is an absolute necessity, even if our mind falls short of the truth, failing to match the greatness of the ideas, that we should still ensure by all the zeal for the Word of which we are capable that we do not appear to disregard the Lord's command. Let us therefore search the Scripture lying before us to the best of our ability. For surely he who has given the command to search the Scriptures will also give us the ability to do so, as it is written, "The Lord will give a word to those who preach good news with great power."[11] HOMILIES ON ECCLESIASTES 1.[12]

ECCLESIASTES IS ABOUT THE CHURCH AND THE ONE WHO LEADS IT. GREGORY OF NYSSA: Now the teaching of this book looks exclusively to the conduct of the church and gives instruction in those things by which one would achieve the life of virtue. For the object of what is said here is to raise the mind above sensation, to persuade it to abandon all that seems to be great and splendid in the world of existence, to catch a glimpse through the eyes of the soul of those things which are unattainable by sense perception, and to conceive a desire for those things to which sense does not attain.

---

[7]PTA 25:3-7. [8]CCL 72:250. [9]PTA 25:17-19. [10]Jn 5:39. [11]Ps 67:12 LXX. [12]GNHE 32-33**.

Perhaps the title of the book also envisages the one who leads the church (*ekklēsia*). For the true Ecclesiast [is] he who collects into one body what has been scattered and assembles (*ekklēsiazon*) into one whole those who have been led astray in many ways by various deceits.[13] Who else would he be but the true King of Israel, the Son of God, to whom Nathanael said, "You are the Son of God, you are the King of Israel"?[14] If therefore these are words of the King of Israel, and this same one is also the Son of God, as the gospel says, then the same one is called Ecclesiast (Assembler). Perhaps we may not unreasonably give this sense to the expression used in the title, so that we may learn by this that the meaning of these words has reference to him who established the church forever through the gospel message. Words, it says, of the Ecclesiast, the Son of David. And Matthew so names him at the beginning of his gospel, calling the Lord "Son of David."[15] HOMILIES ON ECCLESIASTES 1.[16]

CHRIST THE AUTHOR OF TRUE KNOWLEDGE. EVAGRIUS OF PONTUS: The church is [the assembly] of pure souls. It is the true knowledge of the ages and worlds and about their judgment and provision. Ecclesiastes is Christ, the author of that knowledge. Or, Ecclesiastes is one who, having purified the soul by moral contemplation, leads his or her soul to the contemplation of the physical [world]. SCHOLIA ON ECCLESIASTES 1.1.1.[17]

1:2 Vanity of Life

VANITY MEANS FUTILITY. GREGORY OF NYSSA: The insubstantial is deemed "futile," that which has existence only in the utterance of the word. No substantial object is simultaneously indicated when the term is used, but it is a kind of idle and empty sound, expressed by syllables in the form of a word, striking the ear at random without meaning, the sort of word people make up for a joke but which means nothing. This then is one sort of futility. Another sense of "futility" is the pointlessness of things done earnestly to no purpose, like the sandcastles children build, and shooting arrows at stars, and chasing the winds, and racing against one's own shadow and trying to step on its head, and anything else of the same kind which we find done pointlessly. All these activities are included in the meaning of "futility." . . . [And] so also "futility of futilities" indicates the absolute extreme of what is futile. HOMILIES ON ECCLESIASTES 1.[18]

THIS PRESENT WORLD IS NOT THE ULTIMATE END. EVAGRIUS OF PONTUS: To those who have entered into the church of the mind and marvel in contemplation of what has come into being, the text says, Do not think that this is the ultimate end or that these are the promises that have been stored up for you. For all these things are [only] vanity of vanities before the knowledge of one's God. For, just as it is futile for medicine [to seek] a final cure, so is it useless [to seek] after knowledge of the Holy Trinity in the ideas of the [present] ages and worlds. SCHOLIA ON ECCLESIASTES 2.1.2.[19]

DIFFERENT KINDS OF VANITIES. DIDYMUS THE BLIND: There is a difference between vanities; there are those that are especially so, and others that are not. . . .

Question: [Does Ecclesiastes speak] about one and the same [kind of vanity]?

Answer: About both, about the things that are just vanity as well as about those that are a vanity of vanities. Both the things that most clearly belong to the sphere of vanity and the less obvious vanities are altogether vain in comparison with actual truth. The newborn, the little child and the boy are imperfect. Of course, they are imperfect in comparison with an adolescent, and they are all imperfect in comparison with a man. . . .

---

[13]Jn 11:52. [14]Jn 1:49. [15]Mt 1:1. [16]GNHE 34. [17]SC 397:58. [18]GNHE 34, 36**. [19]SC 397:58-60.

Question: Does he not mean by "vanity of vanities" the visible and the perceivable?

Answer: Yes, but the layperson and the astronomer do not perceive the sun in the same way. The perception of the sun by an astronomer and by a scientist is far inferior to the seeing of the invisible God and it is inferior to the knowledge that comes from God. COMMENTARY ON ECCLESIASTES 10.13.[20]

WHY VANITY OF VANITIES? JEROME: If everything that God made is very good, then how can everything be vanity—and not only vanity, but even vanity of vanities? As one song in the Song of Songs is shown to excel above all songs, so also is the magnitude of vanity demonstrated by the expression "vanity of vanities." COMMENTARY ON ECCLESIASTES I.2.[21]

IMPORTANCE OF RISING ABOVE THIS WORLD. AMBROSE: David, who had experienced those very glances which are dangerous for a man, aptly says that the person is blessed whose every hope is in the name of God.[22] For such a one does not have regard to vanities and follies who always strives toward Christ and always looks upon Christ with his inner eyes. For this reason David turned to God again and said, "Turn away my eyes, that they may not see vanity."[23] The circus is vanity, because it is totally without profit; horse racing is vanity, because it is counterfeit as regards salvation;[24] the theater is vanity, every game is vanity. "All things are vanity!" as Ecclesiastes said, all things that are in this world. Accordingly, let the person who wishes to be saved ascend above the world, let him seek the Word who is with God, let him flee from this world and depart from the earth. For a man cannot comprehend that which exists and exists always, unless he has first fled from here. FLIGHT FROM THE WORLD 1.4.[25]

VANITY BECAUSE OF THE FALL OF HUMANITY. AUGUSTINE: By this perversity of the soul, due to sin and punishment, the whole corporeal creation becomes, as Solomon says: "Vanity of them that are vain, all is vanity. What advantage has man in all his labor which he does under the sun?" Not for nothing does he say, "of them that are vain," for if you take away vain persons who pursue that which is last as if it were first, matter will not be vanity but will show its own beauty in its own way, a low type of beauty, of course, but not deceptive. When man fell away from the unity of God the multitude of temporal forms was distributed among his carnal senses, and his sensibilities were multiplied by the changeful variety. So abundance became laborious, and his needs, if one may say so, became abundant, for he pursues one thing after another, and nothing remains permanently with him. So what with his corn and wine and oil, his needs are so multiplied that he cannot find the one thing needful, a single and unchangeable nature, seeking which he would not err and attaining which he would cease from grief and pain. For then he would have as a consequence the redemption of his body, which no longer would be corrupted. As it is, the corruption of the body burdens the soul, and its earthly habitation forces it to think of many things; for the humble beauty of material objects is hurried along in the order in which one thing succeeds another. The reason why corporeal beauty is the lowest beauty is that its parts cannot all exist simultaneously. Some things give place and others succeed them, and all together complete the number of temporal forms and make of them a single beauty. OF TRUE RELIGION 21.41.[26]

VANITY IS THE POSSESSION OF MATERIAL BODIES. ORIGEN: Let us see what is the "vanity" to which the creation was subjected. My own opinion is, that this is nothing else than the possession of bodies, for even though the stars are composed of ether they are nevertheless material. This, it seems to me, is the reason why Solomon

---

[20]PTA 25:37-41. [21]CCL 72:252. [22]Cf. Ps 40:4 (39:5 LXX). [23]Ps 119:37 (118:37 LXX). [24]Cf. Ps 33:17 (32:17 LXX). [25]FC 65:282-83*. [26]LCC 6:244-45.

arraigns the whole bodily universe as being in a way burdensome and as impeding the activity of spirits, thus: "Vanity of vanities, all is vanity, said the Preacher; all is vanity." "For," he adds, "I looked and I saw all things that are under the sun, and behold, all is vanity." ON FIRST PRINCIPLES 1.7.5.[27]

VANITY IS THE PURSUIT OF WORLDLY PLEASURES. VALERIAN: What is that vanity, if not devotion to riches and the pursuit of worldly pleasures? This is confirmed through Solomon, who says, "Vanity of vanities, and all is vanity." Therefore, dearly beloved, let no one put his confidence in the vanity of this world. That vanity, as you see, is something standing with insecure footing. Devotion to it is short-lived and empty, and its beauty is like smoke in a wind. The comeliness of its countenance is like that which you see when you look on the beauty of that vine which had its early summer blossoms in well-constituted abundance yet cannot bring forth the actual fruit of the promised grape harvest. While it brings forth too much, it incurs the reproach of perpetual sterility. HOMILY 6.7.[28]

VANITY IS BEING BUSIED ABOUT VAIN THINGS. CHRYSOSTOM: What is vanity of mind? It is the being busied about vain things. And what are those vain things, but all things in the present life? Of them the Preacher says, "Vanity of vanities, all is vanity." But a person will say, If they be vain and vanity, for what purpose were they made? If they are God's works, how are they vain? And great is the dispute concerning these things. But listen, beloved: it is not the works of God that he calls vain; God forbid! The heaven is not vain, the earth is not vain—God forbid!—nor the sun, nor the moon and stars, nor our own body. No, all these are "very good."[29] But what is vain? Let us hear the Preacher himself, what he says: "I planted vineyards, I got men singers and women singers, I made pools of water, I had great possessions of herds and flocks, I gathered me

also silver and gold, and I saw that these are vanity."[30] HOMILIES ON EPHESIANS 12.[31]

1:3 Vanity of Human Labor

PROSPERITY DOES NOT PROFIT OUR LIFE. AUGUSTINE: So this is what the rich should do: not be haughty in their ideas, nor set their hopes on the uncertainty of riches, but on the living God, who bestows all things on us abundantly for our enjoyment; that is what they must do. But what are they to do with what they have? Let me tell you what: "Let them be rich in good works, let them be easy givers."[32] After all, they have the wherewithal. Poverty is difficult and grim. "Let them be easy givers"; they have the wherewithal. Let them share, that is, take some notice of their fellow mortals. "Let them share, let them store up for themselves a good foundation for the future." "You see," he says, "just because I say 'Let them be easy givers, let them share,' it doesn't mean I want them looted, want them stripped naked, want them left empty. I am teaching them how to make a profit, when I point out, 'Let them store up for themselves.' I'm not telling them to do this so that they can lose it; I'm showing them where to transfer the account. 'Let them store up for themselves a good foundation for the future, so that they lay hold of true life.'"[33] So this one is a false life; let them lay hold of true life. After all, "Vanity of vanities, and all is vanity. What is this great abundance for man in all his toil, at which he toils under the sun?" So true life is to be laid hold of, our investments are to be transferred to the place of true life, so that we may find there what we give here. The one who transforms us also transforms those investments. SERMON 61.11.[34]

WE SHOULD NOT WORK FOR PERISHABLE THINGS. AUGUSTINE: If it is a vain thing to do good works for the sake of human praise, how

---

[27]OFP 63-64. [28]FC 17:341-42. [29]Gen 1:31. [30]Cf. Eccles 2:4-8. [31]NPNF 1 13:109*. [32]1 Tim 6:18. [33]1 Tim 6:18-19. [34]WSA 3 3:147.

much more vain for the sake of getting money, or increasing it, or retaining it, and any other temporal advantage, which comes unto us from without? Since "all things are vanity: what is man's abundance, with all his toil, wherein he labors under the sun?" For our temporal welfare itself finally we ought not to do our good works but rather for the sake of that everlasting welfare which we hope for, where we may enjoy an unchangeable good, which we shall have from God, nay, what God himself is unto us. For if God's saints were to do good works for the sake of this temporal welfare, never would the martyrs of Christ achieve a good work. EXPLANATIONS OF THE PSALMS 119.38.[35]

THOSE WHO TOIL FOR THE ETERNAL GAIN MUCH. DIDYMUS THE BLIND: Those who are rich in things that are valued in the realm of the natural do not gain anything. They do not gain longevity. Rich and poor are in the same situation: they go through life quickly and do not stay for a long time. Thus "from all the toil at which they toil under the sun" one does not gain anything, no increase in natural qualities. But the one who toils and strives for things that lead to the eternal and to the invisible gains something: A human being becomes a god, an uncertain human being becomes a strong one, a coward becomes courageous. COMMENTARY ON ECCLESIASTES 11.18.[36]

1:4 Stability of the Earth and Instability of Human Life

STABILITY OF THE EARTH DEPENDS ON THE WILL OF GOD. AMBROSE: By the will of God, therefore, the earth remains immovable. "The earth stands forever," according to Ecclesiastes, yet it is moved and nods according to the will of God. It does not therefore continue to exist because based on its own foundations. It does not stay stable because of its own props. The Lord established it by the support of his will, because "in his hand are all the ends of the earth."[37] The

simplicity of this faith is worth all the proffered proofs. SIX DAYS OF CREATION 1.6.22.[38]

ERROR OF THOSE WHO THINK THAT THEY CAN POSSESS THE EARTH. GREGORY OF NYSSA: What good does the possessor of many acres gain in the end, except that the foolish person thinks his own that which never belongs to him? Seemingly, in his greed he is ignorant that "the earth is the Lord's, and the fullness thereof,"[39] and that "God is king of all the earth."[40] It is the passion of having which gives people a false title of lordship over that which can never belong to them. "The earth," says the wise Preacher, "abides for ever," ministering to every generation, first one, then another, that is born upon it. People, though they are so little even their own masters, because they are brought into life without knowing it by their Maker's will and before they wish are withdrawn from it, nevertheless in their excessive vanity think that they are life's lords and think that they, now born, now dying, rule that which remains continually. ON VIRGINITY 4.[41]

GENERATIONS GO AND COME. DIDYMUS THE BLIND: The sun has existed since it was created and will exist and be one and the same as long as God wants it. But if I say . . . that humankind remains forever, I do not mean one and the same human being but the whole succession of generations. The same is true for other mortal beings and plants. . . . One generation goes and one generation comes. The generation that goes is destroyed by death; the one that comes is the one that is born. COMMENTARY ON ECCLESIASTES.[42]

1:5 Sunrise and Sunset

A SECOND ENLIGHTENMENT AT SUNRISE. DIDYMUS THE BLIND: The sun of righteousness rises in the soul. The beginning of its rise is preparatory. It

---

[35]NPNF 1 8:566. [36]PTA 25:45-47. [37]Ps 95:4 (94:4 LXX). [38]FC 42:22. [39]Ps 24:1 (23:1 LXX). [40]Ps 47:7 (46:8 LXX). [41]NPNF 2 5:349**. [42]PTA 25:49-53.

is a preparatory enlightenment. But when it circles around the whole soul and enlightens it altogether so that nothing is outside the light any more, then the soul is in perfect enlightenment. For often it sets in order to rise again. Sunset and sunrise are in accordance with its progress. And sunset and sunrise are united with respect to its location. The second enlightenment means sunset with respect to the previous enlightenment, but it means sunrise with respect to the enlightenment now beginning. COMMENTARY ON ECCLESIASTES 13.12.[43]

EVEN THE SUN IS VANITY. OLYMPIODORUS: The great sun, when compared with the Sun of righteousness, is vanity. COMMENTARY ON ECCLESIASTES 1.5.[44]

1:6 The Wind Blows

WIND AND SUN. OLYMPIODORUS: According to the narrative he calls the sun wind, due to the speed of its movement. COMMENTARY ON ECCLESIASTES 1.6.[45]

1:7 The Rivers and the Sea

PATTERN OF THE SEA INDICATES OUR JOURNEY THROUGH LIFE. GREGORY OF NYSSA: The sea is a receptacle for the confluence of waters from every direction, and neither does the confluence cease, nor does the sea increase. What is the point of the activity as far as the waters are concerned, always filling what is not filled? To what end does the sea receive the inflow of the waters, remaining unincreased by what is added? He says these things so that from the very elements among which a person's life is spent he might explain in advance the unreality of the things sought among us.

For if this urgent cycle of the sun has no end, and the successive changes of light and darkness never cease, and the earth, condemned to immobility, remains unmoved in its fixed place, and the rivers toil without effect, being swallowed up by the insatiable nature of the sea, and in vain the sea receives the inflow of the waters, taking to its bosom without increase what forever pours into it—if these things are in this condition, what is likely to be the state of the humanity which spends its life among them? Why are we surprised if generation goes and generation comes, and this cycle does not leave aside its natural rhythm, as the generation of humankind constantly arriving expels its predecessor and is expelled by the one succeeding?

What then does the Word here proclaim to the church? He says, "You human beings, as you look upon the universe, recognize your own nature. What you see in the sky and the earth, what you observe in the sun, what you notice in the sea, let this interpret to you your own nature too." For there is a rising and a setting of our nature corresponding to that of the sun. There is one path for all things, one cycle for the journey through life. HOMILIES ON ECCLESIASTES 1.[46]

THE SALTINESS OF THE SEA. EPHREM THE SYRIAN: The waters that the earth drank on the first day were not salty. Even if these waters were like the deep on the surface of the earth, they were not yet seas. For it was in the seas that these waters, which were not salty before being gathered together, became salty. When they were sent throughout the entire earth for the earth to drink they were sweet, but when they were gathered into seas on the third day, they became salty, lest they become stagnant due to their being gathered together, and so that they might receive the rivers that enter into them without increasing. For the quantity that a sea requires for nourishment is the measure of the rivers that flow down into it. Rivers flow down into seas lest the heat of the sun dry them up. The saltiness [of the seas] then swallows up [the rivers] lest they increase, rise up and cover the earth. Thus the rivers turn into nothing, as it were, because the saltiness of the sea swallows them up. COMMENTARY ON GENESIS 1.10.2.[47]

---

[43]PTA 25:57. [44]PG 93:481. [45]PG 93:484. [46]GNHE 38-39. [47]FC 91:82-83.

THE AWESOME POWER OF GOD MANIFESTED.
GREGORY OF NAZIANZUS: As for the sea, if I had
felt no wonder at its size, I should have felt it for
its stillness, at the way it stands free within its
proper limits. If its stillness had not moved my
admiration, its size must have done. Since both
aspects move me, I shall praise the power
involved in both. What binding force brought the
sea together? What causes it to swell yet stay in
position, as if in awe of the land its neighbor?
How can it take in all rivers and stay the same
through sheer excess of quantity?—I know no
other explanation. Why does so great an element
have sand as its frontier?[48] Can natural philosophers, with their futile cleverness, give any
account of it, when they actually take the sea's
vast measurements with pint size pots of their
own ideas? Or shall I give you the short answer
from Scripture, the one more credible, more real,
than their long arguments? "He made his command a boundary for the face of the waters."[49]
This command is what binds the elemental water.
What makes it carry the sailor in his little boat
with a little wind—do you not find it a marvelous
sight, does not your mind stand amazed at it?—
to bind land and sea with business and commerce
and unify for humanity such very different
things? What springs do the first springs have?
Look for them and see if you, a man, can discover
or track one down. Who parted plains and hills
with rivers and gave them free course? How do
we get a miracle from opposites—from a sea that
does not get out and rivers that do not stand still?
What feeds the waters, what different kinds of
food do they get? Some are nourished with rain,
others drink with their roots—if I may use a rich
metaphor to describe the richness of God. ON
THEOLOGY, THEOLOGICAL ORATION 2(28).27.[50]

THE SEA NEVER EXCEEDS ITS CAPACITY.
GREGORY OF NYSSA: You, whose period of struggle is short, do not become more lifeless than the
earth, do not become more unthinking than the
insensible, for you are endowed with thought and
directed by reason toward life. Instead, as the

apostle says, "Continue in the things you have
learned and been convinced of,"[51] in that steadfast
and immoveable stability, since this also is one of
the divine commands, that you "be steadfast and
immoveable."[52] Let your sobriety abide unshaken,
your faith firm, your love constant, your stability
in every good thing unmoved, so that the earth in
you may stand to eternity.

But if any one, yearning for greater possessions
and letting his desire become as boundless as a
sea, has an insatiable greed for the streams of gain
flowing in from every side, let him treat his disease by looking at the real sea. For . . . the sea
does not exceed its boundary with the innumerable streams of water flowing into it but remains at
the same volume, just as though it were receiving
no new water from streams. In the same way
human nature too, restricted by specific limits in
the enjoyment of what comes to it, cannot
enlarge its appetite to match the extent of its
acquisitions; while the intake is endless, the
capacity for enjoyment is kept within its set limit.
HOMILIES ON ECCLESIASTES 1.[53]

1:8 Insatiability of Human Nature

**SINFUL HUMAN NATURE CANNOT BE SATIS-
FIED.** AMBROSE: Therefore incline to him of
whom the psalmist says, "He has not taken his
soul in vain."[54] To speak now of the troubles of
this life, the person has taken his soul in vain who
is constructing the things of the world and building the things of the body. We arise each day to
eat and drink; yet no one is filled so that he does
not hunger and thirst after a short time. Daily we
seek profit, and to greed there is set no limit.
"The eye will not be satisfied with seeing, nor the
ear with hearing." He that loves silver will not be
satisfied with silver. There is no limit to toil, and
there is no profit in abundance. We desire each
day to know what is new, and what is knowledge

---

[48]Jer 5:22. [49]Job 26:10 LXX. [50]FGFR 240-41*. [51]2 Tim 3:14. [52]1 Cor
15:58. [53]GNHE 40-41*. [54]Ps 24:4 (23:4 LXX).

itself but our daily sorrow and abasement? DEATH AS A GOOD 7.28.[55]

THE WRITTEN WORD. OLYMPIODORUS: All writings, both of secular and of divine wisdom, yield instruction when effort is applied. COMMENTARY ON ECCLESIASTES 1.8.[56]

1:9 Nothing Is New Under the Sun

REPETITION OF CYCLES IS AN ERROR OF PAGAN BELIEF. AUGUSTINE: There are some people who want to twist even a famous passage in the book of Solomon, called Ecclesiastes, into a defense of these recurring cycles of universal dissolution and re-evocation of the past: "What is it that has been? The same thing that shall be. What is it that has been done? The same that shall be done. Nothing under the sun is new, neither is anyone able to say, 'Behold, this is new,' for it has already gone before in the ages that were before us." But here Solomon was speaking either of things he had just been discussing—the succession of generations, the revolution of the sun, the course of rivers—or, at any rate, of those creatures in general that come to life and die. For example, there were people before us, they are with us now, and they shall come after us. And the same is true of animals and plants. Even monstrosities that are abnormal at birth, different as they are among themselves and, in certain cases, unique, nevertheless, inasmuch as they come under the heading of prodigies and monsters, have existed before and will exist again. Consequently, it is nothing new or even of recent date that a monster should be born under the sun. However, there are some who interpret the words to mean that what Solomon had in mind was that, in the predestination of God, everything is already a fact and, in that sense, there is nothing new under the sun.

Far be it from us Christians, however, to believe that these words of Solomon refer to those cycles by which, as these philosophers suppose, the same periods of time and sequence of events will be repeated. For example, the philosopher Plato having taught in a certain age at the school of Athens called the Academy, even so, through innumerable ages of the past at long but definite intervals, this same Plato and the same city, the same school and the same disciples all existed and will all exist again and again through innumerable ages of the future. Far be it from us, I say, to believe this.

For Christ died once for our sins; and "having risen from the dead, dies now no more, death shall no longer have dominion over him."[57] And we after the resurrection "shall ever be with the Lord,"[58] to whom we say, as the holy psalmist reminds us, "You, Oh Lord, will preserve us: and keep us from this generation forever."[59] And the verse that follows, I think, may be suitably applied to these philosophers: "The wicked walk round about." These words do not mean that their life will repeatedly recur in cycle after cycle as they think but that here and now the way of their errors, that is, their false doctrine, goes around in circles. CITY OF GOD 12.14.[60]

GOD EXERCISED HIS CREATIVE POWER. ORIGEN: It is probably in this way that, so far as our weakness allows, we shall maintain a reverent belief about God, neither asserting that his creatures were unbegotten and coeternal with him nor that he turned to the work of creation to do good when he had done nothing good before. For the saying that is written, "In wisdom you have made all things,"[61] is a true one. And certainly if "all things have been made in wisdom," then since wisdom has always existed, there have always existed in wisdom, by a prefiguration and preformation, those things which afterwards have received substantial existence. This is, I believe, the thought and meaning of Solomon when he says in Ecclesiastes, "What is it that has been made? The same that is to be. And what is it that has been created? The same that

---

[55]FC 65:91. [56]PG 93:485. [57]Rom 6:9. [58]1 Thess 4:17. [59]Ps 12:7 (11:8 LXX). [60]FC 14:268-69*. [61]Ps 104:24 (103:24 LXX).

is destined to be created. And there is nothing fresh under the sun. If one should speak of anything and say, Behold, this is new: it already has been, in the ages that were before us." If then particular things which are "under the sun" have already existed in the ages which were before us—since "there is nothing fresh under the sun"—then all universal categories[62] have forever existed, and some would say even individual things; but either way, it is clear that God did not begin to create after spending a period in idleness. ON FIRST PRINCIPLES 1.4.5.[63]

ON THE AGES BEYOND THIS AGE. ORIGEN: We say that not then for the first time did God begin to work when he made this visible world; but as, after its destruction, there will be another world, so also we believe that others existed before the present came into being. And both of these positions will be confirmed by the authority of Holy Scripture. For that there will be another world after this is taught by Isaiah, who says, "There will be new heavens, and a new earth, which I shall make to abide in my sight, says the Lord."[64] And that before this world others also existed[65] is shown by Ecclesiastes, in the words "What is that which has been? Even that which shall be. And what is that which has been created? Even this which is to be created: and there is nothing altogether new under the sun. Who shall speak and declare, Lo, this is new? It has already been in the ages which have been before us." By these testimonies it is established both that there were ages before our own and that there will be others after it. It is not, however, to be supposed that several worlds existed at once but that, after the end of this present world, others will take their beginning. ON FIRST PRINCIPLES 3.5.3.[66]

DISTINCTION BETWEEN WHAT IS AND WHAT IS MADE. GREGORY OF NYSSA: Let none of those listening think that there is a longwinded and meaningless repetition of words in the distinction between what has come to be and what has been made. The text points out in each of the expressions the difference between the soul and the flesh. The soul has come to be, and the body has been made. It is not because the words have two different meanings that the text uses this distinction of terminology for each of the things referred to. But [it does so] to enable you to reckon what is advantageous in each case. The soul came to be in the beginning the same as it will again appear hereafter, when it has been purified. The body shaped by the hands of God was made what the resurrection of the dead in due time will reveal it to be. For such as you may see it after the resurrection of the dead, just such it was made at the first. The resurrection of the dead is nothing but the complete restoration of the original state. HOMILIES ON ECCLESIASTES 1.[67]

1:11 No Remembrance of Things Past

AT THE FINAL RESTORATION ALL MEMORY OF EVIL WILL UTTERLY VANISH. GREGORY OF NYSSA: If oblivion has overtaken things which were, do not be surprised; for those that now are will also be veiled in oblivion. When our nature inclined to evil we became forgetful of the good; when we are set free again for the good, evil in turn will be veiled in oblivion. For I think this is the meaning of the text, in which he says, "There is no memory for the first, and indeed for those who come last there will be no memory of them." It is as if he were saying that the memory of events which followed our blessed state at the beginning, through which humanity has come to be among evils, will be obliterated by what again supervenes at the end. For "there will be no memory of them with those who have come to be at the last." That means, the final restoration will make the memory of evil things utterly vanish in our nature, in Jesus Christ our Lord, to whom be the glory forever and ever. HOMILIES ON ECCLESIASTES 1.[68]

---

[62]Presumably, genera and species. [63]OFP 42-43*. [64]Is 65:17. [65]See the previous passage. [66]OFP 238-39**. [67]GNHE 45. [68]GNHE 46.

1:12 King Over Israel in Jerusalem

A KINGLY BIRTH TEMPORAL AND ETERNAL.
GREGORY OF NYSSA: We have learned who the Ecclesiast is, he who unites what has gone astray and has been scattered abroad, and makes it all one church and one flock, that none may be deaf to the shepherd's kindly voice, which gives life to all. For "the words which I speak," he says, "are spirit and are life."[69] This is the one who calls himself Ecclesiast, just as he calls himself "Physician," and "Life," and "Resurrection," and "Light," and "Way," and "Door," and "Truth," and all the names of his love for humankind.[70] . . .

What does the Ecclesiast say? "I have become King over Israel in Jerusalem." When is this? Surely when "he was set up as king by him on Mount Zion, his holy mountain, proclaiming the Lord's commandment."[71] To him the Lord said, "You are my Son," and "Today I have begotten you."[72] He says that today he has begotten the Maker of all, the Father of the ages, so that by applying a temporal term to the moment of his birth, the text might demonstrate not his existence before the ages but his fleshly birth in time, for the salvation of humankind. HOMILIES ON ECCLESIASTES 2.[73]

---

[69]Jn 6:63. [70]Mt 9:12; Jn 14:6; 11:25; 12:46; 10:7. [71]Ps 2:6-7 LXX. [72]Ps 2:7. [73]GNHE 48-49*.

1:13-18 AN INVESTIGATION OF WISDOM

[13]And I applied my mind* to seek and to search out by wisdom all that is done under heaven; it is an unhappy business that God has given to the sons of men to be busy with. [14]I have seen everything that is done under the sun; and behold, all is vanity and a striving after wind.[b†]

[15]What is crooked cannot be made straight,
and what is lacking cannot be numbered.

[16]I said to myself, "I have acquired great wisdom, surpassing all who were over Jerusalem before me; and my mind‡ has had great experience of wisdom and knowledge." [17]And I applied my mind to know wisdom and to know madness and folly. I perceived that this also is but a striving after wind.§

[18]For in much wisdom is much vexation,#
and he who increases knowledge increases sorrow.

b Or a feeding on wind. See Hos 12.1　*LXX heart (kardia)　†LXX presumption of spirit (pneuma)　‡LXX heart　§LXX And my heart knew much—wisdom, and knowledge, parables and understanding; I perceived this is also a waywardness of spirit.　#LXX is abundance of knowledge

---

OVERVIEW: Useless human toil is not necessarily God's fault (GREGORY THAUMATURGUS). To assist human beings in their search for wisdom was the purpose of the incarnation (GREGORY OF NYSSA). Poverty of spirit is the opposite of vanity, whereas wisdom begins in the fear of the Lord (AUGUSTINE, GREGORY OF NAZIANZUS). Wisdom is true knowledge (CLEMENT OF ALEXANDRIA), which is manifested in a love for eternity (AUGUSTINE). Vanity, by contrast, is the result of materiality (ORIGEN), it is caused by abuse of God's gift of freedom (GREGORY OF NYSSA), and its charm is short-lived (JOHN OF DAMASCUS). The better way is to direct one's endeavors positively, toward the middle way of virtue, between excess and deficiency (BASIL). After all, God's way of numbering is not our own (EVAGRIUS). Wisdom shows us the way back to the good, as Solomon found (GREGORY OF NYSSA).

1:13 *The Search for Wisdom*

USELESS HUMAN TOIL. GREGORY THAUMATURGUS: I thoughtfully examined and wisely learned the nature of everything on earth. I discovered that it was all very complex, because human beings are allowed to toil away on earth, wallowing about uselessly in various kinds of pretentious effort at various times. PARAPHRASE OF ECCLESIASTES 1.13.[1]

THE PURPOSE OF THE INCARNATION IS TO ASSIST HUMANS IN THEIR SEARCH FOR WISDOM. GREGORY OF NYSSA: These are the things which the true Ecclesiast recounts as he teaches, so I believe, the great mystery of salvation, the reason why God was revealed in flesh. "I gave my heart," he says, "to enquiring into and investigating by wisdom all that had come about under the heaven." This is the reason for the Lord's fleshly coming to dwell with humankind, to give his heart to investigating in his own wisdom what has come about under the heaven. What is above the heaven had no need of investigation, just as there is no need of a medical attendant for what is not in the grip of illness.[2] So because the evils were on earth—for the creeping animal, the serpent which "crawls on its breast and on its belly," makes the earth its food, eating nothing from heaven; as it crawls on trodden ground it always looks at what treads on it, "watching for the traveler's heel"[3] and injecting its venom into those who have lost "the power to tread upon serpents"[4]—for this reason he gave his "heart to enquiring into and investigating all that has come about under the heaven." HOMILIES ON ECCLESIASTES 2.[5]

1:14 *All Human Works Are Vanity*

VANITY IS CONTRADICTED BY POVERTY OF SPIRIT. AUGUSTINE: We read in Scripture concerning the striving after temporal things, "All is vanity and presumption of spirit," but presumption of spirit means audacity and pride. Usually also the proud are said to have great spirits, and rightly, inasmuch as the wind also is called spirit. And hence it is written, "Fire, hail, snow, ice, spirit of tempest."[6] But, indeed, who does not know that the proud are spoken of as puffed up, as if swelled out with wind? And hence also that expression of the apostle, "Knowledge puffs up, but charity edifies."[7] And "the poor in spirit" are rightly understood here, as meaning the humble and God-fearing, that is, those who have not the spirit which puffs up. Nor ought blessedness to begin at any other point whatever, if indeed it is to attain unto the highest wisdom. "But the fear of the Lord is the beginning of wisdom";[8] for, on the other hand also, "pride" is entitled "the beginning of all sin."[9] Let the proud, therefore, seek after and love the kingdoms of the earth, but "blessed are the poor in spirit, for theirs is the kingdom of heaven."[10] SERMON ON THE MOUNT 1.1.3.[11]

VANITY IS THE RESULT OF THE MATERIALITY OF THIS WORLD. ORIGEN: This then is the "vanity" to which the creation was subjected, and above all that creation which is certainly the greatest thing in this world and which holds a distinguished preeminence by reason of its function. That is, the sun, moon and stars are said to have been subjected to vanity, because they were clothed with bodies and set to perform the task of giving light to the human race. And this creation, Scripture says, was subjected to vanity "not of its own will."[12] For it did not undertake a service to vanity by the exercise of free will but in obedience

---

[1]*GTPE* 19. [2]Lk 5:31. [3]Gen 3:14-15. [4]Lk 10:19. [5]*GNHE* 49. [6]Ps 148:8. [7]1 Cor 8:1. [8]Ps 111:10 (110:10 LXX). [9]Sir 10:13. [10]Mt 5:3. [11]NPNF 1 6:4*. [12]Rom 8:20.

to the wish of him who was subjecting it, because he who subjected it promised those who were being given over unwillingly to vanity that on the fulfillment of their splendid work of service they should be delivered from this bondage of corruption and vanity, when the time of redemption "of the glory of the sons of God"[13] should have come. Having received this hope, and looking for the fulfillment of this promise, the entire creation now in the meantime "groans together" with us (for it even has sympathy with those whom it serves) and "is in pain together,"[14] while in patience it hopes for what has been promised. ON FIRST PRINCIPLES 1.7.5.[15]

VANITY IS CAUSED BY ABUSE OF GOD'S GIFT OF FREEDOM. GREGORY OF NYSSA: He came, then, to enquire by his own wisdom what has come about under the sun, what the confusion is of things here on earth, how being became the slave of nonbeing, how the unreal dominates being. And he saw that evil distress God gave to the sons of man, for them to be distressed with. This does not mean, as one might assume at first glance, that it is devout to think that God gave evil distress to people, for then the responsibility for ills would be laid on him. . . .

What the more devout understanding is disposed to think is this: that the good gift of God, that is, freedom of action, became a means to sin through the sinful use humankind made of it. For unfettered free will is good by nature, and nobody would reckon among good things anything that was constrained by the yoke of necessity. But that free impulse of the mind rushing unschooled toward the choice of evil became a source of distress for the soul, as it was dragged down from the sublime and honorable toward the urges of the natural passions. . . .

[Therefore] a correct understanding does not conclude that anything bad has been put in human nature by God but blames our capacity to choose, which is in itself a good thing. [It is] a gift of God granted to our nature, but through folly it has become a force tipping the balance the oppo-

site way. HOMILIES ON ECCLESIASTES 2.[16]

REJECTION OF VANITY. JOHN OF DAMASCUS: So, following the teachings of these blessed saints, we utterly renounce these corruptible and perishable things of life, wherein may be found nothing stable or constant, or that continues in one stay. But all things are vanity and vexation of spirit, and many are the changes that they bring in a moment, for they are slighter than dreams and a shadow, or the breeze that blows the air. Small and short-lived is their charm, that is after all no charm, but illusion and deception of the wickedness of the world; which world we have been taught to love not at all but rather to hate with all our heart. Yes, and truly it is worthy of hatred and abhorrence; for whatsoever gifts it gives to its friends, these in turn in passion it takes away and shall hand over its victims, stripped of all good things, clad in the garment of shame, and bound under heavy burdens, to eternal tribulation. And those again whom it exalts, it quickly abases to the utmost wretchedness, making them a footstool and a laughing stock for their enemies. Such are its charms, such its bounties. BARLAAM AND JOSEPH 12.109-10.[17]

WE HAVE TO ASCEND TO THINGS THAT ARE FIRM AND IMMOVABLE. GREGORY OF NAZIANZUS: "I have seen everything," says Ecclesiastes. I have reviewed in my mind all human things, wealth, luxury, power, glory that is not stable, wisdom that eludes us more often than it is mastered; again pleasure, again wisdom, often returning full circle to the same things, delights of the belly, orchards, numbers of slaves, a multitude of possessions, male and female table servants, singing men and singing women, arms, henchmen, nations at one's feet, revenues flowing in, the pride of royalty, all life's superfluities and necessities, in which I surpassed all the kings who were before me. And after all this what is his judgment? "All is vanity of vanities, all is vanity and

---

[13]Rom 8:21. [14]Rom 8:22. [15]OFP 64. [16]GNHE 50-51. [17]LCL 34:185.

vexation of spirit," that is, a kind of irrational impulse of soul and distraction of man who has been condemned to this perhaps because of the original fall. But "hear all the conclusion of my discourse," he says; "fear God."[18] Through this he ceases from perplexity. And this alone is your gain from life here, to be brought through the confusion of things that are seen and unstable to things which are firm and immovable. ON HIS BROTHER ST. CAESARIUS, ORATION 7.19.[19]

1:15 Avoiding Excess and Deficiency

THE NATURE OF EXCESS AND DEFICIENCY. BASIL THE GREAT: He is upright in heart who does not have his mind inclined to excess or to deficiency but directs his endeavors toward the mean of virtue. He who has turned aside from valor to something less becomes crooked through cowardice, but he who has strained on to greater things inclines toward temerity. Therefore the Scripture calls those "crooked" who go astray from the middle way by excess or by deficiency. For, as a line becomes crooked when its straight-forward direction is deflected, now convexly, now concavely, so also a heart becomes crooked when it is at one time exalted through boastfulness, at another dejected through afflictions and humiliations. Wherefore Ecclesiastes says, "The crooked will not be kept straight." HOMILIES ON THE PSALMS 11.7 (PSALM 7).[20]

GOD'S WAY OF NUMBERING. EVAGRIUS OF PONTUS: The number by which God numbers the saints displays a certain and determined spiritual order, as it is said, "He numbers the multitudes of stars; and calls them all by name."[21] . . . Now, if David says, the understanding of God is without number,[22] it is not as though it were unworthy of God's essence that it cannot be numbered, or because the nature of such a number cannot be comprehended. For, just as the word *invisible* has two meanings: first, when applied to something that by its very nature is invisible (e.g., God), and second, when applied to something that may be

visible yet is not normally seen, like the ocean floor because it is hidden under waters; similarly, "innumerable" has two meanings: what cannot be numbered by nature and what cannot be numbered for some other reason. SCHOLIA ON ECCLESIASTES 6.1.15.[23]

1:16 Wisdom of Solomon

WISDOM AS TRUE KNOWLEDGE. CLEMENT OF ALEXANDRIA: Therefore it is written in Ecclesiastes, "And I added wisdom above all who were before me in Jerusalem; and my heart saw many things; and besides, I knew wisdom and knowledge, parables and understanding. And this also is the choice of the spirit, because in abundance of wisdom is abundance of knowledge." He who is conversant with all kinds of wisdom will be preeminently reliant upon knowledge. Now it is written, "Abundance of the knowledge of wisdom will give life to him who is of it."[24] And again, what is said is confirmed more clearly by this saying, "All things are in the sight of those who understand"—all things, both hellenic and barbarian; but the one or the other is not all. "They are right to those who wish to receive understanding. Choose instruction, and not silver, and knowledge above tested gold," and prefer also sense to pure gold; "for wisdom is better than precious stones, and no precious thing is worth it."[25] STROMATEIS 1.13.[26]

THE WAY BACK TOWARD THE GOOD. GREGORY OF NYSSA: What is the way back for the wanderer, and the way of escape from evil, and toward good, we learn next. For he "who has had experience like us in all things, without sin,"[27] speaks to us from our own condition. "He took our weaknesses upon him,"[28] and through these very weaknesses of our nature he shows us the way out of the reach of evil. Now note, please,

---

[18]Eccles 12:13. [19]FC 22:19-20. [20]FC 46:176-77**. [21]Ps 147:4 LXX. [22]Cf. Ps 146:5 LXX. [23]SC 397:66-68. [24]Eccles 7:12 LXX. [25]Prov 8:9-11. [26]ANF 2:313*. [27]Heb 4:15. [28]Mt 8:17.

that Wisdom speaks to us through Solomon himself after the flesh, and speaks about those things by which we may most readily be led to despise the things which are pursued by people. HOMILIES ON ECCLESIASTES 2.[29]

1:17 The Experience of Solomon

SOLOMON'S LIFE CORRESPONDED TO HIS EXPERIENCE. GREGORY OF NYSSA: It is Solomon who speaks these words. This Solomon was the third king of Israel, after King Saul and David, the chosen of the Lord. He succeeded his father on the throne and was proclaimed king when the power of the Israelites had already reached its height; he did not go on wearing his people out with war and fighting but lived in peace as far as lay in his power, making it his task not to acquire what did not belong to him but to enjoy what he already had in abundance. . . .

Such is the order he adopts in his account, that first in the early years of his life he devotes his time to education and does not take the easy course in the face of the hard work such study involves but uses the choice of his spirit, that is, his natural impulse, for the accumulation of knowledge, even though his goal was achieved by hard work. And thus, when he has matured in wisdom, he does not merely theoretically observe the passionate and irrational deception of mankind in the matter of bodily enjoyments but through the actual experience of each of the things they pursue recognizes their futility. HOMILIES ON ECCLESIASTES 2.[30]

1:18 Relationship of Wisdom to Sorrow

THOSE WHO LIVE IN THE SPIRIT HAVE WISDOM THAT DOES NOT BRING SORROW. AUGUSTINE: People are accustomed to set a high value on the knowledge of earthly and celestial things. But they are certainly better who prefer the knowledge of themselves to this knowledge. And a mind to which even its own weakness is known is more deserving of praise than one that . . . is igno-

rant of the course by which it must proceed to reach its own true health and strength. But one who has been aroused by the warmth of the Holy Spirit . . . has already awakened to God. In his love for [God, such a person] has already felt his own unworthiness and is willing but is not yet strong enough to come to him. And through the light received from [God, this person] takes heed to himself and finds that his own defilement cannot mingle with his purity. [This person] feels it sweet to weep and to beseech God that he may again and again have pity until he has cast off all his misery. [This person also prays] with confidence as having already received the free gift of salvation through his only Savior and enlightener of humankind. For one who so acts and laments, knowledge does not puff up because charity edifies. He has preferred the one knowledge to the other knowledge; he has preferred to know his own weakness more than to know the walls of the world, the foundations of the earth, and the heights of the heavens. And by acquiring this knowledge he has acquired sorrow, the sorrow arising from his wandering away from the desire of his own true country, and from its founder, his own blessed God. ON THE TRINITY 4, PREFACE.[31]

KNOWLEDGE OF THE LAW MAKES US GUILTY OF SIN. AUGUSTINE: It is evident, then, that the oldness of the letter, in the absence of the newness of the spirit, instead of freeing us from sin, rather makes us guilty by the knowledge of sin. [Thus] it is written in another part of Scripture, "He that increases knowledge, increases sorrow." [It is] not that the law is itself evil, but because the commandment has its good in the demonstration of the letter, not in the assistance of the spirit. And if this commandment is kept from the fear of punishment and not from the love of righteousness, it is kept in a servile manner, not freely, and therefore it is not kept at all. For no fruit is good which does not grow from the root of love. ON THE SPIRIT AND THE LETTER 26.[32]

---

[29]GNHE 53*. [30]GNHE 53-54. [31]FC 45:129-30*. [32]NPNF 1 5:94*.

2:1-11 THE VANITY OF PLEASURE AND WEALTH

[1]*I said to myself, "Come now, I will make a test of pleasure; enjoy yourself." But behold, this also was vanity.* [2]*I said of laughter, "It is mad," and of pleasure, "What use is it?"* [3]*I searched with my mind how to cheer my body with wine—my mind still guiding me with wisdom—and how to lay hold on folly, till I might see what was good for the sons of men to do under heaven during the few days of their life.* [4]*I made great works; I built houses and planted vineyards for myself;* [5]*I made myself gardens and parks, and planted in them all kinds of fruit trees.* [6]*I made myself pools from which to water the forest of growing trees.* [7]*I bought male and female slaves, and had slaves who were born in my house; I had also great possessions of herds and flocks, more than any who had been before me in Jerusalem.* [8]*I also gathered for myself silver and gold and the treasure of kings and provinces; I got singers, both men and women, and many concubines,[c] man's delight.*

[9]*So I became great and surpassed all who were before me in Jerusalem; also my wisdom remained with me.* [10]*And whatever my eyes desired I did not keep from them; I kept my heart from no pleasure, for my heart found pleasure in all my toil, and this was my reward for all my toil.* [11]*Then I considered all that my hands had done and the toil I had spent in doing it, and behold, all was vanity and a striving after wind, and there was nothing to be gained under the sun.*

c The meaning of the Hebrew word is uncertain

OVERVIEW: Excessive laughter is not appropriate to a life of wisdom and is contrasted with real joy in the Lord (BASIL, LEANDER). Works that have no useful end do not benefit God's kingdom (CHRYSOSTOM), whereas a house built upon good deeds is really built upon Christ as the rock (DIDYMUS), and a person who has transcended this world, especially in concern for the poor, is freed of all care and anxieties (AMBROSE, BEDE). It is not the acuity of the mind but rather the disposition of the soul that is to be praised or condemned (OLYMPIODORUS). Wine leads to drunkenness, slavery is wrong, gold is useless, and usury is pointless. Even activity that is enjoyable disappears when it is accomplished (GREGORY OF NYSSA). Nonetheless, every actualization of potential is a move toward perfection, although the desire for visible things should be appropriate but not consuming. Toil in pursuit of virtue does have its reward, but toil is useful if only to know what one is rejecting (DIDYMUS).

2:1 Pleasure Is Tested but Found Wanting

THE TEST. GREGORY OF NYSSA: He condemns pleasures as futile. For he says, "I said in my heart, Come hither, I will test you in merriment, and also in good, and this too is futility." For he did not give himself to this kind of experience straight away or slide into partaking of pleasures without having tasted the austere and more devout life. Rather, after training himself with these things and achieving in his character the severity and determination through which the lessons of wisdom come most readily to those who pursue them, he then descends to things considered agreeable to the senses. [He does this] not because he is drawn down to them by passion but in order to investigate whether the sensual experience of them makes any contribution to the knowledge of true Good.

That is why he makes his own what he had originally regarded as alien, laughter, and calls the condition dizziness, in that it is equivalent in meaning to "frenzy" or "madness"; for what else would anyone properly call laughter? It is neither speech nor activity directed to any end but an unseemly loss of bodily control. HOMILIES ON ECCLESIASTES 2.[1]

2:2 Madness of Laughter

IMMODERATE LAUGHTER IS UNBECOMING. BASIL THE GREAT: Those who live under discipline should avoid very carefully even such intemperate action as is commonly regarded lightly. Indulging in unrestrained and immoderate laughter is a sign of intemperance, of a want of control over one's emotions, and of failure to repress the soul's frivolity by a stern use of reason. It is not unbecoming, however, to give evidence of merriment of soul by a cheerful smile, if only to illustrate that which is written: "A glad heart makes a cheerful countenance,"[2] but raucous laughter and uncontrollable shaking of the body are not indicative of a well-regulated soul, or of personal dignity, or self-mastery. This kind of laughter Ecclesiastes also reprehends as especially subversive of firmness of soul in the words: "Laughter I counted error," and again, "As the crackling of thorns burning under a pot, so is the laughter of fools."[3] Moreover, the Lord appears to have experienced those emotions that are of necessity associated with the body, as well as those that betoken virtue, as, for example, weariness and compassion for the afflicted; but, so far as we know from the story of the gospel, he never laughed. On the contrary, he even pronounced those unhappy who are given to laughter.[4] THE LONG RULES 17.[5]

REAL JOY IN THE LORD. LEANDER OF SEVILLE: Let your rejoicing of the heart in God be calm and moderate, in accordance with the words of the apostle: "Rejoice in the Lord always; again, I say, rejoice."[6] In another place, he says, "The fruit of the spirit is joy."[7] Such happiness does not disturb the mind with the base act of laughter but lifts the soul to the place of rest that is above where you can hear "Enter into the joy of your master."[8] One can usually tell what is in a nun's heart by her laughter. A nun would not laugh impudently if her heart were pure. A man's face is the mirror of his heart: a nun does not laugh wantonly unless she is wanton in her heart. "Out of the abundance of the heart," says the Lord, "the mouth speaks";[9] likewise, the face of a nun laughs from the abundance of a vain heart. See what is written about this: "Of laughter I said: 'Mad!' and of mirth: 'What good does this do?'" And again, in the same place: "Let laughter be mingled with sadness, and the end of joy may be sorrow."[10] And the Lord says, "Blessed are they who mourn, for they shall be comforted."[11] And the apostle spoke the truth to those insanely joyful: "Let your laughter be turned into mourning."[12] Flee laughter, therefore, sister, as a sin and change temporal joy into mourning, that you may be blessed if you grieve that you are a sojourner in the world; for those who mourn, according to God, are blessed and shall be comforted. THE TRAINING OF NUNS 21.[13]

2:3 The Search for the Good

EQUALITY OF WISH AND FULFILLMENT. GREGORY OF NYSSA: But I, he says, sought the true good, which is equally good at any age and every time of life, and of which satiety is not expected or fullness found. Appetite for it and partaking of it are exactly matched, and longing flourishes together with enjoyment and is not limited by the attainment of what is desired. The more it delights in the good, the more desire flames up with

---

[1]GNHE 56. [2]Prov 15:13. [3]Eccles 7:6. [4]Lk 6:25. [5]FC 9:271. [6]Phil 4:4. [7]Gal 5:22. [8]Mt 25:21. [9]Mt 12:34. [10]Prov 14:13. [11]Mt 5:4. [12]Jas 4:9. [13]FC 62:214-15.

delight; the delight matches the desire, and at each stage of life it is always a lovely thing to those who partake of it. Amid the changes of age and time the good alters not at all; when our eyes are closed and when they are open, when we are happy and when we are sorrowful, by day and by night, on land and on the sea, active and at rest, ruling and serving—for every person alive [the good] is equally absolutely good, since the accidents inflicted on one by chance make it neither worse nor better, nor smaller nor larger.

This, as I understand it, is the good that truly is, the thing Solomon sought to see, which people will do under the sun throughout all the number of the days of their life. This seems to me to be none other than the work of faith, the performance of which is common to all, available on equal terms to those who wish for it, lasting in full strength continuously throughout life. This is the good work, which I pray may be done in us too, in Christ Jesus our Lord, to whom be the glory forever and ever. HOMILIES ON ECCLESIASTES 2.[14]

NOT THE MIND BUT THE SOUL. OLYMPIODORUS: It is not the acuity of the mind but rather the disposition of the soul, being employed beneficially or shamefully in making use of the gift, which is to be praised or condemned. COMMENTARY ON ECCLESIASTES 2.3.[15]

2:4 *Vanity of Worldly Labor*

SOLOMON'S INVOLVEMENT IN WORLDLY PLEASURE. GREGORY OF NYSSA: Whether [Solomon] really did these things or made the story up for our benefit, so that the argument might reach its logical conclusion, I cannot say precisely. Nevertheless he does speak of things with which nobody who was aiming at virtue would willingly be associated. However, whether it is by benevolent design that he discusses things that had not happened as if they had, and condemns them as though he had experienced them, in order that we might turn away from desire for what is con-

demned before the experience, or whether he deliberately lowered himself to the enjoyment of such things, so as to train his senses rigorously by using alien things, it is for each to decide freely for himself, whichever conjecture he likes to pursue.

If however anyone were to say that Solomon really was involved in the practical experience of pleasures, I would agree. HOMILIES ON ECCLESIASTES 3.[16]

VAIN IS THAT WHICH HAS NO USEFUL END. CHRYSOSTOM: "Vanity of vanities, all things are vanity." Hear also what the prophet says, "He heaps up riches and knows not who shall gather them."[17] Such is "vanity of vanities," your splendid buildings, your vast and overflowing riches, the herds of slaves that bustle along the public square, your pomp and vainglory, your high thoughts and your ostentation. For all these are vain; they came not from the hand of God but are of our own creating. But why then are they vain? Because they have no useful end. Riches are vain when they are spent upon luxury; but they cease to be vain when they are "dispersed and given to the needy."[18] HOMILIES ON EPHESIANS 12.[19]

ON VANITY AND THE KINGDOM. CHRYSOSTOM: Hear what Solomon says, who knew the present world by actual experience. "I built houses, I planted vineyards, I made gardens, and orchards and pools of water. I gathered also silver and gold. I got myself men singers and women singers, and flocks and herds." There was no one who lived in greater luxury or higher glory. There was no one so wise or so powerful, no one who saw all things so succeeding to his heart's desire. What then? He had no enjoyment from all these things. What after all does he say of it himself? "Vanity of vanities, all is vanity." Vanity not simply but superlatively. Let us believe him, and lay hold on that in which there is no vanity, in which there is truth;

---

[14]*GNHE* 58*. [15]PG 93:493. [16]*GNHE* 61*. [17]Ps 39:6 (38:7 LXX). [18]Ps 112:9 (111:9 LXX). [19]NPNF 1 13:109*.

and what is based upon a solid rock, where there is no old age or decline but all things bloom and flourish, without decay, or waxing old, or approaching dissolution. Let us, I beseech you, love God with genuine affection, not from fear of hell but from desire of the kingdom. For what is comparable to seeing Christ? Surely nothing! What to the enjoyment of those good things? Surely nothing! Well may there be nothing [comparable]; for "eye has not seen, nor ear heard, neither have entered into the heart of man the things which God has prepared for them that love him."[20] HOMILIES ON 1 TIMOTHY 15.[21]

HOMES BUILT UPON GOOD DEEDS ARE BUILT UPON CHRIST AS THE ROCK. DIDYMUS THE BLIND: If one wants to understand houses as good deeds, then every good deed is the house of its owner. Those who "hear the words of Jesus and do them" . . . build their foundation on a rock.[22] Since virtue as a whole is one, one who strives after it builds one house, establishing it upon the rock, upon God's unbreakable Word, that is, upon Christ. COMMENTARY ON ECCLESIASTES 35.29.[23]

REAL JOY COMES WITH TEARS. CHRYSOSTOM: Serve God with tears, that you may be able to wash away your sins. I know that many mock us, saying, "Shed tears." Therefore it is a time for tears. I know also that they are disgusted, who say, "Let us eat and drink, for tomorrow we die."[24] "Vanity of vanities, all is vanity." It is not I that say it, but he who had had the experience of all things says thus: "I built for me houses, I planted vineyards, I made me pools of water, [I had] men servants and women servants." And what then after all these things? "Vanity of vanities, all is vanity."

Let us mourn therefore, beloved, let us mourn in order that we may laugh indeed, that we may rejoice indeed in the time of unmixed joy. For with this joy [here] grief is altogether mingled, and never is it possible to find it pure. But that is simple and undeceiving joy: it has nothing treacherous, nor any admixture. On

THE EPISTLE TO THE HEBREWS 15.9.[25]

VINEYARDS AND DRUNKENNESS. GREGORY OF NYSSA: The confession about planting vines encompasses a great catalogue of effects on the person. The text includes in its meaning the full extent and nature of the effects caused by wine. Who in the world does not know that once wine immoderately exceeds what is necessary, it is tinder for licentiousness, the means to self-indulgence, injury to youth, deformity to age, dishonor for women, a poison inducing madness, sustenance for insanity, destruction to the soul, death to the understanding, estrangement from virtue? From it comes unjustified mirth, lamentation without reason, senseless tears, unfounded boasting, shameless lying, craving for the unreal, expectation of the impracticable, monstrous threats, groundless fear, unawareness of what is really to be feared, unreasonable jealousy, excessive bonhomie, the promise of impossible things—not to mention the unseemly nodding of the head, the shaky, topheavy gait, the indecency due to immoderate intake, uncontrolled movement of the limbs, the bending of the neck which can no longer support itself on the shoulders, when the flabbiness brought about by the wine relaxes the neck muscles.

What caused the unlawful heinous act of incest with daughters? What distracted Lot's mind from what was happening, when he both committed the heinous act and was ignorant of what he committed?[26] Who invented, like a riddle, the weird names of those children? How did the mothers of the accursed progeny become the sisters of their own children? How did the boys have the same man both as father and grandfather? Who was it who muddled their identity by breaking the law? Was it not wine, exceeding moderation, which caused this unbelievable tragedy? Was it not drunkenness that shaped such a myth into history, one which surpasses real myths in its mon-

---

[20]1 Cor 2:9. [21]NPNF 1 13:462*. [22]Mt 7:24. [23]PTA 25:169. [24]Is 22:13; 1 Cor 15:32. [25]NPNF 1 14:442*. [26]Gen 19:30-38.

strosity? HOMILIES ON ECCLESIASTES 3.[27]

2:6 Pools for Water

ALLEGORICAL MEANING OF POOLS THAT SOLOMON MADE. AMBROSE: With reference to the natural sense, you find it said in Ecclesiastes, "I made for myself pools of water to water from them a flourishing woodland." And do not be concerned that he said "pools" instead of "a well," because Moses said "the Well of Room-enough." For the man who has transcended this world with a pious mind is freed of all care and anxieties. There Ecclesiastes says "pools" with reason, for he sees that there is no abundance under the sun,[28] but if anyone wishes to abound, let him abound in Christ.[29] There remains for us the well in the mystical sense, and we find it in the Canticle of Canticles, where the Scripture says, "the fountain of gardens, the well of living water which runs with a strong stream from Lebanon."[30] Indeed if you pursue the depth of the mysteries, the well appears to you to be mystical wisdom set in the deep, as it were. ISAAC, OR THE SOUL 4.25-26.[31]

2:7 Male and Female Slaves

WHY SLAVERY IS WRONG. GREGORY OF NYSSA: What is such a gross example of arrogance in the matters enumerated above—an opulent house, and an abundance of vines, and ripeness in vegetable plots, and collecting waters in pools and channeling them in gardens—as for a human being to think himself the master of his own kind? "I got me slaves and slave girls," he says, and "homebred slaves were born for me." Do you notice the enormity of the boast? This kind of language is raised up as a challenge to God. For we hear from prophecy that "all things are the slaves" of the power that transcends all.[32] So, when someone turns the property of God into his own property and arrogates dominion to his own kind, so as to think himself the owner of men and women, what is he doing but overstepping his

own nature through pride, regarding himself as something different from his subordinates? . . . You have forgotten the limits of your authority and that your rule is confined to control over things without reason. For it says "let them rule over" winged creatures and fishes and four-footed things and creeping things.[33] Why do you go beyond what is subject to you and raise yourself up against the very species that is free, counting your own kind on a level with four-footed things and even footless things? . . . But by dividing the human species in two with "slavery" and "ownership" you have caused it to be enslaved to itself and to be the owner of itself. . . .

He who knew the nature of humankind rightly said that the whole world was not worth giving in exchange for a human soul. Whenever a human being is for sale, therefore, nothing less than the owner of the earth is led into the sale room. Presumably, then, the property belonging to him is up for auction too. That means the earth, the islands, the sea, and all that is in them. What will the buyer pay, and what will the vendor accept, considering how much property is entailed in the deal? . . .

In what respect have you something extra, tell me, that you who are human think yourself the master of a humble being, and say, "I got me slaves and slave girls," like herds of goats or pigs. For when he said, "I got me slaves and slave girls," he added that abundance in flocks of sheep and cattle came to him. For he says, "and much property in cattle and sheep became mine," as though both cattle and slaves were subject to his authority to an equal degree. HOMILIES ON ECCLESIASTES 4.[34]

2:8 Silver and Gold

GOLD INDICATES THINGS OF THE SPIRIT, SILVER THE SPOKEN WORD AND ITS VIRTUE. DIDYMUS THE BLIND: In many places of the

---

[27]GNHE 67-68. [28]See Eccles 9:6. [29]1 Cor 1:31. [30]Song 4:15. [31]FC 65:26. [32]Ps 119:91 (118:91 LXX). [33]Gen 1:26. [34]GNHE 73-75*.

divine teaching the Spirit and spiritual things are expressed by the image of gold, the spoken word and its virtue by the image of silver. "The tongue of the righteous is choice silver,"[35] that is, his spoken word and everything which he teaches by this spoken word. In the same way the following saying is to be understood: "The promises[36] of the Lord are promises that are pure, silver refined in a furnace on the ground."[37] But the spirit is gold. COMMENTARY ON ECCLESIASTES 39.19.[38]

THE USELESSNESS OF GOLD. GREGORY OF NYSSA:

What hope is there, that someone who lives amid so much gold will thereby become wise, sagacious, reflective, learned, a friend of God, prudent, pure, passion-free, detached and aloof from all that draws him toward evil? Or, alternatively, physically strong, pleasant to look at, extending life for many centuries, free from aging, disease and pain, and all the things sought for in the life of the flesh? But nobody is so absurd or so unobservant of our common humanity as to think that these things would come to human beings, if only money were poured out before everyone in vast quantities on demand. Even now one may see many of those already better endowed with much wealth living in a pitiful state of health, so that if their servants were not at hand they would not be able to go on living. If, therefore, the abundance of gold proposed in our argument offers no benefit in body or in soul, it is far more likely that when it is available on a small scale it will prove useless to those who possess it.

What benefit would there be to its owner in the substance itself, which is inert to taste and smell and hearing and which feels to the touch of the same value as all its rivals? Let nobody put as an objection the food or clothing obtained by purchase with gold. For someone who buys bread or clothes with gold gets something useful in exchange for something useless and lives because he has made bread his food, not gold. But if a person gathers this stuff for himself through such transactions as these, what joy does he have of his money? What practical advice does he get from it?

What training in public affairs? What prediction of the future? What comfort for the pains of the body? He gets it, he counts it, he stows it away, he stamps it with his seal, he refuses it when asked, he even swears by it when disbelieved. That is the blessedness, that is the object of endeavor, that is the benefit, that is the extent of the happiness. HOMILIES ON ECCLESIASTES 4.[39]

THE CASE AGAINST USURY. GREGORY OF NYSSA:

If therefore something brings no benefit to those who pursue it, whether in terms of beauty or of physical well-being or of the relief of pains, for what reason is it pursued? And what is the affection of those who have set their heart on the stuff, when they come to be aware of such a possession? Do they congratulate themselves because they have gained something? If someone were to ask them whether they would welcome the chance to have their nature changed into it, and themselves to become what is honored among them with such affection, would they choose the change? [Would they choose to be] transformed from humanity into gold and be proved no longer rational, intelligent or able to use the sense organs for living, but yellow and heavy and speechless, lifeless and senseless, as gold is? I do not think that even those who set their desire passionately on the stuff would choose this.

If, therefore, for right-thinking people it would be a kind of curse to acquire the properties of this inanimate stuff, what is the mindless frenzy over the acquisition of things whose goal is futility, so that for this reason those who are driven mad with the desire for riches even commit murders and robbery? And not only these things, but also the pernicious idea of interest which one might call another kind of robbery or bloodshed without being far from the truth. What is the difference between getting someone else's property by seizing it through covert housebreaking or taking possession of the goods of a

---

[35]Prov 10:20. [36]Gk *logia*. [37]Ps 12:6 (11:7 LXX). [38]PTA 25:189. [39]GNHE 76-77.

passer-by by murdering him and acquiring what is not one's own by exacting interest? . . .

If someone takes someone else's money by force or steals it secretly, he is called a violent criminal or a burglar or something like that. But the one who advertises his felony in financial agreements, and who provides evidence of his own cruelty, and who enforces his crime by contracts, is called a philanthropist and a benefactor and a savior and all the worthiest of names. And the profit from thieving is called loot, but the person who strips his debtor naked by this kind of compulsion gives his harshness the euphemism *philanthropy*. This is what they call the damage done to those in distress.

"I gathered for me both silver and gold." Yes, but the reason why the one who trains humankind wisely includes this also in the lists of things confessed is that human beings may learn, from one who has formed the judgment from experience, that this is one of the things condemned as wrong, and may guard before the experience against the onslaught of evil. HOMILIES ON ECCLESIASTES 4.[40]

HARMONY COMES FROM THE CHOIR DIRECTOR WHO IS THE SAVIOR OF SOLOMON. DIDYMUS THE BLIND: As the choir directors assign a place and a pitch to each male and female member of the choir so that a harmony of sound emerges, so those who sing to God and do so in harmony have the Savior himself as choir director. Or the [choir director could also be the] wise man, who here is Solomon, if we understand him in his role as wise man. COMMENTARY ON ECCLESIASTES 41.10.[41]

2:9 Greater Excellence Than Before

ACTUALIZATION OF POTENTIALITY IS MOVING TOWARD PERFECTION. DIDYMUS THE BLIND: The wise person always finds himself "increasing" when he prospers. But in life, it is the last and the first thing to reach perfection. In Scripture it is said, "When human beings have finished, they are just beginning."[42] Of course, even if human beings reach the perfection possible in this life, still, as it is said, "We know only in part."[43] In the activity of "increasing" there is always something virtuous. . . . [The prophets and Moses] prophesied what Jesus would do and teach. But Jesus fulfilled the prophecy. The actualization of potentialities is always an "increase." These prepared the way, but he has perfected the way when he declared about himself: "I am the way, the truth."[44] And he says to his disciples: "Unless your righteousness exceeds that of the scribes and Pharisees."[45] In this you see that Jesus' disciples had more righteousness than the previous ones. COMMENTARY ON ECCLESIASTES 42.24.[46]

2:10 My Heart Rejoiced

DESIRE FOR VISIBLE THINGS SHOULD BE APPROPRIATE BUT NOT CONSUMING. DIDYMUS THE BLIND: In the literal sense the following is meant: If I desired something among the things in the visible world, I did not keep my eyes from them. I got everything that I longed for. John says in his letter: "The desire of the flesh, the desire of the eyes, the pride in riches comes not from the Father but from the world."[47] Even if they do "not come from the Father" as the gifts of grace and of the Spirit, they are nevertheless from God. Desire for visible things, however, should not be consuming but should instead be appropriate to that which is desired. COMMENTARY ON ECCLESIASTES 43.23.[48]

THE HEART INDICATES REASON. DIDYMUS THE BLIND: "Heart" does not here signify the organ but reason. In a different passage [we read]: "Blessed are the pure in heart."[49] This means with regard to reason. And: "Listen to me, you stubborn of heart."[50] The heart thus understood does not need to be "kept from pleasure." It derives

---

[40]GNHE 78-80*.　[41]PTA 25:197.　[42]Sir 18:7.　[43]1 Cor 13:9.　[44]Jn 14:6.　[45]Mt 5:20.　[46]PTA 25:205-7.　[47]1 Jn 2:16.　[48]PTA 25:211.　[49]Mt 5:8.　[50]Is 46:12.

pleasure from appropriate views and meditations based on knowledge. By knowledge I mean knowledge that is in accordance with God. COMMENTARY ON ECCLESIASTES 44.17.[51]

TOIL IN THE PURSUIT OF VIRTUE HAS ITS REWARD. DIDYMUS THE BLIND: As is well known, the person who toils for something in his heart suffers if he does not succeed with it. Ecclesiastes thus wants to say: I did not fail in any of the things I hoped for in my toil. Further: The person who strives for knowledge and pursues virtue "toils.". . . The person who toils for the things that are useful for the soul and that adorn the inner person says about himself: "I found pleasure in all my toil." COMMENTARY ON ECCLESIASTES 44.23.[52]

SELF-INDULGENCE. BEDE: They nourish their hearts in self-indulgence who, according to the word of Ecclesiastes, do not prevent their heart from enjoying every wish and from delighting itself in the things which they have prepared. And they count it their due if they themselves make use of their own labors, having no care for the support and solace of the poor. COMMENTARY ON JAMES 5.5.[53]

2:11 *All Things Considered*

TOIL CAN BE USEFUL IF ONLY TO KNOW WHAT ONE IS REJECTING. DIDYMUS THE BLIND: My hands are busy and tools fit for work. They toil and are active. And I saw that all that has been created by these visible hands and their activities, was vanity. . . . This kind of toil is to be rejected indeed—it is vanity. And still, most human beings act vainly. Ecclesiastes counts himself among these people; he is himself a human being. I said it already: No one who talks against wealth is heard if he is poor himself. But one who teaches this needs to have experienced all these human things himself. A teaching thus only reaches its goal and is successful if he who

delivers it is acquainted with what he is rejecting. He thereby shows that he himself is able to handle them in an appropriate way. COMMENTARY ON ECCLESIASTES 45.4.[54]

"UNDER THE SUN" AND "IN THE SUN." DIDYMUS THE BLIND: A person who is enlightened by the "sun of righteousness" is not "under" it but "in" it. Thus it is said in the Gospel: "The righteous will shine like the sun in the kingdom of their Father,"[55] not "under" the sun. If a person says about himself that he is a Christian and enlightened by the true light, by the "sun of righteousness," and still concentrates his actions on earthly things and strives after them (and we all are for the most part like these people) this person is "under the sun." If he is "under the sun" in this way, he has no gain. Even if he quotes much from Scripture but does not act accordingly, he has no gain. COMMENTARY ON ECCLESIASTES 46.7.[56]

A SUMMARY THAT ENDS IN FUTILITY. GREGORY OF NYSSA: People who write in water are engaged in drawing the shapes of the letters in the liquid by writing with the hand, but nothing remains of the shape of the letters, and the interest in the writing consists solely in the act of writing (for the surface of the water continually follows the hand, obliterating what is written). In the same way all enjoyable interest and activity disappears with its accomplishment. When the activity ceases the enjoyment too is wiped out, and nothing is stored up for the future, nor is any trace or remnant of happiness left to the pleasure takers when the pleasant activity passes away. This is what the text means when it says "there is no advantage under the sun" for those who labor for such things, whose end is futility. HOMILIES ON ECCLESIASTES 4.[57]

---

[51]PTA 25:215. [52]PTA 25:215-17. [53]CS 82:57. [54]PTA 25:217-19. [55]Mt 13:43. [56]PTA 25:225. [57]GNHE 84.

2:12-26 THE CONTRAST BETWEEN WISDOM AND FOLLY

¹²*So I turned to consider wisdom and madness and folly; for what can the man do who comes after the king? Only what he has already done.* ¹³*Then I saw that wisdom excels folly as light excels darkness.* ¹⁴*The wise man has his eyes in his head, but the fool walks in darkness; and yet I perceived that one fate comes to all of them.* ¹⁵*Then I said to myself, "What befalls the fool will befall me also; why then have I been so very wise?" And I said to myself that this also is vanity.* ¹⁶*For of the wise man as of the fool there is no enduring remembrance, seeing that in the days to come all will have been long forgotten. How the wise man dies just like the fool!* ¹⁷*So I hated life, because what is done under the sun was grievous to me; for all is vanity and a striving after wind.*

¹⁸*I hated all my toil in which I had toiled under the sun, seeing that I must leave it to the man who will come after me;* ¹⁹*and who knows whether he will be a wise man or a fool? Yet he will be master of all for which I toiled and used my wisdom under the sun. This also is vanity.* ²⁰*So I turned about and gave my heart up to despair over all the toil of my labors under the sun,* ²¹*because sometimes a man who has toiled with wisdom and knowledge and skill must leave all to be enjoyed by a man who did not toil for it. This also is vanity and a great evil.* ²²*What has a man from all the toil and strain with which he toils beneath the sun?* ²³*For all his days are full of pain, and his work is a vexation; even in the night his mind does not rest. This also is vanity.*

²⁴*There is nothing better for a man than that he should eat and drink and find enjoyment in his toil. This also, I saw, is from the hand of God;* ²⁵*for apart from him*^d *who can eat or who can have enjoyment?** ²⁶*For to the man who pleases him God gives wisdom and knowledge and joy; but to the sinner he gives the work of gathering and heaping, only to give to one who pleases God. This also is vanity and a striving after wind.*

d Gk Syr: Heb *apart from me*   *LXX *or who shall drink*

OVERVIEW: Evil is deprivation of the Good and the same as nonexistence (GREGORY OF NYSSA). As far as light excels darkness, so wisdom excels foolishness (CHRYSOSTOM), but the love of money is a foolishness that will never satisfy (AMBROSE). Those who are wise will not share the fate of those who are foolish (GREGORY THAUMATURGUS). The kingdom of heaven and its virtues are worth far more than the lure of temporal possessions (ATHANASIUS). Far better it is to care for the orphan and the widow (APOSTOLIC CONSTITUTIONS).

2:12 Wisdom and Madness and Folly

EVIL IS DEPRIVATION OF THE GOOD AND THE SAME AS NONEXISTENCE. GREGORY OF NYSSA: He therefore teaches what human wisdom is, that to follow the real wisdom—which he also calls counsel, which brings about what truly is and has substance, and is not thought of as among futile things—to follow that is the sum of human wisdom. But real wisdom and counsel, on my reckoning, is none other than the Wisdom that is conceived of as before the universe. It is that wisdom by which God made all things, as the prophet says, "by wisdom you made all things"[1] and "Christ is the power of God and the wisdom of God,"[2] by which all things came to be and were set in order. . . .

When I saw these things, he says, and weighed, as in a balance, what is against what is not, I found that the difference between wisdom and folly was the same as one would find if light were measured against the dark. I think it is appropriate that he uses the analogy of light in the discernment of the good. Since darkness is in its own nature unreal (for if there were nothing to obstruct the sun's rays, there would be no darkness), whereas light is of itself, perceived in its own essence, he shows by this analogy that evil does not exist by itself. [Instead evil] arises from deprivation of the good, whereas good is always as it is, stable and steadfast, and does not arise from the deprivation of anything which is prior to it. What is perceived as essentially opposed to good, is not; for what in itself is not, does not exist at all; for evil is the deprivation of being, and not something that exists. Thus the difference is the same between light and darkness and between wisdom and folly. HOMILIES ON ECCLESIASTES 5.[3]

2:13 Light Is to Darkness As Wisdom Is to Folly

LOVE OF MONEY AS DARKNESS. CHRYSOSTOM: And what is the use of understanding, you will say, to the poor person? As might be expected you are ignorant; for neither does the blind person know what is the advantage of light. Listen to Solomon, saying, "As far as light excels darkness, so does wisdom excel folly."

But how shall we instruct him that is in darkness? For the love of money is darkness, permitting nothing that is to appear as it is, but otherwise. For much as one in darkness, though he should see a golden vessel, though a precious stone, though purple garments, supposes them to be nothing, for he does not see their beauty. So

also he that is covetous, knows not as he ought the beauty of those things that are worthy of our care. Disperse then I pray you the mist that arises from this passion, and then will you see the nature of things.

But nowhere do these things so plainly appear as in poverty, nowhere are those things so disproved which seem to be, and are not, as in self-denial. HOMILIES ON THE GOSPEL OF MATTHEW 83.3.[4]

2:14 The Eyes of the Wise Person

ON THE CONSTRUCTION OF THE HUMAN BODY. AMBROSE: Let us make note of the fact that the body of a person is constructed like the world itself. As the sky is preeminent over air, earth and sea, which serve as members of the world, so we observe that the head has a position above the other members of our body. In the same way, the sky stands supreme among the other elements, just as a citadel amid the other outposts in a city's defense. In this citadel dwells what might be called regal Wisdom, as stated in the words of the prophet: "The eyes of a wise man are in his head." That is to say, this position is better protected than the others and from it strength and prevision are brought to bear on all the rest. SIX DAYS OF CREATION 6.9.55.[5]

CHRIST AND THE WISE PERSON. DIDYMUS THE BLIND: If we think about "eyes" in the visible sense, then (one can say) that both the foolish and the wise have eyes in their head. The wise [person], insofar as he is wise, turns upwards to Christ, his head. Thus it is written: "Christ is the head of every man."[6] The head of the wise is the mind; therefore it is written: "But we have the mind of Christ."[7] COMMENTARY ON ECCLESIASTES 48.23.[8]

2:16 No Memory Endures of the Wise or of the Foolish

---

[1]Ps 104:24 (103:24 LXX). [2]1 Cor 1:24. [3]GNHE 88**. [4]NPNF 1 10:500*. [5]FC 42:268*. [6]1 Cor 11:3. [7]1 Cor 2:16. [8]PTA 25:239-41.

THE WISE DO NOT SHARE THE FATE OF THE STUPID. GREGORY THAUMATURGUS: A wise person and a foolish person have nothing in common, either in terms of human remembrance or in terms of divine recompense. As for human works, the end already overtakes them all while they still seem to be beginning. But a wise person never shares the same fate as a stupid person. PARAPHRASE OF ECCLESIASTES 2.16.[9]

2:17 Hatred of This Life

WE SHALL NEVER BE SATISFIED. AMBROSE: Therefore incline to him of whom the psalmist says, "He has not taken his soul in vain."[10] To speak now of the troubles of this life, the person has taken his soul in vain who is constructing the things of the world and building the things of the body. We arise each day to eat and drink; yet no one is filled so that he does not hunger and thirst after a short time. Daily we seek profit, and to greed there is set no limit. "The eye will not be satisfied with seeing, nor the ear with hearing."[11] He that loves silver will not be satisfied with silver. There is no limit to toil, and there is no profit in abundance. DEATH AS A GOOD 7:28.[12]

2:18 Bequeathed to the One Who Follows

WEALTH PERISHABLE AND ETERNAL. ATHANASIUS: If the whole earth is not worth the kingdom of heaven, surely he who has left a few fields leaves nothing, as it were; even if he has given up a house or much gold, he ought not to boast nor grow weary. Moreover, we should consider that if we do not relinquish these things for virtue's sake, we leave them behind later when we die and often, as Ecclesiastes reminds us, to those to whom we do not wish to leave them. Why, then, do we not relinquish them for the sake of virtue, so that we may inherit a kingdom? LIFE OF ST. ANTHONY 17.[13]

2:25 Eat and Enjoy

PRAISE GOD FOR ALL GIFTS. APOSTOLIC CONSTITUTIONS: We exhort, therefore, the widows and orphans to partake of those things that are bestowed upon them with all fear and all pious reverence, and to return thanks to God who gives food to the needy, and to lift up their eyes to him. For, "Which of you shall eat, or who shall drink without him? For he opens his hand and fills every living thing with his kindness: giving wheat to the young men, and wine to the maidens, and oil for the joy of the living, grass for the cattle, and green herb for the service of men, flesh for the wild beasts, seeds for the birds, and suitable food for all creatures."[14] Wherefore the Lord says, "Consider the fowls of heaven, that they sow not, neither do they reap nor gather into barns, and your Father feeds them. Are not you much better than they? Be not therefore solicitous, saying, What shall we eat? or what shall we drink? For your Father knows that you have need of all these things."[15] Since you therefore enjoy such a providential care from him and are partakers of the good things that are derived from him, you ought to return praise to him that receives the orphan and the widow, to Almighty God, through his beloved Son Jesus Christ our Lord; through whom glory be to God in spirit and truth forever. CONSTITUTIONS OF THE HOLY APOSTLES 4.1.5.[16]

---

[9]GTPE 43. [10]Ps 24:4 (23:4 LXX). [11]Eccles 1:8. [12]FC 65:91*. [13]FC 15:151. [14]Ps 144:16 LXX; Zech 9:17 LXX; Ps 104:14-15 (103:14-15 LXX). [15]Mt 6:26, 31-32. [16]ANF 7:434*.

3:1-9 A SEASON FOR EVERYTHING

¹*For everything there is a season, and a*
time for every matter under heaven:
²*a time to be born, and a time to die;*
a time to plant, and a time to pluck up
what is planted;
³*a time to kill, and a time to heal;*
a time to break down, and a time to build
up;
⁴*a time to weep, and a time to laugh;*
a time to mourn, and a time to dance;
⁵*a time to cast away stones, and a time to*
gather stones together;
a time to embrace, and a time to refrain
from embracing;
⁶*a time to seek, and a time to lose;*
a time to keep, and a time to cast away;
⁷*a time to rend, and a time to sew;*
a time to keep silence, and a time to
speak;
⁸*a time to love, and a time to hate;*
a time for war, and a time for peace.
⁹*What gain has the worker from his toil?*

OVERVIEW: Everyone has its own time, just as there was an appropriate time for the apostles to proclaim Jesus as Messiah (BASIL, CYRIL OF ALEXANDRIA). At all times you should be engaged upon the work of your salvation, because every time is suitable for a life pleasing to God (GREGORY OF NAZIANZUS). Every time is also suitable for prayer and continual remembrance, although theological discussions should be reserved for times that are proper (BASIL, GREGORY OF NAZIANZUS). Also there are times to rejoice and times to weep, a time to live and a time to die (CAESARIUS, ATHANASIUS), and weeping and laughing each have different meanings (DIDYMUS). After all, death follows birth, as Exodus follows Genesis. Just as mourning is for the body and dancing for the soul, so now is more a time for weeping and the future a time for laughter (GREGORY OF NYSSA). In baptism death and birth coincide at the same time (CYRIL OF JERUSALEM), and this can be seen also in Jesus' birth and death (GREGORY OF ELVIRA), whereas in marriage there is a time for love and a time for abstinence (TWELVE PATRIARCHS). Even the story of Jerusalem, like a booth in a vineyard, is an example of a time to keep and a time to cast away

(GREGORY OF ELVIRA). To cast off the law, likewise, can be seen as a parallel to death by martyrdom (DIDYMUS). Every time, however, is the right time to seek the Lord (GREGORY OF NYSSA), and one can always embrace wisdom (DIDYMUS). There is also a time for silence and a time to speak (AMBROSE, GREGORY THE GREAT), although the way to wisdom is through silence (BEDE). We should be silent about God's being, but we can speak about God's activity. We must love God and hate evil, but remember that virtues and vices can at times be loved and at other times be hated (GREGORY OF NYSSA). Every soul, after all, has a reprehensible companion and a praiseworthy one (DIDYMUS).

3:1 Everything Has Its Time

EVERY TIME IS SUITABLE FOR PRAYER. BASIL THE GREAT: It is necessary to bear in mind that for certain other tasks a particular time is allotted, according to the words of Ecclesiastes: "All things have their season." For prayer and psalmody, however, as also, indeed, for some other duties, every hour is suitable, that, while our hands are busy at their tasks, we may praise

God sometimes with the tongue (when this is possible or, rather, when it is conducive to edification); or, if not, with the heart, at least, in psalms, hymns and spiritual canticles, as it is written.[1] Thus in the midst of our work we can fulfill the duty of prayer, giving thanks to him who has granted strength to our hands for performing our tasks and cleverness to our minds for acquiring knowledge, and for having provided the materials, both that which is in the instruments we use and that which forms the matter of the arts in which we may be engaged, praying that the work of our hands may be directed toward its goal, the good pleasure of God. THE LONG RULES 37.[2]

WHY THE APOSTLES WAITED TO PROCLAIM JESUS AS MESSIAH. CYRIL OF ALEXANDRIA: When, however, the disciple had professed his faith, he charged them, it says, and commanded them to tell it to no one: "for the Son of man," he said, "is about to suffer many things, and be rejected, and killed, and the third day he shall rise again."[3] And yet how was it not rather the duty of disciples to proclaim him everywhere? For this was the very business of those appointed by him to the apostleship. But as the sacred Scripture says, "There is a time for everything." There were things yet unfulfilled which must also be included in their preaching of him, such as were the cross, the passion, the death in the flesh, the resurrection from the dead, that great and truly glorious sign by which testimony is borne of him that Emmanuel is truly God and by nature the Son of God the Father. For that he utterly abolished death, and effaced destruction, and spoiled hell, and overthrew the tyranny of the enemy, and took away the sin of the world, and opened the gates above to the dwellers upon earth, and united earth to heaven; these things proved him to be, as I said, in truth God. He commanded them, therefore, to guard the mystery by a seasonable silence until the whole plan of the dispensation should arrive at a suitable fulfillment. COMMENTARY ON LUKE, HOMILY 49.[4]

THEOLOGICAL DISCUSSIONS SHOULD BE DONE IN PROPER TIME. GREGORY OF NAZIANZUS: We ought to think of God even more often than we draw our breath; and if the expression is permissible, we ought to do nothing else. Yea, I am one of those who entirely approve that Word which bids us meditate day and night, and tell at eventide and morning and noon day, and praise the Lord at every time;[5] or, to use Moses' words, whether a person lie down, or rise up, or walk by the way, or whatever else he is doing[6]—and by this recollection we are to be molded to purity. So that it is not the continual remembrance of God that I would hinder, but only the talking about God; nor even that as in itself wrong, but only when unreasonable; nor all teaching, but only want of moderation. As of even honey, repletion and satiety, though it be of honey, produce vomiting. As Solomon says and I think, there is a time for everything, and that which is good ceases to be good if it be not done in a good way; just as a flower is quite out of season in winter, and just as a man's dress does not become a woman, nor a woman's a man; and as geometry is out of place in mourning, or tears at a carousal. Shall we in this instance alone disregard the proper time, in a matter in which most of all due season should be respected? Surely not, my friends and brethren (for I will still call you brethren, though you do not behave like brothers). Let us not think so nor yet, like hot-tempered and hard-mouthed horses, throwing off our rider reason, and casting away reverence, that keeps us within due limits, run far away from the turning point. But let us philosophize within our proper bounds and not be carried away into Egypt, nor be swept down into Assyria, nor sing the Lord's song in a strange land.[7] By this I mean before any kind of audience, strangers or kindred, hostile or friendly, kindly or the reverse, who watch what we do with great care, and would like the spark of what is wrong in us to become a flame, and secretly kindle and fan

---

[1]Col 3:16. [2]FC 9:308. [3]Lk 9:22. [4]CGSL 221*. [5]Ps 1:2; 55:17 (54:18 LXX); 34:1 (33:1 LXX). [6]Deut 6:7; 11:19. [7]Ps 137:4 (136:4 LXX).

it and raise it to heaven with their breath and make it higher than the Babylonian flame which burned up everything around it. For since their strength lies not in their own dogmas, they hunt for it in our weak points. And therefore they apply themselves to our, shall I say "misfortunes" or "failings," like flies to wounds. But let us at least be no longer ignorant of ourselves or pay too little attention to the due order in these matters. And if it be impossible to put an end to the existing hostility, let us at least agree upon this, that we will utter mysteries under our breath and holy things in a holy manner, and we will not cast to profane ears that which may not be uttered, nor give evidence that we possess less gravity than those who worship demons, and serve shameful fables and deeds; for they would sooner give their blood to the uninitiated than certain words. But let us recognize that as in dress and diet and laughter and demeanor there is a certain decorum, so there is also in speech and silence; since among so many titles and powers of God, we pay the highest honor to the Word. Let even our disputings then be kept within bounds. AGAINST THE EUNOMIANS, THEOLOGICAL ORATION 1(27).5.[8]

EVERY TIME IS SUITABLE FOR LIFE PLEASING TO GOD. GREGORY OF NAZIANZUS: Sow in good season, and gather together, and open your barns when it is the time to do so; and plant in season, and let the clusters be cut when they are ripe, and launch boldly in spring, and draw your ship on shore again at the beginning of winter, when the sea begins to rage. And let there be to you also a time for war and a time for peace; a time to marry, and a time to abstain from marrying; a time for friendship, and a time for discord, if this be needed; and in short a time for everything, if you will follow Solomon's advice. And it is best to do so, for the advice is profitable. But the work of your salvation is one upon which you should be engaged at all times; and let every time be to you the definite one for baptism. If you are always passing over today and waiting for tomorrow, by your little procrastinations you will be cheated without knowing it by the evil one, as his manner is. Give to me, he says, the present, and to God the future; to me your youth, and to God old age; to me your pleasures, and to him your uselessness. How great is the danger that surrounds you. How many the unexpected mischances. War has expended you, or an earthquake overwhelmed you, or the sea swallowed you up. Or a wild beast carried you off, or a sickness killed you, or a crumb going the wrong way (a most insignificant thing, but what is easier than for a man to die, though you are so proud of the divine image), or a too freely indulged drinking bout. Or a wind knocked you down, or a horse ran away with you, or a drug maliciously scheming against you, or perhaps was found to be deleterious when meant to be wholesome. Or [there was] an inhuman judge, or an inexorable executioner, or any of the things which make the change swiftest and beyond the power of human aid.

But if you would fortify yourself beforehand with the seal and secure yourself for the future with the best and strongest of all aids, being signed both in body and in soul with the unction, as Israel was of old with that blood and unction of the firstborn at night that guarded him,[9] what then can happen to you, and what has been wrought out for you? Listen to the Proverbs: "If you sit," he says, "you shall be without fear; and if you sleep, your sleep shall be sweet."[10] And listen to David giving you the good news: "you shall not be afraid for the terror by night, for mischance or noonday demon."[11] This, even while you live, will greatly contribute to your sense of safety (for a sheep that is sealed is not easily snared, but that which is unmarked is an easy prey to thieves), and at your death a fortunate shroud, more precious than gold, more magnificent than a sepulcher, more reverent than fruitless libations, more seasonable than ripe firstfruits, which the dead bestow on the dead, making a law out of custom. No, if all things forsake you or be taken violently away from you;

---

[8]LCC 3:130-31*. [9]Ex 12:22. [10]Prov 3:24. [11]Ps 91:5 (90:5 LXX).

money, possessions, thrones, distinctions, and everything that belongs to this early turmoil, yet you will be able to lay down your life in safety, having suffered no loss of the helps which God gave you unto salvation. ON HOLY BAPTISM, ORATION 40.14-15.[12]

TIME TO FIND A PEARL OF GREAT PRICE. ORIGEN: "To everything then is its season, and a time for everything under heaven," a time to gather the goodly pearls, and a time after their gathering to find the one precious pearl, when it is fitting for a person to go away and sell all that he has in order that he may buy that pearl. COMMENTARY ON MATTHEW 10.10.[13]

GRADUAL ADVANCEMENT IN SPIRITUAL LIFE. TERTULLIAN: What, then, is the Paraclete's administrative office but this: the direction of discipline, the revelation of the Scriptures, the reformation of the intellect, the advancement toward the "better things"? Nothing is without stages of growth: all things await their season. In short, the Preacher says, "A time to everything." Look how creation itself advances little by little to fruitfulness. First comes the grain, and from the grain arises the shoot, and from the shoot struggles out the shrub. Thereafter boughs and leaves gather strength, and the whole that we call a tree expands. Then follows the swelling of the germen, and from the germen bursts the flower, and from the flower the fruit opens. That fruit itself, rude for a while, and unshapely, little by little, keeping the straight course of its development, is trained to the mellowness of its flavor. So, too, righteousness—for the God of righteousness and of creation is the same—was first in a rudimentary state, having a natural fear of God. From that stage it advanced, through the law and the prophets, to infancy. From that stage it passed, through the gospel, to the fervor of youth; now, through the Paraclete, it is settling into maturity. ON THE VEILING OF VIRGINS 1.[14]

3:2 A Time to Be Born and a Time to Die

THE LINKAGE OF DEATH TO BIRTH. GREGORY OF NYSSA: It is right that at the start he makes this tight bond linking death to birth; for death inevitably follows birth, and everything born dissolves in decay. He intends, through the demonstration that death and birth are connected, by using the reference to death as a goad, to wake from sleep those who are sunk deep in fleshly existence and love this present life, and to rouse them in awareness of the future.

This insight Moses, the friend of God, used secretly in the first books of Scripture, writing Exodus immediately after Genesis, so that those who read what has been written may learn what affects them even through the very arrangement of the books; for it is impossible to hear of a birth ("genesis") without also envisaging a departure ("exodus"). Here also the great Ecclesiast, having noticed this, points it out, classing death with birth. HOMILIES ON ECCLESIASTES 6.[15]

A TIME TO LIVE AND A TIME TO DIE. ATHANASIUS: This is written in the Scriptures and is manifest to all. For although it be hidden and unknown to all, what period of time is allotted to each, and how it is allotted; yet every one knows this, that as there is a time for spring and for summer, and for autumn and for winter, so, as it is written, there is a time to die, and a time to live. DEFENSE OF HIS FLIGHT 14.[16]

DEATH AND BIRTH IN BAPTISM. CYRIL OF JERUSALEM: For as our Savior passed three days and three nights in the bowels of the earth, so you by your first rising out of the water represented Christ's first day in the earth, and by your descent the night. For as in the night one no longer sees, while by day one is in the light, so you during your immersion, as in a night, saw nothing, but on coming up found yourselves in the day. In the same moment you were dying and being born, and that saving water was at once

---

[12]NPNF 2 7:364. [13]ANF 9:418. [14]ANF 4:27-28*. [15]GNHE 103*.
[16]NPNF 2 4:260*.

your grave and your mother. What Solomon said in another context is applicable to you: "A time for giving birth, a time for dying," although for you, contrariwise, it is a case of "a time for dying and a time for being born." One time brought both, and your death coincided with your birth. MYSTAGOGICAL LECTURES 2.4.[17]

THE INCARNATE LORD WAS BORN AND DIED AND ROSE AGAIN AS A MAN. GREGORY OF ELVIRA: "A time to live and a time to die": you can see, therefore, beloved brothers, that this was said concerning the time of the Lord's birth and death. Thus you must accept his virgin birth if we are to believe not only that the Word in the beginning who was called "is" was born, but, as I said, also that the humanity which he adopted and put on was born, both Lord and man. For it says, "what is born of the flesh is flesh, and what is born of the spirit is spirit."[18] Yet, what suffered, died, was buried, and resurrected was not God but man, since he raised man to God, not God to man. EXPOSITION OF ECCLESIASTES, FRAGMENT 1.[19]

3:4 Time to Weep and Time to Laugh

WHEN REJOICING IS APPROPRIATE. CAESARIUS OF ARLES: Let no one believe that he possesses any happiness or true joy in this world. Happiness can be prepared for, but it cannot be possessed here. Two times succeed each other in their own order, "a time to weep, and a time to laugh." Let no one deceive himself, brethren; there is no time to laugh in this world. I know, indeed, that everyone wants to rejoice, but people do not all look for joy in the place where it should be sought. True joy never did exist in this world, it does not do so now, and it never will. For thus the Lord himself warned his disciples in the Gospel when he said: "You will suffer in the world,"[20] and again, "While the world rejoices, you will grieve for a time, but your grief will be turned into joy."[21] For this reason, with the Lord's help let us do good in this life through labor and sorrow, so that in the future life we may be able to

gather the fruits of our good deeds with joy and exultation according to that sentence: "Those that sow in tears shall reap rejoicing."[22] SERMON 215.2.[23]

NOW IS MORE A TIME FOR WEEPING THAN FOR LAUGHING. GREGORY OF NYSSA: Now, therefore, is the moment for weeping, but the moment for laughing is in store for us through hope; for the present sorrow will become mother of the joy that is hoped for. Who would not spend all his life in lamentation and sadness, if he actually becomes acquainted with himself and knows his condition, what he once had and what he has lost, and the state his nature was in at the beginning and the state it is in at present? Then there was no death, disease was absent; "mine" and "yours," those wicked words, were far away from the life of the first humans. As the sun was shared, and the air was shared, and above all the grace and praise of God were shared, so too participation in everything good was freely available on equal terms, and the disease of acquisitiveness was unknown, and there was no resentment over inferiority against superiors (for there was no such thing as superiority), and there were thousands of other things besides these, which no one could describe in words, since they utterly exceed in magnificence those mentioned—I mean equality in honor with the angels, freedom to speak before God, the contemplation of the good things in the realms above, our own adornment with the unspeakable beauty of the blessed nature, when we show in ourselves the divine image, glistening with beauty of soul. HOMILIES ON ECCLESIASTES 6.[24]

WEEPING AND LAUGHING HAVE DIFFERENT MEANINGS. DIDYMUS THE BLIND: Since weeping has different meanings, laughing needs to be understood accordingly; for weeping does not

---

[17]FC 64:164-65. [18]Jn 3:6. [19]CCL 69:263. [20]Jn 16:33. [21]Jn 16:20. [22]Ps 126:5 (125:5 LXX). [23]FC 66:114*. [24]GNHE 108.

have only one meaning, nor does laughing. And since laughing is split in two meanings—sometimes praiseworthy, sometimes reprehensible—even weeping must be seen in this way, so that praiseworthy laughing corresponds to praiseworthy weeping and the same with reprehensible laughing and weeping.

Often, thus, a life which is prone more to lust than to the love of God is laughing in such a way that the laughter itself is made into a god. And as some consider their stomachs divine and others consider them mammon, so a third person who loves entertainment and wants to be witty and so on, builds altars for laughter by making it divine so that he sacrifices to it. One sacrifices to it if one teaches what is suitable for laughing or what excites laughter.

That kind of laughter is reprehensible. It is blissful to abandon this kind of laughter and to devote one's self to the weeping opposed to it. This is what the virtuous one was striving for when he said, "Every night I flood my bed with tears; I drench my couch with my weeping."[25]

There is, however, also a praiseworthy laughter. It is said that God "will yet fill your mouth with laughter"[26]—with (of course) praiseworthy laughter. This corresponds to the fruit of the Spirit, which is joy, for "The fruit of the Spirit is love, joy, peace."[27] Laughter, therefore, that corresponds with joy is praiseworthy.

Any weeping that is opposed to this kind of laughter and to the condition that opposes the joy of the Holy Spirit is reprehensible. That kind of weeping did not help Jerusalem.[28] . . . And why was that so? It is because it did not repent at the time when it should have repented, but after it was too late. . . .

Now, we want to look for the spiritual meaning: The ascetical life, which is appropriate for pious people, is called weeping; the uninhibited life, however, which is prone more to lust than to the love of God, is laughter. Those who weep in this life will laugh later on, so that they are even blessed: "Blessed are you who weep now."[29] . . . But those who have laughed here, because they lived

prone more to lust than to the love of God, will weep, after the punishment that will follow, so that the following is said to them: "There will be weeping and gnashing of teeth."[30] Those, however, who here greatly weep out of repentance pray to God with the words: "You have fed them with the bread of tears, and given them tears to drink in full measure."[31] COMMENTARY ON ECCLESIASTES 71.4.[32]

MOURNING IS FOR THE BODY, DANCING FOR THE SOUL. GREGORY OF NYSSA: Passionate and profound lamentation is called "mourning" in Scripture. Similarly, dancing also indicates the strength of joy, as we learn in the gospel, where it says, "We played to you, and you did not dance; we lamented, and you did not mourn."[33] In the same way history relates that the Israelites mourned at Moses' death[34] and that David danced as he went at the front of the procession of the ark, when he carried it away from the foreigners, not appearing in his usual clothes. It says that he sang, playing an accompaniment on his musical instrument, and moved to the rhythm with his feet, and by the rhythmic movement of the body made public his devotion.[35]

Since, then, a human being is twofold, I mean made of soul and of body, and correspondingly twofold also the life operating in each of them within us, it would be a good thing to mourn in our bodily life—and there are many occasions for lamentation in this life—and prepare for our soul the harmonious dance. For the more life is made miserable with sadness, the more occasions for joy accumulate in the soul. Self-control is gloomy, humility is dreary, being punished is a grief, not being equal with the powerful is a reason for sorrow, but "the one who humbles himself will be lifted up,"[36] and the one who struggles in poverty will be crowned, and the one covered with sores, who exhibits his life as thoroughly lamentable,

---

[25]Ps 6:6 (6:7 LXX). [26]Job 8:21. [27]Gal 5:22. [28]See Lk 19:41, 23:28. [29]Lk 6:21. [30]Mt 8:12; 13:42, 50; 22:13; 24:51; 25:30; Lk 13:28. [31]Ps 80:5 (79:6 LXX). [32]PTA 22:33-39. [33]Mt 11:17. [34]Deut 34:8. [35]2 Sam 6:14-17. [36]Lk 14:11.

will rest in the bosom of the patriarch.[37] May we too rest in it, through the mercy of our Savior Jesus Christ, to whom be the glory forever. HOMILIES ON ECCLESIASTES 6.[38]

3:5a Throwing Stones and Gathering Them

THOUGHTS DIRECTED TO BETTER THINGS ARE DESTRUCTIVE OF WORSE THINGS. GREGORY OF NYSSA: Those who look only to the literal meaning and support the superficial interpretation of the words perhaps fit the law of Moses to the text before us. In cases where the law enjoins the pelting with stones of persons convicted of a felony,[39] we have learned examples from the scriptural account itself in the case of sabbath breakers,[40] and the one who had stolen sacred things,[41] and other offenses, for which the law imposed a penalty of stoning.[42] For my part, if the Ecclesiast had not claimed that collecting stones was also something timely, about which no law directs and no event in biblical history suggests a comparable precept, I might agree with those who interpret the passage through the law, that the moment for throwing stones is when someone has broken the sabbath or stolen something dedicated. But as it is, the addition of the requirement to collect stones again, which is prescribed by no law, leads us to a different interpretation, so that we may learn what kind of stones it is which after being thrown must again become the property of the thrower. . . .

We certainly ought to consider that thoughts destructive of evil are the very stones accurately aimed by the Ecclesiast, which must be continually cast and collected. [They are] cast to put an end to the one who rises in pride against our life and collected to keep the soul's lap always full of such missiles, ready to be thrown at the enemy, whenever he may plan some fresh assault on us.

Where, then, are we to collect stones, with which we shall stone the enemy to death? I have heard the prophecy that said, "holy stones roll about on the ground."[43] These might be the words which come down to us from the divinely inspired writings, which we should collect in our soul's lap, to use at the right moment against those who vex us, and which when they are thrown destroy the enemy and yet do not leave the hand of the thrower. The one who pelts with the stone of self-control the unbridled thought which gathers fuel for the fire through the pleasures defeats it with his attack and always keeps his weapons in his hand. Thus justice both becomes the stone against injustice and defeats it and is kept in the lap of the one who throws it. In the same way all thoughts directed to better things are destructive of worse things and do not leave the one who lives rightly in virtue. This, in my opinion, is "throwing stones at the right moment" and "collecting them at the right moment," so that we always cast good volleys of stones for the destruction of what is bad, and the supply of such weapons never runs out. HOMILIES ON ECCLESIASTES 7.[44]

THE PURPOSE OF THROWING STONES. DIDYMUS THE BLIND: In the literal sense the following is said: The law prescribes that Israel's judges have to investigate the behavior of the people; and if someone was found to have done prohibited things, he was to be convicted to be stoned. . . .

Now, we relate the verse to rebuke instead of stoning. The wise teacher knows whom he has to rebuke and whom not, and in a certain way he throws the rebuke like stones in order to dissuade the rebuked from a bad way of life. If the person improves through the rebuke, the rebuke is gathered in and no more stones are thrown against him. Paul indicates this when he says, "Convince, rebuke and encourage!"[45] By rebuking and convincing he was throwing stones. After seeing the one who was rebuked improve, he encourages and gathers the stones together. The following is meant: There is a time to punish and a time not to punish. COMMENTARY ON ECCLESIASTES 73.22.[46]

---

[37]Lk 16:22. [38]GNHE 109-10. [39]See Ex 19:13; Lev 20:2; Deut 17:5. [40]Num 15:32-36. [41]Josh 7:10-25. [42]Lev 24:10-23. [43]Zech 9:16 LXX. [44]GNHE 111-12, 115-16*. [45]2 Tim 4:2. [46]PTA 22:47-49.

3:5b Marriage and Abstinence

MARRIAGE AND ABSTINENCE HAVE TO BE OBSERVED. ANONYMOUS: For there is a season for a man to embrace his wife, and a season to abstain from embrace for his prayer. So then there are two commandments; and unless they be done in due order, they bring about sin. So also is it with the other commandments. Be wise in God, then, and prudent, understanding the order of the commandments, and the laws of every work, that the Lord may love you. TESTAMENTS OF THE TWELVE PATRIARCHS 8.8.[47]

A TIME FOR MARRYING AND A TIME FOR CONTINENCE. AUGUSTINE: Now this propagation of children which among the ancient saints was a most bounden duty for the purpose of begetting and preserving a people for God, among whom the prophecy of Christ's coming must have had precedence over everything, now has no longer the same necessity. For from among all nations the way is open for an abundant offspring to receive spiritual regeneration, from whatever quarter they derive their natural birth. So that we may acknowledge that the Scripture which says there is "a time to embrace, and a time to refrain from embracing," is to be distributed in its clauses to the periods before Christ and since. The former was the time to embrace, the latter to refrain from embracing. ON MARRIAGE AND CONCUPISCENCE 14.[48]

EXCELLENCE OF VIRGINITY. AUGUSTINE: As for you, you both have children and live in that end of the world when the time has already come not "to scatter stones but to gather; not to embrace but to refrain embraces." [This is a time] when the apostle cries out, "But this I say, brethren, the time is short; it remains that those who have wives be as if they had none."[49] Surely, if you had sought a second marriage, it would not have been in obedience to a prophecy or a law, or even the desire of the flesh for offspring, but merely a sign of incontinence. You would have followed the advice of the apostle, when, after having said, "It is good for them if they so remain, even as I," he immediately added, "But if they do not have self-control, let them marry, for I prefer them to marry rather than to burn."[50] THE EXCELLENCE OF WIDOWHOOD 8.11.[51]

GATHERING STONES. GREGORY THE GREAT: According to Solomon's words, there is "a time to scatter stones and a time to gather them." Because the end of the world presses upon us, it is necessary to gather living stones for the heavenly building, in order to make our Jerusalem grow to its full stature. DIALOGUE 3.37.[52]

DEEPER MEANING OF EMBRACING AND AVOIDING AN EMBRACE. GREGORY OF NYSSA: "A moment for embracing and a moment for avoiding an embrace." These ideas cannot possibly become clear to us unless the passage has first been interpreted through the Scripture, so that it has become clear to us in what connection the divinely inspired word consciously uses the word *embrace*. Great David exhorts us in the words of the psalm, "Circle Zion and embrace her,"[53] and even Solomon himself, when he was describing poetically the spiritual marriage of the one in love with Wisdom, mentions a number of ways in which union with virtue becomes ours and adds this: "Honor her, so that she may embrace you."[54] If, then, David tells us to embrace Zion, and Solomon says that those who honor Wisdom are embraced by her, perhaps we have not missed the correct interpretation if we have identified the object which it is timely to embrace. For Mount Zion rises above the upper city of Jerusalem. Thus the one who urges you to embrace her is bidding you to attach yourself to high principles, so that you hasten to reach the very citadel of the virtues, which he indicates allegorically by the name Zion. And the one who makes you live with wisdom announces the good news of the embrace

---

[47]ANF 8:28*. [48]NPNF 1 5:269*. [49]1 Cor 7:29. [50]1 Cor 7:9. [51]FC 16:290. [52]FC 39:185. [53]Ps 48:12 (47:13 LXX). [54]Prov 4:8 LXX.

she will give you in the future. Therefore there is a moment for embracing Zion and for being embraced by Wisdom, since the name Zion denotes the pinnacle of conduct and Wisdom in herself means every instance of virtue.

If we have learned through these words the right moment for embracing, we have been taught through the same words in what cases separation is more beneficial than union. For he says, "A moment for avoiding an embrace." The one who has become familiar with virtue is a stranger to the state of evil. . . . So when the loving disposition clings to the good—that is the "right moment"—the result is surely estrangement from its opposite. If you really love self-control, then of course you hate its opposite. If you look with love at purity, you obviously loathe the stink of filth. If you have become attached to the good, you surely avoid attachment to evil. HOMILIES ON ECCLESIASTES 7.[55]

ONE CAN ALWAYS EMBRACE WISDOM. DIDYMUS THE BLIND: "A time to embrace, and a time to refrain from embracing." In the literal sense this means men who live together with their wives have a time when they get together with them and a time when they do not. . . . When it is time for prayer, when it is a day on which one has to remain clean and send up prayers, one has to avoid embraces. When the days of prayer are over, they come together and embrace. . . .

According to a superficial explanation, but perhaps also against it, the following remark is valid. "The appointed time has grown short," Paul writes; "from now on, let even those who have wives be as though they had none."[56] He says, Since time has grown short and humankind has increased to a large number, it is not necessary any more to increase it; one has to cease. . . . When it was necessary that humankind increase, it was a time to embrace. But after the population had become numerous and the begetting of the faithful spread, one needed to avoid embracing. . . .

In the spiritual sense this is the meaning: Some have acquired God's wisdom as a wife, like the one who says, "I became enamored of her beauty"[57] and took her home as a spouse. About her it is said: "She will honor you if you embrace her."[58] Then wisdom embraces the wise by communicating to him her character, and the wise man embraces her.

When therefore this wife is with a person from whom she can beget insight and thoughts and works of insight—for "wisdom begets insight for a man"[59]—then it is the time to embrace. This time, however, is not interrupted by breaks. One can always embrace wisdom. This time is eternal. COMMENTARY ON ECCLESIASTES 75.4.[60]

3:6 A Time to Keep and a Time to Cast Away

THE RIGHT TIME TO SEEK THE LORD. GREGORY OF NYSSA: Do you want to learn, too, the right moment to seek the Lord? To put it briefly—all your life. In this case alone the one moment to pursue it is the whole state of life. For it is not at a fixed moment and an appointed time that it is good to seek the Lord, but never to cease from continual search—that is the real timeliness. HOMILIES ON ECCLESIASTES 7.[61]

JERUSALEM LIKE A BOOTH IN A VINEYARD. GREGORY OF ELVIRA: Jerusalem, therefore, was abandoned "like a booth in a vineyard"[62] because the guardian angels left it along with the Lord when Christ had suffered. A crop in the field is guarded by the Lord not for its own sake but only for the grain it yields, such that the stalk is permitted to be destroyed once its fruit is harvested. So also it was not principally for its own sake that Jerusalem was guarded temporarily, but on account of Jesus Christ our Lord, who was born according to the flesh within its borders. But when its fruit had been harvested, that is, the body of Christ, whence came the heavenly bread of life, then Jerusalem was abandoned like a field

---

[55]GNHE 116-17. [56]1 Cor 7:29. [57]Wis 8:2. [58]Prov 4:8. [59]Prov 10:23 LXX. [60]PTA 22:53-57. [61]GNHE 118. [62]Is 1:8.

after the harvest, like a booth in a vineyard after its grapes had been gathered. This, then, is why it was said here in the divine Scriptures, "There is a time for guarding and a time for casting aside," for there was a time when Jerusalem was guarded and a time when it was being cast aside. EXPOSITION OF ECCLESIASTES, FRAGMENT 2.[63]

CASTING OFF THE LAW. DIDYMUS THE BLIND: Before the good things were found (for example, the knowledge of truth), people were in ignorance. For them it was the time of losing. But this time was preceded by the time of seeking; for when some one seeks the good, the time has come to lose what in his case had been before the good. Likewise people lived according to the law before Christ's life on earth, and they looked for the letter. But when the "Sun of righteousness" rose and truth finally had come, the time also had come to lose the letter and to supersede it.

This is how one can sometimes lose in a good way. The Savior in the Gospel says: "Those who want to save their soul will lose it, and those who lose their soul will find it."[64] One [can also] understand this as referring to martyrdom and to the time of persecution: Those who want to save their soul on the day of judgment and at the time of reward must lose it by offering themselves up to death; to lose the soul here means death, the dying for truth in martyrdom. COMMENTARY ON ECCLESIASTES 77.18.[65]

3:7 Silence and Speech

VALUE OF SILENCE. AMBROSE: Ought we to be dumb? Certainly not. For "there is a time to keep silence and a time to speak." If, then, we are to give account for an idle word, let us take care that we do not have to give it also for an idle silence. For there is also an active silence, such as Susanna's was, who did more by keeping silence than if she had spoken. For in keeping silence before others she spoke to God and found no greater proof of her chastity than silence. Her conscience spoke where no word was heard, and she sought

no judgment for herself at the hands of men, for she had the witness of the Lord. She therefore desired to be acquitted by the One who she knew could not be deceived in any way.[66] The Lord himself in the gospel worked out in silence the salvation of humankind.[67] David rightly therefore enjoined on himself not constant silence but watchfulness. DUTIES OF THE CLERGY 1.3.9.[68]

WAY TO WISDOM IS THROUGH SILENCE. BEDE: Let anyone who loves wisdom, therefore, first beg this from God, then let the humble hearer seek out a teacher of truth, and all the while let him not only most carefully restrain his tongue from idle conversations but also hold back from preaching the very truth which he has recently learned. Hence Solomon, writing about differences of times, says, "There is a time for keeping silence and a time for speaking." Hence the Pythagoreans, who were endowed with the capacity to teach natural knowledge, order their listeners to keep silence for five years and thus at last they allow them to preach. The truth is more safely heard than preached, for when it is heard humility is safeguarded, but when it is preached it is difficult for the preacher to escape some minimal boasting. COMMENTARY ON JAMES 1.19.[69]

A TIME TO BE SILENT AND A TIME TO SPEAK. JEROME: I believe that the Pythagoreans, whose discipline it was to remain silent for five years and to speak with erudition afterwards, drew their practice from this principle. We too should learn to be silent before opening our mouths to speak. Let us remain still for an established time, meditating on the words of the Teacher, for nothing should seem right to us except what we have learned. In this way, only after much silence will we be made teachers from the disciples. As it is currently, for the sake of those who are falling into the worst wickedness of the world, we daily teach in the churches what we do not know. And

---

[63]CCL 69:263. [64]Mt 16:25. [65]PTA 22:65-67. [66]Sus 35. [67]See Mt 26:63. [68]NPNF 2 10:2*. [69]CS 82:17-18.

if we provoke the people's applause by our choice of words or by the instigation of the devil, who is the patron of errors, we bear witness against our own conscience that we are doing the very thing against which we are able to warn others. COMMENTARY ON ECCLESIASTES 3.7[70]

WHEN TO KEEP SILENCE AND WHEN TO SPEAK.

GREGORY THE GREAT: The tongue, therefore, should be discreetly curbed, not tied up fast. For it is written, "A wise man will hold his tongue until the time,"[71] in order, assuredly, that when he considers it opportune, he may relinquish the censorship of silence and apply himself to the service of utility by speaking such things as are fit. And again it is written, "A time to keep silence and a time to speak." For, indeed, the times for changes should be discreetly weighed, lest either, when the tongue ought to be restrained, it run loose to no profit in words, or, when it might speak with profit, it slothfully restrain itself. Considering which thing well, the psalmist says, "Set a watch, O Lord, on my mouth, and a door round about my lips."[72] PASTORAL CARE 3.14.[73]

BE SILENT ABOUT GOD'S BEING, SPEAK ABOUT GOD'S ACTIVITY.

GREGORY OF NYSSA: In words about things concerning God, when the discussion is about his being, that is the "moment for keeping silent." But when it is about some good activity [of God], of which the knowledge reaches down even to us, then is the moment for speaking of the powers, to proclaim the wonders, to recount the works, to use language thus far. In matters that lie beyond, it is the moment not to allow the creation to overstep its boundaries but to be content to know itself. HOMILIES ON ECCLESIASTES 7.[74]

3:8 Love and Hate, War and Peace

LOVE GOD AND HATE EVIL.

GREGORY OF NYSSA: What truly exists is the one and only intrinsically Lovable, of whom also the rule of the Ten Commandments says, "You shall love the Lord your God with all your heart and with all your soul and with all your mind."[75] And again the only thing to be hated in truth is the inventor of evil, the enemy of our life, about whom the law says, "You shall hate your enemy."[76]

The love of God becomes a strength for the one who loves, but the disposition to evil brings destruction on the one who loves [what is] evil. HOMILIES ON ECCLESIASTES 8.[77]

VIRTUES AND VICES CAN BE LOVED OR HATED.

GREGORY OF NYSSA: If you make a distinction in your mind between things thought of as virtue and vice, you will recognize the moment for the right attitude to each of them. Restraint and pleasure, self-control and indulgence, humility and pride, goodwill and crookedness, and all that are regarded as opposites of one another, are plainly set out for you by the Ecclesiast, so that by adopting attitudes about them in your soul you may make profitable decisions. Thus there is a moment for loving restraint and for hating pleasure, so that you do not become pleasure-loving rather than God-loving, and likewise in all the other cases, quarrel-loving, gain-loving, glory-loving, and all the rest, which through the use of affection for improper ends separate us from the disposition to good. HOMILIES ON ECCLESIASTES 8.[78]

THE TWO COMPANIONS OF EVERY SOUL.

DIDYMUS THE BLIND: Every soul has a reprehensible companion and a praiseworthy one: the bridegroom, which is the Logos, and the adulterer, which is the devil. If the devil is present, one should not give him room; one should not let him in, as Judas did. This kind of companion needs to be hated. But a "time to love" has come when the true bridegroom is present. He is worthy of love, so much so that one of the saints has said, "My love has been crucified." But love is

[70]CCL 72:276. [71]Sir 20:7. [72]Ps 141:3 (140:3 LXX). [73]NPNF 2 12:38. [74]GNHE 126-27*. [75]Deut 6:5, Mt 22:37 and parallels. [76]Mt 5:43. [77]GNHE 133-34. [78]GNHE 135*.

intensified desire. Further, we have a commandment to love our enemies[79] and to approach those who hate us in such a way that we even send a prayer to heaven for them. Insofar as we desire that they be helped and do not want ourselves to be troubled by hostility, we love our enemies; but insofar as we do not imitate them and do not accept the same things or want to be enemies as they want to be, we hate them. COMMENTARY ON ECCLESIASTES 81.4.[80]

THE ARMY OF GOD'S PEACE. GREGORY OF NYSSA: If we have learned, then, whom we should go to war with and how to carry on the fight, we must also learn the other part of the lesson, with whom the Scripture solemnly warns us to make a peaceful alliance. What is the good army, with which I am to join forces through peace? Who is the king of such an army? It is clear, from what we are taught by the inspired

Scriptures, that it is the array of the angels of the host of heaven. HOMILIES ON ECCLESIASTES 8.[81]

NECESSITY TO FIGHT. DIDYMUS THE BLIND: If powers, forces, rulers of the world of darkness and evil spirits tempt us, we are not supposed to take issue with them or make peace with them, but we must fight them. But when we have subdued them and are given power "to tread on snakes and scorpions,"[82] then it is a time for peace. Thus, first the devil has to be crushed under the feet of the saints. When it is time for war, one has to tread on "all the power of the enemy."[83] But when we have broken them down, we can live in enduring peace, our thinking is free from confusion, and we have a time for peace. COMMENTARY ON ECCLESIASTES 81.21.[84]

---

[79]Mt 5:43-45. [80]PTA 22:81-83. [81]GNHE 139*. [82]Lk 10:19. [83]Lk 10:19. [84]PTA 22:85.

3:10-22 THE TASK THAT GOD HAS APPOINTED

[10]*I have seen the business that God has given to the sons of men to be busy with.* [11]*He has made everything beautiful in its time; also he has put eternity into man's mind, yet so that he cannot find out what God has done from the beginning to the end.* [12]*I know that there is nothing better for them than to be happy and enjoy themselves as long as they live;* [13]*also that it is God's gift to man that every one should eat and drink and take pleasure in all his toil.* [14]*I know that whatever God does endures for ever; nothing can be added to it, nor anything taken from it; God has made it so, in order that men should fear before him.* [15]*That which is, already has been; that which is to be, already has been; and God seeks what has been driven away.*

[16]*Moreover I saw under the sun that in the place of justice, even there was wickedness, and in the place of righteousness, even there was wickedness.* [17]*I said in my heart, God will judge the righteous and the wicked, for he has appointed a time for every matter, and for every work.* [18]*I said in my heart with regard to the sons of men that God is testing them to show them that they are but beasts.* [19]*For the fate of the sons of men and the fate of beasts is the same; as one dies, so dies the other. They all have the same breath, and man has no advantage over the beasts; for all is vanity.*

²⁰All go to one place; all are from the dust, and all turn to dust again. ²¹Who knows whether the spirit of man goes upward and the spirit of the beast goes down to the earth? ²²So I saw that there is nothing better than that a man should enjoy his work, for that is his lot; who can bring him to see what will be after him?

OVERVIEW: God made everything beautiful and for a transcendent purpose (DIONYSIUS OF ALEXANDRIA, AMBROSE). Thus even material things can be used in spiritual contemplation (EVAGRIUS). God's image is obliterated by the evil one, not by God (GREGORY THAUMATURGUS). But neither should the stomach be substituted for God. God's primary creation is invisible, but creation is also made so that we know God is its ruler (DIDYMUS). Even those who are not yet born already exist for God (PETER CHRYSOLOGUS), for human beings have reason and a soul (DIDYMUS). But in this world that is passing away, the wicked are intermingled with the righteous (BEDE). Nothing in this world is permanent (JOHN CASSIAN), and at the end God will judge between believers and unbelievers (AUGUSTINE). God's judgment has different places for the godly and the ungodly (GREGORY THAUMATURGUS). A person, unlike a beast, is destined for life everlasting (GREGORY THE GREAT) and should therefore heed the spiritual (OLYMPIODORUS), but a person can also reject that life and sink to a lower state (SHENOUTE). In this present life, in fact, it is difficult to distinguish between the righteous and the ungodly (EVAGRIUS), but Ecclesiastes guides us upward to the other life (OLYMPIODORUS). The resurrection and the existence of soul and spirit are designed by God (AMBROSE, AUGUSTINE).

3:11 God Made Everything Beautiful

BOTH BEAUTY AND PURPOSE IN EVERYTHING. DIONYSIUS OF ALEXANDRIA: Of all these things there is not one either idle or useless. Not even the meanest of them—the hair, or the nails, or such like—is so; but all have their service to do, and all their contribution to make, some of them to the soundness of bodily constitution and others of them to beauty of appearance. For Providence cares not only for the useful but also for the seasonable and beautiful. FRAGMENT 1.4.[1]

MATERIAL THINGS CAN BE USED IN SPIRITUAL CONTEMPLATION. EVAGRIUS OF PONTUS: I have seen, he says, the material world that preoccupies human minds, that which God gave to the human race prior to its cleansing so that they would occupy themselves. He means here that the beauty of the material world is temporal, not eternal. For, after cleansing, the one who is pure no longer needs to view material things only as a diversion of the mind. Rather, he can also use them in spiritual contemplation. SCHOLIA ON ECCLESIASTES 15.3.10-13.[2]

THE EVIL ONE OBLITERATES GOD'S IMAGE. GREGORY THAUMATURGUS: Indeed, an evil observer of the times has this age in his jaws and strives with a great effort to wipe out the image of God, having chosen to fight against him from the beginning until the end. PARAPHRASE OF ECCLESIASTES 3.11.[3]

3:13 Everyone Should Eat and Drink and Take Pleasure

BUT DO NOT TAKE YOUR STOMACH TO BE YOUR GOD. DIDYMUS THE BLIND: Whoever eats in a way that he takes his stomach to be God does not find anything good in eating and drinking, but rather ungodliness: "Such people do not serve our Lord Christ but their own stomach."[4] COMMENTARY ON ECCLESIASTES 86.2.[5]

---

[1]ANF 6:88*. [2]SC 397:80-82. [3]GTPE 65. [4]Rom 16:18. [5]PTA 22:105.

3:14 Whatever God Does Endures Forever

GOD'S PRIMARY CREATION IS INVISIBLE. DIDY-MUS THE BLIND: In the spiritual and higher sense one can also say the following: The invisible things are God's creations in the real sense. They are eternal. The timely and visible things are secondary and accidental and created for the sake of the eternal ones. These visible things have come into being for the sake of humankind, which by nature is invisible regarding the soul and the inner being. The visible things cannot primarily be called God's creations. God certainly has created them, but for the purpose of other things. COMMENTARY ON ECCLESIASTES 87.6.[6]

CREATION IS MADE SO THAT WE KNOW GOD IS ITS RULER. DIDYMUS THE BLIND: God has made creation so that human beings, through an outward picture of the greatness and beauty of created things,[7] might [understand] that God exists. He himself manages the cosmos and looks after it so that we—while the whole cosmos is orderly guided by one commander and provider and ruler and charioteer and king—get the outward picture that there is someone who rules the cosmos. When you see a ship which is piloted and holds its course, you perceive the idea of a helmsman even if he is not visible. And if you see a chariot which travels orderly, you get the idea of a charioteer. Likewise the Creator is known by his works and the order of his providence. COMMENTARY ON ECCLESIASTES 88.29.[8]

3:15 God Requires an Account of What Is Past

THOSE NOT YET REBORN ALREADY EXIST FOR GOD. PETER CHRYSOLOGUS: "Our Father." No one should be astonished that one not yet born[9] calls God Father. With God, beings who will be born are already born; with God future beings have been made. "The things that shall be," Scripture says, "have already been." [Thus] it is that while John was still in the womb[10] he perceived his

creator, and he who was unaware of his own life served as a messenger to his mother. [Thus] too we read that Jacob waged war before he was born and triumphed before he lived.[11] [Thus] too, those who do not yet exist themselves are existent for God, that is, those who were chosen before the foundation of the world. SERMON 70.[12]

INSIGHT INTO THE KNOWLEDGE OF CREATED THINGS. EVAGRIUS OF PONTUS: If those are "blessed who are persecuted for righteousness' sake, for theirs is the kingdom of heaven"[13] and at the same time the kingdom of heaven is the totality of the ideas[14] of the things that have been and will come into being, then it follows that the persecuted are blessed because they have insight into the knowledge of created things. SCHOLIA ON ECCLESIASTES 19.3.15.[15]

3:16 Time for Judgment

GOD'S JUDGMENT SETS DIFFERENT PLACES. GREGORY THAUMATURGUS: I saw in the lower regions a pit of punishment awaiting the ungodly but a different place set apart for the godly. PARAPHRASE OF ECCLESIASTES 3.16.[16]

GOD WILL JUDGE THE RIGHTEOUS AND THE WICKED. BEDE: "The shape of this world passes away,"[17] not its substance; just as with our bodies too, the shape will be changed. The substance does not perish when "what is sowed as a physical body rises as a spiritual body."[18] But we read nothing of this sort about the fire and the water. Rather we have in the book of Revelation, "And the sea is now no longer,"[19] and in the prophets, "And the light of the lamp shall shine for you no more."[20] "We wait for his promises," he says, "in which righteousness dwells."[21] Righteousness dwells in the future age, because then the crown

---

[6]PTA 22:111. [7]See Wis 13:5. [8]PTA 22:119. [9]A catechumen not yet reborn through baptism. [10]Lk 1:44. [11]Gen 25:21-24. [12]FC 17:120. [13]Mt 5:10. [14]Gk *logoi*. [15]SC 397:88. [16]GTPE 72. [17]1 Cor 7:31. [18]1 Cor 15:44. [19]Rev 21:1. [20]Rev 18:23. [21]2 Pet 3:13.

of righteousness will be given to each of the faithful in accord with the measure of their struggle. This is a thing that cannot at all happen in this life, according to the saying of Solomon, "I have seen beneath the sun wickedness in place of judgment and iniquity in place of righteousness and I said in my heart, 'God will judge the righteous and the wicked, and there will be a time for everything.'" And again he says, "I saw the deceit that goes on beneath the sun and the tears of the innocent and that there was no comforter, nor were those deprived of the help of all able to resist their power, and I praised the dead rather than the living."[22] COMMENTARY ON 2 PETER 3:13.[23]

3:17 God Will Judge

THERE WILL BE NO EXCUSE FOR UNBELIEF.
AUGUSTINE: I ask you, then, are we to suppose that the only decree of God that will not come to pass, the only decree of God, will be the one which we read in those same writings as being about to judge between believers and unbelievers, when everything else that we read has happened as it was foretold? On the contrary, it will come to pass as all those other prophecies came to pass. Then there will be no person of our times who will be able at that judgment to find an excuse for unbelief when everyone shall call on Christ: the upright for justice, the perjurer for deceit, the king for power and the soldier for battle, the husband to maintain his authority and the wife to show her submission, the father for command and the son for obedience, the master for his right to rule and the servant for his subjection, the humble for piety and the proud for ambition, the rich man to distribute and the poor to receive, the drunkard at his wine cups and the beggar at the gate, the good person that he may excel in virtue and the bad one that he may cheat, the Christian worshiper and the pagan sycophant. All have the name of Christ upon their lips, and, with whatever intention and formula they invoke him, without doubt they shall render an account of it to him whom they invoke. LETTER 232.[24]

NOTHING IN THIS WORLD IS A PERMANENT GOOD. JOHN CASSIAN: In Ecclesiastes the divine wisdom has indicated that there is an appropriate time for everything—that is, for all things, whether they be fortunate or be considered unfortunate and sad. As it says, "There is a time for all things, and a time for everything under heaven."... And a little later it says that "there is a time for everything and for every deed."

It has therefore been determined that none of these things is a permanent good, except when it is carried out at the right time and in correct fashion. Thus the very things that turn out well now, since they were done at the right time, are found to be disadvantageous and harmful if they are tried at an inopportune or inappropriate moment. The only exception to this is those things that are essentially and of themselves either good or bad and that can never be turned to their contraries, such as justice, prudence, fortitude, temperance, and the other virtues, and, on the other hand, the vices, which can never be understood differently. But if they can sometimes have different effects, so that they are found to be good or bad in accordance with the character of those who are exercising them, they are perceived not in absolute terms relative to their nature but as sometimes advantageous and sometimes harmful in keeping with the disposition of the one exercising them and with the opportuneness of the moment. CONFERENCE 21.12.3-4.[25]

3:19 Like Beasts

PEOPLE HAVE THE ABILITY TO GO WHERE THERE IS LIFE. GREGORY THE GREAT: In describing the pleasures of the flesh, he puts all cares out of his mind and states that it is good to eat and drink. Later, he finds fault with this view from the standpoint of reason and says it is better to go to the house of mourning than to the house of feasting. Likewise, from purely carnal consider-

---

[22]Eccles 4:1-2. [23]CS 82:151-52*. [24]FC 32:170-71*. [25]ACW 57:728-29.

ations he advises a young man to find his pleasure in his youth, and later, modifying this statement, he blames youth and its pleasures as fleeting. So, too, when he speaks from the minds of the infirm, our Preacher voices an opinion based on suspicion. "For the lot of man and of beast," he says, "is one lot; the one dies as well as the other. Both have the same life breath, and man has no advantage over the beast." Later, however, he presents conclusions drawn from reason and says, "What has the wise man more than the fool? and what the poor man, but to go where there is life?"[26] So, after he says, "Man has no advantage over the beast," he again specifies that the wise person has an advantage not only over the beast but also over the foolish person, namely, his ability to go "where there is life." DIALOGUE 4.4.[27]

HUMAN BEINGS ALSO HAVE REASON AND A SOUL. DIDYMUS THE BLIND: Animals are mortal beings without reason, angels are immortal beings with reason, human beings are mortal beings with reason. Regarding mortality the human being is grouped together with beings without reason. Regarding reason [the human being] is grouped together with the immortal beings, since angels also have reason. Regarding its senses . . . the human being is of the same kind as the beings without reason. But the human being is receptive to something to which no other mortal being is receptive: its soul can become perfect, as far as this can be achieved, and become like God, as far as it is possible. . . .

Thus, when he says that "the fate of humans and the fate of animals is the same," he does not mean what happens to reason but what happens to the outward body. . . . The general judgment which enacts promises and punishments does not judge what human beings have in common with animals but what humans have in common with angels. As humans can be led into the kingdom of heaven and remain in heaven, so it is with angels; and as humans can be judged, so can angels be judged. . . .

If one investigates the nature of death, then the death of animals is not like the death of humans. Human death divides the soul from the body, and after the division the soul remains. But the death of animals destroys soul and body, since they have been created simultaneously. COMMENTARY ON ECCLESIASTES 99.1.[28]

THEREFORE HEED THE SPIRITUAL. OLYMPIODORUS: Ecclesiastes teaches us from this not to attend to our physical needs but to our spiritual existence. COMMENTARY ON ECCLESIASTES 3.19.[29]

PEOPLE LIKENED TO A BEAST OR WORSE. SHENOUTE: Why did he write, "What advantage does man have over beast?" Perceive now what had happened. Understand now the scorn toward us when he saw that humanity had recognized gods other than the Lord God alone and had not obeyed this utterance, "No foreign god shall be in your midst, nor shall you worship a strange god."[30] Then, when he saw humanity had acted wickedly by [doing] what is contrary to nature, with abominable deeds, with pernicious deeds that no one should be able to mention [and] to which no one should be able to listen, he said this. For if a person does not recognize his value, not only is he reckoned with the beast but the beast is more esteemed than he, when it is said, "An ox knows its owner, and the ass its master's crib."[31] FRAGMENT ON ECCLESIASTES.[32]

NO DIFFERENCE IN THIS LIFE BETWEEN THE RIGHTEOUS AND THE UNGODLY. EVAGRIUS OF PONTUS: By "fate" he means everything that is part of the life of anyone in this world, whether that person is righteous or unrighteous—things such as life, death, sickness, health, affluence, poverty, loss of limbs, of wives, children or possessions. In all these it is impossible to discern between the righteous and unrighteous before the last judgment. He also says that both have in common the fact that they are taken from dust and will return to dust. They also have one soul, not by number but by

---

[26]Eccles 6:8. [27]FC 39:194-95*. [28]PTA 22:153-59. [29]PG 93:521. [30]Ps 81:9 (80:10 LXX). [31]Is 1:3. [32]CMWM 172.

nature. For the Spirit, he says, "is one [and the same] in all." Here he calls a man, who was born in honor, a beast instead of labeling him as someone of understanding. It is because of his foolish desires that he is compared with the senseless beasts and that he ends up becoming like them.[33] And not even through their acts can the righteous and unrighteous be clearly distinguished before the day of judgment, because a good number of the unrighteous become righteous and are elevated, while a good number of the righteous abandon virtue and are debased. "What is the advantage of the righteous over the ungodly?" In this present time, he says, there is no advantage. Everything is vanity except for the spiritual joy that naturally occurs to each according to his deeds and virtues. SCHOLIA ON ECCLESIASTES 21.3.19-22.[34]

3:20 From Dust to Dust

ON THE RESURRECTION. AMBROSE: The resurrection as a fact is not to be rejected because of an exceptional situation. Yet, since all things earthly return and crumble into the earth, I wonder how there can be any doubt even concerning the instances noted. For the most part, the sea itself also casts up on neighboring shores whatever human bodies it has swallowed. And if this were not so, it surely would not be difficult for God to join what has been scattered and to unite again what has been dispersed. Could it be maintained for a moment that God, whom the universe and the silent elements obey and nature serves, did not perform a greater miracle in giving life to clay than in joining it together? ON HIS BROTHER SATYRUS 2.58.[35]

GOD'S ABILITY TO CHANGE. PSEUDO-CLEMENT OF ROME: Yea, even a person, who is dust, he changed by the inbreathing of his breath[36] into flesh, and changed him back again into dust. And was not Moses, who himself was flesh, converted into the grandest light, so that the sons of Israel could not look him in the face?[37] Much more, then, is God completely able to convert himself into whatsoever he wishes. HOMILY 20.6.[38]

SOUL AND SPIRIT. AUGUSTINE: In order, indeed, that you may have the fullest and clearest assurance that what is the *soul* is in the usage of the Holy Scriptures also called *spirit*, the soul of a brute animal has the designation of spirit. And of course cattle have not that spirit which you, my beloved brother, have defined as being distinct from the soul. It is therefore quite evident that the soul of a brute animal could be rightly called "spirit" in a general sense of the term; as we read in the book of Ecclesiastes, "Who knows the spirit of the sons of men, whether it goes upward; and the *spirit of the beast*, whether it goes downward into the earth?" In like manner, touching the devastation of the deluge, the Scripture testifies, "All flesh died that moved upon the earth, both of fowl, and of cattle, and of beast, and of every creeping thing that creeps upon the earth, and every man: and all things which have the spirit of life."[39] Here, if we remove all the windings of doubtful disputation, we understand the term *spirit* to be synonymous with *soul* in its general sense. Of so wide a signification is this term, that even God is called "a spirit";[40] and a stormy blast of the air, although it has material substance, is called by the psalmist the "spirit" of a tempest.[41] For all these reasons, therefore, you will no longer deny that what is the soul is called also spirit. I have, I think, adduced enough from the pages of Holy Scripture to secure your assent in passages where the soul of the very brute beast, which has no understanding, is designated spirit. ON THE SOUL AND ITS ORIGIN 4.37.[42]

3:21 The Other Life May Be Upward or Downward

THE FUTURE CAN BE POSITIVE. OLYMPIODORUS: Ecclesiastes, instructing us through enigmas, guides us to the other life. COMMENTARY ON ECCLESIASTES 3.21.[43]

---

[33]See Ps 48:13-21 LXX. [34]SC 397:92-94. [35]FC 22:221. [36]Gen 2:7. [37]Ex 34:29. [38]ANF 8:341*. [39]Gen 7:21-22. [40]Jn 4:24. [41]Ps 55:8 (54:9 LXX). [42]NPNF 1 5:370*. [43]PG 93:524.

4:1-8 THE VANITY OF TOIL FOR ONESELF

¹*Again I saw all the oppressions that are practiced under the sun. And behold, the tears of the oppressed, and they had no one to comfort them! On the side of their oppressors there was power, and there was no one to comfort them. ²And I thought the dead who are already dead more fortunate than the living who are still alive; ³but better than both is he who has not yet been, and has not seen the evil deeds that are done under the sun.*

⁴*Then I saw that all toil and all skill in work come from a man's envy of his neighbor. This also is vanity and a striving after wind.*

⁵*The fool folds his hands, and eats his own flesh.*

⁶*Better is a handful of quietness than two hands full of toil and a striving after wind.**

⁷*Again, I saw vanity under the sun:* ⁸*a person who has no one, either son or brother, yet there is no end to all his toil, and his eyes are never satisfied with riches, so that he never asks, "For whom am I toiling and depriving myself of pleasure?" This also is vanity and an unhappy business.*

*LXX *presumption of spirit.*

OVERVIEW: It is a greater burden to live for sin than to die in sin, because at death sin ceases (AMBROSE). The death of the innocent, who have not toiled for their own advancement, betokens their reward of everlasting happiness (BEDE). Intimacy with our neighbors can generate envy in ourselves (BASIL), and even Satan can be jealous (EVAGRIUS), just as assistance to the idle does no good (APOSTOLIC CONSTITUTIONS). Idleness in the spiritual life is not commendable, just as quietness is often better than eloquence. (AMBROSE). And those who teach are often the ones in need of instruction (JOHN CASSIAN), for wisdom also can be foolish (EVAGRIUS).

4:1 Sufferings of the Oppressed

IT IS A GREATER BURDEN TO LIVE FOR SIN THAN TO DIE FOR SIN. AMBROSE: We desire each day to know what is new, and what is knowledge itself but our daily sorrow and abasement? All things that are have already been, and "nothing is new under the sun," but "all is vanity. Therefore I hated the whole of this life," said

Ecclesiastes. He who hated his life certainly commended death. And so he praised the dead rather than the living and judged him happy that did not come into this life nor take up this vain toil. "My heart took a circuit to know the joy of the impious man and to examine carefully and to seek wisdom and a mode of calculating and to know joy through the impious man and trouble and disquietude, and I find that it is bitterer than death"[1]—not because death is bitter, but because it is bitter for the impious one. And yet life is bitterer than death. For it is a greater burden to live for sin than to die in sin, because the impious person increases his sin as long as he lives, but if he dies, he ceases to sin. DEATH AS A GOOD 7.28.[2]

THE DEATH OF THE INNOCENT AND THE REWARD OF EVERLASTING HAPPINESS. BEDE: He praised the innocent dead rather than the living because the latter were still engaged in the struggle but the former had been given their reward of everlasting happiness. He complained

---

[1]Eccles 7:25-26 LXX. [2]FC 65:91-92.

that he had seen deceit beneath the sun because he knew that above the sun there is a just judge "who dwells on high and looks down upon humble things."[3] Above the sun there are dwelling places in which the righteous receive due rewards for their righteousness. COMMENTARY ON 2 PETER 3:13.[4]

4:4 Envy of a Neighbor

THE CLOSEST NEIGHBORS ARE THE OBJECTS OF ENVY. BASIL THE GREAT: Wise, therefore, was he who forbids us even to dine in company with an envious person, and in mentioning this companionship at table, he implies a reference to all other social contacts as well. Just as we are careful to keep material which is easily inflammable as far away as possible from fire, so we must refrain insofar as we can from contracting friendships in circles of which envious persons are members. By so doing, we place ourselves beyond the range of their shafts. We can be caught in the toils of envy only by establishing intimacy with it. In the words of Solomon, "A man is exposed to envy from his neighbor." And so it is. The Scythian is not envious of the Egyptian, but each of them envies a fellow countryman. Among members of the same nation, the closest acquaintances and not strangers are objects of envy. Among acquaintances, neighbors and fellow workmen, or those who are otherwise brought into close contact, are envied, and among these again, those of the same age and kinsmen and brothers. In short, as the red blight is a common pest to corn, so envy is the plague of friendship. HOMILY CONCERNING ENVY.[5]

THE JEALOUSY OF SATAN. EVAGRIUS OF PONTUS: I have seen, he says, every sort of wickedness and boldness in the one who is evil. For, such a one [as Satan] thinks he is brave even when in [his] ungodliness he oppresses the poor[6] or again, sees himself as a "creature" who was "made to be mocked by the angels"[7] of God. Also I have seen all the jealousy that he has acquired towards human beings, which is vain and governs his heart,[8] since God certainly "will become all in all."[9] And when God does so, this will fulfill the prayer of Christ, which said, "Grant that they also may be one in us, as you and I are one, Father."[10] SCHOLIA ON ECCLESIASTES 25.4.4.[11]

4:5 Foolishness of Idle People

THE IDLE DO NOT DESERVE ASSISTANCE. APOSTOLIC CONSTITUTIONS: But if any one is in want by gluttony, drunkenness or idleness, he does not deserve any assistance or to be esteemed a member of the church of God. For the Scripture, speaking of such persons, says, "The slothful hides his hand in his bosom and is not able to bring it to his mouth again."[12] And again, "The sluggard folds up his hands, and eats his own flesh." "For every drunkard and whoremonger shall come to poverty, and every drowsy person shall be clothed with tatters and rags."[13] And in another passage [we read], "If you give your eyes to drinking and cups, you shall afterwards walk more naked than a pestle."[14] For certainly idleness is the mother of famine. CONSTITUTIONS OF THE HOLY APOSTLES 2.2.4.[15]

IDLENESS IN THE SPIRITUAL LIFE. AMBROSE: Let one who still doubts hear the testimony of the Gospel, for the Son of God said, "We have played for you, and you have not danced."[16] The Jews who did not dance and knew not how to clap their hands were abandoned, but the Gentiles were called and applauded God in spirit. "The fool folds his hands together and eats his own flesh," that is, he becomes involved in the concerns of the body and eats his own flesh, just as does all-powerful death. And such a one will not find eternal life. But the wise person who lifts up his works that they may shine before his Father who is in heaven has not consumed his flesh; instead, he has raised it to the

---

[3]Ps 113:5-6 (112:5-6 LXX). [4]CS 82:152*. [5]FC 9:468-69. [6]See Prov 28:3. [7]Job 40:19 LXX. [8]Eccles 8:11. [9]1 Cor 15:28. [10]Jn 17:21-22. [11]SC 397:100. [12]Prov 19:24 LXX. [13]Prov 23:21. [14]Prov 23:31 LXX. [15]ANF 7:397*. [16]Mt 11:17.

grace of the resurrection. This is the wise person's honorable dance which David danced, mounting by the loftiness of his spiritual dance to the throne of Christ that he may see and hear the Lord saying to his Lord, "Sit at my right hand."[17] LETTER 28, TO BISHOP SABINUS.[18]

4:6 *Quietness Is Better Than Eloquence*

TEACHERS NEED INSTRUCTION. JOHN CASSIAN: According to the words of Solomon, "A single handful with repose is better than two handfuls with toil and presumption of spirit." All those who are very weak are inevitably entangled in these illusions and losses. Even though their own salvation is in doubt and they still stand in need of others' teaching and instruction, they are prompted by diabolical illusions to convert and to govern others. And even if they have been able to acquire some gain and to make some conversions, they will lose whatever they got because of their impatience and their immoderate behavior. CONFERENCE 24.13.5.[19]

A HANDFUL OF VIRTUE IS SUPERIOR TO FOOLISH WISDOM. EVAGRIUS OF PONTUS: The "chasing after wind," I believe, refers to the will of the soul caught up with passions. That is why a handful of virtue is better than two handfuls of wickedness, ignorance and "chasing after wind." . . . It is as if someone said it is better to learn contemplation of one spiritual thing than to have numerous visions of foolish wisdom. SCHOLIA ON ECCLESIASTES 27.4.6.[20]

---

[17]Ps 110:1 (109:1 LXX). [18]FC 26:146*. [19]ACW 57:836*. [20]SC 397:102-4.

4:9-16 COMPANIONSHIP LIGHTENS THE HUMAN LOAD

[9]*Two are better than one, because they have a good reward for their toil.* [10]*For if they fall, one will lift up his fellow; but woe to him who is alone when he falls and has not another to lift him up.* [11]*Again, if two lie together, they are warm; but how can one be warm alone?* [12]*And though a man might prevail against one who is alone, two will withstand him. A threefold cord is not quickly broken.*

[13]*Better is a poor and wise youth than an old and foolish king, who will no longer take advice,* [14]*even though he had gone from prison to the throne or in his own kingdom had been born poor.* [15]*I saw all the living who move about under the sun, as well as that[f] youth, who was to stand in his place;* [16]*there was no end of all the people; he was over all of them. Yet those who come later will not rejoice in him. Surely this also is vanity and a striving after wind.*

f *Heb the second*

OVERVIEW: Christ sent his disciples two by two, and it is dangerous to lead the spiritual life alone, whether one is a monk or not (PETER CHRYSOLO-GUS, SYMEON, BASIL). Christ was not raised by the power of someone else (AMBROSE), but most of us do need a good spiritual guide (GREGORY OF

NYSSA). In fact, in such matters, even three are stronger than two (AMBROSE, GREGORY THE GREAT).

4:10 Spiritual Guidance and Support

NEED FOR A GOOD SPIRITUAL GUIDE. GREGORY OF NYSSA: Since the majority of persons who intend to lead a life of virginity are still young and immature, they must concern themselves with this before all: the finding of a good guide and teacher on this path, lest, on account of their ignorance, they enter upon trackless places and wander away from the straight road. For, as Ecclesiastes says, "Two are better than one." The one is easily overcome by the enemy lying in ambush on the divine road, and truly, "woe to the solitary man, for if he should fall he has no one to lift him up." In the past, certain people have made an auspicious beginning in their desire for this life, but, although they have attained perfection in their intention, they have been tripped up because of their vanity. They deceived themselves, through some craziness, into thinking that that was fair toward which their own thought inclined. Among these, there are those called "the slothful"[1] in the Book of Wisdom, who strew their path with thorns, who consider harmful to the soul a zeal for deeds in keeping with the commandments of God, the demurrers against the apostolic injunctions, who do not eat their own bread with dignity but, fawning on others, make idleness the art of life. Then there are the dreamers who consider the deceits of dreams more trustworthy than the teachings of the Gospels, calling fantasies revelations. Apart from these, there are those who stay in their own houses, and still others who consider being unsociable and brutish a virtue without recognizing the command to love and without knowing the fruit of long-suffering and humility. ON VIRGINITY 23.[2]

CHRIST RAISED HIMSELF BY HIS OWN POWER. AMBROSE: Fittingly does Ecclesiastes say, "For if one falls, he raises up his companion." He himself is not raised up, for Christ was not raised up by another's help and power, but he himself raised himself. Indeed, he said, "Destroy this temple, and in three days I will raise it up. This he said of the temple of his body."[3] It is well that he who did not fall should not be raised by another, for one who is raised by another has fallen, and one who falls needs help to be raised up. Additional words also teach this when Scripture says, "Woe to him that is alone: for when he falls, he has none to lift him up. And if two lie together, they shall warm one another." We have died with Christ, and we live together with him.[4] Christ died with us to warm us, and he said, "I have come to cast fire upon the earth."[5] LETTER 58, TO HIS CLERGY.[6]

THE DANGER OF SOLITARY LIFE FOR A MONK. BASIL THE GREAT: In the solitary life, what is at hand becomes useless to us and what is wanting cannot be provided, since God the Creator decreed that we should require the help of one another, as it is written, so that we might associate with one another. Again, apart from this consideration, the doctrine of the charity of Christ does not permit the individual to be concerned solely with his own private interests. "Charity," says the apostle, "seeks not her own."[7] But a life passed in solitude is concerned only with the private service of individual needs. This is openly opposed to the law of love, which the apostle fulfilled, who sought not what was profitable to himself but to many that they might be saved.[8] Furthermore, a person living in solitary retirement will not readily discern his own defects, since he has no one to admonish and correct him with mildness and compassion. In fact, admonition even from an enemy often produces in a prudent person the desire for amendment. But the cure of sin is wrought with understanding by him who loves sincerely. Holy Scripture says, "for he that loves, at times corrects."[9] Such a one it is very difficult to find in solitude, if in one's prior

---

[1]Prov 15:19. [2]FC 58:70-71*. [3]Jn 2:19, 21. [4]Rom 6:8. [5]Lk 12:49. [6]FC 26:318*. [7]1 Cor 13:5. [8]1 Cor 10:33. [9]Prov 13:24.

state of life one had not been associated with such a person. The solitary, consequently, experiences the truth of the saying, "Woe to him that is alone, for when he falls he has none to lift him up." Moreover, the majority of the commandments are easily observed by several persons living together, but not so in the case of one living alone, for while he is obeying one commandment, the practice of another is being interfered with. For example, when he is visiting the sick, he cannot show hospitality to the stranger, and in the imparting and sharing of necessities (especially when the ministrations are prolonged), he is prevented from giving zealous attention to [other] tasks. As a result, the greatest commandment and the one especially conducive to salvation is not observed, since the hungry are not fed nor the naked clothed. Who, then, would choose this ineffectual and unprofitable life in preference to that which is both fruitful and in accordance with the Lord's command? THE LONG RULES 7.[10]

CHRIST SENT DISCIPLES TWO BY TWO. PETER CHRYSOLOGUS: "And he began to send them forth two by two." He sent them two by two that no one of them, being abandoned and alone, might fall into a denial, like Peter, or flee, like John.[11] Human frailty quickly falls if it proudly relies on itself, despises companions and is unwilling to have a colleague. As Scripture says, "Woe to him that is alone, for when he falls, he has none to lift him." The same Scripture testifies how much one is strengthened by another's aid, when it states, "A brother that is helped by his brother is like a strong city."[12] SERMON 170.[13]

THE DANGER OF LIVING THE SPIRITUAL LIFE ALONE. SYMEON THE NEW THEOLOGIAN: Do

not follow the wolf instead of the shepherd,[14] or enter into a flock that is diseased.[15] Do not be alone by yourself, lest you be seen carried off by the wolf who destroys souls or succumb to one disease after the other and so die spiritually, or, as you succumb, you attain to that woe. He who gives himself in the hand of a good teacher will have no such worries but will live without anxiety and be saved in Christ Jesus our Lord, to whom be glory forever. Amen. DISCOURSE 20.7.[16]

4:12 Three Are Stronger Than Two

AN EXAMPLE OF A THREEFOLD ROPE.
AMBROSE: Paul fled too, that he might pass out through a window and be lowered in a basket.[17] Yes, he knew that the triple-stranded rope could not break, but he fled so that he might preach the gospel of the Lord in the entire world,[18] and consequently he was taken up into paradise.[19] Let us also flee through the window while heeding the Lord's precepts and keeping them with steady vision and chaste eyes. FLIGHT FROM THE WORLD 9.54.[20]

BY THE CORD FAITH IS EXPRESSED.
GREGORY THE GREAT: By a "cord," faith is expressed, as Solomon witnesses, who says, "A threefold cord is not easily broken" because the faith in truth that is woven by the mouth of preachers from the knowledge of the Trinity remains firm in the elect. It is broken only in the heart of the reprobate. MORALS ON THE BOOK OF JOB 6.33.18.[21]

---

[10]FC 9:248-49. [11]Mk 14:66-72, 50-52. [12]Prov 18:19. [13]FC 17:280. [14]Mt 7:15. [15]Ezek 34:4. [16]SNTD 237. [17]2 Cor 11:32-33. [18]See 1 Cor 9:16-18. [19]2 Cor 12:2-4. [20]FC 65:321. [21]LF 31:573-74*.

5:1-7 FEAR GOD AND KEEP YOUR VOWS

[1g]Guard your steps when you go to the house of God; to draw near to listen is better than to offer the sacrifice of fools; for they do not know that they are doing evil. [2h]Be not rash with your mouth, nor let your heart be hasty to utter a word before God, for God is in heaven, and you upon earth; therefore let your words be few.

[3]For a dream comes with much business, and a fool's voice with many words.

[4]When you vow a vow to God, do not delay paying it; for he has no pleasure in fools. Pay what you vow. [5]It is better that you should not vow than that you should vow and not pay. [6]Let not your mouth lead you into sin, and do not say before the messenger[i] that it was a mistake; why should God be angry at your voice, and destroy the work of your hands?

[7]For when dreams increase, empty words grow many:[j] but do you fear God.

g Ch 4.17 in Heb h Ch 5.1 in Heb i Or angel j Or For in a multitude of dreams there is futility, and ruin in a flood of words

OVERVIEW: Our words to God in prayer should be few in number (EVAGRIUS). We should guard our mouth by humility (THEODORE OF TABENNESI), especially when discussing theology (ORIGEN). We should remember that God regards us from heaven and that his nature transcends our intelligence (ORIGEN, GREGORY OF NYSSA). Our faith without works would be like words without deeds (CAESARIUS), but it is better not to vow at all than to vow and then not to pay what we have promised (JOHN CASSIAN). Vows of virginity, especially, should not be undertaken rashly (APOSTOLIC CONSTITUTIONS).

5:2 Watching the Mouth

OUR WORDS TO GOD IN PRAYER SHOULD BE FEW IN NUMBER. EVAGRIUS OF PONTUS: "We do not know how to pray as we ought."[1] He is not so much talking [about prayer] at this point as issuing a command not to theologize thoughtlessly. Indeed, anyone who belongs to this material world and whose thoughts have their origin in this world cannot speak about God without error—or on other matters that elude the senses. That is why he says, "And let your words be few,"

that is, they should be true and well chosen. I think also that "few" means the same as in the following texts: "Better a little with righteousness than an abundance of riches with sinners."[2] And, "Better is the receiving of a little with righteousness."[3] But to those who do not observe this, he says, "For as a dream comes when there are many cares, so is the fool's voice with many words."...

He also talks about "the voice of a fool," coming up with false words and beguiling the soul. This is "the voice of the slanderer and reviler."[4] He is also able to apply this to the voice of the fool who "by a multitude of words you will not escape sin."[5] SCHOLIA ON ECCLESIASTES 35.5.1-2.[6]

GUARD OUR MOUTHS BY HUMILITY. THEODORE OF TABENNESI: Truly, if a person guards his mouth[7] and acquires humility, the angels will be his friends here below; his soul will be a perfume poured out; the angels will carry his remembrance before God day and night, whether he is a monk or a secular. Besides, many persons in the

[1]Rom 8:26. [2]Ps 37:16 (36:16 LXX). [3]Prov 16:8 (15:29 LXX). [4]Ps 44:16 (43:17 LXX). [5]Prov 10:19 LXX. [6]SC 397:116-18. [7]Jas 1:26.

world are watchful on this point. As for me, I know many who have acquired a great humility and have watched themselves not to speak evil of anyone. On the contrary, they underestimate themselves constantly and praise the others, saying, "It is within the power of God that we should find a little place in heaven." FRAGMENT 2.[8]

WE SHOULD NOT HASTEN TO DISCUSS THEOLOGY. ORIGEN: [It might be that] a person dedicates himself rashly, without comprehending what is esoteric of the wisdom of God and of the Word who is "in the beginning with God"[9] and who is himself God. And . . . it is by means of the Word and God and by means of the wisdom with him that one must examine and discover these things. [Then] it must happen that he, by falling into myths and nonsense and fictions, submits himself to the danger that surrounds impiety. For that reason one must remember also the commandment from Solomon in Ecclesiastes concerning such things, which says, "Do not hasten to express a word before the face of God. For God is in the heaven above, and you are on the earth below. Therefore let your words be few." FRAGMENTS ON JEREMIAH 1.1.[10]

THOSE ON EARTH AND IN HEAVEN. ORIGEN: The passage in Ecclesiastes, "Be not hasty to utter a word before the face of God; for God is in heaven above, and you upon earth below," is intended to make clear the distance between those who are in "the body of lowness,"[11] and him who is with the angels, elevated by the help of the Word, and with the holy powers, or with Christ himself. It is not absurd that he, allegorically termed "heaven," should properly be the "throne of the Father," and that his church, termed "earth," should be the footstool for his feet.[12] ON PRAYER 23.4.[13]

GOD'S NATURE TRANSCENDS OUR INTELLIGENCE. GREGORY OF NYSSA: Listen to the Preacher exhorting not to be hasty to utter anything before God, "for God," (says he), "is in heaven above, and you upon earth beneath."

He shows, I think, by the relation of these elements to each other, or rather by their distance, how far the divine nature is above the speculations of human reason. For that nature which transcends all intelligence is as high above earthly calculation as the stars are above the touch of our fingers, or rather, many times more than that.

Knowing, then, how widely the divine nature differs from our own, let us quietly remain within our proper limits. For it is both safer and more reverent to believe the majesty of God to be greater than we can understand, than, after circumscribing his glory by our misconceptions, to suppose there is nothing beyond our conception of it. ANSWER TO EUNOMIUS'S SECOND BOOK.[14]

5:4 Vows Before God

FAITH WITHOUT WORKS IS LIKE WORDS WITHOUT DEEDS. CAESARIUS OF ARLES: It does a person no good to say that he possesses faith if he neglects to fulfill in deed what he promises in word. As the Scriptures say, "If you have vowed anything to God, defer not to pay it. For an unfaithful and foolish promise displeases him. It is much better not to vow than after a vow not to perform the things promised." In order that we may understand these facts clearly from our relations with our servants, let someone tell me whether it is enough for him if his servant says all day that he is his lord and ceases not to commend him with praises but refuses to do what has been commanded. Therefore, if words without deeds do not please us, how much more can faith without works fail to benefit us in the sight of God? Above all, we must fear lest someone believes so strongly that he will receive God's mercy that he does not dread his justice. If a person does this, he has no faith. Likewise, if he dreads God's justice so much that he despairs of his mercy, there is no faith. Since God is not only merciful but also just, let us believe in both. Let

---

[8]CS 47:133*. [9]Jn 1:1. [10]FC 97:277*. [11]Phil 3:21. [12]Mt 5:34-35. [13]ACW 19:79-80. [14]NPNF 2 5:260*.

us not despair of his mercy because we fear his justice or love his mercy so much that we disregard his justice. Therefore we should neither hope wrongly nor despair wickedly. SERMON 12.5.[15]

WE HAVE TO FOLLOW THE VOWS THAT WE MADE. JOHN CASSIAN: This will be fulfilled by each one of us in this way. We pray when we renounce this world and pledge that, dead to every earthly deed and to an earthly way of life, we will serve the Lord with utter earnestness of heart. We pray when we promise that, disdaining worldly honor and spurning earthly riches, we will cling to the Lord in complete contrition of heart and poverty of spirit. We pray when we promise that we will always keep the most pure chastity of body and unwavering patience, and when we vow that we will utterly eliminate from our heart the roots of death-dealing anger and sadness. When we have been weakened by sloth and are returning to our former vices and are not doing these things, we shall bear guilt for our prayers and vows and it will be said of us, "It is better not to vow than to vow and not to pay." According to the Greek this can be said, "It is better for you not to pray than to pray and not to pay." CONFERENCE 9.12.2.[16]

5:5 Better Not to Vow

REWARDS OF THOSE WHO WERE NOT DILIGENT. JOHN CASSIAN: For as unbounded glory hereafter is promised to those who faithfully serve God and cleave to him according to the rule of this system, so the severest penalties are in store for those who have carried it out carelessly and coldly and have failed to show to him fruits of holiness corresponding to what they professed or what they were believed by people to be. For "it is better," as Scripture says, "that one should not vow rather than to vow and not pay"; and "Cursed is he that does the work of the Lord carelessly."[17] INSTITUTES 4.33.[18]

ON THOSE WHO TAKE VOWS OF VIRGINITY. APOSTOLIC CONSTITUTIONS: Concerning virginity we have received no commandment,[19] but we leave it to the power of those that are willing, as a vow. [We exhort] them so far in this matter that they do not promise anything rashly, since Solomon says, "It is better not to vow than to vow and not pay." Let such a virgin, therefore, be holy in body and soul, as the temple of God,[20] as the house of Christ, as the habitation of the Holy Spirit. For she that vows ought to do such works as are suitable to her vow, and to show that her vow is real, and made on account of leisure for piety, not to cast a reproach on marriage. Let her not be one who wanders idly around, or one that rambles about unseasonably; not double-minded, but grave, continent, sober, pure, avoiding the conversation of many, and especially of those that are of ill reputation. CONSTITUTIONS OF THE HOLY APOSTLES 4.2.14.[21]

---

[15]FC 31:71-72*. [16]ACW 57:337. [17]Jer 48:10. [18]NPNF 2 11:230*. [19]See 1 Cor 7:25. [20]See 1 Cor 7:34. [21]ANF 7:436**.

5:8—6:12 THE VANITY OF THE
SELF-SEEKING LIFE

[8]*If you see in a province the poor oppressed and justice and right violently taken away, do not be amazed at the matter; for the high official is watched by a higher, and there are yet higher ones over them. [9]But in all, a king is an advantage to a land with cultivated fields.[k]*

[10]*He who loves money will not be satisfied with money; nor he who loves wealth, with gain: this also is vanity.*

[11]*When goods increase, they increase who eat them; and what gain has their owner but to see them with his eyes?*

[12]*Sweet is the sleep of a laborer, whether he eats little or much; but the surfeit of the rich will not let him sleep.*

[13]*There is a grievous evil which I have seen under the sun: riches were kept by their owner to his hurt, [14]and those riches were lost in a bad venture; and he is father of a son, but he has nothing in his hand. [15]As he came from his mother's womb he shall go again, naked as he came, and shall take nothing for his toil, which he may carry away in his hand. [16]This also is a grievous evil: just as he came, so shall he go; and what gain has he that he toiled for the wind, [17]and spent all his days in darkness and grief,[l] in much vexation and sickness and resentment?*

[18]*Behold, what I have seen to be good and to be fitting is to eat and drink and find enjoyment in all the toil with which one toils under the sun the few days of his life which God has given him, for this is his lot. [19]Every man also to whom God has given wealth and possessions and power to enjoy them, and to accept his lot and find enjoyment in his toil—this is the gift of God. [20]For he will not much remember the days of his life because God keeps him occupied with joy in his heart.*

6 *There is an evil which I have seen under the sun, and it lies heavy upon men: [2]a man to whom God gives wealth, possessions, and honor, so that he lacks nothing of all that he desires, yet God does not give him power to enjoy them, but a stranger enjoys them; this is vanity; it is a sore affliction. [3]If a man begets a hundred children, and lives many years, so that the days of his years are many, but he does not enjoy life's good things, and also has no burial, I say that an untimely birth is better off than he. [4]For it comes into vanity and goes into darkness, and in darkness its name is covered; [5]moreover it has not seen the sun or known anything; yet it finds rest rather than he. [6]Even though he should live a thousand years twice told, yet enjoy no good—do not all go to the one place?*

[7]*All the toil of man is for his mouth, yet his appetite is not satisfied.* * [8]*For what advantage has the wise man over the fool? And what does the poor man have who knows how to conduct himself before the living? [9]Better is the sight of the eyes than the wandering of desire; this also is vanity and a striving after wind.*

[10]*Whatever has come to be has already been named, and it is known what man is, and that he is*

not able to dispute with one stronger than he. [11]The more words, the more vanity, and what is man the better? [12]For who knows what is good for man while he lives the few days of his vain life, which he passes like a shadow? For who can tell man what will be after him under the sun?

k Or *The profit of the land is among all of them; a cultivated field has a king*   l Gk: Heb *all his days also he eats in darkness*   *Vg *but his soul will not be filled*

OVERVIEW: The well-cultivated soul has the Logos as its king (DIDYMUS). The desire to increase one's wealth is like a trap or a noose (GREGORY THE GREAT), and God grants suffering to the greedy but peace to those who are good. Evil can be revealed in wealth (EVAGRIUS), and it is certain that wealth does not profit the rich after their death (AMBROSE). In fact, more restful is the sleep of a poor laborer than that of a wealthy person (CHRYSOSTOM). Since all wealth comes to us from God and riches bring merely torment, we should not be slaves to wealth (DIDYMUS). True richness consists in virtue and faith (AMBROSE). We should work only for that which we can take with us after death (AMBROSE, ATHANASIUS), when true life begins (GREGORY THE GREAT). In fact, the enormity of a voracious appetite is an antecedent to the corrupting power of riches (TERTULLIAN). Far better it is for Christians to be forever hungry for God's Word, for that kind of appetite is, quite properly, never satisfied (JEROME). Not only are money and possessions gifts from God, but so also is wisdom (DIDYMUS).

5:9 The Advantage of Having a King

A SOUL THAT IS WELL CULTIVATED HAS THE LOGOS AS ITS KING. DIDYMUS THE BLIND: Regarding the literal interpretation: No one is lord, owner and ruler over a field that lies fallow where thorns and thistles grow; but the field that is well tilled has a king. Thereby the owner is called a king. . . .

When the defenders of the teaching that God's providence rules over everything argue that there is providence, they generally say, Like a weave clearly shows that there is a weaver—whether or not he is seen—in the same way he who sees a well tilled field gets the impression that it has

someone who leads and rules over it. . . .

When you, therefore, see a soul that is well tilled, that sows with tears and is ready to reap with shouts of joy,[1] then this tilled field has a king, the Logos, who leads, rules and reigns. COMMENTARY ON ECCLESIASTES 145.2.[2]

5:10 No Satisfaction in Increasing Wealth

TRAP FOR THOSE WHO LOVE MONEY. GREGORY THE GREAT: When they are intent on increasing money, let them hear what is written: "The covetous man is not filled with money, and he that loves riches shall not reap fruit thereof." For indeed he would reap fruit of them, were he minded, not loving them, to disperse them well. But whoever in his affection for them retains them shall surely leave them behind here without fruit. When they burn to be filled at once with all manner of wealth, let them hear what is written: "He that makes haste to be rich shall not be innocent."[3] For certainly he who goes about to increase wealth is negligent in avoiding sin; and, being caught after the manner of birds, while looking greedily at the bait of earthly things, he is not aware in what a noose of sin he is being strangled. PASTORAL CARE 3.20.[4]

GOD GRANTS SUFFERING TO THE GREEDY BUT PEACE TO THOSE WHO ARE GOOD. EVAGRIUS OF PONTUS: If, he says, you see among people those on the one hand who are oppressed and those on the other who do wrong in judgment, and still others who practice justice, do not be amazed that this occurs as if there were no divine foresight. Rather, know that God guards everything through

---

[1]See Ps 126:5 (125:5 LXX). [2]PTA 13:3-5. [3]Prov 28:20. [4]NPNF 2 12:46*.

Christ and that he also exercises his provision over everything through his holy angels, who excel in their knowledge of earthly events.[5] God is the ruler of the world that he created,[6] and he allots suffering to those who prefer greed and the vanity of this life to knowledge of Christ. But to those who live their lives in goodness, conduct themselves with courage and serve justly, he grants the knowledge of God and a peaceful rest. He grants this whether their knowledge was small or great here, for "we know in part and we prophesy in part."[7] But in the end, he will receive these, while those who were filled with wickedness will find no rest from the worm produced by their evil. SCHOLIA ON ECCLESIASTES 38.5.7-11.[8]

5:12-13 Prosperity Brings No Peace, for Wealth Is Vain that Is Not Used for Good

EVIL CAN BE REVEALED IN WEALTH. EVAGRIUS OF PONTUS: An abundance of evil can be revealed in wealth. But this type of evil should be viewed as more of a weakness. Therefore, everyone who guards his wealth for himself does not know the wisdom of God, nor is his heart inclined to insight, nor to instructing his children. He has neither received the words of God's commandments nor has he hidden them in his heart. SCHOLIA ON ECCLESIASTES 39.5.12-13.[9]

NO PROFIT AFTER DEATH. AMBROSE: Ecclesiastes sees that riches are kept for ill by one who possesses them, for their loss causes a very great anxiety and disquiet. Indeed they are lost, for they are left here and can be of no advantage to one who is dead. And so, the dead man felt anxiety in regard to them and could not find rest; he left what would bring him shame and did not take with himself what he could keep.[10] He was far different from him of whom it is written, "Blessed is the man that has filled his desire with them; he shall not be confounded when he speaks to his enemies in the gate."[11] His inheritance is the Lord, his reward is from the offspring of the Virgin Mary, and he is extolled with praises in the going forth of wisdom. THE PRAYER OF JOB AND DAVID 2.4.12.[12]

DO NOT BE A SLAVE TO WEALTH. DIDYMUS THE BLIND: Of what use is wealth that belongs to someone? He is obviously lord over his wealth. The wealth somebody owns is his amenity and he himself is lord over his wealth. As he himself can use wealth well by being lord over it and not its slave, so also wealth can become lord over him who owns it. Woe to that person. That is the case if he is greedy and becomes a slave of mammon. COMMENTARY ON ECCLESIASTES 155.11.[13]

WEALTH CAN BE AN EXCUSE. DIDYMUS THE BLIND: People use their children as an excuse for gathering riches. At times they do injustice, rob and do similar things, saying: "I'm doing this for my children.". . . I have seen a person who struggled to become rich, but his riches were of no use. He did not enjoy them himself, nor did his son receive them, but he remained poor and in the same state as he had entered the world. After all, he was not born with money or with clothes. . . .

Only the soul's goods can be taken away into heaven. . . . If he has done good with his money, if he has a good reputation and honor, and if he has tried to help the weak, then he takes with him something of what he has labored for, namely, that he has done good. COMMENTARY ON ECCLESIASTES 156.15.[14]

ADVANTAGE IN SLEEP OF SERVANTS OVER MASTERS. CHRYSOSTOM: The same thing happens as every one may perceive with regard to sleep. For not a soft couch, or a bedstead overlaid with silver, or the quietness that exists throughout the house, or anything else of this kind are so generally likely to make sleep sweet and pleasant, as labor and fatigue, and the need of sleep, and drowsiness when one lies down. And to this partic-

---

[5]See 2 Sam 14:20. [6]See Jn 1:10. [7]1 Cor 13:9. [8]SC 397:128-30. [9]SC 397:132. [10]See Lk 12:20-21, 33. [11]Ps 127:5 (126:5 LXX). [12]FC 65:359. [13]PTA 13:23. [14]PTA 13:25-27.

ular the experience of facts, nay, before actual experience, the assertion of the Scriptures bears witness. For Solomon, who had passed his life in luxury, when he wished to make this matter evident, said, "The sleep of a laboring man is sweet, whether he eat little or much." Why does he add, "whether he eat little or much"? Both these things usually bring sleeplessness, namely, indigence and excess of food; the one drying up the body, stiffening the eyelids and not suffering them to be closed; the other straitening and oppressing the breath and inducing many pains. But at the same time so powerful a persuasive is labor, that though both these things should befall them, servants are able to sleep. For since throughout the whole day, they are running about everywhere, ministering to their masters, being knocked about and hard pressed, and having but little time to take breath, they receive a sufficient recompense for their toils and labors in the pleasure of sleeping. And thus it has happened through the goodness of God toward humanity, that these pleasures are not to be purchased with gold and silver but with labor, with hard toil, with necessity, and every kind of discipline. Not so the rich. On the contrary, while lying on their beds, they are frequently without sleep through the whole night; and though they devise many schemes, they do not obtain such pleasure. But the poor person, when released from his daily labors, having his limbs completely tired, falls almost before he can lie down into a slumber that is sound, and sweet, and genuine, enjoying this reward, which is not a small one, of his fair day's toils. Since therefore the poor person sleeps, and drinks, and eats with more pleasure than the rich person, what further value is left to riches, now deprived of the one advantage they seemed to have over poverty? HOMILIES CONCERNING THE STATUES 2.23.[15]

TRUE RICHES CONSIST IN VIRTUE AND FAITH. AMBROSE: Wherefore Ecclesiastes says, "There is a grievous illness which I have seen under the sun: riches kept to the hurt of the owner.". . . If you are desirous of treasure, take the invisible and the intangible which is to be found in the heavens on high, not that which is in the deepest veins of the earth. Be poor in spirit and you will be rich, no matter what your worldly goods are.[16] "A man's life does not consist in the abundance of his possessions,"[17] but in his virtue and in his faith. This richness will enrich you if you are rich in your relations to God. CAIN AND ABEL 1.5.21.[18]

5:19 Money and Possessions Are Gifts from God

BUT SO ALSO IS WISDOM. DIDYMUS THE BLIND: This is the literal interpretation. If someone has much money, if he has lots of good food and many wines, he still cannot eat and drink all of it. But he doubtless has a gift: whatever he can consume, if he has enough food to satisfy him and enough drink, this is a gift from God. But when someone eats and drinks more than necessary, then it is not a gift from God but a gift from desire.

Regarding the spiritual interpretation: God gives wisdom along with the riches and capabilities inherent in wisdom, that is, wisdom's insights, so that people eat and drink from the things they have received: the bread of wisdom, its water, the wine, which he mingled into a cup. This is a gift from God. If one takes the spiritual in the right way, it is, finally, the grace of his lot. COMMENTARY ON ECCLESIASTES 164.1.[19]

6:2 Wealth Is Given to Us by God

WE SHOULD WORK FOR WHAT WE CAN TAKE WITH US AFTER DEATH. ATHANASIUS: Let none of us entertain the desire for possessions, for what gain is it to acquire those things which we cannot take with us? Why not rather acquire those that we can take: prudence, justice, temperance, fortitude, understanding, charity, love of

---

[15]NPNF 1 9:352*. [16]See Mt 5:3. [17]Lk 12:15. [18]FC 42:379-80. [19]PTA 13:41.

the poor, faith in Christ, gentleness, hospitality? If we obtain these, we shall find them there before us preparing a welcome for us in the land of the meek. LIFE OF ST. ANTHONY 17.[20]

RICHES BRING TORMENT. AMBROSE: What good is there for a person in this life? He lives in darkness and cannot be satisfied in his desires. And if he is sated with riches, he loses the enjoyment of his rest, because he is forced to guard the possessions he has acquired through his wretched greed. Thus he possesses them in greater wretchedness, seeing that they can do him no good. For what is more wretched than to be tormented with guarding them and derive no advantage from their abundance? DEATH AS A GOOD 2.4.[21]

6:7 All Labor Is for One's Mouth

RELATIONSHIP OF TOIL TO APPETITE. JEROME: Everything that human labor produces in this world is consumed by the mouth, ground by the teeth, and sent to the stomach for digestion. Even when a bite to eat delights the palate, it seems to give pleasure only for as long as it remains in the mouth, for when it passes into the belly, it can no longer be distinguished from other food. The soul of the diner is afterwards not fulfilled, because he will again desire what he has just eaten, since neither the wise nor the foolish is able to live without food, and the poor seeks nothing other than to sustain his frail body and to avoid starvation. Moreover, the soul derives no benefit from the refreshment of the body. Food is common to both the wise and the foolish, and the poor tend to go where they perceive wealth. It is better to understand this teaching as referring to the ecclesiastical person whose labor is in his mouth because he is learned in the heavenly Scriptures but whose soul is not fulfilled because he desires always to learn more. COMMENTARY ON ECCLESIASTES 6.7.[22]

FED BY RICHES. TERTULLIAN: To the corrupting power of riches [the Lord] made the enormity of

voracious appetite antecedent; indeed, the former generates the latter. ON FASTING 6.[23]

THE FATE OF THOSE WHO ARE KNOWLEDGEABLE BUT NOT RIGHTEOUS. GREGORY THE GREAT: The rich man reveals the great burning in his tongue when he says, "Send Lazarus to dip the end of his finger in water and cool my tongue, since I am tormented in this flame."[24] The unbelieving people keep the words of the law in their mouths but refuse to act on them. The burning will be greater in the place where they manifested that they knew what to do, but that they were unwilling to do it. Solomon said concerning those who are knowledgeable but remiss, "All the toil of a man is in his mouth, but his soul will not be filled." Whoever labors only for this, to know what he should say, fasts with an empty heart from the nourishment that should provide him with knowledge. FORTY GOSPEL HOMILIES 40.[25]

TRUE LIFE BEGINS AFTER BODILY DEATH. GREGORY THE GREAT: A person's true life is not found here on earth, for he claims that it is found elsewhere. This, then, is the great advantage humankind has over the animal: The animal does not live on after death, while a person begins to live only when he has completed this visible life through bodily death. DIALOGUE 4.4.[26]

6:10 The Vanity of Names

TWO SORTS OF NAMES, AND THE VANITY OF ASKING QUESTIONS. EVAGRIUS OF PONTUS: There are two sorts of names: some names designate those things which by nature have a body; others designate those which by nature are without a body. The names of those with a body designate the characteristics of such a being, such as its size, color and structure. . . . The names of those without a body reveal a quality of their state of existence, such as their being worthy of

---

[20]FC 15:151**. [21]FC 65:72. [22]CCL 72:298-99. [23]ANF 4:105**. [24]Lk 16:24. [25]CS 123:373. [26]FC 39:195*.

praise or condemnation. But if the first class of names is applied in a straightforward manner, such is not the case with the second class. [With the second class] there are two options: the being has the ability of self-determination of either to incline toward virtue and honor in its knowledge of the Creator, which is the case with angels, archangels, thrones and dominions;[27] or to incline toward evil and increase in its ignorance of the Creator, as is the case with Satan and any other world ruler of the present darkness.[28]. . .

Let us not ask, "Why was I placed in this body? Or why was I not made an angel? Does not God show partiality?[29] Do we not have free will?"

All these questions simply multiply vanity. How can the creature say to its Creator, "Why did you make me like this?" Or, how can a creature answer back to God? Let all those kinds of discussions cease. Instead, let those discussions prevail which guide us towards virtue and knowledge. All that is present in this age of shadows is called vanity and shadows, and all that belongs to this life will be covered with the darkness, becoming obsolete upon departing this life. SCHOLIA ON ECCLESIASTES 52.6.10-12.[30]

---

[27]See Col 1:16. [28]See Eph 6:12. [29]See Rom 2:11. [30]SC 397:150-52.

7:1-29 THE VALUES OF PRACTICAL WISDOM AND RELATIVE GOOD

[1]A good name is better than precious ointment;
  and the day of death, than the day of birth.
[2]It is better to go to the house of mourning
  than to go to the house of feasting;
for this is the end of all men,
  and the living will lay it to heart.
[3]Sorrow is better than laughter,
  for by sadness of countenance the heart is made glad.
[4]The heart of the wise is in the house of mourning;
  but the heart of fools is in the house of mirth.
[5]It is better for a man to hear the rebuke of the wise
  than to hear the song of fools.
[6]For as the crackling of thorns under a pot,
  so is the laughter of the fools,
  this also is vanity.
[7]Surely oppression makes the wise man foolish,
  and a bribe corrupts the mind.
[8]Better is the end of a thing than its beginning;

and the patient in spirit is better than the proud in spirit.
⁹*Be not quick to anger,*

for anger lodges in the bosom of fools.
¹⁰*Say not, "Why were the former days better than these?"*

For it is not from wisdom that you ask this.
¹¹*Wisdom is good with an inheritance,*

an advantage to those who see the sun.
¹²*For the protection of wisdom is like the protection of money;*

and the advantage of knowledge is that wisdom preserves the life of him who has it.
¹³*Consider the work of God;*

who can make straight what he has made crooked?
¹⁴*In the day of prosperity be joyful, and in the day of adversity consider; God has made the one as well as the other, so that man may not find out anything that will be after him.*

¹⁵*In my vain life I have seen everything; there is a righteous man who perishes in his righteousness, and there is a wicked man who prolongs his life in his evil-doing.* ¹⁶*Be not righteous overmuch, and do not make yourself overwise; why should you destroy yourself?** ¹⁷*Be not wicked overmuch, neither be a fool; why should you die before your time?* ¹⁸*It is good that you should take hold of this, and from that withhold not your hand; for he who fears God shall come forth from them all.*

¹⁹*Wisdom gives strength to the wise man more than ten rulers that are in a city.*

²⁰*Surely there is not a righteous man on earth who does good and never sins.*

²¹*Do not give heed to all the things that men say, lest you hear your servant cursing you;* ²²*your heart knows that many times you have yourself cursed others.*

²³*All this I have tested by wisdom; I said, "I will be wise"; but it was far from me.* ²⁴*That which is, is far off, and deep, very deep; who can find it out?* ²⁵*I turned my mind to know and to search out and to seek wisdom and the sum of things, and to know the wickedness of folly and the foolishness which is madness.* ²⁶*And I found more bitter than death† the woman whose heart is snares and nets, and whose hands are fetters; he who pleases God escapes her, but the sinner is taken by her.* ²⁷*Behold, this is what I found, says the Preacher, adding one thing to another to find the sum,* ²⁸*which my mind has sought repeatedly, but I have not found. One man among a thousand I found, but a woman among all these I have not found.* ²⁹*Behold, this alone I found, that God made man upright, but they have sought out many devices.*

---

*LXX *lest you be struck dumb*   †LXX *My heart took circuit to know the joy of the impious man and to examine carefully and to seek wisdom and a mode of calculating and to know joy through the impious man and trouble and disquietude, and I find that it is bitterer than death.*

OVERVIEW: A good name consists in a virtuous life. Just as death is better than birth (DIDYMUS), so death in Christ is better than birth in evil and ignorance (EVAGRIUS). If one wishes to ascend to God, it is better to be sorrowful than to rejoice, to mourn than to feast, to weep than to dance (AMBROSE, CHRYSOSTOM). There is a spiritual blessing that comes from mourning (EVAGRIUS), which is better than feasting. Indeed, sorrow even in the sense of anger is good if its purpose is good (DIDYMUS). Anger is the rejection of wisdom, and arrogance the contrast to patience (GREGORY THE GREAT, JOHN CASSIAN). Flattery, however, is more often deceptive than helpful. Although God's providence is manifest in creation, crookedness is caused by personal moral decision, not by God's misleading, and a distinction must be made between corporate righteousness and that which is personal (DIDYMUS). Total love is reserved for God alone (ORIGEN). Apart from Jesus, there is no one in this world without sin (BEDE, GREGORY THE GREAT, ORIGEN, AUGUSTINE). Wisdom was a great distance even from Solomon, who was the wisest of all (GREGORY OF NAZIANZUS, ATHANASIUS, JOHN CASSIAN). Even for the impious, death would be better than life, because in life their sin increases (AMBROSE, ATHANASIUS). Many human schemes obscure the face that God has created (DIDYMUS). Humanity was created good by the good God; by our own decision we became bad, but God can make us good again (AUGUSTINE, BEDE).

7:1 A Good Name Is Better Than Ointment and Death Better Than Birth

A GOOD NAME IS A VIRTUOUS LIFE. DIDYMUS THE BLIND: The good name consists in a virtuous life. It is acquired with labor, effort and sweat. What, however, is pleasant in the moment oftentimes is gained without labor and one's own effort. . . .

Those who really make progress regarding their inner person and who lead a spotless life, they have a good name. This is better than ointment, better than pleasantness. COMMENTARY ON ECCLESIASTES 196.22.[1]

WHY DEATH IS BETTER THAN BIRTH. DIDYMUS THE BLIND: Whoever does not focus attention on perishable goods and does not think highly of them but knows that "it is better to be with Christ after death" thinks that the day of

death is better than the day of birth. The latter is the beginning of many evils; the former, however, the end and termination of evil. COMMENTARY ON ECCLESIASTES 197.14.[2]

DEATH IN CHRIST IS BETTER THAN BIRTH IN EVIL AND IGNORANCE. EVAGRIUS OF PONTUS: If the death by which the righteous die with Christ[3] is praiseworthy because it separates the soul from evil and ignorance, then such a death is the opposite of the birth that unites the soul with evil and ignorance. Therefore, such a death is much more honorable than such a birth. SCHOLIA ON ECCLESIASTES 54.7.1.[4]

7:2 Better Mourning Than Feasting

SORROW BETTER THAN REJOICING. AMBROSE: If anyone wants to ascend, let him seek not the joys of the world or the pleasant things or the delights but whatever is filled with pain and weeping; for it is better to go into a house of sorrow than into a house of rejoicing. Indeed, Adam would not have come down from paradise unless he had been beguiled by pleasure. FLIGHT FROM THE WORLD 1.3.[5]

THE SPIRITUAL BLESSING THAT COMES FROM MOURNING. EVAGRIUS OF PONTUS: The final end of human beings is a state of blessedness. If the Lord in the Gospel calls those who mourn "blessed"—"Blessed are those who mourn, for they shall be comforted"[6]—then Solomon quite rightly calls mourning the end of every human being, because those who live in that state of mourning are filled with an abundance of spiritual blessings. SCHOLIA ON ECCLESIASTES 55.7.2.[7]

WHY MOURNING IS BETTER THAN FEASTING. DIDYMUS THE BLIND: Where there is mourning, there is no moral superficiality. Happiness and laughter are avoided; the calamity prohibits it.

---

[1]PTA 16:3-5. [2]PTA 16:5. [3]See Rom 6:8. [4]SC 397:154-56. [5]FC 65:282. [6]Mt 5:4. [7]SC 397:156.

Sometimes we refrain from appearing happy out of regard for those who mourn and for those who experience harm. In the house of feasting, however, the opposite happens: Dances and songs bring reproof, since they indicate a disorderly life. . . .

The "house," however, signifies a condition or an attitude, not a location. . . . The one who goes to the house of mourning knows that everyone dies in the end. Once he knows that he has to die, he will not think about and dedicate his effort to owning something, if it is a possession that is lost in death such as wealth, reputation and honor. . . .

One can understand "the living" in the following way: one who lives according to God's will. Those people were Abraham and his descendents. COMMENTARY ON ECCLESIASTES 197.19—198.22.[8]

A HARD SAYING. CHRYSOSTOM: "It is better," we read, "to go into the house of mourning than into the house of laughter." But, likely enough, you do not like the saying and want to evade it. Let us however see what sort of man Adam was in paradise, and what he was afterwards; what sort of man Cain was before, and what he was afterwards. HOMILIES ON THE ACTS OF THE APOSTLES 16.[9]

7:3 Sorrow Better Than Laughter

WEEPING BETTER THAN DANCING. CHRYSOSTOM: Is it better to go where there is weeping, lamentation, and groans, and anguish, and so much sadness, than where there is the dance, the cymbals, and laughter, and luxury, and full eating and drinking? Yes, truly, [Solomon] replies. And tell me why it is so, and for what reason? Because, at the former place, insolence is bred; at the latter, sobriety. And when a person goes to the banquet of one who is more opulent, he will no longer behold his own house with the same pleasure, but he comes back to his wife in a discontented mood. In discontent he partakes of his own table and is peevish toward his own servants, and his own children, and everybody in his house, perceiving his own poverty the more forcibly by the wealth of others. And this is not the only evil. But he also often envies him who has invited him to the feast and returns home having received no benefit at all. But with regard to the house of mourning, nothing of this sort can be said. On the contrary, much spiritual wisdom is to be gained there, as well as sobriety. For when once a person has passed the threshold of a house which contains a corpse and has seen the departed one lying speechless, and the wife tearing her hair, mangling her cheeks, and wounding her arms, he is subdued; his countenance becomes sad. And every one of those who sit down together can say to his neighbor but this: "We are nothing, and our wickedness is inexpressible!" What can be more full of wisdom than these words, when we both acknowledge the insignificance of our nature and accuse our own wickedness and account present things as nothing? Giving utterance, though, in different words, to that very sentiment of Solomon—that sentiment which is so marvelous and pregnant with divine wisdom—"Vanity of vanities, all is vanity." He who enters the house of mourning indeed weeps for the departed, even though he is an enemy. Do you not see how much better that house is than the other? For there, though he is a friend, he envies; but here, though he is an enemy, he weeps. HOMILIES CONCERNING THE STATUES 15.5.[10]

SORROW IS GOOD IF ITS PURPOSE IS GOOD. DIDYMUS THE BLIND: Take the case that someone has subjects, for example, children or slaves. If he is angry[11] with them and in a fury so that he limits the evil, then his anger is good, not anger as such, but the anger of a father over his child, of a guardian's anger over his charge. . . .

He calls that kind of anger good that prevents sins from becoming so big that punishment has to follow. COMMENTARY ON ECCLESIASTES 199.22.[12]

---

[8]PTA 16:7-11. [9]NPNF 1 11:104. [10]NPNF 1 9:440*. [11]Sorrow (Eccles 7:3) being understood as anger. [12]PTA 16:13-15.

7:5-8 Contrasts for the Better

FLATTERY IS MORE OFTEN DECEPTIVE THAN HELPFUL. DIDYMUS THE BLIND: For most people it seems to be right to avoid the critique of a wise man, especially if they like to sin. Whoever desires amusement and sin avoids the person who wants to hinder it. Whoever has no insight is pleased with flatterers, preferring flattery to critique. It is the characteristic of the wise man that he criticizes the one he loves. . . . The flatterers sing in a certain way. Even when they give ethical speeches, they want to make their audience happy instead of looking out for their best interests. Such song is a speech that gives joy, but a rebuke helps one to find the right way. COMMENTARY ON ECCLESIASTES 202.2.[13]

THE LAUGHTER OF FOOLS. DIDYMUS THE BLIND: Thorns that burn under a pot make loud crackling noises. This is like the laughing of the foolish. It makes noise and is crackling, but not because it educates the soul. . . . As the thorns produce noise when they as plants are burned under a pot, in the same way the laughter of the foolish comes out of a bad soul that is burning. . . . Thorns are earthly worries, shameful desires and uncurbed joys. COMMENTARY ON ECCLESIASTES 203.3.[14]

THE IDEAL OF A TEACHER WHO IS PATIENT. DIDYMUS THE BLIND: The end of words is more likely to be good than their beginning. . . . A speech is given in order to actualize something. . . . Oftentimes someone who teaches has with patience led someone who is not highly intelligent to learning. He does not give up after the first or second admonition but tries to heal him in every case. Such a patient teacher is better than an arrogant one, or someone proud in spirit. COMMENTARY ON ECCLESIASTES 204.22.[15]

7:9 Anger in Fools

ANGER THE REJECTION OF WISDOM. GREGORY THE GREAT: When the peace of the mind is lashed with anger, torn and rent, as it were, it is thrown into confusion, so that it is not in harmony with itself and loses the force of the inward likeness. Let us consider, then, how great the sin of anger is, by which, while we part with mildness, the likeness of the image of the Most High is spoiled. By anger, wisdom is cast off, so that we are left wholly in ignorance of what to do and in what order to do it. MORALS ON THE BOOK OF JOB 1.5.78.[16]

PATIENCE CONTRASTED WITH ARROGANCE. GREGORY THE GREAT: When a person does not put up with being disregarded in this world, he tries to display what good points he may have. And so impatience leads him on to arrogance, and being unable to tolerate contempt, he ostentatiously boasts in advertising himself. Wherefore it is written, "Better is the patient man than the presumptuous." Indeed, the patient person suffers any evil rather than that his hidden good qualities become known through the evil of ostentation. On the contrary, the arrogant person prefers that good should be attributed to him even falsely, rather than that he should suffer the slightest evil. PASTORAL CARE 3.9.[17]

THE EFFECTS OF THE DEADLY POISON OF ANGER. JOHN CASSIAN: The deadly poison of anger has to be utterly rooted out from the inmost corners of our soul. For as long as this remains in our hearts and blinds with its hurtful darkness the eye of the soul, we can neither acquire right judgment and discretion nor gain the insight which springs from an honest gaze, or ripeness of counsel. Nor can we be partakers of life, or retentive of righteousness, or even have the capacity for spiritual and true light, "for," says one, "mine eye is disturbed by reason of anger."[18] Nor can we become partakers of wisdom, even

---

[13]PTA 16:19. [14]PTA 16:23-25. [15]PTA 16:27-29. [16]LF 18:303*. [17]ACW 11:108*. [18]Ps 31:9 (30:10 LXX).

though we are considered wise by universal consent, for "anger rests in the bosom of fools." INSTITUTES 8.1.[19]

7:13 The Ways of God's Providence

THE WORKING OF GOD'S PROVIDENCE IS MANIFEST IN HIS CREATION. DIDYMUS THE BLIND: Even among the Greeks there were many opponents to those who claimed that the cosmos came into being by itself. . . . Since providence of necessity is concerned with the details and God is providence, his providence concerns the cosmos that he himself has created. Now admit even something else: God watches over the cosmos that he himself has created out of providence, so that it might go well. . . . God knows the reasons for everything that came into being, and he knows why they are hidden. . . . In no way do you have sufficient knowledge of God's creations, if you take offence at them, because you are not reasonable. Watch God's creatures! What for others is a reason for offence will be for you knowledge of the Creator and of the created. COMMENTARY ON ECCLESIASTES 209.26.[20]

CROOKEDNESS CAUSED BY PERSONAL MORAL DECISION. DIDYMUS THE BLIND: God does not make crooked by causing destruction but by showing that someone is crooked. . . . It is written, "Those who turn to crooked ways, the Lord will lead away together with those who have committed injustice."[21] It is not God himself who leads them away against their will together with those who have committed injustice, but he has shown that those who turn from the way after their own moral decision are such people. COMMENTARY ON ECCLESIASTES 212.12.[22]

7:15 The Mystery of Life

DISTINCTION BETWEEN ABSOLUTE AND INDIVIDUAL RIGHTEOUSNESS. DIDYMUS THE BLIND: There is an absolute righteousness and a righteousness that is only righteous for one. . . .

A righteous person can get lost in what is only righteous for him. Those, however, who are really righteous . . . do not remain in what is righteous for them alone and do not trust in this as their own right. This is why he does not perish in absolute righteousness, as the psalmist says: "In your righteousness I will live."[23] Paul, for example, who was a great man who lived in Christ and for whom truth was revealed, said, "I am not aware of anything against myself, but I am not thereby acquitted."[24] COMMENTARY ON ECCLESIASTES 213.23.[25]

7:16 Do Not Be Overly Righteous or Overly Wise

TOTAL LOVE IS RESERVED FOR GOD ALONE. ORIGEN: Neither those who love too much nor those who hate, abide by the rule of truth. The former lie through love; the latter lie through hatred. It is right to place a bridle even on charity and to permit it freedom to roam only insofar as it does not rush headlong over a cliff. Scripture says, in Ecclesiastes, "Do not be righteous in excess, nor think yourself more than you are, lest perhaps you should be struck dumb." Following this, I can say something similar. Do not love a man "with your whole heart and with your whole soul and with all your strength." Do not love an angel "with your whole heart and with your whole soul and with all your strength." In accord with the Savior's words, keep this command in respect to God alone. For, he says, "You shall love the Lord your God with your whole heart and with your whole soul and with all your strength."[26] HOMILIES ON THE GOSPEL OF LUKE 25.6.[27]

LOCAL POSITION. GREGORY OF NYSSA: No one can say that he has strayed from ignorance into some silly fancy of separating, locally, the supreme from that which is below, and assigning

---

[19]NPNF 2 11:257. [20]PTA 16:43-47. [21]Ps 125:5 (124:5 LXX). [22]PTA 16:51. [23]See Ps 119:40 (118:40 LXX). [24]1 Cor 4:4. [25]PTA 16:55-57. [26]Lk 10:27. [27]FC 94:107*.

to the Father as it were the peak of some hill, while he seats the Son lower down in the hollows. No one is so childish as to conceive of differences in space, when the intellectual and spiritual is under discussion. Local position is a property of the material, but the intellectual and immaterial is confessedly removed from the idea of locality. What, then, is the reason why he says that the Father alone has supreme being? For one can hardly think it is from ignorance that he wanders off into these conceptions, being one who, in the many displays he makes, claims to be wise, even "making himself overwise," as the Holy Scripture forbids us to do. AGAINST EUNOMIUS 1.14.[28]

7:17 Do Not Be Overly Wicked

LET MERCY ABOUND. AMBROSE: One is victorious who hopes for the grace of God, not he who presumes upon his own strength. For why do you not rely upon grace, since you have a merciful Judge in the contest? "For the Lord is merciful and just, and our God shows mercy."[29] Mercy is mentioned twice, but justice once. Justice is in the middle, enclosed by a double wall of mercy. Sins superabound. Therefore let mercy superabound. With the Lord there is an abundance of all powers, for he is the Lord of hosts. Yet there is neither justice without mercy, nor without the exercise of mercy is there justice, for it is written, "Be not overjust." What is above measure, you cannot endure, even if it is good. Preserve measure, that you may receive according to the measure. ON THE DEATH OF THEODOSIUS 25.[30]

MERCY ESSENTIAL TO RIGHTEOUSNESS. AMBROSE: He who endeavors to amend the faults of human weakness ought to bear this very weakness on his own shoulders, let it weigh upon himself, not cast it off. For we read that the Shepherd in the Gospel carried the weary sheep and did not cast it off.[31] And Solomon says, "Be not overmuch righteous," for restraint should temper righteousness. For how shall he offer himself to you for healing whom you despise, who thinks

that he will be an object of contempt, not of compassion, to his physician? CONCERNING REPENTANCE 1.1.2.[32]

DEATH AND RIGHTEOUSNESS. ATHANASIUS: And as God promises to them that serve him truly, "I will fulfill the number of your days,"[33] Abraham dies "full of days," and David called on God, saying, "Take me not away in the midst of my days."[34] And Eliphaz, one of the friends of Job, being assured of this truth, said, "You shall come to your grave. . . like as a shock of corn comes in its season."[35] And Solomon confirming his words, says, "The souls of the unrighteous are taken away untimely."[36] And therefore he exhorts in the book of Ecclesiastes, saying, "Be not overmuch wicked, neither be hard: why should you die before your time?" DEFENSE OF HIS FLIGHT 14.[37]

7:19 Wisdom Is the Strength of the Wise

FEED THE MIND BEFORE THE STOMACH. CAESARIUS OF ARLES: Perhaps a person possesses no bread to extend as an alms to the needy, but still greater is what a person who has a tongue is able to give. It is more important to refresh a mind that will live forever with the food of the word than to satisfy with earthly food the stomach of a body that is going to die. Therefore, brethren, do not take from your neighbors the alms of the word. Paul says, "If we have sown for you spiritual things, is it a great matter if we reap from you carnal things?"[38] "Do good to the just, and you shall find great recompense: and if not of him, assuredly of God."[39] "It is good that you should hold up the just, and from him withdraw not your hand, for he that fears God neglects nothing." SERMON 8.5.[40]

FROM THE WISDOM OF GOD. ORIGEN: The

---

[28]NPNF 2 5:51. [29]Ps 116:5 (114:5 LXX). [30]FC 22:318*. [31]Lk 15:5. [32]NPNF 2 10:329. [33]Ex 23:26. [34]Ps 102:24 (101:24 LXX). [35]Job 5:26. [36]Prov 10:27. [37]NPNF 2 4:260*. [38]1 Cor 9:11. [39]Sir 12:2. [40]FC 31:53-54*.

inhabited world arises in no other way than in the wisdom of God. For "wisdom gives strength to the wise beyond ten rulers who live in the city." "And the one who despises wisdom and instruction is miserable, and his hope empty, and his labors unprofitable, and his works useless,"[41] says the Book of Wisdom ascribed to Solomon. Hence insofar as possible, since the inhabited world is set aright in the wisdom of God,[42] let us ourselves desire that our inhabited world, which perhaps has fallen, be set aright. For this inhabited world has fallen whenever we went to the place of affliction. This inhabited world has fallen whenever "we sinned, did wrong, acted wickedly,"[43] and it has need of being set aright. HOMILIES ON JEREMIAH 8.1.3.[44]

DIVINE WISDOM NECESSARY FOR SALVATION. DIDYMUS THE BLIND: Look for the might of a general in his wisdom rather than in the size of his troops.... If a city has many mighty men but lacks wisdom, these cannot help the city. In a spiritual exegesis the world is called city, that is, the earthly realm around us. No one can live without harm, if he is not given divine wisdom. If wisdom does not help, the mighty ones cannot do anything, whether you mean angels or holy men. If wisdom does not help, the city will not be saved. One can also see the soul of every human being as a city. Even if one had a thousand earthly thoughts that could help a city, it cannot be helped if God's wisdom is not sent down to help and to create and sustain order. COMMENTARY ON ECCLESIASTES 219.8.[45]

7:20 No One Is Without Sin

THE SINS THAT ARE LESS SERIOUS. BEDE: There are less serious sins about which it has been written that "there is not a righteous person on earth who does what is good and does not sin," and, "No living person will be made righteous in your sight."[46] COMMENTARY ON 2 PETER 1.10.[47]

NO ONE IS FREE FROM MORAL FAULTS. BEDE: The Lord himself gives us sure confidence of

obtaining what we properly ask when he adds, "Therefore if you, although you are evil, know how to give good gifts to your children, how much more will your Father from heaven give his good Spirit to those who ask him?"[48] His disciples were good, as far as human judgment can see. He calls them "evil" because there is surely no one in this life who is capable of being free from moral faults, as Solomon states when he says, "There is not a just person on earth, who does good and does not sin." HOMILIES ON THE GOSPELS 2.14.[49]

THE PROPHET HAS SAID. GREGORY THE GREAT: Because the prophet says, "Behold, I was conceived in iniquity, and in sin did my mother bring me forth,"[50] no one coming into the world with sin can be sinless. That is why the same prophet says, "No one living shall be considered righteous in your sight,"[51] and Solomon, "There is no righteous man on earth, who does good, and does not sin." FORTY GOSPEL HOMILIES 39.[52]

BE NOT DELUDED BY DEMONS. ORIGEN: And it is likely also that in countless other things demons delude us and influence us to act according to their will. And it is possible that, just as no one among us is "clean from defilement,"[53] and there is no "just person on the earth who will do good and will not sin," so also there is no one who has always been free of demons and has never fallen victim to their influence. COMMENTARY ON THE GOSPEL OF JOHN 20.328.[54]

ONLY JESUS IS WITHOUT SIN. ORIGEN: If you wish to recall some other of the saints, the word of Scripture replies to you, saying, "There is no one upon the earth who does good and sins not." Therefore only Jesus rightly "has perfect hands"; who alone "does not sin,"[55] that is, who has per-

[41]Wis 3:11. [42]See Jer 10:12. [43]See Dan 9:5. [44]FC 97:75. [45]PTA 16:73. [46]Ps 143:2 (142:2 LXX). [47]CS 82:129. [48]Mt 7:11. [49]CS 111:132*. [50]Ps 51:5 (50:7 LXX). [51]Ps 143:2 (142:2 LXX). [52]CS 123:365*. [53]Job 14:4. [54]FC 89:274. [55]1 Pet 2:22.

fect and whole works of his hands. HOMILIES ON LEVITICUS 12.3.2.[56]

THE IMPOSSIBILITY OF LIVING WITHOUT SIN. AUGUSTINE: The following is one of the many arguments that Pelagius uses in treating this subject: "Once more I repeat: I say that it is possible for a person to be without sin. And what do you say? That it is impossible for a person to be without sin? But I do not say," he adds, "that there is a person without sin, nor do you say that there is not a person without sin. We are disputing about what is possible and impossible, not about what is and is not." Next he notes that a number of the passages of Scripture which are usually invoked against them do not bear upon the question in dispute, namely, whether or not a person can be without sin: "For there is no one who is free from pollution,"[57] and, "There is no one that does not sin,"[58] and, "There is no just person on the earth," and, "There is no one that does good."[59] "These and other similar texts," he says, "apply to nonexistence, not to impossibility. By examples of this kind it is shown how some persons were at a given time, not that they could not have been something else. For this reason they are justly found to be guilty. For if they were as they were because they could not have been otherwise, then they are free from blame." ON NATURE AND GRACE 8.[60]

7:23 Wisdom Is Far Off

WISDOM A GREAT DISTANCE EVEN FROM SOLOMON. GREGORY OF NAZIANZUS: Now the subject of God is harder to come at, in proportion as it is more perfect than any other, and is open to more objections, and the solutions of them are more laborious. For every objection, however small, stops and hinders the course of our argument and cuts off its further advance, just like people who suddenly check with the rein the horses in full gallop and turn them right around by the unexpected shock. Thus Solomon, who was the wisest of all[61] whether before him or in his own time, to whom God gave breadth of heart, and a flood of contemplation, more abundant than the sand, even he, the more he entered into profundities, the more dizzy he became. And he declared the furthest point of wisdom to be the discovery of how very far away wisdom was from him. ON THEOLOGY, THEOLOGICAL ORATION 2(28).21.[62]

7:24 Wisdom Is Far Off and Deep

I WILL BE WISE. ATHANASIUS: Consider therefore how it is written in the book of Ecclesiastes, "I said, I will be wise, but it was far from me. That which is far off, and exceeding deep, who shall find it out?" [Consider] what is said in the Psalms, "The knowledge of you is too wonderful for me; it is high, I cannot attain unto it."[63] And Solomon says, "It is the glory of God to conceal a thing."[64] [Therefore] I frequently designed to stop and to cease writing; believe me, I did. But lest I should be found to disappoint you, or by my silence to lead into impiety those who have made enquiry of you and are given to disputation, I constrained myself to write briefly, what I have now sent to your piety. LETTERS TO MONKS 1.2.[65]

NO WORTHY RESULT. BASIL THE GREAT: Even if all minds, in fact, should combine their researches and all tongues would concur in their utterance, never, as I have said, could anyone achieve a worthy result in this matter. Solomon, the wisest of all, presents this thought clearly to us when he says, "I have said: I will be wise; and it departed farther from me"; not that it really fled but because wisdom appears unattainable particularly to those to whom knowledge has been given in an exceptionally high degree by the grace of God. CONCERNING FAITH.[66]

---

[56]FC 83:222*. [57]Job 14:4 LXX. [58]1 Kings 8:46. [59]Ps 14:3 (13:3 LXX). [60]FC 86:27-28*. [61]1 Kings 3:12. [62]NPNF 2 7:296*. [63]Ps 139:6 (138:6 LXX). [64]Prov 25:2. [65]NPNF 2 4:563*. [66]FC 9:63*.

THE VASTNESS IS IMMEASURABLE. JOHN CASSIAN: As far in it as the breath of the divine Spirit may have brought us, yet the vastness that opens out before our eyes is ever more immeasurable. In the words of Solomon, "It will become much farther from us than it was, and a great depth. Who shall find it out?" Therefore let us beseech the Lord that the fear of him and the love that cannot fail may remain fixed in us, making us wise in all things and keeping us ever unharmed from the devil's missiles. For with these protections it is impossible for anyone to fall into the snares of death. CONFERENCE 8.25.5-6.[67]

INCREASED KNOWLEDGE INCREASES SORROW. GREGORY OF NAZIANZUS: Who is it, who made all things by his Word,[68] and formed man by his Wisdom, and gathered into one things scattered abroad, and mingled dust with spirit, and compounded an animal visible and invisible, temporal and immortal, earthly and heavenly, able to attain to God but not to comprehend him, drawing near and yet far off? "I said, I will be wise," says Solomon, "but she[69] was far from me beyond what is," and, "Verily, he that increases knowledge increases sorrow."[70] For the joy of what we have discovered is no greater than the pain of what escapes us; a pain, I imagine, like that felt by those who are dragged, while yet thirsty, from the water, or are unable to retain what they think they hold, or are suddenly left in the dark by a flash of lightning. IN DEFENSE OF HIS FLIGHT, ORATION 2.75.[71]

GOD'S MAGNIFICENCE. JEROME: What Ecclesiastes is saying is this: Before I turned my thoughts to ponder over God's work, I was not aware of God's magnificence. I said, I must have wisdom; that is, I must inquire into the nature of every cause; and wisdom withdrew farther away from me than it ever was before. By that I mean, formerly I was not in quest of wisdom because I was unaware of it, and afterwards, when I began to seek it, I could not find it. HOMILIES ON THE PSALMS 21 (PSALM 91).[72]

7:26 Snares and Nets More Bitter Than Death

LIFE MORE BITTER THAN DEATH FOR THE IMPIOUS. AMBROSE: "My heart took a circuit to know the joy of the impious man and to examine carefully and to seek wisdom and a mode of calculating and to know joy through the impious man and trouble and disquietude, and I find that it is bitterer than death"—not because death is bitter, but because it is bitter for the impious one. And yet life is bitterer than death. For it is a greater burden to live for sin than to die in sin, because the impious person increases his sin as long as he lives, but if he dies, he ceases to sin. DEATH AS A GOOD 7.28.[73]

THE MADNESS OF THE IMPIOUS IS MORE BITTER THAN DEATH. ATHANASIUS: Although a perfect apprehension of the truth is at present far removed from us by reason of the infirmity of the flesh, yet it is possible, as the Preacher himself has said, to perceive the madness of the impious, and having found it, to say that it is "more bitter than death." Therefore for this reason, as perceiving this and able to find it out, I have written, knowing that to the faithful the detection of impiety is a sufficient information wherein piety consists. For although it is impossible to comprehend what God is, yet it is possible to say what he is not. LETTERS TO MONKS 1.2.[74]

RUIN THROUGH WOMEN. PSEUDO-CLEMENT OF ROME: Be admonished, O man: for, if such men as these have been brought to ruin through women, what is your righteousness, or what are you among the holy, that you consort with women and with maidens day and night, with much silliness, without fear of God? Not thus, my brethren, not thus let us conduct ourselves; but let us be mindful of that word which is spoken concerning a woman: "Her hands lay snares,

---

[67]ACW 57:312. [68]See Ps 33:6 (32:6 LXX). [69]Wisdom. [70]Eccles 1:18. [71]NPNF 2 7:220*. [72]FC 48:168-69. [73]FC 65:92. [74]NPNF 2 4:563*.

and her heart spreads nets; but the just shall escape from her, while the wicked falls into her hands." Therefore let us, who are consecrated, be careful not to live in the same house with females who have taken the vow. For such conduct as this is not becoming nor right for the servants of God. LETTERS ON VIRGINITY 2.10.[75]

FLEE FROM EVIL WOMEN. CYRIL OF ALEXANDRIA: Solomon seems to me very wise in bestowing upon an indecent woman the face of every heresy and then saying about her that it is necessary to repudiate and to flee such a woman, "who is a hunter's snare, and her heart is a net, and in her hands are bonds." The good man before the face of God will be rescued from her and the sinner will be ensnared by her. LETTER 31.3.[76]

THE SIGNIFICANCE OF FEMALE IMAGERY. DIDYMUS THE BLIND: In many passages of divine instruction, thoughts and mindsets are called "women" of those who have them, both in a positive and in a negative sense. So it is said, for example, "Sophia gives birth to a man's insight,"[77] and, "Your wife is like a good vine, your sons like offshoots of olive trees."[78] Out of this woman male offshoots emerge, nourishment for fire and light, since the blessing from these plants gives nourishment for fire and light. In the negative sense again it is said, "Do not pay attention to a bad woman; honey runs from the lips of every prostitute who makes your throat sweet only for a brief time. Later you will find it more bitter than bile."[79] . . . If you want to understand it in an allegorical sense the bad and frivolous thought is a temptation. It is sophistical and heretical; it is like an evil woman. COMMENTARY ON ECCLESIASTES 227.7.[80]

7:29 Upright by Creation, Fallen by Choice

INCITING TO ZEAL FOR GOOD. EZNIK OF KOLB: But because [God] knows that some humans act according to his will and some do not, for that very reason he proclaims the virtue of the one part in order to incite the others to a zeal for the good from the womb. In the same way too, concerning those others, he proclaims their worthlessness. It is not as if he creates one worthless from the womb, and another useful. And if such were the case, why would it be necessary to praise the worthy and to blame the worthless if he himself is the creator of worthiness and worthlessness? Thus one ought not to be held blameable for that worthlessness if he had created him so from the womb.

And now it is clear that God's saying beforehand, "Jacob I have loved and Esau have I hated"[81] means that this one will become beloved by his conduct, and that one hateful. . . . As it also says elsewhere: "God made man upright, and they thought a thought of evil." ON GOD 248.[82]

MADE TO SEE GOD. ATHANASIUS: For [the soul] is made to see God and to be enlightened by him; but of its own accord in God's stead it has sought corruptible things and darkness, as the Spirit says somewhere in writing, "God made man upright, but they have sought out many inventions." Thus it has been then that people from the first discovered and contrived and imagined evil for themselves. But it is now time to say how they came down to the madness of idolatry, that you may know that the invention of idols is wholly due not to good but to evil. But what has its origin in evil can never be pronounced good in any point—being evil altogether. AGAINST THE HEATHEN 7.5-6.[83]

HUMAN BEINGS CANNOT HEAL THEMSELVES. AUGUSTINE: The reason that we, being bad, have a good Father is in order that we may not always remain bad. No bad person can make a good one. If no bad person can make a good one, how can a bad man make himself good? The only one who can make a good person out of a bad one is the one

---

[75]ANF 8:64*. [76]FC 76:123. [77]Prov 10:23 LXX. [78]Ps 128:3 (127:3 LXX). [79]Prov 5:3-4. [80]PTA 16:105-7. [81]Mal 1:2-3; Rom 9:11, 13. [82]EKOG 139*. [83]NPNF 2 4:7*.

who is always good. "Heal me, Lord," he says, "and I shall be healed; save me, and I shall be saved."[84] Why do they say to me, silly people saying silly things, "You can save yourself if you want to"? "Heal me, Lord, and I shall be healed." We were created good by the good God, seeing that "God made man upright." But by our own decision we became bad. We were able to change from good to bad, and we shall be able to change from bad to good. But it is the one who is always good that can change bad to good, because man, by his own will, cannot heal himself. You don't look for a doctor to wound you; but when you have wounded yourself, you look for one to heal you. SERMON 61.2.[85]

WHAT DISPLEASES GOD SHOULD ALSO DISPLEASE US.

AUGUSTINE: Let us be displeased with ourselves when we sin, because sins displease God. And because we are not in fact without sin, let us at least be like God in this respect, that what displeases him displeases us. Now you are displeased with that in yourself which he also hates who made you. He designed and constructed you; but take a look at yourself and eliminate from yourself everything that does not come from his workshop. For God, as it says, "created man upright." SERMON 19.4.[86]

THE WHOLE IS VITIATED IN ITS ROOT.

AUGUSTINE: There is also a good world consisting of people, but made so out of a bad one. The whole world, you see, if you take the world as meaning people, leaving aside world in the sense of heaven and earth and all things that are in them; if you mean people by world, then the whole world was made bad by the one who first sinned. The whole mass is vitiated in its root. God made man good; that is what Scripture says: "God made man upright, and they themselves have sought out many devices." SERMON 96.6.[87]

THE CATHOLIC TEACHING.

AUGUSTINE: The Manichaeans deny that to a good man the beginning of evil came from free will; the Pelagians say that even a bad man has free will sufficiently to perform the good commandment. The Catholic church condemns both, saying to the former, "God made man upright," and saying to the latter, "If the Son shall make you free, you shall be free indeed." AGAINST TWO LETTERS OF THE PELAGIANS 2.2.[88]

SCHEMES AND THOUGHTS THAT OBSCURE GOD'S FACE.

DIDYMUS THE BLIND: God has created human beings straightforward, that is, morally perfect without anything crooked or oblique. But they themselves found many thoughts. . . . They did not devise one thought but many. Evil, thus, is manifold. . . . There is only one single human form that makes a person like God, but there are many into which he can transform himself. If he is cunning, he has the face of a fox; if he shows a poisonous, dangerous face, he has the face of a snake; if he looks wild, he has the face of a lion; if his face is ungovernable, flattering and desiring pleasures, he has the face of a dog. Generally out of one human being and one form emerge a whole plurality of characters and forms. Thus it is the goal to get rid of all forms—even if some people do not share this opinion—in order to show that he has the face that God created. COMMENTARY ON ECCLESIASTES 231.13.[89]

EVIL IS EXTRANEOUS TO OUR CREATION.

BEDE: Our struggle against the vices has not been naturally implanted in us by God our Father and Creator but is proved to have befallen us from our love of this world, which we preferred to our Creator. For God made human beings upright, and they have involved themselves in endless questions, as Solomon bears witness. Hence James also says, "Let no one, when he is tempted, say that he is tempted by God. For God is not the instigator of evil, for he himself tempts no one. Each one, in fact, is tempted, drawn on and lured by his own concupiscence."[90] COMMENTARY ON 1 JOHN 2.16.[91]

---

[84]Jer 17:14. [85]WSA 3 3:142-43. [86]WSA 3 1:380. [87]WSA 3 4:32. [88]NPNF 1 5:392. [89]PTA 16:121-25. [90]Jas 1:13-14. [91]CS 82:174.

8:1-17 WHO IS LIKE THE WISE MAN?

¹Who is like the wise man?
    And who knows the interpretation of a thing?
  A man's wisdom makes his face shine,
    and the hardness of his countenance is changed.
²Keep^m the king's command, and because of your sacred oath be not dismayed; ³go from his presence, do not delay when the matter is unpleasant, for he does whatever he pleases. ⁴For the word of the king is supreme, and who may say to him, "What are you doing?" ⁵He who obeys a command will meet no harm, and the mind of a wise man will know the time and way. ⁶For every matter has its time and way, although man's trouble lies heavy upon him. ⁷For he does not know what is to be, for who can tell him how it will be? ⁸No man has power to retain the spirit, or authority over the day of death; there is no discharge from war, nor will wickedness deliver those who are given to it. ⁹All this I observed while applying my mind to all that is done under the sun, while man lords it over man to his hurt.

¹⁰Then I saw the wicked buried; they used to go in and out of the holy place, and were praised in the city where they had done such things. This also is vanity. ¹¹Because sentence against an evil deed is not executed speedily, the heart of the sons of men is fully set to do evil. ¹²Though a sinner does evil a hundred times and prolongs his life, yet I know that it will be well with those who fear God, because they fear before him; ¹³but it will not be well with the wicked, neither will he prolong his days like a shadow, because he does not fear before God.

¹⁴There is a vanity which takes place on earth, that there are righteous men to whom it happens according to the deeds of the wicked, and there are wicked men to whom it happens according to the deeds of the righteous. I said that this also is vanity. ¹⁵And I commend enjoyment, for man has no good thing under the sun but to eat and drink and enjoy himself, for this will go with him in his toil through the days of life which God gives him under the sun.

¹⁶When I applied my mind to know wisdom, and to see the business that is done on earth, how neither day nor night one's eyes see sleep; ¹⁷then I saw all the work of God, that man cannot find out the work that is done under the sun. However much man may toil in seeking, he will not find it out; even though a wise man claims to know, he cannot find it out.

m Heb inserts an I

OVERVIEW: Wisdom is needed to recognize a wise person, the sort of wisdom that illuminates the face of the inner person (DIDYMUS). It is not wrong to know evil but to do it or associate with it (AMBROSE, DIDYMUS). It is clear that no one can be deceived by the devil except the person who has chosen to offer him the assent of his own will (JOHN CASSIAN). But God will deal with each as each deserves (ORIGEN). Solomon's ultimate purpose in the book of Ecclesiastes is to lead those who are wise to yearn for another kind of life that is the substantial reality of the One who created the sun. This was foreshadowed in the sacrifices of the Old Testament and is now, for Christians, completed in the table of the Eucharistic sacrifice (AUGUSTINE).

8:1 The Shining Face of the Wise Person

WISDOM IS NEEDED TO RECOGNIZE A WISE PERSON. DIDYMUS THE BLIND: As it is impossible to recognize a white thing if one does not know the color white, and as it is impossible to recognize science if one does not know what science is, so it is also impossible to recognize a wise person by someone who does not know wisdom according to which the wise person is formed and called. COMMENTARY ON ECCLESIASTES 233.5.[1]

INWARDLY, NOT BODILY. DIDYMUS THE BLIND: Here he means that the wisdom of a person makes the face shine, but not the face of the body, not a part of the flesh, but the face of the inner person. . . . The face of the inner person is illuminated by wisdom. But wisdom, light, Logos, truth and the other conceptions are identical when applied to Christ. COMMENTARY ON ECCLESIASTES 233.16.[2]

8:5 Nothing Harmful to Those Who Keep the King's Command

ASSOCIATION WITH WICKEDNESS IS CULPABLE. AMBROSE: And you find in another passage, "For he that keeps the commandment does not know the wicked word" when it is altogether clear that knowledge of wickedness is not culpable, but association with it is. THE PRAYER OF JOB AND DAVID 4.7.27.[3]

TO KNOW THE GOOD IS ALSO TO KNOW EVIL AND TO AVOID IT. DIDYMUS THE BLIND: Whoever knows what is good also knows at the same time what is bad. "To know" here does not mean "to do" but simply "to know about something."

Because when the commandment is given to turn away from evil and do good, we must also know evil in order to be able to turn away from it and to choose good. About these things the apostle writes with the following words: "But test everything; hold fast to what is good; abstain from every form of evil."[4] One sees here that whoever tests everything, knows that the good is to be chosen and obeyed and that the evil is to be avoided. . . . Ecclesiastes means that he who obeys the command does not know an evil word, that is, he does not say that he does not "understand" it, but that he does not "use" it. COMMENTARY ON ECCLESIASTES 236.2.[5]

8:8 Neither the Spirit Nor Death Can Be Regulated by Humans

NO HUMAN CONTROL. DIDYMUS THE BLIND: In the direct and literal sense, there is no person who has power over the spirit[6] so as to understand the movement of air, that is, the wind as breath. The human being has no great power as long as he does not have power over the wind. He can do nothing to cause it and nothing to prevent it when it wants to harm him. Sailors have no power to direct the wind in accordance to their direction, and they cannot stop it when it is fierce and dangerous, even if they are excellent sailors. Thus we have to understand it in this sense in the literal meaning. Since, however, the soul of human beings often is called breath, we also can say: There is no one who has the power to cause the soul to remain within him or who has the power to take it from other living beings. This depends on providence. COMMENTARY ON ECCLESIASTES 240.20.[7]

8:11 A Heart Set to Do Evil

THE DEVIL DECEIVES THOSE WHO ASSENT. JOHN CASSIAN: It is clear, then, that no one can

---

[1]PTA 16:127. [2]PTA 16:129. [3]FC 65:411. [4]1 Thess 5:21-22. [5]PTA 16:139. [6]Gk *pneuma*, understood by Didymus as "wind" or "breath." [7]PTA 16:155.

be deceived by the devil except the person who has chosen to offer him the assent of his will. Ecclesiastes has expressed this plainly in these words: "Because those who do evil are not quickly opposed, therefore the heart of the children of men is full within them, so that they may do evil." Hence it is evident that a person transgresses because, when wicked thoughts attack him, he does not at once resist and oppose them. CONFERENCE 7.8.3.[8]

NO EVIL SHALL DISTURB YOU. JOHN CASSIAN: Up until now, when you never gainsaid him either by your own or by anybody else's response, you gave him leave to have the mastery in you, as Solomon says: "Because those who do evil are not quickly opposed, therefore the heart of the children of men is full within them, so that they may do evil." And therefore, after he has been disclosed, this most wicked spirit will no longer be able to disturb you, nor shall the filthy serpent ever again seize a place to make his lair in you, now that by a salutary confession he has been drawn out from the darkness of your heart into the light. CONFERENCE 2.11.4.[9]

GOD DEALS WITH EACH AS EACH DESERVES. ORIGEN: Let them rest assured that punishment shall be inflicted on the wicked, and rewards shall be bestowed upon the righteous, by him who deals with everyone as each deserves, and who will proportion his rewards to the good that each has done, and to the account of himself that he is able to give. And let all know that the good shall be advanced to a higher state, and that the wicked shall be delivered over to sufferings and torments, in punishment of their licentiousness and depravity, their cowardice, timidity, and all their follies. AGAINST CELSUS 8.52.[10]

8:14 Remarkable Vanities

YEARNING FOR ANOTHER KIND OF LIFE. AUGUSTINE: In fact, Solomon gives over the entire book of Ecclesiastes to suggesting, with such fullness as he judged adequate, the emptiness of this life, with the ultimate objective, to be sure, of making us yearn for another kind of life which is no unsubstantial shadow under the sun but substantial reality under the sun's Creator. For a person becomes as insubstantial as the insubstantiality that surrounds him, and it is by God's righteous decree that he, too, must pass away like a shadow. CITY OF GOD 20.3.[11]

GOD ORDAINS IT. GREGORY THE GREAT: So Solomon bears witness, saying, "There are just men to whom many things happen, as though they had done the deeds of the wicked; and there are wicked, who are as secure as though they had the deeds of the just." God no doubt so ordains it of his inestimable mercy, that scourges should torture the just, lest their doings should elate them, and that the unjust should pass this life at least without punishment, because, by their evil doings, they are hastening onward to those torments that are without end. For that the just are sometimes scourged in no way according to their deserving is shown by this very history that we are considering. MORALS ON THE BOOK OF JOB 5.23.44.[12]

8:15 Enjoyment of Food and Drink

SACRIFICE FORESHADOWED IN THE OLD TESTAMENT. AUGUSTINE: Now, to be made a sharer at the table is to begin to have life, as we see from a text in Ecclesiastes: "There is no good for a man except what he shall eat and drink." How can we reasonably interpret these words save as an allusion to partaking at the table which the Mediator of the New Testament, priest according to the order of Melchizedek, provides with his own body and blood? This sacrifice, indeed, has taken the place of all the sacrifices of the Old Testament that foreshadowed it. CITY OF GOD 17.20.[13]

---

[8]ACW 57:254-55. [9]ACW 57:92. [10]ANF 4:659*. [11]FC 24:254*. [12]LF 23:85*. [13]FC 24:76.

9:1-12 DEATH IS INEVITABLE

[1] *But all this I laid to heart, examining it all, how the righteous and the wise and their deeds are in the hand of God; whether it is love or hate man does not know. Everything before them is vanity,[n]* [2] *since one fate comes to all, to the righteous and the wicked, to the good and the evil,[o] to the clean and the unclean, to him who sacrifices and him who does not sacrifice. As is the good man, so is the sinner; and he who swears is as he who shuns an oath.*

[3] *This is an evil in all that is done under the sun, that one fate comes to all; also the hearts of men are full of evil, and madness is in their hearts while they live, and after that they go to the dead.* [4] *But he who is joined with all the living has hope, for a living dog is better than a dead lion.* [5] *For the living know that they will die, but the dead know nothing, and they have no more reward; but the memory of them is lost.* [6] *Their love and their hate and their envy have already perished, and they have no more for ever any share in all that is done under the sun.*

[7] *Go, eat your bread with enjoyment, and drink your wine with a merry heart; for God has already approved what you do.*

[8] *Let your garments be always white; let not oil be lacking on your head.*

[9] *Enjoy life with the wife whom you love, all the days of your vain life which he has given you under the sun, because that is your portion in life and in your toil at which you toil under the sun.* [10] *Whatever your hand finds to do, do it with your might; for there is no work or thought or knowledge or wisdom in Sheol, to which you are going.*

[11] *Again I saw that under the sun the race is not to the swift, nor the battle to the strong, nor bread to the wise, nor riches to the intelligent, nor favor to the men of skill; but time and chance happen to them all.* [12] *For man does not know his time. Like fish which are taken in an evil net, and like birds which are caught in a snare, so the sons of men are snared at an evil time, when it suddenly falls upon them.*

n Syr Compare Gk: Heb *Everything before them is everything*　　**o** Gk Syr Vg: Heb lacks *and the evil*

OVERVIEW: There is a difference between knowing and merely looking (EVAGRIUS). We are like the brutes except that our belief in Christ promises eternity (JEROME). The living may still correct their lives, whereas the dead cannot (GREGORY THE GREAT). The mystical bread and wine, the oil and the white garments, to which Solomon calls us, all have Christian significance (CYRIL OF JERUSALEM, ORIGEN, JEROME). The white garments and oil on the head can also signify a call to pure works and active charity (BEDE), and our anointing follows because of the anointing of Christ (DIDYMUS). Since we do not know the time of our coming death, and we cannot work after death, we must make best use of the times we now have (GREGORY THE GREAT, PACIAN OF BARCELONA), neither exceeding nor diminishing our ability (DIDYMUS). Thus, we should take care not to put things off from day to day (HORSIESI), and this is especially true as we journey through life making choices for which we shall later be examined (BABAI). We must remember that our days are definitely numbered, and any success we do have comes from God (DIDYMUS). Our Lord as God knew his own time, which he had appointed for himself, but as man he hid himself from it until he was ready for it (ATHANASIUS). Spiritual time, moreover, must be contrasted to chronological time, especially when death is concerned (DIDYMUS).

9:1 Considering in the Heart

KNOWING AND MERELY LOOKING. EVAGRIUS OF PONTUS: One acquaints the heart with what one has decided to investigate. The heart in turn longs to know more about these things, which is why it is said, "I turned my heart to know."[1] Those "spheres"[2] are the matters [of inquiry]. The one who directs the heart by meditating on these spheres causes the heart to know them. However, one should note that those spheres that encircle human beings and those that the heart knows are not the same, because we may look into a lot of things, yet only know a very few of them. SCHOLIA ON ECCLESIASTES 68.9.1.[3]

9:2 The Same Fate for All

CHRIST REDEEMS THE COMMON FATE. JEROME: Except that our belief in Christ raises us up to heaven and promises eternity to our souls, the physical conditions of life are the same for us as for the brutes. LETTER 108.27.[4]

9:4 A Living Dog Better Than a Dead Lion

CORRECTING THE PAST. GREGORY THE GREAT: "Better" by far "is a living dog" in this problem "than a dead lion." For a living saint may correct what had not been corrected by another who came before him. LETTER 127.[5]

9:7 Bread and Enjoyment

THE MYSTICAL BREAD AND WINE. CYRIL OF JERUSALEM: For this reason Solomon also, in Ecclesiastes, covertly alluding to this grace, says,

"Come hither, eat your bread with joy," that is, the mystical bread. "Come hither," he calls, a saving, beatific call. "And drink your wine with a merry heart," that is, the mystical wine. "And let oil be poured out upon your head": you see how he hints also of the mystical chrism. "And at all times let your garments be white, because the Lord approves what you do." It is now that the Lord approves what you do, for before you came to the grace your doings were "vanity of vanities." MYSTAGOGICAL LECTURES 4.8.[6]

9:8 Mystical Meanings

WASHED IN BAPTISM. ORIGEN: No one, therefore, can hear the Word of God unless he has first been sanctified, that is, unless he is "holy in body and spirit,"[7] unless he has washed his garments. For a little later he shall go in to the wedding dinner, he shall eat from the flesh of the lamb, he shall drink the cup of salvation. Let no one go in to this dinner with dirty garments. Wisdom also has commanded this elsewhere, saying, "Let your garments be clean at all times." For your garments were washed once when you came to the grace of baptism; you were purified in body; you were cleansed from all filth of flesh and spirit. HOMILIES ON EXODUS 11.7.[8]

WHITE GARMENTS. JEROME: Walk about adorned in white garments, anoint your head, embrace with joy whatever delights your femininity, pursue this vain, brief life with a vain, brief relish, quickly seize whatever it is that pleases you lest it perish, for you will have nothing more beyond this that you currently enjoy. Neither should you fear the frivolous fantasy that an account will be required in the afterlife for each of your deeds, whether good or evil. For there is no wisdom in death, nor any consciousness after the dissolution of this life. COMMENTARY ON ECCLESIASTES 9.8.[9]

---

[1]Eccles 7:25 LXX. [2]Gk *kykloi*. [3]SC 397:172. [4]LCC 5:378. [5]NPNF 2 13:40. [6]FC 64:184. [7]1 Cor 7:34. [8]FC 71:365. [9]CCL 72:325.

DO NOT PROCRASTINATE. HORSIESI: The Holy Spirit actually teaches us not to put things off from day to day but to do to our soul all the good that is possible. [This we do] to adorn it with every virtue worthy of heaven, so as to clothe it with brilliant vestments according to this agreeable voice: "Let your clothes be brilliant at all times; let your head not lack in oil." INSTRUCTIONS 4.1.[10]

AN EXAMPLE OF TROPOLOGY. BEDE: Tropology (that is, a moral manner of speech) has regard to the establishment and correction of manners, pronounced in words that are either plain or figurative; in plain words, as when John admonishes, saying, "My little children, let us love not in word or speech but in deed and in truth,"[11] or in figurative words, as when Solomon said: "Let your garments be always white and let not oil be lacking on your head," which is to say openly, "At all times let your works be pure and let not charity be lacking from your heart." ON THE TABERNACLE 1.[12]

OUR ANOINTING FOLLOWS FROM THE ANOINTING OF CHRIST. DIDYMUS THE BLIND: "You love righteousness and hate wickedness. Therefore God, your God, has anointed you with the oil of gladness beyond your companions."[13] See, even the companions are anointed. But he himself was anointed before them, since he has not been anointed because of them, but they because of him. After all, they are called "Christ's companions," not Christ their companion. COMMENTARY ON ECCLESIASTES 273.13.[14]

9:9 *Live Joyfully*

OUR DAYS ARE DEFINITELY NUMBERED. DIDYMUS THE BLIND: The time of the days has an end and a definite number. The psalmist as well says, "Lord, let me know my end, and what is the measure of my days; let me know how fleeting my life is."[15] . . .

The days of life which are given under the sun are days of vanity. Even if our lives which we live now are good and filled with illumination, they will be replaced with greater joys, about which God says: "I will satisfy him through the length of the days."[16] COMMENTARY ON ECCLESIASTES 277.7.[17]

VAIN LIFE IS EMPTY EXISTENCE. BABAI: You, who travel on the road of virtue, should be mindful of your departure from your parental home and know how to acquire your salvation with due precaution. For your temporal life is dissipated as a result of neglect during "the days of your empty existence," and everything which is done neglectfully by the discerning during their lifetime brings them to be questioned once they have shaken off dust and corruption and woken up from the sleep of mortality. LETTER TO CYRIACUS 3.[18]

9:10 *Fill Your Remaining Time with Good Work*

NEITHER EXCEED NOR DIMINISH YOUR OWN ABILITY. DIDYMUS THE BLIND: May your action be according to your ability! "Do with your might!" Act, according to the might you have received. . . . That might consists in the gifts of grace from the Holy Spirit. The one who has might and still does not increase his spiritual capacity does not use his might. The one, however, who forcefully does more than is right, not out of real desire, but out of ambition or for another reason, commits a sin. . . .

The beginner acts like a novice, the one who has made progress like one who is on his way, the one who has reached perfection like one who is perfect. Thus, one has to act in accordance with one's ability. If you are not weak, do not act in a way that would diminish your ability to assert your will. On the other hand, do not attempt

---

[10]CS 47:141. [11]1 Jn 3:18. [12]CCL 119A:25. [13]Ps 45:7 (44:8 LXX). [14]PTA 24:3-5. [15]Ps 39:4 (38:5 LXX). [16]Ps 91:16 (90:16 LXX). [17]PTA 24:19-21. [18]CS 101:139*.

something which you cannot do! COMMENTARY ON ECCLESIASTES 278.16.[19]

WAGES OF A GOOD WORK. GREGORY THE GREAT: Since the hours and their moments are running away, see to it, dearly beloved, that they are filled with what will earn the wages of a good work. Listen to what Solomon in his wisdom says: "Do vigorously everything your hand can do, because there will be no work or plan or wisdom or knowledge in the lower world, to which you are hurrying." Since we do not know the time of our coming death and we cannot work after death, it remains for us to seize the time granted us before death. So death itself will be defeated when it comes, if we always fear it before it comes. FORTY GOSPEL HOMILIES 20 (13).[20]

NO CONFESSION AFTER DEATH. PACIAN OF BARCELONA: Remember, my brethren, that there is no confession in the grave; nor can penance be granted when the time for repentance is past. Hurry while you are still alive. ON PENITENTS 12.1.[21]

9:11 The Race Is Not to the Swift Nor the Battle to the Strong

ANY SUCCESS WE HAVE COMES FROM GOD. DIDYMUS THE BLIND: Those who believe that human things are guided by providence do not ascribe anything accomplished by humans to their own effort. "Unless the Lord builds the house, those who build it labor in vain. Unless the Lord guards the city, the guard keeps watch in vain."[22] He does not say that no one should build or no one guard the city but that one should remember: if the Lord does not grant success to the effort, both the effort and those who strive for it will be without success. It is up to us to start, but it is up to God to grant success. We start to build the house; God helps and perfects the construction. We guard our own city and are watchful of that decision to guard it, but God preserves it, undestroyed and undefeated by the aggressors.

This is also expressed in Proverbs: "Keep your heart with all vigilance."[23] But even if you yourself keep your heart with all vigilance, say nevertheless to God: "You, Lord, will guard and preserve us." This thought is also affirmed by Paul, when he says, "So it depends not on human will or exertion, but on God who shows mercy."[24] He does not prohibit running towards the goals of our endeavor and to desire them. But he does prohibit belief that they are reached through one's own effort. Many who have had this expectation have been found without success in their efforts.

Question: How should we understand "the swift?"

Answer: You can understand it clearly in the visible world: Some who are runners run fast, but in spite of that they still do not always escape their pursuers. And the slow are often not caught because the pursuers sometimes stumble. Therefore it is up to God, not to the swift, to finish the race. . . . The strong do not necessarily finish a war victoriously. Goliath was strong, and the war nevertheless did not end well for him.[25] He was struck down like someone unarmed, like one who is not a general or someone inexperienced in war. For David the war ended successfully, although he did not trust in many armed forces. Rather, he defeated this mighty giant "in the name of the Lord." Goliath, on the other hand, who was so proud of himself, had no success in war. COMMENTARY ON ECCLESIASTES 282.1.[26]

9:12 People Do Not Know Their Time

SPIRITUAL TIME CONTRASTED WITH CHRONOLOGICAL TIME. DIDYMUS THE BLIND: Many can know chronological time. Everybody, for example, knows that noon is the time for healthy people to eat lunch. The time, however, which is determined by physicians, is not known to everyone but only to the physician. And since there is

---

[19]PTA 24:25-27. [20]CS 123:156. [21]FC 99:85. [22]Ps 127:1 (126:1 LXX). [23]Prov 4:23. [24]Rom 9:16. [25]1 Sam 17:41-51. [26]PTA 24:41-45.

only one physician for the soul, to whom we say, "O Lord, be gracious to me; heal me, for I have sinned against you,"[27] only this physician knows our time. But the individual does not know his time. The inhabitants of Tyre, for example, who would have been ready to repent if the supernatural miracles had occurred among them[28]—they did not know the time. COMMENTARY ON ECCLESIASTES 286.1.[29]

JESUS, AS GOD, DID KNOW HIS OWN TIME.
ATHANASIUS: Now as these things are written in the Scriptures, the case is clear, that the saints know that a certain time is measured to every person, but that no one knows the end of that time is plainly intimated by the words of David, "Declare unto me the shortness of my days."[30] What he did not know, that he desired to be informed of. Accordingly the rich man also, while he thought that he had yet a long time to live, heard the words, "You fool, this night your soul shall be required of you: then whose shall those things be which you have provided?"[31] And the Preacher speaks confidently in the Holy Spirit, and says, "Man also knows not his time." Wherefore the patriarch Isaac said to his son Esau,

"Behold, I am old, and I know not the day of my death."[32] Our Lord, therefore, although as God and the Word of the Father, both knew the time measured out by him to all and was conscious of the time for suffering, which he himself had appointed also to his own body. Yet since he was made man for our sakes, he hid himself when he was sought after before that time came, as we do; when he was persecuted, he fled; and avoiding the designs of his enemies he passed by, and "so went through the midst of them."[33] But when he had brought on that time which he himself had appointed, at which he desired to suffer in the body for all men, he announces it to the Father, saying, "Father, the hour is come; glorify thy Son."[34] And then he no longer hid himself from those who sought him but stood willing to be taken by them; for the Scripture says, he said to them that came unto him, "Whom do you seek?" And when they answered, "Jesus of Nazareth," he said unto them, "I am he whom you seek."[35] DEFENSE OF HIS FLIGHT 15.[36]

---

[27]Ps 41:4 (40:5 LXX). [28]See Mt 11:21. [29]PTA 24:55-57. [30]Ps 102:23 (101:24 LXX). [31]Lk 12:20. [32]Gen 27:2. [33]Lk 4:30. [34]Jn 17:1. [35]Jn 18:4-5. [36]NPNF 2 4:260*.

9:13 — 10:20 WISDOM AS SUPERIOR TO FOLLY

[13]*I have also seen this example of wisdom under the sun, and it seemed great to me.* [14]*There was a little city with few men in it; and a great king came against it and besieged it, building great siegeworks against it.* [15]*But there was found in it a poor wise man, and he by his wisdom delivered the city. Yet no one remembered that poor man.* [16]*But I say that wisdom is better than might, though the poor man's wisdom is despised, and his words are not heeded.*

[17]*The words of the wise heard in quiet are better than the shouting of a ruler among fools.* [18]*Wisdom is better than weapons of war, but one sinner destroys much good.*

10 *Dead flies make the perfumer's ointment give off an evil odor; so a little folly outweighs wisdom and honor.*

²*A wise man's heart inclines him toward the right,*
   but a fool's heart toward the left.
³*Even when the fool walks on the road, he lacks sense,*
   and he says to every one that he is a fool.
⁴*If the anger* of the ruler rises against you,† do not leave your place,*
   for deference will make amends for great offenses.
⁵*There is an evil which I have seen under the sun, as it were an error proceeding from the ruler:*
⁶*folly is set in many high places, and the rich sit in a low place.* ⁷*I have seen slaves on horses, and princes walking on foot like slaves.*
⁸*He who digs a pit‡ will fall into it;*
   and a serpent will bite him who breaks through a wall.
⁹*He who quarries stones is hurt by them;*
   and he who splits logs is endangered by them.
¹⁰*If the iron is blunt, and one does not whet the edge,*
   he must put forth more strength;
   but wisdom helps one to succeed.
¹¹*If the serpent bites before it is charmed,§*
   there is no advantage in a charmer.

¹²*The words of a wise man's mouth win him favor,*
   but the lips of a fool consume him.
¹³*The beginning of the words of his mouth is foolishness,*
   and the end of his talk is wicked madness.
¹⁴*A fool multiplies words,*
   though no man knows what is to be,
   and who can tell him what will be after him?
¹⁵*The toil of a fool wearies him,*
   so that he does not know the way to the city.

¹⁶*Woe to you, O land,# when your king is a child,*
   and your princes feast in the morning!
¹⁷*Happy are you, O land, when your king is the son of free men,*
   and your princes feast at the proper time,
   for strength, and not for drunkenness!
¹⁸*Through sloth the roof sinks in,*
   and through indolence the house leaks.
¹⁹*Bread is made for laughter,*
   and wine gladdens life,
   and money answers everything.

²⁰Even in your thought, do not curse the king,
nor in your bedchamber curse the rich;
for a bird of the air will carry your voice,
or some winged creature tell the matter.

---

*Heb *ruah;* LXX *pneuma;* Vg *spiritus*   †VL *upon your heart*   ‡VL adds *for his neighbor*   §VL *without hissing*   #LXX *city*

OVERVIEW: Neither riches nor poverty can be evil because they both come from the Lord. (CHRYSOSTOM). Just as dead flies spoil an entire pot of sweet ointment, so even one transgressor can infect the entire church (FULGENTIUS, APOSTOLIC CONSTITUTIONS). The dead flies are like foolishness but the sweet ointment is like wisdom (GREGORY THAUMATURGUS). The bite of a silent snake is especially dangerous (JOHN CASSIAN), and its head, which represents the beginning of sin, is pride (AUGUSTINE). The teacher who charms, in fact, should take care to be without guile (DIDYMUS). Our intellect is not brought into submission until our body is subject to it, and our intellect is not subject to God unless our free will is subject to it (ISAAC OF NINEVEH). The princes of the city of the devil are unwilling to await the true happiness of the world to come, whereas the princes of the city of Christ await in patience the blessedness that is sure to be theirs (AUGUSTINE). A house seldom collapses unless the rot has already set in (JOHN CASSIAN, JEROME), but on this side of death repair can be made by way of repentance (JOHN OF DAMASCUS). Secret utterances are always heard (ATHANASIUS), and one should take special care not to curse the king (DIDYMUS).

9:16 *The Poor Person's Wisdom*

NEITHER RICHES NOR POVERTY CAN BE EVIL. CHRYSOSTOM: If riches and poverty are from the Lord, how can either poverty or riches be an evil? Why then were these things said? They were said under the Old Covenant, where there was much account made of wealth, where there was great contempt of poverty, where the one was a curse and the other a blessing. But now it is no longer

so. ON THE EPISTLE TO THE HEBREWS 18.4.[1]

10:1 *Flies in the Ointment*

THE FLIES ARE LIKE FOOLISHNESS BUT THE OINTMENT LIKE WISDOM. GREGORY THAUMATURGUS: Flies falling into perfume, and drowning, make the appearance and use of that pleasant oil unseemly; so, too, it is improper to have both wisdom and foolishness together in one's mind. PARAPHRASE OF ECCLESIASTES 10.1.[2]

PRINCE OF FLIES. AUGUSTINE: Indeed, it is said that Beelzebub means prince of flies; and it has been written of them, "Dying flies spoil the sweetness of the oil." TRACTATES ON THE GOSPEL OF JOHN 1.14.3.[3]

A DIVINIZED FLY INDICATES A WORTHLESS ENTERPRISE. DIDYMUS THE BLIND: These flies bring death as well as life. For example there is a divinized fly about which Elijah has said, "Is there no God in Israel that you are sending to inquire of the fly, the God of Ekron?"[4] I would be astonished if they really did divinize a fly. Rather he hereby has described the worthlessness of their enterprise. COMMENTARY ON ECCLESIASTES 291.3.[5]

FALSE FAITH AND EVIL WAYS. FULGENTIUS OF RUSPE: What is called the prince of flies is shown to be prince of the wicked; another text of Scripture refers to him by saying, "Dead flies destroy the perfumer's sweet ointment." Who destroy except those who grieve the Holy Spirit either by

---

[1]NPNF 1 14:452.   [2]GTPE 249.   [3]FC 78:54.   [4]See 2 Kings 1:6 LXX.
[5]PTA 24:73-75.

the crime of infidelity or by the filthy obscenity of unclean deeds, while befouling themselves either with a false faith or an evil way of life? LETTER 48, TO SCARILA.[6]

ONE TRANSGRESSOR MAKES A DEN OF THIEVES. APOSTOLIC CONSTITUTIONS: "Dead flies spoil the whole pot of sweet ointment," and "when a king hearkens to unrighteous counsel, all the servants under him are wicked."[7] So one scabbed sheep, if not separated from those that are whole, infects the rest with the same distemper; and a person infected with the plague is to be avoided by all; and a mad dog is dangerous to everyone that it touches. If, therefore, we neglect to separate the transgressor from the church of God, we shall make the "Lord's house a den of thieves."[8] CONSTITUTIONS OF THE HOLY APOSTLES 2.3.17.[9]

10:4 Be Constant in Your Place

THE RULER WILL HAVE POWER IF YOU SUBJECT YOURSELF. DIDYMUS THE BLIND: "If the anger of the ruler rises against you"—if he seems to have power over you, it is only because you have subjected yourself to him. For as "sin reigns in the mortal bodies" of those who want to "obey their passions,"[10] and as someone is ruled over if he is ruled by mammon and has focused his thinking on the desire for money, so he [the ruler] has power over the one who subjects himself as slave. COMMENTARY ON ECCLESIASTES 294.2.[11]

THE DEVIL WANTS TO CARRY YOU AWAY. AMBROSE: Do not say of your God, "He is grievous to me,"[12] or of your position, "It is useless to me," for it is written, "Leave not your place." The devil wishes to take it from you, he wishes to carry you away, for he is jealous of your hope and jealous of your task. LETTER 58, TO HIS CLERGY.[13]

GIVE NO PLACE TO THE DEVIL. BASIL THE GREAT: He who sins gives place to the devil, taking no heed of him who said, "Do not give place to the devil,"[14] or to Ecclesiastes, "If the spirit of him that has power ascends upon you, leave not your place." Let us, then, who are in the Lord and who, as much as we are able, observe closely his wonders, so draw joy to our hearts from the contemplation of them. HOMILIES ON THE PSALMS 15.1 (PSALM 32).[15]

BANISH THE DEVIL'S THOUGHTS. CYRIL OF JERUSALEM: You alone are not the source of the trouble, but there is also one who instigates you, the accursed devil. He makes his suggestions to all, but he does not prevail by force over those who do not give way to him. Therefore Ecclesiastes says, "Should the anger of the ruler burst upon you, forsake not your place." If you shut your door, you will be out of his reach and he will not harm you. But if you are so careless as to admit the lustful thought, reflection will cause it to strike roots within you; it will capture your mind and drag you down into an abyss of sins. CATECHETICAL LECTURES 2.3[16]

SURRENDER TO THE DEVIL IS SIN. JEROME: We also read in Ecclesiastes, "If the spirit of him that has power, ascend upon your heart, leave not your place." From this it is clearly evident that we have committed a sin if we surrender our place to him who ascends upon us and if we have not cast down headlong the enemy ascending upon the walls. However, it seems to me that when you call down upon the heads of your brothers, that is to say, upon your slanderers, eternal fires with the devil, you are not so much dashing your brothers to the ground as you are elevating the devil, since he is to be punished in the same fires as Christians. AGAINST RUFINUS 2.7.[17]

10:7 Servants on Horses and Princes Walking

TEMPORAL DIGNITY. GREGORY THE GREAT: By

---

[6]FC 95:467. [7]Prov 29:12. [8]Mt 21:13. [9]ANF 7:403*. [10]See Rom 6:12. [11]PTA 24:79-81. [12]Wis 2:15. [13]FC 26:320*. [14]Eph 4:27. [15]FC 46:228. [16]FC 61:97. [17]FC 53:112-13*.

the name *horse* is understood temporal dignity, as Solomon witnesses, who says, "I have seen servants upon horses, and princes walking as servants upon the earth." For everyone who sins is the servant of sin, and servants are upon horses when sinners are elated with the dignities of the present life. MORALS ON THE BOOK OF JOB 6.31.43.[18]

FROM PAGANISM TO THE GOSPEL. DIDYMUS THE BLIND: Those who have come from paganism to the gospel—those who were slaves of desire, slaves of sin, slaves of the devil and of death—have become riders on horseback. About them it is said that, in the future, they will ride on divine words like on horses. COMMENTARY ON ECCLESIASTES 299.24.[19]

10:8 A Pitfall to Be Avoided

PURPOSEFUL MISINTERPRETATION. ATHANASIUS: The Jews in their imaginings, and in their agreeing to act unjustly against the Lord, forgot that they were bringing wrath upon themselves. Therefore does the Word lament for them saying, "Why do the people exalt themselves, and the nations imagine vain things?"[20] For vain indeed was the imagination of the Jews, meditating death against the Life, and devising unreasonable things against the Word of the Father. For who that looks upon their dispersion, and the desolation of their city, may not aptly say, "Woe unto them, for they have imagined an evil imagination, saying against their own soul, let us bind the righteous man, because he is not pleasing to us."[21] And full well it is so, my brethren; for when they erred concerning the Scriptures, they knew not that "he who digs a pit for his neighbor falls into it; and he who destroys a hedge, a serpent shall bite him." And if they had not turned their faces from the Lord, they would have feared what was written before in the divine Psalms: "The heathen are caught in the pit which they made; in the snare which they hid is their own foot taken. The Lord is known when executing judgments: by the works of his hands is the sinner taken."[22] FESTAL LETTERS 9.5.[23]

SOME MYSTERIES NOT TO BE SOUGHT. AUGUSTINE: Scripture says that there are deep things that must not under any circumstances be looked into, and the one who searches in a hedge will be bitten by a snake. LETTER 12.10.[24]

TO BREAK THE BOUNDARY HARMS THE CATHOLIC FAITH. VINCENT OF LÉRINS: Once they begin not only to use the divine expressions but also to explain them, not only to present them but also to interpret them, then people will realize how bitter, how sharp, how fierce they are. Then will the poisonous breath of their new ideas be exhaled, then will profane novelties appear in the open, then will you see that "the hedge is broken," that the ancient bounds have been passed,[25] that the dogma of the church is lacerated, that the Catholic faith is harmed. COMMONITORIES 25.[26]

10:11 The Bite of a Silent Snake

SNAKE'S VENOM IN A PERSON'S HEART. JOHN CASSIAN: "If a snake bites without hissing," it says, "there is no abundance for the charmer," indicating that the bite of a silent snake is dangerous. This means that if a diabolical suggestion or thought has not been disclosed by confessing it to the charmer (namely, to a spiritual man, who by the songs of Scripture can heal a wound immediately and draw the snake's harmful venom out of a person's heart), he will not be able to help the one who is in danger and about to perish. CONFERENCE 2.6.[27]

IRRITATED BY GIFTS. JOHN CASSIAN: These silent bites are alone in fending off the medicine of the wise people. This deadly menace is so utterly incurable that it is worsened by soothings, inflamed by serious treatment, and irritated by gifts. CONFERENCE 18.16.[28]

THE TEACHER WHO CHARMS SHOULD BE

---

[18]LF 31:456-57. [19]PTA 24:99. [20]Ps 2:1. [21]Is 3:10 LXX; cf. Wis 2:12. [22]Ps 9:15-16. [23]NPNF 2 4:534-35. [24]FC 81:104. [25]Prov 22:28. [26]FC 7:317. [27]ACW 57:93. [28]JCC 200.

WITHOUT GUILE. DIDYMUS THE BLIND: The snake is powerful, when it spreads its poison secretly. In the one who is tricked, an impression is created that he has received something good which in reality is not good. The teacher who charms should not do so in a superflous way but in a way that accomplishes something. Then he shows his [student] the error, the guile of his seducer. COMMENTARY ON ECCLESIASTES 304.20.[29]

10:13 *The Words of a Fool*

SHUN THE BEGINNING OF SIN. AUGUSTINE: The church was admonished to shun the beginning of sin. Which is that beginning of sin, like the head of a serpent? The beginning of all sin is pride. EXPLANATIONS OF THE PSALMS 74.13.[30]

10:15 *The Heavenly City*

THE TOWN IS REALLY HEAVEN NOT A PLACE. DIDYMUS THE BLIND: By "town" he does not mean a place but the deed according to the law. The fool does "not even know the way to town." But the one who says, "Even if we live on earth, our citizenship is in heaven,"[31] "knows the way to the town" in which he is a true citizen. And further: "As we have heard, so we have received in the city of the Lord of hosts, in the city of our God."[32] COMMENTARY ON ECCLESIASTES 308.1.[33]

UNABLE TO GET TO HEAVEN. JOHN CASSIAN: Thus, having turned aside from the royal path, they are unable to get to that metropolis to which our journeying must ever and unswervingly be directed. Ecclesiastes expressed this quite distinctly when he said, "The toil of fools afflicts those who do not know how to go to the city"— namely, to "that heavenly Jerusalem, which is the mother of us all."[34] CONFERENCE 24.6.[35]

10:16 *Spiritual Immaturity*

THE BODY MUST BE SUBJECT TO THE MIND. ISAAC OF NINEVEH: Our intellect is not brought into submission unless our body is subject to it. The kingship of the intellect is the crucifixion of the body. The intellect is not subject to God unless the free will is subject to reason. It is hard to convey anything sublime to one who is still a beginner and an infant in stature. "Woe to you, O city, when thy king is a child!" ASCETICAL HOMILIES 36.[36]

10:17 *Two Cities Have Two Kings*

FAULTS RAMPANT IN YOUTH. AUGUSTINE: The passage from this book which I gladly quote is one touching the two cities and their kings, the devil and Christ: "Woe to you, O land, when your king is a youth, and when the princes eat in the morning. Blessed is the land whose king is the son of freeborn parents and whose princes eat in due season, in strength and not in confusion." Here, the devil is spoken of as a "youth" because of the foolishness, pride, rashness, unruliness, and other faults usually rampant at that age; and Christ is spoken of as the "son of freeborn parents" because he descended in the flesh from those holy patriarchs who were citizens of the free city. The princes of the devil's city "eat in the morning," that is, before the proper time—in the sense that, being overeager to attain perfect happiness at once in the society of this present world, they are unwilling to await the only true happiness which will come in due time in the world to come. But the princes of the city of Christ await in patience the time of a blessedness which is sure to be theirs. The conclusion, "in strength and not in confusion," means that their hope will not cheat them. CITY OF GOD 17.20.[37]

10:18 *The Results of Sloth*

A TINY LEAK BECOMES A STORMY TEMPEST. JOHN CASSIAN: A house never suddenly collapses

---

[29]PTA 24:117-19. [30]NPNF 1 8:346. [31]See Phil 3:20. [32]See Ps 48:8 (47:9 LXX). [33]PTA 24:131. [34]Gal 4:26. [35]ACW 57:845. [36]*AHSIS* 161-62*. [37]FC 24:76-77*.

except because of some old weakness in the foundation or because of extended disregard by its tenants. Thus the structure of the roof is eventually destroyed by what had begun as a tiny leak but into which, through long neglect, a stormy tempest of rain pours like a river, once a large breach has been made. For "by slothfulness a dwelling will be brought low, and through lazy hands a house will leak." Conference 6.17.1[38]

The House Is Our House. Jerome: Our house, which was built to human stature, along with the habitation we shall have in heaven, will collapse if we are lazy and hesitant to do good works. And every floor that depends upon a rafter for support will crush its inhabitant when it falls to the ground. It is when the assistance of our hands and our strength is lacking that all the storm clouds and violent winds from above burst forth upon us. Moreover, because we translated this verse in the singular, it is better to understand it as pertaining to the church, all of whose sublimity will be ruined through the negligence of its leaders. And where the roof is thought to be strong, there will be found the enticements of wickedness. Commentary on Ecclesiastes 10.18.[39]

Sloth Remedied by Repentance. John of Damascus: But as long as we are among the living, while the foundation of our true faith continues unshattered, even if somewhat of the outer roofwork or inner building be disabled, it is allowed to renew by repentance the part rotted by sins. Barlaam and Joseph 11.94.[40]

10:19 Silence in the Bakery

No Chatting or Shouting. Horsiesi: Let each one do his work without chatting or shouting. Let absolutely no one laugh, so that there will not apply to us the reproach of the Scriptures, "They make bread for laughter." If someone needs to ask his neighbor a question, he must do so quietly, without shouting. Regulations 40.[41]

10:20 Things Spoken in Secret

Secret Utterances Are Always Heard. Athanasius: If then those things, which are spoken in secret against you that are kings, are not hidden, is it not incredible that I should have spoken against you in the presence of a king and of so many bystanders? Defense Before Constantius 3.[42]

Neither Curse the King nor Anyone Else. Didymus the Blind: Generally one is advised not to say bad things about others. A curse is nothing else but a wish for something bad. . . .

The word cautions against slander. Do not even have the intention, he says, of slandering someone—let alone actually slandering someone. Look at how great an evil this is: "Do not love speaking ill [of anyone], lest you be cut off."[43] Thus, he says the following: Not even in your thoughts, not even in your consciousness, should you "curse the king." But if one is not supposed to curse anyone, the king should be cursed even less. Commentary on Ecclesiastes 313.13.[44]

---

[38]ACW 57:234. [39]CCL 72:341-42. [40]LCL 34:159*. [41]CS 46:210. [42]NPNF 2 4:239. [43]Prov 20:13 LXX. [44]PTA 24:153-55.

11:1-8 THE VALUE OF DILIGENCE AND GENEROSITY

¹Cast your bread upon the waters,
   for you will find it after many days.
²Give a portion to seven,* or even to
     eight,*
   for you know not what evil may happen
     on earth.
³If the clouds are full of rain,
   they empty themselves on the earth;
and if a tree falls to the south or to the
     north,
   in the place where the tree falls, there it
     will lie.
⁴He who observes the wind will not sow;
   and he who regards the clouds will not
     reap.

⁵As you do not know how the spirit comes to
the bones in the womb[p] of a woman with child,
so you do not know the work of God who
makes everything.
⁶In the morning sow your seed, and at
evening withhold not your hand; for you do not
know which will prosper, this or that, or
whether both alike will be good.
⁷Light is sweet, and it is pleasant for the
eyes to behold the sun.
⁸For if a man lives many years, let him
rejoice in them all; but let him remember that
the days of darkness will be many. All that
comes is vanity.

p Or *As you do not know the way of the wind, or how the bones grow in the womb*   *LXX has *the*, definite article

---

OVERVIEW: The bread upon the waters is the bread of heaven (AMBROSE), and if it is cast freely it will meet us again in due time (GREGORY OF NAZIANZUS). The seventh day symbolizes the mystery of the law, the Old Testament, whereas the eighth symbolizes the resurrection, the day of the Lord (AMBROSE, DIDYMUS, AUGUSTINE). The north wind indicates evil, the south the good (DIDYMUS). Infancy is in need of teaching and instruction, so that youth may escape sin (PETER OF ALEXANDRIA). Always give more than you are asked for, and do not try to discriminate the worthy from the unworthy (ISAAC OF NINEVEH). Never be hesitant to pray at the hours that are stipulated (FRUCTUOSUS).

11:1 Casting Bread on the Waters

THE BREAD OF HEAVEN. AMBROSE: Tears are

aptly called bread there, where a hunger for justice exists. "Blessed are they who hunger and thirst for justice, for they shall be satisfied."[1] And so there are tears which are bread and which strengthen the human heart.[2] The maxim of Ecclesiastes is also appropriate to this discussion, "Cast your bread on the face of the water." For the bread of heaven is there, where the water of grace is; it is right that those from whose belly rivers of living water flow[3] should receive the support of the Word and a nurture of a mystical kind. THE PRAYER OF JOB AND DAVID 4.2.7.[4]

OUR BREAD WILL MEET US IN DUE TIME. GREGORY OF NAZIANZUS: It happens with most people that they give indeed, but they do not do so freely and readily, which is a greater

---

[1]Mt 5:6. [2]See Ps 104:15 (103:15 LXX). [3]Jn 7:38. [4]FC 65:395.

and more perfect thing than the mere act of offering itself. It is far better to be generous to the unworthy for the sake of the worthy than to deprive the worthy out of fear of the unworthy. This seems to have a bearing on our duty of casting bread upon the waters, not that it may be swept away or perish in the eyes of the just examiner, but that it may come to that place where all our goods will be stored up. And [it will] be there to meet us in due time, even though we may think otherwise. ON THE DEATH OF HIS FATHER, ORATION 18.20.[5]

GIVE GENEROUSLY. ISAAC OF NINEVEH: When you give, give generously, with a joyous countenance, and give more than you are asked for, since it is said, "Send forth your morsel of bread toward the face of the poor man, and soon you will find your recompense." Do not separate the rich from the poor or try to discriminate the worthy from the unworthy, but let all persons be equal in your eyes for a good deed. ASCETICAL HOMILIES 4.[6]

11:2 The Number Eight

AN OCTAVE. AMBROSE: The Old Testament took note of this number eight, called by us in Latin an octave, for Ecclesiastes says, "Give a portion to those seven, and also to those eight." The seven of the Old Testament is the eight of the New, since Christ arose and the day of the new salvation has shed light upon all. It is the day of which the prophet says, "This is the day which the Lord has made; let us be glad and rejoice in it."[7] LETTER 50, TO HORONTIANUS.[8]

THE EIGHTH DAY. AMBROSE: The seventh day symbolizes the mystery of the law, the eighth that of the resurrection, as you have in Ecclesiastes. LETTER 84, TO IRENAEUS.[9]

SIGNIFICANCE OF SEVEN AND EIGHT. DIDYMUS THE BLIND: The one who "gives a part to the seven"[10] commits to the Old Testament, which was before the arrival of the Savior. The number

seven indicates the institution of the sabbath. The one who "gives a part to the eight" is the one who believes in the resurrection of the Savior, since he came after the sabbath.

The Jews who "give a part to the seven" have not "given a part to the eight" and therefore they were not saved. The heretics . . . rejected the law and the Old Testament; since they did not "give a part to the seven," they miss the goal. COMMENTARY ON ECCLESIASTES 317.15.[11]

THE LORD'S DAY. AUGUSTINE: Before the Lord's resurrection there was rest for the departed but resurrection for none: "Rising from the dead he dies no more, death has no more dominion over him."[12] But after such resurrection had taken place in the Lord's body, so that the head of the church might foreshadow what the body of the church hopes for at the end, then the Lord's day—that is the eighth, which is also the first—began to be observed. LETTER 55.[13]

SEVEN OR EIGHT HOURS TO PRAY. FRUCTUOSUS OF BRAGA: They need not be hesitant to pray at their own special hours, that is, the second, fourth, fifth, seventh, eighth, tenth, and eleventh, inasmuch as seven or eight are harmonious with the words of Solomon: "Make seven or eight portions." [This is] in order that they may be able to climb through the sevenfold grace of the Spirit and the eight beatitudes on the day of resurrection with unhampered tread up the ladder of Jacob by its fifteen steps to the region of heaven, where Christ is resplendent above. GENERAL RULE FOR MONASTERIES 10.[14]

11:3 Nature Takes Its Course

READING AND UNDERSTANDING. AMBROSE: He who reads much and also understands is filled; he who has been filled sheds water upon

---

[5]FC 22:134*. [6]*AHSIS* 37*. [7]Ps 118:24 (117:24 LXX). [8]FC 26:266. [9]FC 26:470. [10]"Gives a part" in the sense of "divides." [11]PTA 9:11. [12]Rom 6:9. [13]FC 12:279*. [14]FC 63:191.

others. So Scripture says, "If the clouds be full, they will pour out rain upon the earth." LETTER 15, TO CONSTANTIUS.[15]

THE NORTH WIND INDICATES EVIL, THE SOUTH THE GOOD. DIDYMUS THE BLIND: This sentence obviously is meant in a figurative and spiritual sense. . . .

The south is in many ways distinguished from the north geographically, but also in a spiritual sense: The bride in the Song of Songs says, "Awake, O north wind, and come, O south wind!"[16] So she sends the evil power away. The evil power was within her. When the evil was active, that is, the evil regarding faith and vocation, then she had the north wind living within. When she "turned away from evil"[17] and went to the doing of good, she called for the south wind. Pay attention to the occasion: "Blow upon my garden that its fragrance may be wafted abroad,"[18] [she says to the south wind]; the north wind does not do this. She uses the terms in a quite physical sense, since the "cold wind" is called "north wind." The cold wind closes the openings of the trees, the so-called invisible pores, so that the elements of fragrance are kept inside. But when the warm south wind blows through the garden of the soul, . . . then the pores are widened. COMMENTARY ON ECCLESIASTES 321.1.[19]

11:4 Wind and Clouds

TEMPTATIONS AND DISTRACTIONS. GREGORY THE GREAT: For what is expressed by the wind but the temptation of malignant spirits? And what are denoted by the clouds which are moved of the wind but the oppositions of bad people? The clouds, that is to say, are driven by the winds, because bad people are excited by the blasts of unclean spirits. He, then, that observes the wind sows not, and he that regards the clouds reaps not, because whosoever fears the temptation of malignant spirits, whosoever [fears] the persecution of bad people and does not sow the seed of good work now, neither does he then reap

handfuls of holy recompense. PASTORAL CARE 3.15.[20]

WISDOM AS A STUMBLING BLOCK. ISAAC OF NINEVEH: Let not much wisdom become a stumbling block to your soul and a snare before you. But, trusting in God, manfully make a beginning upon the way that is filled with blood, lest always you be found wanting and naked of knowledge of God. For he who is fearful or watches the winds, sows not. ASCETICAL HOMILIES 6.[21]

11:5 God's Work Unknowable

BEYOND HUMAN UNDERSTANDING. GREGORY THE GREAT: Yet his work is not known, because even those who preach him venerate his impenetrable judgments. They therefore both know him whom they preach, and yet do not know his works: because they know by grace him by whom they were made, but cannot comprehend his judgments that are wrought by him above their understanding. MORALS ON THE BOOK OF JOB 5.27.6.[22]

11:6 Morning and Evening

YOUTH AND OLD AGE. [ATTRIBUTED TO] PETER OF ALEXANDRIA: Let us turn now and ponder the word just as the natural philosopher has said, and let us know its power. "Sow your seed," he said, "in the morning hour and do not cease in the evening hour." And I say according to my dull mind, "The morning hour is the young childhood of man, and the evening hour is old age." For infancy is in need of teaching and instruction for everyone so that they escape sin. Likewise moreover, he will continue to remember the sin into which he has fallen in the morning hour, which is his childhood, and he will not set his heart on his own teaching but will be first to the church, the

---

[15]FC 26:78. [16]Song 4:16. [17]Ps 34:14 (33:15 LXX); cf. 1 Pet 3:11. [18]Song 4:16. [19]PTA 9:27-31. [20]NPNF 2 12:39*. [21]AHSIS 61*. [22]LF 23:202*.

school for little and great, and he will listen to the Scriptures inspired by God, that he might not be unmindful or fall but become new again through repentance. The word extends to us, too, we who are called "bishop" and "presbyter" and "teacher," that we might continue to abide in the word of teaching every day from morning until evening every day, just as it is written, "Speak [and] do not be silent."[23] I am speaking with you, he said, personally, so that you will not be ashamed. I will sow in you the Word of God, the seed of truth and life from the morning hour to the evening hour. HOMILIES ON RICHES 1.6-7.[24]

11:8 Shortness of the Present Life

LIVE WITH PRUDENCE. GREGORY THE GREAT: He shows himself to live with prudence and circumspection. Considering the shortness of the present life, he does not look to the furtherance but to the ending of it, so as to understand from the end, that delights, while life is passing,

amount to nothing. For so it is said by Solomon: "But if a man should live many years and rejoice in them all, yet let him remember the time of darkness, and the days that will be many; and when they come, the past will be convinced of vanity." MORALS ON THE BOOK OF JOB 2.9.92.[25]

YOUNG IN THE WORD OF GOD. DIDYMUS THE BLIND: In the spiritual sense [this saying] is even more valid, for "young men" are those who are strong because they have the Word of God and because they have power against evil. John, for example, writes, "I write to you, young people, because you are strong and the Word of God abides in you, and you have overcome the evil one."[26] He certainly does not write to a certain age group in a physical sense but to a soul made young, since it has "clothed [itself] with the new self."[27] COMMENTARY ON ECCLESIASTES 335.5.[28]

---

[23]Cf. Eccles 3:7. [24]TCH 97-98. [25]LF 18:563*. [26]1 Jn 2:14. [27]Eph 4:24. [28]PTA 9:97.

11:9 — 12:8 VITALITY AND OPTIMISM OF YOUTH

[9]Rejoice, O young man, in your youth, and let your heart cheer you in the days of your youth; walk in the ways of your heart and the sight of your eyes. But know that for all these things God will bring you into judgment.

[10]Remove vexation from your mind,* and put away pain from your body; for youth and the dawn of life are vanity.

12 Remember also your Creator in the days of your youth, before the evil days come, and the years draw nigh, when you will say, "I have no pleasure in them"; [2]before the sun and the light and the moon and the stars are darkened and the clouds return after the rain; [3]in the day when the keepers of the house tremble, and the strong men are bent, and the grinders cease because they are few, and those that look through the windows are dimmed, [4]and the doors on the street are shut; when the sound of the grinding is low, and one rises up at the voice of a bird, and *all the daughters of song are brought low; ⁵they are afraid also of what is high, and terrors are in the way; the almond tree blossoms, the grasshopper drags itself along^q and desire fails; because man goes to his eternal home, and the mourners go about the streets; ⁶before the silver cord is snapped,^r or the golden bowl is broken, or the pitcher is broken at the fountain, or the wheel broken at the cistern, ⁷and the dust returns to the earth as it was, and the spirit returns to God who gave it. ⁸Vanity of vanities, says the Preacher; all is vanity.*

q Or *is a burden*   r Syr Vg Compare Gk: Heb *is removed*   *LXX *heart* (kardia)

OVERVIEW: Youth should rejoice now, before the end of the world comes (GREGORY THE GREAT, CYRIL OF JERUSALEM). Train yourselves, therefore, to be not idle (EPHREM THE SYRIAN), and let not anger become a permanent condition of the heart. At the last, when false teaching ceases and the almond blooms (DIDYMUS), there will be a division of the good and the bad, and a mighty blow will strike everything (GREGORY THAUMATURGUS). Then the broken pitcher will be replaced by living water, and the water wheel at the cistern will no longer be needed (DIDYMUS). This is the meaning of the silver cord and the golden bowl (JEROME, DIDYMUS). The wheel of our life is like a ceaseless advance by which we are continuously moved from the day of our birth right up to death as if by the ever-turning wheel of a carriage (BEDE). At the end, our dust, or flesh, goes to earth and our spirit, or soul, to God, but it would be misleading to conclude from the common properties of our bodies that there is no individuality to our souls (AUGUSTINE, JOHN CASSIAN). Since we possess the body from the earth and the spirit from heaven, it is proper to pray that God's will may be done in both (CYPRIAN). There is, after all, only one salvation (GREGORY THAUMATURGUS). Things which humans create are vain because, ultimately, they have no useful end, as Solomon realized; therefore we should seek truth and love God, in whom there is no vanity (CHRYSOSTOM).

11:9 Rejoice Now, for Judgment Will Come

A TRUE JUDGMENT. GREGORY THE GREAT: One statement is introduced [by Solomon] through his impersonation of the weak, while the other is added from the dictates of reason, for he immediately discusses the dictates of reason and shows the advantage of a house of mourning. "For that is the end of every man," he says, "and the living should take it to heart."[1] And again he writes, "Rejoice, O young man, while you are young." While a little later he adds, "The dawn of youth is fleeting." In criticizing what he has just recommended, he indicates clearly that the former pronouncement proceeded from carnal desires, while the latter was based on a true judgment. DIALOGUE 4.4.[2]

11:10 Remove Sorrow and Evil

SHAMEFUL BOLDNESS. AUGUSTINE: Therefore, if anger has held out with most shameful boldness in the heart of any one of you until these holy days, now at least let it depart. [Thus] your prayer may proceed in peace and . . . may not stumble, tremble, or become mute under the pricking of conscience when it has come to that passage where it must say, "Forgive us our debts, as we forgive also our debtors."[3] SERMON 208.2.[4]

PUT SORROW AWAY. EPHREM THE SYRIAN: Put sorrow far from your flesh and sadness from your thoughts, except only that for your sins you should be constant in sadness. Cease not

---

[1]Eccles 7:2. [2]FC 39:194. [3]Mt 6:12. [4]FC 38:94.

from labor, not even though you are rich, for the slothful person gains manifold guilt by his idleness. HOMILY ON ADMONITION AND REPENTANCE 15.[5]

ANGER MUST NOT BECOME A PERMANENT CONDITION OF THE HEART. DIDYMUS THE BLIND: In Scripture the spirit is continuously called "heart."

The passage therefore means: Even if we sometimes are caught up in anger, this "anger" should not be allowed into the "heart," so that the anger does not become a permanent condition. And when suddenly a desire comes up in the part of the soul which deals with desire, this desire should not be transferred to the spirit and to the part of the soul that deals with reason. Otherwise it becomes a permanent condition and not just an affect or a precondition for this affect, but simply evil. . . . If "anger is banished from your heart," you will not do evil through the members of your body. Whoever is caught by anger often fights and may even decide to kill. Thus, if you "banish anger from your heart," then evil, which comes about through deeds, will vanish as well. COMMENTARY ON ECCLESIASTES 337.20.[6]

12:1 Remember Now Your Creator

PLEASURE AWAITS THOSE WHO HAVE ACTED IN ACCORDANCE WITH GOD'S PROMISES. DIDYMUS THE BLIND: When the punishing evil comes, the years arrive in which you have no pleasure. Nobody has pleasure in being punished. When the years of promise arrive, the good have pleasure in them. They have pleasure in enjoying the promises, since they have acted exactly in accordance with the promises. In a similar way, those who are prone to amusement and only recognize what can be experienced with the senses have not pleasure in the time of hunger, but only in the time of excess. The righteous have pleasure even in the times of retribution. COMMENTARY ON ECCLESIASTES 340.9.[7]

THE PASSING OF WINTER. CYRIL OF JERUSALEM: Ecclesiastes knew of the Lord's coming at the end of the world when he said, "Rejoice, O young man, while you are young." Subsequently [he said], "Ward off grief from your heart, and put away trouble from your presence. Remember your Creator, before the evil days come, before the sun is darkened, and the light, and the moon, and the stars; and they who look through the windows go blind" (this signifies the power of sight). [Remember] "before the silver cord is snapped" (he means the cluster of the stars, silvery in appearance). [Remember before] "the golden fillet shrinks back" (here is indicated the sun with its golden aspect, for the fillet-like flower is a well-known plant, with ray-like shoots of foliage circling it), "and they shall rise up at the voice of the sparrow, and they shall see from the height, and terrors shall be in the way." What shall they see? "Then they will see the Son of man coming upon clouds of heaven,"[8] and they will mourn, tribe by tribe. What happens when the Lord comes? "The almond tree will bloom, and the locust will grow sluggish, and the caper berry will be scattered abroad." According to the interpreters the blooming of the almond tree signifies the passing of winter; our bodies, after the winter, then, are to flourish with a heavenly bloom. CATECHETICAL LECTURES 15.20.[9]

THE WHEEL OF LIFE. BEDE: "The wheel of our life": The ceaseless advance of our earthly life by which we are continuously moved from the day of our birth right up to death as if by the always turning wheel of a carriage. [Thus] Solomon, when he said well, "Remember your Creator in the days of your youth before the time of affliction comes," a little further on added, "And the wheel above the cistern is broken, and the dust returns to the earth it came from." COMMENTARY ON JAMES 3.6.[10]

---

[5]NPNF 2 13:334*. [6]PTA 9:109-11. [7]PTA 9:125. [8]Mt 24:30. [9]FC 64:66. [10]CS 82:40.

12:4 *The Bird and the Daughters*

SYMBOL OF TRUTH AND THE SAVIOR. DIDY-MUS THE BLIND: "Bird" can here mean the Savior in his human nature. . . .

But also the message of truth itself can be called "bird" for this time. It can be compared for this time with a bird that comes from on high, from where truth came to the listeners. Since, however, now even the perfect listeners are lifted up and strive for what is above the earth, the "bird on the roof" calls to them. Standing above the cosmos it has announced the perfect, the encounter with truth "from face to face." COM-MENTARY ON ECCLESIASTES 352.12.[11]

THE DAUGHTERS ARE FALSE TEACHERS. DIDYMUS THE BLIND: "The daughters of song" are false teachers, the daughters only of the voice but not of the spirit, not of wisdom, not of knowledge, not of light. Because of their unmanliness and their feminization in the treatment of the perishable they are called daughters.

They will be brought low. Like darkness ends when light appears, they will be unveiled as nothing when the "call of the bird," that is, of the "market" or the Savior or the divine teacher, the "rising" [human being], is here. It turns out that the teaching [of the daughters of song] is valid only for this present life and that—to say briefly what has been treated extensively by people elsewhere—human wisdom, which promises a program of nice speeches and good rhetoric, lasts only as long as the voice. Since, however, this voice will vanish, because no air is moving any more when they rise above the sphere of the air, they will be brought low. The "daughters of song" will be seen as nothing, since the wise teachers are not called daughters or daughters of song, but "sons of light," and "sons of wisdom." COMMEN-TARY ON ECCLESIASTES 353.26.[12]

12:5 *The Last Things*

THERE WILL BE A DIVISION. GREGORY THAU-

MATURGUS: Cities and their bloodstained leaders will wait for punishment from above. A most bitter and bloody time will arise like a blossoming almond tree, continuous punishments will be imposed like a swarm of flying locusts, and lawbreakers will be thrown out of the way like a black and contemptible caper plant. The good person will enter into his eternal home with rejoicing, but the bad people will fill all their homes with mourning. PARAPHRASE OF ECCLESI-ASTES 12.5.[13]

THE MEANING OF THE ALMOND TREE. DIDY-MUS THE BLIND: Those who have dealt with the world of plants say the following about the almond: Among all the plants it grows leaves in springtime and sheds them not before all the other trees have gotten bare; it is very durable.

This is why it is said about the "priestly rod"[14] that it was of almond wood. It did not last a short time; from Moses until the coming of the Savior it was a visible sign. . . .

This is what we think: Even if there are plants from other teachings, they bloom later, that is, after the true teaching, and cease before it; they vanish when it appears. This rod, there-fore, has extinguished the other rods, those of the false apostles, and of the false prophets. . . .

The sentence "the almond blooms" can be understood in a moral sense. The almond has two layers around the edible kernel: something hard that has to be cracked and something bitter, that is, the outer shell. The outer shell can be seen as the body, since it is bitter, tending to the sensual. The hard part, however, is the soul, since it is strong and big. The edible in the kernel is the spirit. When the sentence of the apostle comes to fruition—"May the God of peace sanctify you, perfect your spirit, your soul, and your body"[15]—then the almond blooms. In its blooming it envel-ops all the three.

The human being blooms, when it progresses

---

[11]PTA 9:187. [12]PTA 9:193-95. [13]GTPE 294. [14]Num 17:8.
[15]1 Thess 5:23.

in virtue, when it transforms its body so that it imitates the body of Christ. COMMENTARY ON ECCLESIASTES 356.10.[16]

12:6 Signs of the End

A MIGHTY BLOW WILL STRIKE EVERYTHING.
GREGORY THAUMATURGUS: Neither stored silver nor tested gold will be of any further use. A mighty blow will strike everything, right down to a water pot standing next to a well, and to a carriage wheel which happens to have been left in the ditch, its time of revolving ceased, and to the life that, by water, has passed through the age of washing. PARAPHRASE OF ECCLESIASTES 12.6.[17]

MEANINGS OF SILVER AND GOLD. DIDYMUS
THE BLIND: By "gold" in Scripture one has to understand the spirit; but if one understands by "silver" the spoken word, we have to understand here by "gold" the thought and by bowl the sphere of reason, since it is the bowl and storage place for gold. When Scripture describes the spoken word and the written word as silver, this means a weaving of the words that fit to each other and a linking of the meaning of the different words among each other. COMMENTARY ON ECCLESIASTES 360.14.[18]

THE SILVER CORD AND THE GOLDEN BOWL.
JEROME: The silver cord indicates a pure life and the inspiration that is given to us from heaven. The return again of the golden band[19] signifies the soul that returns to the place from which it descended. Moreover, there are two remaining [figures] which follow. The shattered pitcher at the spring and the broken wheel at the well, through the use of metaphor, are allegories for death. For if a pitcher is worn through it ceases to draw water, and when a wheel at the well is broken the water it would have drawn is left to become putrid. COMMENTARY ON ECCLESIASTES 12.6[20]

THE PITCHER AT THE FOUNTAIN. DIDYMUS

THE BLIND: Some are able to drink from the fountain without the pitcher. Rebecca, which means steadfastness in the good, stepped down to the fountain and scooped the water with the pitcher in order to give the thirsty servant [of Abraham] to drink; but she herself drank from the fountain without the pitcher. . . .

The imperfect knowledge and the imperfect prophecy[21] are the pitcher filled from the fountain. When the imperfect will pass away,[22] the pitcher is broken. Its content, however, is not lost. . . . When one does not need to drink from the pitcher anymore because the Savior has given to drink and prepared in the person who drinks a spring of living water, then the pitcher is not needed for the person who has the fountain of living water[23] inside. COMMENTARY ON ECCLESIASTES 361.9.[24]

THE WATER WHEEL AT THE CISTERN. DIDYMUS THE BLIND: One can understand the "cistern" accordingly: Inasmuch as it is possible to scoop water from a fountain with a pitcher, it is also possible to pull up water from a cistern with a water wheel. When there is no need any more to pull up water in this way, then the "[water] wheel will break at the cistern." COMMENTARY ON ECCLESIASTES 362.13.[25]

12:7 Dust to Earth and Spirit to God

THE SOUL GOES TO HEAVEN. ANONYMOUS: Do not therefore be afraid of death: for that which is from me—that is to say, the soul—goes to heaven; and that which is from the earth—that is to say, the body—goes to the earth, from which it was taken. REVELATION OF ESDRAS.[26]

WE OURSELVES ARE BODY AND SPIRIT. CYPRIAN: We ask that the will of God may be done

---

[16]PTA 9:205-9, 15. [17]GTPE 296. [18]PTA 9:229. [19]Latin *vitta*, a band worn around the head as a symbol of sacred office. [20]CCL 72:356-57. [21]1 Cor 13:9. [22]1 Cor 13:10. [23]Jn 4:14. [24]PTA 9:235-39. [25]PTA 9:243. [26]ANF 8:574.

both in heaven and in earth, each of which things pertains to the fulfillment of our safety and salvation. For since we possess the body from the earth and the spirit from heaven, we ourselves are earth and heaven; and in both—that is, both in body and spirit—we pray that God's will may be done. THE LORD'S PRAYER 4.16.[27]

THERE IS ONLY ONE SALVATION. GREGORY THAUMATURGUS: For people lying on earth there is one salvation, if their souls acknowledge and fly up to the One by whom they were brought into being. PARAPHRASE OF ECCLESIASTES 12.7.[28]

BODY AND SOUL. AUGUSTINE: Near the end of the book called Ecclesiastes there is a passage about the dissolution of man, brought about by that death through which the soul is separated from the body, where the Scripture says, "And let the dust return into its earth, as it was, and the spirit return to God who gave it." This authoritative statement is unquestionably true and leads no one into error. But if anyone wished to interpret it so as to try to defend the view that there was a posterity of souls and that all the subsequent ones come from that one which God gave to the first man, this passage seems to support him. [This is so] because flesh is there spoken of as dust—obviously, dust and spirit mean nothing else in this passage than flesh and soul—and in that way it declares that the soul returns to God, as if it might be a sort of branch, cut from that soul which God gave to the first man, just as the flesh is returned to the earth, since it is an offshoot of that flesh that in the first man was fashioned of the earth. Thus, he might contend from this that we ought to believe something that is not known about the soul, but is perfectly well known about the body. There is no doubt about the propagation of the flesh, but there is about the soul. LETTER 143.[29]

ORIGIN AND DESTINY OF FLESH AND SPIRIT. JOHN CASSIAN: "Before the dust returns to the earth as it was, and the spirit returns to God,

who gave it." What could be said more clearly than his having declared the stuff of the flesh, which he has called dust because it originated from the seed of man and seems to be sown by his doing, will return to the earth once more just as it was taken from the earth? Whereas he has indicated that the spirit, which is not begotten from the mingling of the sexes but is bestowed particularly by God alone, will return to its Creator? This is clearly expressed, too, by that inbreathing of God by which Adam was first ensouled.[30] CONFERENCE 8.25.3.[31]

12:8 Therefore All Is Vanity

VANITY HAS NO USEFUL END. CHRYSOSTOM: Such is "vanity of vanities," your splendid buildings, your vast and overflowing riches, the herds of your slaves that bustle along the public square, your pomp and vainglory, your high thoughts, your ostentation. For all these are vain; they came not from the hand of God but are of our own creating. But why then are they vain? Because they have no useful end. HOMILIES ON EPHESIANS 12.[32]

SOLOMON KNEW VANITY AND ITS CONSEQUENCES. CHRYSOSTOM: Hear what Solomon says, who knew the present world by actual experience. "I built houses, I planted vineyards, I made gardens, and orchards and pools of water. I gathered also silver and gold. I got men singers and women singers, and flocks and herds."[33] There was no one who lived in greater luxury or higher glory. There was no one so wise or so powerful, no one who saw all things so succeeding to his heart's desire. What then? He had no enjoyment from all these things. What after all does he say of it himself? "Vanity of vanities, all is vanity." Vanity not simply but superlatively. Let us believe him and lay hold on that in which there is no vanity, in which there is truth and what is based

[27]ANF 5:451. [28]GTPE 298. [29]FC 20:156. [30]Gen 2:7. [31]ACW 57:311. [32]NPNF 1 13:109. [33]Eccles 2:4-6, 8.

upon a solid rock, where there is no old age or decline, but all things bloom and flourish, without decay or waxing old, or approaching dissolution. Let us, I beseech you, love God with genuine affection, not from fear of hell but from desire of the kingdom. For what is comparable to seeing Christ? HOMILIES ON 1 TIMOTHY 15.[34]

---

[34]NPNF 1 13:462*.

12:9-14 THE WHOLE DUTY OF HUMANKIND

[9]*Besides being wise, the Preacher also taught the people knowledge, weighing and studying and arranging proverbs with great care.* [10]*The Preacher sought to find pleasing words, and uprightly he wrote words of truth.*

[11]*The sayings of the wise are like goads, and like nails firmly fixed are the collected sayings which are given by one Shepherd.* [12]*My son, beware of anything beyond these. Of making many books there is no end, and much study is a weariness of the flesh.*

[13]*The end of the matter; all has been heard. Fear God, and keep his commandments; for this is the whole duty* of man.*[s] [14]*For God will bring every deed into judgment, with[t] every secret thing, whether good or evil.*

s Or *the duty of all men*   t Or *into the judgment on*   *LXX omits *duty*

OVERVIEW: The words of wisdom are useful to preachers in sermons, and even reproach is sometimes appropriate (AMBROSE, GREGORY THE GREAT, ORIGEN). Nonetheless, the writing of too many books and the fashioning of too many words is a danger that threatens those given to the pursuit of divinity (ORIGEN). Knowledge will pass away, but the whole duty of humanity is to fear God and keep his commandments (SHEPHERD OF HERMAS, CHRYSOSTOM, JEROME, BEDE). The function of Solomon as the Preacher is to bring into harmony the diverse opinions of many and to call them back to a unified way of thinking (GREGORY THE GREAT). Every work will be judged, but God's Word is not a work (APOSTOLIC CONSTITUTIONS, ATHANASIUS).

12:11 The Words of the Wise

SERMON ADVICE. AMBROSE: Therefore let your sermons be flowing, let them be clear and lucid so that by suitable disputation you may pour sweetness into the ears of the people and by the grace of your words may persuade the crowd to follow willingly where you lead. But if in the people, or in some persons, there is any stubbornness or any fault, let your sermons be such as to goad the listener, to sting the person with a guilty conscience. "The words of the wise are as goads." Even the Lord Jesus goaded Saul when he was a persecutor. Consider how salutary was the goad that made of a persecutor an apostle, saying, "It is hard for you to kick against the goad."[1] LETTER 15, TO CONSTANTIUS.[2]

---

[1]Acts 9:5 in some manuscripts. See the KJV. [2]FC 26:78.

REPROACH SOMETIMES APPROPRIATE. GREGORY THE GREAT: Holy preachers are also accustomed to reprove their hearers with sharp words and to rage with strict severity against their sins. As it is written, "The words of the wise are goads, and as nails fastened deep." But their words are properly called nails, since they do not know how to handle the sins of offenders gently, but only how to pierce them. Were not the words of John nails when he said, "O generation of vipers, who has shown you to flee from the wrath to come?"[3] Were not the words of Stephen nails when he said, "You have always resisted the Holy Spirit"?[4] Were not the words of Paul nails when he said, "O senseless Galatians, who has bewitched you?"[5] and again when saying to the Corinthians, "For while there is among you envying and strife, are you not carnal, and do you not walk according to man?"[6] MORALS ON THE BOOK OF JOB 5.24.41.[7]

REPROACH MAY APPEAR DISCORDANT. ORIGEN: All the Scriptures are "words of the wise like goads, and as nails firmly fixed which were given by agreement from one shepherd," and there is nothing superfluous in them. But the Word is the one Shepherd of things rational which may have an appearance of discord to those who have not ears to hear but are truly at perfect concord. COMMENTARY ON MATTHEW 2.[8]

HARMONY OF THE OLD AND NEW COVENANTS. ORIGEN: And likewise it is a pleasant thing to endeavor to understand and exhibit the fact of the concord of the two covenants—of the one before the bodily advent of the Savior and of the new covenant. For among those things in which the two covenants are at concord so that there is no discord between them would be found prayers, to the effect that about anything whatever they shall ask it shall be done to them from the Father in heaven. And if also you desire the third that unites the two, do not hesitate to say that it is the Holy Spirit. For "the words of the wise," whether they be those before the advent, or at the time of the advent, or after it, "are as goads,

and as nails firmly fixed, which were given by agreement from one shepherd." COMMENTARY ON MATTHEW 14.4.[9]

12:12 Of the Making of Many Books

AVOID WRITING MANY BOOKS. ORIGEN: I, for my part, am inclined to shrink from toil and to avoid that danger which threatens from God those who give themselves to writing on divinity; thus I would take shelter in Scripture in refraining from making many books. For Solomon says in Ecclesiastes, "My son, beware of making many books; there is no end of it, and much study is a weariness of the flesh." For we, except that text have some hidden meaning which we do not yet perceive, have directly transgressed the injunction; we have not guarded ourselves against making many books. COMMENTARY ON THE GOSPEL OF JOHN 5, PREFACE.[10]

AVOID TOO MANY WORDS. ORIGEN: First of all, we set forth the command from Ecclesiastes: "My son, beware of making many books." I juxtapose for comparison with this the saying from the Proverbs of the same Solomon, who says, "In a multitude of words you will not escape sins, but you will be wise if you restrain your lips."[11] And I inquire, therefore, if speaking many words, regardless of what they are, is being loquacious, even if the many words are holy and pertain to salvation? For if this is the way things are, and if he who expounds many beneficial things is loquacious, Solomon himself has not escaped the sin. COMMENTARY ON THE GOSPEL OF JOHN 5.4.[12]

12:13 Fear God and Keep His Commandments

THE FEAR ONE MUST HAVE. SHEPHERD OF HERMAS: "Fear the Lord and keep his commandments," he said. So, by keeping God's command-

---

[3]Mt 3:7. [4]Acts 7:51. [5]Gal 3:1. [6]1 Cor 3:3. [7]LF 23:81-82*. [8]ANF 9:413. [9]ANF 9:496. [10]ANF 9:346. [11]Prov 10:19. [12]FC 80:162.

ments you will be powerful in every action, and your action will be beyond criticism. Fear the Lord, then, and you will do everything well; this is the fear you must have to be saved. MANDATE 7.1.[13]

KNOWLEDGE WILL PASS AWAY. CHRYSOSTOM: If fear of God comes from knowledge but knowledge is going to pass away, as Paul says,[14] then we shall be completely destroyed when there is no knowledge. All that we are will be gone, and we shall be in a state no better but much worse than irrational beings. For in knowledge we have the advantage over them, whereas in all other things pertaining to the body they surpass us by far. AGAINST THE ANOMOEANS, HOMILY 1.9.[15]

GOOD COUNSEL. AUGUSTINE: What could be briefer, truer, better for the soul to know? For this is all a person is—a keeper of God's commandments. Not being such, he is, so to say, nothing at all, because instead of being constantly reshaped to the image of the truth, he remains bogged down in the likeness of shadow. CITY OF GOD 20.3.[16]

FOR THIS REASON PEOPLE WERE BORN. JEROME: Let us indeed "fear God and obey his commandments," for each person was born for this purpose, that knowing his Creator, he might venerate him with fear, honor and observance of the commandments. When the time of judgment arrives, whatever we have done will stand under judgment and await the double sentence that each person will receive for his work, whether he has done evil or good. We will be held accountable on the day of judgment for what we were able to do, "for every hidden deed, whether good or evil," as Symmachus and the Septuagint translated it, that is, for every contempt, or at least every negligence, but also for every idle word offered even unknowingly, not willfully. But because fear belongs to slaves and perfect love drives fear away,[17] fear has a double meaning in divine Scripture, for beginners and for the per-

fect. The fear of him who has been perfected in virtue, I believe, is expressed here: "They who fear the Lord lack nothing."[18] Or at least because he is still a man and has not taken God's name, he knows his own nature, that he might fear God while placed in the body. For God will bring each creature, that is, each person, to judgment for every decision he or she made contrary to that which God has arranged and said. "Woe" indeed "to those who call evil good and good evil."[19] COMMENTARY ON ECCLESIASTES 12.13-14.[20]

HUMANITY AS IT TRULY IS. BEDE: Of those who are proud and at the same time treacherous it is said, "The foxes have dens and the birds of the air have nests."[21] And of all people in general it is said, "And man, when he was held in esteem" (that is, made in the image of God), "did not understand; he was like foolish cattle."[22] Solomon, however, shows humanity as it truly is, that is, uncorrupted, when he says, "Fear God and keep his commandments, for this is all there is to man." COMMENTARY ON THE ACTS OF THE APOSTLES 10.12.[23]

THE PURPOSE OF HUMAN BEINGS. BEDE: They have been appointed to this, that is, to this made human beings by nature, that they may believe God and obey his will, as Solomon attests when he says, "Fear God and obey his commandments, for this is [the duty of] every human being." That is, every human being has been naturally made for this purpose, that he may fear God and obey his commandments. COMMENTARY ON 1 PETER 2.8.[24]

SOLOMON'S CONCLUSION. GREGORY THE GREAT: Solomon's book in which these words appear is called Ecclesiastes. Translated, this name means "Preacher." Now, in preaching one expresses sentiments that tend to quiet a noisy

---

[13]FC 1:272. [14]1 Cor 13:8. [15]FC 72:54. [16]FC 24:255. [17]1 Jn 4:18. [18]Ps 34:10 (33:11 LXX). [19]Is 5:20. [20]CCL 72:360-61. [21]Mt 8:20. [22]Ps 49:12 (48:13 LXX). [23]CS 117:98*. [24]CS 82:86*.

crowd. And when there are many people holding opinions of various kinds, they are brought into harmony by the reasoning of the speaker. This book, then, is called "the Preacher" because in it Solomon makes the feelings of the disorganized people his own in order to search into and give expression to the thoughts that come to their untutored minds perhaps by the way of temptation. For the sentiments he expresses in his search are as varied as the individuals he impersonates. But, like a true preacher, he stretches out his arms at the end of his address and calms the troubled sprits of the assembled people, calling them back to one way of thinking. This we see him do at the close of the book, where he says, "Let us all hear together the conclusion of the discourse. Fear God and keep his commandments: for this is the whole duty of man." DIALOGUE 4.4.[25]

12:14 Universal Judgment

RESURRECTION FOR ALL. APOSTOLIC CONSTITUTIONS: Nor is a resurrection declared only for the martyrs, but for all persons, righteous and unrighteous, godly and ungodly, that everyone may receive according to his desert. For God, says the Scripture, "will bring every work into judgment, with every secret thing, whether it be good or whether it be evil." CONSTITUTIONS OF THE HOLY APOSTLES 5.1.7.[26]

GOD'S WORD IS NOT A WORK TO BE JUDGED. ATHANASIUS: Consider how grave an error it is to call God's Word a work. Solomon says in one place in Ecclesiastes that "God shall bring every work into judgment, with every secret thing, whether it be good or whether it be evil." If then the Word is a work, do you mean that he as well as others will be brought into judgment? And what room is there for judgment, when the Judge is on trial? Who will give to the just their blessing, who to the unworthy their punishment, the Lord, as you must suppose, standing on trial with the rest? By what law shall he, the Lawgiver, himself be judged? FOUR DISCOURSES AGAINST THE ARIANS 2.14.6.[27]

---

[25]FC 39:193*. [26]ANF 7:440. [27]NPNF 2 4:351.

The Song of Solomon

1:1-4 THE BRIDE AND THE LOVER

¹*The Song of Songs, which is Solomon's.*

²*O that you*ᵃ *would kiss me with the kisses
    of your*ᵇ *mouth!
For your love* is better than wine,
    ³your anointing oils are fragrant,
    your name is oil poured out;*

*therefore the maidens love you.
⁴Draw me after you,*† *let us make haste.*‡
    *The king has brought me into his
    chambers.
We will exult and rejoice in you;
    we will extol your love more than wine;
    rightly do they love you.*§

a Heb *he*   b Heb *his*   *LXX (*mastoi*) and Vg (*ubera*) *breasts*   †LXX *They have drawn you*   ‡LXX *we will run after you in the odor of your ointments*   §LXX *righteousness loves you*

OVERVIEW: This book can be seen as a sublime wedding song, written by Solomon in his infinite wisdom, that portrays the love of bride and bridegroom, and from this perspective it has no corporeal or fleshly meaning (ORIGEN, GREGORY OF NYSSA, JEROME, GREGORY OF ELVIRA). It is spiritual, not factual (THEODORET OF CYR). Spiritually, it is also a story of Christ and the church, or of the individual soul with the Word of God (ORIGEN). The bride is the church and the bridegroom is Christ, and this book brings out the mystical intercourse between them. Its contents are inherited, not plagiarized, and its purpose was for a wedding (THEODORET OF CYR). "The breasts" are symbolic of "love" or the heart (AMBROSE, GREGORY OF NYSSA, HIPPOLYTUS, BEDE). Just as the church's kiss is a mark of love, so the kiss of God's Word is spiritual and excels any bodily pleasure (AMBROSE, JEROME, THEODORET OF CYR, CASSIODORUS, GREGORY THE GREAT). Such imagery is, nonetheless, profane (PSEUDO-DIONYSIUS). The oil that is poured out has sacred meaning and is even related to the name of Christ (AMBROSE, EUSEBIUS, JEROME, GREGORY THE GREAT). We must also be aware of a discrepancy in the text (ORIGEN). In one sense, all this is a tale of rapture veiled in allegory (AUGUSTINE), but in another sense it represents truth known in the flesh because what we desire is not always what we do (GREGORY THE GREAT). It is also a song among the angels, the sweet savor of the heavenly calling (JEROME, AUGUSTINE). It is also a call to the king's chambers, which represent God's hidden purpose, Christ's mind, the church or the realm of heaven (ORIGEN, THEODORET OF CYR, GREGORY THE GREAT, HIPPOLYTUS, GREGORY OF ELVIRA, BEDE).

1:1 Solomon's Book

A WEDDING SONG. ORIGEN: This book seems to me an epithalamium, that is, a wedding song, written by Solomon in the form of a play, which he recited in the character of a bride who was being married and who burned with a heavenly love for her bridegroom, who is the Word of God. . . .

[Therefore we shall] discuss briefly, first, love itself, which is the chief subject of the book, and next, the order of Solomon's books, among which this book is apparently put in third place. Then we shall also discuss the title of the book itself and why it is called Song of Songs. COMMENTARY ON THE SONG OF SONGS, PROLOGUE.[1]

ANOTHER SOLOMON. GREGORY OF NYSSA: Another Solomon is signified here: one who is also descended from the seed of David according to the flesh, one whose name means peace, the true king of Israel and builder of God's temple. This other Solomon comprehends the knowledge of all things. His wisdom is infinite and his very essence is wisdom, truth, as well as every exalted, divine name and thought. [Christ] used Solomon as an instrument and speaks to us through his voice first in Proverbs and then in Ecclesiastes. After these two books he speaks in the philosophy set forth in the Song of Songs and shows us the ascent to perfection in an orderly fashion. . . .

It is not accidental, I think, that the book is ascribed to Solomon. This serves as an indication to readers to expect something great and divine. . . .

Proverbs teaches in one way and Ecclesiastes in another; the philosophy of the Song of Songs transcends both by its loftier teaching. HOMILIES ON THE SONG OF SONGS 1.[2]

SPECIAL PLACE OF THIS BOOK. ORIGEN: First, let us examine why it is, since the churches of God acknowledge three books written by Solomon, that of them the book of Proverbs is put first, the one called Ecclesiastes second, and the book Song of Songs has third place. . . . We can give them the terms moral, natural and contemplative. . . . The moral discipline is defined as the one by which an honorable manner of life is

equipped and habits conducive to virtue are prepared. The natural discipline is defined as the consideration of each individual thing, according to which nothing in life happens contrary to nature, but each individual thing is assigned those uses for which it has been brought forth by the Creator. The contemplative discipline is defined as that by which we transcend visible things and contemplate something of divine and heavenly things and gaze at them with the mind alone, since they transcend corporeal appearance. . . .

Certain wise men of the Greeks took these ideas from Solomon, since it was long before them in age and time that he first gave these teachings through the Spirit of God. . . . Solomon discovered them before all the rest and taught them through the wisdom he received from God, as it is written, "And God gave Solomon understanding and wisdom beyond measure, and largeness of heart like the sand on the seashore. And his wisdom was made greater than that of all the ancient sons of men and all the wise men of Egypt."[3] Thus Solomon, since he wished to distinguish from one another and to separate what we have called earlier the three general disciplines, that is, moral, natural and contemplative, set them forth in three books, each one in its own logical order.

Thus he first taught in Proverbs the subject of morals, setting regulations for life together, as was fitting, in concise and brief maxims. And he included the second subject, which is called the natural discipline, in Ecclesiastes, in which he discusses many natural things. And by distinguishing them as empty and vain from what is useful and necessary, he warns that vanity must be abandoned and what is useful and right must be pursued. He also handed down the subject of contemplation in the book we have in hand, that is, Song of Songs, in which he urges upon the soul the love of the heavenly and the divine under the figure of the bride and the bridegroom, teaching us that we must attain fellowship with God

---

[1]OSW 217, 219**. [2]GNSS 44, 49, 45. [3]1 Kings 4:29-30.

by the paths of loving affection and of love. . . .

So indeed, this book occupies the last place, so that a person may come to it when he has been purged in morals and has learned the knowledge and distinction of corruptible and incorruptible things. By this preparation he is enabled to receive no harm from those figures by which the love of the bride for her heavenly bridegroom, that is, of the perfect soul for the Word of God, is described and fashioned. For with these preliminaries accomplished by which the soul is purified through its acts and habits and conducted to the discernment of natural things, the soul comes suitably to doctrines and mysteries and is led up to the contemplation of the Godhead by a genuine and spiritual love. COMMENTARY ON THE SONG OF SONGS, PROLOGUE.[4]

THE BRIDE IS THE CHURCH AND THE BRIDEGROOM IS CHRIST. THEODORET OF CYR: Let us, therefore, understand the church as the bride, and Christ as the bridegroom, and as the young girls attending the bride souls that are pious and youthful, who have not yet attained the virtue of the bride and been accorded perfection—hence their attending on the bride but not being called brides. COMMENTARY ON THE SONG OF SONGS, PREFACE.[5]

SOLOMON'S LADDER OF THREE STEPS. THEODORET OF CYR: It is also necessary to say by way of introduction that three works belong to Solomon: Proverbs, Ecclesiastes and the Song of Songs. Proverbs offers those interested moral benefit, while Ecclesiastes comments on the nature of visible realities and thoroughly explains the futility of the present life so that we may learn its transitory character, despise passing realities and long for the future as something lasting. The Song of Songs . . . brings out the mystical intercourse between the bride and the bridegroom, the result being that the whole of Solomon's work constitutes a kind of ladder with three steps—moral, physical and mystical. That is to say, the person approaching a religious way of life must first purify

the mind with good behavior, then strive to discern the futility of impermanent things and the transitory character of what seems pleasant, and then finally take wings and long for the bridegroom, who promises eternal goods. Hence this book is placed third, so the person treading this path comes to perfection. COMMENTARY ON THE SONG OF SONGS, PREFACE.[6]

TO INHERIT IS NOT TO PLAGIARIZE. THEODORET OF CYR: Let us set about the commentary by making this considerable recommendation to those reading it, not to charge us with plagiarism if they find in our commentary something said by the fathers. We admit, in fact, that we have found in them the basis for clear exposition; far from being plagiarism, however, such material is an inheritance from our forebears. Some things that we include we have taken from them, other things we came up with ourselves and added; some things expressed at length by certain commentators we abbreviated, other things requiring further work we developed. COMMENTARY ON THE SONG OF SONGS, PREFACE.[7]

MANY SONGS, THE PURPOSE BEING A WEDDING. THEODORET OF CYR: Let us consider why on earth Solomon the sage called it not Song but "Song of Songs"; after all, the fact that nothing that is the result of the divine Spirit's action is said idly and to no purpose is clear to people of a sober and pious mind. This being the case, the question needs to be asked why the work is called "Song of Songs" and not Song. In fact, we find many songs, psalms, hymns and odes, oral and written, both in blessed David and in the biblical authors before him and after him. . . .

Solomon the sage . . . composed a song that was not for triumph in battle or for morning prayer but for a wedding. . . .

The Song of Songs . . . outlines his wedding and depicts his love for the bride. "Bride" is the term he uses of the people who in the above songs

---

[4]*OSW* 231-32, 234. [5]ECS 2:31. [6]ECS 2:32. [7]ECS 2:32.

have been freed from captivity, have attained their freedom and associated themselves to the king, retaining an indelible memory of his favors, giving evidence of great benevolence and affection for him and constantly attending on him. Then, when the powers on high enquire, "Who is the king of glory?"[8] they long to be with him, unable to bear being separated even for a short space of time from their savior. This is the reason this book is called the Song of Songs, the phrase suggesting that those other songs were composed with a view to this song, and the others lead to this one. . . .

This is the reason, therefore, that the book is called the Song of Songs, in that it teaches us the major forms of God's goodness and reveals to us the innermost recesses and the holiest of holy mysteries of divine loving-kindness. Commentary on the Song of Songs, Preface.[9]

No Corporeal or Fleshly Meaning. Origen: Therefore it is appropriate that in this book, which was to be written about the love of the bridegroom and the bride, there should for this reason be written neither Son of David nor king nor anything else that could be related to a corporeal meaning. And so, the bride now made perfect may worthily say of him, "Even though we once regarded Christ according to the flesh, we know him thus no longer."[10] She says this lest anyone should think she loves anything corporeal or placed in the flesh, and she be thought not to have fallen in love with him spotlessly. That is why, then, it is "the Song of Songs," which is merely "Solomon's" and not the Son of David's or the king of Israel's; absolutely no meaning that might come from a fleshly name is mingled with the themes of the book. Commentary on the Song of Songs, Prologue.[11]

Why Not the Plural Title? Origen: Some write the title of this book Songs of Songs. This is incorrect; for it should not be in the plural, but in the singular, Song of Songs. . . .

Those who have raised the question under-

stand the verse as though it said this is one of Solomon's songs, so that he designates this as one of his many songs. But how shall we accept an interpretation of this kind when neither the church of God has accepted any other songs written by Solomon save this one nor is any other book of Solomon's but the three we also have included in their canon by the Hebrews, by whom the noble words of God have evidently been handed down to us? Commentary on the Song of Songs, Prologue.[12]

The Song That Is the Most Sublime. Gregory of Elvira: For thus is it called the Canticle of Canticles, inasmuch as it is above every canticle that Moses and Mary in Exodus and Isaiah and Habakkuk and others sang. These are better canticles because they give praise to the Lord with joyful mind and soul for the liberation of the people, or for their conversion, or in gratitude for the divine works. Here they are superior also because the voice of the singing church and of God is heard. Because the divine and human are united with one another, therefore, it is called the Canticle of Canticles, that is, the best of the best. Explanation of the Song of Songs 1.2.[13]

This Book Is Spiritual, Not Factual. Theodoret of Cyr: Some commentators misrepresent the Song of Songs, believe it to be not a spiritual book [and] come up instead with some fanciful stories inferior even to babbling old wives' tales and dare to claim that Solomon the sage wrote it as a factual account of himself and the Pharaoh's daughter. . . . Those of a more serious frame of mind, on the contrary, gave the name "royal" to the material, and saw the people referred to as the bride and the groom. . . .

My view is that when they read this composition and noticed in it unguents, kisses, thighs, belly, navel, cheeks, eyes, lilies, apples, nard, ointment, myrrh and the like, in their ignorance of

---

[8]Ps 24:8, 10 (23:8, 10 LXX). [9]ECS 2:33-35. [10]2 Cor 5:16. [11]OSW 241. [12]OSW 243. [13]CCL 69:170.

the characteristics of the divine Scripture they were unwilling to get beyond the surface, penetrate the veil of the expression, gain entrance in spirit and behold the glory of the Lord with face unveiled. Rather, they gave the text a corporeal interpretation and were drawn into that awful blasphemy. COMMENTARY ON THE SONG OF SONGS, PREFACE.[14]

A SWEET MARRIAGE SONG. JEROME: Solomon, a lover of peace and of the Lord, corrects morals, teaches nature, unites Christ and the church, and sings a sweet marriage song to celebrate that holy bridal. LETTER 53.8.[15]

1:2 The Kisses of Your Mouth

THE SONG THAT IS THE SONG OF SONGS. ORIGEN: Now let us ask first what the songs are of which this is said to be the Song of Songs. I think, then, that they are those that were sung of old by the prophets or by the angels. For the law is said to have been "ordained by angels by the hand of an intermediary."[16] Thus all the proclamations made by them were songs that went before, sung by the friends of the bridegroom; but this is the one song that was to be sung in the form of an epithalamium to the bridegroom when he is about to take his bride. In it the bride does not want the song sung to her by the friends of the bridegroom right away, but she longs to hear the words of the bridegroom now present. She says, "Let him kiss me with the kisses of his mouth." This is why it deserves to be placed before all the other songs. For apparently the other songs, which the law and the prophets sang, were recited for the bride when she was still a little girl and had not yet crossed the threshold of a mature age. But this song is recited for her when she is grown up, quite strong, and now able to receive adult power and perfect mystery. COMMENTARY ON THE SONG OF SONGS, PROLOGUE.[17]

DRAMATIC EXCHANGE WITH AN INNER MEANING. ORIGEN: It behooves us to remember the

fact to which we drew attention in our introduction—namely, that this little book which has the semblance of a marriage song is written in dramatic form. And we defined a drama as something in which certain characters are introduced who speak. From time to time some of them arrive upon the scene, while others go or come, so that the whole action consists in interchange between the characters. This book, therefore, will be like that all through; and, reading it along those lines, we shall get from it according to our powers a simple record of events. And the spiritual interpretation too is equally in line with that which we pointed out in our prologue; the appellations of bride and bridegroom denote either the church in relation to Christ or the soul in its union with the Word of God.

Reading it as a simple story, then, we see a bride appearing on the stage, having received for her betrothal and by way of dowry most fitting gifts from a most noble bridegroom. But, because the bridegroom delays his coming for so long, she, grieved with longing for his love, is pining at home and doing all she can to bring herself at last to see her spouse and to enjoy his kisses. We understand further that the bride, seeing that she can neither be quit of her love nor yet achieve what she desires, betakes herself to prayer and makes supplication to God, whom she knows to be her bridegroom's father....

This is the content of the actual story, presented in dramatic form. But let us see if the inner meaning also can be fittingly supplied along these lines. Let it be the church who longs for union with Christ, but ... [it is] the church as a corporate personality who speaks. COMMENTARY ON THE SONG OF SONGS 1.1.[18]

BREASTS BETTER THAN WINE. AMBROSE: But why do we doubt? The church has believed in his goodness all these ages and has confessed its faith in the saying, "Let him kiss me with the kisses of

[14]ECS 2:22, 24. [15]NPNF 2 6:101. [16]Gal 3:19. [17]OSW 236*. [18]ACW 26:58-59**.

his mouth; for your breasts are better than wine," and again, "And your throat is like the goodliest wine." Of his goodness, therefore, he nourishes us with the breasts of the law and grace, soothing our sorrows by telling of heavenly things. And do we then deny his goodness, when he is the manifestation of goodness, expressing in his person the likeness of the eternal bounty, even as we showed above that it was written, that he is the spotless reflection and counterpart of that bounty?[19] On the Christian Faith 2.2.32.[20]

The Breasts Are the Heart Indicating God's Secret Power.

Gregory of Nyssa: "Your breasts are better than wine," signifying by the breasts the heart. Nobody will err if he understands by the heart the hidden, secret power of God. One would rightly suppose that the breasts are the activities of God's power for us by which he nourishes each one's life and bestows appropriate nourishment. Homilies on the Song of Songs 1.[21]

Superiority of Breasts.

Hippolytus: When it says "your breasts are better than wine," it signifies that the commandments of Christ delight the heart like wine. For, as infants suck upon breasts in order to extract some milk, so also all who suck on the law and the gospel obtain the commandments as eternal food. Treatise on the Song of Songs 2.3.[22]

Breasts of Christ Are Better Than the Wine of the Law.

Bede: But if the breasts of Christ, that is, the source of the Lord's revelation, are better than the wine of the law, how much more will the wine of Christ, that is, the perfection of evangelical doctrine, surpass all the ceremonies of the law? If the sacraments of his incarnation vivify, how much more will the knowledge and vision of his divinity glorify? Commentary on the Song of Songs 1.1.1.[23]

The Church's Kiss Is a Mark of Love.

Ambrose: "You gave me no kiss, but she, from the moment she entered, has not ceased to kiss my feet."[24] A kiss is a mark of love. How, then, can a Jew have a kiss, who has not known peace, who has not received peace from Christ when he said, "My peace I give you, my peace I leave unto you"?[25] The synagogue has no kiss, but the church has, for she waited and loved and said, "Let him kiss me with the kiss of his mouth." She wished with his kiss to quench gradually the burning of the long desire that had grown with longing for the Lord's coming; she wished to satisfy her thirst with this boon. Letter 62, To His Sister.[26]

A Holy Kiss.

Jerome: I see two attributes that, by coming together, are made one. Justice and peace have kissed. All this becomes one in the mystery of the Lord Savior, the Son of man and of God who is our truth, kindness, peace, justice, in whom the justice of the first people and the mercy of the second people are joined together into one peace. The apostle says, in fact, "He himself is our peace, he it is who has made both one."[27] This is the mystery for which the church longs and cries out in the Song of Solomon: "Let him kiss me with the kiss of his mouth." This is the kiss of which Paul the apostle says, "Greet one another with a holy kiss."[28] Homilies on the Psalms, Alternate Series 64 (Psalm 84).[29]

Kissing Is Spiritual as Well as Material.

Theodoret of Cyr: Let no earthbound and materially minded person, however, be abashed at the mention of "kisses." Let them, on the contrary, consider that also at the moment of holy communion we receive the bridegroom's limbs, caress and embrace them, press them to our heart with our eyes, imagine a kind of embrace, believe ourselves to be with him, embrace him, caress him, love driving out fear, in the words of the divine Scripture. . . .

[19]Song 7:9. [20]NPNF 2 10:227*. [21]GNSS 52. [22]CSCO 264:26. [23]CCL 119B:191. [24]Lk 7:45. [25]Jn 14:27. [26]FC 26:390*. [27]Eph 2:14. [28]Rom 16:16; 1 Cor 16:20; 2 Cor 13:12; 1 Thess 5:26. [29]FC 57:54.

The Song of Songs introduces the bride saying, "Let him kiss me with kisses of his mouth." Now, by "kiss" we understand not the joining of mouths but the communion of pious soul and divine Word. It is like the bride saying something of this kind, I experienced your words in writing, but I long to hear your very voice as well, I wish to receive the sacred teaching directly from your mouth and to caress it with the lips of my mind. COMMENTARY ON THE SONG OF SONGS 1.[30]

THE CHURCH DEMANDS MANY KISSES.

AMBROSE: But the church does not cease to kiss Christ's feet, and she demands not one but many kisses in the Song of Solomon, since like blessed Mary she listens to his every saying, she receives his every word, when the gospel or prophets are read, and she keeps all these words in her heart.[31] LETTER 62, TO HIS SISTER.[32]

THE DIFFERENCE MADE BY THE REDEEMER.

GREGORY THE GREAT: Holy church, sighing for the coming of the mediator between God and humanity, for the coming of her Redeemer, prays to the Father that he would send the Son and illuminate him with his presence, that he would speak to the church no longer through the mouths of prophets but by his own mouth. COMMENTARY ON THE SONG OF SONGS 12.[33]

THE CHURCH DESERVES CHRIST'S KISS.

CASSIODORUS: In short, you deserve Christ's kiss and the continuance of your virginal glory forever, for these words are spoken to you: "Let him kiss me with the kiss of his mouth, for your breasts are better than wine, smelling sweet of the best ointments," and the other verses which that divine book includes with its mystical proclamation. EXPOSITION OF THE PSALMS, PREFACE.[34]

KISSING THE REDEEMER'S FEET.

GREGORY THE GREAT: The Gentiles who were called did not cease kissing their Redeemer's feet, because they longed for him with uninterrupted love. Hence the bride in the Song of Songs said of this same Redeemer: "Let him kiss me with the kisses of his mouth." It is fitting that she desires her Creator's kiss, as she makes herself ready through her love to obey him. FORTY GOSPEL HOMILIES 33.[35]

THE KISS OF GOD'S WORD EXCELS ANY BODILY PLEASURE.

AMBROSE: Therefore such a soul also desires many kisses of the Word, so that she may be enlightened with the light of the knowledge of God. For this is the kiss of the Word, I mean the light of holy knowledge. God the Word kisses us, when he enlightens our heart and governing faculty with the spirit of the knowledge of God. The soul that has received this gift exults and rejoices in the pledge of wedded love and says, "I opened my mouth and panted."[36] For it is with the kiss that lovers cleave to each other and gain possession of the sweetness of grace that is within, so to speak. Through such a kiss the soul cleaves to God the Word, and through the kiss the spirit of him who kisses is poured into the soul, just as those who kiss are not satisfied to touch lightly with their lips but appear to be pouring their spirit into each other. Showing that she loves not only the appearance of the Word and his face, as it were, but all his inner parts, she adds to the favor of the kisses: "Your breasts are better than wine, and the fragrance of your ointments is above all perfumes." She sought the kiss, God the Word poured himself into her wholly and laid bare his breasts to her, that is, his teachings and the laws of the wisdom that is within, and was fragrant with the sweet fragrance of his ointments. Captive to these, the soul is saying that the enjoyment of the knowledge of God is richer than the joy of any bodily pleasure. ISAAC, OR THE SOUL 3.8-9.[37]

THE SOUL'S HIGHEST DESIRE.

AMBROSE: Having embraced the Word of God, [the soul] desires him above every beauty; she loves him

---

[30]ECS 2:37-39. [31]Cf. Lk 2:51. [32]FC 26:392*. [33]SC 314:88. [34]ACW 51:42*. [35]CS 123:274. [36]Ps 119:131 (118:131 LXX). [37]FC 65:16-17**.

above every joy; she is delighted with him above every perfume; she wishes often to see, often to gaze, often to be drawn to him that she may follow. "Your name," she says, "is as oil poured out," and that is why we maidens love you and vie with one another but cannot attain to you. Draw us that we may run after you, that from the odor of ointments we may receive the power to follow you. LETTER 79, TO LAYMEN.[38]

BUT THE IMAGERY IS PROFANE. PSEUDO-DIONYSIUS: And in the Songs there are those passionate longings fit only for prostitutes. There are too those other sacred pictures boldly used to represent God, so that what is hidden may be brought out into the open and multiplied, what is unique and undivided may be divided up, and multiple shapes and forms be given to what has neither shape nor form. All this is to enable the one capable of seeing the beauty hidden within these images to find that they are truly mysterious, appropriate to God, and filled with a great theological light. LETTER 9.[39]

1:3 Oil Poured Out

OIL OF CHRISMATION. AMBROSE: After this, you went up to the priest. Consider what followed. Was it not that of which David speaks: "Like the ointment upon the head, which went down to the beard, even Aaron's beard"?[40] This is the ointment of which Solomon, too, says, "Your name is ointment poured out, therefore have the maidens loved you and drawn you." How many souls regenerated this day have loved you, Lord Jesus, and have said, "Draw us after you, we are running after the odor of your garments," that they might drink in the odor of your resurrection.

Consider now why this is done, for "the eyes of a wise man are in his head."[41] Therefore the ointment flows down to the beard, that is to say, to the beauty of youth; and therefore, Aaron's beard, that we, too, may become a chosen race, priestly and precious, for we are all anointed with spiritual

grace for a share in the kingdom of God and in the priesthood. ON THE MYSTERIES 6.29-30.[42]

CHRIST'S NAME INDICATES OINTMENT POURED FORTH. EUSEBIUS OF CAESAREA: And as we are examining his name, the seal of all we have said may be found in the oracle of Solomon the wisest of the wise, where he says in the Song of Songs: "Your name is as ointment poured forth." Solomon, being supplied with divine wisdom, and thought worthy of more mystical revelations about Christ and his church, and speaking of him as heavenly bridegroom and her as bride, speaks as if to [Christ] and says, "Your name, O Bridegroom, is ointment," and not simply ointment, but "ointment poured forth." And what name could be more suggestive of ointment poured forth than the name of Christ? For there could be no Christ, and no name of Christ, unless ointment had been poured forth. And in what has gone before I have shown of what nature the ointment was with which Christ was anointed. PROOF OF THE GOSPEL 4.16.[43]

OIL IS ESSENTIAL TO ANOINTING. JEROME: "It is as when the precious ointment upon the head runs down over the beard, the beard of Aaron."[44] Oh, if only there were time to explore together each verse; even a day would not suffice! We have read in Exodus[45] the account of how oil is prepared for the anointing of the priest; we have read, too, of the different kind of balm used to anoint kings. There was still another unguent for prophets. What more is there to say? All these oils of unction were different, each with its own spiritual symbolism. . . . Nothing is ever made sacred except by anointing. It is with this in view that young maidens say in the Song of Solomon, "Your name is a spreading perfume: we will run after you in the odor of your ointments." HOMILIES ON THE PSALMS 45 (PSALM 132).[46]

---

[38]FC 26:441-42*. [39]PDCW 282-83. [40]Ps 133:2 (132:2 LXX). [41]Eccles 2:14. [42]NPNF 2 10:321*. [43]POG 1:216*. [44]Ps 133:2 (132:2 LXX). [45]See Ex 29:7. [46]FC 48:334*.

ANOINTED WITH THIS OIL WHEN HE BECAME MAN. GREGORY THE GREAT: [Jesus] was anointed with this oil[47] when he became incarnate. For it was not that the man existed first, then received the Holy Spirit afterwards. Rather, because he became incarnate by the mediation of the Holy Spirit, the man was anointed with this oil at the moment of his creation. COMMENTARY ON THE SONG OF SONGS 14.[48]

DISCREPANCY IN THE TEXT. ORIGEN: We must not, however, overlook the fact that in certain versions we find written "for your sayings are better than wine," where we read "for your breasts are better than wine." But although it may seem that this gives a plainer meaning in regard to the things about which we have discoursed in the spiritual interpretation, we ourselves keep to what the seventy interpreters wrote in every case. For we are certain that the Holy Spirit willed that the figures of the mysteries should be roofed over the divine Scriptures and should not be displayed publicly and in the open air. COMMENTARY ON THE SONG OF SONGS 1.3.[49]

1:4 Let Us Make Haste

RAPTURE VEILED IN ALLEGORY. AUGUSTINE: The Canticle of Canticles sings a sort of spiritual rapture experienced by holy souls contemplating the nuptial relationship between Christ the King and his queen-city, the church. But it is a rapture veiled in allegory to make us yearn for it more ardently and rejoice in the unveiling as the bridegroom comes into view—the bridegroom to whom the canticle sings, "The righteous love you," and the hearkening bride replies, "There is love in your delights."[50] CITY OF GOD 17.20.[51]

TRUTH KNOWN IN THE FLESH. GREGORY THE GREAT: You see how Truth, having made himself known in the flesh, gave some leaps for us to make us run after him. "He exulted like a giant to run his course,"[52] so that we might tell to him from our hearts, "Draw me after you; let us run

in the fragrance of your ointments." FORTY GOSPEL HOMILIES 29.[53]

WHAT WE DESIRE IS NOT ALWAYS WHAT WE DO. GREGORY THE GREAT: The one who says "draw me" has something in mind that he wants but does not have the ability to obtain it. Human nature wants to follow God, but, overcome by habitual infirmity, as it deserves, it cannot follow. He sees therefore that there is something in himself whereby he yearns, but something else whereby he fails to attain. Rightly, then, does he say "draw me." COMMENTARY ON THE SONG OF SONGS 24.[54]

SWEET SAVOR OF THE HEAVENLY CALLING. AUGUSTINE: Some great thing it is we are to see, since all our reward is seeing; and our Lord Jesus Christ is that very great sight. He who appeared humble, will himself appear great and will rejoice us, as he is even now seen of his angels. . . . Let us love and imitate him; let us run after his ointments, as is said in the Song of Solomon: "Because of the sweet smell of your good ointments, we will run after you." For he came and gave forth a sweet smell that filled the world. Whence was that fragrance? From heaven. Follow then toward heaven, if you do not answer falsely when it is said, "Lift up your hearts." Lift up your thoughts, your love, your hope, that it may not rot upon the earth. . . . "For wherever your treasure is, there will be your heart also."[55] EXPLANATIONS OF THE PSALMS 91.20.[56]

A SONG AMONG THE ANGELS. JEROME: There also—the Lord himself is my witness—when I had shed copious tears and had strained my eyes toward heaven, I sometimes felt myself among angelic hosts and for joy and gladness sang, "Because of the sweet smell of your good ointments, we will run after you." LETTER 22.7.[57]

---

[47]Cf. Ps 45:7 (44:8 LXX). [48]SC 314:90. [49]ACW 26:74. [50]Song 7:6. [51]FC 24:77*. [52]Ps 19:5 (18:6 LXX, Vg). [53]CS 123:234. [54]SC 314:104. [55]Mt 6:21. [56]NPNF 1 8:452*. [57]NPNF 2 6:25*.

DEEPER MEANING OF THE KING'S CHAMBERS.
ORIGEN: But since the reference is either to the church who comes to Christ, or to the soul that cleaves to the Word of God, how should we understand Christ's chamber and the storehouse of the Word of God into which he brings the church or the soul thus cleaving to him—you can take it either way—except as Christ's own secret and mysterious mind? COMMENTARY ON THE SONG OF SONGS 1.5.[58]

THE INNER CHAMBER IS GOD'S HIDDEN PURPOSE. THEODORET OF CYR: She is admitted to the inner chamber, the quarters and rooms of the bridegroom, and boastfully says to her own retinue, "The king introduced me into his chamber," that is, he revealed to me his hidden purposes, the plan concealed from ages and generations he made known to me,[59] the treasuries obscure, hidden, and unseen he opened to me, in keeping with the prophecy of Isaiah.[60] COMMENTARY ON THE SONG OF SONGS 1.[61]

KING'S CHAMBER IS THE CHURCH. GREGORY THE GREAT: The church of God is like the house of a certain king. It has a gate, it has a staircase, it has a dining room, and it has a bedroom. Everyone within the church has faith and has already entered the gate to the house, for, just as the gate opens the way to the rest of the house, so does faith provide entrance to the rest of the virtues. COMMENTARY ON THE SONG OF SONGS 26.[62]

CHRIST IS THE KING. HIPPOLYTUS: "The king introduced me to his treasures." Who is this king, if not Christ himself? And what are these treasures, if not his chambers? This is the people who say, "We will rejoice and delight in you," for he calls everyone. First, it tells us about the past, then it reveals a time of penance in the future: "We will rejoice and delight in you." "I loved your breasts more than wine," not the wine that was mixed by Christ, surely, but the wine whereby

Noah previously languished in drunkenness, the wine that deceived Lot. "We loved your fonts of milk more than this wine" because breasts were the commandments given by Christ; they delight but certainly do not inebriate. For this reason, indeed, the apostle said, "Do not drink so much wine that you become drunk."[63] Therefore the beloved now says, "I loved your breasts more than wine; righteousness loves you," because those who follow the way of righteousness are those who love you, whereas unbelievers hate you and deserve retribution from the judge. TREATISE ON THE SONG OF SONGS 3.1.4.[64]

HIDDEN IN THE REALM OF HEAVEN. GREGORY OF ELVIRA: "The king introduced me to his chambers." This is the church speaking, who confesses Christ the Son of God to be King. But what is the chamber to which Christ the King introduced his queen, the church, if not the mystery of the heavenly kingdom? For who does not know that Christ introduced his church, that is, his own flesh, to that place from which he had descended without flesh, that is, the gates of heaven? We learn that the church is the flesh of Christ from the authority of the apostle, who said "the flesh of Christ, which is the church."[65] EXPLANATION OF THE SONG OF SONGS 1.20.[66]

CHAMBERS OF THE ETERNAL KING. BEDE: The chambers of the eternal King are the interior joys of the heavenly homeland to which the holy church is now introduced by faith, as it awaits a fuller, future introduction to the reality itself. The young maidens of which it speaks are the faithful souls of the church of Christ who were only recently reborn as members of Christ. COMMENTARY ON THE SONGS OF SONGS 1.1.3.[67]

---

[58]ACW 26:84. [59]See Eph 3:9. [60]See Is 45:3. [61]ECS 2:41. [62]SC 314:108. [63]Eph 5:18. [64]CSCO 264:30-31. [65]Col 1:24. [66]CCL 69:176. [67]CCL 119B:194.

1:5-6 BLACK AND BEAUTIFUL

⁵*I am very dark, but comely,*
 O daughters of Jerusalem,
 like the tents of Kedar,
  like the curtains of Solomon.
⁶*Do not gaze at me because I am swarthy,*

because the sun has scorched me.
My mother's sons were angry with me,
 they made me keeper of the vineyards;
 but, my own vineyard I have not kept!

OVERVIEW: There is a superficial meaning and also a mystical exposition for this story. "Dark and comely" can also mean dark and beautiful, black and beautiful, black by lowly origin but beautiful by faith (ORIGEN). Or it can mean black by human frailty and comely by sacramental faith (AMBROSE), black physically and beautiful in merit (CASSIODORUS), dark by nature and beautiful by grace (CAESARIUS OF ARLES, GREGORY THE GREAT), dark through sin but beautiful through love (GREGORY OF ELVIRA, GREGORY OF NYSSA), black from worship of creation rather than Creator, black from the stench of wild beasts but beautiful from expectation of the Lord (THEODORET OF CYR), beautiful but sinful (HIPPOLYTUS), or black by adversity but beautiful by virtue (BEDE). Spiritually, we do all begin in darkness (ORIGEN), as did the church (AMBROSE, JEROME). It is also possible to be black and ugly (ORIGEN). Nonetheless, from a different viewpoint, the literal meaning of Scripture, and thus of this passage, is all there is (THEODORE OF MOPSUESTIA). Reversed is the case, however, with blackness of the soul. Spiritual sunlight is contrasted to visible sunlight (ORIGEN). Although in one sense Christ is the sun (GREGORY OF ELVIRA), it is also he, the true Light, who made the sun (ORIGEN).

1:5 Dark but Comely

BLACK AND BEAUTIFUL. ORIGEN: "I am dark and beautiful, O daughters of Jerusalem, as the tents of Kedar, as the curtains of Solomon." In some copies we read, "I am black and beautiful." Here again the person of the bride is introduced as speaking, but she speaks now not to those maidens who are accustomed to run with her but to the daughters of Jerusalem. To these, since they have spoken slightingly about her as being ugly, she now makes answer, saying, "I am indeed dark—or black—as far as my complexion goes, O daughters of Jerusalem; but, should a person scrutinize the features of my inward parts, then I am beautiful. For the tents of Kedar, which is a great nation," she says, "also are black, and their very name of Kedar means blackness or darkness. The curtains of Solomon likewise are black, but that blackness of his curtains is not considered unbecoming for so great a king in all his glory."[1] . . .

This much is comprehended in the tale enacted and is the superficial meaning of the story here set forth. But let us return to the mystical exposition. This bride who speaks represents the church gathered from among the Gentiles. But the daughters of Jerusalem to whom she addresses herself are . . . the daughters of this earthly Jerusalem who, seeing the church of the Gentiles, despise and vilify her for her ignoble birth. She is baseborn in their eyes, because she cannot count as hers the noble blood of Abraham and Isaac and Jacob. . . .

She answers their objections thus: "I am indeed black, O daughters of Jerusalem, in that I cannot claim descent from famous men, neither have I received the enlightenment of Moses' law.

---

[1]See Mt 6:29.

But I have my own beauty, all the same. For in me too there is that primal thing, the image of God wherein I was created,[2] and, coming now to the Word of God, I have received my beauty." . . .

"I am black indeed by reason of my lowly origin, but I am beautiful through penitence and faith. For I have taken to myself the Son of God, I have received the Word made flesh; I have come to him who is the image of God, the firstborn of every creature[3] and who is the brightness of the glory and the express image of the substance of God,[4] and I have been made fair." . . .

It can be said also of each individual soul that turns to repentance after many sins, that it is black by reason of the sins but beautiful through repentance and the fruits of repentance. COMMENTARY ON THE SONG OF SONGS 2.1.[5]

Spiritually We All Begin in Darkness.

ORIGEN: Thus some such process also happens to us who are in generation. We are dark at the beginning in believing—hence in the beginning of the Canticle of Canticles it is said, "I am very dark and beautiful," and we look like the soul of an Ethiopian at the beginning—then we are cleansed so that we may be more bright according to the passage, "Who is she who comes up whitened?"[6] HOMILIES ON JEREMIAH 11.6.3.[7]

Church Also Began in Darkness.

AMBROSE: It is written, "Ethiopia shall stretch out her hand unto God."[8] In this is signified the appearance of holy church, who says in the Song of Solomon, "I am black and comely, O daughters of Jerusalem": black through sin, comely through grace; black by natural condition, comely through redemption, or certainly, black with the dust of her labors. So it is black while fighting but comely when it is crowned with the ornaments of victory. ON THE HOLY SPIRIT 2.10.112.[9]

Miraculous Change of Complexion.

JEROME: Born, in the first instance, of such parentage we are naturally black. Even when we have repented, so long as we have not scaled the

heights of virtue, we may still say, "I am black but comely, O daughters of Jerusalem." . . . "For this cause shall a man leave his father and his mother and shall be joined unto his wife, and they two shall be" not as is there said, "of one flesh"[10] but "of one spirit." Your bridegroom is not haughty or disdainful; he has "married an Ethiopian woman."[11] When once you desire the wisdom of the true Solomon and come to him, he will avow all his knowledge to you; he will lead you into his chamber with his royal hand.[12] He will miraculously change your complexion so that it shall be said of you, "Who is this that goes up and has been made white?"[13] LETTER 22.1.[14]

Human Frailty and Sacramental Faith.

AMBROSE: The church, having put on these garments through the laver of regeneration,[15] says in the Song of Songs, "I am black and comely, O daughters of Jerusalem." Black through the frailty of its human condition, comely through the sacrament of faith. And the daughters of Jerusalem beholding these garments say in amazement, "Who is this that comes up made white?"[16] She was black; how is she now suddenly made white? ON THE MYSTERIES 7.35.[17]

Black Physically and Beautiful in

Merit. CASSIODORUS: We read in the Song of Songs of the church which bears the image of the Lord Savior, "I am black and beautiful," that is, black physically and beautiful in heavenly merits. He demonstrates why he used the word *beautiful*: as Christ put it, the world was reconciled to God through grace.[18] EXPOSITION OF THE PSALMS 44.3.[19]

Dark by Nature, Beautiful by Grace.

CAESARIUS OF ARLES: It is said concerning the

---

[2]Gen 1:26-27. [3]Col 1:15. [4]Heb 1:3. [5]ACW 26:91-93, 106*. [6]Song 8:5 LXX. [7]FC 97:109. [8]Ps 68:31 (67:32 LXX). [9]NPNF 2 10:129*. [10]Eph 5:31. [11]Num 12:1. [12]See Song 1:4. [13]Song 8:5 LXX. [14]NPNF 2 6:22-23*. [15]The white robes worn by catechumens after baptism. [16]Song 8:5 LXX. [17]NPNF 2 10:321-22*. [18]2 Cor 5:19. [19]ACW 51:442.

church of the Gentiles, "I am dark and beautiful, O daughter of Jerusalem." Why is the church dark and beautiful? She is dark by nature, beautiful by grace. Why dark? "Indeed, in guilt was I born, and in sin my mother conceived me."[20] Why beautiful? "Cleanse me of sin with hyssop, that I may be purified; wash me, and I shall be whiter than snow."[21] SERMON 124.1.[22]

IF THE ONE, THEN HOW THE OTHER? GREGORY OF ELVIRA: It adds, "I was dark and beautiful, O daughters of Jerusalem." I have to confess that I am astonished at how the church is here called dark and beautiful, since it is not possible for what is dark to be beautiful. How can something dark be so beautiful, or something beautiful be so dark? But pay attention to the mystery of the Word and see how elevated is the sense with which the Holy Spirit speaks. The church called herself dark on account of those from the Gentiles who would become believers, all of whom were seen to be blackened with the filthy smoke of idolatry and sepulcher of sacrifices. But they were made beautiful through faith in Christ and the holiness of the Spirit, whom they received. Hence she said, "I was dark" because she had not yet seen herself as the sun. EXPLANATION OF THE SONG OF SONGS 1.23-24.[23]

DARK THROUGH SIN BUT BEAUTIFUL THROUGH LOVE. GREGORY OF NYSSA: The bride further speaks to her pupils of an amazing fact about herself in order that we might learn of the bridegroom's immense love for humankind who added beauty to the beloved [bride] through such love. "Do not marvel," she says, "that righteousness has loved me." Although I have become dark through sin and have dwelt in gloom by my deeds, the bridegroom made me beautiful through his love, having exchanged his very own beauty for my disgrace. After taking the filth of my sins upon himself, he allowed me to share his own purity, and filled me with his beauty. He who first made me lovely from my own repulsiveness has showed his love for me....

The bride says, although the beauty given to me by being loved by righteousness now shines forth, I still realize that in the beginning I was not radiant but black. My former life has created this dark, shadowy appearance. Although I am black, I am now this beautiful form, for the image of darkness has been transformed into beauty....

Then the text adds further words for strengthening the minds of its pupils. The cause of darkness is not ascribed to the Creator, but its origin is attributed to the free will of each person. HOMILIES ON THE SONG OF SONGS 2.[24]

BLACK FROM WORSHIP OF CREATION RATHER THAN OF CREATOR. THEODORET OF CYR: The bride is saying this no longer to the young girls but to those taking pride in the law, glorying and boasting, and reproaching her not only for her foreign origins but also for her former superstition and the black color coming from it. Hence she says to them, "I am not only black but also beautiful: though once blind, I gained my sight, and though once clad in rags, I am now clothed in a vesture of gold, of a rich variety, enjoying the king's regard. I attend on the king, displacing you for raging against the king, delivering him to death, and defiling the bridal chamber with a series of adulteries. So do not reproach me for my black color, nor bring my former vices to the fore: I am black, I admit, but beautiful and pleasing to the bridegroom. ... I too am Ethiopian, then, but the bride of the great lawgiver, daughter of a Midianite priest, an idolatrous man. I forgot my people and my father's house—hence the king desired my beauty."

"So do not gaze on me for my being black, because the sun looked at me; you will see me, black though I now am, made white, and you will cry out, 'Who is this who emerges in her whiteness?' I shall tell you also the reason for this blackness: I became black through worshiping creation instead of the Creator, and adoring this visible sun instead of the sun of

---

[20]Ps 51:5 (50:7 Vg).   [21]Ps 51:7 (50:9 Vg).   [22]FC 47:209.   [23]CCL 69:176-77*.   [24]*GNSS* 60-62*.

righteousness. But I saw the difference between the one and the other, and forsook the creature to worship the Creator. So do not gaze on me for being blackened because the sun looked at me—or, as Symmachus says, fastened upon me.[25] In fact, 'I am black and beautiful, daughters of Jerusalem': black as a result of the former impiety, beautiful as a result of repentance; black as a result of unbelief, beautiful as a result of belief. I was as black 'as the tents of Kedar,' which means darkness; I became beautiful 'like Solomon's curtains.' " COMMENTARY ON THE SONG OF SONGS 1.[26]

BLACK FROM STENCH BUT BEAUTIFUL FROM EXPECTATION OF THE LORD. THEODORET OF CYR: In the Song of Songs the bride cries aloud, "I am black and beautiful, O daughters of Jerusalem"—"black" in the sense of deceived, besmirched by the stench of wild beasts, and "beautiful" in the sense of awaiting for your arrival from heaven as Lord for the sake of my salvation. He suggested at the same time both the gloom of impiety and the charm given by divine grace. COMMENTARY ON PSALM 87.3.[27]

A BEAUTIFUL SINNER. HIPPOLYTUS: "I am black and beautiful, daughters of Jerusalem." I am a sinner, but even more, I am beautiful, because Christ loved me. "I am black and beautiful, daughters of Jerusalem." All nations, come and gather and look at me, the beloved. "Do not marvel at my countenance because I am darkened or because the sun's glance has made me swarthy."... Nor is it because Christ has despised me, since [Scripture] calls him the true sun, for it says, "And the sun of righteousness will appear to you who fear my name."[28] TREATISE ON THE SONG OF SONGS 4.1-2.[29]

DARK IN YOUR JUDGMENT BUT BEAUTIFUL BY GRACE. GREGORY THE GREAT: For we know that in the first days of the church, when the grace of our Redeemer had been preached, some of the Jews believed and others did not. Those who

believed were despised by the unbelievers and suffered persecution as though they had been found guilty of taking the way of the Gentiles. Hence the church in their name cries out against those who had not converted: "I am black but beautiful, daughters of Jerusalem." COMMENTARY ON THE SONG OF SONGS 32.[30]

BLACK BY ADVERSITY BUT BEAUTIFUL BY VIRTUE. BEDE: Black, of course, with the adversity of hardships but beautiful with the adornment of virtue, indeed as much more beautiful in the sight of interior judgment as the vexations of the foolish are greater. It is as though she were befouled with afflictions. The daughters of Jerusalem to whom this speaks are souls imbued with celestial sacraments, yearning for the dwelling of their heavenly homeland. For, consoling them in their tribulations, holy mother said, "I am black but beautiful, daughters of Jerusalem," as if she had said more clearly: I appear most vile indeed to the eyes of my persecutors, but I shine with the glorious profession of truth before God. Hence you who recognize that you are citizens of a homeland above must at least be sorrowful in the labors of this exile while you hasten through adversities to the vision of everlasting peace. COMMENTARY ON THE SONGS OF SONGS 1.1.4.[31]

BUT THE LITERAL MEANING IS ALL THERE IS. THEODORE OF MOPSUESTIA: [Solomon] took Pharaoh's daughter as his wife. But ... she was dark, as all the Egyptian and Ethiopian women are.... The Hebrews and their beautiful wives, and the other princesses as well, ridiculed her on account of her unseemliness, her small height and her dark complexion. To avoid any irritation on her part and so that no hostility would result between him and the Pharaoh, Solomon exclusively built for her a house of valuable stones [and

---

[25]Symmachus is associated with an ancient alternative translation of the Hebrew that would have been available to Theodoret in a copy of the Hexapla. [26]ECS 2:44-45*. [27]FC 102:79*. [28]Mal 4:2. [29]CSCO 264:31. [30]SC 314:118. [31]CCL 119B:195.

decorated it] with gold and silver. During the meals he chanted [the Song of Songs] in her presence in order to honor her, and he made known with it that she was dark yet beautiful and loved by him. Paraphrase of the Commentary of Theodore of Mopsuestia.[32]

1:6 The Rays of the Sun

Blackness of the Soul. Origen: "Look not at me, for that I am darkened; for the sun has looked down on me.". . .

It is commonly said among the whole of the Ethiopian race, in which there is a certain natural blackness inherited by all, that in those parts the sun burns with fiercer rays, and that bodies that have once been scorched and darkened transmit a congenital stain to their posterity. But the reverse is the case with the blackness of the soul. For the soul is scorched, not by being looked at by the sun but by being looked down upon. Its blackness, therefore, is acquired not through birth but through neglect; and, since it comes through sloth, it is repelled and driven away by means of industry. Commentary on the Song of Songs 2.2.[33]

Spiritual Sunlight Contrasted to Visible Sunlight. Origen: Yonder visible sun, then, darkens and burns the bodies that come within its range when it is at the zenith; whereas it keeps within its light and does not burn at all those bodies that are distant and situated further from it when in that position. But the spiritual sun, by contrast, the Sun of Justice in whose wings is healing,[34] we are told, illuminates and surrounds with every brightness those whom he finds upright in heart and standing close to the zenith of his splendor. But [he] must look askance at those who walk contrary to him, and he cannot look on them with favor. It is their own fickleness and instability that brings this about. . . .

For it was not by that visible light of ours that the world was made; that light is itself a part of the world. The world was made by that true Light, who, as we are told, looks askance at us if we walk contrary to it. Commentary on the Song of Songs 2.2.[35]

The Sun Also Is Christ. Gregory of Elvira: "Do not look at me," it says, "because the sun has not regarded me." The prophet Ezekiel proved that the sun is Christ when he said, "upon you who fear the Lord, the sun of righteousness will rise,"[36] who is Christ. For, as I have often said, before the advent of the Son of God, the church of the Gentiles was dark because it had not yet believed in him. But when it was illuminated by Christ the true sun, it was made extremely lovely and decorous, such that the Holy Spirit would say to it through David: "the king desired your beauty."[37] Explanation of the Song of Songs 1.25.[38]

It Is Also Possible to Be Black and Ugly. Origen: We understand, then, why the bride is black and beautiful at one and the same time. But if you do not likewise practice penitence, take heed lest your soul be described as black and ugly, and you be hideous with a double foulness— black by reason of your past sins and ugly because you are continuing in the same vices. Homilies on the Song of Songs 1.6.[39]

Failure to Watch Over One's Affairs. Gregory the Great: The church says of its weak members, "They have put me as a guard in the vineyards; my own vineyard I have not guarded." Our vineyards are our deeds, and we cultivate them by our daily labor. We are put as guards in the vineyards, but we do not cultivate our own. When we are involved with external affairs, we neglect to watch over our own activities. Forty Gospel Homilies 19 (17).[40]

---

[32]TMB 50**. [33]ACW 26:106-7. [34]Mal 4:2. [35]ACW 26:109-10*. [36]Mal 4:2. [37]Ps 45:11 (44:12 LXX). [38]CCL 69:177. [39]ACW 26:276*. [40]CS 123:145.

1:7-8 QUESTIONS IN A DIALOGUE OF LOVE

⁷Tell me, you whom my soul loves,
where you pasture your flock,
where you make it lie down at noon;
for why should I be like one who wanders^c
beside the flocks of your companions?

⁸If you do not know,
O fairest among women,
follow in the tracks of the flock,
and pasture your kids
beside the shepherds' tents.

c Gk Syr Vg: Heb *is veiled*

OVERVIEW: As the bride seeks the bridegroom, so the spouse seeks the shepherd and the church seeks Christ (AUGUSTINE), and they meet at midday. But a noonday meeting and the flocks of companions also portend dangers (JEROME, AUGUSTINE). There are pastors who mislead the faithful (GREGORY THE GREAT), in fact false shepherds (THEODORET OF CYR). Association with multiple shepherds can easily lead to error and confusion (ORIGEN, AUGUSTINE).

1:7 Conversation of Bride and Bridegroom

THE BRIDE SEEKS THE BRIDEGROOM. AUGUSTINE: "Tell me, you whom my soul loves, where do you feed your flock, where you lie down?" Neither we nor they have any doubt that the bride is speaking to the bridegroom, the church to Christ. But listen to all the words of the bride. Why do you want to attribute to the bridegroom a word that is still in the bride's part? Let the bride say everything she says, and then the bridegroom will reply. . . .

Midday is coming, you see, when the shepherds take refuge in the shade; and perhaps where you are feeding your flock and lying down will escape me; and I want you to tell me, lest perchance I go as one veiled, that is, as one concealed and not recognized. I am in fact plain to see, but lest as one veiled, as one hidden, I stumble on the flocks of your companions. SERMON 46.36.[1]

BEWARE THE FLOCKS OF COMPANIONS. AUGUSTINE: Why do I want you to tell me where you graze, where you lie down in the noonday? "Lest I should happen, like a veiled woman, on the flocks of your companions." That is the reason, she says, why I want you to tell me where you graze your flock, where you lie down in the noonday. When I come to you I won't lose my way, lest like a veiled woman I should come upon the flocks of your companions, that is to say, I should stumble on flocks that are not yours but belong to your companions. SERMON 147A.3.[2]

AS SPOUSE TO SHEPHERD, SO CHURCH TO CHRIST. AUGUSTINE: With good reason then to this shepherd of shepherds, does his beloved, his spouse, his fair one, but by him made fair, before by sin deformed, beautiful afterward through pardon and grace, speak in her love and ardor after him, and say to him, "Where do you feed?" And observe how, by what transport this spiritual love is here animated. And far better are they by this transport delighted who have tasted of the sweetness of this love. They bear this properly who love Christ. For in them, and of them, does the church sing this in the Song of Songs. SERMON 88.6.[3]

IN THE MIDDAY SUN. JEROME: I linger long in

---

[1]*WSA 3 2:286-87*. [2]*WSA 3 4:453.* [3]*NPNF 1 6:524*.

the land of the midday sun, for it was there and then that the spouse found her bridegroom at rest. LETTER 108.12.[4]

NOONDAY PROMISE OF HERETICS IS NOT THE LIGHT OF CHRIST. JEROME: You see that it is not in the third hour that the spouse dines or reclines but at midday. Where do you dine, where do you rest, where shall I find you, where do you enjoy delights, where can I find you, O my spouse? Do you want to find me? At noon, in perfect knowledge, in good works, in the bright light. Because we have the noonday, that is why the devil disguises himself as an angel of light[5] and pretends that he has the light, that he has the noonday. When heretics promise any pseudo-mysteries, when they promise the kingdom of heaven, when they promise continence, fasts, sanctity, the renunciation of the world, they promise the noonday. But since their midday is not the light of Christ, it is not the noonday but the noonday demon. HOMILIES ON THE PSALMS 20 (PSALM 90).[6]

PASTORS WHO MISLEAD THE FAITHFUL. GREGORY THE GREAT: That which we said about heretical teachers we can also say about catholics who do not behave properly. For many of the faithful poor within the church seek to live rightly, desire to maintain a just life, and consider the example of the priests who were set over them. Thus, as long as the priests themselves do not live righteous lives, as long as they who preside do not act properly, they who follow also slip into error. This is why the church says, as though in the name of the poor and faithful, "Tell me, you whom my soul loves, where do you pasture, where do you rest at noon?" COMMENTARY ON THE SONG OF SONGS 43.[7]

FALSE SHEPHERDS. THEODORET OF CYR: It is logical for the bride to enquire at the time of midday where the bridegroom takes his rest because when the light of knowledge became stronger, heresies developed which, while bearing the name of Christians, were nevertheless devoid of truth.

This is the reason she is exercised and anxious to learn the spot where the bridegroom rests the sheep, the risk of falling in with the flocks of so-called companions. It should be understood that just as there were the prophets and the false prophets opposed to them, and likewise apostles and false apostles of an opposite mind, so too false Christs are referred to in the divine Scripture. Hence the Lord also says, "Many false prophets will rise up and will lead many people astray."[8] And blessed Paul was in the habit of speaking not only of false brethren but also of false apostles—hence his remark, "For such people are false apostles."[9] The bride begs not to fall in with these people since they give the appearance of shepherds and likewise seem to have flocks and herds. Of such kind are the people who hold the views of Arius, Eunomius, Marcion, Valentinus, Mani and Montanus. While invested with a Christian appearance and name, building churches, reading divine Scriptures to sheep led astray, wrongly tending their followers and thought to be companions of the bridegroom, they are instead pernicious schemers, providing the sheep with poison instead of nourishing draughts. COMMENTARY ON THE SONG OF SONGS 1.[10]

1:8 The Tents of Other Shepherds

LOVE THAT WAVERS. AUGUSTINE: "If you do not know yourself, go out, you, in the tracks of the flocks, and graze your goats in the tents of the shepherds." Go out in the tracks, not of the flock but of the flocks, and graze, not like Peter my sheep but your goats; in the tabernacles, not of the shepherd but of the shepherds; not of unity but of division, not established in the place where there is one flock and one shepherd.

By this answer she has been stiffened, built up, made stronger as the beloved wife, ready to die for her husband and live with her husband. SERMON 138.8.[11]

---

[4]NPNF 2 6:200. [5]2 Cor 11:14. [6]FC 48:160. [7]SC 314:132*. [8]Mt 24:1. [9]2 Cor 11:13. [10]ECS 2:47. [11]WSA 3 4:390*.

ASSOCIATION CAN LEAD TO ERROR. ORIGEN: The passage before us, then, enjoins the soul, under the figure of a woman, that she should know herself. . . .

And for this reason, when a soul has thus neglected knowledge, it is bound to be "carried about with every wind of doctrine"[12] into the deception of errors. It pitches its tent now with one shepherd—that is, with one teacher of the Word—and now with another, and so it is carried hither and thither, tending not sheep, which

are guileless creatures, but goats, that is, wanton, restless, sinful inclinations; for which purpose indeed it has sought these diverse teachers. And this will be the punishment of the fault of the soul who has not tried to know itself and to follow that Shepherd only who lays down his life for the sheep.[13] COMMENTARY ON THE SONG OF SONGS 2.5.[14]

---

[12]Eph 4:14. [13]Jn 10:11. [14]ACW 26:132-33.

1:9-17 SOME DETAILS
OF THE FIRST MEETING

[9]I compare you, my love,
   to a mare of Pharaoh's chariots.
[10]Your cheeks are comely with
      ornaments,*
   your neck with strings of jewels.
[11]We will make you ornaments of gold,
   studded with silver.

[12]While the king was on his couch,
   my nard gave forth its fragrance.
[13]My beloved is to me a bag of myrrh,
   that lies between my breasts.

[14]My beloved† is to me a cluster of henna
      blossoms
   in the vineyards of En-gedi.

[15]Behold, you are beautiful, my love;
   behold, you are beautiful;
   your eyes are doves.
[16]Behold, you are beautiful, my beloved,
      truly lovely.
   Our couch is green;
[17]the beams of our house are cedar,
   our rafters[d] are pine.

d The meaning of the Hebrew word is uncertain *LXX like a turtledove †LXX brother

OVERVIEW: Pharaoh and his chariots stand against God's people (ORIGEN, GREGORY OF ELVIRA, GREGORY THE GREAT), for Pharaoh represents the enemy common to us all (THEODORET OF CYR). A string of jewels for the neck can betoken modesty of disposition (NILUS OF ANCYRA). It can also be deceiving in appearance (JULIAN OF ECLANUM), although certain externals can have

deeper meaning when the shadows are eclipsed by reality (AUGUSTINE, JEROME, BEDE). So also it is with law and gospel (CAESARIUS), with nard and myrrh (NILUS OF ANCYRA), and with the heart's location between the breasts (GREGORY OF NYSSA, THEODORET OF CYR). Indeed, the outcome of the grape harvest was no more certain than that of the crucifixion (NILUS OF ANCYRA). There are many examples to be learned from a dove (ORIGEN, GREGORY OF NYSSA, JEROME, BEDE), whose eyes are particularly reflective of deeper spiritual reality (ORIGEN). Likewise there is deeper meaning in beams of cedar and rafters of pine (AMBROSE, GREGORY OF ELVIRA).

1:9 Pharaoh's Chariots

FOR THE PERSECUTION OF GOD'S PEOPLE. ORIGEN: Let us see now whether, on the mystical interpretation, under the figure of the chariots and four-horse teams of Pharaoh headed and driven by him for the persecution of God's people and the oppression of Israel, he is perhaps describing souls who are under the dominion of the spiritual pharaoh and spiritual wickedness. For it is certain that the evil spirits stir up the temptations and troubles which they arouse against the saints, by means of certain souls who are suitable and convenient for the purpose. Mounting these like chariots, they fiercely attack and assail both the church of God and individual believers. COMMENTARY ON THE SONG OF SONGS 2.6.[1]

IN THE POWER OF THE DEVIL. GREGORY OF ELVIRA: "My horses are with Pharaoh's chariots," it says. The horses of the Lord, that is, the people of the Gentiles, were formerly with Pharaoh's chariots, that is, in the power of the devil, since they had not yet believed in Christ. He forewarns them, therefore, not to submit themselves again to that yoke through contempt of the faith. For, as I have already said, the people of the Gentiles who required horses were held under the Pharaoh's yoke, that is, with the chariots of the devil, before the Lord's advent, even though the Lord already foreknew them to be his own. But there is no doubt that the Pharaoh is the devil, for the devil tyrannizes the world like the Pharaoh did Egypt. Moreover, just as the Pharaoh persecuted the sons of Israel, so does the devil persecute the saints in this world. . . . Yet, now liberated by the grace of Christ from the yoke of tyrannical servi-

tude, having been made sons of God through faith, and destined for celestial glory with a pure heart and true devotion in all holiness and righteousness, let us hold firmly to the same faith through which we live and are saved. EXPLANATION OF THE SONG OF SONGS 2.24-27.[2]

SERVING PHARAOH OR GOD? GREGORY THE GREAT: All who are servants of hedonism, pride, avarice, envy and falsehood are still under Pharaoh's chariot, being like horses under [the control of] Pharaoh's chariot, that is, under the devil's rule. But all who strive for humility, chastity, doctrine and charity have been made horses of our Creator, having been placed in the chariot of God, with God as their driver. COMMENTARY ON THE SONG OF SONGS 45.[3]

PHARAOH REPRESENTS THE ENEMY COMMON TO US ALL. THEODORET OF CYR: Here in figurative fashion he referred by "Pharaoh" to the implacable foe of our nature, the noxious enemy common to us all whom he drowned in the holy waters of baptism like Pharaoh. My mare, then, which I used when I overwhelmed Pharaoh's chariots, I judge you to resemble since you are close to me and have love for me. . . . So from the apostolic words we understand the mystical words of the Song, and hear the bridegroom saying, I declare that you, being close to me, and hence called an intimate, getting the name from the fact, are like my mare, which I used when drowning the spiritual Pharaoh with his chariots, and I granted you freedom. COMMENTARY ON THE SONG OF SONGS 1.[4]

1:10 A Neck with Strings of Jewels

THE CHURCH IS TO CHRIST LIKE A TURTLEDOVE. THEODORET OF CYR: "How beautifully made your cheeks, like those of a turtledove." Zoologists claim that the turtledove not only likes solitude but is also not promiscuous, the

---

[1]ACW 26:140. [2]CCL 69:187-88. [3]SC 314:136. [4]ECS 2:48.

male mating with one female, and the female associating with one male, and at the death of its mate it refrains from mating with another bird. Appropriately, then, he says the church in its relationship to Christ is like her, shunning relations with others, and reluctant after his death to abandon him, awaiting instead the resurrection and looking forward to his second coming. He also says her neck is like a necklace; this is a choker, a kind of ornament beautifying the neck. He is commending her for nicely carrying the yoke of religion, of which the bridegroom says in the Gospels, "Take my yoke upon you, for my yoke is easy and my burden light."[5] COMMENTARY ON THE SONG OF SONGS I.[6]

THE STRINGS OF JEWELS CAN BETOKEN MODESTY OF DISPOSITION. NILUS OF ANCYRA: Wishing to inspire a spirit of humility in her actions, the Word says this: "Your neck is as if circled with jewels." For just as he describes "the stiff neck" of the proud as "a sinew of iron"[7] because of its stiffness, so too he describes the neck of a modest person as a necklace [with strings of jewels]. He thus designates the form of the virtue by its shape. For modest persons (even if such people stand tall) are bent down in the manner of a necklace when they think humbly of themselves and restrain the vanity of pride that accompanies virtue, which is a fact of the weakness of human nature. For the memory of earth and the ancient parentage of clay[8] is sufficient to destroy such vainglory even if the honor of the image and the excellence of the actions may cause an inflation of pride.

And the Word does not call the neck of the humble simply a "necklace," for there are indeed those who by affectation take the appearance of humility while they pursue human glory. To them the Word says, "If you bend your neck like a ring."[9] Wishing to show the difference between them and a perfect soul, he has compared their behavior to the ring of iron which those who are condemned wear in punishment, for virtue contrived for the sake of deception ends by assuming the aspect of punishment. But the virtue of the

bride he has compared to a necklace of gold, letting her [inner] condition be intimated through her appearance while the substance [of that virtue] is thus proven.[10] . . .

If then the necklace indicates humility, such a neck, compared with a necklace that is praiseworthy, also reveals the abundance of virtues and the lowliness pertaining to each of them. For just as the necklace, forged at right angles, is eventually curved to its own given use, so too persons who are perfect in virtue are humbled by submission. Although being upright in their manner of life, they take on a curvature in the disposition of their minds. COMMENTARY ON THE SONG OF SONGS 26.[11]

AN EVALUATION OF EXTERNAL APPEARANCES. JULIAN OF ECLANUM: When the naturally beautiful neck is endowed with the adornment of jewels, such industry undoubtedly increases happiness and, as though they were worthy, the honor of necklaces and the loveliness of necks as well. This is also true with you, therefore, whose generosity is constituted by doctrine, so that discipline would perfect the virtues which nature began. COMMENTARY ON THE SONG OF SONGS, FRAGMENT 9.[12]

1:11-12 Ornaments of Gold

GOLDEN BUT NOT GOLD. THEODORET OF CYR: Logically they said "golden ornaments" and not gold itself, since the bridegroom's presents are greater, and his servants' do not have equal splendor. Hence we show the divine Gospels greater respect, though we also respect the law and the prophets and the writings of the holy apostles. COMMENTARY ON THE SONG OF SONGS I.[13]

A LIFE HIDDEN WITH CHRIST. AUGUSTINE: We may appropriately understand of them, what

---

[5]See Mt 11:29-30. [6]ECS 2:49. [7]Is 48:4. [8]See Job 10:9. [9]See Is 58:5. [10]See 2 Cor 10:18. [11]SC 403:190-94. [12]CCL 88:400. [13]ECS 2:49.

was said to the bride in the Canticle of Canticles: "We shall make you likenesses of gold inlaid with silver while the king is reclining at his table," that is, while Christ is in his secret place, because "your life is hidden with Christ in God. When Christ your life shall appear, then you too will appear with him in glory."[14] On the Trinity 1.8.16.[15]

From Shadow to Reality. Jerome: Let us hear what the bride says before that the bridegroom comes to earth, suffers, descends to the lower world, and rises again. "We will make for you likenesses of gold with ornaments of silver while the king sits at his table." Before the Lord rose again and the gospel shone, the bride had not gold but likenesses of gold. As for the silver, however, which she professes to have at the marriage, she not only had silver ornaments, but she had them in variety—in widows, in the continent and in the married. Then the bridegroom makes answer to the bride and teaches her that the shadow of the old law has passed away and the truth of the gospel has come. Against Jovinianus 1.30.[16]

Mary's Spikenard Was a Type. Bede: There comes about in our case too what follows: "And the house was filled with the fragrance of the ointment."[17] In accord with our capacity will the world be filled with the renown of our devotion, by which we prove that we venerate and love God and our neighbors with a simple and pure heart. There is accomplished what the bride glories of in the canticle of love, "While the king was resting [on his couch], my spikenard gave forth its fragrance." Here it is clearly shown that what Mary did as a type, the entire church and every perfect soul should do always. Homilies on the Gospels 2.4.[18]

1:13-14 Prefigurations of the Savior

Law and Gospel. Caesarius of Arles: For this reason it ought to be clear to your minds that the fig tree was an image of the law, just as it is certain that the cluster of grapes prefigured the Savior, as the church declares in the Canticle of Canticles: "My brother is for me a cluster of henna." Christ, indeed, cannot exist without the law or the law without Christ, for we have said that the law is evidence of the gospel, and the gospel is the fulfillment of the law. Sermon 106.4.[19]

Both Nard and Myrrh. Nilus of Ancyra: She calls him "nard" because of his working of miracles and service of kindness extended to all, and "bag of myrrh" because of his suffering, death and the infamy represented by his cross, when he concentrated the inactive power of his divinity into his body as if in a little bag. For it is not the same to believe in one who works miracles and is glorified as to trust in one who is crucified, buried and taken for dead. The common response of humanity is to recognize his divinity [only] when they enjoy his benefits and are convinced by numerous signs, for the action of the miracle does not so much relieve the judgment as its plausibility. On the contrary, to see him suffer, exposed to banter[20] and enduring the injuries of malefactors[21]—without doubt or perplexity but rather keeping in every circumstance the same judgment: this is the deed of a very small number or perhaps of only one perfect soul. . . .

That he dwells between the breasts of the bride is a sign that he has humbled himself from infancy and has assumed the human sufferings of hunger, thirst, slumber and physical fatigue. Commentary on the Song of Songs 29.[22]

The Heart Between the Breasts. Gregory of Nyssa: The location of the heart is said by experts to lie between the two breasts. Here is where the bride says that she has the sachet in which her treasure is kept. Also, the heart is said to be a source of warmth from which the body's heat is distributed through the arteries. The body's members are thereby heated, ani-

---

[14]Col 3:3-4. [15]FC 45:23. [16]NPNF 2 6:368*. [17]Jn 12:3. [18]CS 111:38. [19]FC 47:129. [20]See Lk 23:36. [21]See Lk 23:39. [22]SC 403:204-6.

mated and nourished by the heart's fire. Therefore the bride has received the good odor of Christ in the governing part of the soul and has made her own heart a kind of sachet for such incense. And so she makes all her actions, like parts of the body, seethe with the breath from her heart so that no iniquity can cool her love for God in any member of her body. HOMILIES ON THE SONG OF SONGS 3.[23]

THE HEART IS LOCATED BETWEEN THE BREASTS. THEODORET OF CYR: "It will lodge between my breasts," that is, in the governing part of my soul, which is located in the heart lying between the breasts. This indicates the fulfillment of the prophecy spoken by God, "I shall dwell and walk about among them, and I shall be their God and they shall be my people, says the Lord almighty."[24] The bridegroom in person also makes the promise, "We shall come, my Father and I, and shall make our abode with him."[25] COMMENTARY ON THE SONG OF SONGS 1.[26]

OUTCOME OF THE GRAPE HARVEST WAS NO MORE CERTAIN THAN THAT OF THE CRUCIFIXION. NILUS OF ANCYRA: The cluster of grapes in bloom, suspended from the branch, is not desired by everyone, because it fails to possess an immediate pleasure. Rare indeed are those who rejoice at postponing pleasures, for people attach themselves naturally to the preference of present enjoyment, just as those pleasures whose utility is not immediate but resides in future hope are reckoned not to have the same usefulness. Now it pertains to the science of agriculture to recognize future utility in the present condition of fruit that has not yet reached maturity, and in the unripe grape to discern whether there is any future and assured maturity.

In the same way also, the Lord hanging upon the cross,[27] as if to say in a public examination before the eyes of all, evoked a great despair in those who saw him. For who therefore would not be perplexed, understandably, seeing the liberator of the human race undergoing the ultimate pun-

ishment, seeing the one who accomplished so many miracles and delivered Lazarus from the bonds of death,[28] nailed to the cross and his life passing over into death? Thus the condemnation inflicted at that time upon the good name which everyone attributed to him induced doubt among those who saw it when compared with the opinion regarding him that everyone entertained then. This was because every eye, filled in an untimely way with the evidence of the suffering by which he was tested and forgetting the miracles, took sides with the suffering it could see. For not only the Jews but also the disciples themselves fell into doubt[29] such that even after learning that "he had been raised from the dead,"[30] they did not believe[31] in his resurrection. COMMENTARY ON THE SONG OF SONGS 31.[32]

1:15 The Eyes of a Dove

CHEEKS AND TURTLEDOVES. ORIGEN: This beauty of the cheeks, however, that is, of modesty and chastity, is compared with turtledoves. They say it is the nature of turtledoves that the male bird never mates with any female but one, and the female similarly will not suffer more than a single mate. If one of the pair is killed and the other left, the survivor's desire for intercourse is extinguished with its mate.[33] The figure of the turtledove is thus fittingly applied to the church, either because it knows no union with any other after Christ or because all the continence and modesty that is in it resembles a flight of many doves. COMMENTARY ON THE SONG OF SONGS 2.7.[34]

PERCEPTIVE POWER OF THE EYES OF A DOVE. ORIGEN: Our eyes [are not] such as the eyes of Christ's beautiful bride must be, of which eyes the bridegroom says, "Your eyes are doves." He is

---

[23]GNSS 86. [24]Lev 26:12. [25]Jn 14:23. [26]ECS 2:51. [27]See Acts 10:39. [28]Jn 11:41-44. [29]See Mt 28:17. [30]Rom 6:9. [31]See Lk 24:11. [32]SC 403:210-12. [33]Commonly believed in the ancient world. [34]ACW 26:146.

hinting, perhaps, at the perceptive power of spiritual people, because the Holy Spirit came upon the Lord as a dove,[35] and the Lord is in each one. Nevertheless, even in our condition, we will not hesitate to examine the words of life that have been spoken, and to attempt to grasp their power which streams forth into him who has apprehended them with faith. COMMENTARY ON THE GOSPEL OF JOHN 10.173.[36]

THE DOVE'S IMAGE IN THE PUPILS OF THE BRIDE'S EYES. GREGORY OF NYSSA: When her own beauty is manifest, the loveliness of her eyes is extolled. The bridegroom says that her eyes are those of a dove that seem to convey this meaning: when the pupils of the eye are clear, the faces of those gazing at them are clearly reflected. Persons skilled in studying natural phenomena say that the eye sees by receiving the impression of images emanating from visible objects. For this reason the beauty of the bride's eyes is praised since the image of a dove appears in her pupils. Whenever a person gazes upon an object he receives in himself the image of that object. He who no longer attends to flesh and blood looks toward the life of the Spirit. As the apostle says, such a person lives in the Spirit, conforms to the Spirit, and by the Spirit puts to death the deeds of the body.[37] This person has become wholly spiritual, neither natural nor carnal. HOMILIES ON THE SONG OF SONGS 4.[38]

BEAUTY SEEKS BEAUTY. JEROME: "Ah, you are beautiful, my beloved, ah, you are beautiful: your eyes are doves!" You who are beautiful and strong, because you resemble him of whom it is sung, "In your beauty and your splendor,"[39] will hear from your spouse, "Forget your people and your father's house. So shall the king desire your beauty."[40] HOMILIES ON THE PSALMS, ALTERNATE SERIES 61 (PSALM 15).[41]

SOME EXAMPLES TO BE LEARNED FROM A DOVE. BEDE: Since the image of a dove is placed before us by God so that we may learn the simplicity favored, let us look diligently at its

nature, so that from each one of its examples of innocence we may take the principles of a more correct life. [The dove] is a stranger to malice. May all bitterness, anger and indignation be taken away from us, together with all malice. It injures nothing with its mouth or talons, nor does it nourish itself or its young on tiny mice or grubs, which almost all smaller birds [do]. Let us see that our teeth are not weapons and arrows, lest gnawing and consuming one another we be consumed by one another. Let us keep our hands from plundering. "He who has now been stealing, let him steal no more; let him labor by working with his hands, which is a good thing, so that he may have something he can bestow upon one who is suffering need."[42] It is also reported that the dove often supplies nourishment to strangers as though they were her own young. She feeds them with the fruits and seeds of the earth. HOMILIES ON THE GOSPELS 1.12.[43]

1:17 Beams of Cedar and Rafters of Pine

THE SUPERSTRUCTURE OF THE CHURCH. AMBROSE: These words point to the beautiful adornment of its pedimental structure, which, as beams do, uphold by their excellent qualities the superstructure of the church and give charm to its façade. SIX DAYS OF CREATION 3.13.53.[44]

THE MEANING OF KEDAR. GREGORY OF ELVIRA: Kedar, from the Hebrew, is translated by the Latin word for dark (accordingly, Kedar among the city of the Gentiles at that time seethed with idolatry), for nothing is more forbidding than serving demons. Thus the Lord scolded the people of Israel through the prophet Jeremiah for abandoning the Lord and for worshiping idols made by Gentiles. . . . And Christ spoke in a prophetic way from the voice of the church that was

---

[35]Mt 3:16; Mk 1:10; Lk 3:22; Jn 1:32. [36]FC 80:294*. [37]Gal 5:25. [38]*GNSS* 93. [39]Ps 45:3 (44:4 LXX, Vg). [40]Ps 45:10-11 (44:11-12 LXX, Vg). [41]FC 57:26. [42]Eph 4:28. [43]CS 110:120-21*. [44]FC 42:108.

to be gathered from the Gentiles, saying, "I am dark like the tents of Kedar,"[45] that is, like the gathering of Gentiles. EXPLANATION OF THE

SONG OF SONGS 1.28.[46]

[45]Cf. Song 1:5. [46]CCL 69:178.

2:1-7 THE ROSE OF SHARON, THE LILY OF THE VALLEYS

¹I am a rose[e] of Sharon,*
  a lily of the valleys.

²As a lily among brambles,
  so is my love among maidens.

³As an apple tree among the trees of the
    wood,
  so is my beloved among young men.
  With great delight I sat in his shadow,
    and his fruit was sweet to my taste,

⁴He brought me to the banqueting house,
    and his banner over me was love.[†]
⁵Sustain me with raisins,
    refresh me with apples;
  for I am sick[‡] with love.
⁶O that his left hand were under my head,
    and that his right hand embraced me!
⁷I adjure you, O daughters of Jerusalem,
    by the gazelles[§] or the hinds[#] of the field,
  that you stir not up nor awaken love
    until it please.

e Heb crocus *LXX, Vg flower of the field †LXX he set love before me ‡LXX wounded §LXX powers #LXX forces

OVERVIEW: Christ is likened to a flower of simplicity and lowliness (AMBROSE), for all people (HIPPOLYTUS), who gives life (AMBROSE), and can be consumed (JEROME), a solitary lily that causes other things to grow (NILUS OF ANCYRA), a lily of the valleys that proclaims life over death (THEODORET OF CYR). A lily can also represent the church (GREGORY THE GREAT, BRAULIO OF SARAGOSA), or virtue among thorns (AMBROSE), such as Christ's mother did (THE PASSING OF MARY). Likewise an apple tree can represent shade for the infirm or shade for the church (AMBROSE). The bride's prescient faith in the grape cluster betokened, indeed, an extraordinary foreknowledge of Deity (NILUS OF ANCYRA). So there is a right order to love (AUGUSTINE, JOHN CASSIAN, BEDE), but

one can also be sick from God's love (BASIL) or wounded by it (AUGUSTINE, AMBROSE, APONIUS, CASSIODORUS). Indeed, the words of preachers are the arrows of God's love (GREGORY THE GREAT). The right hand can represent length of life and the left hand riches and glory (ORIGEN), or the right hand honor and good fortune and the left earthly convenience (AUGUSTINE). One can also interpret the left hand as the old law and the right the gospel (GREGORY OF ELVIRA), or the present on the left and the future on the right (CYRIL OF ALEXANDRIA). One can consider the left hand guidance and the right hand protection (JOHN CASSIAN), or the left this present life and the right eternity (GREGORY THE GREAT). Yet another interpretation is to see the left as honor and glory and the right as length of life (LEANDER OF SEVILLE), or the left earthly pleasures and the right eternal blessings (BEDE). Or the two together can be a figure of wedlock (JEROME). Whatever, the symbolism is profound (THEODORET OF CYR), and some verses provide great difficulty even for a seasoned interpreter (NILUS OF ANCYRA). Finally, an oath is taken to lead the less advanced to a life of virtue (GREGORY OF NYSSA), but love must be continually rekindled (THEODORET OF CYR).

2:1 Christ's Beauty as a Flower in a Field

A FLOWER OF SIMPLICITY AND LOWLINESS. AMBROSE: He says himself, "I am a flower of the field, a lily of the valleys, as a lily among brambles." Consider, then, another place in which the Lord likes to reside, and not only one place but many. He says, "I am a flower of the field," because he often visits the open simplicity of a pure mind; "and the lily of the valleys," for Christ is the bloom of lowliness, not of luxury, voluptuousness, of lasciviousness, but the flower of simplicity and lowliness. "A lily among brambles" as the flower of a good odor is sure to grow in the midst of hard labors and heartfelt sorrow (since God is pleased with a contrite heart). ON VIRGINITY 9.51.[1]

A FLOWER FOR ALL PEOPLE. HIPPOLYTUS: The justified here begins to praise herself and says, "I am the flower of the field" because she was not spread abroad throughout the earth. For, behold, I am a flower to all men through faith in you. TREATISE ON THE SONG OF SONGS 17.1.[2]

A FLOWER THAT GIVES LIFE. AMBROSE: He himself said, "I am the flower of the plain, a lily of the valley." The flower, when cut, keeps its odor, and when bruised increases it, nor if torn off does it lose it. So, too, the Lord Jesus, on the gibbet of the cross, neither failed when bruised nor fainted when torn. And when he was cut by that piercing of the spear, being made more beautiful by the color of the outpoured blood, he, as it were, grew

comely again, not able in himself to die, and breathing forth upon the dead the gift of eternal life. ON THE HOLY SPIRIT 2.38-39.[3]

A SOLITARY LILY THAT CAUSES OTHER THINGS TO GROW. NILUS OF ANCYRA: It is necessary to understand that the valleys where the bride is a lily, as she is called, are comparable to these ravines. For in distinguishing herself in the midst of that which is called "hollow" by reason of actions or thoughts that are base, she who is adorned magnificently stands resplendent among them as a lily. It is also because at the age to come she is going to pass judgment on such souls by comparison with the perfection of her own deeds even though by nature she holds no advantage over them, just as the inhabitants of Nineveh and the Queen of the South pass judgment upon a generation that is faithless.[4] Besides the fact that she became as a lily in the valleys where nothing was possible before, these valleys may have begun to bear fruit out of envy for the beauty of her flower, receiving seeds from the sower who went out to sow,[5] . . . like a land rich and good that causes the seed to multiply.[6] . . .

If the valleys, because they are low, fallow and many in number, designate the Gentiles who have come to knowledge[7] after being in the depths of impiety, then the field may designate Israel made level[8] by the teachings of the prophets and the law in order to be ready for cultivation. . . . For the plow of the cross has not yet opened up the earth: that plow to which the Savior has yoked the apostles like oxen in sending them out to cultivate[9] two-by-two. Nor has the land yet been moistened by the blood of the Savior, being sterile and infertile. COMMENTARY ON THE SONG OF SONGS 39-40.[10]

A LILY OF THE VALLEYS PROCLAIMS LIFE OVER DEATH. THEODORET OF CYR: I was "a

---

[1]AOV 26. [2]CSCO 264:38. [3]NPNF 2 10:119. [4]See Mt 12:41-42. [5]See Mt 13:3-8. [6]See Mt 13:19-23. [7]See Acts 15:17-18; 2 Tim 2:15. [8]See Is 40:3-4. [9]See Lk 10:1. [10]SC 403:234-38.

flower of the countryside," that is, I assumed an earthly body and sprang from the earth, being eternal and exalted or, rather, immeasurable. I became "a lily" not of mountains or hills, or simply of the countryside, but of "valleys": I brought not only the good news of salvation to the living but also resurrection to the dead, descending to the lower parts of the earth to fill everything.[11] This is the reason he calls himself "a flower of the countryside, a lily of the valleys," that is, the dead: to them he both promised and brought into effect a return to life. COMMENTARY ON THE SONG OF SONGS 2.[12]

A FLOWER TO BE CONSUMED. JEROME: This flower has become fruit that we might eat it, that we might consume its flesh. Would you like to know what this fruit is? A Virgin from a virgin, the Lord from the handmaid, God from man, Son from mother, fruit from earth. Listen to what the fruit itself says: "Unless the grain of wheat fall into the ground and die, it cannot bring forth much fruit."[13] HOMILIES ON THE PSALMS 6 (PSALM 66).[14]

CHRIST AS ROSE AND LILY. JEROME: [Christ] himself says in the Song of Songs, "I am the rose of Sharon, and the lily of the valley." Our rose is the destruction of death, and [that rose] died that death itself might die in his dying. LETTER 75.1.[15]

2:2 The Lily Among Brambles

MARY'S SOUL AMONG THE THORNS. ANONYMOUS: And when the Lord's day came, at the third hour, just as the Holy Spirit descended upon the apostles in a cloud, so Christ descended with a multitude of angels, and received the soul of his beloved mother. For there was such splendor and perfume of sweetness, and angels singing the songs of songs, where the Lord says, "As a lily among thorns, so is my love among the daughters," that all who were there present fell on their faces, as the apostles fell when Christ transfigured himself before them on Mount Tabor, and

for a whole hour and a half no one was able to rise. But when the light went away, and at the same time with the light itself, the soul of the blessed virgin Mary was taken up into heaven with psalms, and hymns, and songs of songs. And as the cloud went up the whole earth shook, and in one moment all the inhabitants of Jerusalem openly saw the departure of St. Mary. THE PASSING OF MARY 1.[16]

VIRTUE AMONG THORNS. AMBROSE: "I am the flower of the field, and the lily of the valleys, as a lily among thorns." This is a plain declaration that virtues are surrounded by the thorns of spiritual wickedness, so that no one can gather the fruit who does not approach with caution. CONCERNING VIRGINS 1.8.43.[17]

THORNS ARE ALSO DAUGHTERS. AUGUSTINE: But would you like to know what is said to this lady somewhere else, in the Song of Songs? "Like a lily in the midst of thorns, so is my darling in the midst of the daughters." An extraordinary saying—he called the same people both thorns and daughters. And do those thorns do mightily? They do indeed. Can't you see how these heresies too pray, fast, give alms, praise Christ? SERMON 37.27.[18]

CONTRAST OF LILY AND THORNS. AUGUSTINE: So also strange daughters: daughters, because of the form of godliness; strange, because of their loss of virtue. Be the lily there; let it receive the mercy of God: hold fast the root of a good flower, be not ungrateful for soft rain coming from heaven. Be thorns ungrateful, let them grow by the showers: for the fire they grow, not for the garner. EXPLANATIONS OF THE PSALMS 48.8.[19]

THE LILY IS THE CHURCH. GREGORY THE GREAT: Solomon, in the voice of the bridegroom,

---

[11]See Eph 1:23. [12]ECS 2:55. [13]Jn 12:24. [14]FC 48:47. [15]NPNF 2 6:155*. [16]ANF 8:593. [17]NPNF 2 10:370*. [18]WSA 3 2:199. [19]NPNF 1 8:167.

said of the church, "As a lily among briers, so is my love among the maidens." FORTY GOSPEL HOMILIES 38.[20]

THE CHURCH IS THE LILY. BRAULIO OF SARAGOSA: It is written of the church: "As a lily among thorns, so is my beloved among women." LETTER 42.[21]

2:3 An Apple Tree in the Wood

SHADE FOR THE INFIRM. AMBROSE: To this verdure of grace ever-flourishing in Christ the church refers in saying, "I sat down under his shadow whom I desired." The apostles received this privileged gift of verdure, whose leaves could never fall, so as to provide shade for the healing of the sick. Their fidelity of heart and the superabundance of their merits provided shade for bodily infirmities. SIX DAYS OF CREATION 3.17.71.[22]

SHADE FOR THE CHURCH. AMBROSE: "As an apple tree among the trees of the woods, so is my beloved among young men." And seeing this, the church is glad and rejoices, saying with great delight, "I sat in his shadow, and his fruit was sweet to my taste." ON VIRGINITY 9.52.[23]

2:4 Order in Love

EXTRAORDINARY FOREKNOWLEDGE OF DEITY. NILUS OF ANCYRA: Naturally the bride now demands entry into the house of wine. For she alone had believed beforehand in the grape cluster hanging upon the cross, the grape cluster that was counted for nothing by everyone because while still in flower it had not exhibited to everyone the properties of wine. At that time she alone had believed in advance in this grape cluster, although its identity would become clearly manifest only at a later time. She had established in advance an idea so high, even before the wine season itself, which permitted her to anticipate a mental notion of the wine

even in the flowering vine. Besides this, it permitted her to bear witness to Deity from on high present within the one who hung upon the cross, and thus to conceive of impassibility within suffering, of resurrection within death. She alone had firmly grasped, as though it had already been spoken, the message of the vine upon the cross that would soon be pressed out. And thus she experienced before the outcome of events that which the majority experienced only after their outcome had been realized. Hence she requests, as an exceptional privilege of such discernment, entry into the house of wine. COMMENTARY ON THE SONG OF SONGS 45.[24]

LOVING IN RIGHT ORDER. AUGUSTINE: He didn't abolish love of parents, wife, children, but put them in their right order. He didn't say, "Whoever loves" but "whoever loves above me."[25] That's what the church is saying in the Song of Songs: "He put charity in order for me." Love your father, but not above your Lord; love the one who begot you, but not above the one who created you. SERMON 344.2.[26]

PROPERLY ORDERED LOVE. JOHN CASSIAN: There is a properly ordered love that, while hating no one, loves certain persons more by reason of their good qualities. Although it loves everyone in a general way, nonetheless it makes an exception for itself of those whom it should embrace with a particular affection. CONFERENCE 16.14.3.[27]

LOVE'S PROPER DEGREES. AUGUSTINE: What is, "Set in order love in me"? Make the proper degrees, and render to each what is his due. Do not put what should come before, below that which should come after it. Love your parents but prefer God to them. SERMON 50(100).2.[28]

---

[20]CS 123:345. [21]FC 63:89. [22]FC 42:121. [23]AOV 26. [24]SC 403:254-56. [25]Mt 10:37. [26]WSA 3 10:49-50. [27]ACW 57:565. [28]NPNF 1 6:421.

THE RIGHT MEASURE OF LOVE. BEDE: We ought to love God in the first place, enemies in the last; and the measure of love that ought to be weighed out to our neighbors will vary according to the diversity of their merits. We know that the patriarch Jacob, although he loved all his sons, nevertheless loved Joseph more than the rest because of his singular innocence, as Scripture bears witness.[29] Hence the church says pleasingly of Christ in the Song of Songs: "He brought me into the wine chamber, he set charity in order in me." ON THE TABERNACLE 1.6.[30]

2:5 Sick with Love

FROM GOD'S LOVE. BASIL THE GREAT: What reflection is sweeter than the thought of the magnificence of God? What desire of the soul is so poignant and so intolerably keen as that desire implanted by God in a soul purified from all vice and affirming with sincerity, "I languish with love." Totally ineffable and indescribable are the lightning flashes of divine Beauty. THE LONG RULES 2.[31]

THE WOUND OF LOVE. AUGUSTINE: In the Song of Songs it is said, "I am wounded with love"; that is, of being in love, of being inflamed with passion, of sighing for the bridegroom, from whom she received the arrow of the Word. EXPLANATIONS OF THE PSALMS 45.14.[32]

A WOUND WITHOUT A SORE. AMBROSE: The Word of God inflicts a wound, but it does not produce a sore. There is a wound of righteous love, there are wounds of charity, as she has said, "I am wounded with love." The one who is perfect is wounded with love. Therefore the wounds of the Word are good, and good are the wounds of the lover. ON VIRGINITY 14.91.[33]

A WOUND THAT GIVES HEALTH. AUGUSTINE: The wound of love is health-giving. The bride of Christ sings in the Song of Songs, "I am wounded with charity." When is this wound healed? When our desire is sated with good things. It's called a wound as long as we desire and don't yet have. Love, you see, in that case, is the same as if it were a pain. When we get there, when we have what we desire, the pain disappears, the love doesn't cease. SERMON 298.2.[34]

A WOUND THAT LEADS TO GREATER THINGS. APONIUS: The love of eternal life sprouts from the love of knowledge, as does the ability to endure persecution from the love of eternal life, and the virtue of fortitude from persecution, and the perfected glory of martyrdom from fortitude. EXPOSITION OF SONG OF SONGS 3.44.[35]

DYING AND LIVING. CASSIODORUS: The church proclaims in the Song of Songs, "I am wounded by love." So the holy people pray to be pierced by the fear of the Lord, so that by dying they may live, whereas earlier by living they were dying. EXPOSITION OF THE PSALMS 119.120.[36]

WORDS OF PREACHERS ARE THE ARROWS OF GOD'S LOVE. GREGORY THE GREAT: What do we understand by "arrows" but the words of preachers? For when they are drawn forth by the voice of those leading holy lives, they transfix the hearts of the hearers. With these arrows holy church had been struck, saying "I am wounded with love." MORALS ON THE BOOK OF JOB 34.21.[37]

2:6 God's Embrace

THE LEFT HAND AND THE RIGHT. ORIGEN: Turn with all speed to the life-giving Spirit and, eschewing physical terms, consider carefully what is the left hand of the Word of God, what the right. Also [consider] what his bride's head is— the head, that is to say, of the perfect soul or of the church. Do not suffer an interpretation that has to do with the flesh and the passions to carry you away.

---

[29]Gen 37:3. [30]TTH 18:22. [31]FC 9:234. [32]NPNF 1 8:149. [33]AOV 41*. [34]WSA 3 8:225. [35]CCL 19:87. [36]ACW 53:230. [37]LF 31:633*.

For the bridegroom's right and left hands are the same in this place as those attributed to wisdom in the book of Proverbs, where the writer says, "Length of life is in her right hand, and in her left hand riches and glory."[38] COMMENTARY ON THE SONG OF SONGS 3.9.[39]

THE HANDS OF GOD. AUGUSTINE: As for the right hand of the Father, it isn't meant in the manner of the structure of the human body, as though he is on the Son's left, if the Son in terms of bodily positions and relationships is placed on his right. But the right hand of God means the inexpressible peak of honor and good fortune, as we read it said about wisdom: "His left hand under my head, and his right hand embraces me." If earthly convenience has been lying underneath, then eternal felicity is embracing from above. SERMON 214.8.[40]

LEFT HAND INDICATES THE OLD LAW AND THE RIGHT THE GOSPEL. GREGORY OF ELVIRA: These two hands are the two covenants of the old law and the gospel. When it refers to his left hand, it indicates the old covenant, but the right hand is the preaching of the gospel. The old covenant is inferior because it is placed beneath the head of the church, who is Christ, whereas the right hand embraced the church, meaning that old sins were covered by the sacraments of the gospel. Whoever goes forth in faith, therefore, and serves Christ with devotion, leaves the old person beneath himself and embraces anew the body of Christ, which is the church. EXPLANATION OF THE SONG OF SONGS 3.29.[41]

THE PRESENT LIFE ON THE LEFT, THE FUTURE ON THE RIGHT. CYRIL OF ALEXANDRIA: The law is said to be in his left hand, the gospel in his right. Or, the left hand is to be understood as the present life and the right hand as the future life, which will indeed embrace me after it is said to those on the right: "Come, blessed of my Father."[42] We also read elsewhere: "A long life is in wisdom's right hand and riches and glory in its

left hand."[43] Thus, his right hand is the knowledge[44] of divine realities, from which comes eternal life, but his left hand is the knowledge[45] of human realities, from which come riches and glory. He is saying, therefore, My mind exceeds human realities and divine knowledge covers me. For, it is said again: "Honor her that she will embrace you."[46] . . . Rightly, then, is it said that the right hand embraces and the left hand offers support to the head, for the goods of the present life, however much they are thought to be visible, must be subject to the head of the perfect soul and used only out of necessity, as though they were a pillow for the head. But the goods of the future age, because they exceed human nature, being divine, signify the supernatural through this embrace. Perhaps also, since the hands are symbols of acts, the left hand indicates corporeal deeds, whereas the right hand signifies spiritual work. Because the right hand is more powerful, then, it embraces corporeal necessities. FRAGMENTS IN THE COMMENTARY ON THE SONG OF SONGS 2.6.[47]

GUIDANCE AND PROTECTION. JOHN CASSIAN: Solomon also speaks of the right hand and the left hand in the Song of Songs in the person of the bride: "His left hand is under my head, and his right hand will embrace me." Although she indicates that both are beneficial, yet she puts the former under her head because adversities should be subject to the guidance of the heart. They are beneficial only to the extent that they discipline us for a time, instruct us for salvation and make us perfectly patient. But for being fondled and forever protected she desires the bridegroom's right hand to cling to her and to hold her fast in a saving embrace. CONFERENCE 6.10.9.[48]

MARRIAGE IS SIGNIFIED. JEROME: The hands are here a figure of wedlock. LETTER 22.19.[49]

---

[38]Prov 3:16. [39]ACW 26:200. [40]WSA 3 6:155. [41]CCL 69:198-99. [42]Mt 25:34. [43]Prov 3:16. [44]Gk *epistēmē*. [45]Gk *gnōsis*. [46]Prov 4:8. [47]PG 69:1282-83. [48]ACW 57:227. [49]NPNF 2 6:29.

THE PRESENT AND THE ETERNAL. GREGORY THE GREAT: What indeed does the left side mean except this present life, and what does the right side mean except eternal life? FORTY GOSPEL HOMILIES 21.[50]

HONOR AND GLORY AND LENGTH OF LIFE. LEANDER OF SEVILLE: He who has joined you to his company will not sadden you. With his left hand, in which is honor and glory, under your head, with his right arm, in which is length of life, he will embrace you. THE TRAINING OF NUNS, PREFACE.[51]

SEPARATION FROM EARTHLY PLEASURES. BEDE: Surely the left hand of the bridegroom is placed under the head of the bride because the Lord raises up the minds of the faithful with temporal benefits, separating them from earthly pleasures and longings so that they may desire and hope for eternal blessings. And he shall embrace her with his right hand because by revealing the vision of his majesty he glorifies her without end. ON THE TABERNACLE 1.8.[52]

SYMBOLISM OF THE LEFT AND RIGHT HANDS. THEODORET OF CYR: "His left hand under my head, and his right hand will embrace me." Let us be careful once more, however, not to get involved in corporeal ideas on hearing "left hand" and "right hand." Solomon, in fact, speaks of wisdom, which is a habit and not substance: "Length of life and years of existence are in her right hand, and in her left wealth and glory." Likewise regarding the "embrace" you can find in the Proverbs the saying, "Love her, and she will keep you safe; ring her about with a rampart, and she will exalt you; honor her, and she will embrace you."[53] Let us take occasion from this, then, to understand the references spiritually, believing the so-called embrace to be a communion between the divine Word and the pious soul, and the "right and left hands" should be understood in the way taken by us. So as not to leave its deeper meaning undiscerned, however, let us interpret it this way: God is in the habit of

bestowing both beneficence and punishment, distributing both to those who deserve them. Let us accordingly understand beneficent grace in the case of the right hand, and punishment in the case of the left, and thus listen to the bride saying, "His left hand under my head," that is, "I am beyond punishments, I am not subject to them, on account of my closeness to the bridegroom and my attention to his service"; and "His right hand will embrace me," that is, "He will regale me with his beneficence and fill me with it as though enfolding and embracing me, and satisfying my desire." COMMENTARY ON THE SONG OF SONGS 2.[54]

2:7 Solemn Adjuration

THE SKILLS OF ARCHERY APPLIED TO SCRIPTURAL INTERPRETATION. NILUS OF ANCYRA: "I adjure you, O daughters of Jerusalem, by the powers and the forces of the field, that you arouse and waken love as far as it pleases." This verse is of great difficulty. However, it is often necessary to let the understanding run towards the point of the text, in imitation of those who in the practice of archery release many arrows at the target but can hardly reach it even one time. Indeed, there is a resemblance to archers on the part of those who apply their craft to the divine Scripture as if aiming an arrow directly at the point of a passage. It is not easy to say to which of the characters should be applied the expression "to awaken love." To express this in a better way, the act of wakening love is clearly assigned to the "daughters of Jerusalem," but in whom is love to be awakened? In themselves, in the bridegroom, or in the one who is speaking? This is uncertain. For this reason it is necessary to try to fit the meaning of the passage to each example and whatever one finds in the way of a target that has been hit, whether close to "love" or to "truth," that must be accepted as a successful explanation. COMMENTARY ON THE SONG OF SONGS 49.[55]

---

[50]CS 123:158. [51]FC 62:189. [52]TTH 18:37. [53]Prov 3:16. [54]ECS 2:57-58. [55]SC 403:264.

AN OATH FOR ETERNAL SALVATION. GREGORY OF NYSSA: An oath works in two ways. In the present text, the soul is progressing toward great heights, as we have seen. At the same time she is instructing less advanced souls in the way of perfection. She uses the oath not to assure them of the progress she herself has made but to lead them through their oath to a life of virtue. She adjures them to keep their love alert and watchful until his good will come to fulfillment, that is, until all are saved and come to a knowledge of the truth.[56] HOMILIES ON THE SONG OF SONGS 4.[57]

LOVE MUST BE CONTINUALLY REKINDLED. THEODORET OF CYR: "I adjure you, daughters of Jerusalem, by the powers and forces of the field to stir up and awaken love for as long as he wishes," that is, "Do not allow love for God in us to slumber: stir it up and inflame it, and pour the memory of kindnesses like oil on it lest it be said of us also, 'They fell into a deep sleep, and found nothing.'"[58] In other words, if you do not proclaim day in day out his salvation and recall the marvels he worked, and instead you forget his kindnesses, love will be extinguished and die, as it were. We must, on the contrary, continually rekindle it, stir it up and lift the flame itself on high. COMMENTARY ON THE SONG OF SONGS 2.[59]

---

[56]1 Tim 2:4. [57]*GNSS* 104-5. [58]Ps 76:5 (75:6 LXX). [59]ECS 2:58*.

2:8-17 SONGS AT THE BREAK OF SPRING

[8]*The voice of my beloved!*
  Behold, he comes,
 leaping upon the mountains,
  bounding over the hills.
[9]*My beloved is like a gazelle,*
  or a young stag.
 Behold, there he stands
  behind our wall,
 gazing in at the windows,
  looking through the lattice.
[10]*My beloved* speaks and says to me:*
 "Arise, my love, my fair one,
  and come away;[†]
[11]*for lo, the winter is past,*
  the rain is over and gone.
[12]*The flowers appear on the earth,*
  the time of singing[‡] has come,
 and the voice of the turtledove

 is heard in our land.
[13]*The fig tree puts forth its figs,*
  and the vines are in blossom;
  they give forth fragrance.
 Arise, my love, my fair one,
  and come away.
[14]*O my dove, in the clefts of the rock,*
  in the covert of the cliff,
 let me see your face,
  let me hear your voice,
 for your voice is sweet,
  and your face is comely.
[15]*Catch us the foxes,*
  the little foxes,
 that spoil the vineyards,
  for our vineyards are in blossom."

 [16]*My beloved is mine and I am his,*

> he pastures his flock among the lilies.
> ¹⁷Until the day breathes
>   and the shadows flee,

> turn, my beloved, be like a gazelle,
>   or a young stag upon rugged ^f mountains.

f The meaning of the Hebrew word is unknown   *LXX *kinsman*   †LXX *my dove*   ‡LXX *pruning*

OVERVIEW: The Word of God came leaping over the mountains and bounding over the hills, present already but not yet (CYRIL OF ALEXANDRIA, AMBROSE, JEROME), over everyone and everything (GREGORY OF ELVIRA) and over every rebellious power (GREGORY OF NYSSA), down from heaven and back up again (GREGORY THE GREAT). We too can see him leaping if we wish (ORIGEN). The Word comes as a gazelle or young stag, and we must be attentive if we would follow or seek him resting at noonday (AMBROSE, GREGORY THE GREAT). He can destroy enmity between soul and body (AMBROSE). The winter is now past (ORIGEN, GREGORY OF ELVIRA). This is signified by the approach of the stag and the voice of the dove (AMBROSE, THEODORET OF CYR), signified also by the advent of the gospel (JEROME) and the coming of Christ (CYRIL OF ALEXANDRIA). It is signaled by the fig tree (JEROME) and the confounding of heretics (ORIGEN). But we should beware the little foxes in the vineyard who plot against the church (APOSTOLIC CONSTITUTIONS, GREGORY OF ELVIRA, BEDE), and we must refute them as heretics (THEODORET OF CYR, AUGUSTINE). Such is the nature and blessing of love in the heavenly city (AMBROSE, THEODORET OF CYR). The shadows have receded (AMBROSE), the Lord has risen (APONIUS), useless antiquity is terminated, spiritual meaning has been revealed (AUGUSTINE), heavenly heights are accessible (CYRIL OF ALEXANDRIA), and we face the world that is to come (BEDE). We are indeed passing from shadows to reality (NILUS OF ANCYRA).

2:8 The Leaping Lord

ALREADY PRESENT BUT NOT YET. CYRIL OF ALEXANDRIA: "Behold, he comes leaping upon the mountains and jumping across the hills."... Some things imply that the bridegroom is already present, whereas other things suggest that the bridegroom is being sought by the bride. For we too investigate some problems for which we do not know the solution and some problems, when the bridegroom and Word enlightens our hearts, which we find already solved. Then, in other matters, we doubt again and it is revealed to us anew. This will happen often until we possess the bridegroom fully, when he not only comes to us but also remains within us.... "He comes leaping upon the mountains." He also comes trampling upon the nets cast by the evil demon, breaking them that we too might trample on them contemptuously. FRAGMENTS IN THE COMMENTARY ON THE SONG OF SONGS 2.9.[1]

NOT ABSENT FOR LONG. AMBROSE: As they were speaking with one another, she rested in his shadow,[2] and suddenly the Word departed from her in the middle of their conversation. Yet he was not absent for long, for as she sought him, he came leaping over the mountains and bounding over the hills. Soon after, like a gazelle or hart, while he was speaking to his beloved, he leapt up and left her. ISAAC, OR THE SOUL 6.50.[3]

SPRINGING ACROSS THE MOUNTAINS. JEROME: Let us follow Christ in the mountains since our brother like a gazelle or a young stag came leaping over the hills, springing across the mountains. In truth, Christ after the resurrection did not ascend into heaven from the valley but from the mountain. Unless we are mountains of virtue, we cannot ascend into heaven. HOMILIES ON THE PSALMS 45 (PSALM 132).[4]

OVER EVERYONE AND EVERYTHING. GREGORY

---

[1]PG 69:1283-86. [2]Cf. Song 2:3. [3]FC 65:40. [4]FC 48:339.

of Elvira: The mountains are patriarchs, vast with holiness, robust in faith, founded upon a mass of charity, but the hills are prophets, established for seeing. He is said therefore to be raised higher than every mountain, or patriarch, and to leap over every hill, or prophet, because he is Lord over all, with all things being put under his feet. Explanation of the Song of Songs 4.4.[5]

Over Every Rebellious Power. Gregory of Nyssa: The voice of the bridegroom was heard when God spoke through the prophets. After the voice the Word came leaping over the mountains that stood in his way, and by bounding over the hills, he made every rebellious power subject to himself, both the inferior powers and those that are greater. The distinction between mountains and hills signifies that both the superior adversary and the inferior one are trampled and destroyed by the same power and authority. The lion and the dragon, superior beasts, are trampled; so too are the serpent and the scorpion, which are inferior. Homilies on the Song of Songs 5.[6]

Down from Heaven and Back Again. Gregory the Great: The church speaks through Solomon: "See how he comes leaping on the mountains, bounding over the hills!". . . If I can put it this way, by coming for our redemption the Lord leaped! My friends, do you want to become acquainted with these leaps of his? From heaven he came to the womb, from the womb to the manger, from the manger to the cross, from the cross to the sepulcher, and from the sepulcher he returned to heaven. You see how Truth, having made himself known in the flesh, leaped for us to make us run after him. Forty Gospel Homilies 29.[7]

We Too Can See the Word of God Leaping. Origen: You must understand, however, that at first, before he appeared before her eyes, the bridegroom was recognized by the bride by his voice alone. Afterwards, however, he appeared before her eyes, leaping upon certain mountains near that place where the bride was, and skipping over the hills and mountains, not with great steps so much as with great bounds, after the manner of a hart or roe, and in this manner coming with all speed to his bride.

Understand that when he reached the house wherein the bride was staying, he stood a while behind the house, so that at any rate his presence might be noticed; though as yet he would not enter the house openly and for all to see but, lover-like, would first look through the windows at the bride.

Understand also that near the bride's house some nets and snares had been set, so that if she or one of her companions among the daughters of Jerusalem should chance to go out at any time, they would be caught. The bridegroom, moreover, had come to these nets, certain that he could not be caught in them; and, being stronger than they, he tore them and, having torn them, he stepped over them and also looked through them. And after achieving this work he says to the bride, "Arise, come, my neighbor, my bride, my dove."

And he says this in order to show her by the very fact of what he had done, how boldly she herself should now despise the nets which the enemy had spread out in her path, and that she should not fear the snares which she now sees torn by him. And, in order to urge her still more cogently to hasten to himself, he tells her: The whole time that seemed oppressive is now past, and the winter, whose incidence had been her excuse, has departed, and the unprofitable rains have ceased, and the time of flowers is come. . . .

If, then, we too want to see the Word of God, the bridegroom of the soul, "leaping upon the mountains and skipping over the hills," we must first hear his voice. And then when we have heard him in all things, we shall be able to see him under the same conditions as those under which the bride is said to have seen him here. For

[5]CCL 69:200. [6]*GNSS* 111-12. [7]CS 123:234**.

although she herself saw him before, she did not see him as she sees him now, "leaping upon the mountains and skipping over the hills." Nor did she see him leaning through the windows or looking through the net; but rather it appears that on that first occasion she saw him in the time of winter. For he says now for the first time that the winter is past. . . .

For if you consider how in the space of a short time the Word of God has run through all the world that was possessed of false beliefs, and has recalled it to the knowledge of the true faith, you will understand in what sense he leaps upon the mountains. [He overcomes] some great kingdoms with his leaps, that is to say, and inclines them to receive the knowledge of divine religion—and he springs forth over the hills in that he swiftly subjugates the lesser kingdoms and leads them to the piety of true worship. COMMENTARY ON THE SONG OF SONGS 3.11.[8]

2:9 A Gazelle or Young Stag

FOLLOW THE ONE WHO COMES LEAPING.
AMBROSE: Be a follower of him "who comes leaping upon the mountains, skipping over the hills, looking through the windows," beyond the reach of snares. The bonds of pleasure, which give delight to the eye, charm to the ear, but pollution to the mind, are evil. What pleasure offers is often spurious. CAIN AND ABEL 1.5.15.[9]

BE ALWAYS ATTENTIVE. AMBROSE: Because we ought always to be anxious, always attentive, and because the Word of God leaps forth like the gazelle or the hart, let the soul who searches after him and longs to possess him always be on watch and maintain her defenses. ISAAC, OR THE SOUL 5.38.[10]

SEEK THE STAG RESTING AT NOONDAY. GREGORY THE GREAT: Holy church says to the one she is seeking under the figure of a young stag, "Tell me, you whom my soul loves, where you pasture, where you lie down at noon."[11] The Lord is

referred to as a young stag, an offspring of deer, because of the flesh he assumed as a son of the ancient fathers. Heat increases at noon, and the young stag seeks a shady place not affected by the heat. The Lord rests in hearts not on fire with love of the present age, which are not burnt up by unspiritual desires, and which, if they are on fire, are not dried up by their anxious desires in this world. FORTY GOSPEL HOMILIES 33.[12]

THE STAG DESTROYS ENMITY BETWEEN SOUL AND BODY. AMBROSE: He came then, and at first he is behind the wall, so that he may destroy the enmity between soul and body by removing the wall, which seemed to offer an obstacle to harmony. Then he looks through the windows. Hear the prophet as he tells what the windows are: "The windows are opened from heaven."[13] Thus he means the prophets, through whom the Lord had regard for the race of humankind, before he should come down on earth himself. Today also, if any soul seeks after him much, it will merit much mercy, because very much is owed to the person who seeks much. Therefore if any soul searches for him with greater zeal, it hears his voice from afar and, although it inquires of others, it hears his voice before those from whom it is asking. It sees that he is running, bounding, that is, hastening and running and leaping over those who cannot receive his strength from weakness of heart. Then, by reading the prophets and remembering their words, the soul sees him looking through their riddles,[14] looking, but as if through a window, not yet as if present. ISAAC, OR THE SOUL 4.32-33.[15]

2:10-14 The Winter Is Past

APPROACH OF THE STAG SIGNIFIES THE END OF WINTER. AMBROSE: Good is the stag whose mountain is the house of God. He ran to it with such speed that he anticipated the wishes and longings of the bride. Indeed, where she had seen

---

[8]ACW 26:206-7, 211-13. [9]FC 42:373-74. [10]FC 65:32. [11]Song 1:7. [12]CS 123:275. [13]Is 24:18. [14]See Num 12:8. [15]FC 65:29.

him coming from afar, she suddenly recognized that he was in her presence, and in consequence she also says, "Behold, he is behind our wall, gazing through the windows, standing out through the netting. My cousin answered and said to me, 'Arise, come, my near one, my beautiful one, my dove, for behold! The winter is past, the rain is over, is gone; the flowers have appeared on the earth.' " The winter is the synagogue; the rain, the people of the Jews, which could not look upon the sun; the flowers are the apostles. THE PRAYER OF JOB AND DAVID 4.1.3.[16]

THE BRIDE OR DOVE OR SPIRIT LOCATED IN THE MIDDLE OF THE TWO TESTAMENTS. THEODORET OF CYR: It makes sense, therefore, for the bridegroom to call the bride, mature in virtue as she is, "dove," that is, spiritual and filled with the Holy Spirit. . . .

The bridegroom encourages and consoles his church in its struggle with trials, "peeps through the windows and looks in through the netting," and urges her to stand fast and to fly to him. . . .

He is saying, if you rest in the middle of the two Testaments and draw benefit from both, you will find there the manifold gifts of the Spirit. The bride, accordingly, by accepting the spiritual exhortation and lying between the lots, found the wings coated in silver through which she was bidden fly up to the bridegroom. COMMENTARY ON THE SONG OF SONGS 2.[17]

WINTER FIRST HAD TO BE ENDURED. ORIGEN: Each one of the blessed will first be obliged to travel the narrow and hard way in winter[18] to show what knowledge he has acquired for guiding his life, so that afterwards there may take place what is said in the Song of Songs to the bride when she has safely passed through the winter. For she says, "My beloved answers and says to me, 'Arise and come away, my love, my fair one, my dove; for lo, the winter is past, the rain is over and gone.' " And you must keep in mind that you cannot hear "the winter is past" any other way than by entering the contest of this present win-

ter with all your strength and might and main. And after the winter is past and the rain is over and gone, the flowers will appear that are planted in the house of the Lord and flourish in the courts of our God.[19] EXHORTATION TO MARTYRDOM 31.[20]

NOW THAT WINTER IS PAST, THE DOVE'S VOICE CAN BE HEARD. AMBROSE: "Arise, come, my dearest one," that is, arise from the pleasures of the world, arise from earthly things and come to me, you who still labor and are burdened,[21] because you are anxious about worldly things. Come over the world, come to me, because I have overcome the world. Come near, for now you are fair with the beauty of everlasting life, now you are a dove, that is, you are gentle and mild, now you are filled entirely with spiritual grace. . . .

"Winter is now past"; that is, the Pasch has come, pardon has come, the forgiveness of sins has arrived, temptation has ceased, the rain is gone, the storm is gone, and the affliction. Before the coming of Christ it is winter. After his coming there are flowers. On this account he says, "The flowers appear on the earth." Where before there were thorns, now flowers are there. "The time of pruning has come." Where before there was desert, the harvest is there. "The voice of the dove is heard in our land." ISAAC, OR THE SOUL 4.34-35.[22]

SIGNIFICANCE OF WINTER AND ITS PASSING. GREGORY OF ELVIRA: There is thus no doubt that winter has a double meaning, either that harshness and severity belong to it, or that it is a time for sowing with the coming of the rain. When it says winter, therefore, it refers to the present world, where the Word of God is sowed in this age like a seed of righteousness by prophets and apostles, or priests, and is fertilized by assiduous preaching, as though by rains from heaven. . . .

But with the passing of winter, that is, the

---

[16]FC 65:391. [17]ECS 2:63. [18]See Mt 7:14. [19]Ps 92:13 (91:14 LXX, Vg). [20]OSW 62. [21]Mt 11:28. [22]FC 65:29-30.

tribulations of this world, and the cessation of the rains, that is, the preaching of the Word of God, and the subsequent arrival of the joy of Spring (which designates the coming of Christ's vernal kingdom in great peace), then the bodies of the saints everywhere will emerge from the graves of the earth like flowers—lilies or roses—pure white with holiness and red with passion. EXPLANATION OF THE SONG OF SONGS 4.13, 15.[23]

THE TRUTH OF THE GOSPEL HAS COME.
JEROME: Then the bridegroom makes answer to the bride and teaches her that the shadow of the old law has passed away and the truth of the gospel has come. "Rise up, my love, my fair one, and come away, for lo, the winter is past, the rain is over and gone.". . . "The voice of the turtle [dove] is heard in our land." The turtle [dove], the most chaste of birds, always dwelling in lofty places, is a type of the Savior. AGAINST JOVINIANUS 1.30.[24]

APPROACH OF THE TURTLEDOVE SIGNIFIES THE COMING OF CHRIST. CYRIL OF ALEXANDRIA: Such did the Savior of all become toward us, showing the most perfect gentleness, and like a turtle [dove], moreover, soothing the world and filling his own vineyard, even us who believe in him, with the sweet sound of his voice. For it is written in the Song of Songs, "The voice of the turtle[dove] has been heard in our land." For Christ has spoken to us the divine message of the gospel, which is for the salvation of the whole world. COMMENTARY ON LUKE, HOMILY 3.[25]

THE TIME OF THE PRUNING. CYRIL OF ALEXANDRIA: Also in the Song of Songs we find Christ calling to the bride there described, and who represents the person of the church, in these words: "Arise, come, my neighbor, my beautiful dove. For lo! the winter is past, and the rain is gone; it has passed away. The flowers appear on the ground. The time of the pruning is come.". . . A certain spring-like calm was about to arise for

those who believe in him. COMMENTARY ON LUKE, HOMILY 95.[26]

THE ROCK IS CHRIST. CYRIL OF ALEXANDRIA: The rock is Christ. He is a wall and a shelter to us who believe and a perfect guardian, which is denoted by the wall. When you arrive, he says, you will be protected with every defense. FRAGMENTS IN THE COMMENTARY ON THE SONG OF SONGS 2.14.[27]

SIGNIFICANCE OF THE FIG TREE AND OF THE CLEFT IN THE ROCK. JEROME: Immediately the turtle says to its fellow, "The fig tree has put forth its green figs," that is, the commandments of the old law have fallen, and the blossoming vines of the gospel give forth their fragrance. . . . While you covered your countenance like Moses and the veil of the law remained, I neither saw your face, nor did I condescend to hear your voice. I said, "Yes, when you make many prayers, I will not hear."[28] But now, with unveiled face behold my glory, and shelter yourself in the cleft and steep places of the solid rock. AGAINST JOVINIANUS 1.30.[29]

SWEET VOICE OF THE DOVE IS A CONTRAST TO HERETICS. ORIGEN: "For your voice is sweet." Who would not admit that the voice of the Catholic church is sweet in its confession of the true faith; whereas the voice of the heretics, who speak not the doctrines of the truth but blasphemies against God and iniquity on high, is harsh and unpleasing? In the same way the face of the church is fair but that of heretics is hideous and ugly; if indeed anyone is able to discern this beauty of face—if he is spiritual, that is to say, and a person who knows how to sift all things out. For with ignorant and sensual people the fallacies of falsehood appear more beautiful than do the dogmas of the truth.[30] COMMENTARY ON THE SONG OF SONGS 3.15.[31]

---

[23]CCL 69:202-3. [24]NPNF 2 6:368. [25]CGSL 58. [26]CGSL 381-82*. [27]PG 69:1286. [28]Is 1:15. [29]NPNF 2 6:368-69*. [30]See 1 Cor 2:14. [31]ACW 26:253-54.

2:15 *Foxes in the Vineyard*

Walk with the Wise. Apostolic Constitutions: [Those] who spoil the church of God, as the "little foxes do the vineyard," we exhort you to avoid, lest you lay traps for your own souls. "For he that walks with wise men shall be wise, but he that walks with the foolish shall be known."[32] Constitutions of the Holy Apostles 6.3.18.[33]

Foxes Plot Against the Church. Bede: This animal, which is very shrewd with respect to deceit and craftiness, represents the Jews, Gentiles and heretics, who are always plotting against the church of God, and, as it were, continuously making a racket with their babbling voices. Concerning them the command is given to the guardians of the church: "Catch for us the tiny foxes which are wrecking the vineyards." Commentary on the Acts of the Apostles 19.14.[34]

Foxes Are Heretics Who Harm the Churches. Theodoret of Cyr: "Catch us little foxes that demolish vineyards." Some commentators actually applied "little" to the "vineyards"; but the sense is no different in either case. By "foxes" he refers to those with a deceitful attitude who harm the Lord's churches that are just beginning to flourish—hence his saying "our vines blossom." By "foxes" he is hinting at the heretics warring against people in the church and endeavoring furtively and deceitfully to steal away those not yet made firm in the faith. By persuasiveness in word and by the snares and intricacies of argumentation they lead astray those of simpler disposition and damage the vines. For this reason he bids those exercising the teaching role to hunt them down and ensnare them with the arguments of the truth and rid the blossoming vines of this damage. Commentary on the Song of Songs 2.[35]

Schismatics and Heretics. Bede: The foxes who destroy the vineyards are heretics and schismatics who devour with their crooked teeth the blossoming vineyard of the doctrine of Christ,

that is, the green minds of the faithful. Would that we not know [such destruction]! Commentary on the Songs of Songs 2.2.15.[36]

No Better Because They Are Little. Gregory of Elvira: It calls these foxes "little" because there are also greater ones. Indeed, the ruling powers of the world are greater at raging than the fallacies of the heretics are at seducing. They are both equally evil, but their respective powers to punish are unequal, for the heretic coaxes to destroy, but the Gentile rages to conquer, the former being peacefully deceptive and the latter being cruel in persecution. But the Lord commands that both receive appropriate dispositions from the keepers of the vineyards, that is, from the leaders of the churches. Explanation of the Song of Songs 4.25.[37]

The Meaning of "Catch." Augustine: What does "catch" mean? [This means to] come to grips with them, convince, refute them, so that the vineyards of the church may not be spoiled. What else is catching foxes, but overcoming heretics with the authority of the divine law, and so to say binding and tying them up with the cords provided by the testimonies of the Holy Scriptures? [Samson] catches foxes, ties their tails together and attaches firebrands.[38] What's the meaning of the foxes' tails tied together? What can the foxes' tails be but the backsides of the heretics, whose fronts are smooth and deceptive, their backsides bound, that is condemned, and dragging fire behind them, to consume the crops and works of those who yield to their seductions? Sermon 364.4.[39]

2:16 *The Lover and the Beloved*

Love in the Heavenly City. Ambrose: Joining the daughters of the heavenly city, she seeks

---

[32]Prov 13:20 LXX. [33]ANF 7:457-58*. [34]CS 117:155. [35]ECS 2:65-66. [36]CCL 119B:226. [37]CCL 69:205. [38]Judg 15:4-5. [39]WSA 3 10:278-79*; cf. Caesarius of Arles Sermon 118.4 (FC 47:186, and cf. FC 31:xxiv-xxv).

after the Word; by her search she arouses his love for her, and she knows where to search for him. For she has come to know that he delays among the prayers of his saints and remains close to them, and she understands that he feeds the church and the souls of his just ones among the lilies. ISAAC, OR THE SOUL 6.56.[40]

GOD'S BLESSINGS. THEODORET OF CYR: They who are blessed by the boons of God and have learned to know these passages and others like them, kindled with warm love for their bountiful Master, constantly carry on their lips this his dearest name and cry in the words of the Song of Songs, "My beloved is mine, and I am his." LETTER 146.[41]

2:17 The Passing of the Shadows at the Break of Day

THE SHADOWS RECEDE AT THE WORD'S APPROACH. AMBROSE: In the first stage, that of formation, the soul still sees shadows not yet parted by the revelation of the Word's approach, and therefore hitherto the daylight of the gospel did not shine upon it. In the second, it enjoys sweet fragrances without the confusion of the shadows.[42] ISAAC, OR THE SOUL 8.68.[43]

A FORETELLING OF THE LORD'S RESURRECTION. APONIUS: In this verse, the Lord's resurrection is taught and foretold. Just as the apostles were afraid without him, terrorized by the treachery of the Jews, so also is the soul, which, in a certain sense, is naked and unarmed without the assistance of the Holy Spirit, terrorized by the treachery of demons. EXPOSITION OF SONG OF SONGS 5.4.[44]

USELESS ANTIQUITY TERMINATED AND SPIRITUAL MEANING REVEALED. AUGUSTINE: Since, then, there are in the Old Testament precepts that we who belong to the New Testament are not compelled to observe, why do not the Jews realize that they have remained stationary in use-less antiquity rather than hurl charges against us who hold fast to the new promises, because we do not observe the old? Just as it is written in the Canticle of Canticles: "The day has broken, let the shadows retire," the spiritual meaning has already dawned, the natural action has already ceased. "The God of Gods, the Lord has spoken: and he has called the earth from the rising of the sun to the going down thereof."[45] IN ANSWER TO THE JEWS 6.8.[46]

THE HEAVENLY HEIGHTS. CYRIL OF ALEXANDRIA: With the barren synagogue abandoned, she asks the bridegroom to come to those downtrodden and humiliated and formerly idolatrous souls who will be raised with him to heavenly heights. FRAGMENTS IN THE COMMENTARY ON THE SONG OF SONGS 2.17.[47]

FROM SHADOWS TO REALITY. NILUS OF ANCYRA: He pastures his flocks among the lilies, therefore, although he does so only until the coming day emerges and the shadows begin to move on. Since the majority of people think that the events which are passing and not stable are fixed and will remain, because their faculty of discernment is obscured by the darkness of ignorance, they have need of the daylight in order to see that the shadows of the things of this world dissipate and have no permanence. For all present realities are shadows,[48] drawing their origin from the good things of the heavens yet subsisting like shadows, only resembling the truth of the things there above. But once the night has passed and the dawn has arisen, the nature of things from on high is clearly seen, as if in sunlight. Then people realize: "Our life on the earth is a shadow."[49] Then they say, "My days, as the shadow, are in decline,"[50] indicating how feeble and quick to vanish is temporal success. The one who says, "If there are many gods and many lords, yet for us there is only one God

---

[40]FC 65:45-46. [41]NPNF 2 3:320. [42]See Song 1:12-13. [43]FC 65:56. [44]CCL 19:115. [45]Ps 50:1 (49:1 LXX, Vg). [46]FC 27:400-401. [47]PG 69:1286. [48]See Wis 5:9. [49]Job 8:9. [50]Ps 101:12 (102:12 LXX).

the Father, from whom all things come and for whom we exist, and one Lord Jesus Christ through whom all things come and through whom we exist,"[51] can also say, "My beloved is mine, and I am his," for the meaning is identical in each text. For anyone who renounces both gods and lords lays claim to the one God and Lord, from whom he exists and to whom he returns. "For," it says, "for us there is one God from whom all things come and for whom we exist," thus declaring clearly that "he is mine, and I am his.". . .

Regarding the expression "the shadows move on," it is necessary to consider . . . that it refers to the abrogation of the works of the law. That is the shadow frequently cited by Paul as "the law having the shadow of good things to come and not the very image of the realities,"[52] and again "These are only a shadow of the things to come, but the substance is of Christ,"[53] and again, "They provide a copy and a shadow of the heavenly realities,"[54] meaning the priests that functioned according to the law. Thus it is indicated for certain that, the shadow of the law having

moved on, the truth of grace now governs, established upon the rock against which "the gates of hell shall never prevail."[55]. . . It should also be remarked that it is everywhere necessary for the Word to rest upon the mountains, or at least upon the hills. And if the Word is ever found in the valleys or chasms, he is found there by reason of his great condescension and with the intention to restore those who are down there to the higher realities, on account of his love for humankind. COMMENTARY ON THE SONG OF SONGS 64-66.[56]

A REMINDER OF ESCHATOLOGY. BEDE: "Until the day breathes and the shadows lengthen," that is, until the eternal light of the coming age appears and the shadows of the present life, that is, the ignorance or error whereby even many of us faithful who have the use of the lamp of God's word are temporarily darkened, lengthen and disappear. COMMENTARY ON THE SONGS OF SONGS 2.2.17.[57]

---

[51]1 Cor 8:5-6. [52]Heb 10:1. [53]Col 2:17. [54]Heb 8:5. [55]Mt 16:18. [56]SC 403:314-18, 324. [57]CCL 119B:228.

3:1-5 SEEKING AND NOT FINDING

[1]*Upon my bed by night*
     I sought him whom my soul loves;
I sought him, but found him not;
     I called him, but he gave no answer.[g]
[2]*"I will rise now and go about the city,*
     in the streets and in the squares;
I will seek him whom my soul loves."
     I sought him, but found him not.
[3]*The watchmen found me,*
     as they went about in the city.
"Have you seen him whom my soul loves?"

[4]*Scarcely had I passed them,*
     when I found him whom my soul loves.
I held him, and would not let him go
     until I had brought him into my mother's
          house,
     and into the chamber of her that
          conceived me.
[5]*I adjure you, O daughters of Jerusalem,*
     by the gazelles or the hinds of the field,
that you stir not up nor awaken love
     until it please.

g Gk: Heb lacks this line

OVERVIEW: Christ can be sought by night (AMBROSE, GREGORY THE GREAT) or by day (AMBROSE) inside the secret chamber of the heart (JEROME), which represents the Lord's tomb (CYRIL OF ALEXANDRIA), where wisdom resides (GREGORY OF ELVIRA) and God dwells (GREGORY OF NYSSA). When the beloved is found in his divinity (GREGORY THE GREAT), it means bypassing all created beings to reach the angelic nature (THEODORET OF CYR). This is related to "mother church" and the heavenly Jerusalem (GREGORY OF ELVIRA), because the heavenly mysteries are represented allegorically on earth through the gospel (AMBROSE). "My Mother's house," in fact, is the Jerusalem on high (THEODORET OF CYR).

3:1-4 Seeking the One We Love

SEEKING BY NIGHT. AMBROSE: "In my bed at night I sought him whom my soul loved," as if he had stolen in upon her. Let one who seeks carefully seek while in his bed; let him seek at night. Let there be neither nights nor holiday, let no time be free from pious service, and if one does not find him at first, let him persevere in searching after him. . . .

And because we see the heavenly mysteries represented allegorically on earth through the gospel, let us come to Mary Magdalene and to the other Mary.[1] Let us meditate upon how they sought Christ at night in the bed of his body, in which he lay dead, when the angel said to them, "You seek Jesus, who was crucified. He is not here, for he has risen. Why then do you seek the living one among the dead?"[2] Why do you seek in the tomb him who is now in heaven? Why do you seek in the bonds of the tomb him who frees all men of their bonds? The tomb is not his dwelling, but heaven is. And so one of them says, "I sought him and I did not find him." ISAAC, OR THE SOUL 5.38, 42.[3]

THE CHAMBER IS THE LORD'S TOMB. CYRIL OF ALEXANDRIA: "In my chamber by night I sought him." This refers to the women who came at the beginning of the morning on the sabbath to the tomb of Jesus and did not find him.[4] He is in the chamber, therefore, or away from the chamber. Or perhaps they call their chamber the Lord's tomb because we are buried together with him.[5] But when they did not find him, they heard at once: "He is not here, for he has been raised."[6] And they discovered guardian angels, whom they asked, "Where have you laid the Lord?"[7] Then, when they had left the angels whom they were questioning, the Lord met them and said, "Rejoice."[8] For this reason, it says, "When I had passed by them for a little while, I found him whom I will not let go." She grasped his feet and heard, "Don't hold me."[9] Finally, he called the gathering of the apostles the house of the mother, to whom he announced the resurrection of Christ. FRAGMENTS IN THE COMMENTARY ON THE SONG OF SONGS 3.1.[10]

CHAMBER OF THE HEART WHERE WISDOM RESIDES. GREGORY OF ELVIRA: To what does this bed refer, upon which the church seeks the one whom its soul loves, if not to the bed of its heart in which wisdom rests, where it seeks our Lord and Savior through continuous meditation? If the bed is the secrecy of the heart, then what is the night in which the church sought the Lord but was unable to find him? Surely it means that the God of light was not easily found in darkness. EXPLANATION OF THE SONG OF SONGS 5.2.[11]

WHERE GOD DWELLS. GREGORY OF NYSSA: The chamber is indeed the heart that becomes an acceptable dwelling of God when it returns to that state which it had in the beginning made by "her who conceived me." We would be correct by understanding "mother" as the first cause of our being. HOMILIES ON THE SONG OF SONGS 6.[12]

FOLLOWING BY DAY. AMBROSE: Let us follow him by day, the present day of the church, which

---

[1]See Mt 28:1; Lk 24:3, 10. [2]Mt 28:5-6; Lk 24:5. [3]FC 65:32-34. [4]See Lk 24:1ff. [5]See Rom 6:4. [6]Lk 24:6. [7]Jn 20:15. [8]See Mt 28:9. [9]Jn 20:17. [10]PG 69:1286. [11]CCL 69:207. [12]GNSS 131.

Abraham saw and was glad.[13] This is why we follow Christ during the day; for he will not be found by night. "Upon my bed," Scripture says, "by night I sought him whom my soul loves. I called him, but he gave no answer." On Virginity 8.45.[14]

Search Extends into the City and the Beloved Is Found. Gregory the Great: We seek the one we love upon our beds when we sigh with longing for our Redeemer during our short period of rest during the present life. We seek him during the night, because even though our hearts are already watchful for him, our eyes are still darkened. But it remains for the person who does not find the one he loves to rise and go about the city, that is, he must travel about the holy church of the elect with an inquiring heart. He must seek her through its streets and squares, making his way, that is, through narrow and broad places, on the watch to make inquiries if any traces of her can be found in them, because there are some, even of those leading worldly lives, who have something worth imitating of virtue in their actions. The watchmen who guard the city find us as we search, because the holy fathers who guard the church's orthodoxy come to meet our good efforts, to teach us, by their words of their writings. Scarcely have we passed them by when we find him whom we love. Although in his humility our Redeemer was a human being in the midst of human beings, in his divinity he was above human beings. Therefore once the watchmen have been passed by, the beloved is found. Forty Gospel Homilies 25.[15]

Bypassing All Beings to Reach the Angelic Nature. Theodoret of Cyr: Since the bridegroom is incomprehensible in his being even to the holy angels, and hence they did not give me an answer to my question, teaching me by their silence that he is incomprehensible even to them, the uncreated to created beings, I left them as well, still searching for my beloved.

"It was not long after passing them that I found him whom my soul loved. I laid hold of him." I had scarcely bypassed the creature to reach the angelic nature itself in an effort to find my uncreated beloved, my benefactor as he is, when by faith alone I came upon him, bypassing all beings and with the confirmation from experience itself that the one responsible for everything is above all beings and in his being is seen by no nature, of the senses or the intellect, being superior to them in substance. Commentary on the Song of Songs 3.[16]

I Would Not Let Him Go from My Heart. Jerome: Happy the person in whose heart Jesus sets his feet every day! If only he would set his feet in my heart! If only his footsteps would cling to my heart forever! If only I may say with the spouse, "I took hold of him and would not let him go." Homilies on the Psalms 26 (Psalm 98).[17]

An Interior, Secret Place. Ambrose: What is signified by the house of your mother and her chamber except the interior, secret place of your nature? Keep this house, and cleanse its inmost parts so that, once it is an immaculate house unstained by any sordidness of an adulterous conscience, a spiritual house held together by the cornerstone may rise into a holy priesthood, and the Holy Spirit may dwell in it. One who thus seeks Christ, who entreats him, is not abandoned by him. Rather, that one is frequently visited, for he is with us until the end of the world. On Virginity 13.78.[18]

Mother Church and the Heavenly Jerusalem. Gregory of Elvira: "In my mother's house and in the chamber where she conceived me." This is the voice of the church speaking. If the church is a mother to all, we must ask for the identity of the mother of the church, in whose house and in whose chamber she is said

---

[13]Jn 8:56. [14]AOV 23. [15]CS 123:189. [16]ECS 2:70. [17]FC 48:209. [18]AOV 36.

to have been conceived. I have already shown above what is the church, namely, the body of Christ that consists of his gathering members. The mother of the church, therefore, is the holy heavenly Jerusalem.[19] EXPLANATION OF THE SONG OF SONGS 5.12.[20]

MOTHER'S HOUSE IS THE JERUSALEM ON HIGH. THEODORET OF CYR: She says she found him and did not let him go before bringing him into her mother's house and the inner chamber of the one who conceived her. By "city" she refers to the house of God, which we call church, by "marketplaces" and "streets" the divine Scriptures, by the city's "watchmen" the holy prophets and the sacred apostles, from whom the pious soul learns

in its longing for the divine Word. After these she finds the bridegroom attended by guards and attendants, she lays hold of him, clings to him and is reluctant to leave him before she brings him into her mother's house and the inner chamber of the one who conceived her. Now, we recognize the mother of the pious as the Jerusalem on high, of whom blessed Paul says, "The Jerusalem on high is free in being mother of us all."[21] COMMENTARY ON THE SONG OF SONGS 3.[22]

3:5 Solemn Adjuration

See commentary on Song of Solomon 2:7.

---

[19]Gal 4:26. [20]CCL 69:209. [21]Gal 4:6. [22]ECS 2:71.

3:6-11 THE GROOM AND HIS PARTY

[6]*What is that coming up from the*
  wilderness,
    like a column of smoke,*
  perfumed with myrrh and frankincense,
    with all the fragrant powders of the
      merchant?
[7]*Behold, it is the litter† of Solomon!*
  About it are sixty mighty men
    of the mighty men of Israel,
[8]*all girt with swords*
  and expert in war,
  each with his sword at his thigh,
    against alarms by night.

[9]*King Solomon made himself a*
  palanquin
    from the wood of Lebanon.
[10]*He made its posts of silver,*
  its back of gold, its seat of purple;
  it was lovingly wrought within[b]
    by the daughters of Jerusalem.
[11]*Go forth, O daughters of Zion,*
  and behold King Solomon,
  with the crown with which his mother
    crowned him
  on the day of his wedding,
    on the day of the gladness of his heart.

h The meaning of the Hebrew is uncertain   **VL all white*   *†LXX, Heb (lit.) bed*

OVERVIEW: The true Solomon on his litter is an image of Christ the king of peace (AMBROSE, HIP-

POLYTUS, THEODORET OF CYR, APONIUS, BEDE), and those who attend him guard against carnal desires (GREGORY OF NYSSA). The myrrh is for burial, but the frankincense indicates divinity (CYRIL OF ALEXANDRIA) as well as the absence of spot or wrinkle (ORIGEN). His bed is the divine Scriptures (THEODORET OF CYR), his crown of thorns a crown of mystery (AMBROSE, RUFINUS OF AQUILEIA, CYRIL OF JERUSALEM), his wedding day also the day of his passion (CYRIL OF ALEXANDRIA). But the "crown" could come from either "mother" or "father" because there is neither male nor female in God, and all such terms are therefore inadequate (GREGORY OF NYSSA).

3:6-7 Coming from the Wilderness

MYRRH FOR BURIAL, FRANKINCENSE FOR DIVINITY. CYRIL OF ALEXANDRIA: The myrrh that was mixed with frankincense was used for burying him, but frankincense because whoever rises with Christ shares his divinity. And the ecclesiastical soul is imbued not only with these fragrances but also with various principles of knowledge. For whoever discerns accurately and searches all the way to the highest peak will be said to crush everything and reduce to dust the doctrines of good fragrance, like some perfume with which the bride is now said to be fragrant. Perhaps also the one who does not live according to the flesh but according to the Spirit, whose heart has not been hardened, generating and preserving various sweet smells, renders a good odor from all the herbs which are now called perfumes. Likewise, some will say that the holy and ecclesiastical soul, a daughter formerly destitute of God, ascends from the assembly of the Gentiles, that is, from the desert of those who are remiss in dogmas, words and deeds, having abandoned God, and rises to the things that are of God. FRAGMENTS IN THE COMMENTARY ON THE SONG OF SONGS 3.6.[1]

FRANKINCENSE IS TRANSLATED AS WHITENING. ORIGEN: They also bring "frankincense," translated as "whitening," since they reject every dark condition, so that the words are fitting for them: "Who is she who comes up all white?" For

in this way they will be able to bring praise to the house of the Lord, not having a spot or a wrinkle or any such thing which brings dirt on the church of Christ. FRAGMENTS ON JEREMIAH 11.[2]

APPROACH OF SOLOMON'S LITTER. AMBROSE: For Solomon made himself a bed of wood from Lebanon. Its pillars were of silver, its bottom of gold, its back strewn with gems. CONCERNING VIRGINS 3.5.21.[3]

SPLENDOR OF SOLOMON'S LITTER COMPARED WITH THE LOVE OF CHRIST. AMBROSE: Do you, therefore, grind your faith so that you may be like the soul that excites in itself the love of Christ, that the powers of heaven admire as it mounts up, that it may rise easily and soar above this world with joy and gladness. Like the vine, put forth branches, and like smoke, rise on high, shedding the odor of a holy resurrection and the sweetness of faith, as you have it written: "Who is she that goes up by the desert like a branch of the vine burning with smoke, fragrant with myrrh and frankincense, and with all the powders of the perfumer?" LETTER 77, TO LAYMEN.[4]

SOLOMON ON HIS LITTER IS NONE OTHER THAN CHRIST. HIPPOLYTUS: "Behold the litter of Solomon surrounded by sixty mighty men from the powerful of Israel, each one equipped with a sword and trained for battle." O blessed sight! O litter of sabbath rest! For Solomon's litter reveals nothing other than Christ himself. TREATISE ON THE SONG OF SONGS 27.1.[5]

SOLOMON THE PEACEABLE IS JESUS THE CHRIST. THEODORET OF CYR: We must enquire why on earth they call the bridegroom Solomon. Solomon means "peaceable," as you can find in the Chronicles. God said to David, when he wanted to build the new temple, "Lo, a son is born to you; he will be a man of repose, and I shall give him peace

---

[1]PG 69:1286-87. [2]FC 97:284. [3]NPNF 2 10:384*. [4]FC 26:433. [5]CSCO 264:50.

from all his enemies round about, because his name is Solomon, and I shall give peace and tranquility to Israel in his days. He will build a house for my name, and he will be a son to me, and I shall be a father to him, and I shall assure the throne of his kingdom in Israel forever."[6] . . .

It was not Solomon who had dominion to the ends of the world but he who sprang from Solomon in his humanity, Jesus Christ, and was called Solomon on account of his peaceable and gentle nature and his being the cause of peace. COMMENTARY ON THE SONG OF SONGS 3.[7]

SOLOMON'S BED IS HOLY SCRIPTURE. THEODORET OF CYR: "Lo, it is Solomon's bed." Let us understand the bridegroom's bed to be the divine Scriptures. When the bride reclines on them, as it were, along with the bridegroom, and receives the seeds of teaching, she conceives, bears, is in labor and gives birth to spiritual benefit. COMMENTARY ON THE SONG OF SONGS 3.[8]

THE TRUE SOLOMON IS CHRIST THE KING. APONIUS: Thus he was crowned by the blessed mother who begot him according to the flesh, Christ the King, the true Solomon. This was the day of his wedding and the day of gladness of heart, when the immaculate was joined to the stained. Our Lord Jesus Christ made the church immaculate by the touch of his body and blood and rendered it most beautiful, cleansed from every stain of sin by the most holy washing of baptism, with every wrinkle of heretical inclination wiped away by the salve of doctrine. EXPOSITION OF SONG OF SONGS 5.48.[9]

SIXTY ARMED MEN. GREGORY OF NYSSA: What then is their meaning? Perhaps the loveliness of the divine beauty has something fearful about it as characterized by elements contrary to corporeal beauty. What attracts our desire is pleasant to the sight, soft to the touch, and not associated with anything fearful or terrifying. But that incorruptible beauty is fearful, terrifying and not easily frightened. Since our desire for carnal things in the body's members is subject to passion and defilement, like a band of robbers it ambushes the mind, captivates it and carries away the will. Therefore it becomes God's enemy; as the apostle says, the wisdom of the flesh arises from what is inimical to God.[10] It follows that the love of God arises from what is opposed to carnal desire. If carnal desire consists of weakness, laxity and laziness, the love of God is made up of a fearful, terrifying fortitude. An unrelenting anger scares and puts to flight the ambush resulting from pleasure, thus revealing the soul's beauty as pure and no longer sullied by a desire for carnal pleasure. The king's nuptial bed is therefore surrounded by armed men expert in battle. The sword at the thigh terrorizes and causes fear against dark, nocturnal thoughts and against those who lie in ambush to shoot arrows in the darkness at the upright of heart.[11] The weapons of those standing guard around the bed destroy impure desires. HOMILIES ON THE SONG OF SONGS 6.[12]

THE KING OF PEACE AT THE END OF TIME. BEDE: Solomon's litter, therefore, is the glory of heavenly beatitude in which the King of peace himself rests with his saints, a rest toward which the King's beloved, that is, the church, strains daily through the desert of this world and already partly enjoys, insofar as he gives his faithful a foretaste of their future reward. But they will receive it fully only when, at the end of the age, the founder and king of the heavenly city gathers the elect from the four winds and, as was said elsewhere, "girds himself and makes them recline at table and serves them."[13] COMMENTARY ON THE SONGS OF SONGS 2.3.7.[14]

3:10-11 A Crown for a Wedding

SIGNIFICANCE OF GOLD AND PURPLE. CYRIL OF ALEXANDRIA: We should think that the use of

---

[6]1 Chron 22:9-10. [7]ECS 2:73. [8]ECS 2:73*. [9]CCL 19:138. [10]Rom 8:7. [11]Ps 11:2 (10:2 LXX). [12]GNSS 135. [13]See Lk 12:37. [14]CCL 119B:237-38.

gold denotes spiritual union, which is precious and divine. For, to demonstrate the union of God and humankind, the ark in the desert was also covered within and without by gold.[15] The purple signifies that number of persons who are called to the kingdom. And when someone believes, at that moment Christ is received in the heart, who is a precious pearl. For it says that he made a litter for himself from the daughters of Jerusalem on account of love alone: "For God so loved the world that he sent his only-begotten Son, that all who believe in him would not perish but have eternal life."[16] FRAGMENTS IN THE COMMENTARY ON THE SONG OF SONGS 3.10.[17]

THE WEDDING DAY IS THE DAY OF CHRIST'S PASSION. CYRIL OF ALEXANDRIA: The church forged from the Gentiles says this: "Go forth and see." But what it calls the day of his wedding is the day of his passion, when he married the church by his blood.[18] FRAGMENTS IN THE COMMENTARY ON THE SONG OF SONGS 3.11.[19]

THE NUPTIAL SONG. AMBROSE: Then when the bride has been led to the resting place of her bridegroom, they sing the nuptial song and express love from the daughters of Jerusalem: "Come forth and look upon King Solomon in the crown with which his mother has crowned him on the day of his marriage." They sing the epithalamium and call upon the other heavenly powers or souls to see the love that Christ has toward the daughters of Jerusalem. On this account he deserved to be crowned by his mother, as a loving son, as Paul shows, saying that "God has rescued us from the power of darkness and transferred us into the kingdom of his loving son."[20] ISAAC, OR THE SOUL 5.46.[21]

A CROWN OF THORNS. RUFINUS OF AQUILEIA: It is written that there was put on him a crown of thorns. Of this hear in the Canticles the voice of God the Father marveling at the iniquity of Jerusalem in the insult done to his Son: "Go forth and see, you daughters of Jerusalem, the crown with which his mother has crowned him." COMMENTARY ON THE APOSTLES' CREED 22.[22]

ALSO A CROWN OF MYSTERY. CYRIL OF JERUSALEM: Every king is proclaimed by soldiers. It was fitting that Jesus also, in figure, be crowned by soldiers. For this reason Scripture says in the Canticles: "Daughters of Jerusalem, come forth and look upon King Solomon in the crown with which his mother has crowned him." But the crown was also a mystery, for it was a remission of sins and release from the sentence of condemnation. CATECHETICAL LECTURES 13.17.[23]

ALL TERMS FOR "GOD" ARE INADEQUATE. GREGORY OF NYSSA: No one can adequately grasp the terms pertaining to God. For example, "mother" is mentioned in the Song in place of "father." Both terms mean the same, because there is neither male nor female in God. For how can anything transitory like this be attributed to God? But when we are one in Christ, we are divested of the signs of this difference along with the old person. Therefore every name equally indicates God's ineffable nature; neither can "male" nor "female" defile God's pure nature. Because of this, the father mentioned in the gospel parable prepares a wedding.[24] The prophet says of God, "You have placed on his head a crown of precious stones."[25] Hence the Song says that a crown is placed upon the bridegroom by his mother. Since the nuptials and bride are one, one mother places the crown upon the bridegroom's head. Neither does it make much difference whether one calls the Son of God the only begotten God, or the Son of his love. According to Paul, each name has the capacity to be a bridal escort that leads the bridegroom to dwell in us. HOMILIES ON THE SONG OF SONGS 7.[26]

---

[15]See Ex 25:11. [16]Jn 3:16. [17]PG 69:1287. [18]See Eph 5:27. [19]PG 69:1287. [20]Col 1:13. [21]FC 65:36-37. [22]NPNF 2 3:552. [23]FC 64:16. [24]Mt 22:2. [25]Ps 20:3 LXX. [26]GNSS 145-46*.

4:1-8 THE BRIDEGROOM'S PROPOSAL

¹*Behold, you are beautiful, my love,*
behold, you are beautiful!
Your eyes are doves
behind your veil.
Your hair is like a flock of goats,
moving down the slopes of Gilead.
²*Your teeth are like a flock of shorn ewes*
that have come up from the washing,
all of which bear twins,
and not one among them is bereaved.
³*Your lips are like a scarlet thread,*
and your mouth is lovely.
Your cheeks are like halves of a
pomegranate
behind your veil.
⁴*Your neck is like the tower of David,*
built for an arsenal,ⁱ

whereon hang a thousand bucklers,
all of them shields of warriors.
⁵*Your two breasts are like two fawns,*
twins of a gazelle,
that feed among the lilies.
⁶*Until the day breathes*
and the shadows flee,
I will hie me to the mountain of myrrh
and the hill of frankincense.
⁷*You are all fair, my love;*
there is no flaw in you.
⁸*Come with me from Lebanon, my bride;*
come with me from Lebanon.
Depart^j from the peak of Amana,*
from the peak of Senir and Hermon,
from the dens of lions,
from the mountains of leopards.

i The meaning of the Hebrew word is uncertain   j Or Look   *LXX *from the beginning of faith*

OVERVIEW: The bride comes not from the law but from idols, from Lebanon (CYRIL OF ALEXANDRIA). The church is the bride (AMBROSE) but beauty is in its soul (APONIUS). The bride's eyes are those of a dove (AMBROSE, AUGUSTINE, CASSIODORUS), and her hair like a flock of goats (BEDE). Her teeth are like a flock of ewes (CYRIL OF JERUSALEM), because she is shorn of her sins, as the church is washed in baptism, or shorn of secular burdens, their twins being God and neighbor, law and prophets (AUGUSTINE). However, such teeth may instead indicate an ability to chew the thick dense bread of spiritual food into more delectable pieces (GREGORY OF NYSSA). Thus the bride in her various parts represents either the soul or the church (ORIGEN, GREGORY THE GREAT). Therefore the bridegroom invites her to pass through things temporal and seek true

beauty, assisted by the Holy Spirit (AMBROSE, JEROME).

4:1 The Eyes and Hair

THE CHURCH AS BRIDE. AMBROSE: [The church] mourns in its eyes, that is in its faithful, because it is written, "Your eyes are as doves apart from your reticence," because they see spiritually and know how to keep silent about the mysteries which they have seen. CONSOLATION ON THE DEATH OF EMPEROR VALENTINIAN 7.[1]

FIRST IS THE BEAUTY OF THE SOUL. APONIUS: Having been cleansed from every habit of the vices of the flesh and converted to the one true

[1]FC 22:268.

God from the worship of a multitude of shameful gods, Christ the Lord praises the twin beauty of the church of the Gentiles, both body and soul. For the first beauty of the soul is that it would know its Creator, second that it would know itself, the kind of thing it is or the reason for which it was created. EXPOSITION OF SONG OF SONGS 6.1.[2]

BEAUTIFUL EYES OF A DOVE. AMBROSE: But Christ, beholding his church, for whom he himself, as you find in the book of the prophet Zechariah, had put on filthy garments,[3] now clothed in white raiment, seeing, that is, a soul pure and washed in the laver of regeneration, says, "Behold, you are fair, my love, behold you are fair, your eyes are like a dove's," in the likeness of which the Holy Spirit descended from heaven. The eyes are beautiful like those of a dove, because in the likeness of a dove the Holy Spirit descended from heaven. ON THE MYSTERIES 7.37.[4]

TO SEE WITH THE EYES OF A DOVE. AUGUSTINE: We are not to administer rebukes until we have removed from our eye the beam of envy or malice or pretense, so that we may have clear vision to cast out the speck from a brother's eye. For we shall then see that speck with the eyes of the dove, the kind of eyes that are commended [as belonging to] the spouse of Christ, the glorious church which God has chosen for himself, the church which has neither spot nor wrinkle,[5] that is, the church which is pure without guile. SERMON ON THE MOUNT 2.19.66.[6]

EYES THAT HAVE FAINTED. CASSIODORUS: So they say that these eyes have fainted after the Lord's salvation, because of the holy coming of the incarnation, which they bore with such longing that it could allow them no rest. So they were right to faint, because they had no period of leisure. EXPOSITION OF THE PSALMS 119.123.[7]

HAIR LIKE A FLOCK OF GOATS. BEDE: For if goats and the hair or skins of goats always signi-

fied the foulness of sinners and never the humility of penitents, that animal would by no means have been reckoned among the clean [animals], nor would it have been said in praise of the bride: "Your hair is like a flock of goats." ON THE TABERNACLE 2.3.[8]

4:2 The Teeth

LIKE A FLOCK OF EWES. CYRIL OF JERUSALEM: "Your teeth are like a flock of ewes to be shorn." A sincere confession is a spiritual shearing! And further: "all of them big with twins," signifying the twofold grace, either that perfected by water and the Spirit, or that announced in the Old and in the New Testament. CATECHETICAL LECTURES 3.16.[9]

THE TEETH OF THE CHURCH. AUGUSTINE: The teeth of the church[10] are those through whom she speaks. Of what sort are your teeth? "Like a flock of sheep that are shorn." Why "that are shorn"? Because they have laid aside the burdens of the world. Were not those sheep, of which I was a little before speaking, shorn, whom the bidding of God had shorn when he said, "Go and sell what you have, and give to the poor; and you shall find treasure in heaven: and come and follow me"?[11] They performed this bidding: shorn they came. And because those who believe in Christ are baptized, what is there said "which come up from the washing" means they have come up from cleansing. "Whereof every one bears twins." What twins? Those two commandments, whereupon hang all the law and the prophets.[12] EXPLANATIONS OF THE PSALMS 95.9.[13]

THAT WHICH IS SHORN IS THE SUPERFLUITY OF SINS. AMBROSE: [There is a] pleasing comparison to those that are shorn; for we know that goats both feed in high places without risk and

---

[2]CCL 19:139. [3]Zech 3:3. [4]NPNF 2 10:322*. [5]Eph 5:27. [6]FC 11:176*. [7]ACW 53:232. [8]TTH 18:56. [9]FC 61:118*. [10]Cf. Song 6:6. [11]Mt 19:21. [12]Mt 22:40. [13]NPNF 1 8:469*.

securely find their food in rugged places, and then when shorn are freed from what is superfluous. The church is likened to a flock of these, having in itself the many virtues of those souls which through the laver lay aside the superfluity of sins and offer to Christ the mystic faith and the grace of good living, which speak of the cross of the Lord Jesus. ON THE MYSTERIES 7.38.[14]

SHORN OF SECULAR BURDENS. AUGUSTINE: "Your teeth are like a flock of shorn ewes." What do shorn ewes mean? Those who lay aside secular burdens. What does shorn mean? Those who lay aside their fleeces, like the load of secular burdens. Those persons were your teeth, about whom it is written in the Acts of the Apostles that "they sold all their possessions and laid the proceeds at the feet of the apostles, so that distribution might be made to each, as there was need."[15] You have received the fleeces of your shorn ewes. That flock has come up from the washing of holy baptism. All have given birth, because they have fulfilled the two commandments. SERMON 313B.3.[16]

GOD AND NEIGHBOR, LAW AND PROPHETS. AUGUSTINE: He says to the church, his spouse, "Your teeth are like a flock of sheep that are shorn, which come up from the washing, all with twins, and there is none barren among them." By this twin offspring the twofold object of love is meant, namely, God and the neighbor: "On these two commandments depend all the law and the prophets."[17] LETTER 149.[18]

MAKING SPIRITUAL FOOD MORE EASILY ACCEPTABLE. GREGORY OF NYSSA: Now is the time to examine the beauty attributed to the teeth of shorn sheep. . . . If we look at the literal meaning of this verse, I do not see how teeth can be compared with prolific sheep. . . . What then can we gather from these words? Persons reducing the divine mysteries into small fragments for a clearer interpretation of the text make spiritual food more easily acceptable for the body of

the church. They perform the function of teeth by receiving the thick, dense bread of the text into their mouths. By a more subtle contemplation, they make the food delectable. HOMILIES ON THE SONG OF SONGS 7.[19]

4:5 Two Fawns That Feed Among the Lilies

FIGURATIVE INTERPRETATION. ORIGEN: And in the song of the bride, hair, teeth, lips, cheeks, the neck, and breasts, are praised by the bridegroom. The bride is either the soul of man, which enters into marriage with Christ, or the church. The parts of the body are interpreted figuratively: if they are said of the soul, then they apply to its powers. FRAGMENTS ON LUKE 186.[20]

THE SAINTS FEED AMONG THE LILIES. GREGORY THE GREAT: In order to [gain knowledge of heavenly things], we study the examples of the saints who have gone before. They are said to feed among the lilies. For what is meant by lilies but the conduct of those who say with all truth, "We are unto God a sweet savor of Christ."[21] MORALS ON THE BOOK OF JOB 24.17.[22]

4:7-8 An Invitation

RENOUNCING THE WORLD. AMBROSE: God the Word says to [the church], "You are all fair, my love, and there is no blemish in you," for guilt has been washed away. "Come here from Lebanon, my spouse, come here from Lebanon, from the beginning of faith[23] you will pass through and pass on," because, renouncing the world, she passed through things temporal and passed on to Christ. ON THE MYSTERIES 7.39.[24]

NOT FROM THE LAW BUT FROM LEBANON. CYRIL OF ALEXANDRIA: This teaches us the bride's place of origin, that she comes from the

---

[14]NPNF 2 10:322*. [15]Acts 4:34-35. [16]WSA 3 9:98. [17]Mt 22:40. [18]FC 20:242*. [19]150-51*. [20]FC 94:200. [21]2 Cor 2:15. [22]LF 23:61*. [23]"From the beginning of faith" LXX. [24]NPNF 2 10:322*.

worship of idols. For Mount Lebanon is full of idols, whence you come, it says, hastening past through the law. Without knowing the law, you were taught the mystery of Christ. FRAGMENTS IN THE COMMENTARY ON THE SONG OF SONGS 4.8.[25]

TRUE BEAUTY. AMBROSE: This is indeed true beauty, to which nothing is wanting, which alone is worthy to hear the Lord saying, "You are all fair, my love, and no blemish is in you. Come hither from Lebanon, my spouse, come hither from Lebanon. You shall pass and pass through from the beginning of faith, from the top of Senir and Hermon, from the dens of lions, from the mountains of the leopards." By which references is set forth the perfect and irreproachable beauty of a virgin soul, consecrated to the altars of God, not moved by perishable things amidst the haunts and dens of spiritual wild beasts but intent, by the mysteries of God, on being found worthy of the beloved, whose breasts are full of joy. CONCERNING VIRGINS 1.7.38.[26]

ASK FOR THE HOLY SPIRIT. AMBROSE: You pass through and penetrate from the beginning of faith. That is, you will pass through to fight the world and you will penetrate to Christ to triumph over the world. You have heard that he removes you from the incursions of lions and leopards, that is, of spiritual evils. You have heard that the beauty of your virtues pleases him; you have heard that he prefers the fragrance of your garments, that is, the sweet perfume of integrity, to all other perfumes. You have heard that you are an enclosed garden, full of the products of delightful fruit trees. Ask, therefore, for the Holy Spirit to breathe on you on your couch and to gather the fragrances of a holy mind and spiritual gifts. ON VIRGINITY 12.69.[27]

THE VEIL OF THE SCRIPTURES REVEALED. THEODORET OF CYR: We require prayer, in fact—attentive and earnest prayer—for our eyes to become like doves with the gift of spiritual sight, getting beyond the veil of the letter and distinguishing clearly the hidden mysteries.[28] It is not possible by any other way, you see, to come to know the meaning of the divine Scripture, especially the Song of Songs, than having the very one who inspired those composers illuminate our vision by sending rays of grace and give a glimpse of the hidden sense. COMMENTARY ON THE SONG OF SONGS 4.[29]

A MYSTIC SONG. AMBROSE: "Come hither from Lebanon. You shall pass and pass through." This verse must be often repeated by us, that at least being called by the words of the Lord, she may follow if there be any who will not trust the words of man. We have not formed this power for ourselves, but have received it; this is the heavenly teaching of the mystic song. CONCERNING VIRGINS 2.6.42.[30]

AN INVITATION RENEWED. JEROME: "Come with me from Lebanon, my bride, with me from Lebanon. You shall come and pass on from the beginning of faith, from the top of Senir and Hermon, from the lions' dens, from the mountains of the leopards." Lebanon is, being interpreted, "whiteness." Come then, fairest bride, concerning whom it is elsewhere said, "Who is she that comes up, all in white?"[31] Pass on by way of this world, from the beginning of faith, and from Senir, which is by interpretation, "God of light," as we read in the psalm: "Your word is a lantern unto my feet, and light unto my path,"[32] and "from Hermon," that is, "consecration," and "flee from the lions' dens, and the mountains of the leopards who cannot change their spots." AGAINST JOVINIANUS 1.30.[33]

---

[25]PG 69:1287. [26]NPNF 2 10:369*. [27]AOV 32. [28]See 2 Cor 3:6. [29]ECS 2:80-81. [30]NPNF 2 10:380. [31]Song 8:5 LXX. [32]Ps 119:105 (118:105 LXX, Vg). [33]NPNF 2 6:369*.

4:9 — 5:1 THE ENCLOSED GARDEN

⁹*You have ravished my heart, my sister,*
  my bride,
  you have ravished my heart with a glance
    of your eyes,
  with one jewel of your necklace.
¹⁰*How sweet is your love,* my sister, my bride!*
  how much better is your love than wine,
  and the fragrance of your oils[†] than any
    spice!
¹¹*Your lips distil nectar, my bride;*
  honey and milk are under your tongue;
  the scent of your garments is like the scent
    of Lebanon.
¹²*A garden locked is my sister, my bride,*
  a garden locked, a fountain sealed.
¹³*Your shoots are an orchard of*
    pomegranates
  with all choicest fruits,
  henna with nard,
¹⁴*nard and saffron, calamus and*

  cinnamon,
  with all trees of frankincense,
myrrh and aloes,
  with all chief spices—
¹⁵*a garden fountain, a well of living water,*
  and flowing streams from Lebanon.

¹⁶*Awake, O north wind,*
  and come, O south wind!
Blow upon my garden,
  let its fragrance be wafted abroad.
Let my beloved come to his garden,
  and eat its choicest fruits.[‡]

5 *I come to my garden, my sister, my bride,*
I gather my myrrh with my spice,
I eat my honeycomb[§] with my honey,
I drink my wine with my milk.

Eat, O friends, and drink:
  drink deeply, O lovers!

* LXX breasts   †LXX garments   ‡ LXX Arise, O north wind, and come, O south wind, blow through my garden and let my ointments flow forth. Let my brother come down into his garden and eat the fruit of his apple trees.   § LXX bread

OVERVIEW: There is a "right eye of virginity" that is not related to carnal love and bodily marriage (JEROME). For it, for the bride of Christ, for the church, there is a sealed and enclosed garden with a fountain of pure water in which Scripture has power (AMBROSE, PSEUDO-DIONYSIUS, CYPRIAN) and where we are sealed by the Holy Spirit after baptism (CYRIL OF ALEXANDRIA). Here the Scriptures are distilled in honeycombs by teachers for our benefit, for the letter of Scripture resembles the honeycomb while the sense hidden inside resembles the honey (THEODORET OF CYR). This enclosed garden, which represents virginity (AMBROSE), is protected from evil thoughts (GREGORY OF NYSSA), and from it the pleasure of intercourse is excluded (AMBROSE). The womb of the blessed Virgin typifies it (PETER CHRYSOLOGUS). It smells of the violet, is scented with the olive and is resplendent with the rose (AMBROSE). Its scent of myrrh and aloes recalls also the garden in which Christ was buried (CYRIL OF JERUSALEM), just as the myrrh and aloes indicate Christ's redemption of the saints who preceded him (CYRIL OF ALEXANDRIA). The roots of its trees are dipped in sacred water (AMBROSE), and within it the north and south winds have deeper meanings (APONIUS). This garden symbolizes the church, even though some within it are not part of it and others do not belong that seem to be within it (AUGUSTINE), but here Christ may be sought and found (AMBROSE). The garden is an image of paradise, permeated with frankincense, which indicates divinity (GREGORY OF NYSSA). Especially symbolic of Christ is the association of the bride's clothing with frankincense (THEODORET OF CYR). Thus, this garden is the well of mystical wisdom (AMBROSE), the living water and fountain of life, within this garden is none other than Christ (CYRIL OF JERUSALEM). Likewise, the sealed fountain within the locked garden indicates the sacraments, which are available only to the initiated (THEODORET OF CYR). The garden is therefore closed to outsiders (CYPRIAN, CYRIL OF ALEXANDRIA), undefiled by the filth of heresy (PACIAN OF BARCELONA), and it can be likened to the pomegranate, whose protective covering is tough and bitter but whose inner fruit and juice are sweet (GREGORY OF NYSSA) and representative of love (THEODORET OF CYR). To eat and drink in this garden produces not intoxication but inebriation (JEROME, AMBROSE). This is the living water that irrigates the church (THEODORET OF CYR).

4:9 With the Glance of an Eye

YOU CREATED A HEART FOR US. CYRIL OF ALEXANDRIA: Truly you inflamed us with desire for you by one word of confession, which you rightly possessed, seeing with your interior eyes. For you made a confession by your necklace. These things were said to the bride by friends of the bridegroom, that is, by angelic powers. For, since the power of the visual faculty is twofold, one sees the truth and another wanders astray after vanity. Because the pure eye of the bride is opened only toward the nature of the good but the other is idle, therefore the friends give praise only to one eye, calling her "sister" on account of their kinship with respect to freedom from passion but calling her "bride" on account of her marriage to the Word. Because he says that your eye is one, therefore, insofar as it beholds one thing, likewise is your soul one, insofar as it is not

divided into many dispositions. And your necklace is perfect, given that you imposed the divine yoke upon yourself, for this necklace is surely the yoke of the Lord. For this reason, we confess that you created a heart for us by your wondrous dowry, which is to say that our souls and minds were brought to the contemplation of the light through you. For in you we contemplate the sun of justice as though in a mirror. FRAGMENTS IN THE COMMENTARY ON THE SONG OF SONGS 4.9.[1]

THE RIGHT EYE OF VIRGINITY. JEROME: Flee, he says, from the lions' dens, flee from the pride of devils, that when you have been consecrated to me, I may be able to say unto you, "You have ravished my heart, my sister, my bride, you have ravished my heart with one of your eyes, with one chain of your neck." What he says is something like this—I do not reject marriage: you have a second eye, the left, which I have given to you on account of the weakness of those who cannot see the right. But I am pleased with the right eye of virginity, and if it is blinded, the whole body is in darkness. And that we might not think he had in view carnal love and bodily marriage, he at once excludes this meaning by saying, "You have ravished my heart, my bride, my sister." The name *sister* excludes all suspicion of unhallowed love. "How fair are your breasts with wine," those breasts concerning which he had said above, my beloved is mine, and I am his: "between my breasts shall he lie," that is, in the princely portion of the heart where the Word of God has its lodging. AGAINST JOVINIANUS 1.30.[2]

DO NOT GRIEVE THE LOSS OF BODILY EYES. JEROME: You should not grieve that you are destitute of those bodily eyes which ants, flies and creeping things have as well as do people. Rather you should rejoice that you possess that eye of which it is said in the Song of Songs, "You have ravished my heart, my sister, my spouse; you have ravished my heart with one of your eyes." This is

---

[1]PG 69:1287-90. [2]NPNF 2 6:369*.

the eye with which God is seen and to which Moses refers when he says, "I will now turn aside and see this great sight."[3] LETTER 76.2.[4]

4:10-12 Love Better Than Wine

A GARDEN CLOSED AND A FOUNTAIN SEALED. AMBROSE: Christ, then, feeds his church with these sacraments, by means of which the substance of the soul is strengthened, and seeing the continual progress of her grace, he rightly says to her, "How comely are your breasts, my sister, my spouse, how comely they are made by wine, and the smell of your garments is above all spices. A dropping honeycomb are your lips, my spouse, honey and milk are under your tongue, and the smell of your garments is as the smell of Lebanon. A garden enclosed is my sister, my spouse, a garden enclosed, a fountain sealed." By which he signifies that the mystery ought to remain sealed up with you, that it be not violated by the deeds of an evil life, and pollution of chastity, that it be not made known to you, for whom it is not fitting, nor by garrulous talkativeness it be spread abroad among unbelievers. Your guardianship of the faith ought therefore to be good, that integrity of life and silence may endure unblemished. ON THE MYSTERIES 9.55.[5]

THE SEALED FOUNTAIN INDICATES THE SACRAMENTS. THEODORET OF CYR: He calls her "a garden," not as though bearing a single fruit of piety and virtue, but as one producing many and varied fruits; and "locked" as though sealed off and proof against intrigue.... She is also "a fountain sealed." She is not available to everyone but to those thought worthy of these streams; the Lord in the sacred Gospels also says of this fountain, "Whoever drinks of the water I shall give will not thirst forever, and instead there will be in them a spring of living water gushing up to life eternal."[6] Properly, then, he refers to her as "a fountain sealed" for not being available to everyone but to those thought worthy. The divine sacraments, after all, are available not to the

uninitiated but to the initiated, not to those wallowing in iniquity after initiation but to those living an exact life or purified through repentance. COMMENTARY ON THE SONG OF SONGS 4.[7]

ANOINTED AFTER BAPTISM. CYRIL OF ALEXANDRIA: [This garden] is closed to the world but opened to the heavenly bridegroom. And the fountain where we are anointed after baptism was sealed by the Holy Spirit. FRAGMENTS IN THE COMMENTARY ON THE SONG OF SONGS 4.12.[8]

THE POWER OF THE SCRIPTURES. PSEUDO-DIONYSIUS: The divine and conceptual Scriptures are compared with dew, with water,[9] with milk,[10] with wine,[11] and with honey,[12] for they have the power like water to produce life, like milk to give growth, like wine to revive, like honey both to purify and preserve. LETTER 9.4.[13]

TEACHERS DISTILL THE SCRIPTURES IN HONEYCOMBS. THEODORET OF CYR: "Your lips distill a honeycomb, bride; honey and milk are under your tongue." Here it refers to the teachers of the church, offering religious teaching and, as it were, carrying honeycomb of bees on its lips, and distilling drops of honey, containing not only honey but also milk, and providing to each the appropriate nourishment, both suited to the infants and adapted to the mature.[14] Now, honeycombs borne on the lips of the teachers are the divine Scriptures, which contain bees that make honeycombs and produce honey, the sacred prophets and apostles. These latter fly about the meadows of the Holy Spirit, as it were constructing the honeycombs of the divine Scriptures, filling them with the honey of doctrine and dispatching them to us for our benefit. The letter resembles the honeycomb, while the sense hidden in it resembles the honey; the lips

---

[3]Ex 3:3. [4]NPNF 2 6:157*. [5]NPNF 2 10:325*. [6]Jn 4:14. [7]ECS 2:84*. [8]PG 69:1290. [9]Deut 32:2. [10]1 Cor 3:2; 1 Pet 2:2; Heb 5:12-13. [11]Prov 9:5; Rev 14:10, 16:19, 19:15. [12]Ps 19:10 (18:11 LXX); 119:103 (118:103 LXX); Rev 1:9-10. [13]PDCW 286-87*. [14]See 1 Cor 3:2.

of pious teachers release the drops of this honey. Also, milk flowing from their tongue reaches those in need of milk. Commentary on the Song of Songs 4.[15]

Bride's Clothing of Frankincense Is Symbolic of Christ.

Theodoret of Cyr: "Fragrance of your garments like the fragrance of frankincense." We said before that the bridegroom himself became her garment, and blessed Paul confirms it in the words, "All of you who were baptized into Christ put on Christ."[16] Now, the bridegroom is both God eternal and was born a man from the holy Virgin in the last days. While remaining what he was, he took as well what is ours, and clothed the bride who was formerly left naked—hence his saying to her, "fragrance of your garments like the fragrance of frankincense." She is clothed with Christ, who is both God and man. Now, "frankincense" is a symbol of the true doctrine of God, since under the norms of the old law it was offered to God.[17] Commentary on the Song of Songs 4.[18]

The Enclosed Garden and the Sealed Fountain.

Cyprian: If then this spouse of Christ—which is the church—is a garden enclosed, what is closed cannot be open to the stranger and profane. If the church is a sealed fountain, one who is outside, without access to the fountain, cannot drink from it or be sealed there. If there is but one well of living water—that which is within—then one who is without can have no life or grace from the water which only those within are allowed to use and drink.[19] Letter 69.2.[20]

An Enclosed Fountain.

Pacian of Barcelona: We know, too, that since it is "the well of living water"[21] and "a fountain enclosed," it is defiled with no filth from a heretical abyss; that it is also a garden and filled with herbs great and small alike, some of little value, some precious; and that it is also the eight souls from the ark.[22] Letter 3.21.2.[23]

Enclosed Garden Represents Virginity.

Ambrose: "A garden enclosed" [is virginity] because it is shut in on all sides by the wall of chastity. "A fountain sealed up" is virginity, for it is the fount and wellspring of modesty that keeps the seal of purity inviolate, in whose source there may shine the image of God, since the pureness of simplicity coincides with the chastity of the body. Letter 59, To Priests.[24]

Sealed and Protected from Evil Thoughts.

Gregory of Nyssa: Because a seal protects the inviolability of whatever it guards, it scares off thieves; everything not stolen remains unharmed for the master. Praise of the bride in the Song would then testify to her excellence in virtue because her mind remains safe from enemies and is guarded for her Lord in purity and tranquility. Purity seals this fountain while the radiance and transparency of the bride's heart is unclouded by no mire of evil thoughts. Homilies on the Song of Songs 9.[25]

Pleasure of Intercourse Excluded.

Ambrose: Watch out that the firmness of your mind not be bent and softened by the bodily pleasure of intercourse and thus dissolve into all her embraces and open up her fountain, that ought to have been shut and closed in by zealous intent and reasoned consideration. "You are an enclosed garden, a fountain sealed." For once the firmness of the mind is dissolved, thoughts of bodily pleasure pour forth; they are very harmful and flare up into an unrestrained longing for grave danger. But if careful attention had been devoted to guarding the lively mind, it would have checked them. Isaac, or the Soul 2.2.[26]

Fountain of Pure Water Reflects the Image of God.

Ambrose: In gardens of this

---

[15]ECS 2:83. [16]Gal. 3:27. [17]Lev 2:1-2, 15-16. [18]ECS 2:83-84. [19]Cf. Song 6:9. [20]LCC 5:151. [21]See Jn 4:10-15; 7:37-39. [22]See Gen 6:18; 7:7, 13; 1 Pet 3:20. [23]FC 99:63. [24]FC 26:334. [25] 177. [26]FC 65:12.

kind the water of the pure fountain shines, reflecting the features of the image of God, lest its streams mingled with mud from the wallowing places of spiritual wild beasts should be polluted. For this reason, too, that modesty of virgins fenced in by the wall of the Spirit is enclosed lest it should lie open to be plundered. And so as a garden inaccessible from without smells of the violet, is scented with the olive and is resplendent with the rose, that religion may increase in the vine, peace in the olive and the modesty of consecrated virginity in the rose. CONCERNING VIRGINS 1.9.45.[27]

AN ALLEGORY OF THE CHURCH. AUGUSTINE: This account can be even better read as an allegory of the church, prophetical of what was to happen in the future. Thus the garden is the church itself, as we can see from the Canticle of Canticles; the four rivers are the four Gospels; the fruit-bearing trees are the saints, as the fruits are their works; and the tree of life is, of course, the Saint of saints, Christ. CITY OF GOD 13.21.[28]

VIRGINAL CONCEPTION. PETER CHRYSOLOGUS: He so departed from the abode of the womb that the virginal door did not open, and what is sung in the Canticle of Canticles was fulfilled: "My sister, my spouse, is a garden enclosed, a garden enclosed, a fountain sealed up." SERMON 145.[29]

SOME WITHIN THE CHURCH ARE NOT PART OF IT. AUGUSTINE: Taking all these things, therefore, into consideration, I think that I am not rash in saying that there are some in the house of God after such a fashion as not to be themselves the very house of God, which is said to be built upon a rock.[30] [The church] is called the one dove,[31] which is styled the beauteous bride without spot or wrinkle,[32] and a garden enclosed, a fountain sealed, a well of living water, an orchard of pomegranates with pleasant fruits. [This] house also received the keys, and the power of binding and loosing.[33] ON BAPTISM 7.51.99.[34]

SOME DO NOT BELONG. AUGUSTINE: I think that we have sufficiently shown, both from the canon of Scripture and from the letters of Cyprian himself. [Thus] bad people, while by no means converted to a better mind, can have, and confer, and receive baptism, of whom it is most clear that they do not belong to the holy church of God, though they seem to be within it. [But] they are covetous, robbers, usurers, envious, evil thinkers, and the like; while [the church] is one dove,[35] modest and chaste, a bride without spot or wrinkle,[36] a garden enclosed, a fountain sealed, an orchard of pomegranates with pleasant fruits, with all similar properties that are attributed to her. ON BAPTISM 6.3.5.[37]

4:13-15 Images of the Church

FRANKINCENSE INDICATES DIVINITY AND PARADISE. GREGORY OF NYSSA: When the Word raises his bride to such a point through her ascents, he leads her even further, saying that her garments have the scent of frankincense. Scripture testifies that Christ is clothed with this frankincense.[38] The end of a virtuous life is participation in God, for frankincense manifests the divinity. The soul is not always led by the Word to what is higher by means of honey and milk, but after having been compared with the scent of frankincense, the garden becomes an image of paradise. It is not loosely guarded as with our first parents, but protected from every side by recollection of the bridegroom's command. HOMILIES ON THE SONG OF SONGS 9.[39]

PROTECTED BY THE RIND OF THE POMEGRANATE. GREGORY OF NYSSA: In order that we may know the plants that the Word cultivates in believers, the Song calls the trees he planted "pomegranates." These issue from the bride's mouth. The

---

[27]NPNF 2 10:370. [28]FC 14:331. [29]FC 17:234-35. [30]Mt 16:18. [31]Cf. Song 6:9. [32]Eph 5:27. [33]Mt 16:19. [34]NPNF 1 4:511. [35]Song 6:9. [36]Eph 5:27. [37]NPNF 1 4:480*. [38]See Gal 3:27; Rom 13:14. [39]*GNSS* 178-79*.

pomegranate is difficult for a thief to grasp because of its thorny branches, and its fruit is surrounded and protected by a rind bitter and harsh to the taste. Once the pomegranate ripens in its own good time, and once the rind is peeled off and the inside revealed, it is sweet and appealing to the sight much like honey to the taste; its juice tastes like wine and affords much pleasure to the palate. I think that the issues from the bride's mouth [are] a "garden of pomegranates" present in the souls of those listening to her. We must heed her words and not become soft by indulgence and enjoyment of this present life. Rather we should choose a life that has become toughened by continence. Thus virtue's fruit is inaccessible to thieves and is protected by the bitter covering of self-control. Surrounded by a solemn, austere way of life, it wards off as though by spiny thorns those who approach the fruit with evil intent. HOMILIES ON THE SONG OF SONGS 9.[40]

LOVE IS INDICATED BY THE SEEDS AND LAYERS OF THE POMEGRANATE. THEODORET OF CYR: "Pomegranate" is to be taken figuratively as love, since countless seeds are contained together within the one skin, pressed together without squeezing or ruining one another, remaining fresh unless one of the seeds in the middle goes bad. You can also gain a different insight from the sections in the middle: we see many ranks also among the saved, one of virgins, one of ascetics, one of those drawing the yoke of marriage, and of the affluent, one of those living a life of poverty, one of slaves in love with godliness, one of masters exercising lordship lawfully. The pomegranate, too, then, has walled off compartments, as it were, separating its seeds into certain divisions. This is the reason he compares the presents of the bride to "an orchard of pomegranates." COMMENTARY ON THE SONG OF SONGS 4.[41]

THE LIVING WATER IRRIGATES THE CHURCH. THEODORET OF CYR: [This garden] also contains "a spring" and "a well of water alive and babbling from Lebanon." It contains not only the gospel teaching that flows openly but also the "well" of the law, which is "a well of water alive" that also holds hidden streams that babble, emit a sound and flow from Lebanon. The way of life according to the law blossomed in Jerusalem, which is figuratively called Lebanon, but this well changed direction toward the Lord's bride, the church, and though hidden, it flows with a babble and irrigates the orchard of the church. COMMENTARY ON THE SONG OF SONGS 4.[42]

CLOSED TO OUTSIDERS. CYPRIAN: If the garden enclosed is the spouse of Christ, which is the church, a thing enclosed cannot lie open to outsiders and profane people. And if the fountain is sealed, there is no access to the fountain to anyone placed outside either to drink or to be sealed therewith. The well of living water, also, if it is one, is the same which is within; one who is situated outside cannot be vivified and sanctified by that water of which it is granted only to those who are within to have all use and drink. LETTER 69.2.[43]

MYRRH AND ALOES. CYRIL OF JERUSALEM: The place of his burial was a garden. . . . What is he going to say who was buried in the garden? "I gather my myrrh, and my spices";[44] and again, "Myrrh and aloes with all the finest spices." These were the tokens of his burial, and in the Gospels it is said, "The women came to the tomb, taking the spices they had prepared,"[45] and "there also came Nicodemus, bringing a mixture of myrrh and aloes."[46] CATECHETICAL LECTURES 14.11.[47]

MYRRH AND ALOES INDICATE REDEMPTION OF THE SAINTS WHO PRECEDED CHRIST. CYRIL OF ALEXANDRIA: Virtues are signified by the perfumes and the trees of Lebanon are the prophets. Myrrh and aloes, finally, demonstrate that the buried Christ communed with the saints who preceded him, for, descending to hades, he

---

[40]*GNSS* 179-80*. [41]ECS 2:84-85. [42]ECS 2:85-86*. [43]FC 51:245. [44]Song 5:1. [45]Lk 24:1. [46]Jn 19:39. [47]FC 64:38-39.

led them out. FRAGMENTS IN THE COMMENTARY ON THE SONG OF SONGS 4.15.[48]

THE WELL OF MYSTICAL WISDOM. AMBROSE: We find the well in the mystical sense in the Canticle of Canticles, where the Scripture says, "the fountain of gardens, the well of living water which runs with a strong stream from Lebanon." Indeed if you pursue the depth of the mysteries, the well appears to you to be mystical wisdom set in the deep, as it were. But if you wish to drink the abundance of love, which is greater and richer than faith and hope, then you have your fountain. For love abounds, so that you can drink it in close at hand and water your garden with its abundance, so that the latter overflows with spiritual fruits. ISAAC, OR THE SOUL 4.26.[49]

CHRIST IS THE FOUNTAIN OF LIFE. CYRIL OF JERUSALEM: Now who is the "fountain sealed," or who is signified by the "wellspring of living water"? It is the Savior himself, of whom it is written: "For with you is the fountain of life."[50] CATECHETICAL LECTURES 14.5.[51]

4:16 A Garden Pleasing to Christ

TREES WHOSE ROOTS ARE DIPPED IN SACRED WATER. AMBROSE: For this reason, too, the church, guarding the depth of the heavenly mysteries, repels the furious storms of wind, and calls to it the sweetness of the grace of spring, and knowing that its garden cannot displease Christ, invites the bridegroom, saying, "Arise, O north wind, and come, you south; blow upon my garden, and let my ointments flow down. Let my brother come down to his garden and eat the fruit of his trees." For it has good trees and fruitful, which have dipped their roots in the water of the sacred spring, and with fresh growth have shot forth into good fruits, so as now not to be cut with the axe of the prophet, but to abound with the fruitfulness of the gospel. ON THE MYSTERIES 9.56.[52]

THE CHURCH INVITES US. AMBROSE: Recog-

nize also the voice of the church inviting us when it says, "Arise, O north wind, and come, O south wind, blow through my garden and let my ointments flow forth. Let my brother come down into his garden and eat the fruit of his apple trees." For knowing even then, O holy church, that from these also you would have fruitful works, you promised to your anointed one the fruit from such as these. It was you who first said that you were brought into the king's chamber, loving [Christ's] breasts above wine.[53] For you loved him who loved you, you sought him who nourished you, and you despised dangers for religion's sake. ON HIS BROTHER SATYRUS 2.118.[54]

THE WINDS AND THE REGIONS HAVE DEEPER MEANINGS. APONIUS: By exalting the kingdom of the north above all kingdoms of the world, therefore, Almighty God commands what is [now] the kingdom of the Romans to arise. By inspiring prophets from the south, by revealing his Christ through a Virgin, whom the prophets of the south had celebrated as proceeding from a dense and intact body (as the prophet Habakkuk said, "God will come from the south," that is, the Word of the Father, and "the holy one from a mountain shadowy and dense,"[55] which refers to the assumed humanity), paradise begins to be redolent with fragrances of the deaths of the martyrs, precious and wonderful aromas, and to give great praise to the Lord, the King of heaven, and to all the heavenly host, as the prophet predicted: "Precious in the sight of the Lord is the death of his saints."[56] EXPOSITION OF SONG OF SONGS 7.49.[57]

SEEK CHRIST AND THE SPIRIT. AMBROSE: Having thus learned where to seek out Christ, learn now how to merit that he may be seeking you. Arouse the Holy Spirit by saying, "Awake, O north wind, and come, O south wind! Blow upon my garden, and let its fragrance be wafted abroad.

---

[48]PG 69:1290. [49]FC 65:26**. [50]Ps 36:9 (35:10 LXX). [51]FC 64:35. [52]NPNF 2 10:325*. [53]Song 4:10 LXX. [54]FC 22:252. [55]Hab 3:3. [56]Ps 115:15 (113:23 LXX). [57]CCL 19:175.

Let my beloved come to his garden and eat its choicest fruits." The garden of the Word is the affection of a flourishing soul, and its fruit is the produce of virtue. On Virginity 9.54.[58]

5:1 Eating and Drinking in the Garden

The Concept Is Not Dishonorable.
Jerome: "O my sister, my bride, come." Lest you associate anything base with the concept of bride, the word *sister* is adjoined to preclude any dishonorable love. Come, my sister: love is something sacred and for that reason I call you sister. My bride: I call you my bride that I may have a wife, and from you, my wife, beget sons in number, sons as many as clusters of grapes on the vine. Homilies on the Psalms 42 (Psalm 127).[59]

Christ Dines and Drinks in Us. Ambrose: The bridegroom comes down and takes delight in the diversity of her fruit; he rejoices because he has found a stronger food and one that is sweeter, too.[60] For there is a kind of bread of the word, and a honey, one speech more ardent, another more persuasive. There is also one faith that is more hot like wine, another that is more clear like the taste of milk. Christ dines on such food in us. He drinks such drink in us; with the intoxication of this drink, he challenges us to make a departure from worse things to those that are better and best. Isaac, or the Soul 5.49.[61]

Bread and Honey as the Food of Christ.
Ambrose: "I have eaten my bread with my honey." This solid is gathered from the flowers of various virtues by the cooperative work of those bees that proclaim wisdom. Holy church puts it in honeycombs so that it may be the food of Christ. On Virginity 16.98.[62]

Not the Wine of the Flesh. Jerome: "Come, brethren, drink deeply of love." Wine to cheer the heart of people. The wine of the flesh does not cheer the heart of humankind but overpowers it and produces madness; it is written, in fact, that it is not for kings to drink wine.[63] Homilies on the Psalms 42 (Psalm 127).[64]

Sobering Inebriation. Ambrose: This inebriation makes people sober. This inebriation is one of grace, not of intoxication. It leads to joy, not to befuddlement. In the banquet hall of the church there will be pleasant odors, delightful food, and drink in variety. There will be noble guests and attendants who grace that occasion. It will not be otherwise! What is there that is nobler than to have Christ at the church's banquet, as one who ministers and is ministered unto? Cain and Abel 1.5.19.[65]

---

[58]AOV 27. [59]FC 48:321. [60]See 1 Cor 3:2. [61]FC 65:39-40. [62]AOV 44. [63]Prov 31:4. [64]FC 48:322*. [65]FC 42:377.

5:2—6:3 A DREAM OF LOVE

²I slept, but my heart was awake.
Hark! my beloved is knocking.
"Open to me, my sister, my love,
   my dove, my perfect one;
for my head is wet with dew,
   my locks with the drops of the night."
³I had put off my garment,
   how could I put it on?
I had bathed my feet,
   how could I soil them?
⁴My beloved put his hand to the latch,
   and my heart was thrilled within me.
⁵I arose to open to my beloved,
   and my hands dripped with myrrh,
my fingers with liquid myrrh,
   upon the handles of the bolt.
⁶I opened to my beloved,
   but my beloved had turned and gone.
My soul failed me when he spoke.
I sought him, but found him not;
   I called him, but he gave no answer.
⁷The watchmen found me,
   as they went about in the city;
they beat me, they wounded me,
   they took away my mantle,
   those watchmen of the walls.
⁸I adjure you, O daughters of Jerusalem,
   if you find my beloved,
that you tell him
   I am sick with love.

⁹What is your beloved more than another
     beloved,
   O fairest among women?
What is your beloved more than another
   beloved,
   that you thus adjure us?

¹⁰My beloved is all radiant and ruddy,
   distinguished among ten thousand.
¹¹His head is the finest gold;
   his locks are wavy,
   black as a raven.
¹²His eyes are like doves
   beside springs of water,
bathed in milk,
   fitly set.ᵏ
¹³His cheeks are like beds of spices,
   yielding fragrance.
His lips are lilies,
   distilling liquid myrrh.
¹⁴His arms are rounded gold,
   set with jewels.
His body is ivory work,ˡ
   encrusted with sapphires.ᵐ
¹⁵His legs are alabaster columns,
   set upon bases of gold.
His appearance is like Lebanon,*
   choice as the cedars.
¹⁶His speech is most sweet,
   and he is altogether desirable.
This is my beloved and this is my friend,
   O daughters of Jerusalem.

6 Whither has your beloved gone,
   O fairest among women?
Whither has your beloved turned,
   that we may seek him with you?

²My beloved has gone down to his garden,

> to the beds of spices,
> to pasture his flock in the gardens,
> and to gather lilies.

> [3] I am my beloved's and my beloved is
> mine;
> he pastures his flock among the lilies.

k The meaning of the Hebrew is uncertain   l The meaning of the Hebrew word is uncertain   m Heb *lapis lazuli*   *LXX *Libanus* or *incense*

OVERVIEW: The marriage of the Word and the soul is spiritual, not carnal (AMBROSE), and to sleep while the heart is awake has profound meaning (APONIUS). The soul speaks, for example, while it sleeps (CHRYSOSTOM). During such sleep sin is destroyed (AMBROSE), the heart is pure (GREGORY OF NYSSA), dryness is removed by heavenly dew (AMBROSE), the thoughts of the day come back as the heart watches (BASIL), the garment of corporeal life is removed (AMBROSE), the past is recalled and the future anticipated (BEDE).

A voluntary mortification of bodily passions may even be indicated by the presence of myrrh, a sign of the death of the flesh (GREGORY THE GREAT, GREGORY OF NYSSA). Still, God's Word can pierce as a sharp sword (AMBROSE), and still God can seek us (JOHN CASSIAN). If there is no answer it may well be because of God's utter transcendence, for the soul would not seek that which it could not receive (GREGORY OF NYSSA). For the bride to describe her spouse as "white and ruddy" may indicate some pairing such as white in virginity, ruddy in martyrdom (JEROME). Or it may signify white as divine, ruddy as human (THEODORET OF CYR), or of the Father's brightness but born of the Virgin (AMBROSE). It may also indicate white because of sinlessness and red because he died for us (BEDE). Or it may have still deeper significance (APONIUS, GREGORY OF NYSSA) as is the case with the locks of hair that are wavy and black (JULIAN OF ECLANUM).

The keen vision of the dove provides an image of Christ (THEODORET OF CYR, ORIGEN, CYRIL OF JERUSALEM, GREGORY OF NYSSA, BEDE), as do the alabaster columns and bases of gold (AMBROSE, GREGORY OF NYSSA, CYRIL OF ALEXANDRIA), the two natures being indicated by the incense and the cedar (THEODORET OF CYR). If we agree that there is an analogy from the visible world to the incomprehensible beauty of the infinite (GREGORY OF NYSSA), then it must also be agreed that this has implications for our appearance and conduct here and now (AUGUSTINE). And this, in turn, implies that we should be loyal and faithful to the one church of Christ (LEANDER OF SEVILLE).

5:2-5 The Heart Awake in Sleep

HUMANITY AND DIVINITY, BOTH ASLEEP AND AWAKE. CYRIL OF ALEXANDRIA: I sleep, he says, on the cross, insofar as he suffers death on behalf of humanity. But his heart remains awake because, as God, he plunders hades. FRAGMENTS IN THE COMMENTARY ON THE SONG OF SONGS 5.2.[1]

MARRIAGE OF THE WORD AND SOUL IS SPIRITUAL. AMBROSE: She is now awakened from sleep by him, although she was keeping watch with her heart so that she might hear his voice at once when he knocked. But while she was rising, she experienced a delay, because she could not match the swiftness of the Word. While she was opening the door, the Word passed by.[2] She went out at his word, sought for him through wounds, but wounds of love, and, finally and with difficulty, found him and embraced him, so that she might not lose him. . . .

Even though you are asleep, if only Christ has come to know the devotion of your soul, he comes and knocks at her door and says, "Open to me, my sister." "Sister" is well put, because the marriage of the Word and the soul is spiritual. For souls do not know covenants of wedlock or the ways of bodily union, but they are like the angels in heaven.[3] "Open to me," but close to strangers. Close to the times, close to the world, do not go out of doors to

---

[1] PG 69:1290.   [2] Cf. Song 5:5-6.   [3] Mt 22:30.

material things, do not abandon your own light and search for another's, because material light pours out a dark mist, so that the light of true glory is not seen. "Open," therefore, "to me"; do not open to the adversary or give place to the devil. "Open yourself to me," do not be confined, but expand, and I will fill you. And because, in my passage through the world, I have found very much trouble and vexation and have not readily had a place to rest, do you then open, that the Son of man may rest his head on you, for he has no rest[4] save on one who is humble and quiet.

The soul, hearing "Open to me," and "My head is wet with dew," that is, the soul that was suddenly disturbed by the temptations of the world and was bidden to rise, and indeed is on the point of rising, as it were, speaks: fragrant with aloe and myrrh, signs of burial.[5] ISAAC, OR THE SOUL 6.50-52.[6]

THE DEEPER MEANING OF SUCH SLEEP. APONIUS: "I sleep and my heart remains awake." The divine Word, who is to be understood here under the title of the heart, never sleeps or falls asleep while hidden within the veil of the flesh, but he carries the sleeper. He explains this in a deeply mysterious way to the friends and beloveds who believe in him and whom he invites to partake of the joy of human salvation. [He does this] lest, while they see him detained in the sleep of death according to his humanity, they are deprived of the faith through which they see in him a majesty that is full and ever watchful. I am asleep to you through bodily absence, he says, but I am awake in heart by never withdrawing the presence of my deity from you. EXPOSITION OF SONG OF SONGS 7.59.[7]

THE SOUL SPEAKS WHILE IT SLEEPS. CHRYSOSTOM: Both when I stayed at home and when I departed, when I walked and rested, and wherever I went, I continuously turned your love over in my mind and dreamt about it. I found pleasure in these dreams not only during the day but also at night. The very statement made by Solomon,

"I sleep but my heart is awake," was then happening to me. The necessity for sleep weighed down my eyelids, but the great power of your love chased away the sleep from the eyes of my soul; and constantly I thought that I was speaking with you in my sleep.

At night, it is natural for the soul to see in her dreams all the things that she thinks about in the day, something that I was then experiencing. Although I did not see you with the eyes of my body, I saw you with the eyes of love. In spite of my physical absence, I was close to you in disposition, and my ears always heard your vivacious voice. HOMILIES ON REPENTANCE AND ALMSGIVING 1.3-4.[8]

GOD FEASTS WHEN SIN IS DESTROYED. AMBROSE: "I sleep, but my heart is awake." Let us learn what food and produce God feasts upon and in which ones he takes pleasure. He takes pleasure in this, if anyone dies to his sin, blots out his guilt, and destroys and buries his iniquities. The myrrh represents the burial of the dead, but sins are dead, for they cannot possess the sweetness of life. Moreover, some wounds of sinners are moistened with the ointments of Scripture and the stronger food of the word as with bread,[9] and are treated with the sweeter word like honey. DEATH AS A GOOD 5.20.[10]

HEART IS PURE WHEN SENSES ARE ASLEEP. GREGORY OF NYSSA: Once all the senses have been put to sleep and are gripped by inaction, the heart's action is pure; reason looks above while it remains undisturbed and free from the senses' movement. . . .

If a person pays attention to the senses and is drawn by pleasure in the body, he will live his life without tasting the divine joy, since the good can be overshadowed by what is inferior. For those who desire God, a good not shadowed over by anything awaits them; they realize that what

[4]Lk 9:58. [5]See Jn 19:39. [6]FC 65:40-41. [7]CCL 19:180. [8]FC 96:1-2. [9]See Ps 104:15 (103:15 LXX, Vg). [10]FC 65:86.

enters the senses must be avoided. Therefore, when the soul enjoys only the contemplation of being, it will not arise for those things that effect sensual pleasure. It puts to rest all bodily movement, and by naked, pure insight, the soul will see God in a divine watchfulness. May we be made worthy through this sleep, of which the Song has spoken, to keep our soul vigilant. HOMILIES ON THE SONG OF SONGS 10.[11]

THE MOISTURE OF ETERNAL LIFE. AMBROSE: As the dew from the heavens removes the dryness of the night, so the dew of our Lord Jesus Christ descends as the moisture of eternal life into the nocturnal shadows of the world. This is the head that knows nothing of the dryness caused by the heat of this world. ON VIRGINITY 12.70.[12]

THE VISIONS OF SLEEP. BASIL THE GREAT: According to the counsel of the apostle, the zealous person can do all things for the glory of God, so that every act and every word and every work has in it power of praise. Whether the just person eats or drinks, he does all for the glory of God.[13] The heart of such a one watches when he is sleeping, according to him who said in the Song of Solomon: "I sleep, and my heart watches." For on many occasions the visions seen during sleep are images of our thoughts by day. HOMILIES ON THE PSALMS 16.1 (PSALM 33).[14]

THE LORD DIVESTED HIMSELF FOR US. AMBROSE: In this night of the world the garment of corporeal life is first to be taken off as the Lord divested himself in his flesh that for you he might triumph over the dominions and powers of this world. ON VIRGINITY 9.55.[15]

MYRRH INDICATES MORTIFICATION. GREGORY THE GREAT: Myrrh indicates the death of our flesh, and so the church says of its members who are striving even to death on behalf of God: "My hands dripped with myrrh." FORTY GOSPEL HOMILIES 8 (10).[16]

MYRRH IS VOLUNTARY. GREGORY OF NYSSA: Resurrection is not effected in us unless a voluntary death precedes it. Such a voluntary death is indicated by the drops of myrrh dripping from the bride's hands, for her fingers are filled with this spice. She says that myrrh did not come into her hands from any other source—if this were so, myrrh would mean something accidental and involuntary. Rather her hands (the operative faculties of the soul) drop myrrh, meaning a voluntary mortification of her bodily passions. HOMILIES ON THE SONG OF SONGS 12.[17]

A REMINDER FROM THE PRIMITIVE CHURCH. BEDE: "I sleep" because I enjoy by grace a little tranquility in this life through worshiping him. Nor clearly do I bear as much of the labor of preaching as was delivered to the primitive church. Nor am I as tossed about by conflicts of the faithless as were the innumerable crowds of the nascent church at the beginning. "My heart remains awake" because the more freedom I acquire from external incursions, the more deeply within I see that he is the Lord. COMMENTARY ON THE SONGS OF SONGS 3.5.2.[18]

5:6 He Had Gone

AS PIERCING AS A SHARP SWORD. AMBROSE: "I opened to my beloved, but my beloved had gone." What is this going? Simply that he has penetrated into the center of the mind as it was said to Mary, "And his sword will pierce your soul."[19] For the living Word of God, as piercing as a sharp sword, comprehends both the limits of bodily thoughts and the secret places of the heart. ON VIRGINITY 11.67.[20]

IT IS GOD WHO SEEKS US. JOHN CASSIAN: The Lord seeks us when he says, "I sought, and there was no one. I called, and there was no one

---

[11]*GNSS* 195*. [12]AOV 33. [13]1 Cor 10:31. [14]FC 46:250. [15]AOV 27. [16]CS 123:59*. [17]*GNSS* 214. [18]CCL 119B:274. [19]Lk 2:35. [20]AOV 31.

who responded." And he himself is sought by his bride, who mourns tearfully, "In my chamber at night I sought him whom my soul loved. I sought him, and I did not find him; I called him, and he did not answer me." CONFERENCE 13.12.12.[21]

NO ANSWER BECAUSE GOD IS COMPLETELY TRANSCENDENT.

GREGORY OF NYSSA: The bride says, "I sought him, but found him not." How can the bridegroom be found when he does not reveal anything of himself? He has no color, form, quality, quantity, place, appearance, evidence, comparison or resemblance. Rather, everything we can discover always transcends our comprehension and completely escapes our search. Therefore the bride says, "I have sought him by my soul's capacities of reflection and understanding. He completely transcended them, and he escaped my mind when it drew near to him."

How can that which is always beyond everything we know be designated by a name? For this reason the bride understands every function of a name as a sign of the ineffable good. The significance of each word falls short and shows something inferior to the truth. . . .

The soul thus calls the Word as best it can. It cannot do so as it wishes, for the soul desires more than it is capable of. The soul does not wish what it is incapable of receiving, such as God himself, but its choice is in accord with its wish. Since the one called is unattainable, the bride says, "I called him, but he did not answer." HOMILIES ON THE SONG OF SONGS 12.[22]

5:10 Radiant and Ruddy

ANALOGY FROM THE VISIBLE TO THE INVISIBLE.

GREGORY OF NYSSA: All these elements constituting the bridegroom's beauty are made known for our benefit but do not show his invisible, incomprehensible beauty. . . .

Therefore, whoever looks at the visible world and understands the wisdom that has been made manifest by the beauty of creatures can make an analogy from the visible to invisible beauty, the fountain of beauty whose emanation established all living beings in existence. Similarly, whoever views the world of this new creation in the church sees in it him who is all in all. This person is then led by faith through what is finite and comprehensible to knowledge of the infinite. HOMILIES ON THE SONG OF SONGS 13.[23]

WHILE IN VIRGINITY, RUDDY IN MARTYRDOM.

JEROME: "My beloved is white and ruddy": white in virginity, ruddy in martyrdom. And because he is white and ruddy, therefore it is immediately added, "His mouth is most sweet, yea, he is altogether lovely."[24] AGAINST JOVINIANUS 1.31.[25]

WHITE AS GOD, RUDDY AS A HUMAN.

THEODORET OF CYR: The bride instructs the young women who had enquired as to the features of the bridegroom, saying, "My nephew is white and ruddy," mentioning "white" first and "ruddy" second. He was always God, but he became man as well, not by abandoning what he was or being turned into a man but by putting on a human nature. So he is "white" as God: what could be whiter than light? Now, he is the true light, according to the Gospel saying, "He was the true light, which enlightens every person coming into the world."[26]

He is not only "white," however, but also "ruddy." After all, he is not only God but also man. Now, the term *ruddy* suggests earthly; hence also in Isaiah the divine powers, on seeing him ascending from earth to heaven, pose the question, "Who is this coming from Edom, the red of his garments from Bozrah? He is charming in his vesture, overpowering in his strength."[27] COMMENTARY ON THE SONG OF SONGS 5.[28]

BRIGHTNESS OF THE FATHER.

AMBROSE: "My beloved is white and ruddy." It is fitting, O virgin, that you should fully know him whom you love, and should recognize in him all the mystery of his

---

[21]ACW 57:481. [22]*GNSS* 220*. [23]*GNSS* 235. [24]Song 5:16. [25]NPNF 2 6:370. [26]Jn 1:9. [27]See Is 63:1-9. [28]ECS 2:90.

divine nature and the body which he has assumed. He is white fittingly, for he is the brightness of the Father; and ruddy, for he was born of a Virgin. The color of each nature shines and glows in him. Concerning Virgins 1.9.46.[29]

White Because Sinless, Red Because He Died for Us. Bede: The beloved is white because, when he appeared in the flesh, "he committed no sin, nor was a lie found in his mouth."[30] And he is red because "he washed away our sins with his blood."[31] He is rightly called white first, then red, because the holy one first came into the world from blood and later departed from the world through his bloody passion. Commentary on the Songs of Songs 3.5.10.[32]

Both Colors Have Deeper Significance. Aponius: He is white because he is the light of the world, the Sun of righteousness "who enlightens everyone entering the world,"[33] according to John the Evangelist and the preaching of the prophets. He is red because he would walk on earth in the fleshly clothing derived from the Virgin Mary, a miracle to be offered through angels by rising to heaven, as was said through the mouth of the prophet Isaiah to those who asked him, "Why is your apparel red?"[34] Exposition of Song of Songs 8.34.[35]

The Power of the Most High. Gregory of Nyssa: All flesh implies birth, with marriage as the means for bringing it about. The person, however, who is not subject to a birth of flesh with respect to the mystery of religion does not submit to the actions effected by human nature or to the passions arising from the mind. He understands that the generation of the flesh belongs to all humankind. The bride says that he who partakes of flesh and blood is "white and ruddy." However, by indicating the body's nature by these two colors, she does not say that Christ partakes of that birth common to humankind. Rather, God assumed our human nature from the multitude of people he had begotten. From the

passage of succeeding generations, Christ alone entered this life by a new form of birth. Nature did not cooperate in this birth but served it. Therefore, the bride says that her spouse is "white and ruddy." That is, he dwells in this present life through flesh and blood while having been begotten from virginal purity. His conception is virginal. His birth is undefiled and without pangs. His bridal chamber is the power of the Most High overshadowing the virgin like a cloud. He is a nuptial torch of the Holy Spirit's splendor. His bed is free from passion, and his marriage is incorruptibility.

The bridegroom born under such circumstances as these is rightly called "chosen from myriads." He was free from birth resulting from marriage, for his existence does not come from marriage. No terminology pertaining to human birth can rightly pertain to Christ's incorruptible, painless birth because virginity and childbirth cannot apply to the bridegroom at the same time. As the Son is given to us without a father, the child is thus begotten without birth. Homilies on the Song of Songs 13.[36]

5:11 Locks of Hair

Comparison with the Brilliance of Gold. Julian of Eclanum: Hair is also represented by another comparison, wherein the shape of its locks seems to mimic the brilliance of gold. "His hair is like waves of palms," so that they would surely seem to be curly and golden. Commentary on the Song of Songs, Fragment 10.[37]

5:12 The Dove's Eyes

The Doves on the Water Indicate Baptism. Theodoret of Cyr: "His eyes like doves on pools of water," once again here by mention of the "eyes" admiring his keen sight. Hence her say-

---

[29]NPNF 2 10:370*. [30]1 Pet 2:22. [31]Rev 1:5. [32]CCL 119B:283. [33]Jn 1:9. [34]Is 63:2. [35]CCL 19:194-95. [36]*GNSS* 236-37*. [37]CCL 88:400-401.

ing they are like doves "on pools of water" reminds us of the dove coming down on him in the Jordan.[38] . . . Hence the bride says, "His eyes like doves on pools of water": his eyes are constantly upon the source of baptism, awaiting those being saved and longing for the salvation of everyone. Commentary on the Song of Songs 5.[39]

The Hawk's Shadow Seen by the Dove. Origen: In doves, the eyes are signified. For when it says, "doves over the abundance of the waters," it means this kind of bird when it comes to the waters. There it is accustomed to suffer the attacks of the hawk and to detect its hostile arrival in flight when it sees the shadow of its wings in the waters. And so it escapes the deceit of imminent peril by the keen vision of its eyes. For if you could thus look out for the snares of the devil and avoid them, you would offer "doves" as a sacrifice to God. Homilies on Leviticus 3.8.4.[40]

Christ in the Image of a Dove. Cyril of Jerusalem: Perhaps, as some say, it was to reveal an image that he came down in the likeness of a pure, innocent, simple dove, working with prayers for the sons he begot and for the forgiveness of sins; just as in a veiled manner it was foretold that the beauty of Christ's eyes would be manifested in this way. Catechetical Lectures 17.9.[41]

Eyes Bathed in Milk. Gregory of Nyssa: The eyes "upon the fullness of waters" are compared with doves because of their simplicity and innocence, and the Word says they have been washed in milk. A quality of milk is that it does not reflect any image. Every other liquid is like a mirror whose smooth surface serves to reflect the image of those gazing in it. However, milk lacks such reflective capacity. This is, then, the best praise for the church's eyes. They do not reflect deceptive, shadowy pictures of nonexistent things that are erroneous, vain or contrary to the true nature of reality. They look, rather, at being itself, and do not reflect the false visions and fantasies of life. Thus the perfect soul bathes its eyes in

milk to keep them pure. Homilies on the Song of Songs 13.[42]

The Dove Sees the Hawk's Shadow. Bede: [A dove] is inclined to sit above water so that it may avoid being seized by a hawk coming, since it has seen its shadow beforehand in the water. Let us also be clean, and take care to sit attentively at the cleansing streams of the Scriptures, and, thoroughly instructed by [their] mirrors, may we be capable of distinguishing and guarding ourselves against the snares of the ancient enemy. Homilies on the Gospels 1.12.[43]

5:15 Alabaster Columns and Bases of Gold

Christ Claims the Church as Bride. Ambrose: Who indeed but Christ could dare to claim the church as his bride, whom he alone, and none other, has called from Libanus, saying, "Come here from Lebanon, my bride; come here from Lebanon"?[44] Or of whom else could the church have said, "His throat is sweetness, and he is altogether desirable"?[45] And seeing that we entered upon this discussion from speaking of the shoes of his feet, to whom else but the Word of God incarnate can those words apply? "His legs are pillars of marble, set upon bases of gold." For Christ alone walks in the souls and makes his path in the minds of his saints, in which, as upon bases of gold and foundations of precious stone the heavenly Word has left his footprints ineffaceably impressed. On the Christian Faith 3.10.74.[46]

The Legs Are the Foundation of Truth. Gregory of Nyssa: A pillar must rest on the foundation of truth. Truth is golden, and its bases are the bridegroom's legs adorning his hands and head. The foundation may be interpreted as marble. We understand by the Song's words that the body's legs are marble pillars, that is, those per-

[38]See Mt 3:16. [39]ECS 2:92*. [40]FC 83:67. [41]FC 64:101-2. [42]GNSS 240. [43]CS 110:121*. [44]Song 4:8. [45]Song 5:16. [46]NPNF 2 10:253*.

sons who support and bear the body of the church by exemplary lives and sound words. Through them the base of our faith is firm, the course of virtue is completed, and the entire body is raised on high by our longing for God's promise. Truth and stability guide the church's body. Gold represents truth, which, according to Paul, is called the foundation of the divine edifice.[47]... Christ is the truth upon whom are founded the legs, or pillars of the church. HOMILIES ON THE SONG OF SONGS 14.[48]

THE FOUNDATION OF THE APOSTLES AND PROPHETS. CYRIL OF ALEXANDRIA: "His legs are pillars of marble." These are clearly foundations, for whoever builds does so upon the foundation of the apostles and prophets. He aptly praises the legs after the belly, who says that marble is set upon bases of gold. Peter and John are pillars of the church, for example, who had Christ, called by a golden name, as their foundation.[49] And they are marble, for Paul also calls them a pillar,[50] surely on account of their stability and consistency, sustaining and supporting the common body of the church, moreover, with their enlightened lives and their saving doctrine. But the charity with which we love God with our whole heart and our neighbor as ourselves also supports the common body of the church, as though on pillars of marble. For whoever is perfected in these two commandments becomes a pillar and support of the church, such that the whole body of the church rests upon this double virtue, as though on legs. The golden foundation contains the unwavering and unchanged base of faith and in all things holds fast reasonably to the good. FRAGMENTS IN THE COMMENTARY ON THE SONG OF SONGS 5.15.[51]

INCENSE AND CEDAR INDICATE THE TWO NATURES. THEODORET OF CYR: "His form is like choice incense, like cedars." Here again she makes reference to the fact of two natures, calling the divine nature "incense" since by the law incense was offered to God,[52] and by "cedar"

referring to the human nature in its not being affected by the rottenness of sin, the cedar of all trees not going rotten. COMMENTARY ON THE SONG OF SONGS 5.[53]

5:16 My Beloved and My Friend

GOD IS THE AUTHOR OF THE PURE SOUL. AMBROSE: Such is the concern of the soul that is pure, such is what it perceives within; it discerns God and abounds in all good things. On this account, "his mouth is sweetness, and he is all delight." For God is the author of all good things and all things which are, are his. ISAAC, OR THE SOUL 7.61.[54]

SWEET IN SPEECH AND DESIRABLE. AUGUSTINE: A person of God should so appear and conduct himself that there would be no one who would not desire to see him, no one who would not wish to hear him, no one who, having seen him, would not believe that he was a son of God. In his case the prophetic words would be fulfilled: "His throat is most sweet, and he is all lovely." ON THE CHRISTIAN LIFE 9.[55]

6:3 Reciprocal Belonging

APPLIED TO THE CHURCH. LEANDER OF SEVILLE: So long as Christ wishes there to be one church of all nations, whoever is a stranger to the church is not considered a part of the body of Christ, even though he uses the name of Christian. That heresy which rejects the unity of the Catholic church is to him a concubine and not a wife, in that it loves Christ with an adulterous love, since Scripture says that there are actually two in one flesh, that is, Christ and the church, in which there is no third place for a harlot. "One is my friend, one is my bride, only daughter of her mother."[56] Of whom, likewise, the same church

---

[47]1 Cor 3:11. [48]*GNSS* 252*. [49]See Eph 2:20. [50]See 1 Tim 3:15. [51]PG 69:1290. [52]Lev 2:1-2, 15-16. [53]ECS 2:93. [54]FC 65:51. [55]FC 16:26*. [56]Song 6:9.

speaks, saying, "My lover belongs to me, and I to him." Homily on the Triumph of the Church.[57]

Personal Love of Christ. Leander of Seville: He is, indeed, your true bridegroom. He is also your brother. He is likewise your friend. He is your inheritance. He is your reward. He is God and the Lord. You have in him a bridegroom to love: "For he is fair in beauty above the sons of men."[58] . . . He is a friend of whom you need not

doubt, for he himself says, "You are my only lover." You have in him the inheritance that you may embrace, for he is himself the portion of your inheritance. You have in him the reward that you may recognize, for his blood is your redemption. You have in him God by whom you may be ruled, the Lord to fear and honor. The Training of Nuns, Preface.[59]

---

[57]FC 62:234. [58]Ps 45:2 (44:3 LXX, Vg). [59]FC 62:185*.

6:4-13 THE BRIDEGROOM'S INNER THOUGHTS

[4]*You are beautiful as Tirzah, my love,*
  comely as Jerusalem,
  terrible as an army with banners.
[5]*Turn away your eyes from me,*
  for they disturb me—
  Your hair is like a flock of goats,
  moving down the slopes of Gilead.
[6]*Your teeth are like a flock of ewes,*
  that have come up from the washing,
  all of them bear twins,
  not one among them is bereaved.
[7]*Your cheeks are like halves of a*
    pomegranate
  behind your veil.
[8]*There are sixty queens and eighty*
    concubines,
  and maidens without number.
[9]*My dove, my perfect one, is only one,*
  the darling of her mother,
  flawless to her that bore her.
  The maidens saw her and called her

  happy;
  the queens and concubines also, and they
    praised her.
[10]*"Who is this that looks forth like the dawn,*
  fair as the moon, bright as the sun,
  terrible as an army with banners?"

[11]*I went down to the nut orchard,*
  to look at the blossoms of the valley,
  to see whether the vines had budded,
  whether the pomegranates were in bloom.
[12]*Before I was aware, my fancy set me*
  in a chariot beside my prince."

[13] [o]*Return, return, O Shulammite,*
  return, return, that we may look upon
    you.

  Why should you look upon the
    Shulammite,
  as upon a dance before two armies?[p]

---

n Cn: The meaning of the Hebrew is uncertain   **o** Ch 7.1 in Heb   **p** Or *dance of Mahanaim*

Overview: The beauty of Jerusalem is not the beauty of the perishable body, surpassing comprehension, but sometimes modesty is needed for the sake of others less gifted or fortunate (Ambrose, Theodoret of Cyr). The thick coat of the goat does provide an image of beauty for the bride, and for this reason the Song's comparison with a flock of goats seems appropriate (Gregory of Nyssa). Likewise the teeth are appropriately likened to the shorn sheep, because the latter have laid aside worldly cares and, by human analogy, are cleansed by the sacrament of baptism (Augustine). Pomegranates are an appropriate comparison for the cheeks, because of the sweetness contained therein (Ambrose). Those who are concubines already have their reward in this life (Augustine), and there is a reason why Solomon had sixty queens but eighty concubines (Theodoret of Cyr), although it must be conceded that Solomon had many wives (Origen). The three orders in the church (Aponius) must be considered in relation to its unity, symbolized by the one dove (Rufinus of Aquileia, Cyprian, Bede). There is also a unity in the sense that the church's members should not be divided in their choices of the one good (Gregory of Nyssa). Nonetheless, it should be remembered that hawks are not the same as doves (Augustine), even though the heavenly Jerusalem is our only mother (Jerome). When speaking of the church, analogy with the sun and moon is also appropriate (Augustine, Aponius, Cassiodorus). The moon is to the sun as the church is to Christ, but the bride will shine like a sun (Theodoret of Cyr). Also appropriate is the analogy of the church to the garden of nutmeats inside their shells (Theodoret of Cyr, Bede, Cyril of Jerusalem) or the company of saints focused heavenwards (Ambrose). Indeed, the peacemaker is the bride of the peaceable one (Theodoret of Cyr).

6:4 The Beauty of Jerusalem

Not the Beauty of the Perishable Body.
Ambrose: He who was spoiled by the soldiers, who was wounded by the spear, that he might heal us by the blood of his sacred wounds, will assuredly answer you (for he is meek and lowly of heart, and gentle in aspect): "Arise, O north wind, and come, O south, and blow upon my garden, that my spices may flow out."[1] For from all parts of the world has the perfume of holy religion increased, and the limbs of the consecrated Virgin have glowed. "You are beautiful, O my love, as Tirzah, comely as Jerusalem." So it is not the beauty of the perishable body, which will come to an end with sickness or old age, but the reputation for good deserts, subject to no accidents and never to perish, which is the beauty of virgins. Concerning Virgins 1.9.47.[2]

6:5 Turn Away Your Eyes

Modesty for the Sake of Others.
Ambrose: So he says to her, as if to one who is perfect, . . . "Turn your eyes from me," because she cannot withstand the fullness of his divinity and the splendor of the true light.

Yet we can also take "turn your eyes from me" as follows: "Although you have been perfected, I must still redeem other souls and strengthen them. For you exalt me by looking upon me, but I have descended so that I may exalt all humankind.[3] Although I have risen up and possess the throne of the Father,[4] still I will not leave you orphans[5] bereft of a father's help, but by my presence I will strengthen you. You find this written in the gospel: 'I am with you even unto the consummation of the world.'[6] Turn your eyes from me, therefore, because you exalt me." The more anyone strives toward the Lord, the more he exalts the Lord and is himself exalted. On this account also the psalmist says, "I will extol you, O Lord, because you have upheld me."[7] For the holy person extols the Lord; the sinner brings him low. Therefore he wishes that she turn her eyes away. Otherwise, by contemplating her he

---

[1]Song 4:16. [2]NPNF 2 10:370*. [3]See Jn 6:38-40. [4]See Heb 8:1. [5]See Jn 14:18. [6]Mt 28:20. [7]Ps 30:1 (29:1 LXX, 29:2 Vg).

may be exalted—for now he can attain to the higher regions—and may leave the other souls behind. Likewise in the gospel he showed his glory, not to all the disciples but to those who were more nearly perfect.[8]

Now imagine some teacher who desires to explain an obscure matter to his hearers. Although he is himself an accomplished speaker and well informed, nevertheless let him lower himself to the ignorance of those who do not understand, and let him use simple, rather plain, everyday speech so that he can be understood. Then whoever is more quick-witted among his hearers, and can follow easily, disparages and questions him. Looking on such a one, the teacher restrains him, so that the latter may permit him to spend time rather on those who are more humble and lowly, in order that the rest may also be able to follow. ISAAC, OR THE SOUL 7.57.[9]

LIGHT THAT SURPASSES COMPREHENSION. THEODORET OF CYR: "Turn your eyes away from me because they set me all aflutter." What he means is something like this: the beauty of your eyes, the sharpness of your vision and the clarity of your thinking have drawn me to love of you; but do not gaze at me immoderately lest I take harm from it. After all, I am inaccessible and incomprehensible, surpassing all comprehension, not only human but also angelic. Even if you wish to surpass limits and pry into what is beyond your power, you would not only find nothing but would also impair your sight and render it dull. Such is the nature of light, after all: as it illumines the eye, so it penalizes intemperance with damage. COMMENTARY ON THE SONG OF SONGS 6.[10]

COMPARISON WITH A FLOCK OF GOATS. GREGORY OF NYSSA: A goat is honored because its thick coat provides an image of beauty for the bride. Another reason for praise is that a goat can pass over rocks with a sure foot, agilely turn on mountain peaks, courageously pass through difficult, rough places, and can go safely on the road of virtue. Some would maintain that this animal

is suitable for the comparison with the bride because Moses the lawgiver uses it for many of the sacred functions of the law.[11] HOMILIES ON THE SONG OF SONGS 15.[12]

6:6 Teeth Again

THE TEETH OF THE CHURCH. AUGUSTINE: He praises these sheep also in the Song of Solomon,[13] speaking of some perfect ones as the teeth of his spouse the holy church. EXPLANATIONS OF THE PSALMS 95.9.[14]

TEETH LIKE TO SHORN SHEEP. AUGUSTINE: Separated from the world, to which they were once conformed, they pass over into the members of the church. And rightly therefore are they, through whom such things are done, called teeth like to shorn sheep;[15] for they have laid aside the burdens of earthly cares, and coming up from the bath, from the washing away of the filth of the world by the sacrament of baptism, every one bears twins. For they fulfill the two commandments, of which it is said, "On these two commandments hang all the law and the prophets":[16] loving God with all their heart, and with all their soul and with all their mind, and their neighbor as themselves. EXPLANATIONS OF THE PSALMS 3.7.[17]

6:7 The Cheeks of the Church

CHEEKS LIKE THE HALVES OF A POMEGRANATE. AMBROSE: What are the cheeks of the church of which the Scripture elsewhere says, "Your cheeks are as the bark of pomegranates"? They are the cheeks on which modesty is accustomed to shine, beauty to sparkle, on which there is either the flower of youth or the distinguished mark of perfect age. CONSOLATION ON THE DEATH OF EMPEROR VALENTINIAN 6.[18]

---

[8]See Mt 17:1-8. [9]FC 65:47-48*. [10]ECS 2:96*. [11]Lev 4:23, 9:3. [12]*GNSS* 269*. [13]Song 4:2. [14]NPNF 1 8:469*. [15]Song 4:2. [16]Mt 22:40. [17]NPNF 1 8:6. [18]FC 22:268.

6:8 Queens and Concubines

THE LATTER HAVE THEIR REWARD. AUGUSTINE: The word *queens* refers to the souls that rule in the realm of the intelligible and spiritual. The word *concubines* [refers] to the souls that receive an earthly reward, concerning whom it is said, "They have received their reward."[19] ON EIGHTY-THREE VARIED QUESTIONS 55.[20]

WHY SIXTY QUEENS BUT EIGHTY CONCUBINES. THEODORET OF CYR: Let us examine why on earth he mentioned "sixty queens" but "eighty concubines." The number sixty contains six tens, and while the ten signifies perfection, the six represents the number of the world's creation: in six days the God of all formed the whole creation. Accordingly, by "sixty queens" he referred to the souls in this world who were made perfect in virtue and who longed for the kingdom. The bride lives a way of life above this world, she is outside it, flies beyond it, is totally the bridegroom's and has him constantly in mind, whereas these latter souls live in this world and practice the perfection of virtue to the extent possible while longing to attain the kingdom. But it is through fear that they obey the laws, and so they were called "eighty." The divine Scripture, remember, speaks of the time of judgment as the eighth. In describing judgment in the Psalms, blessed David used the title "On the eighth" and began this way, "Lord, do not censure me in your anger, nor chastise me in your wrath," and shortly after, "Because in death there is no one to remember you, in hades who will confess you?"[21] Thus [he brings] out that at the time of judgment no place for repentance will be given to those who have sinned and have not had a change of heart. COMMENTARY ON THE SONG OF SONGS 6.[22]

SOME PATRIARCHS HAD MANY WIVES. ORIGEN: Scripture recounts that some of the patriarchs had many wives at the same time; others took other wives when previous wives had died.

The purpose of this is to indicate figuratively that some can exercise many virtues at the same time; others cannot begin those which follow before they have brought the former virtues to perfection. Accordingly, Solomon is reported to have had many wives at the same time. HOMILIES ON GENESIS 11.2.[23]

THREE ORDERS IN THE CHURCH. APONIUS: In the present verse, therefore, three orders of merit are indicated to be in the church according to the following enigma. First, clearly, there are teachers, living an immaculate life. Second, there are the teachable, who imitate the lives of their teachers and burn with great desire to understand the content of the teaching and to distinguish sound doctrine from unsound doctrine. But the third order is that of maidens,[24] for whom only belief in the one God helps toward salvation, who are not yet worthy to be joined to the sacred number. Although all of them may have the Word of the Father as King, he who was with the Father in the beginning and always remains God in the Father, the dignity of merit nevertheless escapes them. EXPOSITION OF SONG OF SONGS 9.21.[25]

6:9 The Perfection of the Dove

ONE CHURCH IS CREDAL BELIEF. RUFINUS OF AQUILEIA: Of this church which keeps the faith of Christ entire, hear what the Holy Spirit says in the Canticles, "My dove is one; the perfect one of her mother is one." He then who receives this faith in the church let him not turn aside in the council of vanity, and let him not enter in with those who practice iniquity. COMMENTARY ON THE APOSTLES' CREED 39.[26]

ONE CHURCH IS INDICATED BY ONE DOVE. CYPRIAN: This one church is also intended in the Song of Songs, when the Holy Spirit says, in the

---

[19]Mt 6:2. [20]FC 70:97. [21]Ps 6:1, 5. [22]ECS 2:98. [23]FC 71:171. [24]Latin *adulescentularum.* [25]CCL 19:223. [26]NPNF 2 3:558.

person of the Lord: "My dove, my perfect one, is but one; she is the only one of her mother, the choice one of her that bare her." Can one who does not keep this unity of the church believe that he keeps the faith? Can one who resists and struggles against the church be sure that he is in the church? For the blessed apostle Paul gives the same teaching and declares the same mystery of unity when he says, "There is one body and one Spirit, one hope of your calling, one Lord, one faith, one baptism, one God."[27] THE UNITY OF THE CATHOLIC CHURCH 4.[28]

ONE IN THE CHOICE OF THAT WHICH IS GOOD. GREGORY OF NYSSA: "My dove, my perfect one, is one." The Lord's words in the gospel explain this more clearly . . . that in the diversity of their lives' activities, they should not be divided in their choices of the good. Rather, they should all be one,[29] united into a single good through the unity of the Holy Spirit. . . . All will look to the same goal, and every evil will be destroyed. God will be all in all, and all persons will be united together in fellowship of the Good, Christ Jesus our Lord, to whom be glory and power forever and ever. HOMILIES ON THE SONG OF SONGS 15.[30]

HAWKS ARE NOT THE SAME AS DOVES. AUGUSTINE: "For as regards the fact that to preserve the figure of unity the Lord gave the power to Peter that whatsoever he should loose on earth should be loosed,"[31] it is clear that that unity is also described as one dove without fault. Can it be said, then, that to this same dove belong all those greedy ones, whose existence in the same Catholic church Cyprian himself so grievously bewailed? For birds of prey, I believe, cannot be called doves, but rather hawks. How then did they baptize those who used to plunder estates by treacherous deceit and increase their profits by compound usury, if baptism is only given by that indivisible and chaste and perfect dove, that unity which can only be understood as existing among the good? Is it possible that, by the prayers of the saints who are spiri-

tual within the church, as though by the frequent lamentations of the dove, a great sacrament is dispensed, with a secret administration of the mercy of God? [Thus] their sins also are loosed who are baptized, not by the dove but by the hawk, if they come to that sacrament in the peace of Catholic unity. ON BAPTISM 3.17.22.[32]

THE HEAVENLY JERUSALEM. JEROME: "My dove, my undefiled is but one; she is the only one of her mother, she is the choice one of her that bare her." Now the mother of whom this is said is the heavenly Jerusalem.[33] LETTER 22.24.[34]

NATURE OF THE CHURCH'S UNITY. BEDE: "My dove, my perfect one, is one." [The church] is one because it does not accept a schismatic division. It is one because it is not a collection of various parties, some before the law, some under the law, some under grace, some of the circumcision, and others of the uncircumcised. But just as "there is one Lord, one faith, one baptism, and one God and Father of everyone,"[35] so also is there one Catholic multitude of all the elect throughout every place and every era of the world, subjected to one God and Father. This is why Luke teaches that [the church] should be called Catholic. COMMENTARY ON THE SONGS OF SONGS 4.6.8.[36]

6:10 Fair as the Moon, Bright as the Sun

APPLIED TO THE CHURCH. AUGUSTINE: The church is the sun and the moon and the stars, to which it was said, "Fair as the moon, bright as the sun." By it our Joseph is adored in this world as in Egypt, when he is raised from humble to high estate. LETTER 199.39.[37]

THE MOON IS TO THE SUN AS THE CHURCH IS TO CHRIST. THEODORET OF CYR: "As beautiful

---

[27]Eph 4:4-6. [28]LCC 5:126. [29]Jn 17:22. [30]275-76*. [31]Mt 16:19. [32]NPNF 1 4:443. [33]Gal 4:26. [34]NPNF 2 6:32. [35]Eph 4:5-6. [36]CCL 119B:309. [37]FC 30:387.

as the special moon." The experts in these matters say the moon gets its light from the sun's rays and gets partial light when a small part of it faces the sun. When it is directly opposite and is in full view of the sun, it is completely lit up as though reflecting its face like a kind of mirror and leaving no part of its bulk unlit. The church of Christ likewise, therefore, the congregation of the souls made perfect in virtue, "with unveiled face seeing the glory of the Lord as though reflected in a mirror," in the words of blessed Paul, "is being transformed into the same image from one degree of glory to another, as a work of the Lord, the Spirit."[38] And it becomes so completely luminous as to resemble a moon, and a "special moon," that is, full moon. COMMENTARY ON THE SONG OF SONGS 6.[39]

BUT THE BRIDE WILL ALSO SHINE LIKE A SUN. THEODORET OF CYR: The bride, however, is not only "like a special moon," but also she will shine in the future life "like a sun," astounding all with its brightness. They will marvel not only at her light but also at her orderliness. There is nothing disordered about the Lord's bride, nothing undetermined; she gives practical directions like a kind of plumb line, and regulates her own life by use of norm and rule. COMMENTARY ON THE SONG OF SONGS 6.[40]

THE MOON AND THE SUN. APONIUS: By clinging continually to God the Word, she is made wholly on fire, like a burning coal.[41] Also like a burning coal among a number of dead coals, when joined to the others, she ignites them all. Thus, in the midst of the souls of the dead [destined] for eternal life, she alone, the singular chosen one, vivifies all souls who believe in her, makes them like herself, and draws them to her beauty. Nevertheless, uniquely splendid like the moon, perfect in heaven among the stars, she in their midst is proven to glow with everlasting beauty more than all others. Chosen like the sun in paternal majesty among all the powers of the heavenly hosts, she is proclaimed as one to be admired by all, as

the following verse teaches: "The maidens saw her and called her most blessed; queens and concubines also praised her." EXPOSITION OF SONG OF SONGS 9.30.[42]

A PYRAMID FULL OF HEAVENLY CORN. CASSIODORUS: You are rightly compared with this figure since you raise your precious head over all races, and you transmit the souls of the just like resplendent stars to the kingdom above. You are a pyramid full of heavenly corn, the blessed gathering of saintly people from diverse nations, the shining assembly of bright minds, a structure that cannot be dismantled since it is fashioned from living stones, the eternal happiness of all who are blessed, brighter than the sun, whiter than snow, without spot or wrinkle. Of you it is written in the Song of Songs: "Who is she that comes forth as the morning rising, fair as the moon, bright as the sun, terrible as an army set in array?" EXPOSITION OF THE PSALMS, PREFACE 17.[43]

6:11 Going to the Nut Garden

HIDDEN WITH CHRIST IN GOD. THEODORET OF CYR: By "nut plantation" they refer to the present life, which is harsh, troublesome and laborious but contains hidden in itself the fruit of virtue. The fruit of the nut has a bitter skin on the outside, the second one is tough and resistant, and the edible part is hidden as though deposited in a kind of inner chamber and is not extracted without effort. Such also is the present life, containing as it does harsh pain and grief, containing hardship and effort which, however, are not fruitless, not useless, holding the fruit hidden within them. Hence blessed Paul also says, "Our life is hidden with Christ in God; but when Christ our life is revealed, then we too shall live in him."[44] COMMENTARY ON THE SONG OF SONGS 6.[45]

---

[38]2 Cor 3:18. [39]ECS 2:100. [40]ECS 2:101. [41]See Rom 12:20; Ezek 1:27; Is 44:19. [42]CCL 19:226. [43]ACW 51:42*. [44]Col 3:3-4. [45]ECS 2:102.

A Figure of the Present Church. Bede: Solomon bears witness that a nut is customarily employed as a figure of the present church when in the Song of Songs he speaks in the character of the faithful teachers. . . . For just as a nut has sweet fruit on the inside but does not show it on the outside unless its hard shell can be broken, so in the same way do the righteous maintain the sweetness of spiritual grace in their inmost heart while they are in this present life. Its magnitude cannot be perceived by their neighbors until the time when the bodily dwelling is dissolved and the souls freed from it can gaze upon one another in heavenly light, and they individually shine so much with the grace of the Holy Spirit, and they are loved so much by one another, that absolutely nothing remains hidden. On the Tabernacle 1.8.[46]

A Type of the Passion. Cyril of Jerusalem: You wish to know the place? He says in the Canticles, "I came down to the nut garden"; for it was a garden where he was crucified. Catechetical Lectures 14.5.[47]

6:13 Returning

The Bride of the Peaceable One. Theodoret of Cyr: Just as the work calls Solomon—our Lord, in other words—"peaceable," so too it calls his bride "peacemaker" for attaining peace from him and being freed from the former conflict. The bridegroom's attendants, then, on seeing her driven from the chariot and under attack, comfort her in the words, "Return," peacemaker, "return, return, and we shall look upon you." That is to say, "Do not be afraid of your pursuers but hold fast the doctrine, proclaim the message of the doctrine, have no fear of the chariot, do not be afraid of war, called peacemaker as you are. If fact, if you persist in your preaching, we shall see your kingdom." Commentary on the Song of Songs 6.[48]

Hasten to the Company of Saints on High. Ambrose: Turn to us, O peaceful soul, that you may show your glory to your sisters and that they may begin to console themselves with the security of your repose and happiness. Turn to us once only, that we may see you, and turn again and hasten with all speed to that great Jerusalem, the city of the saints. Or indeed, since Christ says this to the pious soul, he commands it to turn for a little while, that its glory and its future repose with the saints may be manifest to us, and then he commands it to hasten to the company of the saints on high. Consolation on the Death of Emperor Valentinian 65.[49]

---

[46]TTH 18:35. [47]FC 64:35. [48]ECS 2:103. [49]FC 22:292.

7:1-13 THE QUEENLY MAIDEN

[1]How graceful are your feet in sandals,
   O queenly maiden!
   Your rounded thighs are like jewels,
      the work of a master hand.
[2]Your navel is a rounded bowl
      that never lacks mixed wine.

Your belly is a heap of wheat,
*   encircled with lilies.*
[3] *Your two breasts are like two fawns,*
*   twins of a gazelle.*
[4] *Your neck is like an ivory tower.*
Your eyes are pools in Heshbon,
*   by the gate of Bath-rabbim.*
Your nose is like a tower of Lebanon,
*   overlooking Damascus.*
[5] *Your head crowns you like Carmel,*
*   and your flowing locks are like purple;*
a king is held captive in the tresses.[q]

[6] *How fair and pleasant you are,*
*   O loved one, delectable maiden!*[r]
[7] *You are stately*[s] *as a palm tree,*
*   and your breasts are like its clusters.*
[8] *I say I will climb the palm tree*
*   and lay hold of its branches.*
Oh, may your breasts be like clusters of

the vine,
*   and the scent of your breath like apples,*
[9] *and your kisses*[t] *like the best wine*
*   that goes down*[u] *smoothly,*
*   gliding over lips and teeth.*[v]

[10] *I am my beloved's,*
*   and his desire is for me.*
[11] *Come, my beloved,*
*   let us go forth into the fields,*
*   and lodge in the villages;*
[12] *let us go out early to the vineyards,*
*   and see whether the vines have budded,*
*   whether the grape blossoms have opened*
*   and the pomegranates are in bloom.*
There I will give you my love.
[13] *The mandrakes give forth fragrance,*
*   and over our doors are all choice fruits,*
new as well as old,
*   which I have laid up for you, O my beloved.*

q The meaning of the Hebrew word is uncertain r Syr: Heb *in delights* s Heb *This your stature is* t Heb *palate* u Heb *down for my lover* v Gk Syr Vg: Heb *lips of sleepers*

OVERVIEW: Not everyone will agree with the choice of virginity, even if selected voluntarily (JEROME). Peter, the prince of the apostles, gave an example of fleshly mortification (APONIUS). Even the belly and the navel have their mystical significance, when related to wisdom, just as is true of the palm tree when its stature is related to the church (AMBROSE). The turning of the beloved, however, is tantamount to the second advent or the conversion of the Jews (CYRIL OF ALEXANDRIA). The church is a rich field, fecund in diversity, and therefore the unity of marriage should also be preserved (AMBROSE).

7:1 The Steps of Virginity

PRAISE FOR THIS CHOICE. JEROME: The virgin bridegroom, having been praised by the virgin bride, in turn praises the virgin bride and says to her, "How beautiful are your feet in sandals, O daughter of Aminadab," which is, being interpreted, a people that offers itself willingly. For virginity is voluntary, and therefore the steps of the church in the beauty of chastity are praised. This is not the time for me like a commentator to explain all the mysteries of virginity from the Song of Songs. I have no doubt that the fastidious reader will turn up his nose at what has already been said. AGAINST JOVINIANUS 1.31.[1]

THE EXAMPLE OF BLESSED PETER. APONIUS: In every way, then, [the beauty of her feet] seems to me to be understood to follow the first fruits of praise in this people who are imitators of the

---

[1] NPNF 2 6:370.

footsteps of those who follow Christ to heaven by dying in the [steps of the] blessed prince of the apostles. Thus does this people, through its earthly works in the example of blessed Peter, by mortifying its flesh, migrate to heaven, just as it also comes into the light from the shadows of ignorance by following Christ the Head. EXPOSITION OF SONG OF SONGS 10.4-5.[2]

7:2 The Belly and the Navel

MYSTIC SIGNIFICANCE. AMBROSE: Small, too, are the navel and belly of the soul that ascends to Christ. Therefore it is praised in the words of the spouse, who says, "Your navel is like a round bowl never wanting wine, your belly is like a heap of tiny wheat among lilies." It is polished by all kinds of learning, and it is a spiritual draught never failing in fullness and in the knowledge of heavenly secrets. The belly of the soul is mystic, like the navel, and it receives not only strong food to strengthen hearts but sweet and fragrant food by which it is delighted. Perhaps Moses meant that this sacrilege[3] needs to be atoned for by many pious prayers. LETTER 77, TO LAYMEN.[4]

THE NAVEL OF THE SOUL. AMBROSE: "Your navel is like a round bowl, not wanting tempered wine. Your belly is like a heap of wheat, set about with lilies. Your neck is like a tower of ivory. Your eyes are a pool in Heshbon." The good navel of the soul, capable of receiving all virtues, is like a bowl, fashioned by the author of faith himself.[5] For in a bowl wisdom has mixed her wine, saying, "Come, eat my bread and drink the wine which I have mingled for you."[6] This navel, therefore, fashioned with all the beauty of the virtues, does not lack mixed wine. His belly also was filled not only with the wheaten food of justice, as it were, but also with that of grace, and it bloomed with sweetness like a lily.[7] CONSOLATION ON THE DEATH OF EMPEROR VALENTINIAN 69.[8]

7:5 The Crown of the Head

ORDERLY TEACHING COLORED WITH THE BLOOD OF CHRIST. THEODORET OF CYR: "The hair of your head like purple, a king caught in its tresses." Your hair was previously loose and hence was compared with the flocks of goats emerging in Gilead, whereas now it is caught up, and not only caught up but also wondrously dyed, resembling a king clad in purple and hastening in all directions. By the comparison of her fastened hair to royal purple he refers to the teaching proposed in orderly fashion and colored with the blood of Christ. A king clad in purple is not so resplendent as the teacher of religion who carefully composes the proclamation of the knowledge of God and offers it to the devotees of truth. COMMENTARY ON THE SONG OF SONGS 7.[9]

7:6-10 The Church Likened to a Palm Tree

RENUNCIATION OF THINGS TEMPORAL. AMBROSE: The church is beautiful in [those recently baptized]. So that God the Word says to her: "You are all fair, my love, and there is no blemish in you," for guilt has been washed away. "Come here from Lebanon, my spouse, come here from Lebanon, from the beginning of faith you will pass through and pass on,"[10] because, renouncing the world, she passed through things temporal and passed on to Christ. And again, God the Word says to her, "How beautiful and sweet are you made, O love, in your delights! Your stature is become like that of a palm tree, and your breasts like bunches of grapes." ON THE MYSTERIES 7.39.[11]

THE SECOND ADVENT. CYRIL OF ALEXANDRIA: I will offer my beloved praise, and his turning[12] will be toward me. What it calls his turning is either the second advent or the conversion of the Jewish people. FRAGMENTS IN THE COMMENTARY ON THE SONG OF SONGS 7.10.[13]

---

[2]CCL 19:239. [3]The making and adoring of the golden calf. [4]FC 26:434*. [5]Heb 12:2. [6]Prov 9:5. [7]See Is 35:1. [8]FC 22:293-94*. [9]ECS 2:108. [10]Cf. Song 4:7-8. [11]NPNF 2 10:322*. [12]"Turning" in the sense of "desire." [13]PG 69:1291.

Emblems of Victory. Ambrose: The laurel and palm are emblems of victory. The heads of victors are crowned with laurel; the palm adorns the victor's hand. Hence the church, too, says, "I said: I will go up into the palm tree, I will take hold of the heights thereof." Seeing the sublimity of the Word and hoping to be able to ascend to its height and to the summit of knowledge, he says, "I will go up into the palm tree." So he may abandon all things that are low and strive after things that are higher, to the prize of Christ, in order that he may pluck its fruit and taste it, for sweet is the fruit of virtue. Six Days of Creation 3.13.53.[14]

Flourish Like the Palm Tree. Ambrose: Imitate the palm, so that it may be said also to you, "Your stature is like a palm tree." Preserve the verdure of your childhood and of that natural innocence of youth which you have received from the beginning, and may you possess the fruits, prepared in due time, of what was planted along the course of the waters—and may there be no fall to your leaf! . . .

Remain, therefore, planted in the house of the Lord so as to flourish like a palm in his halls, whence the grace of the church may ascend for you and "the odor of your mouth may be like apples and your throat like the best wine," so that you may be inebriated in Christ.[15] Six Days of Creation 3.17.71.[16]

7:12-13 The Church Fecund in Rich Diversity

A Field with Many Fruits. Ambrose: Actually, what has always been condemned by the church is the perverse opinion of those who dare to dissolve the unity of marriage. Listen again to the voice of holy church: "Come, my brother, let us go forth into the fields, and lodge in the villages; let us go out early to the vineyards, and see whether the vines have budded." A field may produce many fruits, but the best field is one richly productive of both fruits and flowers. The church is a field of this sort, fecund in diversity. On Virginity 6.34.[17]

Hidden Mysteries, Made New in Christ. Ambrose: The old things according to the flesh have passed away; all have become new. If the scribe instructed in the kingdom of heaven knows not these things, he is like the householder who brings from his treasure new things and old, not old without new, or new without old.[18] So the church says, "The new and the old I have kept for you." The old have passed away, that is, the hidden mysteries of the law have all been made new in Christ. Letter 73, To Laymen.[19]

---

[14]FC 42:108. [15]Cf. Song 5:1. [16]FC 42:121-22. [17]AOV 19. [18]See Mt 13:52. [19]FC 26:418-19.

8:1-14 STILL YEARNING FOR LOVE

¹O that you were like a brother to me,
    that nursed at my mother's breast!
If I met you outside, I would kiss you,
    and none would despise me.
²I would lead you and bring you

into the house of my mother,
    and into the chamber of her that
        conceived me.ʷ
I would give you spiced wine to drink,
    the juice of my pomegranates.

³O that his left hand were under my head,
  and that his right hand embraced me!
⁴I adjure you, O daughters of Jerusalem,
  that you stir not up nor awaken love
    until it please.

⁵Who is that coming up from the
      wilderness,*
  leaning upon her beloved?

Under the apple tree I awakened you.
There your mother was in travail with you,
  there she who bore you was in travail.

⁶Set me as a seal upon your heart,
  as a seal upon your arm;
for love is strong as death,
  jealousy is cruel as the grave.
Its flashes are flashes of fire,
  a most vehement flame.
⁷Many waters cannot quench love,
  neither can floods drown it.
If a man offered for love
  all the wealth of his house,
    it would be utterly scorned.

⁸We have a little sister,
  and she has no breasts.

What shall we do for our sister,
  on the day when she is spoken for?
⁹If she is a wall,
  we will build upon her a battlement of
      silver;
but if she is a door,
  we will enclose her with boards of cedar.
¹⁰I was a wall,
  and my breasts were like towers;
then I was in his eyes
  as one who brings˟ peace.

¹¹Solomon had a vineyard at Baal-hamon;
  he let out the vineyard to keepers;
cach one was to bring for its fruit a
    thousand pieces of silver.
¹²My vineyard, my very own, is for myself;
  you, O Solomon, may have the thousand,
  and the keepers of the fruit two hundred.

¹³O you who dwell in the gardens,
  my companions are listening for your voice;
  let me hear it.

¹⁴Make haste, my beloved,
  and be like a gazelle
or a young stag
  upon the mountains of spices.

w Gk Syr: Heb *mother; she (or you) will teach me* x Or *finds* *LXX *all white*

OVERVIEW: The church is as a family in its baptismal unity (AMBROSE, JULIAN OF ECLANUM), and "mother's house" is where divine teaching is received (THEODORET OF CYR). From a Christian perspective, the salvation of humankind in the incarnation of Jesus Christ was precisely what the figures in the Song of Solomon had been longing for, and now it has come (ATHANASIUS, CYRIL OF JERUSALEM). All this, in turn, is reflected in the joy and brightness of the celebration of holy baptism, all covered in white (AMBROSE, AUGUSTINE, THEODORET OF CYR, JEROME), and the love that is thereby proclaimed is even stronger than death (AMBROSE, THEODORET OF CYR, FRUCTUOSUS OF BRAGA, GREGORY THE GREAT, AUGUSTINE, JOHN THE SOLITARY). This is why the examples of the myrrh-bearing women and even of the "little sister who had no breasts" find their deepest meaning in the redemption that has been won by Christ (CYRIL OF JERUSALEM, APONIUS, BEDE) and can even be seen as a remedy for spiritual immaturity (THEODORET OF CYR). The bridegroom, therefore, is urged to take flight, and to flee heavenward after the work of redemption is complete (AMBROSE, APONIUS, BEDE).

8:1-4 Like a Brother to Me

TO ATTAIN THE INNERMOST MYSTERIES. AMBROSE: The church answers unto [God the Word], "Who will give you to me, my brother, you who did suck the breasts of my mother? If I find you outside I will kiss you, and indeed they will not despise me. I will take you, and bring you into the house of my mother; and into the secret chamber of her who conceived me. You shall teach me." You see how, delighted with the gifts of grace, she longs to attain to the innermost mysteries and to consecrate all her affections to Christ. She still seeks, she still stirs up his love, and asks of the daughters of Jerusalem to stir it up for her, and desires that by their beauty, which is that of faithful souls, her spouse may be incited to ever richer love for her. ON THE MYSTERIES 7.40.[1]

THE BREAST IS BAPTISM. AMBROSE: What are the breasts of the church except the sacrament of baptism? And well does he say "sucking," as if the baptized were seeking him as a draught of snowy milk. "Finding you without," he says, "I shall kiss you," that is, finding you outside the body, I embrace you with the kiss of mystical peace. No one shall despise you; no one shall shut you out. I will introduce you into the inner sanctuary and hidden places of Mother Church, and into all the secrets of mystery, so that you may drink the cup of spiritual grace. CONSOLATION ON THE DEATH OF EMPEROR VALENTINIAN 75.[2]

IN OUR MIDST, EVEN THOUGH UNSEEN. AMBROSE: Therefore she interceded so that he would go forth from the bosom of the Father, go out of doors like the bridegroom coming out from his chamber, and run his course.[3] She interceded, too, that he would win those who were weak,

would not linger on the distant throne of the Father and in that light, for those without strength cannot follow there. Instead he would be taken up and led into the dwelling of the bride and her chamber, that he would be out of doors for her but within for us, would be in our midst, even though unseen by us.[4] ISAAC, OR THE SOUL 8.69.[5]

TO OPEN THE DOOR TO GOD'S WORD. AMBROSE: "I will take you up and lead you in." It is right to take up the Word of God and lead him in, because he knocks at the soul, that the door may be opened to him, and, unless he finds the door opened to him, he does not enter. But if anyone opens the door, he enters and dines.[6] The bride takes up the Word in such a way that she is taught in the taking up. ISAAC, OR THE SOUL 8.71.[7]

DO NOT SEPARATE LITTLE ONES FROM THE LOVE OF CHRIST. AMBROSE: Neither hold back the maidens of whom it is written, "Thus have the maidens loved you, and they have brought you into the house of their mother." You may not, then, separate the little ones from the love of Christ whom they proclaimed with prophetic exaltation even from their mother's womb. ON VIRGINITY 7.41.[8]

INFANCY IN THE MOTHER'S HOUSE. JULIAN OF ECLANUM: Here are shown many infancies in her, from which we ought to learn. First, it was the Creator of everything that is born from the union of masculine and feminine who fabricated a body from a virgin without the assistance of a man. Next, no sin is congenital to humankind, since it comes forth surrounded by the truth of the flesh and free from stain. Finally, it is impious to ascribe our origin to the works of the devil, since it rejoices that the true God is not only its founder but also its inhabitant. COMMENTARY ON THE SONG OF SONGS, FRAGMENT 11.[9]

---

[1]NPNF 2 10:322*. [2]FC 22:296. [3]Ps 19:5 (18:6 LXX, Vg). [4]See Jn 1:26. [5]FC 65:57. [6]Rev 3:20. [7]FC 65:57. [8]AOV 22. [9]CCL 88:401.

DIVINE TEACHING IN MY MOTHER'S HOUSE.
THEODORET OF CYR: "I shall lead you into my
mother's house and into the chamber of the one
who conceived me." Now, what is the house of the
all-holy Spirit (of whom the bride was born, after
all) if not the divine temple, which resembles the
Jerusalem on high, where they enter to speak with
the bridegroom, having received the status of
bride? And there, she says, "I shall give you some
spiced wine to drink and some juice from my
pomegranates," by "spiced wine" referring to the
teaching redolent of divine grace, as it were spiced
and proving to be fragrant. By "juice of pomegranates" she refers to the benefit deriving from the
fruits of love. COMMENTARY ON THE SONG OF
SONGS 8.[10]

A TYPE OF THE PASSION OF CHRIST. CYRIL OF
JERUSALEM: Again, referring to the wine mingled
with myrrh, the Canticle says, "I will give you a
cup of spiced wine." SERMON ON THE PARALYTIC
11.[11]

GOD APPOINTS THE TIMES AND SEASONS.
ATHANASIUS: Thus the God of all, after the manner of wise Solomon,[12] distributes everything in
time and season, to the end that, at the right
time, the salvation of humankind should be
everywhere spread abroad. In this way, "the Wisdom of God,"[13] our Lord and Savior Jesus Christ
. . . "passed into holy souls, making them friends
of God, and prophets."[14] Although very many
were praying for his coming and saying, "O that
the salvation of God would come out of Sion,"[15]
the spouse also, as it is written in the Song of
Songs, was praying and saying, "O that you were
like a brother to me, that nursed at my mother's
breasts." And the meaning of that prayer is, "O
that you were like humanity and would take on
human nature for our sake." After all, it was God
who set up times and seasons, and he knows our
needs better than we do. Because he loves us, he
exhorts us to do right things at right times so that
we may be healed. Thus, when the appropriate
time had come, the Father sent the Son, just as he
had promised. FESTAL LETTERS 1.1.[16]

8:5 Coming from the Wilderness

LEANING ON CHRIST. AMBROSE: She ascends
leaning on the Word of God. For those who are
more perfect recline upon Christ, just as John
also was reclining at Jesus' bosom.[17] So then she
either rested in Christ or reclined upon him or
even—since I am speaking of a marriage—as if
already given into the power of Christ, she was
led to the bridal couch by the bridegroom. ISAAC,
OR THE SOUL 8.72.[18]

WHITENESS A SIGN OF RENEWAL. AUGUSTINE:
Therefore Christ has given a new commandment
to us: that we love one another as he also has
loved us. This love renews us that we may be new,
heirs of the New Testament, singers of a new
song. This love renewed even then those just persons of ancient times, then the patriarchs and the
prophets, as it did the blessed apostles later. Even
now it also renews the nations, and from the
whole human race, which is scattered over the
whole world, it makes and gathers a new people,
the body of the new spouse, the bride of the Son
of God, the Only Begotten about whom it is said
in the Song of Songs, "Who is this who comes up
in white?"[19] In white, of course, because renewed.
By what, except by the new commandment?
TRACTATES ON THE GOSPEL OF JOHN 65.1.2.[20]

**FORMERLY BLACK BUT NOW COVERED IN
WHITE.** THEODORET OF CYR: "Who is this coming up all covered in white, leaning on her
nephew?" They do not say "white" but "all covered in white," being black, remember. While
the bride said of the bridegroom, "My nephew is
white,"[21] and did not say "covered in white,"
being such by nature, she on the contrary was

---

[10]ECS 2:113-14. [11]FC 64:216. [12]Eccles 3:7. [13]1 Cor 1:24. [14]Wis
7:27. [15]Ps 14:7 (13:7 LXX, Vg). [16]NPNF 2 4:506**. [17]Cf. Jn 13:23.
[18]FC 65:58. [19]"White" LXX. Those recently baptized were to wear
white garments. [20]FC 90:50-51**. [21]Song 5:10.

covered in black (the sun looked on her, remember)[22] and is now covered in white and shares the bridegroom's whiteness. And just as being the light he both made her light and called her so, and being holy he made her holy,[23] and becoming resurrection he accorded her resurrection, so he also gave her a share in his own peculiar whiteness. Hence on seeing her, the young women say, "Who is this coming up all covered in white, leaning on her nephew?" Guided by him and as it were led hand in hand, she makes her ascent into heaven and her departure to her beloved through her firm belief in him. Commentary on the Song of Songs 8.[24]

Resplendent in Faith. Ambrose: She is radiant . . . because she is resplendent in faith and in works. The Prayer of Job and David 4.4.16.[25]

Illuminated That You May Shine. Augustine: Oh, bride of Christ, beautiful among women! Oh, you in white, coming up and leaning upon your beloved! For by his light you are illuminated that you may shine; by his help you are supported that you may not fall! Oh, how well it is sung to you in that Song of Songs, your wedding song, as it were, that "there is love in your delights!"[26] Tractates on the Gospel of John 65.3.2.[27]

We of Ourselves Are Inadequate. Jerome: O mortal, you have now been cleansed in baptism, and it is said of you, "Who is she that comes up, cleansed and leaning upon her beloved?" so that she, indeed, is cleansed, but she is not able to guard her purity, unless she is sustained by the Lord God. You, who but a moment ago were freed from your sins, how is it that you desire to be delivered by the mercy of God, if not in the way I stated, that, when we have done everything, we confess that we of ourselves are insufficient? Against the Pelagians 3.15.[28]

8:6 A Seal on Your Heart and Arm

So That Your Faith and Works May Shine. Ambrose: The Lord Jesus himself, invited by such eager love and by the beauty of comeliness and grace, since now no offences pollute the baptized, says to the church, "Place me as a seal upon your heart, as a signet upon your arm"; that is, you are comely, my beloved, you are all fair, nothing is lacking in you. Place me as a seal upon your heart, so that your faith may shine forth in the fullness of the sacrament. Let your works also shine and set forth the image of God in whose image you were made. Let no persecution lessen your love, which cannot be quenched by many waters nor drowned by many rivers. On the Mysteries 7.41.[29]

The Life of Heavenly Beings. Ambrose: And since you are worthy to be compared not now with humans but with heavenly beings, whose life you are living on earth, receive from the Lord the precepts you are to observe: "Set me as a signet upon your heart, and as a seal upon your arm." [Thus] clearer proofs of your prudence and actions may be set forth, in which Christ the figure of God may shine, who, equaling fully the nature of the Father, has expressed the whole which he took of the Father's Godhead. Whence also the apostle Paul says that we are sealed in the Spirit;[30] since we have in the Son the image of the Father, and in the Spirit the seal of the Son. Let us then, sealed by this Trinity, take more diligent heed, lest either levity of character or the deceit of any unfaithfulness unseal the pledge which we have received in our hearts. Concerning Virgins 1.9.48.[31]

Now Fully Perfect. Ambrose: That we may fully know that this is true you have in the Canticles to the soul, now fully perfect, what I wish the Lord Jesus may say to you, "Put me as a seal upon your arm." May peace glow in your heart, Christ

[22]Song 1:6. [23]Cf. Jn 8:12; Mt 5:14; 1 Pet 1:16. [24]ECS 2:114. [25]FC 65:401. [26]Cf. Song 7:6. [27]FC 90:53. [28]FC 53:372-73*. [29]NPNF 2 10:322*. [30]Eph 1:13. [31]NPNF 2 10:370-71*.

in your works, and may there be formed in you wisdom and justice and redemption. LETTER 80, TO LAYMEN.[32]

CHRIST IS OUR SEAL OF GOD'S LOVE.

AMBROSE: Christ is the seal on the forehead, the seal in the heart—on the forehead that we may always confess him, in the heart that we may always love him, and a sign on the arm that we may always do his work. Therefore let his image shine forth in our profession of faith, let it shine forth in our love, let it shine forth in our works and deeds so that, if it is possible, all his beauty may be represented in us. Let him be our head, because "the head of man is Christ";[33] let him be our eye, that through him we may see the Father; let him be our voice, that through him we may speak to the Father; let him be our right hand, that through him we may bring our sacrifice to God the Father. He is also our seal, which is the mark of perfection and of love, because the Father, loving the Son, set his seal on him, just as we read, "Upon him the Father, God himself, has set his seal."[34]

And so Christ is our love. Good is love, since it has offered itself to death for transgressions; good is love, which has forgiven sins. And so let our soul clothe itself with love,[35] and love of a kind that is "strong as death." For just as death is the end of sins, so also is love, because one who loves the Lord ceases to commit sin. For "charity thinks no evil and does not rejoice over wickedness, but endures all things."[36] For if one does not seek his own goods, how will he seek the goods of another? Strong, too, is that death through the bath[37] through which every sin is buried and every fault forgiven. ISAAC, OR THE SOUL 8.75-76.[38]

THE STRENGTH OF LOVE.

THEODORET OF CYR: Possess "ardor" as well: if you were to acquire it, you would allow no one else to have more importance in your eyes, or yourself to be apathetic, but only her to enjoy your intimacy. "Ardor is harsh," note, and difficult to overcome,

like hades (drawing the name hades from common usage, and applying it also to death). But love is so strong because first of all it has wings, and around its wings it has a fiery flame and emits sparks. What could be more powerful than this when enkindled, especially since its fire is of the kind that is unquenchable? COMMENTARY ON THE SONG OF SONGS 8.[39]

LOVE AS STERN AS DEATH.

FRUCTUOSUS OF BRAGA: "Stern as death is love." Love is compared with the sternness of death, for, doubtless, once it comes, it summons the mind completely away from the love of the world. Accordingly, abbots must be such that they may perfectly love God and their neighbor; they must have their eyes removed from the evil desires of this world, as Adam did in paradise before the fall. GENERAL RULE FOR MONASTERIES 10.[40]

LOVE FOR ETERNITY.

GREGORY THE GREAT: Just as death destroys the body, so ardent desire for eternal life cuts off the love of material things. It renders one whom it has perfectly taken hold of insensible to earthly desires which come from without. FORTY GOSPEL HOMILIES 9 (11).[41]

DEATH CANNOT BE RESISTED.

AUGUSTINE: When death comes, it cannot be resisted. By whatever arts, whatever medicines, you meet it; the violence of death can none avoid who is born mortal; so against the violence of love can the world do nothing. For from the contrary the similitude is made of death; for as death is most violent to take away, so love is most violent to save. Through love many have died to the world, to live to God. EXPLANATIONS OF THE PSALMS 48.12.[42]

LOVE OF GOD STRONGER THAN DEATH.

JOHN OF APAMEA: Let the love of God be stronger than

[32]FC 26:454. [33]1 Cor 11:3. [34]Jn 6:27. [35]Gal 3:27. [36]1 Cor 13:5-7. [37]Tit 3:5. The reference is baptism. [38]FC 65:59-60. [39]ECS 2:115. [40]FC 63:192-93. [41]CS 123:63-64. [42]NPNF 1 8:167-68*.

death in you. If death releases you from the desire for everything, how much more appropriate is it that the love of God should release you from the desire for everything. LETTER 45, TO HESYCHIUS.[43]

DEATH FOR ONE'S FRIENDS. AUGUSTINE: Rightly is [love] said to be "strong as death," either because no one overcomes it as no one overcomes death, or because in this life the measure of charity is unto death, as the Lord said: "Greater love than this no man has, that a man lay down his life for his friends."[44] Or, rather, because as death tears the soul away from the senses of the flesh, so charity tears it away from carnal passions. LETTER 167.11.[45]

8:7 Love Is Stronger Than Many Waters

NOTHING DIMINISHES LOVE. AMBROSE: Love ought to exist in us in such a fashion that we are not called away from Christ by any dangers. For it is written, "Much water cannot shut out love, and floods will not confine it," because the soul of the lover passes through the torrent.[46] No storm, no profound danger, no fear of death or of punishment diminishes the strength of love; in such happenings as we are tested, in them lies the happy life, even though it is deluged by many dangers. For the wise person is not broken by bodily ills nor is he disturbed by misfortunes, but he remains happy even amid troubles. Bodily adversities do not diminish the gift of the happy life or take away anything from its sweetness. For the happiness of life does not lie in bodily pleasure, but in a conscience pure of every stain of sin, and in the mind of the one who knows that the good is also the pleasurable, even though it is harsh, and that what is shameful does not give delight, even though it is sweet. JACOB AND THE HAPPY LIFE 1.7.27.[47]

OVERCOMING SPITE WITH LOVE. THEODORET OF CYR: "If a man gives his whole life for love, they will utterly despise him." Those bereft and devoid of love will despise the one giving his life for love; hence blessed Paul also said, "When reviled we bless, when persecuted we put up with it, when blasphemed we are encouraging, we have become the world's refuse, as it were, everyone's off-scouring to this day."[48] This happens, in fact, to people who are dizzy: though they cannot stand up straight, they think everything else is spinning around; similarly also people bereft of love blaspheme the devotees of love as stupid and foolish. Far from undermining love, however, this even rendered it more ardent. When reviled the apostles gave blessings, when blasphemed they were encouraging, and on becoming the world's refuse, as it were, they claimed to be everyone's off-scouring to this day. COMMENTARY ON THE SONG OF SONGS 8.[49]

EXAMPLE OF THE MYRRH-BEARING WOMEN. CYRIL OF JERUSALEM: Though weak in body the women[50] were courageous in spirit. "Many waters cannot quench charity, neither can floods drown it." He whom they sought was dead, but their hope of the resurrection was not quenched. CATECHETICAL LECTURES 14.13.[51]

8:8 A Little Sister

HER MEANING IN CHRIST. APONIUS: This sister is undoubtedly understood to be the Jewish people (a people that we said was converted to the God of heaven in the final days), who are led out of the prophesied desert before the end of the world. [They are] "ascending from the desert"[52] of unbelief, where God is not worshiped, "leaning upon" the Word of God, "flowing with delights," known by faith in the indivisible Trinity, without which not only are there no delights, but the soul incurs danger of starvation. She is a sister because she descended from the seed of Abraham, from whom came

---

[43]CS 101:92. [44]Jn 15:13. [45]FC 30:41*. [46]Ps 124:4-5 (123:4-5 LXX, Vg). [47]FC 65:137. [48]1 Cor 4:12-13. [49]ECS 2:116. [50]Mt 28:9. [51]FC 64:40. [52]Song 8:5.

Christ according to the flesh and the church according to faith, inasmuch as Abraham would be established by God as a father to the nations.[53] And from these nations comes the church, which is made one body through faith in Christ, just as the soul of Christ is proven to be made one person with the Word, to whom the Word of God the Father united himself. It is the soul of our Lord Jesus Christ which is now understood to say, with pious affection for this very people, "Our sister is little and has no breasts." EXPOSITION OF SONG OF SONGS 12.29.[54]

REMEDY FOR SPIRITUAL IMMATURITY. THEODORET OF CYR: It is the holy authors who were celebrated in the Old Testament who see the bride's spiritual youth and the immaturity and inconspicuous condition of her breasts. In their capacity as go-betweens and marriage brokers [they] say among themselves, "The king is now on the point of taking our sister as his bride, but she is small and without breasts. She is not yet fertile, nor can she provide the milk of instruction or offer developed nourishment to the needy. So we must give thought to what is to be done. Since she is about to be related to the great king and be like a wall of his house, watching and guarding what is within, and being like a door that protects the contents, let us build as if on a wall 'silver parapets.'" That is, [the parapets are] arguments splendid for their reasoning, the Lord's sayings, after all, being "pure sayings, silver tried in the fire, tested in the earth."[55] "So . . . from her position on them she may fire at the enemy and hunt down the schemers. Let us place on her as on a door tablets made of cedar that incur no decay from sin, cedar being incorruptible." COMMENTARY ON THE SONG OF SONGS 8.[56]

NONETHELESS REDEEMED IN CHRIST. BEDE: She is the sister of the Lord our Savior and of all his church gathered from both peoples and of every saint. [This is] not only due to the assumption of her nature, whereby he was made man, but also due to the bestowal of grace

whereby he gives those who believe in him the power to become children of God, so that he who was the only Son of God by nature might become "the firstborn among many brethren" through grace.[57] COMMENTARY ON THE SONGS OF SONGS 5.8.8.[58]

8:10-11 A Wall with Towers

THE WALL IS THE CHURCH. AMBROSE: The wall is the church and the towers are her priests, who have full power to teach both the natural and the moral sciences. SIX DAYS OF CREATION 6.8.49.[59]

THE VINEYARD IS THE CHURCH. CYRIL OF ALEXANDRIA: The vineyard which, it says, was given to the spiritual Solomon is surely the church. And we have already said that Baalhamon means "in believers." For who believed, apart from those who accepted his commandments? FRAGMENTS IN THE COMMENTARY ON THE SONG OF SONGS 8.11.[60]

8:14 Away, My Beloved

TO FLEE ABOVE THE WORLD. AMBROSE: It urges that the bridegroom flee, because already, although it is of earth, it can follow him in his flight. It says this so that it may be like the young deer that escapes the nets; for it desires also to flee and to fly away above the world. DEATH AS A GOOD 5.18.[61]

THE VOICE THAT CHRIST DESIRES TO HEAR. APONIUS: By saying "Flee, my beloved," Christ makes heard the voice that he desires to hear. Through this, it is confessed that he alone on the earth, alone among all humankind (true man, but born in an ineffable manner), alone found to be a foreigner and pilgrim,[62] alone flee-

---

[53]Gen 17:4. [54]CCL 19:280-81. [55]Ps 12:6 (11:7 LXX). [56]ECS 2:117. [57]Rom 8:29. [58]CCL 119B:349. [59]FC 42:262-63. [60]PG 69:1291. [61]FC 65:84. [62]Cf. 1 Pet 2:11.

ing the sordid lifestyle of humanity, alone ascending upon the prophesied "mountains of spices," he alone in every way is made Lord of heaven and earth. It shows that he alone fled both interior and exterior sin. He alone, who would bind the devil, fugitive of heaven, is himself a fugitive of the earth in the midst of a perverse and depraved nation. Exposition of Song of Songs 12.83.[63]

Christ Flees from the Barren Plain. Ambrose: Christ, detested by coiling snakes and beset by reptiles crawling on the earth, flees from the barren plain; he knows no dwelling except the heights of virtue; he knows no home except among those daughters of the church who can say, "We are a sweet fragrance of Christ to God." For some indeed, it is an odor of death, leading to death, for those who perish; but to others, it is an odor of life, leading to life—in those namely, who with living faith, breathe the fragrance of the Lord's resurrection. On Virginity 9.49.[64]

Final Flight Heavenward. Bede: "Flee, my beloved, and be like a goat or a mule upon the mountains of spices." This can be accepted as referring both to the triumph of the Lord's ascension and to those good deeds that are accomplished daily within his holy church. For, the beloved fled after he addressed his bride and sister, when he returned to heaven with the dispensation of our redemption complete. But he is likened to a goat or a mule upon the mountains of spice because he appears frequently through the grace of compunction to the hearts of his faithful, who are the mountains of spice. For they are preserved from the lowest, most contemptible desires by their love of heaven and, having been purged of the fetid stench of vices, they are filled with the fragrance of spiritual virtues, saying with the apostle, "Our citizenship is in heaven."[65] Commentary on the Songs of Songs 5.8.14.[66]

---

[63]CCL 19:305. [64]AOV 25. [65]Phil 3:20. [66]CCL 119B:356.

Early Christian Writers and the Documents Cited

The following table lists all the early Christian documents cited in this volume by author, if known, or by the title of the work. The English title used in this commentary is followed in parentheses with the Latin designation and, where available, the Thesaurus Linguae Graecae (=TLG) digital referenences or Cetedoc Clavis numbers. Printed sources of original language versions may be found in the bibliography of works in original languages.

Acacius of Beroea

Letter to Cyril of Alexandria (*Consilium universale Ephesenum anno*)	TLG 5000.001

Ambrose

Cain and Abel (*De Cain et Abel*)	Cetedoc 0125
Concerning Repentance (*De paenitentia*)	Cetedoc 0156
Concerning Virgins (*De virginibus*)	Cetedoc 0145
Consolation on the Death of Emperor Valentinian (*De obitu Valentiniani*)	Cetedoc 0158
Death as a Good (*De bono mortis*)	Cetedoc 0129
Duties of the Clergy (*De officiis*)	Cetedoc 0144
Flight from the World (*De fuga saeculi*)	Cetedoc 0133
Isaac, or the Soul (*De Isaac vel anima*)	Cetedoc 0128
Jacob and the Happy Life (*De Jacob et vita beata*)	Cetedoc 0130
Letters (*Epistulae*)	Cetedoc 0160
On His Brother Satyrus (*De excessu fratris Satyri*)	Cetedoc 0157
On the Christian Faith (*De fide libri v*)	Cetedoc 0150
On the Death of Theodosius (*De obitu Theodosii*)	Cetedoc 0159
On the Holy Spirit (*De spiritu sancto*)	Cetedoc 0151
On the Mysteries (*De mysteriis*)	Cetedoc 0155
On Virginity (*De virginitate*)	Cetedoc 0147
The Prayer of Job and David (*De interpellatione Job et David*)	Cetedoc 0134
Six Days of Creation (*Exameron*)	Cetedoc 0123

Aphrahat

Demonstrations (*Demonstrationes*)	

Aponius

Exposition of Song of Songs (*In Canticum canticorum expositio*)	Cetedoc 0194

Athanasius

Against the Heathen (*Contra gentes*)	TLG 2035.001
Defense Before Constantius (*Apologia ad Constantium imperatorem*)	TLG 2035.011
Defense of His Flight (*Apologia de fuga sua*)	TLG 2035.012

Defense of the Nicene Definition (*De decretis Nicaenae synodi*)	TLG 2035.003
Deposition of Arius (*Deposition Arii* in *De decretis Nicaenae synodi*)	TLG 2035.003
Festal Letters (*Epistulae festales*)	TLG 2035.x01
Four Discourses Against the Arians (*Orationes tres contra Arianos*)	TLG 2035.042
Letters (*Epistula ad Adelphium*)	TLG 2035.050
Letters to Monks (*Epistula ad monachus*)	TLG 2035.008
Letter to Jovian (*Epistula ad Jovianum*)	TLG 2035.119
Letter to the Bishops of Egypt (*Epistula ad episcopos Aegypti et Libyae*)	TLG 2035.041
Life of St. Anthony (*Vita sancti Antonii*)	TLG 2035.047
Statement of Faith (*See Marcellus, Expositio fidei*)	TLG 2041.004

Athenagorus

A Plea Regarding Christians (*Legatio sive Supplicatio pro Christianis*)	TLG 1205.001

Augustine

Against Julian (*Contra Julianum*)	Cetedoc 0351
Against Two Letters of the Pelagians (*Contra duas epistulas pelagianorum*)	Cetedoc 0346
The Catholic and Manichaean Ways of Life (*De moribus ecclesiae catholicae et de moribus Manichaeorum*)	Cetedoc 0261
Christian Instruction (*De doctrina christiana*)	Cetedoc 0263
City of God (*De civitate Dei*)	Cetedoc 0313
Confessions (*Confessionum libri tredecim*)	Cetedoc 0251
The Correction of the Donatist (*In Epistulae*)	Cetedoc 0262
Enchiridion (*Enchiridion de fide, spe et caritate*)	Cetedoc 0295
The Excellence of Widowhood (*De bono viduitatis*)	Cetedoc 0301
Explanations of the Psalms (*Enarrationes in Psalmos*)	Cetedoc 0283
Holy Virginity (*De sancta virginitate*)	Cetedoc 0300
In Answer to the Jews (*Adversus Judaeos*)	Cetedoc 0315
Letters (*Epistulae*)	Cetedoc 0262
Of True Religion (*De vera religione*)	Cetedoc 0264
On Baptism (*De baptismo*)	Cetedoc 0332
On Eighty-three Varied Questions (*De diversis quaestionibus octoginta tribus*)	Cetedoc 0289
On Faith and the Creed (*De fide et symbolo*)	Cetedoc 0293
On Grace and Free Will (*De gratia et libero arbitrio*)	Cetedoc 0352
On Marriage and Concupiscence (*De nuptiis et concupiscentia*)	Cetedoc 0350
On Nature and Grace (*De natura et gratia*)	Cetedoc 0344
On Patience (*De patientia*)	Cetedoc 0308
On the Christian Life (*De vita christiana*)	Cetedoc 0730
On the Merits and Forgiveness of Sins and on Infant Baptism (*De peccatorum meritis et remissione et de baptismo parvulorum*)	Cetedoc 0342
On the Soul and Its Origin (*De natura et origine animae*)	Cetedoc 0345
On the Spirit and the Letter (*De spiritu et littera*)	Cetedoc 0343
On the Trinity (*De Trinitate*)	Cetedoc 0329
Predestination of the Saints (*De praedestinatione sanctorum*)	Cetedoc 0354
Reply to Faustus the Manichaean (*Contra Faustum*)	Cetedoc 0321

Sermon on the Mount (*De sermone Domini in monte*)	Cetedoc 0274
Sermons (*Sermones*)	Cetedoc 0284
Tractates on the Gospel of John (*In Johannis evangelium tractatus*)	Cetedoc 0278

Babai
Letter to Cyriacus

Basil the Great

Concerning Faith (*Prologus 8 [de fide]*)	TLG 2040.045
Homilies on the Beginning of Proverbs (*Homilia in principium proverbiorum*)	TLG 2040.028
Homilies on the Psalms (*Homiliae super Psalmos*)	TLG 2040.018
Homily Concerning Envy (*Homilia de invidia*)	TLG 2040.027
Homily on the Words "Give Heed to Thyself" (*Homilia in illud: Attende tibi ipsi*)	TLG 2040.006
The Long Rules (*Asceticon magnum sive Quaestiones [regulae fusius tractatae]*)	TLG 2040.048
The Long Rules, Preface (*Prologus 4 [prooemium in asceticum magnum]*)	TLG 2040.047
On Humility (*De humilitate*)	TLG 2040.036
On Mercy and Justice (*Homilia de misericordia et judicio [Sp.]*)	TLG 2040.069
On Renunciation of the World (*Sermo 11 [sermo asceticus et exhortatio de renuntiatione mundi] [Dub.]*)	TLG 2040.041
On the Spirit (*De spiritu sancto*)	TLG 2040.003

Bede

Commentary on the Seven Catholic Epistles (*In epistulam septem catholicas*)	Cetedoc 1362
Commentary on Proverbs (*In proverbia Salomonis libri iii*)	Cetedoc 1351
Commentary on the Acts of the Apostles (*Expositio actuum apostolorum*)	Cetedoc 1357
Commentary on the Songs of Songs (*In Cantica canticorum libri vi*)	Cetedoc 1353
Homilies on the Gospels (*Homiliarum evangelii libri ii*)	Cetedoc 1367
On the Tabernacle (*De tabernaculo et vasis eius ac vestibus sacerdotum libri iii*)	Cetedoc 1345

Benedict

Rule of St. Benedict (*Regula*)	Cetedoc 1852

Besa
Letters (*Epistulae*)
Sermons (*Sermones*)

Braulio of Saragosa
Letters (*Epistulae*)

Caesarius of Arles

Sermons (*Sermones*)	Cetedoc 1008

Cassian, John

Conferences (*Collationes xxiiii*)	Cetedoc 0512
Institutes (*De institutis coenobiorum et de octo principalium vitiorum remediis*)	Cetedoc 0513

Cassiodorus
Expositions of the Psalms (*Expositio Psalmorum*)   Cetedoc 0900

Clement of Alexandria
Christ the Educator (*Paedagogus*)   TLG 0555.002
Stromateis (*Stromata*)   TLG 0555.004

Clement of Rome
1 Clement (*Epistula i ad Corinthios*)   TLG 1271.001

Constitutions of the Holy Apostles (*Constitutiones apostolorum*)   TLG 2894.001

Cyprian
The Dress of Virgins (*De habitu virginum*)   Cetedoc 0040
Letters (*Epistulae*)   Cetedoc 0050
The Lord's Prayer (*De dominica oratione*)   Cetedoc 0043
To Demetrian (*Ad Demetrianum*)   Cetedoc 0046
The Unity of the Catholic Church (*De ecclesiae catholicae unitate*)   Cetedoc 0041
Works and Almsgiving (*De opere et eleemosynis*)   Cetedoc 0047

Cyril of Alexandria
Commentary on Luke (*Commentarii in Lucam [in catenis]*)   TLG 4090.108
Fragments in the Commentary on the Song of Songs (*Fragmenta in Cantica Canticorum*)   TLG 4090.102
Letters (*Epistulae* in *Concilium universale Ephesenum anno*)   TLG 5000.001

Cyril of Jerusalem
Catechetical Lectures (*Catecheses ad illuminandos*)   TLG 2110.003
Mystagogical Lectures (*Mystagogiae*)   TLG 2110.002
Sermon on the Paralytic (*Homilia in paralyticum juxta piscinam jacentem*)   TLG 2110.006

Didache (*Didache xii apostolorum*)   TLG 1311.001

Didymus the Blind
Commentary on Ecclesiastes
  (*Commentarii in Ecclesiasten [1.1-8]*)   TLG 2102.011
  (*Commentarii in Ecclesiasten [3-4.12]*)   TLG 2102.047
  (*Commentarii in Ecclesiasten [5-6]*)   TLG 2102.005
  (*Commentarii in Ecclesiasten [7-8.8]*)   TLG 2102.006
  (*Commentarii in Ecclesiasten [9.8-10.20]*)   TLG 2102.048
  (*Commentarii in Ecclesiasten[11-12]*)   TLG 2102.007
Commentary on the Proverbs of Solomon (*Fragmenta in Proverbia*)   TLG 2102.022

Dionysius of Alexandria
Fragments (*Fragmenta*)   TLG 2952.002

Ephrem the Syrian
Commentary on Genesis (*Commentarii in Genesim*)
Commentary on Tatian's Diatessaron (*In Tatiani Diatessaron*)
Homily on Admonition and Repentance (*Sermones*)
Homily on Our Lord (*Sermo de Domino nostro*)
Hymns on Paradise (*Hymni de paradiso*)
Hymns on the Nativity (*Hymni de nativitate*)
Hymns Preserved in Armenian (*Hymni*)

Epistle of Barnabas (*Barnabae epistula*)   TLG 1216.001

Eusebius of Caesarea
Proof of the Gospel (*Demonstratio evangelica*)   TLG 2018.005

Eustathius of Antioch (*See* Theodoret of Cyr, *Eranistes*)

Evagrius of Pontus
Scholia on Ecclesiastes (*Scholia in Ecclesiasten [fragmenta e catenis]*)   TLG 4110.031
Scholia on Proverbs (*Scholia in Proverbia [fragmenta e catenis]*)   TLG 4110.030

Eznik of Kolb
On God (*De Deo*)

Fructuosus of Braga
General Rule for Monasteries (*Regula Monastica Communis*)
Letters (*Epistola*)
Monastic Agreement (*Consensoria monachorum*)

Fulgentius of Ruspe
Letters (*Epistulae*)   Cetedoc 0817
Letter to Scarila (*Liber de Scarilam de incarnatione filii dei et vilium animalium autore*)   Cetedoc 0822
On the Forgiveness of Sins (*Ad Euthymium de remissione peccatorum libri II*)   Cetedoc 0821

Gerontius
Sayings of the Fathers (*Apophthegmata [collection anonyma]*)   TLG 2742.002

Gregory of Elvira
Explanations of the Song of Songs (*In Canticum canticorum libri quinque*)   Cetedoc 0547
Expositions of Ecclesiastes (*Fragmenta expositiones in Ecclesiasten*)   Cetedoc 0556

Gregory of Nazianzus
Against the Eunomians, Theological Oration 1(27) (*Adversus Eunomianos*)   TLG 2022.007
In Defense of His Flight, Oration 2 (*Apologetica*)   TLG 2022.016
On Holy Baptism, Oration 40 (*In sanctum baptisma*)   TLG 2022.048
On His Brother St. Caesarius, Oration 7 (*Funebris in laudem Caesarii fratris oratio*)   TLG 2022.005

On His Sister St. Gorgiana, Oration 8 (*In laudem sororis Gorgoniae*)   TLG 2022.021
On the Death of His Father, Oration 18 (*Funebris oratio in patrem*)   TLG 2022.031
On the Son, Theological Oration 3 (29), (*De filio*)   TLG 2022.009
On the Son, Theological Oration 4 (30), (*De filio*)   TLG 2022.010
On Theology, Theological Oration 2 (28) (*De theologia*)   TLG 2022.008

Gregory of Nyssa

Against Eunomius (*Contra Eunomium*)   TLG 2017.030
Answer to Eunomius's Second Book (*Contra Eunomium*)   TLG 2017.030
Funeral Oration on Meletius (*Oratio funebris in Meletium episcopum*)   TLG 2017.021
Homilies on Ecclesiastes (*In Ecclesiasten*)   TLG 2017.029
Homilies on the Song of Songs (*In Canticum canticorum*)   TLG 2017.032
On the Lord's Prayer (*De oratione dominica orationes*)   TLG 2017.047
On Virginity (*De virginitate*)   TLG 2017.043

Gregory Thaumaturgus

Paraphrase of Ecclesiastes (*Metaphrasis in Ecclesiasten Salomonis*)   TLG 2063.006

Gregory the Great

Commentary on the Song of Songs (*Expositio in Canticum canticorum*)   Cetedoc 1709
Dialogues (*Dialogorum libri iv*)   Cetedoc 1713
Forty Gospel Homilies (*Homiliarum xl in evangelica*)   Cetedoc 1711
Letters (*Registrum epistularum*)   Cetedoc 1714
Morals on the Book of Job (*Moralia in Job*)   Cetedoc 1708
Pastoral Care (*Regula pastoralis*)   Cetedoc 1712

Hilary of Arles

Life of St. Honoratus (*Vita Honorati*)

Hilary of Poitiers

Homilies on the Psalms (*Tractatus super psalmos I-XCI*)   Cetedoc 0428
On the Trinity (*De Trinitate*)   Cetedoc 0433

Hippolytus

Fragments on Proverbs
    (*Fragmenta in Proverbia*)   TLG 2115.013
    (*Fragmenta in Proverbia [Sp.]*)   TLG 2115.015
    (*Fragmenta in Proverbia*)   TLG 2115.044
Fragments on Song of Songs (*In Canticum canticorum*)   TLG 2115.031
Treatise on the Song of Songs (*In Canticum canticorum [paraphrasis]*)   TLG 2115.049

Horsiesi

Instructions (*Catecheses*)
Regulations (*Regulae*)

Ignatius of Antioch

Epistle to the Ephesians (*Epistulae vii genuinae*)   TLG 1443.001

Isaac of Nineveh

Ascetical Homilies (*De perfectione religiosa*)

Jerome

Against Jovinianus (*Adversus Jovinianum*)   Cetedoc 0610
Against Rufinus (*Apologia adversus libros Rufini*)   Cetedoc 0613
Against the Pelagians (*Dialogi contra Pelagianos libri iii*)   Cetedoc 0615
Commentary on Ecclesiastes (*Commentarius in Ecclesiasten*)   Cetedoc 0583
Homilies on the Psalms (*Tractatus lix in psalmos*)   Cetedoc 0592
Homilies on the Psalms, Alternate Series (*Tractatuum in psalmos series altera*)   Cetedoc 0593
Homily on Obedience (*Tractatus de oboedientia*)   Cetedoc 0605
Letters (*Epistulae*)   Cetedoc 0620
Life of Malchus (*Vita Malchi*)   Cetedoc 0619

John Chrysostom

Against the Anomoeans (*Contra Anomoeos*)
   1-5 (*Contra Anomoeos homiliae 1-5=De incomprehensibili dei natura*)   TLG 2062.012
   6 (*De beato Philogonio*)   TLG 2062.014
Baptismal Instructions (*Ad illuminandos catecheses 1-2 [series prima et secunda]*)   TLG 2062.025
Commentary on Isaiah (*In Isaiam*)   TLG 2062.497
Commentary on the Proverbs of Solomon (*Fragmenta in Proverbia [in catenis]*)   TLG 2062.185
Discourses Against Judaizing Christians (*Adversus Judaeos [orationes 1-8]*)   TLG 2062.021
Homilies Concerning the Statues (*Ad populam Antiochenum homiliae [de statuis]*)   TLG 2062.024
Homilies on Ephesians (*In epistulam ad Ephesios*)   TLG 2062.159
Homilies on Genesis (*In Genesim [homiliae 1-67]*)   TLG 2062.112
Homilies on Repentance and Almsgiving (*De paenitentia [homiliae 1-9]*)   TLG 2062.027
Homilies on Romans (*In epistulam ad Romanos*)   TLG 2062.155
Homilies on the Acts of the Apostles (*In Acta apostolorum [homiliae 1-55]*)   TLG 2062.154
Homilies on the Gospel of John (*In Joannem [homiliae 1-88]*)   TLG 2062.153
Homilies on the Gospel of Matthew (*In Matthaeum [homiliae 1-90]*)   TLG 2062.152
Homilies on 1 Timothy (*In epistulam i ad Timotheum*)   TLG 2062.164
On the Epistle to the Hebrews (*In epistulam ad Hebraeos*)   TLG 2062.168

John of Antioch

Letter to Cyril of Alexandria (In *Concilia Oecumenica*)   TLG 5000.001

John of Apamea

Letter to Hesychius

John of Damascus

Barlaam and Joseph (*Vita Barlaam et Joasaph [Sp.]*)   TLG 2934.066
Orthodox Faith (*Expositio fidei*)   TLG 2934.004

Julian of Eclanum
Commentary on the Song of Songs (*Commentarius in Canticum canticorum*)   Cetedoc 0775

Justin Martyr
Dialogue with Trypho (*Dialogus cum Tryphone*)   TLG 0645.003

Leander of Seville
Homilies on the Triumph of the Church (*Homilia in laudem ecclesiae*)
The Training of Nuns (*Regula, sive liber de institutione virginum et contemptu mundi*)

Leo the Great
Sermons (*Tractatus septem et nonaginta*)   Cetedoc 1657
Tome (*Concilia oecumenica et generalia ecclesiae catholicae Concilium Chalcedonense a. 451*)

Macarius
Fifty Spiritual Homilies (*Homiliae spiritualis 50*)   TLG 2109.002

Macrina *See* **Gregory of Nyssa**
On the Soul and the Resurrection (*Dialogus de anima et resurrectione*)   TLG 2017.056

Marcellus
Statement of Faith (*Expositio fidei*)   TLG 2041.004

Marius Victorinus
Letter to Candidus (*De generatione divini verbi*)   Cetedoc 0096

Maximus of Turin
Sermons (*Collectio sermonum antiqua*)   Cetedoc 0219a

Nilus of Ancyra
Commentary on the Song of Songs (*Commentarius in Canticum canticorum*)

Olympiodorus
Commentary on Ecclesiastes (*Commentarii in Ecclesiasten*)   TLG 2865.002

Origen
Against Celsus (*Contra Celsum*)   TLG 2042.001
Commentary on Matthew
   (*Commentarium in evangelium Matthaei [lib. 10-11]*)   TLG 2042.029
   (*Commentarium in evangelium Matthaei [lib.12-17]*)   TLG 2042.030
   (*Fragmenta ex commentariis in evangelium Matthaei*)   TLG 2042.031
Commentary on the Gospel of John
   (*Commentarii in evangelium Joannis [lib. 1, 2, 4, 5, 6, 10, 13]*)   TLG 2042.005
   (*Commentarii in evangelium Joannis [lib. 19, 20, 28, 32]*)   TLG 2042.079
Commentary on the Song of Songs (*Commentarium in Canticum canticorum*)   Cetedoc 0198, TLG 2042.026

Exhortation to Martyrdom *(Exhortatio ad martyrium)*	TLG 2042.007
Exposition on Proverbs *(Expositio in Proverbia)*	TLG 2042.075
Fragments on Jeremiah	
(Fragmenta in Jeremiam [e *Philocalia])*	TLG 2042.084
(Fragmenta in Jeremiam [in catenis])	TLG 2042.010
Fragments on Luke *(Fragmenta in Lucam* [in catenis])	TLG 2042.017
Homilies on Exodus *(Homiliae in Exodum)*	TLG 2042.023
Homilies on Genesis *(Homiliae in Genesim)*	TLG 2042.022
Homilies on Jeremiah	
(In Jeremiam [homiliae 1-11])	TLG 2042.009
(In Jeremiam [homilae 12-20])	TLG 2042.021
Homilies on Joshua *(In Jesu nave)*	
Homilies on Leviticus *(Homiliae in Leviticum)*	TLG 2042.024
Homilies on the Gospel of Luke *(Homiliae in Lucam)*	TLG 2042.016
Homilies on the Song of Songs *(Homiliae in Canticum canticorum)*	
Letter to Julius Africanus *(Epistula ad Africanum)*	TLG 2042.045
On First Principles	
(De principiis)	TLG 2042.002
(Fragmenta de principiis)	TLG 2042.003
On Prayer *(De oratione)*	TLG 2042.008

Pachomius
Fragments *(Fragmenta)*
Instructions *(Catecheses)*

Pacian of Barcelona
Letters *(Epistulae)*
On Penitents *(De paenitentibus)*

The Passing of Mary *(Tranitus Mariae)*

Paulinus of Milan
Life of St. Ambrose *(Vita S. Ambrosii)*

Peter Chrysologus	
Sermons *(Collectio sermonum)*	Cetedoc 0227+

Peter of Alexandria	
Canonical Epistles *(Epistula canonica)*	TLG 2962.004

[Peter of Alexandria]
Homilies on Riches

Prosper of Aquitaine	
Grace and Free Will *(De gratia Dei et libero arbitrio contra Collatorem)*	Cetedoc 0523

Prudentius
Hymns for Every Day *(Liber Cathemerinon)*   Cetedoc 1438

Pseudo-Clement of Rome
Homilies *(Homiliae [Sp.])*   TLG 1271.006
Letters on Virginity *(Epistulae de virginitate [Sp.])*   TLG 1271.010

Pseudo-Dionysius
Divine Names *(De divinis nominibus)*   TLG 2798.004
Letter *(Epistulae)*   TLG 2798.006-015

Revelation of Esdras (Apocalypsis Esdrae)

Rufinus of Aquileia
Commentary on the Apostles' Creed *(Expositio symboli)*   Cetedoc 0196

Salvian the Presbyter
Four Books of Timothy to the Church *(Ad ecclesiam [sive Adversus avaritiam])*
The Governance of God *(De gubernatione Dei)*   Cetedoc 0485

Shenoute
Fragments on Ecclesiastes *(Fragmenta)*
On Language *(De lingua)*
To the Gentile Philosopher *(Ad philosophum gentilem)*

Shepherd of Hermas *(Hermas, Pastor)*   TLG 1419.001

Symeon the New Theologian
Discourses *(Catecheses)*

Tertullian
Against Hermogenes *(Adversus Hermogenem)*   Cetedoc 0013
Against Praxeas *(Adversus Praxean)*   Cetedoc 0026
On Fasting *(De jejunio adversus psychicos)*   Cetedoc 0029
On Flight in Time of Persecution *(De fuga in persecutione)*   Cetedoc 0025
On Patience *(De patientia)*   Cetedoc 0009
On Prayer *(De oratione)*   Cetedoc 0007
On the Veiling of Virgins *(De virginibus velandis)*   Cetedoc 0027
Prescriptions Against Heretics *(De praescriptione haereticorum)*   Cetedoc 0005

Theodore of Mopsuestia
Paraphrase of the Commentary of Theodore of Mopsuestia

Theodore of Tabennesi
Fragment

Theodoret of Cyr
Commentary on the Psalms *(Interpretatio in Psalmos)*	TLG 4089.024
Commentary on the Song of Songs *(Explanatio in Canticum canticorum)*	TLG 4089.025
Eranistes *(Eranistes)*	TLG 4089.002
Letters *(Ad eos qui in Euphratesia et Osrhoena regione, Syria, Phoeni)*	TLG 4089.034

Theodotus the Valentinian
Excerpts of Theodotus *(See* Clement of Alexandria *Eclogae propheticae)*	TLG 0555.005

Valerian
Homilies *(Homiliae)*

Vincent of Lérins
Commonitories *(Commonitorium)*	Cetedoc 0510

Timeline of Writers of the Patristic Period

Location / Period	British Isles	Gaul	Spain, Portugal	Rome* and Italy	Carthage and Northern Africa
2nd century				Clement of Rome, fl. c. 92-101 (Greek)	
				Shepherd of Hermas, c. 140 (Greek)	
				Justin Martyr (Ephesus, Rome), c. 100/110-165 (Greek)	
		Irenaeus of Lyons, c. 135-c. 202 (Greek)		Valentinus the Gnostic (Rome), fl. c. 140 (Greek)	
				Marcion (Rome), fl. 144 (Greek)	
3rd century				Callistus of Rome, regn. 217-222 (Latin)	Tertullian of Carthage, c. 155/160-c. 225 (Latin)
				Minucius Felix of Rome, fl. 218-235 (Latin)	
				Hippolytus (Rome, Palestine?), fl. 222-235/245 (Greek)	Cyprian of Carthage, fl. 248-258 (Latin)
				Novatian of Rome, fl. 235-258 (Latin)	
				Victorinus of Petovium, 230-304 (Latin)	
4th century				Firmicus Maternus (Sicily), fl. c. 335 (Latin)	
		Lactantius, c. 260- 330 (Latin)		Marius Victorinus (Rome), fl. 355-363 (Latin)	
				Eusebius of Vercelli, fl. c. 360 (Latin)	
		Hilary of Poitiers, c. 315-367 (Latin)	Hosius of Cordova, d. 357 (Latin)	Lucifer of Cagliari (Sardinia), d. 370/371 (Latin)	
			Potamius of Lisbon, fl. c. 350-360 (Latin)	Faustinus (Rome), fl. 380 (Latin)	
			Gregory of Elvira, fl. 359-385 (Latin)	Filastrius of Brescia, fl. 380 (Latin)	
			Prudentius, c. 348-c. 410 (Latin)	Ambrosiaster (Italy?), fl. c. 366-384 (Latin)	
			Pacian of Barcelona, 4th cent. (Latin)	Faustus of Riez, fl. c. 380 (Latin)	
				Gaudentius of Brescia, fl. 395 (Latin)	Paulus Orosius, b. c. 380 (Latin)
				Ambrose of Milan, c. 333-397; fl. 374-397 (Latin)	
				Paulinus of Milan, late 4th early 5th cent. (Latin)	
				Rufinus (Aquileia, Rome), c. 345-411 (Latin)	
				Aponius, fl. 405-415 (Latin)	

*One of the five ancient patriarchates

Alexandria* and Egypt	Constantinople* and Asia Minor, Greece	Antioch* and Syria	Mesopotamia, Persia	Jerusalem* and Palestine	Location Unknown
Philo of Alexandria, c. 20 B.C. – c. A.D. 50 (Greek)				Flavius Josephus (Rome), c. 37-c. 101 (Greek)	
Basilides (Alexandria), 2nd cent. (Greek)	Polycarp of Smyrna, c. 69-155 (Greek)	*Didache* (Egypt?), c. 100 (Greek)			*Second Letter of Clement* (spurious; Corinth, Rome, Alexandria?) (Greek), c. 150
Letter of Barnabas (Syria?), c. 130 (Greek)	Athenagoras (Greece), fl. 176-180 (Greek)	Ignatius of Antioch, c. 35–107/112 (Greek)			
Theodotus the Valentinian, 2nd cent. (Greek)	*Montanist Oracles*, late 2nd cent. (Greek)				
		Theophilus of Antioch, c. late 2nd cent. (Greek)			
Clement of Alexandria, c. 150-215 (Greek)	Gregory Thaumaturgus (Neocaesarea), fl. c. 248-264 (Greek)		Mani (Manichaeans), c. 216-276		Pseudo-Clementines 3rd cent. (Greek)
Sabellius (Egypt), 2nd–3rd cent. (Greek)					
Letter to Diognetus, 3rd cent. (Greek)					
Origen (Alexandria, Caesarea of Palestine), 185-254 (Greek)					
Dionysius of Alexandria, d. 264/5 (Greek)	Methodius of Olympus (Lycia), d. c. 311 (Greek)				
Antony, c. 251-355 (Coptic /Greek)	Theodore of Heraclea (Thrace), fl. c. 330-355 (Greek)	Eustathius of Antioch, fl. 325 (Greek)	Aphrahat (Persia) c. 270-350; fl. 337-345 (Syriac)	Eusebius of Caesarea (Palestine), c. 260/263-340 (Greek)	Commodius, c. 3rd or 5th cent. (Latin)
Peter of Alexandria, d. c. 311 (Greek)	Marcellus of Ancyra, d.c. 375 (Greek)	Eusebius of Emesa, c. 300-c. 359 (Greek)	Jacob of Nisibis, fl. 308-325 (Syriac)	Acacius of Caesarea (Palestine), d. c. 365 (Greek)	
Arius (Alexandria), fl. c. 320 (Greek)	Epiphanius of Salamis (Cyprus), c. 315-403 (Greek)	Ephrem the Syrian, c. 306-373 (Syriac)		Cyril of Jerusalem, c. 315-386 (Greek)	
Alexander of Alexandria, fl. 312-328 (Greek)	Basil (the Great) of Caesarea, b. c. 330; fl. 357-379 (Greek)	Nemesius of Emesa (Syria), fl. late 4th cent. (Greek)			
Pachomius, c. 292-347 (Coptic/Greek?)	Macrina the Younger, c. 327-379 (Greek)	Diodore of Tarsus, d. c. 394 (Greek)			
Theodore of Tabennesi, d. 368 (Coptic/Greek)	Apollinaris of Laodicea, 310-c. 392 (Greek)	John Chrysostom (Constantinople), 344/354-407 (Greek)			
Horsiesi, c. 305-390 (Coptic/Greek)	Gregory of Nazianzus, b. 329/330; fl. 372-389 (Greek)	*Apostolic Constitutions*, c. 375-400 (Greek)			
Athanasius of Alexandria, c. 295-373; fl. 325-373 (Greek)	Gregory of Nyssa, c. 335-394 (Greek)	*Didascalia*, 4th cent. (Syriac)			
Macarius of Egypt, c. 300-c. 390 (Greek)	Amphilochius of Iconium, c. 340/345- c. 398/404 (Greek)	Theodore of Mopsuestia, c. 350-428 (Greek)		Diodore of Tarsus, d. c. 394 (Greek)	
Didymus (the Blind) of Alexandria, 313-398 (Greek)	Evagrius of Pontus, 345-399 (Greek)	Acacius of Beroea c,. 340-c. 436 (Greek)		Jerome (Rome, Antioch, Bethlehem), c. 347-420 (Latin)	
	Eunomius of Cyzicus, fl. 360-394 (Greek)				
	Pseudo-Macarius (Mesopotamia?), late 4th cent. (Greek)				
	Nicetas of Remesiana, d. c. 414 (Latin)				

Timeline of Writers of the Patristic Period

Location	British Isles	Gaul	Spain, Portugal	Rome* and Italy	Carthage and Northern Africa
Period					
5th century	Fastidius (Britain), c. 4th-5th cent. (Latin)	Sulpicius Severus (Bordeaux), c. 360-c. 420/425 (Latin)		Chromatius (Aquileia), fl. 400 (Latin)	Quodvultdeus (Carthage), fl. 430 (Latin)
		John Cassian (Palestine, Egypt, Constantinople, Rome, Marseilles), 360-432 (Latin)		Pelagius (Britain, Rome), c. 354-c. 420 (Greek)	Augustine of Hippo, 354-430 (Latin)
		Vincent of Lérins, d. 435 (Latin)		Maximus of Turin, d. 408/423 (Latin)	Luculentius, 5th cent. (Latin)
		Valerian of Cimiez, fl. c. 422-449 (Latin)		Paulinus of Nola, 355-431 (Latin)	
		Eucherius of Lyons, fl. 420-449 (Latin)		Peter Chrysologus (Ravenna), c. 380-450 (Latin)	
		Hilary of Arles, c. 401-449 (Latin)		Julian of Eclanum, 386-454 (Latin)	
		Eusebius of Gaul, 5th cent. (Latin)		Leo the Great (Rome), regn. 440-461 (Latin)	
		Prosper of Aquitaine, c. 390-c. 463 (Latin)		Arnobius the Younger (Rome), fl. c. 450 (Latin)	
		Salvian the Presbyter of Marseilles, c. 400-c. 480 (Latin)			
		Gennadius of Marseilles, d. after 496 (Latin)			
6th century		Caesarius of Arles, c. 470-543 (Latin)	Paschasius of Dumium (Portugal), c. 515-c. 580 (Latin)	Epiphanius the Latin, late 5th-early 6th cent. (Latin)	Fulgentius of Ruspe, c. 467-532 (Latin)
			Leander of Seville, c. 545-c. 600 (Latin)	Eugippius, c. 460- c. 533 (Latin)	Verecundus, d. 552 (Latin)
			Martin of Braga, fl. 568-579 (Latin)	Benedict of Nursia, c. 480-547 (Latin)	Primasius, fl. 550-560 (Latin)
				Cassiodorus (Calabria), c. 485-c. 540 (Latin)	Facundus of Hermiane, fl. 546-568 (Latin)
				Gregory the Great (Rome), c. 540-604 (Latin)	
7th century				Gregory of Agrigentium, d. 592 (Greek)	
			Isidore of Seville, c. 560-636 (Latin)	Paterius, 6th/7th cent. (Latin)	
			Braulio of Saragossa, c. 585-651 (Latin)		
	Adamnan, c. 624-704 (Latin)		Fructuosus of Braga, d.c. 665 (Latin)		
8th century	Bede the Venerable, c. 672/673-735 (Latin)				

*One of the five ancient patriarchates

Alexandria* and Egypt	Constantinople* and Asia Minor, Greece	Antioch* and Syria	Mesopotamia, Persia	Jerusalem* and Palestine	Location Unknown
Palladius of Helenopolis (Egypt), c. 365-425 (Greek)	Nestorius (Constantinople), c. 381-c. 451 (Greek)	Book of Steps, c. 400 (Syriac)	Eznik of Kolb, fl. 430-450 (Armenian)	Jerome (Rome, Antioch, Bethlehem), c. 347-419 (Latin)	
Cyril of Alexandria, 375-444 (Greek)	Basil of Seleucia, fl. 440-468 (Greek)	Severian of Gabala, fl. c. 400 (Greek)		Hesychius of Jerusalem, fl. 412-450 (Greek)	
Ammonius of Alexandria, c. 460 (Greek)	Diadochus of Photice (Macedonia), 400-474 (Greek)	Nilus of Ancyra, d.c. 430 (Greek)		Euthymius (Palestine), 377-473 (Greek)	
Poemen, 5th cent. (Greek)	Gennadius of Constantinople, d. 471 (Greek)	John of Antioch, d. 441/2 (Greek)		Gerontius of Petra c. 395-c.480 (Syriac)	
		Theodoret of Cyr, c. 393-466 (Greek)			
Besa the Copt, 5th cent.		Pseudo-Victor of Antioch, 5th cent. (Greek)			
Shenoute, c. 350-466 (Coptic)		John of Apamea, 5th cent. (Syriac)			
Olympiodorus early, 6th cent.	Oecumenius (Isauria), 6th cent. (Greek)	Philoxenus of Mabbug (Syria), c. 440-523 (Syriac)	Jacob of Sarug, c. 450-520 (Syriac)	Procopius of Gaza (Palestine), c. 465-530 (Greek)	Pseudo-Dionysius the Areopagite, fl. c. 500 (Greek)
		Severus of Antioch, c. 465-538 (Greek)	Babai the Great, c. 550-628 (Syriac)	Dorotheus of Gaza, fl. 525-540 (Greek)	
		Mark the Hermit (Tarsus), c. 6th cent. (4th cent.?) (Greek)	Babai, early 6th cent. (Syriac)	Cyril of Scythopolis, b. c. 525; d. after 557 (Greek)	
	Maximus the Confessor (Constantinople), c. 580-662 (Greek)	Sahdona/Martyrius, fl. 635-640 (Syriac)	Isaac of Nineveh, d. c. 700 (Syriac)		(Pseudo-) Constantius, before 7th cent.? (Greek)
					Andreas, c. 7th cent. (Greek)
	Theophanes (Nicaea), 775-845 (Greek)	John of Damascus (John the Monk), c. 650-750 (Greek)	John the Elder of Qardu (north Iraq), 8th cent. (Syriac)		
	Cassia (Constantinople), c. 805-c. 848/867 (Greek)		Isho'dad of Merv, d. after 852 (Syriac)		
	Symeon the New Theologian (Constantinople), 949-1022 (Greek)				
	Theophylact of Ohrid (Bulgaria), 1050-1126 (Greek)				

Biographical Sketches & Short Descriptions of Select Anonymous Works

This listing is cumulative, including all the authors and works cited in this series to date.

Acacius of Beroea (c. 340-c. 436). Syrian monk known for his ascetics. He became bishop of Beroea in 378, participated in the council of Constantinople in 381, and played an important role in mediating between Cyril of Alexandria and John of Antioch; however, he did not take part in the clash between Cyril and Nestorius.

Acacius of Caesarea (d. c. 365). Pro-Arian bishop of Caesarea in Palestine, disciple and biographer of Eusebius of Caesarea, the historian. He was a man of great learning and authored a treatise on Ecclesiastes.

Adamnan (c. 624-704). Abbot of Iona, Ireland, and author of the life of St. Columba. He was influential in the process of assimilating the Celtic church into Roman liturgy and church order. He also wrote *On the Holy Sites*, which influenced Bede.

Alexander of Alexandria (fl. 312-328). Bishop of Alexandria and predecessor of Athanasius, on whom he exerted considerable theological influence during the rise of Arianism. Alexander excommunicated Arius, whom he had appointed to the parish of Baucalis, in 319. His teaching regarding the eternal generation and divine substantial union of the Son with the Father was eventually confirmed at the Council of Nicaea (325).

Ambrose of Milan (c. 333-397; fl. 374-397). Bishop of Milan and teacher of Augustine who defended the divinity of the Holy Spirit and the perpetual virginity of Mary.

Ambrosiaster (fl. c. 366-384). Name given by Erasmus to the author of a work once thought to have been composed by Ambrose.

Ammonius (c. fifth century). An Aristotelian commentator and teacher in Alexandria, where he was born and of whose school he became head. Also an exegete of Plato, he enjoyed fame among his contemporaries and successors, although modern critics accuse him of pedantry and banality.

Amphilochius of Iconium (b. c. 340-345, d.c. 398-404). An orator at Constantinople before becoming bishop of Iconium in 373. He was a cousin of Gregory of Nazianzus and active in debates against the Macedonians and Messalians.

Andreas (c. seventh century). Monk who collected commentary from earlier writers to form a catena on various biblical books.

Antony (or Anthony) the Great (c. 251-c. 356). An anchorite of the Egyptian desert and founder of Egyptian monasticism. Athanasius regarded him as the ideal of monastic life, and he has become a model for Christian hagiography.

Aphrahat (c. 270-350 fl. 337-345). "The Persian

Sage" and first major Syriac writer whose work survives. He is also known by his Greek name Aphraates.

Apollinaris of Laodicea (310-c. 392). Bishop of Laodicea who was attacked by Gregory of Nazianzus, Gregory of Nyssa and Theodore for denying that Christ had a human mind.

Aponius/Apponius (fourth–fifth century). Author of a remarkable commentary on Song of Solomon (c. 405-415), an important work in the history of exegesis. The work, which was influenced by the commentaries of Origen and Pseudo-Hippolytus, is of theological significance, especially in the area of Christology.

Apostolic Constitutions (c. 381-394). Also known as *Constitutions of the Holy Apostles* and thought to be redacted by Julian of Neapolis. The work is divided into eight books, and is primarily a collection of and expansion on previous works such as the *Didache* (c. 140) and the *Apostolic Traditions*. Book 8 ends with eighty-five canons from various sources and is elsewhere known as the *Apostolic Canons*.

Arius (fl. c. 320). Heretic condemned at the Council of Nicaea (325) for refusing to accept that the Son was not a creature but was God by nature like the Father.

Arnobius the Younger (fifth century). A participant in christological controversies of the fifth century. He composed *Conflictus cum Serapione*, an account of a debate with a monophysite monk in which he attempts to demonstrate harmony between Roman and Alexandrian theology. Some scholars attribute to him a few more works, such as *Commentaries on Psalms*.

Athanasius of Alexandria (c. 295-373; fl. 325-373). Bishop of Alexandria from 328, though often in exile. He wrote his classic polemics against the Arians while most of the eastern bishops were against him.

Athenagoras (fl. 176-180). Early Christian philosopher and apologist from Athens, whose only authenticated writing, *A Plea Regarding Christians*, is addressed to the emperors Marcus Aurelius and Commodius, and defends Christians from the common accusations of atheism, incest and cannibalism.

Augustine of Hippo (354-430). Bishop of Hippo and a voluminous writer on philosophical, exegetical, theological and ecclesiological topics. He formulated the Western doctrines of predestination and original sin in his writings against the Pelagians.

Babai (c. early sixth century). Author of the Letter to Cyriacus. He should not be confused with either Babai of Nisibis (d. 484), or Babai the Great (d. 628).

Babai the Great (d. 628). Syriac monk who founded a monastery and school in his region of Beth Zabday and later served as third superior at the Great Convent of Mount Izla during a period of crisis in the Nestorian church.

Basil of Seleucia (fl. 444-468). Bishop of Seleucia in Isauria and ecclesiastical writer. He took part in the Synod of Constantinople in 448 for the condemnation of the Eutychian errors and the deposition of their great champion, Dioscurus of Alexandria.

Basil the Great (b. c. 330; fl. 357-379). One of the Cappadocian fathers, bishop of Caesarea and champion of the teaching on the Trinity propounded at Nicaea in 325. He was a great administrator and founded a monastic rule.

Basilides (fl. second century). Alexandrian heretic of the early second century who is said to have believed that souls migrate from body to body and that we do not sin if we lie to protect the body from martyrdom.

Bede the Venerable (c. 672/673-735). Born in Northumbria, at the age of seven he was put under the care of the Benedictine monks of Saints Peter and Paul at Jarrow and given a broad classical education in the monastic tradition. Considered one of the most learned men of his age, he is the author of *An Ecclesiastical History of the English People*.

Benedict of Nursia (c. 480-547). Considered the most important figure in the history of Western monasticism. Benedict founded many monasteries, the most notable found at Montecassino, but his lasting influence lay in his famous Rule. The Rule outlines the theological and inspirational foundation of the monastic ideal while also legislating the shape and organization of the cenobitic life.

Besa the Copt (5th century). Coptic monk, disciple of Shenoute, whom he succeeded as head of the monastery. He wrote numerous letters, monastic catecheses and a biography of Shenoute.

Book of Steps (c. 400). Written by an anonymous Syriac author, this work consists of thirty homilies or discourses which specifically deal with the more advanced stages of growth in the spiritual life.

Braulio of Saragossa (c. 585-651). Bishop of Saragossa (631-651) and noted writer of the Visigothic renaissance. His *Life* of St. Aemilianus is his crowning literary achievement.

Caesarius of Arles (c. 470-543). Bishop of Arles renowned for his attention to his pastoral duties. Among his surviving works the most important is a collection of some 238 sermons that display an ability to preach Christian doctrine to a variety of audiences.

Callistus of Rome (d. 222). Pope (217-222) who excommunicated Sabellius for heresy. It is very probable that he suffered martyrdom.

Cassia (b. c. 805, d. between 848 and 867). Nun, poet and hymnographer who founded a convent in Constantinople.

Cassian, John (360-432). Author of the *Institutes* and the *Conferences*, works purporting to relay the teachings of the Egyptian monastic fathers on the nature of the spiritual life which were highly influential in the development of Western monasticism.

Cassiodorus (c. 485-c. 580). Founder of the monastery of Vivarium, Calabria, where monks transcribed classic sacred and profane texts, Greek and Latin, preserving them for the Western tradition.

Chromatius (fl. 400). Bishop of Aquileia, friend of Rufinus and Jerome and author of tracts and sermons.

Clement of Alexandria (c. 150-215). A highly educated Christian convert from paganism, head of the catechetical school in Alexandria and pioneer of Christian scholarship. His major works, *Protrepticus, Paedagogus* and the *Stromata*, bring Christian doctrine face to face with the ideas and achievements of his time.

Clement of Rome (fl. c. 92-101). Pope whose *Epistle to the Corinthians* is one of the most important documents of subapostolic times.

Commodian (probably third or possibly fifth century). Latin poet of unknown origin (possibly Syrian?) whose two surviving works suggest chiliast and patripassionist tendencies.

Constitutions of the Holy Apostles. See Apostolic Constitutions.

Cyprian of Carthage (fl. 248-258). Martyred bishop of Carthage who maintained that those baptized by schismatics and heretics had no share in the blessings of the church.

Cyril of Alexandria (375-444; fl. 412-444). Patriarch of Alexandria whose extensive exegesis, characterized especially by a strong espousal of the unity of Christ, led to the condemnation of Nestorius in 431.

Cyril of Jerusalem (c. 315-386; fl. c. 348). Bishop of Jerusalem after 350 and author of *Catechetical Homilies*.

Cyril of Scythopolis (b. c. 525; d. after 557). Palestinian monk and author of biographies of famous Palestinian monks. Because of him we have precise knowledge of monastic life in the fifth and sixth centuries and a description of the Origenist crisis and its suppression in the mid-sixth century.

Diadochus of Photice (c. 400-474). Antimonophysite bishop of Epirus Vetus whose work *Discourse on the Ascension of Our Lord Jesus Christ* exerted influence in both the East and West through its Chalcedonian Christology. He is also the subject of the mystical *Vision of St. Diadochus Bishop of Photice in Epirus.*

Didache (c. 140). Of unknown authorship, this text intertwines Jewish ethics with Christian liturgical practice to form a whole discourse on the "way of life." It exerted an enormous amount of influence in the patristic period and was especially used in the training of catechumen.

Didymus the Blind (c. 313-398). Alexandrian

exegete who was much influenced by Origen and admired by Jerome.

Diodore of Tarsus (d. c. 394). Bishop of Tarsus and Antiochene theologian. He authored a great scope of exegetical, doctrinal and apologetic works, which come to us mostly in fragments because of his condemnation as the predecessor of Nestorianism. Diodore was a teacher of John Chrysostom and Theodore of Mopsuestia.

Dionysius of Alexandria (d. c. 264). Bishop of Alexandria and student of Origen. Dionysius actively engaged in the theological disputes of his day, opposed Sabellianism, defended himself against accusations of tritheism and wrote the earliest extant Christian refutation of Epicureanism. His writings have survived mainly in extracts preserved by other early Christian authors.

Dorotheus of Gaza (fl. c. 525-540). Member of Abbot Seridos's monastery and later leader of a monastery where he wrote *Spiritual Instructions.* He also wrote a work on traditions of Palestinian monasticism.

Ephrem the Syrian (b. c. 306; fl. 363-373). Syrian writer of commentaries and devotional hymns which are sometimes regarded as the greatest specimens of Christian poetry prior to Dante.

Epiphanius of Salamis (c. 315-403). Bishop of Salamis in Cyprus, author of a refutation of eighty heresies (the *Panarion*) and instrumental in the condemnation of Origen.

Epiphanius the Latin. Author of the late fifth-century or early sixth century Latin text *Interpretation of the Gospels,* with constant references to early patristic commentators. He was possibly a bishop of Benevento or Seville.

Epistle of Barnabas. See Letter of Barnabas.

Eucherius of Lyons (fl. 420-449). Bishop of Lyons c. 435-449. Born into an aristocratic family, he, along with his wife and sons, joined the monastery at Lérins soon after its founding. He explained difficult Scripture passages by means of a threefold reading of the text: literal, moral and spiritual.

Eugippius (b. 460). Disciple of Severinus and third abbot of the monastic community at Cas-

trum Lucullanum, which was made up of those fleeing from Noricum during the barbarian invasions.

Eunomius (d. 393). Bishop of Cyzicyus who was attacked by Basil and Gregory of Nyssa for maintaining that the Father and the Son were of different natures, one ingenerate, one generate.

Eusebius of Caesarea (c. 260/263-340). Bishop of Caesarea, partisan of the Emperor Constantine and first historian of the Christian church. He argued that the truth of the gospel had been foreshadowed in pagan writings but had to defend his own doctrine against suspicion of Arian sympathies.

Eusebius of Emesa (c. 300-c. 359). Bishop of Emesa from c. 339. A biblical exegete and writer on doctrinal subjects, he displays some semi-Arian tendencies of his mentor Eusebius of Caesarea.

Eusebius of Gaul, or Eusebius Gallicanus (c. fifth century). A conventional name for a collection of seventy-six sermons produced in Gaul and revised in the seventh century. It contains material from different patristic authors and focuses on ethical teaching in the context of the liturgical cycle (days of saints and other feasts).

Eusebius of Vercelli (fl. c. 360). Bishop of Vercelli who supported the trinitarian teaching of Nicaea (325) when it was being undermined by compromise in the West.

Eustathius of Antioch (fl. 325). First bishop of Beroea, then of Antioch, one of the leaders of the anti-Arians at the council of Nicaea. Later, he was banished from his seat and exiled to Thrace for his support of Nicene theology.

Euthymius (377-473). A native of Melitene and influential monk. He was educated by Bishop Otreius of Melitene, who ordained him priest and placed him in charge of all the monasteries in his diocese. When the Council of Chalcedon (451) condemned the errors of Eutyches, it was greatly due to the authority of Euthymius that most of the Eastern recluses accepted its decrees. The empress Eudoxia returned to Chalcedonian orthodoxy through his efforts.

Evagrius of Pontus (c. 345-399). Disciple and

teacher of ascetic life who astutely absorbed and creatively transmitted the spirituality of Egyptian and Palestinian monasticism of the late fourth century. Although Origenist elements of his writings were formally condemned by the Fifth Ecumenical Council (Constantinople II, A.D. 553), his literary corpus continued to influence the tradition of the church.

Eznik of Kolb (early fifth century). A disciple of Mesrob who translated Greek Scriptures into Armenian, so as to become the model of the classical Armenian language. As bishop, he participated in the synod of Astisat (449).

Facundus of Hermiane (fl. 546-568). African bishop who opposed Emperor Justinian's *post mortem* condemnation of Theodore of Mopsuestia, Theodoret of Cyr and Ibas of Ebessa at the fifth ecumenical council. His written defense, known as "To Justinian" or "In Defense of the Three Chapters," avers that ancient theologians should not be blamed for errors tha became obvioust only upon later theological reflection. He continued in the tradition of Chalcedon, although his Christology was supplemented, according to Justinian's decisions, by the theopaschite formula *Unus ex Trinitate passus est* ("Only one of the three suffered").

Fastidius (c. fourth-fifth centuries). British author of *On the Christian Life*. He is believed to have written some works attributed to Pelagius.

Faustinus (fl. 380). A priest in Rome and supporter of Lucifer and author of a treatise on the Trinity.

Faustus of Riez (c. 400-490). A prestigious British monk at Lérins; abbot, then bishop of Riez from 457 to his death. His works include *On the Holy Spirit*, in which he argued against the Macedonians for the divinity of the Holy Spirit, and *On Grace*, in which he argued for a position on salvation that lay between more categorical views of free-will and predestination. Various letters and (pseudonymous) sermons are extant.

The Festal Menaion. Orthodox liturgical text containing the variable parts of the service, including hymns, for fixed days of celebration of the life of Jesus and Mary.

Filastrius (fl. 380). Bishop of Brescia and author of a compilation against all heresies.

Firmicus Maternus (fourth century). An anti-Pagan apologist. Before his conversion to Christianity he wrote a work on astrology (334-337). After his conversion, however, he criticized paganism in *On the Errors of the Profane Religion*.

Fructuosus of Braga (d. c. 665). Son of a Gothic general and member of a noble military family. He became a monk at an early age, then abbot-bishop of Dumium before 650 and metropolitan of Braga in 656. He was influential in setting up monastic communities in Lusitania, Asturia, Galicia and the island of Gades.

Fulgentius of Ruspe (c. 467-532). Bishop of Ruspe and author of many orthodox sermons and tracts under the influence of Augustine.

Gaudentius of Brescia (fl. 395). Successor of Filastrius as bishop of Brescia and author of twenty-one Eucharistic sermons.

Gennadius of Constantinople (d. 471). Patriarch of Constantinople, author of numerous commentaries and an opponent of the Christology of Cyril of Alexandria.

Gerontius (c. 395-c.480). Palestinian monk, later archimandrite of the cenobites of Palestine. He led the resistance to the council of Chalcedon.

Gnostics. Name now given generally to followers of Basilides, Marcion, Valentinus, Mani and others. The characteristic belief is that matter is a prison made for the spirit by an evil or ignorant creator, and that redemption depends on fate, not on free will.

Gregory of Elvira (fl. 359-385). Bishop of Elvira who wrote allegorical treatises in the style of Origen and defended the Nicene faith against the Arians.

Gregory of Nazianzus (b. 329/330; fl. 372-389). Cappadocian father, bishop of Constantinople, friend of Basil the Great and Gregory of Nyssa, and author of theological orations, sermons and poetry.

Gregory of Nyssa (c. 335-394). Bishop of Nyssa and brother of Basil the Great. A Cappadocian father and author of catechetical orations, he was a philosophical theologian of great originality.

Gregory Thaumaturgus (fl. c. 248-264). Bishop of Neocaesarea and a disciple of Origen. There are at least five legendary *Lives* that recount the events and miracles which led to his being called "the wonder worker." His most important work was the *Address of Thanks to Origen,* which is a rhetorically structured panegyric to Origen and an outline of his teaching.

Gregory the Great (c. 540-604). Pope from 590, the fourth and last of the Latin "Doctors of the Church." He was a prolific author and a powerful unifying force within the Latin Church, initiating the liturgical reform that brought about the Gregorian Sacramentary and Gregorian chant.

Hesychius of Jerusalem (fl. 412-450). Presbyter and exegete, thought to have commented on the whole of Scripture.

Hilary of Arles (c. 401-449). Archbishop of Arles and leader of the Semi-Pelagian party. Hilary incurred the wrath of Pope Leo I when he removed a bishop from his see and appointed a new bishop. Leo demoted Arles from a metropolitan see to a bishopric to assert papal power over the church in Gaul.

Hilary of Poitiers (c. 315-367). Bishop of Poitiers and called the "Athanasius of the West" because of his defense (against the Arians) of the common nature of Father and Son.

Hippolytus (fl. 222-245). Recent scholarship places Hippolytus in a Palestinian context, personally familiar with Origen. Though he is known chiefly for *The Refutation of All Heresies,* he was primarily a commentator on Scripture (especially the Old Testament) employing typological exegesis.

Horsiesi (c. 305-c. 390). Pachomius's second successor, after Petronius, as a leader of cenobitic monasticism in Southern Egypt.

Ignatius of Antioch (c. 35-107/112). Bishop of Antioch who wrote several letters to local churches while being taken from Antioch to Rome to be martyred. In the letters, which warn against heresy, he stresses orthodox Christology, the centrality of the Eucharist and unique role of the bishop in preserv-

ing the unity of the church.

Irenaeus of Lyons (c. 135-c. 202). Bishop of Lyons who published the most famous and influential refutation of Gnostic thought.

Isaac of Nineveh (d. c. 700). Also known as Isaac the Syrian or Isaac Syrus, this monastic writer served for a short while as bishop of Nineveh before retiring to live a secluded monastic life. His writings on ascetic subjects survive in the form of numerous homilies.

Isho'dad of Merv (fl. c. 850). Nestorian bishop of Hedatta. He wrote commentaries on parts of the Old Testament and all of the New Testament, frequently quoting Syriac fathers.

Isidore of Seville (c. 560-636). Youngest of a family of monks and clerics, including sister Florentina and brothers Leander and Fulgentius. He was an erudite author of comprehensive scale in matters both religious and sacred, including his encyclopedic *Etymologies.*

Jacob of Nisibis (d. 338). Bishop of Nisibis. He was present at the council of Nicaea in 325 and took an active part in the opposition to Arius.

Jacob of Sarug (c. 450-c. 520). Syriac ecclesiastical writer. Jacob received his education at Edessa. At the end of his life he was ordained bishop of Sarug. His principal writing was a long series of metrical homilies, earning him the title "The Flute of the Holy Spirit."

Jerome (c. 347-420). Gifted exegete and exponent of a classical Latin style, now best known as the translator of the Latin Vulgate. He defended the perpetual virginity of Mary, attacked Origen and Pelagius and supported extreme ascetic practices.

John Chrysostom (344/354-407; fl. 386-407). Bishop of Constantinople who was noted for his orthodoxy, his eloquence and his attacks on Christian laxity in high places.

John of Antioch (d. 441/42). Bishop of Antioch, commencing in 428. He received his education together with Nestorius and Theodore of Mopsuestia in a monastery near Antioch. A supporter of Nestorius, he condemned Cyril of Alexandria, but later reached a compromise with him.

John of Apamea (fifth century). Syriac author of

the early church who wrote on various aspects of the spiritual life, also known as John the Solitary. Some of his writings are in the form of dialogues. Other writings include letters, a treatise on baptism, and shorter works on prayer and silence.

John of Damascus (c. 650-750). Arab monastic and theologian whose writings enjoyed great influence in both the Eastern and Western Churches. His most influential writing was the *Orthodox Faith*.

John the Elder (c. eighth century). A Syriac author who belonged to monastic circles of the Church of the East and lived in the region of Mount Qardu (northern Iraq). His most important writings are twenty-two homilies and a collection of fifty-one short letters in which he describes the mystical life as an anticipatory experience of the resurrection life, the fruit of the sacraments of baptism and the Eucharist.

John the Monk. Traditional name found in *The Festal Menaion*, believed to refer to John of Damascus. *See* John of Damascus.

Josephus, Flavius (c. 37-c. 101). Jewish historian from a distinguished priestly family. Acquainted with the Essenes and Sadducees, he himself became a Pharisee. He joined the great Jewish revolt that broke out in 66 and was chosen by the Sanhedrin at Jerusalem to be commander-in-chief in Galilee. Showing great shrewdness to ingratiate himself with Vespasian by foretelling his elevation and that of his son Titus to the imperial dignity, Josephus was restored his liberty after 69 when Vespasian became emperor.

Julian of Eclanum (c. 385-450). Bishop of Eclanum in 416/417 who was removed from office and exiled in 419 for not officially opposing Pelagianism. In exile, he was accepted by Theodore of Mopsuestia, whose Antiochene exegetical style he followed. Although he was never able to regain his ecclesiastical position, Julian taught in Sicily until his death. His works include commentaries on Job and parts of the Minor Prophets, a translation of Theodore of Mopsuestia's commentary on the Psalms, and various letters. Sympathetic to Pelagius, Julian applied his intel-

lectual acumen and rhetorical training to argue against Augustine on matters such as free will, desire and the locus of evil.

Justin Martyr (c. 100/110-165; fl. c. 148-161). Palestinian philosopher who was converted to Christianity, "the only sure and worthy philosophy." He traveled to Rome where he wrote several apologies against both pagans and Jews, combining Greek philosophy and Christian theology; he was eventually martyred.

Lactantius (c. 260-c. 330). Christian apologist removed from his post as teacher of rhetoric at Nicomedia upon his conversion to Christianity. He was tutor to the son of Constantine and author of *The Divine Institutes*.

Leander (c. 545-c. 600). Latin ecclesiastical writer, of whose works only two survive. He was instrumental in spreading Christianity among the Visigoths, gaining significant historical influence in Spain in his time.

Leo the Great (regn. 440-461). Bishop of Rome whose *Tome to Flavian* helped to strike a balance between Nestorian and Cyrilline positions at the Council of Chalcedon in 451.

Letter of Barnabas (c. 130). An allegorical and typological interpretation of the Old Testament with a decidedly anti-Jewish tone. It was included with other New Testament works as a "Catholic epistle" at least until Eusebius of Caesarea (c. 260/263-340) questioned its authenticity.

Letter to Diognetus (c. third century). A refutation of paganism and an exposition of the Christian life and faith. The author of this letter is unknown, and the exact identity of its recipient, Diognetus, continues to elude patristic scholars.

Lucifer (d. 370/371). Bishop of Cagliari and vigorous supporter of Athanasius and the Nicene Creed. In conflict with the emperor Constantius, he was banished to Palestine and later to Thebaid (Egypt).

Luculentius (fifth century). Unknown author of a group of short commentaries on the New Testament, especially Pauline passages. His exegesis is mainly literal and relies mostly on earlier authors such as Jerome and Augustine. The content of his writing may place it in the fifth century.

Macarius of Egypt (c. 300-c. 390). One of the Desert Fathers. Accused of supporting Athanasius, Macarius was exiled c. 374 to an island in the Nile by Lucius, the Arian successor of Athanasius. Macarius continued his teaching of monastic theology at Wadi Natrun.

Macrina the Younger (c. 327-379). The elder sister of Basil the Great and Gregory of Nyssa, she is known as "the Younger" to distinguish her from her paternal grandmother. She had a powerful influence on her younger brothers, especially on Gregory, who called her his teacher and relates her teaching in *On the Soul and the Resurrection*.

Manichaeans. A religious movement that originated circa 241 in Persia under the leadership of Mani but was apparently of complex Christian origin. It is said to have denied free will and the universal sovereignty of God, teaching that kingdoms of light and darkness are coeternal and that the redeemed are particles of a spiritual man of light held captive in the darkness of matter (*see* Gnostics).

Marcellus of Ancyra (d. c. 375). Wrote a rufutation of Arianism. Later, he was accused of Sabellianism, especially by Eusebius of Caesarea. While the Western church declared him orthodox, the Eastern church excommunicated him. Some scholars have attributed to him certain works of Athanasius.

Marcion (fl. 144). Heretic of the mid-second century who rejected the Old Testament and much of the New Testament, claiming that the Father of Jesus Christ was other than the Old Testament God (*see* Gnostics).

Marius Victorinus (b. c. 280/285; fl. c. 355-363). Grammarian of African origin who taught rhetoric at Rome and translated works of Platonists. After his conversion (c. 355), he wrote against the Arians and commentaries on Paul's letters.

Mark the Hermit (c. sixth century). Monk who lived near Tarsus and produced works on ascetic practices as well as christological issues.

Martin of Braga (fl. c. 568-579). Anti-Arian metropolitan of Braga on the Iberian peninsula.

He was highly educated and presided over the provincial council of Braga in 572.

Martyrius. *See* Sahdona.

Maximus of Turin (d. 408/423). Bishop of Turin. Over one hundred of his sermons survive on Christian festivals, saints and martyrs.

Maximus the Confessor (c. 580-662). Palestinian-born theologian and ascetic writer. Fleeing the Arab invasion of Jerusalem in 614, he took refuge in Constantinople and later Africa. He died near the Black Sea after imprisonment and severe suffering, having his tongue cut off and his right hand mutilated. He taught total preference for God and detachment from all things.

Methodius of Olympus (d. 311). Bishop of Olympus who celebrated virginity in a *Symposium* partly modeled on Plato's dialogue of that name.

Minucius Felix (second or third century). Christian apologist who was an advocate in Rome. His *Octavius* agrees at numerous points with the *Apologeticum* of Tertullian. His birthplace is believed to be in Africa.

Montanist Oracles. Montanism was an apocalyptic and strictly ascetic movement begun in the latter half of the second century by a certain Montanus in Phrygia, who, along with certain of his followers, uttered oracles they claimed were inspired by the Holy Spirit. Little of the authentic oracles remains and most of what is known of Montanism comes from the authors who wrote against the movement. Montanism was formally condemned as a heresy before by Asiatic synods.

Nemesius of Emesa (fl. late fourth century). Bishop of Emesa in Syria whose most important work, *Of the Nature of Man*, draws on several theological and philosophical sources and is the first exposition of a Christian anthropology.

Nestorius (c. 381-c. 451). Patriarch of Constantinople (428-431) who founded the heresy which says that there are two persons, divine and human, rather than one person truly united in the incarnate Christ. He resisted the teaching of *theotokos*, causing Nestorian churches to separate from Constantinople.

Nicetas of Remesiana (fl. second half of fourth

century). Bishop of Remesiana in Serbia, whose works affirm the consubstantiality of the Son and the deity of the Holy Spirit.

Nilus of Ancyra (d. c. 430). Prolific ascetic writer and disciple of John Chrysostom. Sometimes erroneously known as Nilus of Sinai, he was a native of Ancyra and studied at Constantinople.

Novatian of Rome (fl. 235-258). Roman theologian, otherwise orthodox, who formed a schismatic church after failing to become pope. His treatise on the Trinity states the classic western doctrine.

Oecumenius (sixth century). Called the Rhetor or the Philosopher, Oecumenius wrote the earliest extant Greek commentary on Revelation. Scholia by Oecumenius on some of John Chrysostom's commentaries on the Pauline Epistles are still extant.

Olympiodorus (early sixth century). Exegete and deacon of Alexandria, known for his commentaries that come to us mostly in catenae.

Origen of Alexandria (b. 185; fl. c. 200-254). Influential exegete and systematic theologian. He was condemned (perhaps unfairly) for maintaining the preexistence of souls while purportedly denying the resurrection of the body. His extensive works of exegesis focus on the spiritual meaning of the text.

Pachomius (c. 292-347). Founder of cenobitic monasticism. A gifted group leader and author of a set of rules, he was defended after his death by Athanasius of Alexandria.

Pacian of Barcelona (c. fourth century). Bishop of Barcelona whose writings polemicize against popular pagan festivals as well as Novatian schismatics.

Palladius of Helenopolis (c. 363/364-c. 431). Bishop of Helenopolis in Bithynia (400-417) and then Aspuna in Galatia. A disciple of Evagrius of Pontus and admirer of Origen, Palladius became a zealous adherent of John Chrysostom and shared his troubles in 403. His *Lausaic History* is the leading source for the history of early monasticism, stressing the spiritual value of the life of the desert.

Paschasius of Dumium (c. 515-c. 580). Translator of sentences of the Desert Fathers from Greek into Latin while a monk in Dumium.

Paterius (c. sixth-seventh century). Disciple of Gregory the Great who is primarily responsible for the transmission of Gregory's works to many later medieval authors.

Paulinus of Milan (late 4th-early 5th century). Personal secretary and biographer of Ambrose of Milan. He took part in the Pelagian controversy.

Paulinus of Nola (355-431). Roman senator and distinguished Latin poet whose frequent encounters with Ambrose of Milan (c. 333-397) led to his eventual conversion and baptism in 389. He eventually renounced his wealth and influential position and took up his pen to write poetry in service of Christ. He also wrote many letters to, among others, Augustine, Jerome and Rufinus.

Paulus Orosius (b. c. 380). An outspoken critic of Pelagius, mentored by Augustine. His *Seven Books of History Against the Pagans* was perhaps the first history of Christianity.

Pelagius (c. 354-c. 420). Contemporary of Augustine whose followers were condemned in 418 and 431 for maintaining that even before Christ these were people who lived wholly without sin and that salvation depended on free will.

Peter Chrysologus (c. 380-450). Latin archbishop of Ravenna whose teachings included arguments for adherence in matters of faith to the Roman see, and the relationship between grace and Christian living.

Peter of Alexandria (d. c. 311). Bishop of Alexandria. He marked (and very probably initiated) the reaction at Alexandria against extreme doctrines of Origen. During the persecution of Christians in Alexandria, Peter was arrested and beheaded by Roman officials. Eusebius of Caesarea described him as "a model bishop, remarkable for his virtuous life and his ardent study of the Scriptures."

Philo of Alexandria (c. 20 B.C.-c. A.D. 50). Jewish-born exegete who greatly influenced Christian patristic interpretation of the Old Testament. Born to a rich family in Alexandria,

Philo was a contemporary of Jesus and lived an ascetic and contemplative life that makes some believe he was a rabbi. His interpretation of Scripture based the spiritual sense on the literal. Although influenced by Hellenism, Philo's theology remains thoroughly Jewish.

Philoxenus of Mabbug (c. 440-523). Bishop of Mabbug (Hierapolis) and a leading thinker in the early Syrian Orthodox Church. His extensive writings in Syriac include a set of thirteen *Discourses on the Christian Life*, several works on the incarnation and a number of exegetical works.

Poemen (c. fifth century). One-seventh of the sayings in the *Sayings of the Desert Fathers* are attributed to Poemen, which is Greek for shepherd. Poemen was a common title among early Egyptian desert ascetics, and it is unknown whether all of the sayings come from one person.

Polycarp of Smyrna (c. 69-155). Bishop of Smyrna who vigorously fought heretics such as the Marcionites and Valentinians. He was the leading Christian figure in Roman Asia in the middle of the second century.

Potamius of Lisbon (fl. c. 350-360). Bishop of Lisbon who joined the Arian party in 357, but later returned to the Catholic faith (c. 359?). His works from both periods are concerned with the larger Trinitarian debates of his time.

Primasius (fl. 550-560). Bishop of Hadrumetum in North Africa (modern Tunisia) and one of the few Africans to support the condemnation of the Three Chapters. Drawing on Augustine and Tyconius, he wrote a commentary on the Apocalypse, which in allegorizing fashion views the work as referring to the history of the church.

Procopius of Gaza (c. 465-c. 530). A Christian exegete educated in Alexandria. He wrote numerous theological works and commentaries on Scripture (particularly the Hebrew Bible), the latter marked by the allegorical exegesis for which the Alexandrian school was known.

Prosper of Aquitaine (c. 390-c. 463). Probably a lay monk and supporter of the theology of Augustine on grace and predestination. He collaborated closely with Pope Leo I in his doctrinal statements.

Prudentius (c. 348-c. 410). Latin poet and hymn-writer who devoted his later life to Christian writing. He wrote didactic poems on the theology of the incarnation, against the heretic Marcion and against the resurgence of paganism.

Pseudo-Clementines (third-fourth century). A series of apocryphal writings pertaining to a conjured life of Clement of Rome. Written in a form of popular legend, the stories from Clement's life, including his opposition to Simon Magus, illustrate and promote articles of Christian teaching. It is likely that the corpus is a derivative of a number of Gnostic and Judeo-Christian writings. Dating the corpus is a complicated issue.

Pseudo-Dionysius the Areopagite (fl. c. 500). Author who assumed the name of Dionysius the Areopagite mentioned in Acts 17:34, and who composed the works known as the *Corpus Areopagiticum* (or *Dionysiacum*). These writings were the foundation of the apophatic school of mysticism in their denial that anything can be truly predicated of God.

Pseudo-Macarius (fl. c. 390). An anonymous writer and ascetic (from Mesopotamia?) active in Antioch whose badly edited works were attributed to Macarius of Egypt. He had keen insight into human nature, prayer and the inner life. His work includes some one hundred discourses and homilies.

Quodvultdeus (fl. 430). Carthaginian bishop and friend of Augustine who endeavored to show at length how the New Testament fulfilled the Old Testament.

Rufinus of Aquileia (c. 345-411). Orthodox Christian thinker and historian who nonetheless translated and preserved the works of Origen, and defended him against the strictures of Jerome and Epiphanius. He lived the ascetic life in Rome, Egypt and Jerusalem (the Mount of Olives).

Sabellius (fl. 200). Allegedly the author of the heresy which maintains that the Father and Son are a single person. The patripassian variant of this heresy states that the Father suffered on the cross.

Sahdona (fl. 635-640). Known in Greek as Martyrius, this Syriac author was bishop of Beth

Garmai. He studied in Nisibis and was exiled for his christological ideas. His most important work is the deeply scriptural *Book of Perfection* which ranks as one of the masterpieces of Syriac monastic literature.

Salvian the Presbyter of Marseilles (c. 400-c. 480). An important author for the history of his own time. He saw the fall of Roman civilization to the barbarians as a consequence of the reprehensible conduct of Roman Christians. In *The Governance of God* he developed the theme of divine providence.

Second Letter of Clement (c. 150). The so-called *Second Letter of Clement* is an early Christian sermon probably written by a Corinthian author, though some scholars have assigned it to a Roman or Alexandrian author.

Severian of Gabala (fl. c. 400). A contemporary of John Chrysostom, he was a highly regarded preacher in Constantinople, particularly at the imperial court, and ultimately sided with Chrysostom's accusers. He wrote homilies on Genesis.

Severus of Antioch (fl. 488-538). A monophysite theologian, consecrated bishop of Antioch in 522. Born in Pisidia, he studied in Alexandria and Beirut, taught in Constantinople and was exiled to Egypt.

Shenoute (c. 350-466). Abbot of Athribis in Egypt. His large monastic community was known for very strict rules. He accompanied Cyril of Alexandria to the Council of Ephesus in 431, where he played an important role in deposing Nestorius. He knew Greek but wrote in Coptic, and his literary activity includes homilies, catecheses on monastic subjects, letters, and a couple of theological treatises.

Shepherd of Hermas (second century). Divided into five *Visions,* twelve *Mandates* and ten *Similitudes,* this Christian apocalypse was written by a former slave and named for the form of the second angel said to have granted him his visions. This work was highly esteemed for its moral value and was used as a textbook for catechumens in the early church.

Sulpicius Severus (c. 360-c. 420). An ecclesiastical writer from Bordeaux born of noble parents. Devoting himself to monastic retirement, he became a personal friend and enthusiastic disciple of St. Martin of Tours.

Symeon the New Theologian (c. 949-1022). Compassionate spiritual leader known for his strict rule. He believed that the divine light could be perceived and received through the practice of mental prayer.

Tertullian of Carthage (c. 155/160-225/250; fl. c. 197-222). Brilliant Carthaginian apologist and polemicist who laid the foundations of Christology and trinitarian orthodoxy in the West, though he himself was later estranged from the catholic tradition due to its laxity.

Theodore of Heraclea (d. c. 355). An anti-Nicene bishop of Thrace. He was part of a team seeking reconciliation between Eastern and Western Christianity. In 343 he was excommunicated at the council of Sardica. His writings focus on a literal interpretation of Scripture.

Theodore of Mopsuestia (c. 350-428). Bishop of Mopsuestia, founder of the Antiochene, or literalistic, school of exegesis. A great man in his day, he was later condemned as a precursor of Nestorius.

Theodore of Tabennesi (d. 368) Vice general of the Pachomian monasteries (c. 350-368) under Horsiesi. Several of his letters are known.

Theodoret of Cyr (c. 393-466). Bishop of Cyr (Cyrrhus), he was an opponent of Cyril who commented extensively on Old Testament texts as a lucid exponent of Antiochene exegesis.

Theodotus the Valentinian (second century). Likely a Montanist who may have been related to the Alexandrian school. Extracts of his work are known through writings of Clement of Alexandria.

Theophanes (775-845). Hymnographer and bishop of Nicaea (842-845). He was persecuted during the second iconoclastic period for his support of the Seventh Council (Second Council of Nicaea, 787). He wrote many hymns in the tradition of the monastery of Mar Sabbas that were used in the *Paraklitiki.*

Theophilus of Antioch (late second century).

Bishop of Antioch. His only surviving work is *Ad Autholycum*, where we find the first Christian commentary on Genesis and the first use of the term *Trinity*. Theophilus's apologetic literary heritage had influence on Irenaeus and possibly Tertullian.

Theophylact of Ohrid (c. 1050-c. 1108). Byzantine archbishop of Ohrid (or Achrida) in what is now Bulgaria. Drawing on earlier works, he wrote commentaries on several Old Testament books and all of the New Testament except for Revelation.

Valentinus (fl. c. 140). Alexandrian heretic of the mid-second century who taught that the material world was created by the transgression of God's Wisdom, or Sophia (*see* Gnostics).

Valerian of Cimiez (fl. c. 422-439). Bishop of Cimiez. He participated in the councils of Riez (439) and Vaison (422) with a view to strengthening church discipline. He supported Hilary of Arles in quarrels with Pope Leo I.

Verecundus (d. 552). An African Christian writer, who took an active part in the christological controversies of the sixth century, especially in the debate on Three Chapters. He also wrote allegorical commentaries on the nine liturgical church canticles.

Victorinus of Petovium (d. c. 304). Latin biblical exegete. With multiple works attributed to him, his sole surviving work is the *Commentary on the Apocalypse* and perhaps some fragments from *Commentary on Matthew*. Victorinus expressed strong millenarianism in his writing, though his was less materialistic than the millenarianism of Papias or Irenaeus. In his allegorical approach he could be called a spiritual disciple of Origen. Victorinus died during the first year of Diocletian's persecution, probably in 304.

Vincent of Lérins (d. before 450). Monk who has exerted considerable influence through his writings on orthodox dogmatic theological method, as contrasted with the theological methodologies of the heresies.

Bibliography of Works
in Original Languages

This bibliography refers readers to original language sources and supplies Thesaurus Linguae Graecae (=TLG) or Cetedoc Clavis (=Cl.) numbers where available. The edition listed in this bibliography may in some cases differ from the edition found in TLG or Cetedoc databases.

Acacius of Beroea. *Concilium universale Ephesenum anno*. See Cyril of Alexandria.

Ambrose. "De bono mortis." In *Sancti Ambrosii opera*. Edited by Karl Schenkl. CSEL 32, pt. 1, pp. 701-53. Vienna, Austria: F. Tempsky; Leipzig, Germany: G. Freytag, 1897. Cl. 0129.

———. "De Cain et Abel." In *Sancti Ambrosii opera*. Edited by Karl Schenkl. CSEL 32, pt. 1, pp. 337-409. Vienna, Austria: F. Tempsky; Leipzig, Germany: G. Freytag, 1897. Cl. 0125.

———. "De excessu fratris Satyri." In *Sancti Ambrosii opera*. Edited by Otto Faller. CSEL 73, pp. 207-325. Vienna, Austria: Hoelder-Pichler-Tempsky, 1955. Cl. 0157.

———. "De fide libri v." In *Sancti Ambrosii opera*. Edited by Otto Faller. CSEL 78. Vienna, Austria: Hoelder-Pichler-Tempsky, 1962. Cl. 0150.

———. "De fuga saeculi." In *Sancti Ambrosii opera*. Edited by Karl Schenkl. CSEL 32, pt. 2, pp. 161-207. Vienna, Austria: F. Tempsky; Leipzig, Germany: G. Freytag, 1897. Cl. 0133.

———. "De interpellatione Job et David." In *Sancti Ambrosii opera*. Edited by Karl Shenkl. CSEL 32, pt. 2, pp. 209-96. Vienna, Austria: F. Tempsky; Leipzig, Germany: G. Freytag, 1897. Cl. 0134.

———. "De Isaac vel anima." In *Sancti Ambrosii opera*. Edited by Karl Schenkl. CSEL 32, pt. 1, pp. 639-700. Vienna, Austria: F. Tempsky; Leipzig, Germany: G. Freytag, 1897. Cl. 0128.

———. "De Jacob et vita beata." In *Sancti Ambrosii opera*. Edited by Karl Schenkl. CSEL 32, pt. 2, pp. 1-70. Vienna, Austria: F. Tempsky; Leipzig, Germany: G. Freytag, 1897. Cl. 0130.

———. "De mysteriis." In *Sancti Ambrosii opera*. Edited by Otto Faller. CSEL 73, pp. 87-116. Vienna, Austria: Hoelder-Pichler-Tempsky, 1955. Cl. 0155.

———. "De obitu Theodosii." In *Sancti Ambrosii opera*. Edited by Otto Faller. CSEL 73, pp. 371-401. Vienna, Austria: Hoelder-Pichler-Tempsky, 1955. Cl. 0159.

———. "De obitu Valentiniani." In *Sancti Ambrosii opera*. Edited by Otto Faller. CSEL 73, pp. 329-67. Vienna, Austria: Hoelder-Pichler-Tempsky, 1955. Cl. 0158.

———. *De officiis*. In *Ambrosii mediolanensis opera*. Edited by Maurice Testard. Turnhout, Belgium: Brepols, 2000. Cl. 0144.

———. *De paenitentia*. Edited by R. Gryson. SC 179. Paris: Éditions du Cerf, 1971. Cl. 0156.

———. "De spiritu sancto." In *Sancti Ambrosii opera*. Edited by Otto Faller. CSEL 79, pp. 5-222. Vienna, Austria: Hoelder-Pichler-Tempsky, 1964. Cl. 0151.

———. *De virginibus*. Italian and Latin. Translated with introduction, notes and appendixes by Franco Gori. Milan: Biblioteca Ambrosiana; Rome: Città Nuova, 1989. Cl. 0145.

———. *De virginitate*. Edited Egnatius Cazzaniga. Corpus Scriptorum Latinorum Paravianum. Turin: In Aedibus Io. Bapt. Paraviae et Sociorum, 1954. Cl. 0147.

———. "Epistulae; Epistulae extra collectionem traditae." In *Sancti Ambrosii opera*. Edited by Otto Faller and M. Zelzer. CSEL 82. Vienna, Austria: Hoelder-Pichler-Tempsky, 1968. Cl. 0160.

———. "Exameron." In *Sancti Ambrosii opera*. Edited by Karl Schenkl. CSEL 32, pt. 1, pp. 1-261. Vienna,

Austria: F. Tempsky; Leipzig, Germany: G. Freytag, 1897. Cl. 0123.

Aphrahat. "Demonstrationes (IV)" In *Opera omnia*. Edited by R. Graffin. Patrologia Syriaca 1, cols. 137-82. Paris: Firmin-Didor, 1910.

Apocalypsis Esdrae. In *Apocalypses Apocryphae: Mosis, Esdrae, Pauli, Johanni, item Mariae dormitio, additis Evangeliorum et actuum Apocryphorum supplementis*, pp. 24-33. Edited by Konstantin von Tischendorf. Hildesheim, Germany: Georg Olms, 1866.

Aponius. "In Canticum canticorum expositio." In *Apponii: In Canticum Canticorum Expositionem*. Edited by B. de Vregille and L. Neyrand. CCL 19, pp. 1-311. Turnhout, Belgium: Brepols, 1986. Cl. 0194.

Athanasius. "Apologia ad Constantium imperatorem." In *Athanase d'Alexandrie: Apologie à l'empereur Constance; Apologie pour sa fuite*. Edited by Jan M. Szymusiak. SC 56, pp. 88-132. Paris: Éditions du Cerf, 1958. TLG 2035.011.

————. "Apologia de fuga sua." In *Athanase d'Alexandrie: Apologie à l'empereur Constance; Apologie pour sa fuite*. Edited by Jan M. Szymusiak. SC 56, pp. 133-67. Paris: Éditions du Cerf, 1958. TLG 2035.012.

————. "Contra gentes." In *Athanasius: Contra gentes and de incarnatione*, pp. 2-132. Edited by Robert W. Thomson. Oxford: Clarendon Press, 1971. TLG 2035.001.

————. "De decretis Nicaenae synodi." In *Athanasius Werke*. Vol. 2.1, pp. 1-45. Edited by Hans-Georg Opitz. Berlin: Walter de Gruyter, 1940. TLG 2035.003.

————. "Epistula ad Adelphium." In *Opera omnia*. PG 26, cols. 1072-84. Edited by J.-P. Migne. Paris: Migne, 1887. TLG 2035.050.

————. "Epistula ad episcopos Aegypti et Libyae." In *Opera omnia*. PG 25, cols. 537-93. Edited by J.-P. Migne. Paris: Migne, 1857. TLG 2035.041.

————. "Epistula ad Jovianum." In *Opera omnia*. PG 26, cols. 11-526. Edited by J.-P. Migne. Paris: Migne, 1887. TLG 2035.119.

————. "Epistulae ad monachus." In *Athanasius Werke*. Vol. 2.1, pp. 181-82. Edited by Hans-Georg Opitz. Berlin: Walter de Gruyter, 1940. TLG 2035.008.

————. "Epistulae festalis." In *Opera omnia*. PG 26, cols. 1351-444. Edited by J.-P. Migne. Paris: Migne, 1887. TLG 2035.014.

————. "Expositio fidei." *See* Marcellus.

————. "Orationes tres contra Arianos." In *Opera omnia*. PG 26, cols. 813-920. Edited by J.-P. Migne. Paris: Migne, 1887. TLG 2035.042.

————. "Vita sancti Antonii." In *Opera omnia*. PG 26, cols. 835-976. Edited by J.-P. Migne. Paris: Migne, 1857. TLG 2035.047.

Athenagorus. *Legatio sive Supplicatio pro Christianis*. In *Legatio and De Resurrectione*, pp. 2-86. Edited by William R. Schoedel. Oxford: Clarendon Press, 1972.

Augustine. "Adversus Judaeos." In *Opera omnia*. PL 42, cols. 51-64. Edited by J.-P. Migne. Paris, Migne, 1861. Cl. 0315.

————. *Confessionum libri tredecim*. Edited by L. Verheijen. CCL 27. Turnhout, Belgium: Brepols, 1981. Cl. 0251.

————. "Contra duas epistulas pelagianorum." Edited by Karl Franz Urba and Joseph Zycha. CSEL 60, pp. 423-570. Vienna, Austria: F. Tempsky; Leipzig, Germany: G. Freytag, 1913. Cl. 0346.

————. "Contra Faustum." In *Sancti Aurelii Augustini*. Edited by Joseph Zycha. CSEL 25, pp. 249-797. Vienna, Austria: F. Tempsky; Leipzig, Germany: G. Freytag, 1891. Cl. 0321.

————. "Contra Julianum." In *Opera omnia*. Edited by J.-P. Migne. PL 44, cols. 641-874. Paris: Migne, 1861. Cl. 0351.

————. "De bono viduitatis." In *Sancti Aureli Augustini opera*. Edited by J. Zycha. CSEL 41, pp. 303-43. Vienna, Austria: F. Tempsky, 1900. Cl. 0301

————. *De civitate Dei*. In *Aurelii Augustini opera*. Edited by Bernhard Dombart and Alphons Kalb. CCL 47-48. Turnhout, Belgium: Brepols, 1955. Cl. 0313.

————. "De diversis quaestionibus octoginta tribus." In *Aurelii Augustini opera*. Edited by Almut Mutzenbecher. CCL 44A, pp. 11-249. Turnhout, Belgium: Brepols, 1975. Cl. 0289.

————. "De doctrina christiana." In *Aurelii Augustini opera*. Edited by Joseph Martin. CCL 32, pp. 1-167. Turnhout, Belgium: Brepols, 1962. Cl. 0263.

————. "De gratia et libero arbitrio." In *Opera omnia*. PL 44, cols. 881-912. Edited by J.-P. Migne. Paris: Migne, 1861. Cl. 0352.

————. "De natura et gratia." In *Sancti Aurelii Augustini De peccatorum meritis et remissione et de baptismo parvulorum ad Marcellinum libri tres, De spiritu et littera liber unus, De natura et gratia liber unus, De natura et origine animae libri quattuor*. Edited by Karl Franz Urba and Joseph Zycha. CSEL 60, pp. 233-99. Vienna, Austria: F. Tempsky; Leipzig, Germany: G. Freytag, 1913. Cl. 0344.

————. "De praedestinatione sanctorum." In *Opera omnia*. PL 44, cols. 959-92. Edited by J.-P. Migne. Paris: Migne, 1861. Cl. 0354.

————. "De sancta virginitate." In *Sancti Aureli Augustini opera*. Edited by J. Zycha. CSEL 41, pp. 235-302. Vienna, Austria: F. Tempsky, 1900. Cl. 0300.

————. "De sermone Domini in monte." In *Aurelii Augustini opera*. Edited by Almut Mutzenbecher. CCL 35. Turnhout, Belgium: Brepols, 1967. Cl. 0274.

————. "De spiritu et littera." In *Sancti Aurelii Augustini De peccatorum meritis et remissione et de baptismo parvulorum ad Marcellinum libri tres, De spiritu et littera liber unus, De natura et gratia liber unus, De natura et origine animae libri quattuor*. Edited by Karl Franz Urba and Joseph Zycha. CSEL 60, pp. 155-229. Vienna, Austria: F. Tempsky; Leipzig, Germany: G. Freytag, 1913. Cl. 0343.

————. "De Trinitate." In *Aurelii Augustini opera*. Edited by W. J. Mountain. CCL 50-50A. Turnhout, Belgium: Brepols, 1968. Cl. 0329.

————. "De vera religione." In *Aurelii Augustini opera*. Edited by K. D. Daur. CCL 32, pp. 169-260. Turnhout, Belgium: Brepols, 1962. Cl. 0264.

————. "De vita christiana." In *Augustini opera omnia*. PL 40, cols. 1031-46. Edited by J.-P. Migne. Paris: Migne, 1861. Cl. 0730.

————. "Enarrationes in Psalmos." 3 vols. In *Aurelii Augustini opera*. Edited by D. E. Dekkers and John Fraipont. CCL 38, 39 and 40. Turnhout, Belgium: Brepols, 1956. Cl. 0283.

————. "Enchiridion de fide, spe et caritate." In *Aurelii Augustini opera*. Edited by E. Evans. CCL 46, pp. 49-114. Turnhout, Belgium: Brepols, 1969. Cl. 0295.

————. "Epistulae." In *Sancti Aurelii Augustini opera*. Edited by A. Goldbacher. CCL 34, pts. 1, 2. Turnhout, Belgium: Brepols, 1895. Cl. 0262.

————. "In Johannis evangelium tractatus." In *Aurelii Augustini opera*. Edited by R. Willems. CCL 36. Turnhout, Belgium: Brepols, 1954. Cl. 0278.

————. "Sermones." In *Augustini opera omnia*. PL 38 and 39. Edited by J.-P. Migne. Paris: Migne, 1844-1865. Cl. 0284.

Babai. "Letter to Cyriacus." In *Martyànutà d-abāhàta d-ᶜidtä (Admonition of the Fathers of the Church)*. Edited by Sebastian Brock and Metropolitan Mar Yulios Çiçek. Holland: St. Ephrem the Syrian Monastery, 1985.

Basil the Great. *Asceticon magnum sive Quaestiones [regulae fusius tractatae]*. In *Opera omnia*. PG 31, cols. 1052-305. Edited by J.-P. Migne. Paris: Migne, 1885. TLG 2040.050.

————. "De humilitate." In *Opera omnia*. PG 31, cols. 525-40. Edited by J.-P. Migne. Paris: Migne, 1885. TLG 2040.036.

————. *De spiritu sancto*. In *Basile de Césarée: Sur le Saint-Esprit*. Edited by Benoit Pruche. SC 17. Paris:

Éditions du Cerf, 2002. TLG 2040.003.

———. *Homilia de invidia*. In *Opera omnia*. PG 31, cols. 372-85. Edited by J.-P. Migne. Paris: Migne, 1885. TLG 2040.027.

———. *Homilia de misericordia et judicio [Sp.]*. In *Opera omnia*. PG 31, cols. 1705-14. Edited by J.-P. Migne. Paris: Migne, 1885. TLG 2040.069.

———. *Homilia in illud: Attende tibi ipsi*. In *L'homélie de Basile de Césarée sur le mot 'observe-toi toi-même'*, pp. 23-37. Edited by Stig Y. Rudberg. Stockholm: Almqvist & Wiksell, 1962. TLG 2040.006.

———. "Homilia in principium Proverbiorum." In *Opera omnia*. PG 31, cols. 385-424. Edited by J.-P. Migne. Paris: Migne, 1885. TLG 2040.028.

———. *Homiliae super Psalmos*. In *Opera omnia*. PG 29, cols. 209-494. J.-P. Migne. Paris: Migne, 1886. TLG 2040.018.

———. *Prologus 8 [de fide]*. In *Opera omnia*. PG 31, cols. 676-92. Edited by J.-P. Migne. Paris: Migne, 1885. TLG 2040.045.

———. *Prologus 4 [prooemium in asceticum magnum]*. In *Opera omnia*. PG 31, cols. 889-901. Edited by J.-P. Migne. Paris: Migne, 1885. TLG 2040.047.

———. *Sermo 11 (sermo asceticus et exhortatio de renuntiatione mundi) (Dub)*. In *Opera omnia*. PG 31, cols. 625-48. Edited by J.-P. Migne. Paris: Migne, 1885. TLG 2040.041.

Bede. "De tabernaculo et vasis eius ac vestibus sacerdotum libri iii." In *Bedae opera*. Edited by D. Hurst. CCL 119A, pp. 5-139. Cl. 1345.

———. "Expositio actuum apostolorum." In *Bedae opera*. Edited M. L. W. Laistner. CCL 121, pp. 3-99. Turnhout, Belgium: Brepols, 1983. Cl. 1357.

———. "Homiliarum evangelii." In *Bedae opera*. Edited by D. Hurst. CCL 122, pp. 1-378. Turnhout, Belgium: Brepols, 1956. Cl. 1367.

———. "In Cantica canticorum libri vi." In *Bedae opera*. Edited by D. Hurst. CCL 119B, pp. 165-375. Turnhout, Belgium: Brepols, 1983. Cl. 1353.

———. *In epistulam septem catholicas*. In *Bedae opera*. Edited by D. Hurst. CCL 121, pp.181-342. Turnhout, Belgium: Brepols, 1983. Cl. 1362.

———. "In proverbia Salomonis libri iii." In *Bedae opera*. Edited by D. Hurst. CCL 119B, pp. 21-163. Turnhout, Belgium: Brepols, 1983. Cl. 1351.

Benedict (of Nursia). "Regula." In *La règle de saint Benoît*. Edited by Adalbert de Vogüé and Jean Neufville. 2 vols. SC 181, pp. 412-90; SC 182, pp. 508-674. Paris: Éditions du Cerf, 1971-1977. Cl. 1852.

Barnabae epistula. In *Épître de Barnabé*. Edited by Pierre Prigent and Robert A. Kraft. SC 172, pp. 72-218. Paris: Éditions du Cerf, 1971. TLG 1216.001.

Besa. "Epistulae et Sermones." 2 vols. Edited by K. H. Kuhn. CSCO 157, 158 (Scriptores Coptici 21, 22). Louvain, Belgium: Imprimerie Orientaliste L. Durbecq, 1956.

Braulio of Saragosa. "Epistulae." In *Scriptorum ecclesiasticorum, opera omnia*. PL 80, cols. 649-700. Edited by J.-P. Migne. Paris: Migne, 1864.

Caesarius of Arles. *Sermones Caesarii Arelatensis*. 2 vols. Edited by Germain Morin. CCL 103-104. Turnhout, Belgium: Brepols, 1953. Cl. 1008.

Cassian, John. "Collationes xxiii." Edited by Michael Petshenig. CSEL 13. Vienna, Austria: F. Tempsky, 1886. Cl. 0512.

———. "De institutis coenobiorum et de octo principalium vitiorum remediis." In *Johannis Cassiani*. Edited by Michael Petschenig. CSEL 17, pp. 1-231. Vienna, Austria: F. Tempsky; Leipzig, Germany: G. Freytag, 1888. Cl. 0513.

Cassiodorus. *Expositio Psalmorum*, 2 vols. Edited by Marcus Adriaen. CCL 97 and 98. Turnhout: Brepols, 1958. Cl. 0900.

Clement of Alexandria. *Eclogae prophetica*. In *Clemens Alexandrinus*. Vol. 3, 2nd. ed. Edited by Otto Stäh-lin, Ludwig Früchtel and Ursula Treu. GCS 17, pp. 137-55. Berlin: Akademie-Verlag, 1970. TLG 0555.005.

———. "Paedagogus." In *Le pédagogue [par] Clement d'Alexandrie*. 3 vols. Translated by Mauguerite Harl, Chantel Matray and Claude Mondésert. Introduction and notes by Henri-Irénée Marrou. SC 70, 108, 158. Paris: Éditions du Cerf, 1960-1970. TLG 0555.002.

———. "Stromata." In *Clemens Alexandrinus*. Vol. 2, 3rd ed., and vol. 3, 2nd ed. Edited by Otto Stählin, Ludwig Früchtel and Ursula Treu. GCS 15, pp. 3-518 and GCS 17, pp. 1-102. Berlin: Akademie-Ver-lag, 1960-1970. TLG 0555.004.

Clement of Rome. "Epistula i ad Corinthios." In *Clément de Rome: Épître aux Corinthiens*. Edited by Annie Jaubert. SC 167. Paris: Éditions du Cerf, 1971. TLG 1271.001.

"Constitutiones apostolorum." In *Les constitutions apostoliques*. 3 vols. Edited by M. Metzger. SC 320, pp. 100-338; SC 329, pp. 116-394; SC 336, pp. 18-310. Paris: Éditions du Cerf, 1985-1987. TLG 2894.001.

Cyprian. "Ad Demetrianum." In *Sancti Cypriani episcopi opera*. Edited by Manlio Simonetti. CCL 3A, pp. 35-51. Turnhout, Belgium: Brepols, 1976. Cl. 0046.

———. "De dominica oratione." In *Sancti Cypriani episcopi opera*. Edited by C. Moreschini. CCL 3A, pp. 87-113. Turnhout, Belgium: Brepols, 1976. Cl. 0043.

———. "De ecclesiae catholicae unitate." In *Sancti Cypriani episcopi opera*. Edited by Maurice Bévenot. CCL 3, pp. 249-68. Turnhout, Belgium: Brepols, 1972. Cl. 0041.

———. "De habitu virginum." In *S. Thasci Caecili Cypriani opera omnia*. Edited by William Hartel. CSEL 3.1, pp. 185-205. Vienna, Austria: Gerold, 1868. Cl. 0040.

———. "De opera et eleemosynis." In *Sancti Cypriani episcopi opera*. Edited by Manlio Simonetti. CCL 3A, pp. 53-72. Turnhout, Belgium: Brepols, 1976. Cl. 0047.

———. *Epistulae*. Edited by G. F. Diercks. CCL 3B, 3C. Turnhout, Belgium: Brepols, 1994-1996. Cl. 0050.

Cyril of Alexandria. "Commentarii in Lucam (in catenis)." In *Opera omnia*. PG 72, cols. 476-949. Edited by J.-P. Migne. Paris: Migne, 1864. TLG 4090.108.

———. "Epistulae." In *Concilium universale Ephesenum*. Edited by E. Schwartz. Berlin: Walter de Gruyter, 1927. TLG 5000.001.

———. "Fragmenta in Cantica Canticorum." In *Opera omnia*. PG 69, cols. 1277-93. Edited by J.-P. Migne. Paris: Migne, 1859. TLG 4090.102.

Cyril of Jeruslaem. "Catecheses ad illuminandos 1-18." In *Cyrilli Hierosolymorum archiepiscopi opera quae su-persunt omnia*, 1:28-320; 2:2-342. 2 vols. Edited by W. C. Reischl and J. Rupp. Munich: Lentner, 1860 (repr. Hildesheim: Olms, 1967). TLG 2110.003.

———. "Homilia in paralyticum juxta piscinam jacentem." In *Cyrilli Hierosolymorum archiepiscopi opera quae supersunt omnia* 2:405-26. Edited by W. C. Reischl. Munich: Lentner, 1860. TLG 2110.006.

———. "Mystagogiae 1-5 (Sp.)." In *Cyrille de Jérusalem: Catéchèses, mystagogiques*. 2nd ed. SC 126, pp. 82-174. Edited by Auguste Piédagnel. Paris: Éditions du Cerf, 1988. TLG 2110.002.

Didache xii apostolorum. In *Instructions des Apôtres*, pp. 226-42. Edited by J. P. Audet. Paris: Lecoffre, 1958. TLG 1311.001.

Didymus the Blind. *Didymos der Blinde: Kommentar zum Ecclesiates*. 6 vols. PTA 9, 13, 16, 22, 24, 25. Ed-ited by Gerhard Binder, Michael Gronewald, Johannes Kramer, Bärbel Krebber and Leo Liesen-borghs. Bonn: Habelt, 1969-1979. TLG 2102.005-7, 011, 047-48.

———. "Fragmenta in Proverbia," In *Opera omnia*. PG 39, cols. 1621-46. Edited by J.-P. Migne. Paris: Migne, 1863. TLG 2102.022.

Dionysius of Alexandria. "Fragmenta." In *The Letters and Other Remains of Dionysius of Alexandria*, pp. 149-50. Edited by Charles L. Feltoe. Cambridge: Cambridge University Press, 1904. TLG 2952.002.

Ephrem the Syrian. In *Tatiani Diatessaron*. In *Saint Éphrem: Commentaire de l'Évangile Concordant – Text Syriaque* (Ms Chester-Beatty 709), vol. 2. Edited by Louis Leloir. Leuven and Paris: Peeters Press, 1990.

[Ephrem the Syrian]. *Ephraem Syrus: Hymni et Sermones*, vol.1. Edited by Thomas Joseph Lamy. Mechliniae: H. Dessain, 1882-1902.

———. *Des Heiligen Ephraem des Syrers Hymnen de Nativitate (Epiphania)*. Edited by Edmund Beck. CSCO 186 (Scriptores Syri 82). Louvain: Secrétariat du Corpus SCO, 1959.

———. *Des Heiligen Ephraem des Syrers Hymnen de Paradiso und Contra Julianum*. Edited by Edmund Beck. CSCO 174 (Scriptores Syri 78). Louvain: Secrétariat du Corpus SCO, 1957.

———. *Des Heiligen Ephraem Sermo de Domino Nostro*. Edited by Edmund Beck. CSCO 270 (Scriptores Syri 116). Louvain: Impremarie Orientaliste L. Dubecq, 1966.

———. *Hymnes de S. Ephrem conservées en version arménienne*. Edited by Louis Mariès and B. Ch. Mercier. PO 30, fasc. 1. Paris: Firmin-Didot, 1961.

———. *Sancti Ephraem Syri in Genesim et in Exodum Commentarii*. Edited by R. M. Tonneau. CSCO 152 (Scriptores Syri 71). Louvain: Impremarie Orientaliste L. Dubecq, 1955.

———. *Saint Éphrem—Commentaire de l'Évangile Concordant (Version Arménienne)*, Edited by Louis Leloir. CSCO 137 (Scriptores Armeniaci 1). Louvain: Secrétariat du Corpus SCO, 1953.

Eusebius of Caesarea. "Demonstratio evangelica." In *Eusebius Werke*. Vol 6. Edited by Ivar A. Heikel. GCS 23, pp. 1-492. Leipzig: Hinrichs, 1913. TLG 2018.005.

Eustathius of Antioch. *See* Theodoret of Cyr, *Eranistes*.

Evagrius of Pontus. "Scholia in Ecclesiasten (fragmenta e catenis)." See *Évagre le Pontique: Scholies a l'Ecclésiaste*. Edited by Paul Géhin. SC 397. Paris: Éditions du Cerf, 1993. TLG 4110.031.

———. "Scholia in Proverbia (fragmenta e catenis)." See *Évagre le Pontique: Scholies aux Proverbes*. Edited by Paul Géhin. SC 340. Paris: Éditions du Cerf, 1987. TLG 4110.030.

Eznik of Kolb. *De Deo*. Armenian and French. 2 vols. Edited by Louis Mariès and Ch. Mercier. PO 28.3-4. Paris: Firmin-Didot, 1959.

Fructuosus of Braga. *Consensoria monachorum*. In *S. Benedicti, Opera omnia*. PL 66, cols. 993-96. Edited by J.-P. Migne. Paris: Migne, 1866.

———. "Epistola." *See* "Sancti Braulionis Epistolae 43." In *Scriptorum Ecclesiasticorum, opera omnia*. PL 80, cols. 690-92. Edited by J.-P. Migne. Paris: Migne, 1863.

———. *Regulas Monastica Communis*. In *Scriptorum ecclesiasticorum, opera omnia*. PL 87, cols. 1109-30. Edited by J.-P. Migne. Paris: Migne, 1863.

Fulgentius of Ruspe. "Ad Euthymium de remissione peccatorum libri II." In *Opera*. Edited by John Fraipont. CCL 91A, pp. 649-707. Turnhout, Belgium: Brepols, 1968. Cl. 0821.

———. *Epistulae XVIII*. In *Sancti Fulgentii episcopi Ruspensis Opera*, 2 vols. Edited by John Fraipont. CCL 91, pp. 189-280, 311-12, 359-444; and CCL 91A, 447-57, 551-629. Turnhout, Belgium: Brepols, 1968. Cl. 0817.

———. "Liber de Scarilam de incarnatione filii dei et vilium animalium autore." In *Sancti Fulgentii episcopi Ruspensis Opera*. CCL 91, pp. 312-56. Edited by John Fraipont. Turnhout, Belgium: Brepols, 1968. Cl. 0822.

Gerontius. *Apophthegmata (collectio anonyma)*. *See* Vitae Patrum. Books 5-6. In *Vitae Patrum sive historiae ermiticae libri decem*. PG 73, cols. 851-1024. Edited by J.-P. Migne. Paris: Migne, 1860. TLG 2742.002.

Gregory of Elvira. "Fragmenta Expositiones in Ecclesiasten." In *Gregorius Iliberritanus, Faustinus Luciferianus*. CCL 69, pp. 261-63. Edited by Vincent Bulhart. Turnhout, Belgium: Brepols, 1967. Cl. 0557.

———. "In Canticum canticorum libri quinque." In *Gregorius Iliberritanus, Faustinus Luciferianus*. CCL 69, pp. 169-210. Edited by John Fraipont. Turnhout, Belgium: Brepols, 1967. Cl. 0547.

Gregory of Nazianzus. "Adversus Eunomianos (orat. 27)." In *Gregor von Nazianz: Die fünf theologischen Reden*, pp. 38-60. Edited by J. Barbel. Düsseldorf: Patmos-Verlag, 1963. TLG 2022.007.

———. "Apologetica [orat. 2]." In *Opera omnia*. PG 35, cols. 408-513. Edited by J.-P. Migne. Paris: Migne, 1857. TLG 2022.016.

———. "Funebris in laudem Caesarii fratris oratio (orat. 7)." In *Grégoire de Nazianze: Discours funèbres en l'honneur de son frère Césaire et de Basile de Césarée*, pp. 2-56. Edited by F. Boulenger. Paris: Picard, 1908. TLG 2022.005.

———. "Funebris oratio in patrem (orat. 18)." In *Opera omnia*. PG 35, cols. 985-1044. Edited by J.-P. Migne. Paris: Migne, 1857. TLG 2022.031.

———. "In laudem sororis Gorgoniae (orat. 8)." In *Opera omnia*. PG 35, cols. 789-817. Edited by J.-P. Migne. Paris: Migne, 1857. TLG 2022.021.

———. "In sanctum baptisma (orat. 40)." In *Opera omnia*. PG 36, cols. 360-425. Edited by J.-P. Migne. Paris: Migne, 1858. TLG 2022.048.

———. "Orationes 29-31." In *Discours 27-31*. Translated by Paul Gallay. SC 250 pp. 176-343. Paris: Éditions du Cerf, 1978. TLG 2022.008-011.

Gregory of Nyssa. "Contra Eunomium." In *Gregorii Nysseni opera*. Vol. 1.1, pp. 3-409; vol. 2.2, pp. 3-311. Edited by W. Jaeger. Leiden: Brill, 1960. TLG 2017.030.

———. "De oratione dominica orations v." In *Gregor's Bischof's von Nyssa Abhandlung von der Erschaffung des Menschen und fünf Reden auf das Gebet*, pp. 202-314. Edited by F. Oehler. Leipzig: Engelmann, 1859. TLG 2017.047.

———. "De virginitate." In *Grégoire de Nysse: Traité de la virginité*. SC 119, pp. 246-560. Edited by M. Aubineau. Paris: Éditions du Cerf, 1966. TLG 2017.043.

———. "In Canticum canticorum (homiliae 15)." In *Gregorii Nysseni opera*. Vol. 6, pp. 3-469. Edited by H. Langerbeck. Leiden: Brill, 1960. TLG 2017.032.

———. "In Ecclesiasten." In *Gregorii Nysseni opera*. Vol. 5, pp. 277-442. Edited by P. Alexander. Leiden: Brill, 1960. TLG 2017.029.

———. "Oratio funebris in Meletium episcopum." In *Gregorii Nysseni opera*. Vol. 9.1, pp. 441-57. Edited by A. Spira. Leiden: Brill, 1960. TLG 2017.021.

Gregory Thaumaturgus. "Metaphrasis in Ecclesiasten Salomonis." In *Opera omnia*. PG 10, cols. 988-1017. Edited by J.-P. Migne. Paris: Migne, 1857. TLG 2063.006

Gregory the Great. *Commentaire sure le Cantique des cantiques*. Edited by Rodrigur Bélanger. SC 314. Paris: Éditions du Cerf, 1984. Cl. 1709.

———. "Dialogorum libri iv." In *Dialogues*. 3 vols. Translation, introduction and notes by Paul Antin and Adalbert de Vogüé. SC 251, 260, 265. Paris: Éditions du Cerf, 1978-1980. Cl. 1713.

———. "Homiliarum xl in evangelia libri duo." In *Opera omnia*. PL 76, cols 1075-1312. Edited by J.-P. Migne. Paris: Migne, 1857. Cl. 1711.

———. *Moralia in Job*. Edited by Mark Adriaen. CCL 143, 143A and 143B. Turnhout, Belgium: Brepols, 1979-85. Cl. 1708.

———. Regula pastoralis. Edited by Floribert Rommel and R. W. Clement. CCL 141. Turnhout, Belgium: Brepols, 1953. Cl. 1712.

[Gregory the Great]. *S. Gregorii Magni Registrum epistularum*. 2 vols. CCL 140 and 140A. Edited by Dag Norberg. Turnhout, Belgium: Brepols, 1982. Cl. 1714.

Hermas. *Pastor*. In *Die apostolischen Väter 1: Der Hirt des Hermas*. GCS 48, 2nd edition, pp. 1-98. Edited by Molly Whittaker. Berlin: Akademie-Verlag, 1967. TLG 1419.001.

Hilary of Arles. "Vita Honorati." In *Joannis Cassiani, Opera omnia*. PL 50, cols. 1249-72. Edited by J.-P.

Migne. Paris: Migne, 1865.

Hilary of Poitiers. *De trinitate.* Edited by P. Smulders. CCL 62 and 62A. Turnhout, Belgium: Brepols, 1979-1980. Cl. 0433.

———. *Tractatus super psalmos I-XCI.* Edited by Jean Doignon. CCL 61. Turnhout: Brepols, 1997. Cl. 0428.

Hippolytus. "Fragmenta in Proverbia." In *Hippolytus Werke.* Vol. 1. Edited by Hans Achelis. GCS 1, pp. 1-47. Leipzig: Hinrichs, 1897. TLG 2115.013.

———. "Fragmenta in Proverbia (Sp.)." In *Hippolytus Werke.* Vol. 1. Edited by Hans Achelis. GCS 1, pp. 169-75. Leipzig: Hinrichs, 1897. TLG 2115.015.

———. "Fragmenta in Proverbia." In M. Richard. "Les fragments du commentaire de S. Hippolyte sur les proverbs de Salomon" *Muséon* 79 (1966):75-94. TLG 2115.044.

———. "In Canticum canticorum." In *Hippolytus Werke.* Vol. 1. Edited by Hans Achelis and George Nathaniel Bonwetsch. GCS 1. Leipzig: Hinrichs, 1897. TLG 2115.031.

———. "In Canticum canticorum (paraphrasis)." In M. Richard. "Une paraphrase grecque résumée du commentaire d'Hippolyte sure le cantique des cantiques," *Muséon* 77 (1964):140-54. TLG 2115.049.

Horsiesi. *Oeuvres de S. Pachôme et de ses disciples.* Edited by L. Th. Lefort. CSCO 159 (Scriptores Coptici 23). Louvain: Impremerie Orientaliste L. Durbecq, 1956.

Ignatius of Antioch. "Epistulae vii genuinae." In *Ignace d'Antioche: Polycarpe de Smyrne: Lettres: Martyre de Polycarpe.* 4th ed. Edited by P. T. Camelot. SC 10, pp. 56-154. Paris: Éditions du Cerf, 1969. TLG 1443.001.

[Isaac of Nineveh]. *Mar Isaacus Ninivita: De perfectione Religiosa.* Edited by Paul Bedjan. Paris, 1909.

Jerome. "Adversus Jovinianum." In *Opera omnia.* Edited by J.-P. Migne. PL 23, cols. 221-352. Paris: Migne, 1845. Cl. 0610.

———. "Apologia adversus libros Rufini." In *Contra Rufinum.* Edited by Pierre Lardet. CCL 79, pp. 1-72. Turnhout, Belgium: Brepols, 1982. Cl. 0613.

———. "Commentarius in Ecclesiasten." In *S. Hieronymi Presbyteri opera.* CCL 72, pp. 249-361. Edited by Mark Adriaen. Turnhout, Belgium: Brepols, 1959. Cl. 0583.

———. *Dialogus adversus Pelagianos.* Edited by Claudio Moreschini. CCL 80. Turnhout, Belgium: Brepols, 1990. Cl. 0615.

———. *Epistulae.* Edited by I. Hilberg. CSEL 54, 55 and 56. Vienna, Austria: F. Tempsky; Leipzig, Germany: G. F. Freytag, 1910-1918. Cl. 0620.

———. "Tractatus lix in psalmos." In *S. Hieronymi presbyteri opera.* Edited by Germain Morin. CCL 78, pp. 3-352. Turnhout, Belgium: Brepols, 1958. Cl. 0592.

———. "Tractatus de oboedientia." In *S. Hieronymi Presbyteri opera.* Edited by Germain Morin. CCL 78, pp. 552-55. Turnhout, Belgium: Brepols, 1958. Cl. 0605.

———. "Tractatus lix in psalmos." In *S. Hieronymi Presbyteri opera.* Edited by Germain Morin. CCL 78, pp. 3-352. Turnhout, Belgium: Brepols, 1958. Cl. 0592.

———. "Tractatus lix in psalmos, series altera." In *S. Hieronymi Presbyteri opera.* Edited by Germain Morin. CCL 78, pp. 355-447. Turnhout, Belgium: Brepols, 1958. Cl. 0593.

———. "Tractatuum in psalmos series altera." In *S. Hieronymi presbyteri opera.* Edited by Germain Morin. CCL 78, pp. 355-446. Turnhout, Belgium: Brepols, 1958. Cl. 0593.

———. "Vita Malchi." See Charles Christopher Mierow, "Sancti Eusebii Hieronymi Vita Malchi monachi captivi," in *Classical Essays Presented to James A. Kleist,* edited by Richard E. Arnold, pp. 31-60. St. Louis: The Classical Bulletin, St. Louis University, 1946. Cl. 0619.

John Chrysostom. "Ad illuminandos catecheses 1-2 (series prima et secunda)." In *Opera omnia.* Edited by J.-P. Migne. PG 49, cols. 223-40. Paris: Migne, 1862. TLG 2062.025.

———. "Ad populam Antiochenum homiliae (de statuis)." In *Opera omnia*. Edited by J.-P. Migne. PG 49, cols. 15-222. Paris: Migne, 1862. TLG 2062.024.

———. "Adversus Judaeos (orationes 1-8)." In *Opera omnia*. Edited by J.-P. Migne. PG 48, cols. 843-942. Paris: Migne, 1862. TLG 2062.021.

———. "Contra Anomoeos (homiliae 1-5): De incomprehensibili dei natura." In *Jean Chrysostome. Sur l'incompréhensibilité de Dieu*. Edited by F. Cavallera, J. Daniélou and R. Flaceliere. SC 28. Paris: Éditions du Cerf, 1951. TLG 2062.012.

———. "De beato Philogonio." In *Opera omnia*. Edited by J.-P. Migne. PG 48, cols. 747-56. Paris: Migne, 1862. TLG 2062.014.

———. "De paenitentia (homiliae 1-9)." In *Opera omnia*. Edited by J.-P. Migne. PG 49, cols. 277-348. Paris: Migne, 1862. TLG 2062.027.

———. Fragmenta in Proverbia [in catenis]). In *Opera omnia*. Edited by J.-P. Migne. PG 64, cols. 660-740. Paris: Migne, 1862. TLG 2062.185.

———. "In Acta apostolorum (homiliae 1-55)." In *Opera omnia*. Edited by J.-P. Migne. PG 60, cols. 13-384. Paris: Migne, 1862. TLG 2062.154.

———. "In epistulam ad Ephesios." In *Opera omnia*. Edited by J.-P. Migne. PG 62, cols. 9-176. Paris: Migne, 1862. TLG 2062.159.

———. "In epistulam ad Hebraeos (homiliae 1-34)." In *Opera omnia*. Edited by J.-P. Migne. PG 63, cols. 9-236. Paris: Migne, 1862. TLG 2062.168.

———. "In epistulam ad Romanos." In *Opera omnia*. Edited by J.-P. Migne. PG 60, cols. 391-682. Paris: Migne, 1862. TLG 2062.155.

———. "In epistulam i ad Timotheum (homiliae 1-18)." In *Opera omnia*. Edited by J.-P. Migne. PG 62, cols. 501-600. Paris: Migne, 1862. TLG 2062.164.

———. "In Genesim (homiliae 1-67)." In *Opera omnia*. PG 53, cols. 21-384; PG 54, cols. 385-580. Edited by J.-P. Migne. Paris: Migne, 1862. TLG 2062.112.

———. "In Isaiam." In *Jean Chrysostome. Commentaire sur Isaie*. Edited by Jean Dumortier. SC 304, pp. 36-356. Éditions du Cerf, 1983. TLG 2062.497.

———. "In Joannem (homiliae 1-88)." In *Opera Omnia*. Edited by J.-P. Migne. PG 59, cols. 23-482. Paris: Migne, 1862. TLG 2062.153.

———. "In Matthaeum (homiliae 1-90)." In *Opera omnia*. PG 57 and 58. Edited by J.-P. Migne. Paris: Migne, 1862. TLG 2062.152.

John of Antioch. *See Concilia oecumenica*. 7 vols. Edited by Eduard Schwartz. Berlin: Walter de Gruyter, 1927-1929. TLG 5000.001.

John of Apamea. "Letter to Hesychius." In *Briefe von Johannes dem Einsiedler, mit kritischem Apparat, Einleitung und Übersetzung*. Edited by Lars Gosta Rignell. Lund, Sweden: H. Ohlssons Boktryckeri, 1941.

John of Damascus. "Expositio fidei." In *Die Schriften des Johannes von Damaskos*, vol. 2, pp. 3-239. Edited by B. Kotter. Patristische Texte und Studien 12. Berlin: Walter de Gruyter, 1973. TLG 2934.004.

———. "Vita Barlaam et Joasaph." In *Barlaam and Joasaph*. LCL 34. Edited by G. R. Woodward and H. Mattingly. Cambridge, Mass.: Harvard University Press, 1914. Reprint, 1983. TLG 2934.066.

Julian of Eclanum. "Commentarius in Canticum canticorum." In *Juliani Aeclanensis: Expositio libri Job; Tractatus prophetarum Osee, Johel et Amos*. Edited by Luke de Coninck. CCL 88, pp. 398-401. Turnhout, Belgium: Brepols, 1977. Cl. 0775.

Justin Martyr. "Dialogus cum Tryphone" In *Die ältesten Apologeten*, pp. 90-265. Edited by E. J. Goodspeed. Göttingen, Germany: Vandenhoeck & Ruprecht, 1915. TLG 0645.003.

Leander of Seville. "Homilia in laudem ecclesiae." In *Pelagii II, Joannis III, Benedicti I summorum pontificum opera omnia*. PL 72, cols. 893-98. Edited by J.-P. Migne. Paris: Migne, 1849.

————. "Regula, sive liber de institutione virginum et contemptu mundi." In *Pelagii II, Joannis III, Benedicti I summorum pontificum opera omnia*. PL 72, cols. 873-94. Edited by J.-P. Migne. Paris: Migne, 1849.

Leo the Great. *Tractatus septem et nonaginta*. Edited by Antonio Chavasse. CCL 138 and 138A. Turnhout, Belgium: Brepols, 1973. Cl. 1657.

[Leo the Great]. *Concilia oecumenica*. 7 vols. Edited by Eduard Schwartz. Berlin: Walter de Gruyter, 1927-1929. TLG 5000.001.

[Macarius]. *Die 50 geistlichen Homilien des Makarios*. PTS 4. Berlin: Walter de Gruyter, 1964. TLG 2109.002.

Macrina. *See* Gregory of Nyssa, "Dialogus de anima et resurrectione." In *S. P. N. Gregorii*. PG 46, cols. 12-160. Edited by J.-P. Migne. Paris: Migne, 1863. TLG 2017.056.

Marcellus. *Expositio fidei*. In *Athanasiana: Five homilies, Expositio fidei, Sermo maior*. Edited by Henric Nordberg. Helsinki: Centraltryckeriet, 1962.

Marius Victorinus. "De generatione divini verbi." In *Marii Victorini Opera*. Edited by Paul Henry and Pierre Hadot. CSEL 83.1, pp. 15-48. Turnhout, Belgium: Brepols, 1971. Cl. 0096.

Maximus of Turin. "Collectio sermonum antiqua." In *Maximi episcopi Taurinensis sermons*. Edited by Almut Mutzenbecher. CCL 23, pp. 1-364. Turnhout, Belgium: Brepols, 1962. Cl. 0219a.

Nilus of Ancyra. *Commentaire sur le Cantique des cantiques*. Edited by Marie-Gabrielle Guérard. SC 403. Paris: Éditions du Cerf, 1994.

Olympiodorus. "Commentarii in Ecclesiasten." In *Olympiodorus, Hesychius, Leontius*. PG 93, cols. 477-628. Edited by J.-P. Migne. Paris: Migne, 1865. TLG 2865.002.

Origen. "Commentarii in evangelium Joannis (lib. 1, 2, 4, 5, 6, 10, 13)." In *Origene. Commentaire sur saint Jean*, 3 vols. Edited by Cécil Blanc. SC 120, 157, 222. Paris: Éditions du Cerf, 1966-1975. TLG 2042.005.

————. "Commentarii in evangelium Joannis (lib. 19, 20, 28, 32)." In *Origenes Werke*, vol. 4. Edited by Erwin Preuschen. GCS 10, pp. 298-480. Leipzig: Hinrichs, 1903. TLG 2042.079.

————. "Commentarium in Canticum canticorum." In *Origenes Werke*, vol. 8. Edited by W. A. Baehrens. GCS 33, pp. 61-241. Leipzig: Teubner, 1925. Cl. 0198/TLG 2042.026.

————. "Commentarium in evangelium Matthaei [lib.12-17]." In *Origenes Werke*, vols. 10.1 and 10.2. Edited by Erich Klostermann. GCS 40.1, pp. 69-304; GCS 40.2, pp. 305-703. Leipzig: Teubner, 1935-1937. TLG 2042.030.

————. "Contra Celsum." In *Origène Contre Celse*. 4 vols. Edited by M. Borret. SC 132, 136, 147 and 150. Paris: Éditions du Cerf, 1967-1969. TLG 2042.001.

————. "De oratione." In *Origenes Werke*, vol. 2. Edited by Paul Koetschau. GCS 3, pp. 297-403. Leipzig: Hinrichs, 1899. TLG 2042.008.

————. "De principiis." In *Origenes vier Bücher von den Prinzipien*, pp. 462-560, 668-764. Edited by Herwig Görgemanns and Heinrich Karpp. Darmstadt, Germany: Wissenschaftliche Buchgesellschaft, 1976. TLG 2042.002.

————. "Epistula ad Africanum." In *Opera omnia*. PG 11, cols. 48-85. Edited by J.-P. Migne. Paris: Migne, 1857. TLG 2042.045.

————. "Exhortatio ad martyrium." In *Origenes Werke*, vol. 1. Edited by Paul Koetschau. GCS 2, pp. 3-47. Leipzig: Hinrichs, 1899. TLG 2042.007.

————. "Expositio in Proverbia." In *Opera omnia*. PG 17, cols. 161-252. Edited by J.-P. Migne. Paris: Migne, 1862. TLG 2042.075.

————. "Fragmenta de principiis." In *Origenes vier Bücher von den Prinzipien*, passim. Edited by Herwig Görgemanns and Heinrich Karpp. Darmstadt: Wissenschaftliche Buchgesellschaft, 1976. TLG 2042.003.

———. "Fragmenta ex commentariis in evangelium Matthaei." In *Origenes Werke*, vol. 12. Edited by Erich Klostermann and Ernst Benz. GCS 41.1, pp. 3-5. Leipzig: Teubner, 1941. TLG 2042.031.

———. "Fragmenta in Jeremiam (e Philocalia)." In *Origenes Werke*, vol. 3. Edited by Erich Klostermann. GCS 6, pp. 195-98. Leipzig: Hinrichs, 1901. TLG 2042.084.

———. "Fragmenta in Jeremiam (in catenis)." In *Origenes Werke*, vol. 3. Edited by Erich Klostermann. GCS 6, pp. 199-232. Leipzig: Hinrichs, 1901. TLG 2042.010.

———. "Fragmenta in Lucam (in catenis)." In *Origenes Werke*, vol. 9, 2nd Edition. Edited by Max Rauer. GCS 49 (35), pp. 227-336. Berlin: Akademie-Verlag, 1959. TLG 2042.017.

———. "Homiliae in Exodum." In *Origenes Werke*, vol. 6. Edited by W. A. Baehrens. GCS 29, pp. 217-30. Leipzig: Teubner, 1920. Cl. 0198/TLG 2042.023.

———. "Homiliae in Canticum canticorum." In *Origenes Werke*, vol. 8. Edited by W. A. Baehrens. GCS 33, pp. 27-60. Leipzig: Teubner, 1925.

———. "Homiliae in Genesim." In *Origenes Werke*, vol. 6. Edited by W. A. Baehrens. GCS 29, pp. 23-30. Leipzig: Teubner, 1920. Cl. 0198/TLG 2042.022.

———. "Homiliae in Leviticum." In *Origenes Werke*, vol. 6. Edited by W. A. Baehrens. GCS 29, pp. 332-34, 395, 402-7, 409-16 Leipzig: Teubner, 1920. TLG 2042.024.

———. "Homiliae in Lucam." In *Opera omnia*. PG 13, cols. 1799-1902. Edited by J.-P. Migne. Paris: Migne, 1862. TLG 2042.016.

———. "In Jeremiam (homiliae 1-11)." In "Homiliae 2-3." *Origenes Werke*, vol. 8. Edited by W. A. Baehrens. GCS 33, pp. 290-317. Leipzig: Teubner, 1925. TLG 2042.009.

———. "In Jeremiam [homiliae 12-20]." In *Origenes Werke*, vol. 3. Edited by Erich Klostermann. GCS 6, pp. 85-194. Berlin: Akademie-Verlag, 1901. TLG 2042.021.

———. "In Jesu nave." In *Homélies sur Josué*. Edited by Annie Jaubert. SC 71. Paris: Éditions du Cerf, 1960.

[Origin]. *Origène: Commentaire sur l'Évangile selon Matthieu*, vol. 1. Edited by Robert Girod. SC 162. Paris: Éditions du Cerf, 1968. TLG 2042.029.

[Pachomius]. *Oeuvres de s. Pachôme et de ses disciples*. Edited L. T. Lefort. CSCO 159 (Scriptores Coptici 23), pp. 1-26. Louvain: Imprimerie Orientaliste L. Dubecq, 1956.

Pacian of Barcelona. "De paenitentibus." In *Opera omnia*. PL 13, cols. 1081-90. Edited by J.-P. Migne. Paris: Migne, 1845.

[Paulinus of Milan]. *Vita S. Ambrosii Mediolanensis Episcopi a Paulino Eius Notario ad Beatum Augustinum Conscripta: A Revised Text and Commentary with an Introduction and Translation*. Edited by Sister Mary Simplicia Kaniecka. PSt 16. Washington, D.C.: Catholic University of America Press, 1928.

Peter Chrysologus. *Collectio sermonum a Felice episcopo parata sermonibus extravagantibus adjectis*. In *Sancti Petri Chrysologi*. Edited by Alexander Olivar. CCL 24, 24A and 24B. Turnhout, Belgium: Brepols, 1975-1982. Cl. 0227+.

Peter of Alexandria. "Epistula canonica 12." In *Fonti. Fascicolo ix. Discipline générale antique (iie-ixe s.)*, vol. 2 (*Les canons des pères grecs*), pp. 33-57. Edited by P. Joannou. Rome: Tipographia Italo-Orientale "S. Nilo," 1963. TLG 2962.004.

[Peter of Alexandria]. *Two Coptic Homilies Attributed to Saint Peter of Alexandria: On Riches, On the Epiphany*. Translation and commentary by Birger Pearson and Tim Vivian with the assistance of Donald B. Spanel. Roma: C.I.M., 1993.

Prosper of Aquitaine. "De gratia Dei et libero arbitrio contra Collatorem." In *Opera omnia*. Edited by J.-P. Migne. PL 51, cols. 213-76. Paris: Migne, 1861. Cl. 0523.

Prudentius. "Liber Cathemerinon." In *Aurelius Prudentius Clemens*. Edited by Maurice P. Cunningham.

CCL 126, pp. 3-72. Turnhout, Belgium: Brepols, 1966. Cl. 1438.

Pseudo-Clement of Rome. "Epistulae de virginitate (Sp.)." In *Patres apostolici,* vol. 2, 3rd ed., pp. 1-45. Edited by F. X. Funk and Franz Diekamp. Tübingen: Laupp, 1913. TLG 1271.010.

———. "Homiliae (Sp.)." In *Die Pseudoklementinen I. Homilien,* 2nd edition. Edited by Bernhard Rehm, Johannes Irmscher and Franze Paschke. GCS 42, pp. 23-281. Berlin: Akademie-Verlag, 1969. TLG 1271.006.

Pseudo-Dionysius. "De divinis nominibus." In *Opera omnia.* PG 3, cols. 585-984 passim. Edited by J.-P. Migne. Paris: Migne, 1857. TLG 2798.004.

———. "Epistulae." In *Opera omnia.* PG 3, cols. 1065-120. Edited by J.-P. Migne. Paris: Migne, 1857. TLG 2798.006-015.

Rufinus of Aquileia. "Expositio symboli." In *Opera.* Edited by Manlio Simonetti. CCL 20, pp. 125-82. Turnhout, Belgium: Brepols, 1961. Cl. 0196.

Salvian the Presbyter. "Ad ecclesiam (sive Adversus avaritiam)." In *Opera omnia.* PL 53, cols. 173-238. Edited by J.-P. Migne. Paris: Migne, 1865.

———. "De gubernatione Dei." In *Ouvres.* 2 vols. Edited by Georges LaGarrigue. SC 220. Paris: Éditions du Cerf, 1975. Cl. 0485.

Shenoute. "Ad philosophum gentilem." In *Sinuthii archimandritae vita et opera omnia.* Vol. 3. Edited by Johannes Leipoldt. CSCO 42 (Scriptores Coptici 2, Textus), pp. 44-62. Paris: e Typographeo reipublicae, 1908.

———. "Fragmenta." *Coptic Manuscripts from the White Monastery: Works of Shenute.* 2 vols. (Coptic and English). Edited and translated by Dwight W. Young. Vienna, Austria: In Kommission bei Verlag Brüder Hollinek, 1993.

———. "De lingua." In *Sinuthii archimandritae vita et opera omnia,* vol. 3. Edited by Johannes Leipoldt. CSCO 42 (Scriptores Coptici 2, Textus), pp. 113-16. Paris: E Typographeo Reipublicae, 1908.

Symeon the New Theologian. *Catecheses 1-5.* Edited by Basil Krivochéine and Joseph Paramelle. SC 96. Paris: Éditions du Cerf, 1963.

Tertullian. "Adversus Hermogenem." In *Tertulliani opera.* Edited by E. Kroymann. CCL 1, pp. 397-435. Turnhout, Belgium: Brepols, 1954. Cl. 0013.

———. "Adversus Praxean." In *Tertulliani opera.* Edited by E. Kroymann and E. Evans. CCL 2, pp. 1159-205. Turnhout, Belgium: Brepols, 1954. Cl. 0026.

———. "De fuga in persecutione." In *Tertulliani opera.* Edited by J. J. Thierry. CCL 2 pp. 1135-55. Turnhout, Belgium: Brepols, 1954. Cl. 0025.

———. "De jejunio adversus psychicos." In *Tertulliani opera.* Edited by A. Reifferscheid and G. Wissowa. CCL 2, pp. 1257-77. Turnhout, Belgium: Brepols, 1954. Cl. 0029.

———. "De oratione." In *Tertulliani opera.* Edited by G. F. Diercks. CCL 1, pp. 255-74. Turnhout, Belgium: Brepols, 1954. Cl. 0007.

———. "De patientia." In *Tertulliani opera.* Edited by J. G. Ph. Borleffs. CCL 1, pp. 299-317. Turnhout, Belgium: Brepols, 1954. Cl. 0009.

———. "De praescriptione haereticorum." In *Tertulliani opera.* Edited by R. F. Refoulé. CCL 1, pp. 187-224. Turnhout, Belgium: Brepols, 1954. Cl. 0005.

———. "De virginibus velandis." In *Tertulliani opera.* Edited by E. Dekkers. CCL 2, pp. 1209-26. Turnhout, Belgium: Brepols, 1954. Cl. 0027.

Theodore of Mopsuestia. "Expositio in Canticum canticorum." In *Synesii episcopi Cyrenes opera quae extant omnia.* PG 66, cols. 699-700. Edited by J.-P. Migne. Paris: Migne, 1864.

Theodore of Tabennesi. "Fragment." In *Oeuvres de s. Pachôme et de ses disciples.* Edited L. T. Lefort. CSCO 159 (Scriptores Coptici 23), pp. 60-62. Louvain: Imprimerie Orientaliste L. Dubecq, 1956.

Theodoret of Cyr. "Ad eos qui in Euphratesia et Osrhoena regione, Syria, Phoeni." In PG 83, cols. 1416-33. Edited by J.-P. Migne. Paris: Migne, 1859. TLG 4089.034.

———. "Eranistes." Pages 61-266 in *Theodoret of Cyrus: Eranistes*. Edited by G. H. Ettlinger. Oxford: Clarendon Press, 1975. TLG 4089.002.

———. "Explanatio in Canticum canticorum." In *Opera omnia*. Edited by J.-P. Migne. PG 81, cols. 28-213. Paris: Migne, 1864. TLG 4089.025.

———. "Interpretatio in Psalmos." In *Opera omnia*. Edited by J.-P. Migne. PG 80, cols. 857-1997. Paris: Minge, 1864. TLG 4089.024.

Theodotus the Valentinian. *See* Clement of Alexandria, *Eclogae propheticae*.

Transitus Mariae. In *Apocalypses Apocryphae: Mosis, Esdrae, Pauli, Johanni, item Mariae dormitio, additis Evangeliorum et actuum Apocryphorum supplementis*, pp. 113-36. Edited by Konstantin von Tischendorf. Hildesheim, Germany: Georg Olms, 1866.

Valerian. "Homilia i: De bono disciplinae." Edited by J.-P. Migne. PL 52, cols. 691-96. Paris: Migne, 1859.

Vincent of Lérins. "Commonitorium." In *Foebadius, Victricus, Leporius, Vincentius Lerinensis, Evagrius, Rubricius*. Edited by R. Demeulenaere. CCL 64, pp. 147-95. Turnhout, Belgium: Brepols, 1985. Cl. 0510.

Bibliography of Works in English Translation

Acacius of Beroea. "Letter to Cyril of Alexandria." See Cyprian, "Letters 51-110." FC 77. Washington, D.C.: The Catholic University of America Press, 1987.

Ambrose. *Funeral Orations.* Translated by Leo P. McCauley et al. FC 22. Washington, D.C.: The Catholic University of America Press, 1953.

———. *Hexameron, Paradise, and Cain and Abel.* Translated by John J. Savage. FC 42. Washington, D.C.: The Catholic University of America Press, 1961.

———. *Letters. In Early Latin Theology,* pp. 175-278. Translated and edited by S. L. Greenslade. LCC 5. Philadelphia: Westminster, 1956.

———. *Letters.* Translated by Mary Melchior Beyenka. FC 26. Washington, D.C.: The Catholic University of America Press, 1954.

———. *On Virginity.* Translated by Daniel Callam. Toronto: Peregrina Publishing Co., 1996.

———. *Select Works and Letters.* Translated by H. De Romestin. NPNF 10. Series 2. Edited by Philip Schaff and Henry Wace. 14 vols. 1886-1900. Reprint, Peabody, Mass.: Hendrickson, 1994.

———. *Seven Exegetical Works.* Translated by Michael P. McHugh. FC 65. Washington, D.C.: The Catholic University of America Press, 1972.

Aphrahat. "Select Demonstrations." In *Gregory the Great, Ephraim Syrus, Aphrahat,* pp 345-412. Translated by James Barmby. NPNF 13. Series 2. Edited by Philip Schaff and Henry Wace. 14 vols. 1886-1900. Reprint, Peabody, Mass.: Hendrickson, 1994.

Athanasius. "Four Discourses Against the Arians." In *TTC.* Edited by William G. Rusch. Philadelphia: Fortress Press, 1980.

———. "Four Discourses Against the Arians." In *FEF.* Edited by W. A. Jurgens. Collegeville, Minn.: Liturgical Press, 1970.

———. "Life of St. Anthony." *In Early Christian Biographies,* pp. 133-216. Edited by Roy J. Deferrari. FC 15. Washington D.C.: The Catholic University of America Press, 1952.

———. *Selected Works and Letters.* Translated by Archibald Robertson. NPNF 4. Series 2. Edited by Philip Schaff and Henry Wace. 14 vols. 1886-1900. Reprint, Peabody, Mass.: Hendrickson, 1994.

Athenagorus. "A Plea Regarding Christians." In *Early Christian Fathers,* pp. 290-340. Translated and edited by Cyril C. Richardson. LCC 1. Philadelphia: Westminster Press, 1953.

Augustine. *Against Julian.* Translated by Matthew A. Schumacher. FC 35. Washington, D.C.: The Catholic University of America Press, 1957.

———. *Anti-Pelagian Works.* Translated by Peter Holmes and Robert Ernest Wallis. NPNF 5. Series 1. Edited by Philip Schaff. 14 vols. 1886-1889. Reprint, Peabody, Mass.: Hendrickson, 1994.

———. *The Catholic and Manichaean Ways of Life.* Translated by Donald A. Gallagher and Idella J. Gallagher. FC 56. Washington, D.C.: The Catholic University of America Press, 1966.

———. "Christian Instruction." In *Christian Instruction; Admonition and Grace; The Christian Combat; Faith, Hope and Charity,* pp. 3-235. Translated by Bernard M. Peebles. FC 2. Washington, D.C.: The Catholic University of America Press, 1947.

———. The *City of God*. Translated by Demetrius Zema and Gerald G. Walsh. FC 8, 14, 24. Washington, D.C.: The Catholic University of America Press, 1950-1954.

———. *Commentary on the Lord's Sermon on the Mount with Seventeen Related Sermons*. Translated by Denis J. Kavanagh. FC 11. Washington, D.C.: The Catholic University of America Press, 1951.

———. *Confessions and Enchiridion*. Translated and edited by Albert C. Outler. LCC 7. London, SCM, 1955.

———. *Eighty-Three Different Questions*. Translated by David L. Mosher. FC 70. Washington, D.C.: The Catholic University of America Press, 1982.

———. *Expositions on the Book of Psalms*. Edited from the Oxford translation by A. Cleveland Coxe. NPNF 8. Series 1. Edited by Philip Schaff. 14 vols. 1886-1889. Reprint, Peabody, Mass.: Hendrickson, 1994.

———. *Four Anti-Pelagian Writings: On Nature and Grace, On the Preceedings of Pelagius, On the Predestination of the Saints, On the Gift of Perseverance*. Translated by John A. Mourant and William J. Collinge. FC 86. Washington, D.C.: The Catholic University of America Press, 1992.

———. *Letters*. Translated by Sister Wilfrid Parsons and Robert B. Eno. FC 12, 18, 20, 30, 32 and 81. 6 vols. Washington, D.C.: The Catholic University of America Press, 1951-1989.

———. "Of True Religion." In *Earlier Writings*, pp. 218-283. Translated by John H. S. Burleigh. LCC 6. London: SCM Press, 1953.

———. *On Christian Doctrine*. Translated by D. W. Robertson Jr. Library of Liberal Arts. Indianapolis: Bobbs-Merrill, 1958.

———. "[On] Faith and the Creed." In *Earlier Writings*, 349-69. Translated by John H. S. Burleigh. LCC 6. London: SCM Press, 1953.

———. "[On] Grace and Free Will." In *The Teacher, The Free Choice of the Will, Grace and Free Will*, pp. 243-308. Translated by Robert P. Russell. FC 59. Washington, D.C.: The Catholic University of America Press, 1968.

———. "On the Trinity." In *Augustine: Later Works*, pp. 17-181. Translated by John Burnaby. LCC 8. London: SCM Press, 1955.

———. *Sermon on the Mount, Harmony of the Gospels, Homilies on the Gospels*. Translated by William Findlay, S. D. F. Salmond and R. G. MacMullen. NPNF 6. Series 1. Edited by Philip Schaff. 14 vols. 1886-1889. Reprint, Peabody, Mass.: Hendrickson, 1994.

———. *Sermons*. Translated by Edmund Hill. WSA 1, 2, 3, 4, 5, 6, 7, 8, 9 and 10. Part 3. Edited by John E. Rotelle. New York: New City Press, 1990-1995.

———. *Sermons on the Liturgical Seasons*. Translated by Mary Sarah Muldowney. FC 38. Washington, D.C.: The Catholic University of America Press, 1959.

———. *Tractates on the Gospel of John, 1-124*, 4 vols. Translated by John W. Rettig. FC 78, 88, 90 and 92. Washington, D.C.: The Catholic University of America Press, 1988-1995.

———. *Treatises on Marriage and Other Subjects*. Translated by Charles T. Wilcox et al. FC 27. Washington, D.C.: The Catholic University of America, 1955.

———. *Treatises on Various Subjects*. Translated by Mary Sarah Muldowny et al. FC 16. Washington, D.C.: The Catholic University of America, 1952.

———. *The Trinity*. Translated by Stephen McKenna. FC 45. Washington, D.C.: The Catholic University of America, 1963.

———. *The Writings Against the Manichaeans, and Against the Donatists*. Translated by J. R. King. NPNF 4. Series 1. Edited by Philip Schaff. 14 vols. 1886-1889. Reprint, Peabody, Mass.: Hendrickson, 1994.

Basil the Great. *Ascetical Works*. Translated by M. Monica Wagner. FC 9. New York: Fathers of the Church, Inc., 1950.

———. "Homilies on the Psalms." In *Exegetic Homilies*, pp. 151-359. Translated by Agnes C. Way. FC 46. Washington, D.C.: The Catholic University of America Press, 1963.

———. "On the Spirit." In *Letters and Select Works*, pp. 1-50. Translated by Blomfield Jackson. NPNF 8. Series 2. Edited by Philip Schaff and Henry Wace. 14 vols. 1886-1900. Reprint, Peabody, Mass.: Hendrickson, 1994.

Bede. *Commentary on the Acts of the Apostles*. Translated, with an Introduction and Notes by Lawrence T. Martin. CS 117. Kalamazoo, Mich.: Cistercian Publications, 1989.

———. *Commentary on the Seven Catholic Epistles*. Translated by David Hurst. CS 82. Kalamazoo, Mich.: Cistercian Publications, 1985.

———. *Homilies on the Gospels*. 2 vols. Translated by Lawrence T. Martin and David Hurst. CS 110-11. Kalamazoo, Mich.: Cistercian Publications, 1991.

———. *On the Tabernacle*. Translated with notes and introduction by Arthur G. Holder. TTH 18. Liverpool: Liverpool University Press, 1994.

Benedict. *Rule of St. Benedict*. In *Western Asceticism*, pp. 290-337. Translated by Owen Chadwick. LCC 12. Philadelphia: Westminster Press, 1958.

[Braulio of Saragossa]. "Braulio of Saragossa." In *Iberian Fathers (Volume 2): Braulio of Saragossa, Fructuosus of Braga*, pp. 3-142. Translated by Claude W. Barlow. FC 63. Washington, D.C.: The Catholic University of America Press, 1969.

Caesarius of Arles. *Sermons*. Translated by Mary Magdeleine Mueller. 3 vols. FC 31, 47 and 66. Washington, D.C.: The Catholic University of America Press, 1956-1973.

Cassian, John. "Conferences." In *Western Asceticism*, pp. 190-289. Translated by Owen Chadwick. LCC 12. Philadelphia: Westminster Press, 1958.

———. *Conferences*. Translated by Colm Luibheid. The Classics of Western Spirituality. New York: Paulist Press, 1985.

———. *The Conferences*. Translated and annotated by Boniface Ramsey. ACW 57. New York: Paulist Press, 1997.

———. "Institutes." In *Sulpitius Severus, Vincent of Lérins, John Cassian*, pp. 201-90. Translated by Edgar C. S. Gibson. NPNF 11. Series 2. Edited by Philip Schaff and Henry Wace. 14 vols. 1886-1900. Reprint, Peabody, Mass.: Hendrickson, 1994.

Cassiodorus. *Explanation of the Psalms*. Translated by P. G. Walsh. 3 vols. ACW 51, 52 and 53. New York: Paulist Press, 1990-1991.

Clement of Alexandria. *Christ the Educator*. Translated by Simon P. Wood. FC 23. Washington, D.C.: The Catholic University of America Press, 1954.

———. *Stromateis: Books 1-3*. Translated by John Ferguson. FC 85. Washington, D.C.: The Catholic University of America Press, 1991.

[Clement of Alexandria]. *Fathers of the Second Century: Hermas, Tatian, Athenagoras, Theophilus, and Clement of Alexandria*. Translated by F. Crombie et al. ANF 2. Edited by Alexander Roberts and James Donaldson. 10 vols. 1885-1887. Reprint, Peabody, Mass.: Hendrickson, 1994.

Clement of Rome. "First Letter to the Corinthians." In *The Apostolic Fathers*, pp. 9-58. Translated by Francis X. Glimm et al. FC 1. New York: Christian Heritage, Inc., 1947.

———. "The Letter of the Church of Rome to the Church of Corinth, Commonly Called Clement's First Letter." In *Early Christian Fathers*, pp. 33-73. Translated by Cyril C. Richardson. LCC 1. Philadelphia: The Westminster Press, 1953.

Constitutions of the Holy Apostles. In *Lactantius, Venantius, Asterius, Victorinus, Dionysius, Apostolic Teaching and Constitutions, 2 Clement, Early Liturgies*, pp. 391-505. Edited with notes by James Donaldson. ANF 7. Edited by Alexander Roberts and James Donaldson. 10 vols. 1885-1887. Reprint, Peabody, Mass.:

Hendrickson, 1994.

Cyprian. *Letters 1-81*. Translated by Rose Bernard Donna. FC 51. Washington, D.C.: The Catholic University of America Press, 1964.

———. *Treatises*. Translated and edited by Roy J. Deferrari. FC 36. Washington, D.C.: The Catholic University of America Press, 1958.

———. *Treatises*. In *Fathers of the Third Century: Hippolytus, Cyprian, Caius, Novatian, Appendix*, pp. 421-557. Translated by J. H. MacMahon et al. ANF 5. Edited by Alexander Roberts and James Donaldson. 10 vols. 1885-1887. Reprint, Peabody, Mass.: Hendrickson, 1994.

———. "The Unity of the Catholic Church." In *Early Latin Theology*, pp. 119-42. Translated and edited by S. L. Greenslade. LCC 5. Philadelphia: Westminster, 1956

Cyril of Alexandria. *Commentary on the Gospel of Saint Luke*. Translated by R. Payne Smith. Long Island, N.Y.: Studion, 1983.

———. *Letters 1-110*. Translated by John I. McEnerney. 2 vols. FC 76-77. Washington, D.C.: The Catholic University of America Press, 1985.

Cyril of Jerusalem. "Catechetical Lectures." In *Cyril of Jerusalem and Nemesius of Emesa*, pp. 64-199. Edited by William Telfer. LCC 4. Philadelphia: Westminster, 1955.

[Cyril of Jerusalem]. *The Works of Saint Cyril of Jerusalem*. Translated by Leo P. McCauley and Anthony A. Stephenson. 2 vols. FC 61 and 64. Washington, D.C.: The Catholic University of America Press, 1969-1970.

Didache. See "A Church Manual." In *Early Christian Fathers*, pp. 159-79. Translated by Cyril C. Richardson. LCC 1. Philadelphia: Westminster, 1953.

[Dionysius of Alexandria]. "Dionysius the Great." In *Gregory Thaumaturgus, Dionysius the Great, Julius Africanus, Anatolius and Minor Writers, Methodius, Arnobius*, pp. 75-120. Translated by S. D. F. Salmond. ANF 6. Edited by Alexander Roberts and James Donaldson. 10 vols. 1885-1887. Reprint, Peabody, Mass.: Hendrickson, 1994.

Ephrem the Syrian. "Homily on Admonition and Repentance." In *Part 2: Gregory the Great, Ephraim Syrus, Aphrahat*, pp.330-36. Translated by A. Edward Johnston. NPNF 13. Series 2. Edited by Philip Schaff and Henry Wace. 14 vols. 1886-1900. Reprint, Peabody, Mass.: Hendrickson, 1994.

———. "Hymns on Paradise." Translated by Sebastian Brock. Crestwood, N.Y.: St. Vladimir's Seminary Press, 1990.

———. "Hymns Preserved in Armenian." In *The Syriac Fathers on Prayer and the Spiritual Life*, pp. 36-38. CS 101. Kalamazoo, Mich.: Cistercian Publications, 1987.

———. *Selected Prose Works*. Translated by Edward G. Mathews and Joseph P. Amar. FC 91. Washington, D.C.: The Catholic University of America Press, 1994.

Epistle of Barnabas. In *The Apostolic Fathers*, pp. 191-222. Translated by Francis X. Glimm. FC 1. New York: Christian Heritage, Inc., 1947.

Eusebius of Caesarea. *Proof of the Gospel*. 2 vols. Translated by W. J. Ferrar. London: SPCK, 1920. Reprint, Grand Rapids, Mich.: Baker, 1981.

Eustathius of Antioch. See "Eranistes" in *Theodoret of Cyrus: Eranistes*. Translated by Gerard H. Ettlinger. FC 106. Washington, D.C.: The Catholic University of America Press, 2003.

Eznik of Golb. *On God*. Translated by Monica J. Blanchard and Robin Darling Young. Leuven: Peeters, 1998.

[Fructuosus of Braga]. "Writings of Fructuosus of Braga." In *Iberian Fathers*, vol. 2. Translated by Claude W. Barlow. FC 63. Washington, D.C.: The Catholic University of America Press, 1969.

Fulgentius of Ruspe. *Selected Works*. Translated by Robert B. Eno. FC 95. Washington, D.C.: The Catholic University of America Press, 1997.

Gerontius. See "The Sayings of the Fathers." In *Western Asceticism*, pp. 33-189. Translated by Owen Chadwick. LCC 12. Philadelphia: Westminster Press, 1958.

Gregory of Nazianzus. "Orations" In *Cyril of Jerusalem, Gregory of Nazianzen*. Translated by Charles Gordon Browne et al. NPNF 7. Series 2. Edited by Philip Schaff and Henry Wace. 14 vols. 1886-1900. Reprint, Peabody, Mass.: Hendrickson, 1994.

———. "Orations." In *Funeral Orations* by Saint Gregory Nazianzen and Saint Ambrose, pp. 5-156. Translated by Leo P. McCauley et al. FC 22. Washington, D.C.: The Catholic University of America Press, 1953.

———. "Orations." In *Faith Gives Fullness to Reasoning: The Five Theological Orations of Gregory Nazianzen*. Edited by F. W. Norris. Leiden and New York: E. J. Brill, 1991.

———. "The Theological Orations." Translated by Charles Gordon Browne and James Edward Swallow. In *Christology of the Later Fathers*, pp. 128-214. Edited by Edward Rochie Hardy. LCC 3. Philadelphia: Westminster Press, 1954.

Gregory of Nyssa. "On the Lord's Prayer." In *St. Gregory of Nyssa: The Lord's Prayer and The Beatitudes*. Translated by Hilda C. Graef. ACW 18. Westminster, Md.: Newman Press, 1954.

———. "On Virginity." In *Ascetical Works*, pp. 3-75. Translated by Virginia Woods Callahan. FC 58. Washington, D.C.: The Catholic University of America Press, 1967.

[Gregory of Nyssa]. *Gregory of Nyssa Homilies on Ecclesiastes: An English Version with Supporting Studies*. Translated by Stuart George Hall and Rachel Moriarty. Proceedings of the Seventh International Colloquium on Gregory of Nyssa (St. Andrews, September 5-10, 1990). Berlin: Walter de Gruyter, 1993.

———. *Saint Gregory of Nyssa. Commentary on the Song of Songs*. Translated by Casimir McCambley. Brookline MA: Hellenic College Press, 1987.

———. *Select Writings and Letters of Gregory, Bishop of Nyssa*. Translated by William Moore and Henry Austin Wilson. NPNF 5. Series 2. Edited by Philip Schaff and Henry Wace. 14 vols. 1886-1900. Reprint, Peabody, Mass.: Hendrickson, 1994.

———. See also, "Eranistes," by Theodoret of Cyr in *Theodoret of Cyrus: Eranistes*. Translated by Gerard H. Ettlinger. FC 106. Washington, D.C.: The Catholic University of America Press, 2003.

[Gregory Thaumaturgus]. *Gregory Thaumaturgos' Paraphrase of Ecclesiastes*. Translated by John Jarick. Society of Biblical Literature, Septuagint and Cognate Studies Series no. 29. Atlanta, GA: Scholars Press, 1990.

Gregory the Great. *Dialogues*. Translated by Odo John Zimmerman. FC 39. Washington, D. C.: The Catholic University of America Press, 1959.

———. *Forty Gospel Homilies*. Translated by David Hurst. CS 123. Kalamazoo, Mich.: Cistercian, 1990.

———. "Letters." In *Leo the Great, Gregory the Great*, pp. 73-243, and *Part II: Gregory the Great, Ephraim Syrus, Aphrahat*, pp. 1-116. Translated by James Barmby. 2 vols. NPNF 12, 13. Series 2. Edited by Philip Schaff and Henry Wace. 14 vols. 1886-1900. Reprint, Peabody, Mass.: Hendrickson, 1994.

———. *Morals on the Book of Job*. Translated by Members of the English Church. 4 vols. LF 18, 21, 23 and 31. Oxford: John Henry Parker, 1844-1850.

———. *Pastoral Care*. Translated by Henry Davis. ACW 11. New York: Newman Press, 1950.

———. *Pastoral Rule and Selected Epistles*. Translated by James Barmby. NPNF 12. Series 2. Edited by Philip Schaff and Henry Wace. 14 vols. 1886-1900. Reprint, Peabody, Mass.: Hendrickson, 1994.

Hilary of Arles. "Life of St. Honoratus." In *Early Christian Biographies*, pp. 352-94. Translated by Roy J. Defarrari. FC 15. Washington, D.C.: The Catholic University of America Press, 1952.

Hilary of Poitiers. "Homilies on the Psalms." In *Select Works*, pp. 235-48. Translated by E. W. Watson et al. NPNF 9. Series 2. Edited by Philip Schaff and Henry Wace. 14 vols. 1886-1900. Reprint, Peabody, Mass.: Hendrickson, 1994.

———. *The Trinity.* Translated by Stephen McKenna. FC 25. Washington, D.C.: The Catholic University of America Press, 1954.

[Hippolytus]. "Hippolytus." In *Fathers of the Third Century: Hippolytus, Cyprian, Caius, Novatian, Appendix,* pp. 9-266. Translated by J. H. MacMahon et al. ANF 5. Edited by Alexander Roberts and James Donaldson. 10 vols. 1885-1887. Reprint, Peabody, Mass.: Hendrickson, 1994.

[Horsiesi (Horsiesios)]. "The *Instructions of Horsiesios.*" In *Pachomian Koinonia: Volume Three, Instructions, Letters, and Other Writings of Saint Pachomius and His Disciples,* pp. 135-52. Translated by Armand Veilleux. CS 47. Kalamazoo, Mich.: Cistercian, 1982.

———. "The Regulations of Horsiesios." In *Pachomian Koinonia: Volume Two, Pachomian Chronicles and Rules,* 197-223. CS 46. Kalamazoo, Mich.: Cistercian, 1981.

Ignatius of Antioch. "Epistle to the Ephesians." In *The Letters of St. Ignatius of Antioch,* pp. 81-143. Translated by Gerald G. Walsh. FC 1. New York: Christian Heritage, 1947.

Isaac of Nineveh. *The Ascetical Homilies of Saint Isaac the Syrian.* Edited by Dana Miller. Translated by the Holy Transfiguration Monastery, 1984.

Jerome. *Dogmatic and Polemical Works.* Translated by John N. Hritzu. FC 53. Washington, D.C.: The Catholic University of America Press, 1965.

———. "Letters." In *Early Latin Theology,* pp. 279-389. Translated and edited by S. L. Greenslade. LCC 5. Philadelphia: Westminster Press, 1956.

———. *Letters and Select Works.* Translated by W. H. Fremantle. NPNF 6. Series 2. Edited by Philip Schaff and Henry Wace. 14 vols. 1886-1900. Reprint, Peabody, Mass.: Hendrickson, 1994.

———. "Life of Malchus." In *Early Christian Biographies,* pp. 281-97. Translated by Marie Liguori Ewald. FC 15. Washington, D.C.: The Catholic University of America Press, 1952.

[Jerome]. *The Homilies of Saint Jerome.* Translated by Marie Liguori Ewald. 2 vols. FC 48 and 57. Washington, D.C.: The Catholic University of America Press, 1964, 1966.

John Chrysostom. "Against the Anomoeans." In *On the Incomprehensible Nature of God.* Translated by Paul W. Harkins. FC 72. Washington, D.C.: The Catholic University of America Press, 1984.

———. *Baptismal Instructions.* Translated by Paul W. Harkins. ACW 31. New York: Newman Press, 1963.

———. *Discourses Against Judaizing Christians.* Translated by Paul W. Harkins. FC 68. Washington, D.C.: The Catholic University of America Press, 1979.

———. *Homilies on Galatians, Ephesians, Philippians, Colossians, Thessalonians, Timothy, Titus, and Philemon.* Translated by Gross Alexander et al. NPNF 13. Series 1. Edited by Philip Schaff. 14 vols. 1886-1889. Reprint, Peabody, Mass.: Hendrickson, 1994.

———. *Homilies on Genesis.* Translated by Robert C. Hill. 2 vols. FC 74, 82. Washington, D.C.: The Catholic University of America Press, 1986-1990.

———. *[Homilies] On Repentance and Almsgiving.* Translated by Gus George Christo. FC 96. Washington, D.C.: The Catholic University of America Press, 1998.

———. *Homilies on the Acts of the Apostles and the Epistle to the Romans.* Translated by J. Walker, J. Sheppard and H. Browne. NPNF 11. Series 1. Edited by Philip Schaff. 14 vols. 1886-1889. Reprint, Peabody, Mass.: Hendrickson, 1994.

———. *Homilies on the Epistles of Paul to the Corinthians.* Translated by Talbot W. Chambers. NPNF 12. Series 1. Edited by Philip Schaff. 14 vols. 1886-1889. Reprint, Peabody, Mass.: Hendrickson, 1994.

———. "Homilies on the Gospel of John." In *Saint John Chrysostom: Commentary on Saint John the Apostle and Evangelist.* Translated by Thomas Aquinas Goggin. 2 vols. FC 33, 41. Washington, D.C.: The Catholic University of America Press, 1957-1959.

———. *Homilies on the Gospel of Saint John and the Epistle to the Hebrews.* Translated by Frederic Gardiner. NPNF 14. Series 1. Edited by Philip Schaff. 14 vols. 1886-1889. Reprint, Peabody, Mass.: Hendrickson, 1994.

———. *Homilies on the Gospel of Saint Matthew.* The Oxford translation. NPNF 10. Series 1. Edited by Philip Schaff. 14 vols. 1886-1889. Reprint, Peabody, Mass.: Hendrickson, 1994.

———. *On the Priesthood, Ascetic Treatises, Select Homilies and Letters, Homilies on the Statues.* Translated by W. R. W. Stephens et al. NPNF 9. Series 1. Edited by Philip Schaff. 14 vols. 1886-1889. Reprint, Peabody, Mass.: Hendrickson, 1994.

John of Antioch. "Letter to Cyril of Alexandria." In *St. Cyril of Alexandria: Letters 51-110,* pp. 184-87. Translated by John I. McEnerney. FC 77. Washington, D.C.: The Catholic University of America Press, 1987.

John of Apamea. "Letter to Hesychius." In *The Syriac Fathers on Prayer and the Spiritual Life,* pp. 77-100. Translated by Sebastian Brock. CS 101. Kalamazoo, Mich.: Cistercian, 1987.

John of Damascus. *Barlaam and Joasaph.* Translated by G. R. Woodward. LCL 34. London: William Heinemann, 1914. Reprint Cambridge, Mass.: Harvard University Press, 1937.

———. "The Orthodox Faith." In *Writings,* pp. 165-406. Translated by Frederic H. Chase Jr. FC 37. Washington, D.C.: The Catholic University of America Press, 1958.

Justin Martyr. "Dialogue with Trypho." In *Writings of Saint Justin Martyr,* pp. 137-366. Translated by Thomas B. Falls. FC 6. New York: Christian Heritage, Inc., 1948.

[Leander of Seville]. "Writings of Leander of Seville." In *Iberian Fathers,* 1: 173-235. Translated by Claude W. Barlow. FC 62. Washington, D.C.: The Catholic University of America Press, 1969.

Leo the Great. *Sermons.* Translated by Jane P. Freeland and Agnes J. Conway. FC 93. Washington, D.C.: The Catholic University of America Press, 1996.

[Leo the Great]. "The Tome of Leo." Translated by William Bright. In *Christology of the Later Fathers,* pp. 359-70. Edited by Edward Rochie Hardy. LCC 3. Philadelphia: Westminster Press, 1954.

Macarius. *Intoxicated with God: The Fifty Spiritual Homilies of Macarius.* Translated by George A. Maloney. Denville, N.J.: Dimension Books, 1978.

Macrina. See Gregory of Nyssa, "On the Soul and the Resurrection." In *Ascetical Works,* pp. 193-272. Translated by Virginia Woods Callahan. FC 58. Washington, D.C.: The Catholic University of America Press, 1967.

Marius Victorinus. "Letter to Candidus." In *Marius Victorinus: Theological Treatises on the Trinity,* pp. 59-83. Translated by Mary T. Clark. FC 69. Washington, D.C.: The Catholic University of America Press, 1981.

[Maximus of Turin]. *The Sermons of St. Maximus of Turin.* Translated and annotated by Boniface Ramsey. ACW 50. New York: Newman, 1989.

Origen. "Commentaries of Origen." In *Gospel of Peter, Diatessaron, Testament of Abraham, Epistles of Clement, Origen, Miscellaneous Works,* pp. 289-512. Translated by John Patrick. ANF 9. Edited by Allan Menzies. 10 vols. 1885-1887. Reprint, Peabody, Mass.: Hendrickson, 1994.

———. *Commentary on the Gospel According to John.* Translated by Ronald E. Heine. 2 vols. FC 80, 89. Washington, D.C.: The Catholic University of America Press, 1989-1993.

———. *An Exhortation to Martyrdom, Prayer and Selected Works.* Translated by Rowan A. Greer. The Classics of Western Spirituality. New York: Paulist Press, 1979.

———. *Homilies on Genesis and Exodus.* Translated by Ronald E. Heine. FC 71. Washington, D.C.: The Catholic University of America Press, 1982.

———. *Homilies on Jeremiah, Homilies on I Kings 28.* Translated by John Clark Smith. FC 97. Washington, D.C.: The Catholic University of America Press, 1998.

———. *Homilies on Joshua.* Translated by Barbara J. Bruce. FC 105. Washington, D.C.: The Catholic

University of America Press, 2002.

———. *Homilies on Leviticus 1-16.* Translated by Gary Wayne Barkley. FC 83. Washington, D.C.: The Catholic University of America Press, 1990.

———. *Homilies on Luke; Fragments on Luke.* Translated by Joseph T. Lienhard. FC 94. Washington, D.C.: The Catholic University of America Press, 1996.

———. *On First Principles.* Translated by G. W. Butterworth. London: SPCK, 1936; Reprint, Gloucester, Mass.: Peter Smith, 1973.

———. "On Prayer." In *Prayer; Exhortation to Martyrdom,* pp. 15-140. Translated by John J. O'Meara. ACW 19. Westminster, Md.: Newman Press, 1954.

———. *The Song of Songs Commentary and Homilies.* Translated by R. P. Lawson. ACW 26. Westminster, Md.: Newman Press, 1957.

[Origen]. "Works of Origen." In *Tertullian (IV); Minucius Felix; Commodian; Origen (I and III),* 221-669. Translated by Frederick Crombie. ANF 4. Edited by Alexander Roberts and James Donaldson. 10 vols. 1885-1887. Reprint, Peabody, Mass.: Hendrickson, 1994.

[Pachomius]. *Pachomian Koinonia.* Vol. 3. Translated by Armand Veilleux. CS 47. Kalamazoo, Mich.: Cistercian Publications, 1982.

[Pacian of Barcelona]. "Pacian of Barcelona." In *Iberian Fathers,* vol 3. Translated by Craig L. Hanson. FC 99. Washington, D.C.: The Catholic University of America Press, 1999.

The Passing of Mary. In *The Twelve Patriarchs, Excerpts and Epistles, The Clementina, Apocrypha, Decretals, Memoirs of Edessa and Syriac Documents, Remains of the First Ages,* pp. 592-98. Translated by Alexander Walker. ANF 8. Edited by Alexander Roberts and James Donaldson. 10 vols. 1885-1887. Reprint, Peabody, Mass.: Hendrickson, 1994.

Paulinus of Milan. "Life of St. Ambrose." In *Early Christian Biographies,* pp. 25-66. Translated by John A. Lacy. FC 15. Washington, D.C.: The Catholic University of America, 1952.

Peter Chrysologus. "Sermons." In *Saint Peter Chrysologus: Selected Sermons and Saint Valerian: Homilies,* pp. 25-282. Translated by George E. Ganss. FC 17. New York: Fathers of the Church, Inc., 1953.

Peter of Alexandria. "The Canonical Epistle." In *Gregory Thaumaturgus, Dionysius the Great, Julius Africanus, Anatolius and Minor Writers, Methodius, Arnobius,* pp. 269-79. Translated by James B. H. Hawkins. ANF 6. Edited by Alexander Roberts and James Donaldson. 10 vols. 1885-1887. Reprint, Peabody, Mass.: Hendrickson, 1994.

[Peter of Alexandria]. "Homilies on Riches." In *Two Coptic Homilies Attributed to Saint Peter of Alexandria: On Riches, On the Epiphany.* Translation and commentary by Birger Pearson and Tim Vivian with the assistance of Donald B. Spanel. Roma: C.I.M., 1993.

Prosper of Aquitaine. "Grace and Free Will." In *Niceta of Remesiana, Sulpicius Severus, Vincent of Lérins and Prosper of Aquitaine,* pp. 333-418. Translated by J. Reginald O'Donnell. FC 7. New York: Fathers of the Church, 1949.

Prudentius. "Hymns for Every Day." In *The Poems of Prudentius,* pp. 1-92. Translated by M. Clement Eagan. FC 43. Washington, D.C.: The Catholic University of America, 1962.

[Pseudo-Clement of Rome]. "Two Epistles Concerning Virginity" and "Pseudo-Clementine Literature." In *The Twelve Patriarchs, Excerpts and Epistles, The Clementina, Apocrypha, Decretals, Memoirs of Edessa and Syriac Documents, Remains of the First Ages,* pp. 51-346. Translated by B. P. Patten, et. al. ANF 8. Edited by Alexander Roberts and James Donaldson. 10 vols. 1885-1887. Reprint, Peabody, Mass.: Hendrickson, 1994.

[Pseudo-Dionysius]. *The Complete Works.* Translated by Colm Luibheid. The Classics of Western Spirituality. New York: Paulist, 1980.

Revelation of Esdras. In *The Twelve Patriarchs, Excerpts and Epistles, The Clementina, Apocrypha, Decretals,*

Memoirs of Edessa and Syriac Documents, Remains of the First Ages, pp. 571-74. Translated by Alexander Walker. ANF 8. Edited by Alexander Roberts and James Donaldson. 10 vols. 1885-1887. Reprint, Peabody, Mass.: Hendrickson, 1994.

Rufinus of Aquileia. "Commentary on the Apostles' Creed." In *Theodoret, Jerome, Gennadius, Rufinus: Historical Writings etc.*, pp. 541-63. Translated by William Henry Fremantle. NPNF 3. Series 2. Edited by Philip Schaff and Henry Wace. 14 vols. 1886-1900. Reprint, Peabody, Mass.: Hendrickson, 1994.

[Salvian the Presbyter]. *The Writings of Salvian the Presbyter*. Translated by Jermiah F. O'Sullivan. FC 3. Washington, D.C.: The Catholic University of America Press, 1962.

The Shepherd of Hermas. In *The Apostolic Fathers*, pp. 225-352. Translated by Joseph M. F. Marique. FC 1. New York: Christian Heritage, 1947.

Symeon the New Theologian. *The Discourses*. Translated by C. J. de Catanzaro. Classics of Western Spirituality. New York: Paulist, 1980.

Tertullian. *Disciplinary, Moral and Ascetical Works*. Translated by Edwin A. Quain. FC 40. Washington, D.C.: The Catholic University of America, 1959.

———. "The Prescriptions Against Heretics." In *Early Latin Theology*, pp. 25-64. Translated by S. L. Greenslade. LCC 5. Philadelphia: Westminster Press, 1956.

[Tertullian]. *Latin Christianity: Its Founder, Tertullian*, Translated by S. Thelwall et al. ANF 3. Edited by Alexander Roberts and James Donaldson. 10 vols. 1885-1887. Reprint, Peabody, Mass.: Hendrickson, 1994.

———. "Tertullian." In *Tertullian (IV); Minucius Felix; Commodian; Origen (I and III)*, pp. 5-166. Translated by S. Thelwall. ANF 4. Edited by Alexander Roberts and James Donaldson. 10 vols. 1885-1887. Reprint, Peabody, Mass.: Hendrickson, 1994.

The Testaments of the Twelve Patriarchs. In *The Twelve Patriarchs, Excerpts and Epistles, The Clementina, Apocrypha, Decretals, Memoirs of Edessa and Syriac Documents, Remains of the First Ages*, pp. 1-38. Translated by Alexander Walker. ANF 8. Edited by Alexander Roberts and James Donaldson. 10 vols. 1885-1887. Reprint, Peabody, Mass.: Hendrickson, 1994.

[Theodore of Mopsuestia]. See Dimitri Z. Zaharopoulos. *Theodore of Mopsuestia on the Bible: A Study of His Old Testament Exegesis*. New York: Paulist Press, 1989.

Theodore of Tabennesi. "Fragments." In *Pachomian Koinonia*, 3: 91-134. Translated by Armand Veilleux. CS 47. Kalamazoo, Mich.: Cistercian Publications, 1982.

Theodoret of Cyr. *Commentary on the Psalms, 1-150*. 2 vols. Translated by Robert C. Hill. FC 101-102. Washington, D.C.: The Catholic University of America, 2000-2001.

———. *Commentary on the Song of Songs*. Translated by Robert C. Hill. ECS 2. Brisbane: Australian Catholic University, 2001.

———. "Letters." In *Theodoret, Jerome, Gennadius, Rufinus: Historical Writings, Etc.*, pp. 250-348. Translated by Blomfield Jackson. NPNF 3. Series 2. Edited by Philip Schaff and Henry Wace. 14 vols. 1886-1900. Reprint, Peabody, Mass.: Hendrickson, 1994.

[Theodotus the Valentinian]. "Excerpts of Theodotus." In *The Twelve Patriarchs, Excerpts and Epistles, The Clementina, Apocrypha, Decretals, Memoirs of Edessa and Syriac Documents, Remains of the First Ages*, pp. 39-50. Translated by William Wilson. ANF 8. Edited by Alexander Roberts and James Donaldson. 10 vols. 1885-1887. Reprint, Peabody, Mass.: Hendrickson, 1994.

Valerian. "Homilies." In *Saint Peter Chrysologus, Selected Sermons, and Saint Valerian, Homilies*, pp. 299-435. Translated by George E. Ganss. FC 17. Washington, D.C.: The Catholic University of America Press, 1962.

Vincent of Lérins. "Commonitories." In *Niceta of Remesiana, Sulpicius Severus, Vincent of Lérins, Prosper of Aquitaine*, pp. 257-332. Translated by Rudolph E. Morris. FC 7. New York: Fathers of the Church, 1949.

Authors/Writings Index

Subject Index

427

Scripture Index